| | |
|---|---|
| Course | Managerial Accounting |
| Course Number | **Business 207** |
| | LaSalle University |
| | **School of Business** |

http://create.mheducation.com

ISBN-10: 1121240496    ISBN-13: 9781121240490

# Contents

# Credits

# CHAPTER 13

# Statement of Cash Flows

© AP Photo/mark Lennihan

## Learning Objectives

**AFTER STUDYING THIS CHAPTER, YOU SHOULD BE ABLE TO:**

**LO1** Explain the purposes and uses of a statement of cash flows.

**LO2** Describe how cash transactions are classified in a statement of cash flows.

**LO3** Compute the major cash flows relating to operating activities.

**LO4** Compute the cash flows relating to investing and financing activities.

**LO5** Distinguish between the direct and indirect methods of reporting operating cash flows.

**LO6** Explain why net income differs from net cash flows from operating activities.

**LO7** Compute net cash flows from operating activities using the *indirect* method.

**LO8** Discuss the likely effects of various business strategies on cash flows.

**LO8** Explain how a worksheet may be helpful in preparing a statement of cash flows.

## LOWE'S

Cash is sometimes referred to as the "lifeblood" of a company, implying that companies require cash to be successful and to even continue to exist. Cash is required on a daily basis to meet current obligations and to position the company for future success. Cash requirements include activities as broad ranging as meeting payroll requirements for employees, purchasing inventory to meet the shopping needs of customers, repaying debt when it is due, paying dividends to stockholders, and from time to time expanding the business by acquiring plant assets or even entire other businesses.

Cash flow is particularly important for large companies like Lowe's as it continuously seeks to expand its markets. Lowe's 2009 annual report includes three-year comparative statements of cash flows for 2009, 2008, and 2007. These statements are presented in three major categories: operating activities, investing activities, and financing activities. Lowe's shows over $4 billion from operating cash flows for each year presented. This cash was used for many purposes, including major acquisitions, repurchasing the company's common stock, paying dividends to stockholders, and retiring debt.

Efficiently managing cash flows of this magnitude is an important responsibility of the company's leadership and is critical for the company's continued success. ■

Cash flow information about a company is helpful to investors and creditors in judging future cash flows. If the company itself does not have strong cash flow, it is unlikely that the company will be in a cash position to provide strong cash flows to its investors and creditors. We introduced in Chapter 2 the idea of a financial statement that describes cash flows, and in Chapter 13 we go into greater depth regarding this important financial statement. The statement of cash flows shows how the company's cash changed during the period and explains how the company managed its cash in terms of its operating, investing, and financing activities.

## Statement of Cash Flows

### PURPOSES OF THE STATEMENT

**Learning Objective**

**L01** Explain the purposes and uses of a statement of cash flows.

The objective of a statement of cash flows is to provide information about the *cash receipts* and *cash payments* of a business entity during the accounting period. The term **cash flows** includes both cash receipts and payments. In a statement of cash flows, information about cash receipts and cash payments is classified in terms of the company's operating activities, investing activities, and financing activities. The statement of cash flows assists investors, creditors, and others in assessing such factors as:

- The company's ability to generate positive cash flows in future periods.
- The company's ability to meet its obligations and to pay dividends.
- The company's need for external financing.
- Reasons for differences between the amount of net income and the related net cash flows from operating activities.
- Both the cash and noncash aspects of the company's investment and financing transactions for the period.
- Causes of the change in the amount of cash and cash equivalents between the beginning and the end of the accounting period.

Stated simply, a statement of cash flows helps users of financial statements evaluate a company's ability to have sufficient cash—both on a short-run and on a long-run basis. For this reason, the statement of cash flows is useful to virtually everyone interested in the company's financial health: short- and long-term creditors, investors, management—and both current and prospective competitors.

### EXAMPLE OF A STATEMENT OF CASH FLOWS

An example of a statement of cash flows appears in Exhibit 13–1. Cash outflows are shown in parentheses.[1]

### CLASSIFICATION OF CASH FLOWS

**Learning Objective**

**L02** Describe how cash transactions are classified in a statement of cash flows.

The cash flows shown in the statement are presented in three major categories: (1) **operating activities,** (2) **investing activities,** and (3) **financing activities.**[2] We will now look briefly at the way cash flows are classified among these three categories.

**Operating Activities**   The operating activities section shows the *cash effects* of revenue and expense transactions. Stated another way, the operating activities section of the statement of cash flows includes the cash effects of those transactions reported in the continuing operations section of the income statement. To illustrate this concept, consider the effects

---

[1] In this illustration, net cash flows from operating activities are determined by the *direct method.* An alternative approach, called the *indirect method,* is illustrated later in this chapter.

[2] To reconcile to the ending cash balance, "effects of changes in exchange rates on cash" is used in the cash flow statements of companies with foreign currency holdings. This classification, as well as other complexities, is discussed in more advanced accounting courses.

Exhibit 13–1

**ALLISON CORPORATION
STATEMENT OF CASH
FLOWS**

| ALLISON CORPORATION STATEMENT OF CASH FLOWS FOR THE YEAR ENDED DECEMBER 31, 2011 | | |
|---|---:|---:|
| **Cash flows from operating activities:** | | |
| Cash received from customers . . . . . . . . . . . . . . . . . . . . . . . . . . . . | $ 870,000 | |
| Interest and dividends received . . . . . . . . . . . . . . . . . . . . . . . . . . | 10,000 | |
|    Cash provided by operating activities . . . . . . . . . . . . . . . . . . . . | | $880,000 |
| Cash paid to suppliers and employees . . . . . . . . . . . . . . . . . . . . . | $(764,000) | |
| Interest paid . . . . . . . . . . . . . . . . . . . . . . . . . . . . . . . . . . . . . . . | (28,000) | |
| Income taxes paid . . . . . . . . . . . . . . . . . . . . . . . . . . . . . . . . . . . | (38,000) | |
|    Cash disbursed for operating activities . . . . . . . . . . . . . . . . . . | | (830,000) |
| Net cash flows from operating activities . . . . . . . . . . . . . . . . . . . . . . | | $ 50,000 |
| **Cash flows from investing activities:** | | |
| Purchases of marketable securities . . . . . . . . . . . . . . . . . . . . . . . | $ (65,000) | |
| Proceeds from sales of marketable securities . . . . . . . . . . . . . . . | 40,000 | |
| Loans made to borrowers . . . . . . . . . . . . . . . . . . . . . . . . . . . . . . | (17,000) | |
| Collections on loans . . . . . . . . . . . . . . . . . . . . . . . . . . . . . . . . . | 12,000 | |
| Purchases of plant assets . . . . . . . . . . . . . . . . . . . . . . . . . . . . . | (160,000) | |
| Proceeds from sales of plant assets . . . . . . . . . . . . . . . . . . . . . | 75,000 | |
| Net cash flows from investing activities . . . . . . . . . . . . . . . . . . . . | | (115,000) |
| **Cash flows from financing activities:** | | |
| Proceeds from short-term borrowing. . . . . . . . . . . . . . . . . . . . . . | $ 45,000 | |
| Payments to settle short-term debts . . . . . . . . . . . . . . . . . . . . . . | (55,000) | |
| Proceeds from issuing bonds payable . . . . . . . . . . . . . . . . . . . | 100,000 | |
| Proceeds from issuing capital stock . . . . . . . . . . . . . . . . . . . . . | 50,000 | |
| Dividends paid. . . . . . . . . . . . . . . . . . . . . . . . . . . . . . . . . . . . | (40,000) | |
| Net cash flows from financing activities . . . . . . . . . . . . . . . . . . . | | 100,000 |
| **Net increase (decrease) in cash** . . . . . . . . . . . . . . . . . . . . . . . . . | | $ 35,000 |
| Cash and cash equivalents, Jan. 1, 2011 . . . . . . . . . . . . . . . . . . . | | 20,000 |
| Cash and cash equivalents, Dec. 31, 2011 . . . . . . . . . . . . . . . . . | | $ 55,000 |

of credit sales. Credit sales are reported in the income statement in the period when the sales occur. But the cash effects occur later—when the receivables are collected in cash. For many credit sales, cash will be received in the same financial reporting period. If these events occur in different accounting periods, however, the income statement and the operating activities section of the statement of cash flows will differ. Similar differences may exist between the recognition of an expense and the related cash payment. Consider, for example, the expense of postretirement benefits earned by employees during the current period. If this expense is not funded with a trustee, the cash payments may not occur for many years—after today's employees have retired.

Cash flows from operating activities include:

| Cash Receipts | Cash Payments |
|---|---|
| Collections from customers for sales of goods and services | Payments to suppliers of merchandise and services, including payments to employees |
| Interest and dividends received | |
| Other receipts from operations; for example, proceeds from settlement of litigation | Payments of interest |
| | Payments of income taxes |
| | Other expenditures relating to operations; for example, payments in settlement of litigation |

Notice that receipts of *interest and dividends* and payments of *interest* are classified as operating activities, not as investing or financing activities.

### Investing Activities
Cash flows relating to investing activities present the cash effects of transactions involving plant assets, intangible assets, and investments. They include:

| Cash Receipts | Cash Payments |
| --- | --- |
| Cash proceeds from selling investments and plant and intangible assets | Payments to acquire investments and plant and intangible assets |
| Cash proceeds from collecting principal amounts on loans | Amounts advanced to borrowers |

### Financing Activities
Cash flows classified as financing activities include the following items that result from debt and equity financing transactions:

| Cash Receipts | Cash Payments |
| --- | --- |
| Proceeds from both short-term and long-term borrowing | Repayment of amounts borrowed (excluding interest payments) |
| Cash received from owners (for example, from issuing stock) | Payments to owners, such as cash dividends |

Repayment of amounts borrowed refers to repayment of *loans,* not to payments made on accounts payable or accrued liabilities. Payments of accounts payable and of accrued liabilities are payments to suppliers of merchandise and services related to revenues and expenses and are classified as cash outflows from operating activities. Also, remember that all interest payments are classified as operating activities.

### Why Are Receipts and Payments of Interest Classified as Operating Activities?
A case can be made that interest and dividend receipts are related to investing activities, and that interest payments are related to financing activities. The Financial Accounting Standards Board (FASB) considered this point of view but decided instead to require companies to present interest and dividend receipts and interest payments as operating activities. The FASB position reflects the view that cash flows from operating activities should include the cash effects of the revenue and expense transactions entering into the determination of net income. Because dividend and interest revenue and interest expense enter into the determination of net income, the FASB decided that the related cash flows should be presented as operating activities in the statement of cash flows. Payments of dividends, however, *do not* enter into the determination of net income. Therefore, dividend payments are classified as financing activities.

**INTERNATIONAL** CASE IN POINT

Both the Financial Accounting Standards Board in the United States and the International Accounting Standards Board require companies to present a statement of cash flows organized into three categories: operating activities, investing activities, and financing activities. One difference in these two sets of financial reporting standards is the classification of interest received on investments and interest paid on debt financing. As you have learned in this chapter, the FASB requires these to be presented as part of operating cash flows. IASB standards, on the other hand, allow interest received to be classified as either operating or investing and interest paid to be classified as either operating or financing.

**Cash and Cash Equivalents**   For purposes of preparing a statement of cash flows, cash is defined as including *both cash and cash equivalents*. **Cash equivalents** are short-term, highly liquid investments, such as money market funds, commercial paper, and Treasury bills that will mature within 90 days from the acquisition date.

If an item is determined to not be a cash equivalent, its cash flows are presented in the investing activities section of the statement of cash flows. The amount shown as *cash and cash equivalents* in the balance sheet must be the same as the amount shown on the statement of cash flows. Transfers of money between a company's bank accounts and these cash equivalents are *not viewed as cash receipts or cash payments*. Money is considered cash regardless of whether it is held in currency, in a bank account, or in the form of cash equivalents. Interest received from holding cash equivalents is included in cash receipts from operating activities.

Marketable securities, such as investments in the stocks and bonds of other companies, *do not qualify as cash equivalents*. Therefore, purchases and sales of marketable securities *do* result in cash flows that are reported in the statement of cash flows as investing activities.

In the long run, a company must have a strategy that generates positive net cash flows from its operating activities if it is to be successful. A business with negative cash flows from operations will not be able to raise cash from other sources indefinitely. In fact, the ability of a business to raise cash through financing activities is highly dependent on its ability to generate cash from its normal business operations. Creditors and stockholders are reluctant to invest in a company that does not generate enough cash from operating activities to ensure prompt payment of maturing liabilities, interest, and dividends.

Similarly, companies cannot expect to survive indefinitely on cash provided by investing activities. At some point, plant assets, investments, and other assets available for sale will be depleted.

**Cash versus Accrual Information**   The items in an income statement and a balance sheet represent the balances of specific general ledger accounts. Notice, however, that the captions used in the statement of cash flows *do not* correspond to specific ledger accounts. A statement of cash flows summarizes *cash transactions* during the accounting period. The general ledger, however, is maintained on the **accrual basis** of accounting, not the cash basis. Thus an amount such as "Cash received from customers . . . $870,000" does not appear as the balance in a specific ledger account, but it is derived from one or more such accounts.

In a small business, it may be practical to prepare a statement of cash flows directly from the special journals for cash receipts and cash payments. For most businesses, however, it is easier to prepare the statement of cash flows by examining the income statement and the *changes* during the period in all of the balance sheet accounts *except for* Cash. This approach is based on the double-entry system of accounting; any transaction affecting cash must also affect some other asset, liability, or owners' equity account.[3] The change in these *other accounts* determines the nature of the cash transaction, as we see in the example that follows.

## Preparing a Statement of Cash Flows

Earlier in this chapter we illustrated the statement of cash flows of Allison Corporation. We will now show how this statement was developed from the company's accrual-basis accounting records.

Basically, a statement of cash flows can be prepared from the information contained in an income statement and *comparative* balance sheets at the beginning and end of the period. It is also necessary, however, to have some detailed information about the *changes* occurring during the period in certain balance sheet accounts. Shown in Exhibit 13–2 is Allison's income statement, and in Exhibit 13–3 the firm's comparative balance sheets for the current year are presented.

**Additional Information**   An analysis of changes in the balance sheet accounts of Allison Corporation provides the following information about the company's activities in the current

---

[3] Revenue, expenses, and dividends represent changes in owners' equity and, therefore, may be regarded as owners' equity accounts.

**Exhibit 13–2**

**ALLISON CORPORATION INCOME STATEMENT**

### ALLISON CORPORATION INCOME STATEMENT FOR THE YEAR ENDED DECEMBER 31, 2011

**Revenue and gains:**

| | | |
|---|---|---|
| Net sales | | $900,000 |
| Dividend revenue | | 3,000 |
| Interest revenue | | 6,000 |
| Gain on sales of plant assets | | 31,000 |
| Total revenue and gains | | $940,000 |

**Costs, expenses, and losses:**

| | | |
|---|---|---|
| Cost of goods sold | $500,000 | |
| Operating expenses (including depreciation of $40,000) | 300,000 | |
| Interest expense | 35,000 | |
| Income tax expense | 36,000 | |
| Loss on sales of marketable securities | 4,000 | |
| Total costs, expenses, and losses | | 875,000 |
| Net income | | $ 65,000 |

year. To assist in the preparation of a statement of cash flows, we have classified this information into the categories of operating activities, investing activities, and financing activities.

## OPERATING ACTIVITIES

1. Accounts receivable increased by $30,000 during the year.
2. Dividend revenue is recognized on the cash basis, but interest revenue is recognized on the accrual basis. Accrued interest receivable decreased by $1,000 during the year.
3. Inventory increased by $10,000 and accounts payable increased by $15,000 during the year.
4. During the year, short-term prepaid expenses increased by $3,000 and accrued expenses payable (other than for interest or income taxes) decreased by $6,000. Depreciation for the year amounted to $40,000.
5. The accrued liability for interest payable increased by $7,000 during the year.
6. The accrued liability for income taxes payable decreased by $2,000 during the year.

## INVESTING ACTIVITIES

7. Analysis of the Marketable Securities account shows debit entries of $65,000, representing the cost of securities purchased, and credit entries of $44,000, representing the cost of securities sold. (No marketable securities are classified as cash equivalents.)
8. Analysis of the Notes Receivable account shows $17,000 in debit entries, representing cash loaned by Allison Corporation to borrowers during the year, and $12,000 in credit entries, representing collections of notes receivable. (Collections of interest were recorded in the Interest Revenue account and are considered cash flows from operating activities.)
9. Allison's plant asset accounts increased by $116,000 during the year. An analysis of the underlying transactions indicates the following:

| | Effect on Plant Asset Accounts |
|---|---|
| Purchased $200,000 in plant assets, paying $160,000 cash and issuing a long-term note payable for the $40,000 balance | $200,000 |
| Sold for $75,000 cash plant assets with a book value of $44,000 | (44,000) |
| Recorded depreciation expense for the period | (40,000) |
| Net change in plant asset controlling accounts | $116,000 |

| ALLISON CORPORATION COMPARATIVE BALANCE SHEETS DECEMBER 31, 2011 AND 2010 | | |
|---|---|---|
| | **2011** | **2010** |
| **Assets** | | |
| **Current assets:** | | |
| Cash and Cash Equivalents | $ 55,000 | $ 20,000 |
| Marketable Securities | 85,000 | 64,000 |
| Notes Receivable | 17,000 | 12,000 |
| Accounts Receivable | 110,000 | 80,000 |
| Accrued Interest Receivable | 2,000 | 3,000 |
| Inventory | 100,000 | 90,000 |
| Prepaid Expenses | 4,000 | 1,000 |
| Total current assets | $373,000 | $270,000 |
| **Plant and Equipment (net of accumulated depreciation)** | 616,000 | 500,000 |
| Total assets | $989,000 | $770,000 |
| **Liabilities & Stockholders' Equity** | | |
| **Current liabilities:** | | |
| Notes Payable (short-term) | $ 45,000 | $ 55,000 |
| Accounts Payable | 76,000 | 61,000 |
| Interest Payable | 22,000 | 15,000 |
| Income Taxes Payable | 8,000 | 10,000 |
| Other Accrued Expenses Payable | 3,000 | 9,000 |
| Total current liabilities | $154,000 | $150,000 |
| **Long-term liabilities:** | | |
| Notes Payable (long-term) | 40,000 | –0– |
| Bonds Payable | 400,000 | 300,000 |
| Total liabilities | $594,000 | $450,000 |
| **Stockholders' equity:** | | |
| Capital Stock | $ 60,000 | $ 50,000 |
| Additional Paid-in Capital | 140,000 | 100,000 |
| Retained Earnings | 195,000 | 170,000 |
| Total stockholders' equity | $395,000 | $320,000 |
| Total liabilities & stockholders' equity | $989,000 | $770,000 |

**Exhibit 13–3**

**ALLISON CORPORATION BALANCE SHEETS**

## FINANCING ACTIVITIES

10. During the year, Allison Corporation borrowed $45,000 cash by issuing short-term notes payable to banks. Also, the company repaid $55,000 in principal amounts due on these loans and other notes payable. (Interest payments are classified as operating activities.)

11. The company issued bonds payable for $100,000 cash.

12. The company issued 1,000 shares of $10 par value capital stock for cash at a price of $50 per share.

13. Cash dividends declared and paid to stockholders amounted to $40,000 during the year.

## CASH AND CASH EQUIVALENTS

14. Cash and cash equivalents as shown in Allison Corporation's balance sheets amounted to $20,000 at the beginning of the year and $55,000 at year-end—a net increase of $35,000.

Using this information, we will now illustrate the steps in preparing Allison Corporation's statement of cash flows and a supporting schedule disclosing the noncash investing and financing activities. In our discussion, we will often refer to these items of additional information by citing the paragraph numbers shown in the list just described.

The distinction between accrual-basis measurements and cash flows is fundamentally important in understanding financial statements and other accounting reports. To assist in making this distinction, we use two colors in our illustrated computations. We show in blue the accrual-based data from Allison Corporation's income statement and the preceding numbered paragraphs. The cash flows that we compute from these data are shown in red.

## CASH FLOWS FROM OPERATING ACTIVITIES

**Learning Objective**
**LO8  Compute the major cash flows relating to operating activities.**

As shown in our statement of cash flows in Exhibit 13–1, the net cash flows from operating activities are determined by combining certain cash inflows and subtracting certain cash outflows. The inflows are cash received from customers and interest and dividends received; the outflows are cash paid to suppliers and employees, interest paid, and income taxes paid.

In computing each of these cash flows, our starting point is an income statement amount, such as net sales, cost of goods sold, or interest expense. As you study each computation, be sure that you *understand why* the income statement amount must be increased or decreased to determine the related cash flows. You will find that an understanding of these computations will do more than show you how to compute cash flows; it will also strengthen your understanding of the income statement and the balance sheet.

**Cash Received from Customers**    To the extent that sales are made for cash, there is no difference between the amount of cash received from customers in the statement of cash flows and the amount recorded as sales revenue in the income statement. Differences arise, however, when sales are made on account. If accounts receivable increase during the year, credit sales will have exceeded collections of cash from accounts receivable. Therefore, we *deduct the increase* in accounts receivable from net sales to determine the amount of cash received during the year. If accounts receivable decrease, collections of these accounts will have exceeded credit sales. Therefore, we *add the decrease* in accounts receivable to net sales to determine the amount of cash received during the year. The relationship between cash received from customers and net sales is summarized below:

$$\begin{matrix} \text{Cash Received} \\ \text{from Customers} \end{matrix} = \begin{matrix} \text{Net} \\ \text{Sales} \end{matrix} \left\{ \begin{matrix} + \text{ Decrease in Accounts Receivable} \\ \text{or} \\ - \text{ Increase in Accounts Receivable} \end{matrix} \right\}$$

In our Allison Corporation example, paragraph **1** of the additional information tells us that accounts receivable *increased* by $30,000 during the year. The income statement shows net sales for the year of $900,000. Therefore, the amount of cash received from customers is computed as follows:

| | |
|---|---:|
| Net sales (accrual basis) | $900,000 |
| Less: Increase in accounts receivable | 30,000 |
| Cash received from customers | $870,000 |

**Interest and Dividends Received**    Our next step is to determine the amounts of cash received during the year from dividends and interest on the company's investments. As explained in paragraph **2** of the additional information, dividend revenue is recorded on the cash basis. Therefore, the $3,000 shown in the income statement also represents the amount of cash received as dividends.

Interest revenue, on the other hand, is recognized on the accrual basis. We have already shown how to convert one type of revenue, net sales, from the accrual basis to the cash basis. We use the same approach to convert interest revenue from the accrual basis to the **cash basis.** Our formula for converting net sales to the cash basis may be modified to convert interest revenue to the cash basis as follows:

$$\text{Interest Received} = \text{Interest Revenue} \begin{Bmatrix} + \text{ Decrease in Interest Receivable} \\ \text{or} \\ - \text{ Increase in Interest Receivable} \end{Bmatrix}$$

The income statement for Allison Corporation shows interest revenue of $6,000, and paragraph **2** states that the amount of accrued interest receivable *decreased* by $1,000 during the year. Thus the amount of cash received as interest is computed as follows:

| | |
|---|---|
| Interest revenue (accrual basis) | $6,000 |
| Add: Decrease in accrued interest receivable | 1,000 |
| Interest received (cash basis) | $7,000 |

The amounts of interest and dividends received in cash are combined for presentation in the statement of cash flows:

| | |
|---|---|
| Interest received (cash basis) | $ 7,000 |
| Dividends received (cash basis) | 3,000 |
| Interest and dividends received | $10,000 |

## CASH PAYMENTS FOR MERCHANDISE AND FOR EXPENSES

The next item in the statement of cash flows, "Cash paid to suppliers and employees," includes all cash payments for purchases of merchandise and for operating expenses (excluding interest and income taxes). Payments of interest and income taxes are listed as separate items in the statement. The amounts of cash paid for purchases of merchandise and for operating expenses are computed separately.

**Cash Paid for Purchases of Merchandise**  An accrual basis income statement reflects the *cost of goods sold* during the year, regardless of whether the merchandise was acquired or paid for in that period. The statement of cash flows, on the other hand, reports the *cash paid* for merchandise during the year, even if the merchandise was acquired in a previous period or remains unsold at year-end. The relationship between cash payments for merchandise and the cost of goods sold depends on the changes during the period in *two* related balance sheet accounts: inventory and accounts payable to suppliers of merchandise. This relationship may be stated as follows:

$$\text{Cash Payments for Purchases} = \text{Cost of Goods Sold} \begin{Bmatrix} + \text{ Increase in Inventory} \\ \text{or} \\ - \text{ Decrease in Inventory} \end{Bmatrix} \text{and} \begin{Bmatrix} + \text{ Decrease in Accounts Payable} \\ \text{or} \\ - \text{ Increase in Accounts Payable} \end{Bmatrix}$$

Using information from the Allison Corporation income statement and paragraph **3**, the cash payments for purchases may be computed as follows:

| | |
|---|---|
| Cost of goods sold | $500,000 |
| Add: Increase in inventory | 10,000 |
| Net purchases (accrual basis) | $510,000 |
| Less: Increase in accounts payable to suppliers | 15,000 |
| Cash payments for purchases of merchandise | $495,000 |

Here is the logic behind this computation: If a company is increasing its inventory, it is *buying more merchandise than it sells* during the period. If the company is increasing its accounts payable to merchandise creditors, it is *not paying cash* for all of these purchases in the current period. Some portion of the purchases will be paid for in the next period.

**Cash Payments for Expenses**   Expenses, as shown in the income statement, represent the cost of goods and services used up during the period. However, the amounts shown as expenses may differ from the cash payments made during the period. Consider, for example, depreciation expense. Recording depreciation expense *requires no cash payment,* but it does increase total expenses measured on the accrual basis. Thus, in converting accrual-basis expenses to the cash basis, we deduct depreciation expense and any other noncash expenses from our accrual-basis operating expenses. Other noncash expenses—expenses not requiring cash outlays—include amortization of intangible assets, any unfunded portion of postretirement benefits expense, and amortization of bond discount.

A second type of difference arises from short-term *timing differences* between the recognition of expenses and the actual cash payments. Expenses are recorded in accounting records when the related goods or services are used. However, the cash payments for these expenses might occur (1) in an earlier period, (2) in the same period, or (3) in a later period. Let us briefly consider each case.

1. If payment is made in advance, the payment creates an asset, termed a prepaid expense, or, in our formula, a "prepayment." Thus, to the extent that prepaid expenses increase over the year, cash payments *exceed* the amount recognized as expense.
2. If payment is made in the same period, the cash payment is equal to the amount of expense.
3. If payment is made in a later period, the payment reduces a liability for an accrued expense payable. Thus, to the extent that accrued expenses payable decrease over the year, cash payments exceed the amount recognized as expense.

The relationship between cash payments for expenses and accrual-basis expenses is summarized below:

$$\begin{matrix} \text{Cash Payments} \\ \text{for Expenses} \end{matrix} = \text{Expenses} \left\{ \begin{matrix} \\ - \text{ Depreciation} \\ \text{and Other} \\ \text{Noncash} \\ \text{Expenses} \\ \\ \end{matrix} \right\} \text{ and } \left\{ \begin{matrix} \text{Increase in} \\ + \text{ Related} \\ \text{Prepayments} \\ \text{or} \\ \text{Decrease in} \\ - \text{ Related} \\ \text{Prepayments} \end{matrix} \right\} \text{ and } \left\{ \begin{matrix} \text{Decrease in} \\ + \text{ Related Accrued} \\ \text{Liabilities} \\ \text{or} \\ \text{Increase in} \\ - \text{ Related Accrued} \\ \text{Liabilities} \end{matrix} \right\}$$

In a statement of cash flows, cash payments for interest and for income taxes are shown separately from cash payments for operating expenses. Using information from Allison Corporation's income statement and from paragraph **4,** we may compute the company's cash payments for operating expenses as follows:

| | | |
|---|---|---|
| Operating expenses (including depreciation) | | $300,000 |
| Less: Noncash expenses (depreciation) | | 40,000 |
| Subtotal | | $260,000 |
| Add: Increase in short-term prepayments | $3,000 | |
| Decrease in accrued liabilities | 6,000 | 9,000 |
| Cash payments for operating expenses | | $269,000 |

**Cash Paid to Suppliers and Employees**   The caption used in our cash flow statement, "Cash paid to suppliers and employees," includes cash payments for both purchases of merchandise and for operating expenses. This cash outflow may now be computed by combining the two previous calculations:

| | |
|---|---|
| Cash payments for purchases of merchandise | $495,000 |
| Cash payments for operating expenses | 269,000 |
| Cash payments to suppliers and employees | $764,000 |

### Cash Payments for Interest and Taxes

Interest expense and income taxes expense may be converted to cash payments with the same formula we used to convert operating expenses. Allison Corporation's income statement shows interest expense of $35,000, and paragraph **5** states that the liability for interest payable increased by $7,000 during the year. The fact that the liability for unpaid interest *increased* over the year means that *not all of the interest expense shown in the income statement was paid in cash* in the current year. To determine the amount of interest actually paid, we *subtract* from total interest expense the portion that has been financed through an increase in the liability for interest payable. The computation is as follows:

| | |
|---|---|
| Interest expense | $35,000 |
| Less: Increase in related accrued liability | 7,000 |
| Interest paid | $28,000 |

Similar reasoning is used to determine the amount of income tax paid by Allison Corporation during the year. The accrual-based income tax expense reported in the income statement amounts to $36,000. However, paragraph **6** states that the company has reduced its liability for income taxes payable by $2,000 over the year. Incurring income tax expense increases the tax liability; making cash payments to tax authorities reduces it. Thus, if the liability *decreased* over the year, cash payments to tax authorities *must have been greater* than the income tax expense for the current year. The amount of the cash payments is determined as follows:

| | |
|---|---|
| Income tax expense | $36,000 |
| Add: Decrease in related accrued liability | 2,000 |
| Income tax paid | $38,000 |

### A Quick Review

We have now shown the computation of each cash flow relating to Allison Corporation's operating activities. In Exhibit 13–1 we illustrated a complete statement of cash flows for the company. For your convenience, we again show the operating activities section of that statement, illustrating the information developed in the preceding paragraphs.

| **Cash flows from operating activities:** | | |
|---|---|---|
| Cash received from customers | $ 870,000 | |
| Interest and dividends received | 10,000 | |
| Cash provided by operating activities | | $ 880,000 |
| Cash paid to suppliers and employees | $(764,000) | |
| Interest paid | (28,000) | |
| Income taxes paid | (38,000) | |
| Cash disbursed for operating activities | | (830,000) |
| Net cash flows from operating activities | | $ 50,000 |

## CASH FLOWS FROM INVESTING ACTIVITIES

Paragraphs **7** through **9** in the additional information for our Allison Corporation example provide most of the information necessary to determine the cash flows from investing activities. In the following discussion, we illustrate the presentation of these cash flows and explain the sources of the information contained in the numbered paragraphs.

Much information about investing activities can be obtained simply by looking at the changes in the related asset accounts during the year. Debit entries in these accounts represent purchases of the assets, or cash outlays. Credit entries represent sales of the assets, or cash receipts. However, credit entries in asset accounts represent the *cost* (or *book value*) of the assets sold. To determine the cash proceeds from these transactions, we must adjust the amount of the credit entries for any gains or losses recognized on the sales.

**Learning Objective**
Compute the cash flows relating to investing and financing activities.

LO4

**Purchases and Sales of Securities**  To illustrate, consider paragraph **7,** which summarizes the debit and credit entries to the Marketable Securities account. As explained earlier in this chapter, the $65,000 in debit entries represents purchases of marketable securities. The $44,000 in credit entries represents the *cost* of marketable securities sold during the period. However, the income statement shows that these securities were sold at a *$4,000 loss.* Thus the cash proceeds from these sales amounted to only *$40,000* ($44,000 cost, minus $4,000 loss on sale). In the statement of cash flows, these investing activities are summarized as follows:

| | |
|---|---:|
| Purchases of marketable securities . . . . . . . . . . . . . . . . . . . . . . . . . . . . . . . . . . . . . . . . | $(65,000) |
| Proceeds from sales of marketable securities . . . . . . . . . . . . . . . . . . . . . . . . . . . | 40,000 |

**Loans Made and Collected**  Paragraph **8** provides all the information necessary to summarize the cash flows from making and collecting loans:

| | |
|---|---:|
| Loans made to borrowers. . . . . . . . . . . . . . . . . . . . . . . . . . . . . . . . . . . . . . . . . . . . . . . . . | $(17,000) |
| Collections on loans . . . . . . . . . . . . . . . . . . . . . . . . . . . . . . . . . . . . . . . . . . . . . . . . . . . . . | 12,000 |

This information comes directly from the Notes Receivable account. Debit entries in the account represent new loans made during the year; credit entries indicate collections of the *principal* amount on outstanding notes (loans). (Interest received is credited to the Interest Revenue account and is included among the cash receipts from operating activities.)

> **YOUR TURN**      **You as a Sales Manager**
>
> Assume you are a regional sales manager for Wiggins Foods, Inc., a distributor of bulk food products to schools, nursing homes, hospitals, prisons, and other institutions. Recently, the purchasing agent for Baggins Preschools, Inc., tells you the company will likely have to forgo its normal monthly order because of cash flow problems. The purchasing agent tells you other companies are helping it through the cash flow squeeze and asks if your company could loan the payment to Baggins. The purchasing agent suggests you could record the sale as revenue and increase notes receivable (rather than accounts receivable) by the same amount. Baggins is one of your largest customers. Without its order, you will not meet your sales goals for the month—so you are tempted to say yes. However, on reflection you wonder if it might be unethical for the company to lend its customer money to finance purchases. What should you do?
>
> (See our comments on the Online Learning Center Web site.)

**Cash Paid to Acquire Plant Assets**  Paragraph **9** states that Allison Corporation purchased plant assets during the year for $200,000, paying $160,000 in cash and issuing a long-term note payable for the $40,000 balance. Notice that *only the $160,000 cash payment* appears in the statement of cash flows. However, one objective of this financial statement is to show all of the company's *investing and financing activities* during the year. Therefore, the *noncash aspects* of these transactions are shown in a supplementary schedule, as follows:

| Supplementary Schedule of Noncash Investing and Financing Activities | |
|---|---:|
| Purchases of plant assets. . . . . . . . . . . . . . . . . . . . . . . . . . . . . . . . . . . . . . . . . . . . . . . . . . | $200,000 |
| Less: Portion financed through issuance of long-term debt . . . . . . . . . . . . . . . . . . | 40,000 |
| Cash paid to acquire plant assets . . . . . . . . . . . . . . . . . . . . . . . . . . . . . . . . . . . . . . . . | $160,000 |

This supplementary schedule accompanies the statement of cash flows.

### Proceeds from Sales of Plant Assets

Assume that an analysis of the plant asset accounts shows net credit entries totaling $44,000 in the year. ("Net credit entries" means all credit entries, net of related debits to accumulated depreciation when assets were sold.) These net credit entries represent the *book value* of plant assets sold during the year. However, the income statement shows that these assets were sold at a *gain of $31,000*. Therefore, the *cash proceeds* from sales of plant assets amounted to $75,000, as follows:

| | |
|---|---:|
| Book value of plant assets sold | $44,000 |
| Add: Gain on sales of plant assets | 31,000 |
| Proceeds from sales of plant assets | $75,000 |

The amount credited to the Accumulated Depreciation account during the year is not a cash flow and is not included in the statement of cash flows.

### A Quick Review

We have now shown the computation of each cash flow related to Allison Corporation's investing activities. In Exhibit 13–1 we illustrated a complete statement of cash flows for the company. For your convenience, we again show the investing activities section of that statement, illustrating the information developed in the preceding paragraphs.

| **Cash flows from investing activities:** | | |
|---|---:|---:|
| Purchases of marketable securities | $ (65,000) | |
| Proceeds from sales of marketable securities | 40,000 | |
| Loans made to borrowers | (17,000) | |
| Collections on loans | 12,000 | |
| Purchases of plant assets | (160,000) | |
| Proceeds from sales of plant assets | 75,000 | |
| Net cash flows from investing activities | | $(115,000) |

An important feature of the investing activities section of a statement of cash flows is that increases and decreases in cash from similar transactions are presented separately rather than being combined and netted against each other. For example, in this illustration the negative cash flow from purchasing marketable securities ($65,000) is shown separately from the positive cash flow from the sales of marketable securities ($40,000) rather than netting the two to a single negative figure of $25,000 ($65,000 − $40,000).

## CASH FLOWS FROM FINANCING ACTIVITIES

Cash flows from financing activities are determined by analyzing the debit and credit changes recorded during the period in the related liability and stockholders' equity accounts. Cash flows from financing activities are more easily determined than those relating to investing activities, because financing activities seldom involve gains or losses.[4] Thus the debit or credit changes in the balance sheet accounts usually are equal to the amounts of the related cash flows.

Credit changes in such accounts as Notes Payable and the accounts for long-term debt and paid-in capital usually indicate cash receipts; debit changes indicate cash payments.

### Short-Term Borrowing Transactions

To illustrate, consider paragraph **10,** which provides the information supporting the following cash flows:

| | |
|---|---:|
| Proceeds from short-term borrowing | $45,000 |
| Payments to settle short-term debts | (55,000) |

---

[4] An early retirement of debt is an example of a financing transaction that may result in a gain or a loss.

Both the proceeds from short-term borrowing of $45,000 (a positive cash flow) and the payments to settle short-term debts of $55,000 (a negative cash flow) are presented in the statement of cash flows. Presenting both directions of the changes in cash, rather than combining the two and presenting a net amount of $10,000 ($55,000 − $45,000), is an important feature of the statement of cash flows. Presenting both positive and negative cash flows is referred to as presenting *gross* cash flows rather than presenting *net* cash flows.

Is it possible to determine the proceeds of short-term borrowing transactions throughout the year without carefully reviewing each cash receipt? The answer is yes—the proceeds from short-term borrowing are equal to the *sum of the credit entries* in the short-term *Notes Payable* account. Payments to settle short-term debts are equal to the *sum of the debit entries* in this account.

### Proceeds from Issuing Bonds Payable and Capital Stock
Paragraph **11** states that Allison Corporation received cash of $100,000 by issuing bonds payable. This amount was determined by summing the credit entries in the Bonds Payable account. The Bonds Payable account included no debit entries during the year; thus, no bonds were retired.

Paragraph **12** states that during the year Allison Corporation issued capital stock for $50,000. The proceeds from issuing stock are equal to the sum of the credit entries made in the Capital Stock and Additional Paid-in Capital accounts ($10,000 + $40,000).

### Cash Dividends Paid to Stockholders
Paragraph **13** states that Allison Corporation declared and paid cash dividends of $40,000 during the year. If dividends are both declared and paid during the same year, the cash payments are equal to the related debit entries in the Retained Earnings account.

If the balance sheet includes a liability for dividends payable, the amounts debited to Retained Earnings represent dividends *declared* during the period, which may differ from the amount of dividends *paid*. To determine cash dividends paid, we adjust the amount of dividends declared by adding any decrease (or subtracting any increase) in the Dividends Payable account over the period.

### A Quick Review
We have now shown the computation of each cash flow related to Allison Corporation's financing activities. In Exhibit 13–1 we illustrated a complete statement of cash flows for the company. For your convenience, we again show the financing activities section of that statement, illustrating the information developed in the preceding paragraphs.

| Cash flows from financing activities: | | |
|---|---|---|
| Proceeds from short-term borrowing | $ 45,000 | |
| Payments to settle short-term debts | (55,000) | |
| Proceeds from issuing bonds payable | 100,000 | |
| Proceeds from issuing capital stock | 50,000 | |
| Dividends paid | (40,000) | |
| Net cash flows from financing activities | | $100,000 |

## RELATIONSHIP BETWEEN THE STATEMENT OF CASH FLOWS AND THE BALANCE SHEET

The first asset appearing in the balance sheet is Cash and Cash Equivalents. The statement of cash flows explains in some detail the change in this asset from one balance sheet date to the next. The last three lines in the statement of cash flows illustrate this relationship, as shown in our Allison Corporation example:

| | |
|---|---|
| Net increase (decrease) in cash and cash equivalents | $35,000 |
| Cash and cash equivalents, beginning of year | 20,000 |
| Cash and cash equivalents, end of year | $55,000 |

This is referred to as a reconciliation of the beginning and ending cash balances.

> ### CASE IN POINT
>
> Successful companies sometimes experience reductions in cash. Often these reductions are intentional in order to more productively use the company's cash in different ways. For example, in the year ending June 30, 2009, **Microsoft Corporation** reported a *decrease* in cash in excess of $4 billion! Does this mean that the company was experiencing extreme financial difficulty? Not necessarily. That year, operations provided over $19 billion. The overall decline was due to approximately $7.5 billion being used in financing activities, primarily for paying cash dividends to stockholders and purchasing treasury stock. In addition, the company used almost $16 billion in investing activities, primarily to
>
> © ImagineChina via AP Images
>
> purchase investments in other companies. In fact, that year the company did very well, with a net income of more than $14 billion. By comparison, the previous year resulted in a cash *increase* of $4,228 million.
>
> Lessons to be learned from this example are twofold. First, a decrease in cash does not necessarily signal financial problems, and second, a company's cash position may change in ways very different from its net income.

## REPORTING OPERATING CASH FLOWS BY THE INDIRECT METHOD

In determining cash flows from operating activities for Allison Corporation, we have followed what is commonly referred to as the direct method. To this point in our study of the statement of cash flows, we have emphasized the direct method because we consider it to be the more informative and more readily understood approach. The direct method is recommended by the FASB, although companies are permitted to use either the direct or indirect method. Before completing our Allison Corporation illustration of preparing a statement of cash flows, we first look more carefully at the indirect method.

Exhibit 13–4 includes a comparison of the direct and indirect methods of determining net cash provided by operating activities for Allison Corporation. The direct method is the same as discussed earlier in this chapter. The two methods are more similar than it may appear at first glance. Both methods are based on the same underlying information and they result in the same net cash flow amount—in Allison Corporation's case, $50,000. Both methods convert information originally prepared on the accrual basis to information prepared on the cash basis. In Exhibit 13–4, accrual-based data appear in blue: cash flows are shown in red.

To illustrate the similarity in the computations, look briefly at the formulas for computing the cash inflows and outflows shown under the direct method (pages 570–572). Each formula begins with an income statement amount and then adds or subtracts the change during the period in related balance sheet accounts. Now look at our illustration of the indirect method in Exhibit 13–4. Notice that this computation also focuses on the net changes during the period in balance sheet accounts.

The difference between the two methods lies only in approach. However, the two approaches provide readers of the statement of cash flows with different types of information. The direct method informs these readers of the nature and dollar amounts of the *specific cash inflows and outflows* comprising the operating activities of the business. The indirect method, in contrast, *explains why* the net cash flows from operating activities differ from another measurement of performance—net income.

**Exhibit 13-4**

**COMPARISON OF DIRECT AND INDIRECT METHODS**

| **Direct Method** | | |
|---|---|---|
| Cash flows from operating activities: | | |
|   Cash received from customers | $ 870,000 | |
|   Interest and dividends received | 10,000 | |
|     Cash provided by operating activities | | $880,000 |
|   Cash paid to suppliers and employees | $(764,000) | |
|   Interest paid | (28,000) | |
|   Income taxes paid | (38,000) | |
|     Cash disbursed for operating activities | | (830,000) |
| Net cash provided by operating activities | | $ 50,000 |

| **Indirect Method** | | |
|---|---|---|
| Net income | | $ 65,000 |
| Add: Depreciation expense | | 40,000 |
|   Decrease in accrued interest receivable | | 1,000 |
|   Increase in accounts payable | | 15,000 |
|   Increase in accrued interest liabilities | | 7,000 |
|   Nonoperating loss on sales of marketable securities | | 4,000 |
| Subtotal | | $132,000 |
| Less: Increase in accounts receivable | $30,000 | |
|   Increase in inventory | 10,000 | |
|   Increase in prepaid expenses | 3,000 | |
|   Decrease in accrued operating expenses payable | 6,000 | |
|   Decrease in accrued income taxes payable | 2,000 | |
|   Nonoperating gain on sales of plant assets | 31,000 | 82,000 |
| Net cash provided by operating activities | | $ 50,000 |

**Learning Objective**

**L05**   Distinguish between the direct and indirect methods of reporting operating cash flows.

## RECONCILING NET INCOME WITH NET CASH FLOWS

**Learning Objective**

**L06**   Explain why net income differs from net cash flows from operating activities.

To further your understanding of the indirect method, we now discuss common adjustments required to reconcile net income with net cash flows from operating activities. The nature and dollar amounts of these adjustments are determined by an accountant using a worksheet or a computer program; they are *not* entered in the company's accounting records.

1. *Adjusting for Noncash Expenses*

   Depreciation is an example of a noncash expense—that is, depreciation expense reduces net income but does not require any cash outlay during the period. (The cash outflow related to depreciation resulted when the asset was purchased and was presented as an investing activity at that time—before any depreciation was ever recognized.) Depreciation causes expenses on the accrual basis to exceed cash payments, and net income for the period is less than net cash flows. To reconcile net income with net cash flows, we add back to net income the amount of depreciation and any other noncash expenses. (Other noncash expenses included unfunded pension expense, amortization of intangible assets, depletion of natural resources, and amortization of bond discount.)

2. *Adjusting for Timing Differences*

   Timing differences between elements of net income and net cash flows arise whenever revenue or expenses are recognized by debiting or crediting an account *other than* Cash. Changes over the period in the balances of these asset and liability accounts represent differences between the amount of revenue or expenses recognized in the income statement on the accrual basis and the net cash flows from operating activities. The balance sheet accounts that give rise to these timing differences include Accounts Receivable, Inventories, Prepaid Expenses, Accounts Payable, and Accrued Expenses Payable.

3. *Adjusting for Nonoperating Gains and Losses*

   Nonoperating gains and losses include gains and losses from sales of investments, plant assets, and discontinued operations (which relate to investing activities); and gains and losses on early retirement of debt (which relate to financing activities).

In a statement of cash flows, cash flows are classified as operating activities, investing activities, or financing activities. Nonoperating gains and losses, by definition, do not affect *operating activities*. However, these gains and losses do enter into the determination of net income. Therefore, in converting net income to net cash flows from operating activities, we *add back any nonoperating losses* and *deduct any nonoperating gains* included in net income. The full cash effect of the transaction is then presented as an investing activity (for example, sale of a building) or as a financing activity (for example, retirement of debt) in the statement of cash flows.

## THE INDIRECT METHOD: A SUMMARY

The adjustments to net income explained in our preceding discussion are summarized as follows:

|  |  |
|---|---|
| Net income | |
| **Add:** | Depreciation |
| | Decrease in accounts receivable |
| | Decrease in inventories |
| | Decrease in prepaid expenses |
| | Increase in accounts payable |
| | Increase in accrued expenses payable |
| | Increase in deferred income taxes payable |
| | Nonoperating losses deducted in computing net income |
| **Deduct:** | Increase in accounts receivable |
| | Increase in inventories |
| | Increase in prepaid expenses |
| | Decrease in accounts payable |
| | Decrease in accrued expenses payable |
| | Decrease in deferred income taxes payable |
| | Nonoperating gains added in computing net income |
| Net cash provided by (used in) operating activities | |

**Learning Objective**

Compute net cash flows from operating activities using the *indirect* method.

L07

## INDIRECT METHOD MAY BE REQUIRED IN A SUPPLEMENTARY SCHEDULE

The FASB recommends use of the *direct method* in presenting net cash flows from operating activities. The majority of companies, however, elect to use the indirect method. One reason is that the FASB requires companies opting for the direct method to meet an additional reporting requirement.

Companies using the direct method are required to provide a *supplementary schedule* showing the computation of net cash flows from operating activities by the indirect method. However, no supplementary computations are required of companies that present the indirect method computations in their cash flow statements because this same information is already presented in the body of the statement.

## THE STATEMENT OF CASH FLOWS: A SECOND LOOK

We have now completed our explanation of Allison Corporation's statement of cash flows. We have analyzed each type of cash flow by reconciling amounts included in the other two financial statements—the income statement and the balance sheet—to determine the amounts of individual operating, investing, and financing cash flows. In computing cash flows from operating activities, we began by using the direct method, in which major categories of both positive and negative cash flows were determined and presented.

We also illustrated the indirect method to determine the amount of operating cash flows. Rather than adjusting each individual operating cash flow category for changes in balance sheet accounts, these same adjustments were made to net income.

Exhibit 13–5 includes an expanded statement of cash flows for Allison Corporation. This statement uses the direct method for operating activities and includes two supplementary schedules.

*Supplementary Schedule A* in Exhibit 13–5 illustrates the determination of net cash flows from operating activities by the *indirect method. Supplementary Schedule B* in Exhibit 13–5

**Exhibit 13–5**

**ALLISON CORPORATION (EXPANDED) STATEMENT OF CASH FLOWS**

## ALLISON CORPORATION
## STATEMENT OF CASH FLOWS
### FOR THE YEAR ENDED DECEMBER 31, 2011

**Cash flows from operating activities:**

| | | |
|---|---|---|
| Net cash provided by operating activities (see Supplementary Schedule A) | | $ 50,000 |

**Cash flows from investing activities:**

| | | |
|---|---|---|
| Purchases of marketable securities | $ (65,000) | |
| Proceeds from sales of marketable securities | 40,000 | |
| Loans made to borrowers | (17,000) | |
| Collections on loans | 12,000 | |
| Cash paid to acquire plant assets (see Supplementary Schedule B) | (160,000) | |
| Proceeds from sales of plant assets | 75,000 | |
| Net cash used in investing activities | | (115,000) |

**Cash flows from financing activities:**

| | | |
|---|---|---|
| Proceeds from short-term borrowing | $ 45,000 | |
| Payments to settle short-term debts | (55,000) | |
| Proceeds from issuing bonds payable | 100,000 | |
| Proceeds from issuing capital stock | 50,000 | |
| Dividends paid | (40,000) | |
| Net cash provided by financing activities | | 100,000 |
| Net increase (decrease) in cash | | $ 35,000 |
| Cash and cash equivalents, Jan. 1, 2011 | | 20,000 |
| Cash and cash equivalents, Dec. 31, 2011 | | $ 55,000 |

### Supplementary Schedule A: Net Cash Provided by Operating Activities

| | | |
|---|---|---|
| Net income | | $ 65,000 |
| Add: Depreciation expense | | 40,000 |
| Decrease in accrued interest receivable | | 1,000 |
| Increase in accounts payable | | 15,000 |
| Increase in accrued liabilities | | 7,000 |
| Nonoperating loss on sales of marketable securities | | 4,000 |
| Subtotal | | $ 132,000 |
| Less: Increase in accounts receivable | $ 30,000 | |
| Increase in inventory | 10,000 | |
| Increase in prepaid expenses | 3,000 | |
| Decrease in accrued liabilities | 8,000 | |
| Nonoperating gain on sales of plant assets | 31,000 | 82,000 |
| Net cash provided by operating activities | | $ 50,000 |

### Supplementary Schedule B: Noncash Investing and Financing Activities

| | |
|---|---|
| Purchases of plant assets | $ 200,000 |
| Less: Portion financed through issuance of long-term debt | 40,000 |
| Cash paid to acquire plant assets | $ 160,000 |

**Notice this supplementary schedule illustrates the indirect method of determining cash flows from operations**

discloses any noncash aspects of the company's investing and financing activities. This type of supplementary schedule is required whenever some aspects of the company's investing and financing activities do not coincide with cash flows occurring within the current period.

How would the statement of cash flows in Exhibit 13–5 differ if the indirect method were used? The information included in Supplementary Schedule A would be moved up into the "Cash flows from operating activities" section of the financial statement and would no longer be required as a supplemental disclosure. In fact, this is one reason for the popularity of the indirect method. Because the indirect method calculation is required to be disclosed if the direct method is used, many companies simply prefer to include the reconciliation of net income to net cash from operating activities in the body of the statement of cash flows and avoid the need for the supplemental disclosure of that same information.

Preparing a Statement of Cash Flows

## Financial Analysis and Decision Making

The users of a statement of cash flows are particularly interested in the *net cash flows from operating activities*. Is the amount large enough to provide for necessary replacements of plant assets and maturing liabilities? And if so, is there enough left for the current dividend to look secure—or even be increased?

Consider two competitors in the import craft supplies business, Gonzalez, Inc., and Alvarez Company. These companies have approximately the same size assets, liabilities, and sales. Selected information from their most recent statements of cash flows follows:

| | Beginning Cash Balance | Net Cash Flow from (in thousands) | | | Ending Cash Balance |
| --- | --- | --- | --- | --- | --- |
| | | Operating Activities | Investing Activities | Financing Activities | |
| Gonzalez | $150 | $600 | $(500) | $400 | $650 |
| Alvarez | 150 | 50 | 500 | (50) | 650 |

Which company is in the stronger cash flow position? Although both have the same beginning and ending cash balances ($150,000 and $650,000, respectively), Gonzalez is in the stronger position because of its strong operating cash flows of $600,000. Gonzalez has been able to invest $500,000 in operating assets, while financing only $400,000, and still has a $650,000 ending cash balance. Alvarez, on the other hand, has generated only a small amount of cash from operations ($50,000) and has sold assets to generate cash ($500,000) to support its ending cash balance. Whether Alvarez will be able to sustain its cash position over time, and be able to meet its recurring obligations in the future, is questionable.

Even more important than net cash flows from operating activities in any one year is the *trend* in cash flows over a period of years—and the *consistency* of that trend from year to year. The best results are net cash flows from operating activities that increase each year by a substantial—but also predictable—percentage.[5]

**Free Cash Flow** Many analysts compute an amount called **free cash flow.** Free cash flow represents the cash flow available to management for discretionary purposes, *after* the company has met all of its basic obligations relating to business operations. The term *free cash flow* is widely cited within the business community. Different analysts compute this measure in different ways. For example, are all expenditures for plant assets "basic obligations," or only those expenditures made to maintain the current level of productive capacity?

One common method of computing free cash flow is to deduct from the net cash flows from operating activities net cash used to purchase plant assets and any dividends paid. This computation follows, using information from the Allison Corporation statement of cash flows shown earlier.

This computation suggests that Allison Corporation *did not* generate enough cash from operations to meet its basic obligations. Thus, management had to raise cash from other sources. But, of course, an analyst always should look behind the numbers. For example, was Allison's purchase of plant assets during the year a basic obligation, or did it represent a discretionary expansion of the business?

| | | |
| --- | --- | --- |
| Net cash flows from operating activities | | $ 50,000 |
| Less: Net cash used for acquiring plant assets ($160,000 − $75,000 proceeds) | $85,000 | |
| Dividends paid | 40,000 | 125,000 |
| Free cash flow | | $(75,000) |

 **What's left for discretionary purposes?**

---

[5] Percentage change is the dollar amount of change from one year to the next, expressed as a percentage of (divided by) the amount from the *earlier* of the two years. For example, if net cash provided by operating activities was $100,000 in the first year and $120,000 in the second year, the percentage increase is 20 percent, computed as follows: ($120,000 − $100,000) ÷ $100,000.

(*continued*)

You are working for the same stock market research firm as in Chapter 12, but unlike your previous boss (who tended to focus on growth and relative value, both based on reported earnings), your new boss focuses primarily on free cash flow and dividends in choosing stocks.

Your new boss is interested in stocks where free cash flow equals at least 50 percent of cash flow from operations. He also wants dividends to be 25 percent or more of cash flow from operations. You are considering the same stocks as before: Home Depot, Intel, Coca-Cola, and Amazon. Your new boss provides you with the following information and asks you to recommend which stocks are consistent with his investment criteria.

| Company | In Millions | | |
| --- | --- | --- | --- |
| | Cash Flow from Operations (CFO) | Net Capital Expenditures | Dividends |
| Home Depot.................. | $ 5,125 | $ 966 | $1,525 |
| Intel ....................... | 11,170 | 4,515 | 3,108 |
| Coca-Cola ................... | 8,186 | 1,993 | 3,800 |
| Amazon ..................... | 3,293 | 373 | — |

He also tells you that a potential new client is going to be calling you this afternoon. This potential client is an elderly widow who is quite wealthy, and she is curious as to why the relative levels of free cash flow and dividends are important metrics. She also doesn't understand why all firms don't pay dividends. Your boss tells you to answer this prospective client's questions.

(See our comments on the Online Learning Center Web site.)

## Managing Cash Flows

Management can do much to influence the cash flows of a particular period. In fact, it has a responsibility to manage cash flows. No business can afford to run out of cash and default on its obligations. Even being a few days late in meeting payrolls, or paying suppliers or creditors, can severely damage important business relationships. Thus, one of management's most basic responsibilities is to ensure that the business has enough cash to meet its obligations as they come due.

### BUDGETING: THE PRIMARY CASH MANAGEMENT TOOL

The primary tool used by management to anticipate and shape future cash flows is a *cash budget*. A **cash budget** is a *forecast* of future cash receipts and payments. This budget is *not* a financial statement and is not widely distributed to people outside of the organization. To managers, however, it is among the most useful of all accounting reports.

In many ways, a cash budget is similar to a statement of cash flows. However, the budget shows the results *expected in future periods,* rather than those achieved in the past. Also, the cash budget is more *detailed,* usually showing expected cash flows month-by-month and separately for every department within the organization.

Cash budgets serve many purposes. Among the most important are:

- Encouraging managers to plan and coordinate the activities of their departments in advance.
- Providing managers with advance notice of the resources at their disposal and the results they are expected to achieve.
- Providing targets useful in evaluating departmental performance.
- Providing advance warnings of potential cash shortages.

## WHAT PRIORITY SHOULD MANAGERS GIVE TO INCREASING NET CASH FLOWS?

Creditors and investors look to a company's cash flows to protect their investment and provide future returns. Trends in key cash flows (such as from operations and free cash flow) affect a company's credit rating, stock price, and access to additional investment capital. For these reasons, management is under constant pressure to improve the key measures of cash flow. Unfortunately, the pressure to report higher cash flows in the current period may *conflict* with managers' long-run responsibilities.

**Learning Objective**
Discuss the likely effects of various business strategies on cash flows.  LO8

### Short-Term Results versus Long-Term Growth

Often, short-term operating results can be improved at the expense of long-term growth. For example, reducing expenditures for developing new products will increase earnings and net cash flows in the current period. But over time, this strategy may lessen the company's competitiveness and long-term profitability.

### One-Time Boosts to Cash Flows

Some strategies can increase the net cash flows of the current period, but *without having much effect* on future cash flows. Such strategies include collecting receivables more quickly and reducing the size of inventory.

Assume, for example, that a company offers 60-day terms to its credit customers. Thus credit sales made in January are collected in March, and credit sales made in February are collected in April. Notice that in each month, the company is collecting about *one month's amount* of credit sales.

Now assume that on March 1 the company changes its policies to allow only *30-day* credit terms. In April, the company will collect *two months* of credit sales—those made in February (under the former 60-day terms) *and* those made in March (under the new 30-day terms).

This significantly increases the cash received from customers for the month of April. But it does not signal higher cash flows for the months ahead. In May, the company will collect only those credit sales made in April. Thus it quickly returns to the pattern of collecting about *one month's* credit sales in the current month. Shortening the collection period provided only a one-time boost in cash receipts.

A similar one-time boost may be achieved by reducing the size of inventory. This reduces the need for purchasing merchandise, *but only while inventory levels are falling.* Once the company stabilizes the size of its inventory at the new and lower level, its monthly purchases must return to approximately the quantity of goods sold during the period.

## SOME STRATEGIES FOR PERMANENT IMPROVEMENTS IN CASH FLOW

Several strategies may improve cash flows in *both* the short and long term. These are *deferring income taxes, peak pricing,* and developing an *effective product mix.*

### Deferring Income Taxes

*Deferring* income taxes means using accounting methods for income tax purposes that legally postpone the payment of income taxes. An example is using an *accelerated depreciation method* for income tax purposes.

Deferring taxes may benefit a growing business *every year.* Thus, it is an effective and popular cash management strategy.[6]

---

[6] The Modified Accelerated Cost Recovery System (MACRS) is an accelerated method widely used for income tax purposes. Deferred income taxes were discussed briefly in Chapter 10. The reason a growing business can benefit from deferred taxes *every year* is that each year it defers a *greater amount* than comes due from the past.

584    **Chapter 13** Statement of Cash Flows

**Peak Pricing**    Some businesses have more customers than they can handle—at least at certain times of the day or year. Examples of such businesses include popular restaurants, resort hotels, telephone companies, and providers of electricity.

**Peak pricing** is a strategy of using sales prices both to increase revenue and to ration goods and services when total demand exceeds supply (or capacity). A higher price is charged during the peak periods of customer demand and a lower price during off-peak periods. Peak pricing has two related goals. First, it *increases the seller's revenue* during the periods of greatest demand. Second, it *shifts* some of the demand to off-peak periods, when the business is better able to service additional customers.

Peak pricing may make goods and services available to customers who otherwise could not afford them. Also, peak pricing may prevent systems, such as cellular telephones, from becoming so overloaded that they simply cannot function. Peak pricing is *not always appropriate*. For example, we would not expect hospitals or physicians to raise their prices during epidemics or natural disasters. The alternative to peak pricing is a single price all the time.

**Develop an Effective Product Mix**    Another tool for increasing revenue and cash receipts is the mix of products offered for sale. The dual purposes of an effective **product mix** are to (1) increase total sales and (2) increase gross margins (that is, the excess of the selling price over the cost of the product).

Some products complement one another, meaning the customer who buys one product often may purchase the other. Common examples of **complementary products** include french fries at a hamburger restaurant, snacks at a movie theater, and a car wash connected to a gas station.

© PunchStock/Brand X Pictures/DAL

## Ethics, Fraud & Corporate Governance

As discussed in this chapter, cash flow from operations is the subtotal on the statement of cash flows that is most closely scrutinized by financial statement readers. A large and growing cash flow from operations is viewed positively for at least three reasons. First, companies pay bills with cash, not with earnings. Second, a company with significant cash flows from operations is better positioned to fund future growth with its own cash flows rather than having to borrow additional monies or issue more stock. Third, the quality of a company's earnings is viewed as better if cash flow from operations closely matches reported net income.

Although it may be difficult to manipulate cash flows from operations, it is not impossible, as the Securities and Exchange Commission (SEC) enforcement action involving Dynergy, Inc., illustrates. Dynergy produces and delivers energy, including natural gas, electricity, and coal, to customers throughout North America and Europe, and its shares are traded on the New York Stock Exchange. Dynergy entered into a structured transaction (hereafter referred to as Project Alpha) that resulted in Dynergy reporting $300 million in cash flow from operations that should have been reported as cash flow from financing activities.

A primary motivation for Dynergy's involvement with Project Alpha was to bring cash flow from operations closer to reported net income.

Project Alpha had a five-year term and worked as follows. Dynergy sponsored a special-purpose entity, ABG Supply, to sell Dynergy natural gas. In the first year of the five-year term of Project Alpha, ABG Supply sold Dynergy gas at below-market prices. Dynergy then sold this gas at a $300 million profit and reported the resulting cash flow in the operating activities portion of the statement of cash flows. In the remaining four years of Project Alpha's life, Dynergy was obligated to buy gas from ABG Supply at above-market prices. These purchases at above-market prices would be sufficient to pay back the $300 million, plus interest. In substance, the original sale of gas to Dynergy in year 1 at $300 million below market prices represented a loan, and transactions in years 2 to 5 would result in the loan being repaid with interest. As such, the $300 million cash flow in Year 1 should have been reported in the financing activities portion of the statement of cash flows—not in the operating activities portion of the statement.

Three midlevel Dynergy tax executives were largely responsible for Project Alpha's structure, and they

*(continued)*

participated in an active scheme to hide the details of the structure from **Dynergy**'s outside auditors. Two of these executives pled guilty to federal *criminal* charges and testified against the third executive. The third executive, Jamie Olis, was convicted of criminal charges and was sentenced to over 20 years in federal prison (although this sentence was reduced substantially on appeal). This case clearly illustrates the personal risk of violating securities laws, particularly when there is an active scheme to hide the true nature of transactions from auditors, investors, and other outside parties.

Some complementary products are *essential* to satisfying the customer. (Would you be happy at a sports stadium that didn't sell food?) Others increase sales by *attracting customers* who also purchase other types of merchandise.

Some complementary products appear to be only incidental to the company's main product lines. But, in reality, these incidental items may *be* the company's most important products.

## A Worksheet for Preparing a Statement of Cash Flows

A statement of cash flows is developed by *systematically analyzing all changes in the noncash balance sheet accounts.* This process can be formalized and documented through the preparation of a specially designed worksheet. The worksheet also provides the accountant with visual assurance that the changes in balance sheet accounts have been fully explained.

**Learning Objective**
Explain how a worksheet may be helpful in preparing a statement of cash flows. **LO9**

### DATA FOR AN ILLUSTRATION

We will illustrate the worksheet approach using the 2011 financial data of Auto Supply Co.[7] Shown in Exhibit 13–6 are the balances in Auto's balance sheet accounts at the beginning and

| AUTO SUPPLY CO. COMPARATIVE BALANCE SHEETS | | |
|---|---|---|
| | **December 31, 2010** | **2011** |
| **Assets** | | |
| Cash | $ 50,000 | $ 45,000 |
| Marketable Securities | 40,000 | 25,000 |
| Accounts Receivable | 320,000 | 330,000 |
| Inventory | 240,000 | 235,000 |
| Plant and Equipment (net of accumulated depreciation) | 600,000 | 640,000 |
| Totals | $1,250,000 | $1,275,000 |
| **Liabilities & Stockholders' Equity** | | |
| Accounts Payable | $ 150,000 | $ 160,000 |
| Accrued Expenses Payable | 60,000 | 45,000 |
| Mortgage Note Payable (long-term) | –0– | 70,000 |
| Bonds Payable (due in 2020) | 500,000 | 350,000 |
| Capital Stock (no par value) | 160,000 | 160,000 |
| Retained Earnings | 380,000 | 490,000 |
| Totals | $1,250,000 | $1,275,000 |

**Exhibit 13–6**

**AUTO SUPPLY CO. BALANCE SHEETS**

Changes in the noncash accounts are the key to identifying cash flows

---

[7] Our example involving Allison Corporation was quite comprehensive. Therefore, a worksheet for Allison Corporation would be too long and detailed for use as an introductory illustration of a worksheet for the statement of cash flows.

end of 2011. (Notice in this illustration that the account balances at the end of the current year appear in the *right-hand* column. This format also is used in the worksheet.)

### Additional Information

The following information also is used in the preparation of the worksheet. (Accrual-based measurements appear in blue, cash flows in red.)

1. Net income for the year amounted to *$250,000*. Cash dividends of *$140,000* were declared and paid.
2. Auto's only noncash expense was depreciation, which totaled *$60,000*.
3. Marketable securities costing *$15,000* were sold for *$35,000* cash, resulting in a *$20,000* nonoperating gain.
4. The company purchased plant assets for *$100,000*, making a *$30,000* cash down payment and issuing a *$70,000* mortgage note payable for the balance of the purchase price.

### THE WORKSHEET

Auto Supply Co. reports cash flows from operating activities by the *indirect method.*[8] A worksheet for preparing a statement of cash flows appears in Exhibit 13–7.

To set up the worksheet, the company's balance sheet accounts are listed in the top portion of the worksheet, with the beginning balances in the first column and the year-end balances in the last (right-hand) column. (For purposes of illustration, we have shown these accounts and account balances in **black.**)

The two middle columns are used to (1) explain the changes in each balance sheet account over the year and (2) indicate how each change affected cash.

### Entries in the Two Middle Columns

The entries in the *top portion of the worksheet* summarize the transactions recorded in the account over the year. (Because these entries summarize transactions recorded on the accrual basis, they are shown in blue.)

For each summary entry in the top portion of the worksheet, we make an offsetting entry (in the opposite column) in the *bottom portion* of the worksheet indicating the *cash effects* of the transactions. These cash effects are classified as operating, investing, or financing activities and are explained with a descriptive caption. (Entries representing the *cash effects* of transactions and the related descriptive captions appear in red.)

Entries in the two middle columns may be made in any sequence, but we recommend the following approach:

1. Explain the change in the Retained Earnings account.
2. Account for depreciation expense (and any other noncash expenses).
3. Account for timing differences between net income and cash flows from operating activities.
4. Explain any remaining changes in balance sheet accounts *other than Cash.* (Hint: Changes in asset accounts represent investing activities; changes in liability and equity accounts represent financing activities.)
5. Compute and record the net increase or decrease in cash.

Using this approach, we next explain the entries in our illustrated worksheet.

### ENTRY

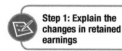

**Step 1: Explain the changes in retained earnings**

1. Auto's net income explains a $250,000 *credit* to the Retained Earnings account. In the bottom portion of the working paper, an offsetting entry is made in the *Sources* column and is classified as an operating activity.[9]
2. Cash dividends of $140,000 caused a *debit* to the Retained Earnings account during 2011. The offsetting entry falls into the *Uses* column; payments of dividends are classified as a financing activity.

---

[8] If the worksheet utilizes the direct method, numerous subclassifications are required within the operating activities section. Such worksheets are illustrated in more advanced accounting courses.

[9] When the *indirect method* is used, net income serves as the *starting point* for computing net cash flows from operating activities.

A Worksheet for Preparing a Statement of Cash Flows

**587**

Exhibit 13-7

**WORKSHEET FOR A STATEMENT OF CASH FLOWS**

**AUTO SUPPLY CO.**
**WORKSHEET FOR A STATEMENT OF CASH FLOWS**
**FOR THE YEAR ENDED DECEMBER 31, 2011**

| Balance sheet effects: | Beginning Balance | Effects of Transactions Debit Changes | Effects of Transactions Credit Changes | Ending Balance |
|---|---|---|---|---|
| **Assets** | | | | |
| Cash and Cash Equivalents ....... | 50,000 | | (x)  5,000 | 45,000 |
| Marketable Securities ........... | 40,000 | | (8)  15,000 | 25,000 |
| Accounts Receivable ........... | 320,000 | (4)  10,000 | | 330,000 |
| Inventory ................... | 240,000 | | (5)  5,000 | 235,000 |
| Plant and Equipment (net of accumulated depreciation) .... | 600,000 | (9) 100,000 | (3)  60,000 | 640,000 |
| Totals ................... | 1,250,000 | | | 1,275,000 |
| **Liabilities & Stockholders' Equity** | | | | |
| Accounts Payable.............. | 150,000 | | (6)  10,000 | 160,000 |
| Accrued Expenses Payable ....... | 60,000 | (7)  15,000 | | 45,000 |
| Mortgage Note Payable ......... | –0– | | (9)  70,000 | 70,000 |
| Bonds Payable................ | 500,000 | (10) 150,000 | | 350,000 |
| Capital Stock ................. | 160,000 | | | 160,000 |
| Retained Earnings ............. | 380,000 | (2) 140,000 | (1) 250,000 | 490,000 |
| Totals ................... | 1,250,000 | 415,000 | 415,000 | 1,275,000 |

| Cash effects: | Sources | Uses |
|---|---|---|
| **Operating activities:** | | |
| Net income ...................... | (1) 250,000 | |
| Depreciation expense............. | (3)  60,000 | |
| Increase in accounts receivable ........... | | (4)  10,000 |
| Decrease in inventory................. | (5)  5,000 | |
| Increase in accounts payable.............. | (6)  10,000 | |
| Decrease in accrued expenses payable ..... | | (7)  15,000 |
| Gain on sales of marketable securities ............. | | (8)  20,000 |
| **Investing activities:** | | |
| Proceeds from sales of marketable securities ....... | (8)  35,000 | |
| Cash paid to acquire plant assets ...................... | | (9)  30,000 |
| **Financing activities:** | | |
| Dividends paid .................... | | (2) 140,000 |
| Payments to retire bonds payable .......... | | (10) 150,000 |
| Subtotals...................... | 360,000 | 365,000 |
| Net decrease in cash ....... | (x)  5,000 | |
| Totals ..................... | 365,000 | 365,000 |

Up here we summarize the changes in each noncash account

Down here we identify and classify the related cash effects of these changes

Cash provided by operations— $280,000

Cash provided by investing activities— $5,000

Cash used in financing activities— $290,000

With these first two entries, we have explained how Auto's Retained Earnings account increased during 2011 from $380,000 to $490,000.

3. Auto's only noncash expense was depreciation. In the top portion of the worksheet, depreciation explains a $60,000 credit (decrease) in Plant and Equipment (which includes the Accumulated Depreciation accounts). The offsetting entry in the

**Step 2: Account for noncash expenses**

bottom of the worksheet is placed in the Sources column. We have explained that depreciation is not really a source of cash, but that it *is added back* to net income as a step in computing the cash flows from operating activities.

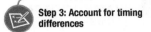

**Step 3: Account for timing differences**

4–7. Fluctuations in current assets and current liabilities create *timing differences* between net income and the net cash flows from operating activities. In the top portion of the worksheet, entries (4) through (7) summarize the changes in these current asset and current liability accounts. In the bottom portion, they show how these changes affect the computation of cash flows from operating activities.

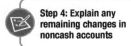

**Step 4: Explain any remaining changes in noncash accounts**

8. In 2011, Auto sold marketable securities with a cost of $15,000 for $35,000 cash, resulting in a $20,000 nonoperating gain. In the top portion of the worksheet, the entry explains the $15,000 credit change in the Marketable Securities account. In the bottom portion, it reports cash proceeds of $35,000. The difference? The $20,000 nonoperating gain, which is *removed from the Operating Activities section* of the worksheet and included instead within the amount reported as "Proceeds from sales of marketable securities" in the Investing Activities category.

9. Auto purchased $100,000 in plant assets, paying $30,000 cash and issuing a $70,000 note payable. These events explain a $100,000 debit in Plant and Equipment and the $70,000 credit change in Mortgage Note Payable; they involved a cash outlay of $30,000, which is classified as an investing activity. (The $70,000 financed by issuance of a note payable is a *noncash* investing and financing activity.)

**Exhibit 13–8**

**AUTO SUPPLY CO. STATEMENT OF CASH FLOWS**

**Compare the content of this statement with the worksheet in Exhibit 13–7**

| AUTO SUPPLY CO. STATEMENT OF CASH FLOWS FOR THE YEAR ENDED DECEMBER 31, 2011 | | |
|---|---:|---:|
| **Cash flows from operating activities:** | | |
| Net income . . . . . . . . . . . . . . . . . . . . . . . . . . . . . . . . . . . | | $ 250,000 |
| Add: Depreciation expense . . . . . . . . . . . . . . . . . . . . . . . . | | 60,000 |
|     Decrease in inventory . . . . . . . . . . . . . . . . . . . . . . . | | 5,000 |
|     Increase in accounts payable. . . . . . . . . . . . . . . . . . . | | 10,000 |
| Subtotal . . . . . . . . . . . . . . . . . . . . . . . . . . . . . . . . . . . . . . | | $ 325,000 |
| Less: Increase in accounts receivable . . . . . . . . . . . . . . . | $ 10,000 | |
|     Decrease in accrued expenses payable . . . . . . . . . . . . | 15,000 | |
|     Gain on sales of marketable securities . . . . . . . . . . . . | 20,000 | 45,000 |
| Net cash provided by operating activities . . . . . . . . . . . . . . . | | $ 280,000 |
| **Cash flows from investing activities:** | | |
| Proceeds from sales of marketable securities. . . . . . . . . . . | $ 35,000 | |
| Cash paid to acquire plant assets (see supplementary schedule below) . . . . . . . . . . . . . . . . . . . | (30,000) | |
| Net cash provided by investing activities . . . . . . . . . . . . . . . | | 5,000 |
| **Cash flows from financing activities:** | | |
| Dividends paid. . . . . . . . . . . . . . . . . . . . . . . . . . . . . . . . . | $ (140,000) | |
| Payments to retire bonds payable . . . . . . . . . . . . . . . . . . | (150,000) | |
| Net cash used for financing activities . . . . . . . . . . . . . . . . . | | (290,000) |
| Net decrease in cash . . . . . . . . . . . . . . . . . . . . . . . . . . . . . | | $ (5,000) |
| Cash and cash equivalents, Jan. 1, 2011 . . . . . . . . . . . . . . . | | 50,000 |
| Cash and cash equivalents, Dec. 31, 2011 . . . . . . . . . . . . . . | | $ 45,000 |
| **Supplementary Schedule: Noncash Investing and Financing Activities** | | |
| Purchases of plant assets. . . . . . . . . . . . . . . . . . . . . . . . . | | $ 100,000 |
| Less: Portion financed through issuance of long-term debt . . . . . . . . . . . . . . . . . . . . . . . . . . . . . . . | | 70,000 |
| Cash paid to acquire plant assets. . . . . . . . . . . . . . . . . . . . | | $ 30,000 |

10. The $150,000 debit change in Auto's Bonds Payable account indicates that this amount of the liability has been repaid—that is, $150,000 in bonds has been retired. This is included in the financing activities category.

At this point, we should check to determine that our entries in the two middle columns *fully explain* the differences between the beginning and ending balance of each noncash balance sheet account. If the top portion of the worksheet explains the changes in every noncash account, the bottom section should include all of the cash flows for the year.

   (x)  We now total the Sources (cash increases) and Uses (cash decreases) columns in the bottom portion of the worksheet. The difference between these column subtotals represents the *net increase or decrease* in cash. In our example, the Sources column totals $360,000, while the Uses column totals $365,000, indicating a *$5,000 decrease* in cash over the period. Notice that this is exactly the amount by which Cash decreased during 2011: $50,000 − $45,000 = $5,000. Our last entry, labeled *(x)*, explains the credit change in the Cash account at the top of the worksheet and brings the bottom of the worksheet into balance.

**Step 5: Compute and record the net change in cash**

The formal statement of cash flows, reporting the cash flows from operating activities by the indirect method, can be prepared directly from the bottom portion of this worksheet. In Exhibit 13–8, amounts appearing in accrual-based accounting records are shown in blue; cash flows appear in red.

## Concluding Remarks

In this chapter, we have discussed the importance of cash flow information for investors and creditors and how that information is arranged and presented in the statement of cash flows. We delayed in-depth coverage of this important topic to this point because of the importance of understanding accounting for assets, liabilities, and stockholders' equity as a forerunner to understanding how cash flow information differs from accrual accounting information.

As stated earlier, companies have an option of presenting cash flow from operations information by either the direct or the indirect method. Although we have presented both in this chapter, our emphasis has been on the direct method despite the fact that most companies employ the indirect method in their financial reporting. We have done this for two reasons. First, we believe the direct method is more readily understood by students and others who are learning for the first time how cash-based and accrual-based information relate. Second, and perhaps more important, investors appear to generally favor the direct method, as evidenced by the following quote from the former chief accountant of the Securities and Exchange Commission, speaking to a group of certified public accountants:

> I've heard many investors express a strong preference for use of the direct method of preparing the statement of cash flows. It's widely understood and believed by many to be a more informative presentation. We are not requiring a change, but it is an action you could consider to promote transparency given the importance to investors of cash flow information.[10]

In the next chapter, we take a broader look at financial statement analysis, including how information about cash flows is combined with information from the other financial statements, to better understand a company's financial activities. Managers and investors alike must look beyond short-term changes in earnings and cash flows from one period to the next. They must consider factors that cause these changes and how they may affect future operations. Throughout this text, we have introduced simple financial analysis techniques that are useful in analyzing a company. In Chapter 14, we bring those techniques together into a comprehensive model for analyzing financial statements in a way that assists informed decision makers in understanding a company's business activities and in anticipating the long-term effects of business strategies.

---

[10] Donald T. Nicolaisen in a speech entitled, "Remarks before the 2003 Thirty-First AICPA National Conference on Current SEC Developments," December 11, 2003.

# END-OF-CHAPTER REVIEW

## SUMMARY OF LEARNING OBJECTIVES

**LO1** **Explain the purposes and uses of a statement of cash flows.** The primary purpose of a statement of cash flows is to provide information about the cash receipts and cash payments of the entity and how they relate to the entity's operating, investing, and financing activities. Readers of financial statements use this information to assess the liquidity of a business and to evaluate its ability to generate positive cash flows in future periods, pay dividends, and finance growth.

**LO2** **Describe how cash transactions are classified in a statement of cash flows.** Cash flows are classified as (1) operating activities, (2) investing activities, or (3) financing activities. Receipts and payments of interest are classified as operating activities.

**LO3** **Compute the major cash flows relating to operating activities.** The major operating cash flows are (1) cash received from customers, (2) cash paid to suppliers and employees, (3) interest and dividends received, (4) interest paid, and (5) income taxes paid. These cash flows are computed by converting the income statement amounts for revenue, cost of goods sold, and expenses from the accrual basis to the cash basis. This is done by adjusting the income statement amounts for changes occurring over the period in related balance sheet accounts.

**LO4** **Compute the cash flows relating to investing and financing activities.** Cash flows from investing and financing activities are determined by examining the entries in the related asset and liability accounts, along with any related gains or losses shown in the income statement. Debit entries in asset accounts represent purchases of assets (an investing activity). Credit entries in asset accounts represent the cost of assets sold. The amount of these credit entries must be adjusted by any gains or losses recognized on these sales transactions.

Debit entries to liability accounts represent repayment of debt, while credit entries represent borrowing. Both types of transactions are classified as financing activities. Other financing activities include the issuance of stock (indicated by credits to the paid-in capital accounts) and payment of dividends (indicated by a debit change in the Retained Earnings account).

**LO5** **Distinguish between the direct and indirect methods of reporting operating cash flows.** The direct and indirect methods are alternative formats for reporting net cash flows from operating activities. The *direct* method shows the specific cash inflows and outflows comprising the operating activities of the business. By the *indirect* method, the computation begins with accrual-based net income and then makes adjustments necessary to arrive at net cash flows from operating activities. Both methods result in the same dollar amount of net cash flows from operating activities. When the direct method is used, the indirect method must also be disclosed.

**LO6** **Explain why net income differs from net cash flows from operating activities.** Net income differs from net operating cash flows for several reasons. One reason is noncash expenses, such as depreciation and the amortization of intangible assets. These expenses, which require no cash outlays when they are recognized, reduce net income but do not require cash payments. Another reason is the many timing differences existing between the recognition of revenue and expense and the occurrence of the underlying cash flows. Finally, nonoperating gains and losses enter into the determination of net income, but the related cash flows are classified as investing or financing activities, not operating activities.

**LO7** **Compute net cash flows from operating activities using the *indirect* method.** The indirect method uses net income (as reported in the income statement) as the starting point in the computation of net cash flows from operating activities. Adjustments to net income necessary to arrive at net cash flows from operating activities are described in three categories: noncash expenses, timing differences, and nonoperating gains and losses. Adjustments reconcile net income (accrual basis) to net cash flows from operating activities. Specific adjustments from each category are illustrated in the summary analysis of the indirect method on page 579.

**LO8** **Discuss the likely effects of various business strategies on cash flows.** It is difficult to predict the *extent* to which a business strategy will affect cash flows. However, an informed decision maker should understand the *direction* in which a strategy is likely to affect cash flows— both in the short term and over a longer term.

**LO9** **Explain how a worksheet may be helpful in preparing a statement of cash flows.** A worksheet can be used to analyze the changes in balance sheet accounts other than Cash and, thereby, determine the related cash flows. In the top portion of the worksheet, entries are made summarizing the changes in each noncash account. In the bottom half, offsetting entries are made to represent the cash effects of the transactions summarized in the top portion. The entries in the bottom half of the worksheet are classified into the same categories as in a statement of cash flows—operating, investing, and financing. The statement of cash flows then is prepared from the data in the bottom portion of the worksheet.

## Key Terms Introduced or Emphasized in Chapter 13

**accrual basis** (p. 567)  A method of summarizing operating results in terms of revenue earned and expenses incurred, rather than cash receipts or cash payments.

**cash basis** (p. 570)  The practice of summarizing operating results in terms of cash receipts and cash payments, rather than revenue earned or expenses incurred.

**cash budget** (p. 582)  A detailed forecast of expected future cash receipts, usually organized department by department and month by month for the coming year.

**cash equivalents** (p. 567)  Highly liquid short-term investments, such as Treasury bills, money market funds, and commercial paper. For purposes of preparing a statement of cash flows, money held in cash equivalents is considered the same as cash. Thus transfers between a bank account and cash equivalents are not considered receipts or disbursements of cash.

**cash flows** (p. 564)  A term describing both cash receipts (inflows) and cash payments (outflows).

**complementary products** (p. 584)  Products that "fit together"—that tie in with a company's other products. As a result, customers attracted to one product may also purchase others.

**financing activities** (p. 564)  Transactions such as borrowing, repaying borrowed amounts, raising equity capital, or making distributions to owners. The cash effects of these transactions are reported in the financing activities section of the statement of cash flows. Noncash aspects of these transactions are disclosed in a supplementary schedule.

**free cash flow** (p. 581)  The portion of the annual net cash flows from operating activities that remains available for discretionary purposes after the basic obligations of the business have been met. Can be computed in several different ways.

**investing activities** (p. 564)  Transactions involving acquisitions or sales of investments or plant assets and making or collecting loans. The cash aspects of these transactions are shown in the investing activities section of the statement of cash flows. Noncash aspects of these transactions are disclosed in a supplementary schedule to this financial statement.

**operating activities** (p. 564)  Transactions entering into the determination of net income, with the exception of gains and losses relating to financing or investing activities. The category includes such transactions as selling goods or services, earning investment income, and incurring costs and expenses, such as payments to suppliers and employees, interest, and income taxes. The cash effects of these transactions are reflected in the operating activities section of the statement of cash flows.

**peak pricing** (p. 584)  The strategy of charging a higher price during periods of high demand, and a lower price during periods of slack demand. Intended to both maximize revenue and shift excess demand to periods in which it can be more easily accommodated.

**product mix** (p. 584)  The variety and relative quantities of goods and services that a company offers for sale.

## Demonstration Problem

You are the chief accountant for Electro Products, Inc. Your assistant has prepared an income statement for the current year and has developed the following additional information by analyzing changes in the company's balance sheet accounts.

### ELECTRO PRODUCTS, INC.
### INCOME STATEMENT
### FOR THE YEAR ENDED DECEMBER 31, 2011

| | | |
|---|---:|---:|
| **Revenue:** | | |
| Net sales | | $9,500,000 |
| Interest income | | 320,000 |
| Gain on sales of marketable securities | | 70,000 |
| Total revenue and gains | | $9,890,000 |
| **Costs and expenses:** | | |
| Cost of goods sold | $4,860,000 | |
| Operating expenses (including depreciation of $700,000) | 3,740,000 | |
| Interest expense | 270,000 | |
| Income tax expense | 300,000 | |
| Loss on sales of plant assets | 90,000 | |
| Total costs, expenses, and losses | | 9,260,000 |
| Net income | | $ 630,000 |

Changes in the company's balance sheet accounts over the year are summarized as follows:

1. Accounts Receivable decreased by $85,000.

2. Accrued Interest Receivable increased by $15,000.

3. Inventory decreased by $280,000, and Accounts Payable to suppliers of merchandise decreased by $240,000.

4. Short-term prepayments of operating expenses decreased by $18,000, and accrued liabilities for operating expenses increased by $35,000.

5. The liability for Accrued Interest Payable decreased by $16,000 during the year.

6. The liability for Accrued Income Taxes Payable increased by $25,000 during the year.

7. The following schedule summarizes the total debit and credit entries during the year in other balance sheet accounts:

|  | Debit Entries | Credit Entries |
|---|---|---|
| Marketable Securities.................................... | $ 120,000 | $ 210,000 |
| Notes Receivable (cash loans made to others) .............. | 250,000 | 190,000 |
| Plant Assets (see paragraph **8**) ......................... | 3,800,000 | 360,000 |
| Notes Payable (short-term borrowing) .................... | 620,000 | 740,000 |
| Bonds Payable.......................................... |  | 1,100,000 |
| Capital Stock........................................... |  | 50,000 |
| Additional Paid-in Capital (from issuance of stock) .............. |  | 840,000 |
| Retained Earnings (see paragraph **9**) ..................... | 320,000 | 630,000 |

8. The $360,000 in credit entries to the Plant Assets account is net of any debits to accumulated depreciation when plant assets were retired. Thus, the $360,000 in credit entries represents the *book value* of all plant assets sold or retired during the year.

9. The $320,000 debit to Retained Earnings represents dividends declared and paid during the year. The $630,000 credit entry represents the net income for the year.

10. All investing and financing activities were cash transactions.

11. Cash and cash equivalents amounted to $448,000 at the beginning of the year and to $330,000 at year-end.

### Instructions

You are to prepare a statement of cash flows for the current year, following the format illustrated in Exhibit 13–1. Cash flows from operating activities are to be determined by the *direct method*. Place brackets around dollar amounts representing cash outlays. Show separately your computations of the following amounts:

a.   Cash received from customers.

b.   Interest received.

c.   Cash paid to suppliers and employees.

d.   Interest paid.

e.   Income taxes paid.

f.   Proceeds from sales of marketable securities.

g.   Proceeds from sales of plant assets.

h.   Proceeds from issuing capital stock.

## Solution to the Demonstration Problem

### ELECTRO PRODUCTS, INC.
### STATEMENT OF CASH FLOWS
### FOR THE YEAR ENDED DECEMBER 31, 2011

**Cash flows from operating activities:**

| | | |
|---|---|---|
| Cash received from customers **(a)** | $ 9,585,000 | |
| Interest received **(b)** | 305,000 | |
| Cash provided by operating activities | | $9,890,000 |
| Cash paid to suppliers and employees **(c)** | $(7,807,000) | |
| Interest paid **(d)** | (286,000) | |
| Income taxes paid **(e)** | (275,000) | |
| Cash disbursed for operating activities | | (8,368,000) |
| Net cash provided by operating activities | | $1,522,000 |

**Cash flows from investing activities:**

| | | |
|---|---|---|
| Purchases of marketable securities | $ (120,000) | |
| Proceeds from sales of marketable securities **(f)** | 280,000 | |
| Loans made to borrowers | (250,000) | |
| Collections on loans | 190,000 | |
| Cash paid to acquire plant assets | (3,800,000) | |
| Proceeds from sales of plant assets **(g)** | 270,000 | |
| Net cash used for investing activities | | (3,430,000) |

**Cash flows from financing activities:**

| | | |
|---|---|---|
| Proceeds from short-term borrowing | $ 740,000 | |
| Payments to settle short-term debts | (620,000) | |
| Proceeds from issuing bonds payable | 1,100,000 | |
| Proceeds from issuing capital stock **(h)** | 890,000 | |
| Dividends paid | (320,000) | |
| Net cash provided by financing activities | | 1,790,000 |
| Net increase (decrease) in cash | | $ (118,000) |
| Cash and cash equivalents, Jan. 1, 2011 | | 448,000 |
| Cash and cash equivalents, Dec. 31, 2011 | | $ 330,000 |

**Supporting computations:**

**a.** Cash received from customers:

| | |
|---|---|
| Net sales | $9,500,000 |
| Add: Decrease in accounts receivable | 85,000 |
| Cash received from customers | $9,585,000 |

**b.** Interest received:

| | |
|---|---|
| Interest income | $ 320,000 |
| Less: Increase in accrued interest receivable | 15,000 |
| Interest received | $ 305,000 |

**c.** Cash paid to suppliers and employees:

Cash paid for purchases of merchandise:

| | |
|---|---|
| Cost of goods sold | $4,860,000 |
| Less: Decrease in inventory | 280,000 |
| Net purchases | $4,580,000 |
| Add: Decrease in accounts payable to suppliers | 240,000 |
| Cash paid for purchases of merchandise | $4,820,000 |

### ELECTRO PRODUCTS, INC. (continued)
### STATEMENT OF CASH FLOWS
### FOR THE YEAR ENDED DECEMBER 31, 2011

|  |  |  |
|---|---:|---:|
| Cash paid for operating expenses: |  |  |
| Operating expenses . . . . . . . . . . . . . . . . . . . . . . . . . . . . . . . . . . . . . . . . . . |  | $3,740,000 |
| Less: Depreciation (a "noncash" expense) . . . . . . . . . . . . . . | $700,000 |  |
| Decrease in prepayments . . . . . . . . . . . . . . . . . . . . . . . . . | 18,000 |  |
| Increase in accrued liabilities for operating expenses . . . . . . . . . . . . . . . . . . . . . . . . . . | 35,000 | 753,000 |
| Cash paid for operating expenses . . . . . . . . . . . . . . . . . . . . . . . . . . . | | $2,987,000 |
| Cash paid to suppliers and employees ($4,820,000 + $2,987,000) . . . . . . . . . . . . . . . . . . . . . . . . . . . . . . . | | $7,807,000 |
| **d.** Interest paid: |  |  |
| Interest expense . . . . . . . . . . . . . . . . . . . . . . . . . . . . . . . . . . . . . . . . . | | $ 270,000 |
| Add: Decrease in accrued interest payable . . . . . . . . . . . . . . . . . . . . . | | 16,000 |
| Interest paid . . . . . . . . . . . . . . . . . . . . . . . . . . . . . . . . . . . . . . . . . | | $ 286,000 |
| **e.** Income taxes paid: |  |  |
| Income tax expense . . . . . . . . . . . . . . . . . . . . . . . . . . . . . . . . . . . . . . | | $ 300,000 |
| Less: Increase in accrued income taxes payable . . . . . . . . . . . . . . . . . . | | 25,000 |
| Income taxes paid . . . . . . . . . . . . . . . . . . . . . . . . . . . . . . . . . . . . . . | | $ 275,000 |
| **f.** Proceeds from sales of marketable securities: |  |  |
| Cost of marketable securities sold (credit entries to the Marketable Securities account) . . . . . . . . . . . . . . . . . . . . . . . . . . . . . . | | $ 210,000 |
| Add: Gain reported on sales of marketable securities . . . . . . . . . . . . . . | | 70,000 |
| Proceeds from sales of marketable securities . . . . . . . . . . . . . . . . . . . . | | $ 280,000 |
| **g.** Proceeds from sales of plant assets: |  |  |
| Book value of plant assets sold (paragraph **8**) . . . . . . . . . . . . . . . . . . . . | | $ 360,000 |
| Less: Loss reported on sales of plant assets . . . . . . . . . . . . . . . . . . . . . | | 90,000 |
| Proceeds from sales of plant assets . . . . . . . . . . . . . . . . . . . . . . . . . . . | | $ 270,000 |
| **h.** Proceeds from issuing capital stock: |  |  |
| Amounts credited to the Capital Stock account . . . . . . . . . . . . . . . . . . . . | | $ 50,000 |
| Add: Amounts credited to Additional Paid-in Capital account . . . . . . . . . . | | 840,000 |
| Proceeds from issuing capital stock . . . . . . . . . . . . . . . . . . . . . . . . . . . | | $ 890,000 |

## Self-Test Questions

*The answers to these questions appear on page 618.*

1. The statement of cash flows is designed to assist users in assessing each of the following, *except:*

   **a.** The ability of a company to remain liquid.

   **b.** The major sources of cash receipts during the period.

   **c.** The company's profitability.

   **d.** The reasons why net cash flows from operating activities differ from net income.

2. Which of the following is *not* included in the statement of cash flows, or in a supplementary schedule accompanying the statement of cash flows?

   **a.** Disclosure of investing or financing activities that did not involve cash.

   **b.** A reconciliation of net income to net cash flows from operating activities.

   **c.** Disclosure of the amount of cash invested in money market funds during the accounting period.

   **d.** The amount of cash and cash equivalents owned by the business at the end of the accounting period.

3. Cash flows are grouped in the statement of cash flows into the following major categories:

   **a.** Operating activities, investing activities, and financing activities.

   **b.** Cash receipts, cash disbursements, and noncash activities.

   **c.** Direct cash flows and indirect cash flows.

   **d.** Operating activities, investing activities, and collecting activities.

4. The following is a list of various cash payments and cash receipts:

| | |
|---|---|
| Cash paid to suppliers and employees . . . . . . . . | $420,000 |
| Dividends paid . . . . . . . . . . . . . . . . . . . . . . . . | 18,000 |
| Interest paid . . . . . . . . . . . . . . . . . . . . . . . . . . | 12,000 |
| Purchases of plant assets . . . . . . . . . . . . . . . . | 45,000 |
| Interest and dividends received . . . . . . . . . . . . | 17,000 |
| Payments to settle short-term bank loans . . . . . | 29,000 |
| Income taxes paid . . . . . . . . . . . . . . . . . . . . . . | 23,000 |
| Cash received from customers . . . . . . . . . . . . . | 601,000 |

Based only on the above items, net cash flows from operating activities are:

a. $138,000

b. $91,000

c. $120,000

d. $163,000

5. During the current year, two transactions were recorded in the Land account of Duke Industries. One involved a debit of $320,000 to the Land account; the second was a $210,000 credit to the Land account. Duke's income statement for the year reported a loss on sale of land in the amount of $25,000. All transactions involving the Land account were cash transactions. These transactions would be shown in the statement of cash flows as:

a. $320,000 cash provided by investing activities, and $210,000 cash disbursed for investing activities.

b. $185,000 cash provided by investing activities, and $320,000 cash disbursed for investing activities.

c. $235,000 cash provided by investing activities, and $320,000 cash disbursed for investing activities.

d. $210,000 cash provided by investing activities, and $320,000 cash disbursed for investing activities.

6. Which of the following business strategies is *most likely* to increase the net cash flows of a software developer in the short run but *reduce* them over a longer term?

a. Develop software that is more costly to create but easier to update and improve.

b. Lower the price of existing versions of products as customer demand begins to fall.

c. Reduce expenditures for the purpose of developing new products.

d. Purchase the building in which the business operates (assume the company currently rents this location).

---

**ASSIGNMENT MATERIAL**  **Discussion Questions**

1. Briefly state the purposes of a statement of cash flows.

2. Does a statement of cash flows or an income statement best measure the profitability of a financially sound business? Explain.

3. Give two examples of cash receipts and two examples of cash payments that fit into each of the following classifications:

   a. Operating activities.

   b. Investing activities.

   c. Financing activities.

4. Why are payments and receipts of interest classified as operating activities rather than as financing or investing activities?

5. In the long run, is it more important for a business to have positive cash flows from its operating activities, investing activities, or financing activities? Why?

6. Of the three types of business activities summarized in a statement of cash flows, which type is *least* likely to show positive net cash flows in a successful, growing business? Explain your reasoning.

7. Identify three factors that may cause net income to differ from net cash flows from operating activities.

8. Briefly explain the difference between the *direct* and *indirect methods* of computing net cash flows from operating activities. Which method results in higher net cash flows?

9. Moss, Inc., acquired land by issuing $665,000 of capital stock. No cash changed hands in this transaction. Will the transaction be disclosed in the company's statement of cash flows? Explain.

10. The only transaction recorded in the plant assets account of Pompei Company in the current year was a $220,000 credit to the Land account. Assuming that this credit resulted from a cash transaction, does this entry indicate a cash receipt or a cash payment? Should this $220,000 appear in the statement of cash flows, or is some adjustment necessary?

11. During the current year, the following credit entries were posted to the paid-in capital accounts of Crawford Shipyards:

| | |
|---|---|
| Capital Stock . . . . . . . . . . . . . . . . . . . . . | $12,000,000 |
| Additional Paid-in Capital . . . . . . . . . . . | 43,500,000 |

Explain the type of cash transaction that probably caused these credit changes, and illustrate the presentation of this transaction in a statement of cash flows.

12. At the beginning of the current year, Callifax Corporation had dividends payable of $1,500,000. During the current year, the company declared cash dividends of $4,300,000, of which $900,000 appeared as a liability at year-end. Determine the amount of cash dividends *paid* during this year.

13. Define the term *free cash flow*. Explain the significance of this measurement to (1) short-term creditors, (2) long-term creditors, (3) stockholders, and (4) management.

14. Explain the concept of *peak pricing* and provide an example from your own experience.

15. Explain why speeding up the collection of accounts receivable provides only a one-time increase in cash receipts.

## Brief Exercises

**L03**  **BRIEF EXERCISE 13.1**

Cash Flows from Operations (Direct)

Olympic, Inc., had the following positive and negative cash flows during the current year:

| Positive cash flows: | |
|---|---|
| Received from customers | $240,000 |
| Interest and dividends | 50,000 |
| Sale of plant assets | 330,000 |
| **Negative cash flows:** | |
| Paid to suppliers and employees | $127,000 |
| Purchase of investments | 45,000 |
| Purchase of treasury stock | 36,000 |

Determine the amount of cash provided by or used for operating activities by the direct method.

**L07**  **BRIEF EXERCISE 13.2**

Cash Flows from Operations (Indirect)

Garagiola Company had net income in the current year of $430,000. Depreciation expense for the year totaled $67,000. During the year the company experienced an increase in accounts receivable (all from sales to customers) of $35,000 and an increase in accounts payable (all to suppliers) of $56,000. Compute the amount of cash provided by or used for operating activities by the indirect method.

**L03**  **BRIEF EXERCISE 13.3**

Cash Flows from Operations (Direct)

Georgia Products Co. had the following positive cash flows during the current year: received cash from customers of $750,000; received bank loans of $35,000; and received cash from the sale of common stock of $145,000. During the same year, cash was paid out to purchase inventory for $335,000, to employees for $230,000, and for the purchase of plant assets of $190,000. Calculate the amount of cash provided by or used for operating activities by the direct method.

**L07**  **BRIEF EXERCISE 13.4**

Cash Flows from Operations (Indirect)

Patterson Company reported net income for the current year of $666,000. During the year the company's accounts receivable increased by $50,000, inventory decreased by $23,000, accounts payable decreased by $55,000, and accrued expenses payable increased by $14,000. Determine the amount of cash provided by or used for operating activities by the indirect method.

**L04**  **BRIEF EXERCISE 13.5**

Cash Flows from Investing

Old Alabama Company purchased investments for $45,000 and plant assets for $127,000 during the current year, during which it also sold plant assets for $66,000, at a gain of $6,000. The company also purchased treasury stock for $78,000 and sold a new issue of common stock for $523,000. Determine the amount of cash provided by or used for investing activities for the year.

**L04**  **BRIEF EXERCISE 13.6**

Cash Flows from Financing Activities

Texas, Inc., sold common stock for $560,000 and preferred stock for $36,000 during the current year. In addition, the company purchased treasury stock for $35,000 and paid dividends on common and preferred stock for $24,000. Determine the amount of cash provided by or used for financing activities during the year.

**L03**  **BRIEF EXERCISE 13.7**

Cash Payment for Merchandise

Dane, Inc., reported cost of goods sold of $100,100 during the current year. Following are the beginning and ending balances of merchandise inventory and accounts payable for the year:

| | Beginning | Ending |
|---|---|---|
| Merchandise inventory | $35,000 | $43,000 |
| Accounts payable | 23,000 | 30,000 |

Determine the amount of cash payments for purchases during the year.

**L02**   **BRIEF**
**EXERCISE 13.8**
Determining Beginning
Cash Balance

Tyler, Inc.'s cash balance at December 31, 2011, the end of its financial reporting year, was $155,000. During 2011, cash provided by operations was $145,000, cash used in investing activities was $67,000, and cash provided by financing activities was $10,000. Calculate the amount of Tyler's beginning cash balance at January 1, 2011.

**L06**   **BRIEF**
**EXERCISE 13.9**
Reconciling Net
Income to Cash from
Operations

Zephre Company reported net income for the year of $56,000. Depreciation expense for the year was $12,000. During the year, accounts receivable increased by $4,000, inventory decreased by $6,000, accounts payable increased by $3,000, and accrued expenses payable decreased by $2,000. Reconcile the amount of net income to the amount of cash provided by or used for operating activities.

**L02**   **BRIEF**
**EXERCISE 13.10**
Preparing Statement
of Cash Flows

Watson, Inc., had a cash balance at the beginning of the year of $89,000. During the year, the following cash flows occurred:

| | |
|---|---:|
| From operating activities | $136,000 |
| From investing activities | (56,000) |
| From financing activities | (34,000) |

Prepare an abbreviated statement of cash flows, including a reconciliation of the beginning and ending cash balances for the year.

## Exercises

 **L01**   **EXERCISE 13.1**
Using a Statement
of Cash Flows

**L02**

Wallace Company's statement of cash flows for the current year is summarized as follows:

| | |
|---|---:|
| Cash provided by operating activities | $200,000 |
| Cash used in investing activities | (120,000) |
| Cash provided by financing activities | 88,000 |
| Increase in cash during the year | $168,000 |
| Cash balance, beginning of the year | 75,000 |
| Cash balance, end of the year | $243,000 |

**a.** Briefly explain what is included in each of the first three categories listed (i.e., the cash from operating, investing, and financing activities categories).

**b.** On the basis of the limited information presented above, describe the company's change in cash position during the year and your interpretation of the strength of the company's current (end-of-year) cash position.

 **L01**   **EXERCISE 13.2**
Using a Statement
of Cash Flows

**L02**

 **L06**

Auto Supply Company's 2011 statement of cash flows appears in Exhibit 13–8. Study the statement and respond to the following questions:

**a.** What was the company's free cash flow in 2011?

**b.** What were the major sources and uses of cash from financing activities during 2011? Did the net effect of financing activities result in an increase or a decrease in cash during the year?

**c.** What happened to the total amount of cash and cash equivalents during the year? Assuming 2011 was a typical year, is the firm in a position to continue its dividend payments in the future? Explain.

**d.** Look at the reconciliation of net income to net cash provided by operating activities, and explain the following:

1. Net loss (gain) from the sale of marketable securities.

2. Increase in accounts receivable.

**LO4**

**EXERCISE 13.3**

Computing Cash Flows

An analysis of the Marketable Securities control account of Prosper Products, Inc., shows the following entries during the year:

| | |
|---|---|
| Balance, Jan. 1 | $ 290,000 |
| Debit entries | 125,000 |
| Credit entries | (140,000) |
| Balance, Dec. 31 | $ 275,000 |

In addition, the company's income statement includes a $35,000 loss on sales of marketable securities. None of the company's marketable securities is considered a cash equivalent.

Compute the amounts that should appear in the statement of cash flows as:

**a.** Purchases of marketable securities.

**b.** Proceeds from sales of marketable securities.

**LO3**

**LO6**

**EXERCISE 13.4**

Comparing Net Sales and Cash Receipts

During the current year, Tachnic, Inc., made cash sales of $285,000 and credit sales of $460,000. During the year, accounts receivable decreased by $32,000.

**a.** Compute for the current year the amounts of:

1. Net sales reported as revenue in the income statement.

2. Cash received from collecting accounts receivable.

3. Cash received from customers.

**b.** Write a brief statement explaining *why* cash received from customers differs from the amount of net sales.

**LO3**

**EXERCISE 13.5**

Computing Cash Paid for Purchases of Merchandise

The general ledger of MPX, Inc., provides the following information relating to purchases of merchandise:

| | End of Year | Beginning of Year |
|---|---|---|
| Inventory | $820,000 | $780,000 |
| Accounts payable to merchandise suppliers | 430,000 | 500,000 |

The company's cost of goods sold during the year was $2,975,000. Compute the amount of cash payments made during the year to suppliers of merchandise.

**LO3**

**LO6**

**EXERCISE 13.6**

Reporting Lending Activities and Interest Revenue

During the current year, Maine Savings and Loan Association made new loans of $15 million. In addition, the company collected $36 million from borrowers, of which $30 million was interest revenue. Explain how these cash flows will appear in the company's statement of cash flows, indicating the classification and the dollar amount of each cash flow.

**LO2**

**EXERCISE 13.7**

Format of a Statement of Cash Flows

The accounting staff of Wyoming Outfitters, Inc., has assembled the following information for the year ended December 31, 2011:

| | |
|---|---:|
| Cash and cash equivalents, Jan. 1. . . . . . . . . . . . . . . . . . . . . . . . . . . . . . . . . . . . . | $ 35,800 |
| Cash and cash equivalents, Dec. 31 . . . . . . . . . . . . . . . . . . . . . . . . . . . . . . . . . . | 74,800 |
| Cash paid to acquire plant assets . . . . . . . . . . . . . . . . . . . . . . . . . . . . . . . . . . . | 21,000 |
| Proceeds from short-term borrowing . . . . . . . . . . . . . . . . . . . . . . . . . . . . . . . . | 10,000 |
| Loans made to borrowers . . . . . . . . . . . . . . . . . . . . . . . . . . . . . . . . . . . . . . . . | 5,000 |
| Collections on loans (excluding interest) . . . . . . . . . . . . . . . . . . . . . . . . . . . . . . | 4,000 |
| Interest and dividends received . . . . . . . . . . . . . . . . . . . . . . . . . . . . . . . . . . . | 27,000 |
| Cash received from customers . . . . . . . . . . . . . . . . . . . . . . . . . . . . . . . . . . . . | 795,000 |
| Proceeds from sales of plant assets . . . . . . . . . . . . . . . . . . . . . . . . . . . . . . . . . | 9,000 |
| Dividends paid . . . . . . . . . . . . . . . . . . . . . . . . . . . . . . . . . . . . . . . . . . . . . . | 55,000 |
| Cash paid to suppliers and employees . . . . . . . . . . . . . . . . . . . . . . . . . . . . . . | 635,000 |
| Interest paid . . . . . . . . . . . . . . . . . . . . . . . . . . . . . . . . . . . . . . . . . . . . . . . | 19,000 |
| Income taxes paid . . . . . . . . . . . . . . . . . . . . . . . . . . . . . . . . . . . . . . . . . . . | 71,000 |

Using this information, prepare a statement of cash flows. Include a proper heading for the financial statement, and classify the given information into the categories of operating activities, investing activities, and financing activities. Determine net cash flows from operating activities by the direct method. Place brackets around the dollar amounts of all cash disbursements.

**L08**

**EXERCISE 13.8**

Effects of Business Strategies

Indicate how you would expect the following strategies to affect the company's net cash flows from *operating activities* (1) in the near future and (2) in later periods (after the strategy's long-term effects have "taken hold"). *Fully explain your reasoning.*

**a.** A successful pharmaceutical company substantially reduces its expenditures for research and development.

**b.** A restaurant that previously sold only for cash adopts a policy of accepting bank credit cards, such as Visa and MasterCard.

**c.** A manufacturing company reduces by 50 percent the size of its inventories of raw materials (assume no change in inventory storage costs).

**d.** Through tax planning, a rapidly growing real estate developer is able to defer significant amounts of income taxes.

**e.** A rapidly growing software company announces that it will stop paying cash dividends for the foreseeable future and will instead distribute stock dividends.

**L06**

**EXERCISE 13.9**

An Analysis of Possible Reconciling Items

**L07**

An analysis of the annual financial statements of Conner Corporation reveals the following:

**a.** The company had a $5 million extraordinary loss from insurance proceeds received due to a tornado that destroyed a factory building.

**b.** Depreciation for the year amounted to $8 million.

**c.** During the year, $2 million in cash was transferred from the company's checking account into a money market fund.

**d.** Accounts receivable from customers increased by $4 million over the year.

**e.** Cash received from customers during the year amounted to $167 million.

**f.** Prepaid expenses decreased by $1 million over the year.

**g.** Dividends declared during the year amounted to $7 million; dividends paid during the year amounted to $6 million.

**h.** Accounts payable (to suppliers of merchandise) increased by $2.5 million during the year.

**i.** The liability for accrued income taxes payable amounted to $5 million at the beginning of the year and $3 million at year-end.

In the computation of net cash flows from operating activities by the *indirect method*, explain whether each of the above items should be *added to net income, deducted from net income,* or *omitted from the computation.* Briefly explain your reasons for each answer.

**EXERCISE 13.10**
Computation of Net
Cash Flows from
Operating Activities—
Indirect Method

The following data are taken from the income statement and balance sheet of Keaner Machinery, Inc.:

| | Dec. 31, 2011 | Jan. 1, 2011 |
|---|---|---|
| **Income statement:** | | |
| Net Income . . . . . . . . . . . . . . . . . . . . . . . . . . . . . . . . . . . . . . . . | $385,000 | |
| Depreciation Expense. . . . . . . . . . . . . . . . . . . . . . . . . . . . . . . . | 125,000 | |
| Amortization of Intangible Assets . . . . . . . . . . . . . . . . . . . . . . . | 40,000 | |
| Gain on Sale of Plant Assets . . . . . . . . . . . . . . . . . . . . . . . . . | 90,000 | |
| Loss on Sale of Investments . . . . . . . . . . . . . . . . . . . . . . . . . . | 35,000 | |
| **Balance sheet:** | | |
| Accounts Receivable. . . . . . . . . . . . . . . . . . . . . . . . . . . . . . . . . . | $335,000 | $380,000 |
| Inventory. . . . . . . . . . . . . . . . . . . . . . . . . . . . . . . . . . . . . . . . . . . | 503,000 | 575,000 |
| Prepaid Expenses. . . . . . . . . . . . . . . . . . . . . . . . . . . . . . . . . . . | 22,000 | 10,000 |
| Accounts Payable (to merchandise suppliers) . . . . . . . . . . . . . . . | 379,000 | 410,000 |
| Accrued Expenses Payable . . . . . . . . . . . . . . . . . . . . . . . . . . . . | 180,000 | 155,000 |

Using this information, prepare a partial statement of cash flows for the year ended December 31, 2011, showing the computation of net cash flows from operating activities by the *indirect* method.

 **EXERCISE 13.11**
Classifying Cash
Flows

Among the transactions of Beeler, Inc., were the following:

**a.** Made payments on accounts payable to merchandise suppliers.

**b.** Paid the principal amount of a note payable to First Bank.

**c.** Paid interest charges relating to a note payable to First Bank.

**d.** Issued bonds payable for cash; management plans to use this cash in the near future to expand manufacturing and warehouse capabilities.

**e.** Paid salaries to employees in the finance department.

**f.** Collected an account receivable from a customer.

**g.** Transferred cash from the general bank account into a money market fund.

**h.** Used the cash received in **d**, above, to purchase land and a building suitable for a manufacturing facility.

**i.** Made a year-end adjusting entry to recognize depreciation expense.

**j.** At year-end, purchased for cash an insurance policy covering the next 12 months.

**k.** Paid the quarterly dividend on preferred stock.

**l.** Paid the semiannual interest on bonds payable.

**m.** Received a quarterly dividend from an investment in the preferred stock of another corporation.

**n.** Sold for cash an investment in the preferred stock of another corporation.

**o.** Received cash upon the maturity of an investment in cash equivalents. (Ignore interest.)

**Instructions**

Most of the preceding transactions should be included among the activities summarized in a statement of cash flows. For each transaction that should be included in this statement, indicate whether the transaction should be classified as an operating activity, an investing activity, or a financing activity. If the transaction *should not be included* in the current year's statement of cash flows, briefly explain why not. (Assume that net cash flows from operating activities are determined by the *direct method*.)

 **EXERCISE 13.12**
Classifying Cash
Flows

Among the transactions of Marvel Manufacturing were the following:

**1.** Made payments on accounts payable to office suppliers.

**2.** Paid the principal amount of a mortgage to Seventh Bank.

**3.** Paid interest charges relating to a mortgage to Seventh Bank.

**4.** Issued preferred stock for cash; management plans to use this cash in the near future to purchase another company.

5. Paid salaries to employees in the finance department.

6. Collected an account receivable from a customer.

7. Transferred cash from the general bank account into a money market fund.

8. Used the cash received in **4**, above, to purchase Moran Manufacturing Co.

9. Made a year-end adjusting entry to recognize amortization expense.

10. At year-end, purchased for cash an advertising spot on a local radio station for the next eight months.

11. Paid the annual dividend on preferred stock.

12. Paid the semiannual interest on bonds payable.

13. Received a semiannual dividend from an investment in the common stock of another corporation.

14. Sold for cash an investment in the common stock of another corporation.

15. Received cash upon the maturity of an investment in cash equivalents. (Ignore interest.)

### Instructions

Most of the preceding transactions should be included among the activities summarized in a statement of cash flows. For each transaction that should be included in this statement, indicate whether the transaction should be classified as an operating activity, an investing activity, or a financing activity. If the transaction *should not be included* in the current year's statement of cash flows, briefly explain why not. (Assume that net cash flows from operating activities are determined by the *direct method*.)

**L04**

**EXERCISE 13.13**

Cash Flows from Investing Activities

Wofford Company provides the following information related to its investing and financing activities for the current year:

| Cash receipts: | |
| --- | --- |
| Sale of common stock | $250,000 |
| Sale of equipment (at $34,000 loss) | 156,000 |
| Sale of land (at $50,000 gain) | 160,000 |
| **Cash payments:** | |
| Purchase of equipment | $178,000 |
| Purchase of treasury stock | 45,000 |
| Retirement of debt | 36,500 |
| Dividends on preferred and common stock | 75,000 |

a. Calculate the net amount of cash provided by or used for investing activities for the year.

b. What impact, if any, do the following facts have on your calculation? (**1**) Equipment was sold at a loss, and (**2**) land was sold at a gain.

c. Briefly explain your decision to exclude any of the items listed above if they were not included in your calculation in part **a**.

**L04**

**EXERCISE 13.14**

Cash Flows from Financing Activities

Shepherd Industries had the following cash flows by major categories during the current year:

| Cash provided by: | |
| --- | --- |
| Receipts from customers | $560,000 |
| Sale of bonds | 400,000 |
| Sale of treasury stock | 34,000 |
| Interest and dividends received | 56,000 |
| Sale of equipment (at a $56,000 loss) | 236,000 |
| **Cash used for:** | |
| Payments to employees | $135,000 |
| Payments to purchase inventory | 190,000 |
| Dividends on common stock | 60,000 |
| Purchase of treasury stock | 20,000 |
| Interest expense | 78,000 |

**602**     Chapter 13 Statement of Cash Flows

a.  Calculate the net amount of cash provided by or used for financing activities for the year.

b.  Briefly justify why you excluded any of the above items in your calculation in part **a**.

c.  Briefly explain your treatment of interest expense in your calculation in part **a**.

**LO1**
**LO2**
**LO4**

**EXERCISE 13.15**

Home Depot, Inc.

Using a Statement
of Cash Flows

Statements of cash flow for Home Depot, Inc., for 2009, 2008, and 2007 are included in Appendix A of this text.

a.  Focus on the information for 2009 (year ending January 31, 2010). How does net earnings compare with net cash provided by or used in operations, and what accounts for the primary difference between the two amounts?

b.  What are the major uses of cash, other than operations, and how have these varied over the three-year period presented?

c.  Cash flows from both investing and financing activities have been mostly negative for all three years presented. Considering Home Depot's overall cash flows, including its cash flows from operations, would you say that this leads to a negative interpretation of Home Depot's cash position at January 31, 2010? Why or why not?

d.  Calculate the amount of free cash flow for each of 2007, 2008, and 2009, and comment briefly on your conclusion concerning this information.

## Problem Set A

**LO2**
**through**
**LO4**

**PROBLEM 13.1A**

Format of a Statement
of Cash Flows

The accounting staff of Harris Company has assembled the following information for the year ended December 31, 2011:

| | |
|---|---:|
| Cash sales | $ 800,000 |
| Credit sales | 2,500,000 |
| Collections on accounts receivable | 2,200,000 |
| Cash transferred from the money market fund to the general bank account | 250,000 |
| Interest and dividends received | 100,000 |
| Purchases (all on account) | 1,800,000 |
| Payments on accounts payable to merchandise suppliers | 1,500,000 |
| Cash payments for operating expenses | 1,050,000 |
| Interest paid | 180,000 |
| Income taxes paid | 95,000 |
| Loans made to borrowers | 500,000 |
| Collections on loans (excluding receipts of interest) | 260,000 |
| Cash paid to acquire plant assets | 3,100,000 |
| Book value of plant assets sold | 660,000 |
| Loss on sales of plant assets | 80,000 |
| Proceeds from issuing bonds payable | 2,500,000 |
| Dividends paid | 120,000 |
| Cash and cash equivalents, Jan. 1 | 489,000 |

### Instructions

Prepare a statement of cash flows in the format illustrated in Exhibit 13–1. Place brackets around amounts representing cash outflows. Use the *direct method* of reporting cash flows from operating activities.

Some of the items above will be listed in your statement without change. However, you will have to combine certain given information to compute the amounts of (1) collections from customers, (2) cash paid to suppliers and employees, and (3) proceeds from sales of plant assets. (Hint: Not every item listed is used in preparing a statement of cash flows.)

**LO4**

**PROBLEM 13.2A**

Reporting Investing
Activities

An analysis of the income statement and the balance sheet accounts of Headrick, Inc., at December 31, 2011, provides the following information:

| Income statement items: | |
| --- | --- |
| Gain on Sale of Marketable Securities . . . . . . . . . . . . . . . . . . . . . . . . . . . . . . . . . | $ 42,000 |
| Loss on Sales of Plant Assets . . . . . . . . . . . . . . . . . . . . . . . . . . . . . . . . . . . . . . . | 33,000 |
| **Analysis of balance sheet accounts:** | |
| **Marketable Securities account:** | |
| Debit entries . . . . . . . . . . . . . . . . . . . . . . . . . . . . . . . . . . . . . . . . . . . . . . . . . . . | $ 75,000 |
| Credit entries . . . . . . . . . . . . . . . . . . . . . . . . . . . . . . . . . . . . . . . . . . . . . . . . . . | 90,000 |
| **Notes Receivable account:** | |
| Debit entries . . . . . . . . . . . . . . . . . . . . . . . . . . . . . . . . . . . . . . . . . . . . . . . . . . | 210,000 |
| Credit entries . . . . . . . . . . . . . . . . . . . . . . . . . . . . . . . . . . . . . . . . . . . . . . . . . . | 162,000 |
| **Plant and Equipment accounts:** | |
| Debit entries to plant asset accounts . . . . . . . . . . . . . . . . . . . . . . . . . . . . . . . . | 196,000 |
| Credit entries to plant asset accounts . . . . . . . . . . . . . . . . . . . . . . . . . . . . . . . . | 120,000 |
| Debit entries to accumulated depreciation accounts . . . . . . . . . . . . . . . . . . . . | 75,000 |

### Additional Information

1. Except as noted in **4** below, payments and proceeds relating to investing transactions were made in cash.

2. The marketable securities are not cash equivalents.

3. All notes receivable relate to cash loans made to borrowers, not to receivables from customers.

4. Purchases of new equipment during the year ($196,000) were financed by paying $60,000 in cash and issuing a long-term note payable for $136,000.

5. Debits to the accumulated depreciation accounts are made whenever depreciable plant assets are retired. Thus, the book value of plant assets retired during the year was $45,000 ($120,000 − $75,000).

### Instructions

a. Prepare the investing activities section of a statement of cash flows. Show supporting computations for the amounts of (1) proceeds from sales of marketable securities and (2) proceeds from sales of plant assets. Place brackets around numbers representing cash outflows.

b. Prepare the supporting schedule that should accompany the statement of cash flows in order to disclose the noncash aspects of the company's investing and financing activities.

c. Assume that Headrick's management expects approximately the same amount of cash to be used for investing activities next year. In general terms, explain how the company might generate cash for this purpose.

**L04  PROBLEM 13.3A**
Reporting Investing
Activities

An analysis of the income statement and the balance sheet accounts of Hayes Export Co. at December 31, 2011 provides the following information:

| Income statement items: | |
| --- | --- |
| Gain on Sale of Plant Assets . . . . . . . . . . . . . . . . . . . . . . . . . . . . . . . . . . . . . . . | $ 12,000 |
| Loss on Sales of Marketable Securities . . . . . . . . . . . . . . . . . . . . . . . . . . . . . . . | 16,000 |
| **Analysis of balance sheet accounts:** | |
| **Marketable Securities account:** | |
| Debit entries . . . . . . . . . . . . . . . . . . . . . . . . . . . . . . . . . . . . . . . . . . . . . . . . . . | $ 78,000 |
| Credit entries . . . . . . . . . . . . . . . . . . . . . . . . . . . . . . . . . . . . . . . . . . . . . . . . . . | 62,000 |
| **Notes Receivable account:** | |
| Debit entries . . . . . . . . . . . . . . . . . . . . . . . . . . . . . . . . . . . . . . . . . . . . . . . . . . | 55,000 |
| Credit entries . . . . . . . . . . . . . . . . . . . . . . . . . . . . . . . . . . . . . . . . . . . . . . . . . . | 60,000 |
| **Plant and Equipment accounts:** | |
| Debit entries to plant asset accounts . . . . . . . . . . . . . . . . . . . . . . . . . . . . . . . . | 150,000 |
| Credit entries to plant asset accounts . . . . . . . . . . . . . . . . . . . . . . . . . . . . . . . . | 140,000 |
| Debit entries to accumulated depreciation accounts . . . . . . . . . . . . . . . . . . . . | 100,000 |

### Additional Information

1. Except as noted in **4** below, payments and proceeds relating to investing transactions were made in cash.

2. The marketable securities are not cash equivalents.

3. All notes receivable relate to cash loans made to borrowers, not to receivables from customers.

4. Purchases of new equipment during the year ($150,000) were financed by paying $50,000 in cash and issuing a long-term note payable for $100,000.

5. Debits to the accumulated depreciation accounts are made whenever depreciable plant assets are sold or retired. Thus, the book value of plant assets sold or retired during the year was $40,000 ($140,000 − $100,000).

### Instructions

a. Prepare the investing activities section of a statement of cash flows. Show supporting computations for the amounts of (1) proceeds from sales of marketable securities and (2) proceeds from sales of plant assets. Place brackets around amounts representing cash outflows.

b. Prepare the supplementary schedule that should accompany the statement of cash flows in order to disclose the noncash aspects of the company's investing and financing activities.

c. Does management have *more* control or *less* control over the timing and amount of cash outlays for investing activities than for operating activities? Explain.

L03
L08

**PROBLEM 13.4A**

Reporting Operating Cash Flows by the Direct Method

The following income statement and selected balance sheet account data are available for Treece, Inc., at December 31, 2011:

| TREECE, INC. INCOME STATEMENT FOR THE YEAR ENDED DECEMBER 31, 2011 | | |
|---|---:|---:|
| **Revenue:** | | |
| Net sales | | $2,850,000 |
| Dividend income | | 104,000 |
| Interest income | | 70,000 |
| Gain on sales of marketable securities | | 4,000 |
| Total revenue and gains | | $3,028,000 |
| **Costs and expenses:** | | |
| Cost of goods sold | $1,550,000 | |
| Operating expenses | 980,000 | |
| Interest expense | 185,000 | |
| Income tax expense | 90,000 | |
| Total costs and expenses | | 2,805,000 |
| Net income | | $ 223,000 |

| | End of Year | Beginning of Year |
|---|---:|---:|
| **Selected account balances:** | | |
| Accounts receivable | $ 650,000 | $ 720,000 |
| Accrued interest receivable | 9,000 | 6,000 |
| Inventories | 800,000 | 765,000 |
| Short-term prepayments | 20,000 | 15,000 |
| Accounts payable (merchandise suppliers) | 570,000 | 562,000 |
| Accrued operating expenses payable | 65,000 | 94,000 |
| Accrued interest payable | 21,000 | 12,000 |
| Accrued income taxes payable | 22,000 | 35,000 |

### Additional Information

1. Dividend revenue is recognized on the cash basis. All other income statement amounts are recognized on the accrual basis.
2. Operating expenses include depreciation expense of $115,000.

### Instructions

a. Prepare a partial statement of cash flows, including only the *operating activities* section of the statement and using the *direct method*. Place brackets around numbers representing cash payments. Show supporting computations for the following:

1. Cash received from customers
2. Interest and dividends received
3. Cash paid to suppliers and employees
4. Interest paid
5. Income taxes paid

b. Management of Treece, Inc., is exploring ways to increase the cash flows from operations. One way that cash flows could be increased is through more aggressive collection of receivables. Assuming that management has already taken all the steps possible to increase revenue and reduce expenses, describe two other ways that cash flows from operations could be increased.

---

**L08**
**L07**
**PROBLEM 13.5A**
Reporting Operating Cash Flows by the Indirect Method

Using the information presented in Problem **13.4A,** prepare a partial statement of cash flows for the current year, showing the computation of net cash flows from operating activities by the *indirect method*. Explain why the decline in accounts receivable over the year was *added* to net income in computing the cash flows from operating activities.

---

**L02**
**through**
**L04**
**L06**
**L08**
**PROBLEM 13.6A**
Preparing a Statement of Cash Flows: A Comprehensive Problem without a Worksheet

You are the controller for 21st Century Technologies. Your staff has prepared an income statement for the current year and has developed the following additional information by analyzing changes in the company's balance sheet accounts.

| 21st CENTURY TECHNOLOGIES INCOME STATEMENT FOR THE YEAR ENDED DECEMBER 31, 2011 | | |
|---|---|---|
| **Revenue:** | | |
| Net sales........................................ | | $3,200,000 |
| Interest revenue ..................................... | | 40,000 |
| Gain on sales of marketable securities ................... | | 34,000 |
| Total revenue and gains............................ | | $3,274,000 |
| **Costs and expenses:** | | |
| Cost of goods sold ................................ | $1,620,000 | |
| Operating expenses (including depreciation of $150,000) ..................................... | 1,240,000 | |
| Interest expense.................................... | 42,000 | |
| Income tax expense ................................ | 100,000 | |
| Loss on sales of plant assets ......................... | 12,000 | |
| Total costs, expenses, and losses .................... | | 3,014,000 |
| Net income....................................... | | $ 260,000 |

### Additional Information

1. Accounts receivable increased by $60,000.
2. Accrued interest receivable decreased by $2,000.

3.  Inventory decreased by $60,000, and accounts payable to suppliers of merchandise decreased by $16,000.

4.  Short-term prepayments of operating expenses increased by $6,000, and accrued liabilities for operating expenses decreased by $8,000.

5.  The liability for accrued interest payable increased by $4,000 during the year.

6.  The liability for accrued income taxes payable decreased by $14,000 during the year.

7.  The following schedule summarizes the total debit and credit entries during the year in other balance sheet accounts:

|  | Debit Entries | Credit Entries |
| --- | --- | --- |
| Marketable Securities . . . . . . . . . . . . . . . . . . . . . . . . . . . . . . . . . . . . . . . | $ 60,000 | $ 38,000 |
| Notes Receivable (cash loans made to borrowers) . . . . . . . . . . . . . . . | 44,000 | 28,000 |
| Plant Assets (see paragraph **8**) . . . . . . . . . . . . . . . . . . . . . . . . . . . . . | 500,000 | 36,000 |
| Notes Payable (short-term borrowing) . . . . . . . . . . . . . . . . . . . . . . . . | 92,000 | 82,000 |
| Capital Stock . . . . . . . . . . . . . . . . . . . . . . . . . . . . . . . . . . . . . . . . . . . . . |  | 20,000 |
| Additional Paid-in Capital—Capital Stock . . . . . . . . . . . . . . . . . . . . . |  | 160,000 |
| Retained Earnings (see paragraph **9**) . . . . . . . . . . . . . . . . . . . . . . . . | 120,000 | 260,000 |

8.  The $36,000 in credit entries to the Plant Assets account is net of any debits to Accumulated Depreciation when plant assets were retired. Thus, the $36,000 in credit entries represents the book value of all plant assets sold or retired during the year.

9.  The $120,000 debit to Retained Earnings represents dividends declared and paid during the year. The $260,000 credit entry represents the net income shown in the income statement.

10. All investing and financing activities were cash transactions.

11. Cash and cash equivalents amounted to $244,000 at the beginning of the year and to $164,000 at year-end.

### Instructions

a.  Prepare a statement of cash flows for the current year. Use the *direct method* of reporting cash flows from operating activities. Place brackets around dollar amounts representing cash out-flows. Show separately your computations of the following amounts:

1.  Cash received from customers

2.  Interest received

3.  Cash paid to suppliers and employees

4.  Interest paid

5.  Income taxes paid

6.  Proceeds from sales of marketable securities

7.  Proceeds from sales of plant assets

8.  Proceeds from issuing capital stock

b.  Explain the *primary reason* why:

1.  The amount of cash provided by operating activities was substantially greater than the company's net income.

2.  There was a net decrease in cash over the year, despite the substantial amount of cash provided by operating activities.

c.  As 21st Century's controller, you think that through more efficient cash management, the company could have held the increase in accounts receivable for the year to $10,000, with-out affecting net income. Explain how holding down the growth in receivables affects cash. Compute the effect that limiting the growth in receivables to $10,000 would have had on the company's net increase or decrease in cash (and cash equivalents) for the year.

Problem Set A

**PROBLEM 13.7A**

LO1 through LO9

Prepare and Analyze a Statement of Cash Flows with a Worksheet

eXcel

Satellite 2010 was founded in 2010 to apply a new technology for efficiently transmitting closed-circuit (cable) television signals without the need for an in-ground cable. The company earned a profit of $115,000 in 2010, its first year of operations, even though it was serving only a small test market. In 2011, the company began dramatically expanding its customer base. Management expects both sales and net income to more than triple in each of the next five years.

Comparative balance sheets at the end of 2010 and 2011, the company's first two years of operations, follow. (Notice that the balances at the end of the current year appear in the right-hand column.)

**Additional Information**

The following information regarding the company's operations in 2011 is available in either the company's income statement or its accounting records:

1. Net income for the year was $440,000. The company has never paid a dividend.
2. Depreciation for the year amounted to $147,000.
3. During the year the company purchased plant assets costing $2,200,000, for which it paid $1,850,000 in cash and financed $350,000 by issuing a long-term note payable. (Much of the cash used in these purchases was provided by short-term borrowing, as described below.)
4. In 2011, Satellite 2010 borrowed $1,450,000 against a $6 million line of credit with a local bank. In its balance sheet, the resulting obligations are reported as notes payable (short-term).
5. Additional shares of capital stock (no par value) were issued to investors for $500,000 cash.

| SATELLITE 2010 COMPARATIVE BALANCE SHEETS | | |
|---|---|---|
| | **December 31,** | |
| | **2010** | **2011** |
| **Assets** | | |
| Cash and cash equivalents . . . . . . . . . . . . . . . . . . . . . . . . . . . . | $ 80,000 | $ 37,000 |
| Accounts receivable . . . . . . . . . . . . . . . . . . . . . . . . . . . . . . . | 100,000 | 850,000 |
| Plant and equipment (net of accumulated depreciation) . . . . . . . . . . . . . . . . . . . . . . . . . . . . . . . . | 600,000 | 2,653,000 |
| Totals . . . . . . . . . . . . . . . . . . . . . . . . . . . . . . . . . . . . . . . | $780,000 | $3,540,000 |
| **Liabilities & Stockholders' Equity** | | |
| Notes payable (short-term) . . . . . . . . . . . . . . . . . . . . . . . . . . | $ –0– | $1,450,000 |
| Accounts payable . . . . . . . . . . . . . . . . . . . . . . . . . . . . . . . . | 30,000 | 63,000 |
| Accrued expenses payable . . . . . . . . . . . . . . . . . . . . . . . . . . | 45,000 | 32,000 |
| Notes payable (long-term) . . . . . . . . . . . . . . . . . . . . . . . . . . | 390,000 | 740,000 |
| Capital stock (no par value) . . . . . . . . . . . . . . . . . . . . . . . . . | 200,000 | 700,000 |
| Retained earnings . . . . . . . . . . . . . . . . . . . . . . . . . . . . . . . | 115,000 | 555,000 |
| Totals . . . . . . . . . . . . . . . . . . . . . . . . . . . . . . . . . . . . . . | $780,000 | $3,540,000 |

**Instructions**

a. Prepare a worksheet for a statement of cash flows, following the general format illustrated in Exhibit 13–7. (*Note:* If this problem is completed as a group assignment, each member of the group should be prepared to explain in class all entries in the worksheet, as well as the group's conclusions in parts **c** and **d**.)

b. Prepare a formal statement of cash flows for 2011, including a supplementary schedule of noncash investing and financing activities. (Follow the format illustrated in Exhibit 13–8. Cash provided by operating activities is to be presented by the *indirect method.*)

c. Briefly explain how operating activities can be a net *use* of cash when the company is operating so profitably.

d. Because of the expected rapid growth, management forecasts that operating activities will be an even greater use of cash in the year 2012 than in 2011. If this forecast is correct, does Satellite 2010 appear to be heading toward illiquidity? Explain.

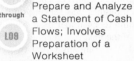

**PROBLEM 13.8A**

L01 through L08

Prepare and Analyze a Statement of Cash Flows; Involves Preparation of a Worksheet

eXcel

Miracle Tool, Inc., sells a single product (a combination screwdriver, pliers, hammer, and crescent wrench) exclusively through television advertising. The comparative income statements and balance sheets are for the past two years.

**Additional Information**

The following information regarding the company's operations in 2011 is available from the company's accounting records:

1. Early in the year the company declared and paid a $4,000 cash dividend.

2. During the year marketable securities costing $15,000 were sold for $14,000 cash, resulting in a $1,000 nonoperating loss.

3. The company purchased plant assets for $20,000, paying $2,000 in cash and issuing a note payable for the $18,000 balance.

4. During the year the company repaid a $10,000 note payable, but incurred an additional $18,000 in long-term debt as described in **3.**

5. The owners invested $15,000 cash in the business as a condition of the new loans described in paragraph **4.**

### MIRACLE TOOL, INC.
### COMPARATIVE INCOME STATEMENT
### FOR THE YEARS ENDED DECEMBER 31, 2010 AND 2011

|  | 2010 | 2011 |
|---|---|---|
| Sales | $500,000 | $350,000 |
| Less: Cost of goods sold | 200,000 | 140,000 |
| Gross profit on sales | $300,000 | $210,000 |
| Less: Operating expenses (including depreciation of $34,000 in 2010 and $35,000 in 2011) | 260,000 | 243,000 |
| Loss on sale of marketable securities | –0– | 1,000 |
| Net income (loss) | $ 40,000 | ($ 34,000) |

### MIRACLE TOOL, INC.
### COMPARATIVE BALANCE SHEETS

|  | December 31, 2010 | 2011 |
|---|---|---|
| **Assets** |  |  |
| Cash and cash equivalents | $ 10,000 | $ 60,000 |
| Marketable securities | 20,000 | 5,000 |
| Accounts receivable | 40,000 | 23,000 |
| Inventory | 120,000 | 122,000 |
| Plant and equipment (net of accumulated depreciation) | 300,000 | 285,000 |
| Totals | $490,000 | $495,000 |
| **Liabilities & Stockholders' Equity** |  |  |
| Accounts payable | $ 50,000 | $ 73,000 |
| Accrued expenses payable | 17,000 | 14,000 |
| Note payable | 245,000 | 253,000 |
| Capital stock (no par value) | 120,000 | 135,000 |
| Retained earnings | 58,000 | 20,000 |
| Totals | $490,000 | $495,000 |

**Instructions**

a. Prepare a worksheet for a statement of cash flows, following the general format illustrated in Exhibit 13–7. (*Note:* If this problem is completed as a group assignment, each member of the group should be prepared to explain in class all entries in the worksheet, as well as the group's conclusions in parts **c, d,** and **e.**)

b. Prepare a formal statement of cash flows for 2011, including a supplementary schedule of noncash investing and financing activities. (Use the format illustrated in Exhibit 13–8. Cash provided by operating activities is to be presented by the *indirect method.*)

c. Explain how Miracle Tool, Inc., achieved positive cash flows from operating activities, despite incurring a net loss for the year.

d. Does the company's financial position appear to be improving or deteriorating? Explain.

e. Does Miracle Tool, Inc., appear to be a company whose operations are growing or contracting? Explain.

f. Assume that management *agrees* with your conclusions in parts **c, d,** and **e.** What decisions should be made and what actions (if any) should be taken? Explain.

## Problem Set B

 **L02** **PROBLEM 13.1B**
*through*
**L04** Format of a Statement of Cash Flows

The accounting staff of Best Company has assembled the following information for the year ended December 31, 2011:

| | |
|---|---:|
| Cash sales ................................................. | $ 230,000 |
| Credit sales .............................................. | 3,450,000 |
| Collections on accounts receivable ................................... | 2,810,000 |
| Cash transferred from the money market fund to the general bank account ....................................................... | 200,000 |
| Interest and dividends received ...................................... | 40,000 |
| Purchases (all on account) ........................................... | 1,822,000 |
| Payments on accounts payable to merchandise suppliers................. | 1,220,000 |
| Cash payments for operating expenses................................ | 930,000 |
| Interest paid ........................................................ | 130,000 |
| Income taxes paid .................................................. | 65,000 |
| Loans made to borrowers ........................................... | 690,000 |
| Collections on loans (excluding receipts of interest) .................... | 300,000 |
| Cash paid to acquire plant assets .................................... | 1,700,000 |
| Book value of plant assets sold ...................................... | 520,000 |
| Loss on sales of plant assets ........................................ | 30,000 |
| Proceeds from issuing bonds payable ................................ | 2,000,000 |
| Dividends paid ...................................................... | 250,000 |
| Cash and cash equivalents, Jan. 1.................................... | 115,000 |

**Instructions**

Prepare a statement of cash flows in the format illustrated in Exhibit 13–1. Place brackets around amounts representing cash outflows. Use the *direct method* of reporting cash flows from operating activities.

Some of the items above will be listed in your statement without change. However, you will have to combine certain given information to compute the amounts of (1) collections from customers, (2) cash paid to suppliers and employees, and (3) proceeds from sales of plant assets. (Hint: Not every item listed above is used in preparing a statement of cash flows.)

**L04** **PROBLEM 13.2B**
Reporting Investing Activities

An analysis of the income statement and the balance sheet accounts of Schmatah Fashions at December 31, 2011, provides the following information:

| Income statement items: | |
|---|---|
| Gain on Sales of Marketable Securities ............................... | $ 15,000 |
| Loss on Sales of Plant Assets ...................................... | 10,000 |
| **Analysis of balance sheet accounts:** | |
| **Marketable Securities account:** | |
| Debit entries .......................................... | 65,000 |
| Credit entries ......................................... | 74,000 |
| **Notes Receivable account:** | |
| Debit entries .......................................... | 175,000 |
| Credit entries ......................................... | 50,000 |
| **Plant and Equipment accounts:** | |
| Debit entries to plant asset accounts ............................... | 220,000 |
| Credit entries to plant asset accounts .............................. | 150,000 |
| Debit entries to accumulated depreciation accounts ................... | 60,000 |

### Additional Information

1. Except as noted in **4,** payments and proceeds relating to investing transactions were made in cash.

2. The marketable securities are not cash equivalents.

3. All notes receivable relate to cash loans made to borrowers, not to receivables from customers.

4. Purchases of new equipment during the year ($220,000) were financed by paying $70,000 in cash and issuing a long-term note payable for $150,000.

5. Debits to the accumulated depreciation accounts are made whenever depreciable plant assets are retired. Thus, the book value of plant assets retired during the year was $90,000 ($150,000 − $60,000).

### Instructions

a. Prepare the investing activities section of a statement of cash flows. Show supporting computations for the amounts of (1) proceeds from sales and marketable securities and (2) proceeds from sales from plant assets. Place brackets around numbers representing cash outflows.

b. Prepare the supporting schedule that should accompany the statement of cash flows in order to disclose the noncash aspects of the company's investing and financing activities.

c. Assume that Schmatah Fashions's management expects approximately the same amount of cash to be used for investing activities next year. In general terms, explain how the company might generate cash for this purpose.

**L04**   **PROBLEM 13.3B**
Reporting Investing
Activities

An analysis of the income statement and the balance sheet accounts of RPZ Imports at December 31, 2011, provides the following information:

| Income statement items: | |
|---|---|
| Gain on Sales of Plant Assets ...................................... | $ 6,000 |
| Loss on Sales of Marketable Securities ............................... | 8,000 |
| **Analysis of balance sheet accounts:** | |
| **Marketable Securities account:** | |
| Debit entries .......................................... | 59,000 |
| Credit entries ......................................... | 60,000 |
| **Notes Receivable account:** | |
| Debit entries .......................................... | 40,000 |
| Credit entries ......................................... | 31,000 |
| **Plant and Equipment accounts:** | |
| Debit entries to plant asset accounts ............................... | 140,000 |
| Credit entries to plant asset accounts .............................. | 100,000 |
| Debit entries to accumulated depreciation accounts ................... | 75,000 |

### Additional Information

1. Except as noted in **4,** payments and proceeds relating to investing transactions were made in cash.
2. The marketable securities are not cash equivalents.
3. All notes receivable relate to cash loans made to borrowers, not to receivables from customers.
4. Purchases of new equipment during the year ($140,000) were financed by paying $50,000 in cash and issuing a long-term note payable for $90,000.
5. Debits to the accumulated depreciation accounts are made whenever depreciable plant assets are retired. Thus, the book value of plant assets sold or retired during the year was $25,000 ($100,000 − $75,000).

### Instructions

a. Prepare the investing activities section of a statement of cash flows. Show supporting computations for the amounts of (1) proceeds from sales and marketable securities and (2) proceeds from sales from plant assets. Place brackets around numbers representing cash outflows.

b. Prepare the supplementary schedule that should accompany the statement of cash flows in order to disclose the noncash aspects of the company's investing and financing activities.

c. Does management have *more* control or *less* control over the timing and amount of cash outlays for investing activities than for operating activities? Explain.

**L03**  **PROBLEM 13.4B**

Reporting Operating  
**L08**  Cash Flows by the  
Direct Method

The following income statement and selected balance sheet account data are available for Royce Interiors, Inc., at December 31, 2011:

| ROYCE INTERIORS, INC. INCOME STATEMENT FOR THE YEAR ENDED DECEMBER 31, 2011 | | |
|---|---|---|
| **Revenue:** | | |
| Net sales | | $2,600,000 |
| Dividend income | | 55,000 |
| Interest income | | 40,000 |
| Gain on sales of marketable securities | | 3,000 |
| Total revenue and gains | | $2,698,000 |
| **Costs and expenses:** | | |
| Cost of goods sold | $1,300,000 | |
| Operating expenses | 300,000 | |
| Interest expense | 60,000 | |
| Income tax expense | 110,000 | |
| Total costs and expenses | | $1,770,000 |
| Net income | | $ 928,000 |

| | End of Year | Beginning of Year |
|---|---|---|
| **Selected account balances:** | | |
| Accounts receivable | $ 450,000 | $ 440,000 |
| Accrued interest receivable | 7,000 | 3,000 |
| Inventories | 575,000 | 550,000 |
| Short-term prepayments | 9,000 | 8,000 |
| Accounts payable (merchandise suppliers) | 415,000 | 410,000 |
| Accrued operating expenses payable | 86,000 | 90,000 |
| Accrued interest payable | 10,000 | 8,000 |
| Accrued income taxes payable | 20,000 | 22,000 |

### Additional Information

1. Dividend revenue is recognized on the cash basis. All other income statement amounts are recognized on the accrual basis.
2. Operating expenses include depreciation expense of $49,000.

### Instructions

a. Prepare a partial statement of cash flows, including only the *operating activities* section of the statement and using the *direct method*. Place brackets around numbers representing cash payments. Show supporting computations for the following:

1. Cash received from customers
2. Interest and dividends received
3. Cash paid to suppliers and employees
4. Interest paid
5. Income taxes paid

b. Management of Royce Interiors, Inc., is exploring ways to increase the cash flows from operations. One way that cash flows could be increased is through more aggressive collection of receivables. Assuming that management has already taken all the steps possible to increase revenue and reduce expenses, describe two other ways that cash flows from operations could be increased.

---

**LO6**   **PROBLEM 13.5B**

**LO7**   Reporting Operating Cash Flows by the Indirect Method

Using the information presented in Problem **13.4B,** prepare a partial statement of cash flows for the current year, showing the computation of net cash flows from operating activities using the *indirect method*. Explain why the increase in accounts receivable over the year was *subtracted* from net income in computing the cash flows from operating activities.

---

**LO2**   **PROBLEM 13.6B**

**through**

**LO4**   Preparing a Statement of Cash Flows: A Comprehensive Problem without a Worksheet

**LO6**

**LO8**

You are the controller for Foxboro Technologies. Your staff has prepared an income statement for the current year and has developed the following additional information by analyzing changes in the company's balance sheet accounts.

| FOXBORO TECHNOLOGIES INCOME STATEMENT FOR THE YEAR ENDED DECEMBER 31, 2011 | | |
|---|---:|---:|
| **Revenue:** | | |
| Net sales | | $3,400,000 |
| Interest income | | 60,000 |
| Gain on sales of marketable securities | | 25,000 |
| Total revenue and gains | | $3,485,000 |
| **Costs and expenses:** | | |
| Cost of goods sold | $1,500,000 | |
| Operating expenses (including depreciation of $75,000) | 900,000 | |
| Interest expense | 27,000 | |
| Income tax expense | 115,000 | |
| Loss on sales of plant assets | 8,000 | |
| Total costs, expenses, and losses | | 2,550,000 |
| Net income | | $ 935,000 |

## Additional Information

1. Accounts receivable increased by $60,000.

2. Accrued interest receivable decreased by $5,000.

3. Inventory decreased by $30,000, and accounts payable to suppliers of merchandise decreased by $22,000.

4. Short-term prepayments of operating expenses increased by $8,000, and accrued liabilities for operating expenses decreased by $9,000.

5. The liability for accrued interest payable increased by $4,000 during the year.

6. The liability for accrued income taxes payable decreased by $10,000 during the year.

7. The following schedule summarizes the total debit and credit entries during the year in other balance sheet accounts:

| | Debit Entries | Credit Entries |
| --- | --- | --- |
| Marketable Securities . . . . . . . . . . . . . . . . . . . . . . . . . . . . . . . . . . . . . | $ 50,000 | $ 40,000 |
| Notes Receivable (cash loans made to borrowers) . . . . . . . . . . . . . . | 30,000 | 27,000 |
| Plant Assets (see paragraph 8) . . . . . . . . . . . . . . . . . . . . . . . . . . . . . | 350,000 | 30,000 |
| Notes Payable (short-term borrowing) . . . . . . . . . . . . . . . . . . . . . . . . | 70,000 | 56,000 |
| Capital Stock . . . . . . . . . . . . . . . . . . . . . . . . . . . . . . . . . . . . . . . . . . . . | | 60,000 |
| Additional Paid-in Capital—Capital Stock . . . . . . . . . . . . . . . . . . . . . | | 100,000 |
| Retained Earnings (see paragraph 9) . . . . . . . . . . . . . . . . . . . . . . . . | 300,000 | 935,000 |

8. The $30,000 in credit entries to the Plant Assets account is net of any debits to Accumulated Depreciation when plant assets were retired. Thus the $30,000 in credit entries represents the book value of all plant assets sold or retired during the year.

9. The $300,000 debit to Retained Earnings represents dividends declared and paid during the year. The $935,000 credit entry represents the net income shown in the income statement.

10. All investing and financing activities were cash transactions.

11. Cash and cash equivalents amount to $20,000 at the beginning of the year and to $473,000 at year-end.

## Instructions

a. Prepare a statement of cash flows for the current year. Use the *direct method* of reporting cash flows from operating activities. Place brackets around dollar amounts representing cash out-flows. Show separately your computations of the following amounts:

   1. Cash received from customers
   2. Interest received
   3. Cash paid to suppliers and employees
   4. Interest paid
   5. Income taxes paid
   6. Proceeds from sales of marketable securities
   7. Proceeds from sales of plant assets
   8. Proceeds from issuing capital stock

b. Explain why cash paid to suppliers is so much higher than cost of goods sold.

c. Does the fact that Foxboro's cash flows from both investing and financing activities are nega-tive indicate that the company is in a weak cash position?

**LO1**
**through**
**LO9**
**PROBLEM 13.7B**
Prepare and Analyze
a Statement of Cash
Flows

LGIN was founded in 2010 to apply a new technology for the Internet. The company earned a profit of $190,000 in 2010, its first year of operations. Management expects both sales and net income to more than double in each of the next four years.

   Comparative balance sheets at the end of 2010 and 2011, the company's first two years of operations, appear below. (Notice that the balances at the end of the current year appear in the right-hand column.)

| LGIN COMPARATIVE BALANCE SHEETS | | |
| --- | --- | --- |
| | **December 31,** | |
| | **2010** | **2011** |
| **Assets** | | |
| Cash and cash equivalents . . . . . . . . . . . . . . . . . . . . . . . . . . . . . . | $ 45,000 | $ 42,000 |
| Accounts receivable . . . . . . . . . . . . . . . . . . . . . . . . . . . . . . . . . . . | 15,000 | 880,000 |
| Plant and equipment (net of accumulated depreciation) . . . . . . . . . . . . . . . . . . . . . . . . . . . . . . . . . . | 680,000 | 3,140,000 |
| Totals . . . . . . . . . . . . . . . . . . . . . . . . . . . . . . . . . . . . . . . . . . | $740,000 | $4,062,000 |
| **Liabilities and Stockholders' Equity** | | |
| Notes payable (short-term). . . . . . . . . . . . . . . . . . . . . . . . . . . . . . | $ 0 | $1,490,000 |
| Accounts payable. . . . . . . . . . . . . . . . . . . . . . . . . . . . . . . . . . . . . | 45,000 | 82,000 |
| Accrued expenses payable . . . . . . . . . . . . . . . . . . . . . . . . . . . . | 55,000 | 38,000 |
| Notes payable (long-term) . . . . . . . . . . . . . . . . . . . . . . . . . . . . . | 200,000 | 785,000 |
| Capital stock (no par value) . . . . . . . . . . . . . . . . . . . . . . . . . . . | 250,000 | 915,000 |
| Retained earnings . . . . . . . . . . . . . . . . . . . . . . . . . . . . . . . . . . . | 190,000 | 752,000 |
| Totals . . . . . . . . . . . . . . . . . . . . . . . . . . . . . . . . . . . . . . . . . . | $740,000 | $4,062,000 |

### Additional Information

The following information regarding the company's operations in 2011 is available in either the company's income statement or its accounting records:

1. Net income for the year was $562,000. The company has never paid a dividend.
2. Depreciation for the year amounted to $125,000.
3. During the year the company purchased plant assets costing $2,585,000, for which it paid $2,000,000 in cash and financed $585,000 by issuing a long-term note payable. (Much of the cash used in these purchases was provided by short-term borrowing, as described below.)
4. In 2011, LGIN borrowed $1,490,000 against a $5 million line of credit with a local bank. In its balance sheet, the resulting obligations are reported as notes payable (short-term).
5. Additional shares of capital stock (no par value) were issued to investors for $665,000 cash.

### Instructions

a. Prepare a formal statement of cash flows for 2011, including a supplementary schedule of noncash investing and financing activities. (Follow the format illustrated in Exhibit 13–8. Cash provided by operating activities is to be presented by the *indirect method.*)

b. Briefly explain how operating activities can be a net *use* of cash when the company is operating so profitably.

c. Because of the expected rapid growth, management forecasts that operating activities will include an even greater use of cash in the year 2012 than in 2011. If this forecast is correct, does LGIN appear to be heading toward insolvency? Explain.

**L01** **PROBLEM 13.8B**
**through**   Prepare and Analyze
**L08**   a Statement of Cash
Flows; Involves
Preparation of a
Worksheet

Extra-Ordinaire, Inc., sells a single product (Pulsa) exclusively through newspaper advertising. The comparative income statements and balance sheets are for the past two years.

## EXTRA-ORDINAIRE, INC.
## COMPARATIVE INCOME STATEMENT
## FOR THE YEARS ENDED DECEMBER 31, 2010 AND 2011

|  | 2010 | 2011 |
|---|---|---|
| Sales | $640,000 | $ 410,000 |
| Less: Cost of goods sold | 310,000 | 190,000 |
| Gross profit on sales | 330,000 | 220,000 |
| Less: Operating expenses (including depreciation of $28,000 in 2010 and $29,000 in 2011) | 260,000 | 250,000 |
| Loss on sale of marketable securities | 0 | 4,000 |
| Net income (loss) | $ 70,000 | $ (34,000) |

## EXTRA-ORDINAIRE, INC.
## COMPARATIVE BALANCE SHEETS

|  | December 31, 2010 | December 31, 2011 |
|---|---|---|
| **Assets** |  |  |
| Cash and cash equivalents | $ 22,000 | $ 60,000 |
| Marketable securities | 27,000 | 12,000 |
| Accounts receivable | 40,000 | 35,000 |
| Inventory | 120,000 | 128,000 |
| Plant and equipment (net of accumulated depreciation) | 250,000 | 241,000 |
| Totals | $459,000 | $476,000 |
| **Liabilities & Stockholders' Equity** |  |  |
| Accounts payable | 50,000 | 70,000 |
| Accrued expenses payable | 16,000 | 14,000 |
| Notes payable | 235,000 | 237,000 |
| Capital stock (no par value) | 108,000 | 143,000 |
| Retained earnings | 50,000 | 12,000 |
| Totals | $459,000 | $476,000 |

## Additional Information

The following information regarding the company's operations in 2011 is available from the company's accounting records:

1. Early in the year the company declared and paid a $4,000 cash dividend.

2. During the year marketable securities costing $15,000 were sold for $11,000 cash, resulting in a $4,000 nonoperating loss.

3. The company purchased plant assets for $20,000, paying $8,000 in cash and issuing a note payable for the $12,000 balance.

4. During the year the company repaid a $10,000 note payable, but incurred an additional $12,000 in long-term debt as described in 3, above.

5. The owners invested $35,000 cash in the business as a condition of the new loans described in paragraphs 3 and 4, above.

## Instructions

a. Prepare a worksheet for a statement of cash flows, following the example shown in Exhibit 13–7.

b. Prepare a formal statement of cash flows for 2011, including a supplementary schedule of noncash investing and financing activities. (Use the format illustrated in Exhibit 13–8. Cash provided by operating activities is to be presented by the *indirect method.*)

c. Explain how Extra-Ordinaire, Inc., achieved positive cash flows from operating activities, despite incurring a net loss for the year.

**616**

**d.** Does the company's financial position appear to be improving or deteriorating? Explain.

**e.** Does Extra-Ordinaire, Inc., appear to be a company whose operations are growing or contracting? Explain.

**f.** Assume that management *agrees* with your conclusions in parts **c, d,** and **e.** What decisions should be made and what actions (if any) should be taken? Explain.

# Critical Thinking Cases

**L01 CASE 13.1**
Another Look at Allison Corporation

This case is based on the statement of cash flows for Allison Corporation, illustrated in Exhibit 13–1. Use this statement to evaluate the company's ability to continue paying the current level of dividends—$40,000 per year. The following information also is available:

1. The net cash flows from operating activities shown in the statement are relatively normal for Allison Corporation. Net cash flows from operating activities have not varied by more than a few thousand dollars in any of the past three years.

2. The net outflow for investing activities was unusually high, because the company modernized its production facilities during the year. The normal investing cash outflow is about $45,000 per year, the amount required to replace existing plant assets as they are retired. Over the long run, marketable securities transactions and lending transactions have a very small impact on Allison's net cash flows from investing activities.

3. The net cash flows from financing activities were unusually large in the current year because of the issuance of bonds payable and capital stock. These securities were issued to finance the modernization of the production facilities. In a typical year, financing activities include only short-term borrowing transactions and payments of dividends.

## Instructions

**a.** Solely on the basis of the company's past performance, do you believe that the $40,000 annual dividend payments are secure? That is, does the company appear able to pay this amount in dividends every year without straining its cash position? Do you think it more likely that Allison Corporation will increase or decrease the amount of dividends that it pays? Explain fully.

**b.** Should any of the unusual events appearing in the statement of cash flows for the current year affect your analysis of the company's ability to pay future dividends? Explain.

**L01 CASE 13.2**
**L08**
Cash Budgeting for You as a Student

Individuals generally do not prepare statements of cash flows concerning their personal activities. But they do engage in cash budgeting—if not on paper, then at least in their heads.

Assume it is December 29—a Monday. While you are in school, you share a small apartment with another student and work part-time, both near your school to minimize expenses. In two days your rent for January, $200, will be due. You now have $140 in the bank; every Friday you receive a paycheck for $100. You probably see the problem. And it probably doesn't look too serious; you can find a way to deal with it. That's what *budgeting* is all about.

Let's take this example a step further. In addition to the facts given above, your weekly cash payments include meals, $30; entertainment, $20; and gasoline, $10.

## Instructions

**a.** Using the following cash budget, compute your cash balance at the end of weeks 2, 3, and 4.

| | Week | | | |
| --- | --- | --- | --- | --- |
| | 1 | 2 | 3 | 4 |
| Beginning cash balance | $ 140 | $(20) | $ ? | $ ? |
| Expected cash receipts | 100 | 100 | 100 | 100 |
| Less: Expected cash outlays: | | | | |
| Monthly rent | (200) | | | |
| Meals | (30) | | | |
| Entertainment | (20) | | | |
| Gasoline | (10) | | | |
| Ending cash balance | $ (20) | $ ? | $ ? | $ ? |

**b.** Evaluate your financial situation.

### CASE 13.3
Lookin' Good?

It is late summer and General Wheels, Inc., an auto manufacturer, is facing a financial crisis. A large issue of bonds payable will mature next March, and the company must issue stock or new bonds to raise the money to retire this debt. Unfortunately, profits and cash flows have been declining over recent years. Management fears that if cash flows and profits do not improve in the current year, the company will not be able to raise the capital needed to replace the maturing bonds. Therefore, members of management have made the following proposals to improve the cash flows and profitability that will be reported in the financial statements dated this coming December 31.

1. Switch from the LIFO method to the FIFO method of valuing inventories. Management estimates that the FIFO method will result in a lower cost of goods sold but in higher income taxes for the current year. However, the additional income taxes will not actually be paid until early next year.

2. Switch from the 150 percent declining-balance method of depreciation to the straight-line method and lengthen the useful lives over which assets are depreciated. (These changes would be made only for financial reporting purposes, not for income tax purposes.)

3. Pressure dealers to increase their inventories—in short, to buy more cars. (The dealerships are independently owned; thus dealers are the customers to whom General Wheels sells automobiles.) Management estimates that this strategy could increase sales for the current year by 5 percent. However, any additional sales in the current year would be almost entirely offset by fewer sales in the following year.

4. Require dealers to pay for purchases more quickly. Currently, dealers must pay for purchases of autos within 60 days. Management is considering reducing this period to 30 days.

5. Pass up cash discounts offered by suppliers for prompt payment (that is, 2/10, n/30), and do not pay any bills until the final due date.

6. Borrow at current short-term interest rates (about 10 percent) and use the proceeds to pay off long-term debt bearing an interest rate of 13 percent.

7. Substitute stock dividends for the cash dividends currently paid on capital stock.

#### Instructions

a. Prepare a schedule with four columns. The first column is to be headed "Proposals" and is to contain the paragraph numbers of the seven proposals listed above. The next three columns are to be headed with the following financial statement captions: (1) "Net Income," (2) "Net Cash Flows from Operating Activities," and (3) "Cash."

   For each of the seven proposals in the left-hand column, indicate whether you expect the proposal to "Increase," "Decrease," or have "No Effect" in the current year on each of the financial statement captions listed in the next three columns. (*Note:* Only a few months remain in the current year. Therefore, you are to determine the *short-term* effects of these proposals.)

b. For each of the seven proposals, write a short paragraph explaining the reasoning behind your answers to part **a.**

### CASE 13.4
Peak Pricing

"Peak pricing is unfair. It makes goods and services available only to the wealthy and prices the average person out of the market."

#### Instructions

a. Comment on the extent to which you agree or disagree with the preceding statement.

b. What is the alternative to peak pricing?

c. Explain how peak pricing might be applied by:

   1. A hotel in Palm Springs, California. (Palm Springs is a winter resort in southern California with wonderful golf facilities. In the summer months, however, temperatures are well over 100 degrees and the tourist business slows dramatically.)

   2. Movie theaters.

d. Both in general terms and using specific examples, describe the conditions (if any) under which you might regard peak pricing as *unethical.*

618 **Chapter 13** Statement of Cash Flows

**CASE 13.5**

Improving the Statement of Cash Flows

The Securities and Exchange Commission (SEC) is an important governmental organization that exists primarily for the protection of the interests of investors in the U.S. securities markets. The SEC provides a wealth of information through its Web site, www.sec.gov.

**Instructions**

**a.** Access the SEC's Web site at the above address. Generally review the site to become familiar with the types of information provided.

**b.** Enter the section of the Web site identified as "About the SEC," then proceed to the section on "Commissioners." Within that section, maneuver around until you are able to access speeches made by the SEC and its staff.

**c.** Locate the following speech given by Scott A. Taub, former Deputy Chief Accountant, Office of the Chief Accountant of the SEC, in the second quarter of 2004: "Remarks at the University of Southern California, Leventhal School of Accounting, SEC and Financial Reporting Conference."

**d.** Peruse that entire speech, and then read carefully Mr. Taub's conclusion. Write a paragraph that captures what Mr. Taub had to say about how financial reporting could be improved in general, and how he specifically believes the statement of cash flows could be improved.

**INTERNET CASE 13.6**

through

Comparing Cash Flow Information from Two Companies

In the long run, a company must generate positive net cash flows from operating activities to survive. A business that has negative cash flows from operations will not be able to raise cash indefinitely from other sources and will eventually cease existing. Many creditors and stockholders are reluctant to invest in companies that do not generate positive cash flows from operations. However, some investors will invest in companies with negative cash flows from operations due to an optimistic future outlook for the company. Thus, investors have invested millions of dollars in Internet companies that have negative cash flows from operations.

**Instructions**

**a.** Visit Coca-Cola's Internet site (www.coke.com) and select "Investors." Under "Financial Information," select the most recent SEC 10K filing or annual report. View the Consolidated Statements of Cash Flows.

**b.** Visit Amazon.com's Internet site (www.amazon.com) and select "Investor Relations" at the bottom of the page, then click "SEC Filings." Select the most recent SEC 10K filing or annual report and view the Cash Flow Statement.

**c.** Compare the Net Cash Provided by Operating Activities for each company. Which company has higher Net Cash Provided by Operating Activities? Speculate why one company has much higher Net Cash Provided by Operating Activities than the other.

**d.** What type of company may have Negative Net Cash Provided from Operating Activities?

**e.** What type of company may have large Positive Net Cash Provided from Operating Activities?

*Internet sites are time and date sensitive. It is the purpose of these exercises to have you explore the Internet. You may need to use the Yahoo! search engine http://www.yahoo.com (or another favorite search engine) to find a company's current Web address.*

## Answers to Self-Test Questions

1. c  2. c  3. a  4. d ($601,000 − $420,000 − $12,000 + $17,000 − $23,000)
5. b  6. c

**CHAPTER 14**

# Financial Statement Analysis

© BananaStock/PictureQuest/DAL

**AFTER STUDYING THIS CHAPTER, YOU SHOULD BE ABLE TO:**

Learning Objective

**LO1** Explain the uses of dollar and percentage changes, trend percentages, component percentages, and ratios.

**LO2** Discuss the quality of a company's earnings, assets, and working capital.

**LO3** Explain the nature and purpose of classifications in financial statements.

**LO4** Prepare a classified balance sheet and compute widely used measures of liquidity and credit risk.

**LO5** Prepare a multiple-step and a single-step income statement and compute widely used measures of profitability.

**LO6** Put a company's net income into perspective by relating it to sales, assets, and stockholders' equity.

**LO7** Compute the ratios widely used in financial statement analysis and explain the significance of each.

**LO8** Analyze financial statements from the viewpoints of common stockholders, creditors, and others.

# JOHNSON & JOHNSON

Johnson & Johnson is the world's most comprehensive and broadly based manufacturer of health care products and related services. In 2009 it had over $50 billion in sales. Other measures of Johnson & Johnson's size include the facts that it has over $94 billion in assets and conducts business in virtually all countries of the world.

How does one get a handle on the financial performance of a huge company such as Johnson & Johnson? Financial statements, including the balance sheet, income statement, and statement of cash flows, provide a wealth of information that is helpful in performing this significant task. Financial statement analysis involves taking key items from these financial statements and gleaning as much useful information as possible from them. For example, we can determine that the amount of Johnson & Johnson's 2009 net income ($12,266 million) represented a return of approximately 13 percent on the total assets used to generate that income. Is a return on assets of 13 percent satisfactory or unsatisfactory? This is a difficult question to answer. To make this judgment we would need more information than we have at this point. For example, we would like to know the trend in various financial measures for Johnson & Johnson for several years. We would also like to know comparative information about other companies with similar operating characteristics (i.e., in the same industry). We will study all of this and more in this chapter as we look at the interesting and challenging subject of financial statement analysis. ■

Financial measures are used often to evaluate corporate performance. As a result, the Securities and Exchange Commission, the Financial Accounting Standards Board, the financial press, and the accounting profession are committed to high-quality financial reporting. Throughout this text, we emphasize the importance of integrity in financial reporting as a means of protecting the interests of investors and creditors. This chapter explores financial statement analysis in depth, building on the introductory sections of this important subject in preceding chapters.

Our discussion of financial statement analysis is presented in three sections. First, we consider general tools of analysis that emphasize comparing information about enterprises with relevant benchmarks. Second, we consider measures of liquidity and credit risk, followed by a consideration of profitability. Third, we present and discuss a comprehensive illustration in which we analyze a company's financial statements from the perspective of three important users of information—common stockholders, long-term creditors, and short-term creditors. Throughout this chapter, we draw on information that was covered in earlier chapters and we use new information that is presented here for the first time.

## FINANCIAL STATEMENTS ARE DESIGNED FOR ANALYSIS

In today's global economy, investment capital is always on the move. Through organized capital markets such as the New York Stock Exchange, investors each day shift billions of investment dollars among different companies, industries, and nations. Capital flows to those areas in which investors expect to earn the greatest returns with the least risk. How do investors forecast risk and potential returns? One of the most important ways is by analyzing accounting information for a specific company in the context of its unique industry setting.

The goal of accounting information is to provide economic decision makers with useful information. The financial statements generated through the accounting process are designed to assist users in identifying key relationships and trends. The financial statements of most publicly owned companies are classified and are presented in comparative form. Often, the word *consolidated* appears in the headings of the statements. Users of financial statements should have a clear understanding of these terms.

Most business organizations prepare **classified financial statements,** meaning that items with certain characteristics are placed together in a group, or classification. The purpose of these classifications is to *develop useful subtotals* that will assist users of the statements in their analyses. These classifications and subtotals are standardized throughout most of American business, a practice that assists decision makers in comparing the financial statements of different companies. An example of a classified financial statement is a balance sheet that separates assets and liabilities into current and noncurrent categories.

In **comparative financial statements,** the financial statement amounts *for several time periods* appear side by side in vertical columns. This assists investors in identifying and evaluating significant changes and trends.

Most large corporations own other companies through which they conduct some of their business activities. A corporation that owns other businesses is the **parent company,** and the owned companies are called divisions or **subsidiaries.** For example, PepsiCo, which makes Pepsi-Cola, also owns and operates the companies that make Frito-Lay, Quaker Foods, Gatorade, and Tropicana products. In essence, these subsidiaries are part of the organization generally known as PepsiCo. **Consolidated financial statements** present the financial position and operating results of the parent company and its subsidiaries *as if they were a single business organization.*

**For Example . . .**    At this point, take a brief look at the financial statements of Home Depot, Inc., which appear in Appendix A at the end of the text. These financial statements illustrate all of the concepts discussed; they are classified and presented in comparative form, and they describe a consolidated business entity. These financial statements also have been *audited* by KPMG LLP, an international public accounting firm.

Tools of Analysis

## Tools of Analysis

Significant changes in financial data are easier to see when financial statement amounts for two or more years are placed side by side in adjacent columns. Such a statement is called a *comparative financial statement*. The amounts for the most recent year are usually placed in the left-hand money column, closest to the words that describe the item. The balance sheet, income statement, and statement of cash flows are often prepared in the form of comparative statements. A highly condensed comparative income statement covering three years is shown in Exhibit 14–1.

| BENSON CORPORATION<br>COMPARATIVE INCOME STATEMENT<br>FOR THE YEARS ENDED DECEMBER 31, 2011, 2010, 2009<br>(IN THOUSANDS OF DOLLARS) | | | |
|---|---|---|---|
| | **2011** | **2010** | **2009** |
| Net sales | $600 | $500 | $400 |
| Cost of goods sold | 370 | 300 | 235 |
| Gross profit | $230 | $200 | $165 |
| Expenses | 194 | 160 | 115 |
| Net income | $ 36 | $ 40 | $ 50 |

**Exhibit 14–1**

**COMPARATIVE INCOME STATEMENT**

Comparative statements place important financial information in a context that is useful for gaining better understanding. For example, knowing that Benson Corporation had sales of $600,000 in 2011 after years in which sales were $500,000 (2010) and $400,000 (2009) is helpful in understanding Benson's sales trend.

Few figures in a financial statement are highly significant in and of themselves. It is their relationship to other quantities or the amount and direction of change that is important. Analysis is largely a matter of establishing significant relationships and identifying changes and trends. Four widely used analytical techniques are (1) dollar and percentage changes, (2) trend percentages, (3) component percentages, and (4) ratios.

### DOLLAR AND PERCENTAGE CHANGES

The dollar amount of change from year to year is significant, and expressing the change in percentage terms adds perspective. For example, if sales this year have increased by $100,000, the fact that this is an increase of 10 percent over last year's sales of $1 million puts it in a different perspective than if it represented a 1 percent increase over sales of $10 million for the prior year.

The dollar amount of any change is the difference between the amount for a *comparison* year and the amount for a *base* year. The percentage change is computed by dividing the amount of the dollar change between years by the amount for the base year. This is illustrated in the following tabulation, using data from the comparative income statement shown in Exhibit 14–1.

**Learning Objective**

Explain the uses of dollar and percentage changes, trend percentages, component percentages, and ratios. **LO1**

| | In Thousands | | | Increase or (Decrease) | | | |
|---|---|---|---|---|---|---|---|
| | | | | 2011 over 2010 | | 2010 over 2009 | |
| | Year 2011 | Year 2010 | Year 2009 | Amount | % | Amount | % |
| Net sales | $600 | $500 | $400 | $100 | 20% | $100 | 25% |
| Net income | 36 | 40 | 50 | (4) | (10) | (10) | (20) |

Dollar and percentage changes

Although net sales increased $100,000 in both 2010 and 2011, the percentage change differs because of the change in the base from 2009 to 2010. These calculations present no problems when the figures for the base year are positive amounts. If a negative amount or a zero amount appears in the base year, however, a percentage change cannot be computed. Thus, if Benson Corporation had incurred a net loss in 2010, the percentage change in net income from 2010 to 2011 could not have been calculated.

### Evaluating Percentage Changes in Sales and Earnings

Computing the percentage changes in sales, gross profit, and net income from one year to the next gives insight into a company's rate of growth. If a company is experiencing growth in its economic activities, sales and earnings should increase at *more than the rate of inflation*. Assume, for example, that a company's sales increase by 6 percent while the general price level rises by 10 percent. The entire increase in the dollar amount of sales may be explained by inflation, rather than by an increase in sales volume (the number of units sold). In fact, the company may well have sold *fewer* goods than in the preceding year.

In measuring the dollar or percentage change in *quarterly* sales or earnings, it is customary to compare the results of the current quarter with those of the *same quarter in the preceding year*. Use of the same quarter of the preceding year as the base period prevents our analysis from being distorted by seasonal fluctuations in business activity.

### Percentages Become Misleading When the Base Is Small

Percentage changes may create a misleading impression when the dollar amount used as a base is unusually small. Occasionally we hear a television newscaster say that a company's profits have increased by a very large percentage, such as 900 percent. The initial impression created by such a statement is that the company's profits must now be excessively large. But assume, for example, that a company had net income of $100,000 in its first year, that in the second year net income drops to $10,000, and that in the third year net income returns to the $100,000 level. In this third year, net income has increased by $90,000, representing a 900 percent increase over the profits of the second year. What needs to be added to the news commentary is that this 900 percent increase in profits in the third year follows a very small profit in the second year and *exactly offsets* the 90 percent decline in profits in the second year.

## TREND PERCENTAGES

The changes in financial statement items from a base year to following years are often expressed as *trend percentages* to show the extent and direction of change. Two steps are necessary to compute trend percentages. First, a base year is selected and each item in the financial statements for the base year is given a weight of 100 percent. The second step is to express each item in the financial statements for following years as a percentage of its base-year amount. This computation consists of dividing an item such as sales in the years after the base year by the amount of sales in the base year.

For example, assume that 2006 is selected as the base year and that sales in the base year amounted to $300,000, as shown in the following table. The trend percentages for sales are computed by dividing the sales amount of each following year by $300,000. Also shown in the illustration are the yearly amounts of net income. The trend percentages for net income are computed by dividing the net income amount for each following year by the base-year amount of $15,000.

| Dollar Amounts | 2011 | 2010 | 2009 | 2008 | 2007 | 2006 |
| --- | --- | --- | --- | --- | --- | --- |
| Sales............ | $450,000 | $360,000 | $330,000 | $321,000 | $312,000 | $300,000 |
| Net income....... | 22,950 | 14,550 | 21,450 | 19,200 | 15,600 | 15,000 |
| **Trend Percentages** | **2011** | **2010** | **2009** | **2008** | **2007** | **2006** |
| Sales............ | 150% | 120% | 110% | 107% | 104% | 100% |
| Net income........ | 153 | 97 | 143 | 128 | 104 | 100 |

These trend percentages indicate a modest growth in sales in the early years and accelerated growth in 2010 and 2011. Net income also shows an increasing growth trend with the exception of the year 2010, when net income declined despite a solid increase in sales. The problem was overcome in 2011 with a sharp rise in net income. Overall the trend percentages give a picture of a profitable, growing enterprise.

## COMPONENT PERCENTAGES

Component percentages indicate the *relative size* of each item included in a total. For example, each item in a balance sheet could be expressed as a percentage of total assets. This shows quickly the relative importance of each type of asset as well as the relative amount of financing obtained from current creditors, long-term creditors, and stockholders. By computing component percentages for several successive balance sheets, we can see which items are increasing in importance and which are becoming less significant.

Another application of component percentages is to express all items in an income statement as a percentage of net sales. Such a statement is called a *common size income statement.* See the condensed income statement in dollars and in common size form in Exhibit 14–2.

**Income Statement**

| | Dollars | | Component Percentages | |
|---|---|---|---|---|
| | **2011** | **2010** | **2011** | **2010** |
| Net sales.......................... | $1,000,000 | $600,000 | 100.0% | 100.0% |
| Cost of goods sold ................... | 700,000 | 360,000 | 70.0 | 60.0 |
| Expenses (including income taxes) ........................... | 250,000 | 180,000 | 25.0 | 30.0 |
| Net income ......................... | $ 50,000 | $ 60,000 | 5.0% | 10.0% |

**Exhibit 14–2**

**COMPONENT PERCENTAGES**

Are the year-to-date changes favorable?

Looking only at the component percentages, we see that the increase in cost of goods sold (60 percent to 70 percent) was only partially offset by the decrease in expenses as a percentage of net sales, causing net income to decrease from 10 percent to 5 percent of net sales.

## RATIOS

A ratio is a simple mathematical expression of the relationship of one item to another. Every percentage may be viewed as a ratio—that is, one number expressed as a percentage of another.

Ratios may be stated in several ways. To illustrate, let us consider the current ratio, which expresses the relationship between a company's most liquid assets (current) and its liabilities that require payment soon (current). If current assets are $240,000 and current liabilities are $80,000, we may say either that the current ratio is 3 to 1 (which is written as 3:1) or that current assets are 300 percent of current liabilities. Either statement correctly summarizes the relationship—that is, that current assets are three times as large as current liabilities.

Ratios are particularly important in understanding financial statements because they permit us to compare information from one financial statement with information from another financial statement. For example, we might compare net income (taken from the income statement) with total assets (taken from the balance sheet) to see how effectively management is using available resources to earn a profit. For a ratio to be useful, however, the two amounts being compared must be logically related. In subsequent sections of this chapter, we will make extensive use of ratios to better demonstrate important dimensions of an enterprise's financial activities.

## STANDARDS OF COMPARISON

In using dollar and percentage changes, trend percentages, component percentages, and ratios, financial analysts constantly search for some standard of comparison against which to judge whether the relationships they have found are favorable or unfavorable. Two such standards are (1) the past performance of the company and (2) the performance of other companies in the same industry. For internal management purposes, another important comparison is with expected or budgeted numbers.

**Past Performance of the Company**   Comparing financial information for a current period with similar information for prior years affords some basis for judging whether the condition of the business is improving or worsening. This comparison of data over time is sometimes called *horizontal analysis,* to express the idea of reviewing data for a number of consecutive periods. It is distinguished from *vertical,* or *static,* analysis, which refers to the review of the financial information within a single accounting period.

In addition to determining whether the situation is improving or becoming worse, horizontal analysis may aid in making estimates of future prospects. Because changes may reverse their direction at any time, however, projecting past trends into the future always involves risk.

A weakness of horizontal analysis is that comparison with the past does not afford any basis for evaluation in absolute terms. The fact that net income was 2 percent of sales last year and is 3 percent of sales this year indicates improvement, but if there is evidence that net income *should be* 7 percent of sales, the record for both years is unfavorable.

**Industry Standards**   The limitations of horizontal analysis may be overcome to some extent by finding appropriate benchmarks against which to measure a particular company's performance. The benchmarks used by most analysts are the performance of comparable companies and the average performance of several companies in the same industry.[1]

Assume, for example, that the revenue of Alpha Airlines drops by 8 percent during the current year. If the revenue for the airlines industry had dropped an average of 15 percent during this year, Alpha's 8 percent decline might be viewed as a *favorable* performance. As another example, assume that Omega Co. earns a net income equal to 3 percent of net sales. This would be substandard if Omega were a pharmaceutical company, but it would be satisfactory performance if it were a retail grocery chain because of the difference in earnings expected in the two industries.

When we compare a given company with its competitors or with industry averages, our conclusions are valid only if the companies in question are comparable. Because of the large number of diversified companies formed in recent years, the term *industry* is difficult to define, and even companies that fall roughly within the same industry may not be comparable in many respects. For example, one company may engage only in the marketing of oil products; another may be a fully integrated producer from the well to the gas pump; yet both are said to be in the oil industry.

## QUALITY OF EARNINGS

**Learning Objective**

**L02**  **Discuss the quality of a company's earnings, assets, and working capital.**

Profits are the lifeblood of a business entity. No entity can survive indefinitely and accomplish its other goals unless it is profitable. Continuous losses drain assets from the business, consume owners' equity, and leave the company at the mercy of creditors. In assessing the prospects of a company, we are interested not only in the total *amount* of earnings but also in the *rate* of earnings on sales, on total assets, and on owners' equity. In addition, we must look at the *stability* and *source* of earnings. An erratic earnings performance over a period of years, for example, is less desirable than a steady level of earnings. A history of increasing earnings is preferable to a flat earnings record.

A breakdown of sales and earnings by *major product lines* may be useful in evaluating the future performance of a company. Publicly owned companies include with their financial statements supplementary schedules showing sales and profits by product line and by geographical area. These schedules assist financial analysts in forecasting the effect on the company of changes in consumer demand for particular types of products.

---

[1] Industry data are available from a number of sources. For example, Robert Morris Associates publishes *Annual Statement Studies,* which includes data from many thousands of annual reports, grouped into several hundred industry classifications. Industry classifications are subdivided further by company size. Dun & Bradstreet, Inc., annually publishes *Key Business Ratios* for more than 800 lines of business.

Financial analysts often express the opinion that the earnings of one company are of higher quality than the earnings of other similar companies. This concept of *quality of earnings* arises because each company's management can choose from a variety of accounting principles and methods, all of which are considered generally acceptable. A company's management often is under pressure to report rising earnings or to meet previously stated earnings projections, and accounting policies may be tailored toward these objectives. We have already pointed out the impact on current reported earnings of the choice between the LIFO and FIFO methods of inventory valuation and the choice of depreciation policies. In judging the quality of earnings, the financial analyst should consider whether the accounting principles and methods selected by management lead to a conservative measurement of earnings (high quality) or tend to inflate reported earnings (low quality).

## QUALITY OF ASSETS AND THE RELATIVE AMOUNT OF DEBT

Although a satisfactory level of earnings may be a good indication of the company's long-run ability to pay its debts and dividends, we must also look at the composition of assets, their condition and liquidity, the timing of repayment of liabilities, and the total amount of debt outstanding. A company may be profitable and yet be unable to pay its liabilities on time; sales and earnings may appear satisfactory, but plant and equipment may be deteriorating because of poor maintenance policies; valuable patents may be expiring; substantial losses may be imminent due to slow-moving inventories and past-due receivables. Companies with large amounts of debt often are vulnerable to increases in interest rates and are particularly vulnerable to declines in profitability and operating cash flows.

## Measures of Liquidity and Credit Risk

*Liquidity* refers to a company's ability to meet its continuing obligations as they arise. For example, a company that has borrowed money must make interest and principal payments to a financial institution. A company that has purchased its inventory and other necessities on credit may be required to pay the seller within 30 days of the purchase date. Transactions like these require a company to maintain a close watch on its liquidity.

We emphasize throughout this text the importance to investors, creditors, and other users of financial statements of information that permits them to assess the amount, timing, and uncertainty of future cash flows from the enterprise to them. As a result, analyzing an enterprise's liquidity and its credit risk is very important and is a natural place for us to start our study of analyzing financial statements.

In this section we learn about ways to assess liquidity, starting with the classified balance sheet and then looking at a number of ratios commonly used to glean information about liquidity from the financial statements.

### A CLASSIFIED BALANCE SHEET

In a classified balance sheet, assets usually are presented in three groups: (1) current assets, (2) plant and equipment, and (3) other assets. Liabilities are classified into two categories: (1) current liabilities and (2) long-term or noncurrent liabilities. A classified balance sheet for Computer City appears in Exhibit 14–3.

**Learning Objective**
Explain the nature and
purpose of classifications
in financial statements.

**LO3**

The classifications *current assets* and *current liabilities* are especially useful in evaluating a company's liquidity.

**Current Assets**   **Current assets** represent relatively liquid resources. This category includes cash, investments in marketable securities, receivables, inventories, and prepaid expenses. To qualify as a current asset, an asset must already be cash or must be capable of *being converted into cash* or used up within a relatively short period of time, without interfering with normal business operations.

Current assets are tied to an enterprise's **operating cycle.** Most companies have several operating cycles within a year. This means that they take cash and purchase inventory, sell the inventory, and collect the receivable in cash several times within a year. For these companies, the time period used to identify current assets is one year, so any asset that is expected to be

Exhibit 14–3

**COMPUTER CITY CLASSIFIED BALANCE SHEET**

### COMPUTER CITY
### BALANCE SHEET
### DECEMBER 31, 2011

#### Assets

**Current assets:**

| | | |
|---|---|---|
| Cash | | $ 30,000 |
| Marketable securities | | 11,000 |
| Notes receivable | | 5,000 |
| Accounts receivable | | 60,000 |
| Inventory | | 70,000 |
| Prepaid expenses | | 4,000 |
| Total current assets | | $180,000 |

**Plant and equipment:**

| | | | |
|---|---|---|---|
| Land | | $151,000 | |
| Building | $120,000 | | |
| Less: Accumulated depreciation | 9,000 | 111,000 | |
| Sales Fixtures and equipment | $ 45,000 | | |
| Less: Accumulated depreciation | 27,000 | 18,000 | |
| Total plant and equipment | | | 280,000 |

**Other assets:**

| | |
|---|---|
| Land held as a future building site | 170,000 |
| Total assets | $630,000 |

#### Liabilities & Stockholders' Equity

**Current liabilities:**

| | |
|---|---|
| Notes payable (due in 6 months) | $ 10,000 |
| Accounts payable | 62,000 |
| Income taxes payable | 13,000 |
| Sales taxes payable | 3,000 |
| Accrued expenses payable | 8,000 |
| Unearned revenue and customer deposits | 4,000 |
| Total current liabilities | $100,000 |

**Long-term liabilities:**

| | |
|---|---|
| Mortgage payable (due in 10 years) | 110,000 |
| Total liabilities | $210,000 |

**Stockholders' equity:**

| | | |
|---|---|---|
| Capital stock (15,000 shares issued and outstanding) | $150,000 | |
| Retained earnings | 270,000 | |
| Total stockholders' equity | | 420,000 |
| Total liabilities & stockholders' equity | | $630,000 |

**Learning Objective**

**L04** Prepare a classified balance sheet and compute widely used measures of liquidity and credit risk.

converted into cash within one year is classified as a current asset in the enterprise's balance sheet. Some enterprises, however, have relatively long operating cycles. For example, a company that constructs very large items (for example, airplanes or ships) may have a production period that extends well beyond one year. In these cases, the length of the company's operating cycle is used to define those assets that are classified as current. While most current assets are expected to be converted into cash, we also include as current assets those that will be used up or consumed during the year or operating cycle, if longer. For example, prepaid expenses are classified as current assets on the basis that their having been paid in advance preserves cash that otherwise would have to be paid in the current period. Combining these ideas, we can define current assets as assets that are already cash, or are expected to be converted into cash or used up within the next year or operating cycle, whichever is longer.

In a balance sheet, current assets are listed in order of liquidity. (The closer an asset is to becoming cash, the greater its liquidity.) Thus cash always is listed first among the current assets, usually followed by investments in marketable securities, receivables, inventory, and prepaid expenses, in that order.

**Current Liabilities**   **Current liabilities** are *existing obligations* that are expected to be paid by using the enterprise's current assets. Among the most common current liabilities are notes payable (due within one year), accounts payable, unearned revenue, and accrued expenses, such as income taxes payable, salaries payable, or interest payable. In the balance sheet, notes payable usually are listed first, followed by accounts payable; other types of current liabilities may be listed in any sequence.

The *relationship* between current assets and current liabilities is as important as the total dollar amount in either category. Current liabilities must be paid in the near future, and the cash to pay these liabilities is expected to come from current assets. Thus, decision makers evaluating the liquidity of a business often compare the relative amounts of current assets and current liabilities, whereas an evaluation of *long-term* credit risk requires a comparison of total assets to total liabilities.

We will now use Computer City's classified balance sheet to examine some widely applied measures of short-term liquidity and long-term credit risk.

## WORKING CAPITAL

Working capital is a measurement sometimes used to express the relationship between current assets and current liabilities. **Working capital** is the *excess* of current assets over current liabilities. Computer City's working capital is *$80,000,* computed as follows:

| | |
|---|---|
| Current assets | $180,000 |
| Less: Current liabilities | 100,000 |
| Working capital | $ 80,000 |

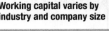

Working capital varies by industry and company size

Recall that current assets are expected to convert into cash (or be used up) within a relatively short period of time, and that current liabilities require a prompt cash payment. Thus, working capital measures a company's potential excess *sources* of cash over its upcoming *uses* of cash.

The amount of working capital that a company needs to satisfy its liabilities as they come due varies with the size of the organization and the nature of its business activities. An analyst familiar with the nature of a company's operations usually can determine from the amount of working capital whether the company is in a sound financial position or is heading for financial difficulties.

## CURRENT RATIO

A widely used measure of short-term debt-paying ability is the **current ratio.** This ratio is computed by *dividing* total current assets by total current liabilities.

In the illustrated balance sheet of Computer City, current assets amount to $180,000 and current liabilities total $100,000. Therefore, Computer City's current ratio is *1.8 to 1,* computed as follows:

| | |
|---|---|
| Current assets | $180,000 |
| Current liabilities | $100,000 |
| Current ratio ($180,000 ÷ $100,000) | 1.8 to 1 |

A widely used measure of liquidity

A current ratio of 1.8 to 1 means that the company's current assets are 1.8 times as large as its current liabilities.

**630** Chapter 14 Financial Statement Analysis

The *higher* the current ratio, the more liquid the company appears to be. Historically, some bankers and other short-term creditors have believed that a company should have a current ratio of 2 to 1 or higher to qualify as a good credit risk. Such rules of thumb are questionable, however, because many successful businesses have current ratios of less than 2 to 1 because their receivables and inventory convert into cash quickly relative to the amount and timing of their payables. Likewise, it is possible for financially weak businesses to have high current ratios as a result of slow turnover in receivables and inventory. In other words, care must be taken in interpreting all ratios, including the current ratio, to ensure that inappropriate conclusions are not reached as a result of superficial analysis. Confirming the information communicated via one ratio by looking at other financial measures is often a good way to help ensure a valid interpretation.

## QUICK RATIO

Inventory and prepaid expenses are the *least liquid* of the current assets. In a business with a long operating cycle, it may take several months to convert inventory into cash. Therefore, some short-term creditors prefer the **quick ratio** (sometimes called the acid-test ratio) to the current ratio as a measure of short-term liquidity.

The quick ratio compares only the *most liquid* current assets—called **quick assets**—with current liabilities. Quick assets include cash, marketable securities, and receivables—the current assets that can be converted most quickly into cash. Computer City's quick ratio is *1.06 to 1,* computed as follows:

| | |
|---|---|
| Quick assets (cash, marketable securities, and receivables)..................... | $106,000 |
| Current liabilities....................................................... | $100,000 |
| Quick ratio ($106,000 ÷ $100,000) ....................................... | 1.06 to 1 |

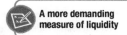
**A more demanding measure of liquidity**

Quick ratios are especially useful in evaluating the liquidity of companies that have inventories of slow-moving merchandise (such as real estate) or inventories that have become excessive in size.

## DEBT RATIO

If a business fails and must be liquidated, the claims of creditors take priority over those of the owners. But if the business has a great deal of debt, there may not be enough assets even to make full payment to all creditors.

A basic measure of the safety of creditors' claims is the **debt ratio,** which states total liabilities as a *percentage* of total assets. A company's debt ratio is computed by dividing total liabilities by total assets, as shown below for Computer City:

| | |
|---|---|
| Total liabilities........................................................ | $210,000 |
| Total assets .......................................................... | $630,000 |
| Debt ratio ($210,000 ÷ $630,000) ....................................... | 33⅓% |

The debt ratio is not a measure of short-term liquidity. Rather, it is a measure of creditors' *long-term* risk. The smaller the portion of total assets financed by creditors, the smaller the risk that the business may become unable to pay its debts. From the creditors' point of view, the *lower* the debt ratio, the *safer* their position.

Many financially sound American companies traditionally have maintained debt ratios under 50 percent. But again, the financial analyst must be familiar with industry characteristics. Banks, for example, may have very high debt ratios—often over 90 percent.

## EVALUATING FINANCIAL RATIOS

We caution users of financial statements *against* placing too much emphasis on rules of thumb, such as *a current ratio should be at least 2 to 1, a quick ratio should be at least 1 to 1,* or *a debt ratio should be under 50 percent.* To interpret any financial ratio properly, the decision maker must first understand the characteristics of the company and the industry in which it operates.

Retailers, for example, tend to have higher current ratios than do wholesalers or manufacturing companies. Service-type businesses—which have no inventory—generally have lower current ratios than merchandising or manufacturing companies. Large businesses with good credit ratings and reliable sources of cash receipts are able to operate with lower current ratios than are small companies whose continuous inflow of cash may be less predictable.

Although a high current ratio is one indication of strong debt-paying ability, an extremely high ratio—say, 4 or 5 to 1—may indicate that *too much* of the company's resources are tied up in current assets. In maintaining such a highly liquid position, the company may be using its financial resources inefficiently and not earning the return that could be earned if the assets were invested in a more productive way.

**Standards for Comparison**   Financial analysts generally use two criteria in evaluating the reasonableness of a financial ratio. One criterion is the *trend* in the ratio over a period of years. By reviewing this trend, analysts are able to determine whether a company's performance or financial position is improving or deteriorating. Second, analysts often compare a company's financial ratios with those of *similar companies* and with *industrywide averages*. These comparisons assist analysts in evaluating a particular ratio in light of the company's current business environment.

**Annual Reports**   Publicly owned corporations issue **annual reports** that provide a great deal of information about the company. For example, annual reports include comparative financial statements that have been audited by a firm of independent public accountants. They also include 5- or 10-year *summaries* of key financial data and **management's discussion and analysis** of the company's operating results, liquidity, and financial position. This is where management identifies and discusses favorable and unfavorable trends and events that may affect the company in the future.

Annual reports are mailed directly to all stockholders of the corporation. They are also available to the public either through the Internet, in libraries, or by writing or calling the stockholder relations department of the corporation.

**Industry Information**   Financial information about *entire industries* is available through financial publications (such as Dun & Bradstreet, Inc.) and through online databases (such as Media General Financial Services). Such information allows investors and creditors to compare the financial health of an individual company with the industry in which that company operates.

**Usefulness and Limitations of Financial Ratios**   A financial ratio expresses the relationship of one amount to another. Most users of financial statements find that certain ratios assist them in quickly evaluating the financial position, profitability, and future prospects of a business. A comparison of key ratios for several successive years usually indicates whether the business is becoming stronger or weaker. Ratios also provide a way to compare quickly the financial strength and profitability of different companies.

Users of financial statements should recognize, however, that ratios have several limitations. For example, management may enter into year-end transactions that temporarily improve key ratios—a process called **window dressing.**

**INTERNATIONAL** CASE IN POINT

Two issues confront accountants analyzing international companies. First, there is great variation in accounting measurement, disclosure, and audit quality across countries. Second, obtaining the information necessary to conduct cross-border accounting analyses is frequently difficult and sometimes not possible. Financial reporting in China is a case in point. Until recent years China did not have active stock markets requiring financial reporting. In addition, there was no external auditing in forms that would be familiar to Westerners. Dealing with these differences is one of the primary objectives of establishing international financial accounting standards.

To illustrate, the December 31, 2011, balance sheet of Computer City (Exhibit 14–3) includes current assets of $180,000 and current liabilities of $100,000, indicating a current ratio of *1.8 to 1*. What would happen if, shortly before year-end, management used $20,000 of the company's cash to pay accounts payable that are not due until January 2012? This transaction would reduce current assets to $160,000 ($180,000 − $20,000) and current liabilities to $80,000 ($100,000 − $20,000), resulting in an increase in the current ratio to a more impressive 2 to 1 ($160,000 ÷ $80,000). Is the company really better off as a result of having simply paid $20,000 of liabilities a few days early? The answer is probably no, although looking only at the current ratio one might think it is stronger after paying the $20,000 than before. Such steps to improve the company's appearance in its financial statements are common and, within reason, are a natural part of financial reporting. The astute reader of financial statements needs to be aware of this, however, and should look for instances where there is evidence that steps have been taken to artificially improve a company's appearance. Usually this can be done by looking at multiple financial measures rather than focusing on a single financial measure.

Financial statement ratios contain the same limitations as do the dollar amounts used in financial statements. For example, some assets are reported at historical cost rather than current market value. Also, financial statement ratios express only *financial* relationships. They give no indication of a company's progress in achieving nonfinancial goals, such as improving customer satisfaction or worker productivity. A thorough analysis of investment opportunities involves more than merely computing and comparing financial ratios.

## LIQUIDITY, CREDIT RISK, AND THE LAW

Accountants view a business entity as separate from the other economic activities of its owners, regardless of how the business is organized. The law, however, draws an important distinction between *corporations* and *unincorporated* business organizations. Users of financial statements should understand this legal distinction, as it may affect both creditors and owners.

Under the law, the owners of unincorporated businesses (sole proprietorships and partnerships) are *personally liable* for any and all debts of the business organization. Therefore, creditors of unincorporated businesses often base their lending decisions on the financial position of the *owners,* rather than the financial strength of the business entity.[2]

If a business is organized as a corporation, however, the owners (stockholders) are *not* personally responsible for the liabilities of the business. Creditors may look *only to the business entity* in seeking payment of their claims. Therefore, the liquidity of the business entity becomes much more important if the business is organized as a corporation.

**Small Corporations and Loan Guarantees**   Small corporations often do not have sufficient financial resources to qualify for the credit they need. In such cases, creditors may require that one or more of the company's stockholders personally guarantee (or co-sign) specific debts of the business entity. By co-signing debts of the corporation, the individual stockholders *do* become personally liable for the debt if the corporation fails to make payment.

## Measures of Profitability

Measures of a company's *profitability* are of interest to equity investors and management and are drawn primarily from the income statement. The measures that we discuss in this chapter include percentage changes in key measurements, gross profit rates, operating income, net income as a percentage of sales, earnings per share, return on assets, and return on equity.

---

[2] In a *limited* partnership, only the *general partners* are personally responsible for the debts of the business. Every limited partnership must have one or more general partners.

Measures of Profitability

**633**

Public opinion polls show that many people believe that most businesses earn a profit equal to 30 percent or more of the sales price of their merchandise. Actually, this is far from true. Most successful companies earn a net income that is between 5 percent and, in unusual cases, 15 percent of sales revenue.

## CLASSIFICATIONS IN THE INCOME STATEMENT

An income statement may be prepared in either the *multiple-step* or the *single-step* format. The multiple-step income statement is more useful in illustrating accounting concepts because it provides more detailed information than the single-step format. A multiple-step income statement for Computer City is shown in Exhibit 14–4.

**Exhibit 14–4**

**COMPUTER CITY INCOME STATEMENT (MULTIPLE-STEP)**

| COMPUTER CITY INCOME STATEMENT FOR THE YEAR ENDED DECEMBER 31, 2011 | | | |
|---|---|---|---|
| **Net sales** | | | $900,000 |
| Less: Cost of goods sold (including transportation-in) | | | 540,000 |
| **Gross profit** | | | $360,000 |
| Less: Operating expenses: | | | |
| Selling expenses: | | | |
| Sales salaries and commissions | $64,800 | | |
| Advertising | 42,000 | | |
| Delivery service | 14,200 | | |
| Depreciation: store equipment | 9,000 | | |
| Other selling expenses | 6,000 | | |
| Total selling expenses | | $136,000 | |
| General and administrative expenses: | | | |
| Administrative and office salaries | $93,000 | | |
| Utilities | 3,100 | | |
| Depreciation: building | 3,000 | | |
| Other general and administrative expenses | 4,900 | | |
| Total general and administrative expenses | | 104,000 | |
| **Total operating expenses** | | | 240,000 |
| Operating income | | | $120,000 |
| Less (add): Nonoperating items: | | | |
| Interest expense | $12,000 | | |
| Purchase discounts lost | 1,200 | | |
| Interest revenue | (3,200) | | 10,000 |
| Income before income taxes | | | $110,000 |
| Income tax expense | | | 38,000 |
| **Net income** | | | $ 72,000 |
| Earnings per share | | | $4.80 |

A knowledge of accounting does not enable you to say what the level of corporate earnings *should be;* however, it does enable you to read audited financial statements that show what corporate earnings *actually are.* Moreover, you are aware that the information in published financial statements of corporations has been audited by CPA firms and has been periodically reviewed in detail by government agencies, such as the Securities and Exchange Commission (SEC). Consequently, you have some assurance that the profits reported in these published financial statements are reliable; they have been determined in accordance with generally accepted accounting principles and verified by independent experts.

| YOUR TURN | You as a Member of the House of Representatives |

Assume you are a member of the U.S. House of Representatives. Because of the financial frauds at Enron, WorldCom, and other public companies, the Congress passed, and President Bush signed, the Sarbanes-Oxley Act of 2002. The Sarbanes-Oxley Act significantly expanded the compliance burden, particularly related to financial reporting, on public companies. Certain of your business constituents argue that the compliance burden is excessive and that smaller public companies will go private, and that private businesses that need capital to expand will not go public because of the increased compliance burden. Your constituents also argue that the economy will grow more slowly, creating fewer jobs for your constituents, if companies are excluded from the capital markets because of the compliance burden imposed by the Sarbanes-Oxley Act. How would you respond?

(See our comments on the Online Learning Center Web site.)

## MULTIPLE-STEP INCOME STATEMENTS

**Learning Objective**

**LO5** Prepare a multiple-step and a single-step income statement and compute widely used measures of profitability.

A multiple-step income statement draws its name from the *series of steps* in which costs and expenses are deducted from revenue and other nonoperating items are incorporated into the income statement. As a first step, the cost of goods sold is deducted from net sales to determine the subtotal *gross profit*. As a second step, operating expenses are deducted to obtain a subtotal called **operating income** (or income from operations). As a final step, income tax expense and other nonoperating items are taken into consideration to arrive at *net income*.

Notice that the income statement is divided into four major sections: (1) revenue, (2) cost of goods sold, (3) operating expenses, and (4) nonoperating items. Multiple-step income statements are noted for their numerous sections and the development of significant subtotals.

**The Revenue Section**   In a merchandising company, the revenue section of the income statement usually contains only one line, entitled *net sales*. (Other types of revenue, if any, appear in the final section of the statement.)

Investors and managers are vitally interested in the *trend* in net sales. As one means of evaluating this trend, they often compute the percentage change in net sales from year to year. As discussed earlier in this chapter, a **percentage change** is the dollar amount of the *change* in a financial measurement, expressed as a percentage. It is computed by dividing the dollar amount of increase or decrease by the dollar amount of the measurement *before* the change occurred. (Dollar changes *cannot* be expressed as percentages if the financial statement amount in the earlier period is zero or has changed from a negative amount to a positive amount.)

In our economy, most prices increase over time. The average increase in prices during the year is called the *rate of inflation*. Because of inflation, a company's net sales may increase slightly from year to year even if the company is not selling greater amounts of merchandise. If a company's physical sales volume is increasing, net sales usually will grow faster than the rate of inflation.

If a company's sales grow faster than the *industry average,* the company increases its **market share**—that is, its share of total industry sales.

Publicly owned corporations include in their annual reports schedules summarizing operating data—such as net sales—for a period of 5 or 10 years. This information is also readily available through several online databases.

**The Cost of Goods Sold Section**   The second section of a merchandising company's income statement shows cost of goods sold for the period. Cost of goods sold usually appears as a single dollar amount, which includes such incidental items as freight costs and normal shrinkage losses.

**Gross Profit: A Key Subtotal**   In a multiple-step income statement, gross profit appears as a subtotal. This makes it easy for users of the income statement to compute the company's *gross profit rate* (or profit margin).

The gross profit rate is gross profit expressed as a *percentage of net sales.* In 2011, Computer City earned an average gross profit rate of *40 percent,* computed as follows:

| | |
|---|---:|
| Dollar amount of gross profit | $360,000 |
| Net sales | $900,000 |
| Gross profit rate ($360,000 ÷ $900,000) | 40% |

In evaluating the gross profit rate of a particular company, the analyst should consider the rates earned in prior periods, as well as the rates earned by *other companies* in the same industry. For most merchandising companies, gross profit rates are often between 20 percent and 50 percent, depending on the types of products they sell. These rates usually are lowest on fast-moving merchandise, such as groceries, and highest on specialty and novelty products.

Under normal circumstances, a company's gross profit rate tends to remain *reasonably stable* from one period to the next. Significant changes in this rate may provide investors with an early indication of changing consumer demand for the company's products.

### The Operating Expenses Section

Operating expenses are incurred for the purpose of *producing revenue.* These expenses often are subdivided into the classifications of *selling expenses* and *general and administrative expenses.* Subdividing operating expenses into functional classifications aids management and other users of the statements in separately evaluating different aspects of the company's operations. For example, selling expenses often rise and fall in concert with changes in net sales. Administrative expenses, on the other hand, usually remain more constant from one period to the next.

### Operating Income: Another Key Subtotal

Some of the revenue and expenses of a business result from activities other than the company's basic business operations. Common examples include interest earned on investments and income tax expense.

*Operating income* (or income from operations) shows the relationship between revenue earned from customers and expenses incurred in producing this revenue. In effect, operating income measures the profitability of a company's *basic or core business operations* and leaves out other types of revenue and expenses.

### Nonoperating Items

Revenue and expenses that are not directly related to the company's primary business activities are listed in a final section of the income statement following operating income.

Two significant nonoperating items are interest expense and income tax expense. Interest expense results from the manner in which assets are *financed,* not the manner in which these assets are used in business operations. Income tax expense is not included among the operating expenses because paying income taxes *does not directly contribute to the production of revenue.* Nonoperating revenues, such as interest and dividends earned on investments, also are listed in this section of the income statement.

### Net Income

Many equity investors consider net income (or net loss) to be the most important figure in a company's financial statements. This amount usually represents the overall increase (or decrease) in owners' equity resulting from all profit-directed activities during the period.

Financial analysts often compute net income as a *percentage of net sales* (net income divided by net sales). This measurement provides an indication of management's *ability to control expenses* and to retain a reasonable portion of its revenue as profit.

The normal ratio of net income to net sales varies greatly by industry. In some industries, companies may be successful by earning a net income equal to only 2 percent or 3 percent of net sales. In other industries, net income may be much higher. In 2011, Computer City's net income amounts to *8 percent* of net sales.

| | |
|---|---:|
| Net income | $ 72,000 |
| Net sales | $900,000 |
| Net income as a percentage of net sales ($72,000 ÷ $900,000) | 8% |

**Learning Objective**
Put a company's net income into perspective by relating it to sales, assets, and stockholders' equity.    **LO6**

## EARNINGS PER SHARE

Ownership of a corporation is evidenced by *shares* of capital stock. What does the net income of a corporation mean to someone who owns, say, 100 shares of a corporation's capital stock? To assist individual stockholders in relating the corporation's net income to *their ownership shares,* public companies compute **earnings per share** and show these amounts at the bottom of their income statements.[3]

In the simplest case, earnings per share is net income, expressed on a per-share basis. For example, the balance sheet in Exhibit 14–3 indicates that Computer City has 15,000 shares of capital stock outstanding.[4] Assuming these shares had been outstanding all year, earnings per share amounts to *$4.80:*

| | |
|---|---:|
| Net income . . . . . . . . . . . . . . . . . . . . . . . . . . . . . . . . . . . . . . . . . . . . . . . . . . . | $72,000 |
| Shares of capital stock outstanding . . . . . . . . . . . . . . . . . . . . . . . . . . . . . . . . . . | 15,000 |
| Earnings per share ($72,000 ÷ 15,000 shares) . . . . . . . . . . . . . . . . . . . . . . . . . . | $4.80 |

Earnings per share is one of the most widely used of all accounting ratios. The *trend* in earnings per share and the expected earnings in future periods are *major factors* affecting the market value of a company's shares.

## PRICE-EARNINGS RATIO

**Learning Objective**

**L07**    Compute the ratios widely used in financial statement analysis and explain the significance of each.

Financial analysts express the relationship between the market price of a company's stock and the underlying earnings per share as a **price-earnings (p/e) ratio.** This ratio is computed by dividing the current market price per share of the company's stock by annual earnings per share. (A p/e ratio cannot be computed for a period in which the company incurs a net loss.)

To illustrate, assume that, at the end of 2011, Computer City's capital stock is trading among investors at a market price of *$96* per share. The p/e ratio of the company's stock is computed as follows:

| | |
|---|---:|
| Current market price per share of stock . . . . . . . . . . . . . . . . . . . . . . . . . . . . . . . . . | $96 |
| Earnings per share (for the last 12 months) . . . . . . . . . . . . . . . . . . . . . . . . . . . . . . | $4.80 |
| Price-earnings ratio ($96 ÷ $4.80) . . . . . . . . . . . . . . . . . . . . . . . . . . . . . . . . . . . . . | 20 |

Technically, this ratio is 20 to 1. But it is common practice to omit the "to 1" and merely describe a p/e ratio by the first number. The p/e ratios of many publicly owned corporations are quoted daily in the financial pages of many newspapers.

The p/e ratio reflects *investors' expectations* concerning the company's *future performance.* The more optimistic these expectations, the higher the p/e ratio is likely to be.

A p/e ratio of 10 or less often indicates that investors expect earnings to *decline* from the current level. It could also mean, however, that the stock is *undervalued.* Likewise, a stock with a p/e ratio of 30 or more usually means that investors expect earnings to *increase* from the current level. However, it may also signal that the stock is *overvalued.*

One word of caution. If earnings decline to *very low levels,* the price of the stock usually does not follow the earnings all the way down. Therefore, a company with *very low earnings* may have a *high p/e ratio* even if investors are not optimistic about future earnings. From this discussion, it should be obvious that significant judgment is required in interpreting the p/e and other financial statement ratios.

---

[3] Only publicly held corporations are *required* to report earnings on a per-share basis. For small businesses, such as Computer City, the reporting of earnings per share is optional.

[4] Assume that all 15,000 shares have been outstanding throughout the year. Computation of earnings per share in more complex situations is addressed in Chapter 12.

Measures of Profitability

## SINGLE-STEP INCOME STATEMENTS

In their annual reports, many publicly owned corporations present their financial statements in a highly condensed format. For this reason, the *single-step* income statement is widely used in annual reports. The 2011 income statement of Computer City in Exhibit 14–5 has been revised to a single-step format.

| COMPUTER CITY<br>INCOME STATEMENT<br>FOR THE YEAR ENDED DECEMBER 31, 2011 | | |
|---|---:|---:|
| **Revenue:** | | |
| Net sales | | $900,000 |
| Interest earned | | 3,200 |
| Total revenue | | $903,200 |
| **Less: Costs and expenses:** | | |
| Cost of goods sold | $540,000 | |
| Selling expenses | 136,000 | |
| General and administrative expenses | 104,000 | |
| Interest expense | 12,000 | |
| Purchase discounts lost | 1,200 | |
| Income tax expense | 38,000 | |
| Total costs and expenses | | 831,200 |
| Net income | | $ 72,000 |
| Earnings per share | | $4.80 |

**Exhibit 14–5**

**COMPUTER CITY
INCOME STATEMENT
(SINGLE-STEP)**

The single-step form of income statement takes its name from the fact that all costs and expenses are deducted from total revenue in a single step. No subtotals are shown for gross profit or for operating income, although the statement provides investors with enough information to compute these subtotals on their own. Notice that the amounts of net income and earnings per share are the same in the multiple-step and single-step income statements.

## EVALUATING THE ADEQUACY OF NET INCOME

How much net income must a business earn to be considered successful? Obviously, the dollar amount of net income that investors consider adequate depends on the *size of the business*. An annual net income of $1 million might seem impressive for an automobile dealership but would represent poor performance for a company the size of Ford, Procter & Gamble, or Home Depot.

Investors usually consider two factors in evaluating a company's profitability: (1) the trend in earnings and (2) the amount of current earnings in relation to the amount of the resources needed to produce the earnings.

Some investors regard the *trend* in earnings from year to year as more important than the amount of net income in the current period. Equity investors stand to benefit from the company's performance over the long run. Years of steadily increasing earnings may increase the value of the stockholders' investment manyfold.

In evaluating the current level of earnings, many investors use *return on investment* analysis.

© Stone/Getty Images

## RETURN ON INVESTMENT (ROI)

We have emphasized throughout this text that a basic purpose of accounting is to assist decision makers in efficiently allocating and using economic resources. In deciding where to invest their money, equity investors want to know how efficiently companies utilize resources. A common method of evaluating the efficiency with which financial resources are employed is to compute the rate of return earned on these resources. This rate of return is called the *return on investment,* or *ROI,* and is sometimes referred to as return on assets.

Mathematically, computing return on investment is simple: the annual return (or profit) generated by the investment is stated as a *percentage* of the average amount invested throughout the year. The basic idea is illustrated by the following formula:

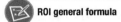

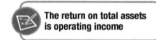 ROI general formula

$$\text{Return on Investment (ROI)} = \frac{\text{Return}}{\text{Average Amount Invested}}$$

The return is earned throughout the period. Therefore, it is logical to express this return as a percentage of the *average* amount invested during the period, rather than the investment at year-end. The average amount invested usually is computed by adding the amounts invested as of the beginning and end of the year, and dividing this total by 2. If the investment is relatively stable over time, the year-end balance may be used instead of an average.

The concept of ROI is applied in many different situations, such as evaluating the profitability of a business, a branch location, or a specific investment opportunity. As a result, a number of variations in the basic ROI ratio have been developed, each suited to a particular type of analysis. These ratios differ in the manner in which return and average amount invested are defined. We will discuss two common applications of the ROI concept: *return on assets* and *return on equity.*

## RETURN ON ASSETS (ROA)

This ratio is used in evaluating whether management has earned a reasonable return with the assets under its control. In this computation, return usually is defined as *operating income,* since interest expense and income taxes are determined by factors other than the manner in which assets are used. The **return on assets** is computed as follows:

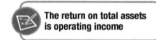 The return on total assets is operating income

$$\text{Return on Assets (ROA)} = \frac{\text{Operating Income}}{\text{Average Total Assets}}$$

Let us now determine the return on assets earned by the management of Computer City in 2011. Operating income, as shown in the income statement in Exhibit 14–4, amounts to *$120,000.* Assume that Computer City's assets at the beginning of 2011 totaled $570,000. The illustrated balance sheet in Exhibit 14–3 shows total assets of $630,000 at year-end. Therefore, the company's *average* total assets during the year amounted to *$600,000* [($570,000 + $630,000) ÷ 2]. The return on assets in 2011 is *20 percent,* determined as follows:

$$\frac{\text{Operating Income}}{\text{Average Total Assets}} = \frac{\$120,000}{\$600,000} = 20\%$$

Most successful businesses earn a return on average total assets of, perhaps, 15 percent or more. At this writing, businesses must pay interest rates of between 3 percent and 8 percent to borrow money. However, interest rates are at historic lows in the United States and are likely to rise in the future. If a business is well managed and has good future prospects, management should be able to earn a return on assets that is higher than the company's cost of borrowing.

## RETURN ON EQUITY (ROE)

The return on assets that we calculated above measures the efficiency with which management has utilized the assets under its control, regardless of whether these assets were financed with debt or equity capital. The **return on equity** ratio, in contrast, looks only at the return earned by management on the stockholders' investment—that is, on *owners' equity.*

The return to stockholders is *net income,* which represents the return from all sources, both operating and nonoperating. Thus, return on equity is computed as follows:

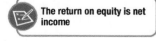 The return on equity is net income

$$\text{Return on Equity (ROE)} = \frac{\text{Net Income}}{\text{Average Total Stockholders' Equity}}$$

To illustrate, let us again turn to the 2011 financial statements of Computer City. The company earned net income of *$72,000.* The year-end balance sheet (Exhibit 14–3) shows total stockholders' equity of $420,000. To enable us to complete our computation, we will assume

Comprehensive Illustration: Seacliff Company                                               **639**

that the stockholders' equity at the *beginning* of the year amounted to $380,000. Therefore, the *average* stockholders' equity for the year amounts to *$400,000* [($380,000 + $420,000) ÷ 2]. The return on stockholders' equity in 2011 is *18 percent,* computed as follows:

$$\frac{\text{Net Income}}{\text{Average Total Stockholders' Equity}} = \frac{\$72,000}{\$400,000} = 18\%$$

Traditionally, stockholders have expected to earn an average annual return of 12 percent or more from equity investments in large, financially strong companies. Annual returns on equity of 30 percent or more are not uncommon, especially in rapidly growing companies with new or highly successful products.

The return on equity may be higher or lower than the overall return on assets, depending on how the company has financed its assets and on the amounts of its nonoperating revenue and expenses. A company that suffers a net loss provides its stockholders with a *negative* return on stockholders' equity.

## Comprehensive Illustration: Seacliff Company

Now that we have presented several techniques that are useful in better understanding an enterprise's financial statements, we will show the comprehensive analysis of a company. This illustration draws from material presented in this chapter as well as from information presented earlier in the text. We take a comprehensive look at the analysis of financial statements from the perspectives of three important groups: common stockholders, long-term creditors, and short-term creditors.

The basic information for our analysis is contained in a set of condensed two-year comparative financial statements for Seacliff Company shown in Exhibits 14–6 through 14–10. Summarized statement data, together with computations of dollar increases and decreases, and component percentages where applicable, have been compiled. For convenience in this illustration, relatively small dollar amounts have been used in the Seacliff Company financial statements.

© Digital Vision/Getty Images/DAL

## Exhibit 14–6 SEACLIFF INCOME STATEMENTS

| | | | | | | |
|---|---|---|---|---|---|---|
| **SEACLIFF COMPANY** | | | | | | |
| **COMPARATIVE INCOME STATEMENT** | | | | | | |
| **FOR THE YEARS ENDED DECEMBER 31, 2011, AND DECEMBER 31, 2010** | | | | | | |
| | | | Increase or (Decrease) | | Percentage of Net Sales | |
| | 2011 | 2010 | Dollars | % | 2011 | 2010 |
| Net sales.......................................... | $900,000 | $750,000 | $150,000 | 20.0 | 100.0 | 100.0 |
| Cost of goods sold ........................... | 530,000 | 420,000 | 110,000 | 26.2 | 58.9 | 56.0 |
| Gross profit on sales......................... | $370,000 | $330,000 | $ 40,000 | 12.1 | 41.1 | 44.0 |
| Operating expenses: | | | | | | |
| Selling expenses............................. | $117,000 | $ 75,000 | $ 42,000 | 56.0 | 13.0 | 10.0 |
| General and administrative expenses..................... | 126,000 | 95,000 | 31,000 | 32.6 | 14.0 | 12.7 |
| Total operating expenses............................ | $243,000 | $170,000 | $ 73,000 | 42.9 | 27.0 | 22.7 |
| Operating income ............................. | $127,000 | $160,000 | $ (33,000) | (20.6) | 14.1 | 21.3 |
| Interest expense ............................... | 24,000 | 30,000 | (6,000) | (20.0) | 2.7 | 4.0 |
| Income before income tax .................. | $103,000 | $130,000 | $ (27,000) | (20.8) | 11.4 | 17.3 |
| Income tax expense .......................... | 28,000 | 40,000 | (12,000) | (30.0) | 3.1 | 5.3 |
| Net income ...................................... | $ 75,000 | $ 90,000 | $ (15,000) | (16.7) | 8.3 | 12.0 |
| Earnings per share of common stock ..................... | $ 13.20 | $ 20.25 | $ (7.05) | (34.8) | | |

Exhibit 14–7 **SEACLIFF STATEMENTS OF RETAINED EARNINGS**

**SEACLIFF COMPANY**
**STATEMENT OF RETAINED EARNINGS**
**FOR THE YEARS ENDED DECEMBER 31, 2011, AND DECEMBER 31, 2010**

| | 2011 | 2010 | Increase or (Decrease) Dollars | % |
|---|---|---|---|---|
| Retained earnings, beginning of year | $176,000 | $115,000 | $ 61,000 | 53.0 |
| Net income | 75,000 | 90,000 | (15,000) | (16.7) |
| | $251,000 | $205,000 | $ 46,000 | 22.4 |
| Less: Dividends on common stock ($5.00 per share in 2010, $4.80 per share in 2011) | $ 24,000 | $ 20,000 | $ 4,000 | 20.0 |
| Dividends on preferred stock ($9 per share) | 9,000 | 9,000 | | |
| | $ 33,000 | $ 29,000 | $ 4,000 | 13.8 |
| Retained earnings, end of year | $218,000 | $176,000 | $ 42,000 | 23.9 |

Exhibit 14–8 **SEACLIFF BALANCE SHEETS**

**SEACLIFF COMPANY**
**CONDENSED COMPARATIVE BALANCE SHEET***
**DECEMBER 31, 2011, AND DECEMBER 31, 2010**

| Assets | 2011 | 2010 | Increase or (Decrease) Dollars | % | Percentage of Total Assets 2011 | 2010 |
|---|---|---|---|---|---|---|
| Current assets | $390,000 | $288,000 | $102,000 | 35.4 | 41.1 | 33.5 |
| Plant and equipment (net) | 500,000 | 467,000 | 33,000 | 7.1 | 52.6 | 54.3 |
| Other assets (loans to officers) | 60,000 | 105,000 | (45,000) | (42.9) | 6.3 | 12.2 |
| Total assets | $950,000 | $860,000 | $ 90,000 | 10.5 | 100.0 | 100.0 |
| **Liabilities & Stockholders' Equity** | | | | | | |
| Liabilities: | | | | | | |
| Current liabilities | $112,000 | $ 94,000 | $ 18,000 | 19.1 | 11.8 | 10.9 |
| 12% long-term note payable (due in 7 years) | 200,000 | 250,000 | (50,000) | (20.0) | 21.1 | 29.1 |
| Total liabilities | $312,000 | $344,000 | $ (32,000) | (9.3) | 32.9 | 40.0 |
| Stockholders' equity: | | | | | | |
| 9% preferred stock, $100 par | $100,000 | $100,000 | — | — | 10.5 | 11.6 |
| Common stock, $50 par | 250,000 | 200,000 | $ 50,000 | 25.0 | 26.3 | 23.2 |
| Additional paid-in capital | 70,000 | 40,000 | 30,000 | 75.0 | 7.4 | 4.7 |
| Retained earnings | 218,000 | 176,000 | 42,000 | 23.9 | 22.9 | 20.5 |
| Total stockholders' equity | $638,000 | $516,000 | $122,000 | 23.6 | 67.1 | 60.0 |
| Total liabilities & stockholders' equity | $950,000 | $860,000 | $ 90,000 | 10.5 | 100.0 | 100.0 |

*In order to focus attention on important subtotals, this statement is highly condensed and does not show individual asset and liability items. These details will be introduced as needed in the text discussion. For example, a list of Seacliff Company's current assets and current liabilities appears in Exhibit 14–18.

Comprehensive Illustration: Seacliff Company                                           **641**

### Exhibit 14–9 SEACLIFF STATEMENT OF CASH FLOWS

| SEACLIFF COMPANY<br>CONDENSED COMPARATIVE STATEMENT OF CASH FLOWS<br>FOR THE YEARS ENDED DECEMBER 31, 2011, AND DECEMBER 31, 2010 | | | Increase<br>or (Decrease) | |
|---|---|---|---|---|
| | 2011 | 2010 | Dollars | % |
| Cash flows from operating activities: | | | | |
| Net cash flows from operating activities | $ 19,000 | $ 95,000 | $(76,000) | (80.0) |
| Cash flows from investing activities: | | | | |
| Purchases of plant assets | (63,000) | (28,000) | (35,000) | 125.0 |
| Collections of loans from officers | 45,000 | (35,000) | 80,000 | N/A* |
| Net cash used by investing activities | $(18,000) | $(63,000) | $ 45,000 | (71.4) |
| Cash flows from financing activities: | | | | |
| Dividends paid | $(33,000) | $(29,000) | $ (4,000) | 13.8 |
| Repayment of long-term debt | (50,000) | –0– | (50,000) | N/A* |
| Proceeds from issuing capital stock | 80,000 | –0– | 80,000 | N/A* |
| Net cash used by financing activities | $ (3,000) | $(29,000) | $ 26,000 | (89.7) |
| Net increase (decrease) in cash and cash equivalents | $ (2,000) | $ 3,000 | $ (5,000) | N/A* |
| Cash and cash equivalents, January 1, 2011 | 40,000 | 37,000 | 3,000 | 8.1 |
| Cash and cash equivalents, December 31, 2011 | $ 38,000 | $ 40,000 | $ (2,000) | (5.0) |

*N/A indicates that computation of the percentage change is not appropriate. Percentage changes cannot be determined if the base year is zero or if a negative amount (cash outflow) changes to a positive amount (cash inflow).

### Exhibit 14–10

**SEACLIFF NOTES TO FINANCIAL STATEMENTS**

| SEACLIFF COMPANY<br>NOTES TO FINANCIAL STATEMENTS<br>FOR THE YEARS ENDED DECEMBER 31, 2011, AND DECEMBER 31, 2010 |
|---|

**Note 1—Accounting Policies**

*Inventories*   Inventories are determined by the LIFO method.

*Depreciation*   Depreciation is computed by the straight-line method. Buildings are depreciated over 40 years, and equipment and fixtures over periods of 5 or 10 years.

**Note 2—Unused Lines of Credit**

The company has a confirmed line of credit in the amount of $35,000. None was in use at December 31, 2011.

**Note 3—Contingencies and Commitments**

As of December 31, 2011, the company has no material commitments or noncancellable obligations. There currently are no loss contingencies known to management.

**Note 4—Current Values of Financial Instruments**

All financial instruments appear in the financial statements at dollar amounts that closely approximate their current values.

**Note 5—Concentrations of Credit Risk**

The company engages in retail sales to the general public from a single location in Seattle, Washington. No individual customer accounts for more than 2% of the company's total sales or accounts receivable. Accounts receivable are unsecured.

## ANALYSIS BY COMMON STOCKHOLDERS

Common stockholders and potential investors in common stock look first at a company's earnings record. Their investment is in shares of stock, so *earnings per share* and *dividends per share* are of particular interest.

### Earnings per Share of Common Stock

As indicated in Chapter 12, earnings per share of common stock are computed by dividing the income applicable to the common stock by the weighted-average number of shares of common stock outstanding during the year. Any preferred dividend requirements must be subtracted from net income to determine income applicable to common stock, as shown in the computations for Seacliff Company in Exhibit 14–11.

**Exhibit 14–11**

**EARNINGS PER SHARE OF COMMON STOCK**

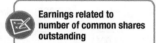

Earnings related to number of common shares outstanding

|  | | 2011 | 2010 |
|---|---|---|---|
| Net income . . . . . . . . . . . . . . . . . . . . . . . . . . . . . . . . . . . . . . . . . . . . . . . . . . |  | $75,000 | $90,000 |
| Less: Preferred dividend requirements . . . . . . . . . . . . . . . . . . . . . . . |  | 9,000 | 9,000 |
| Income applicable to common stock . . . . . . . . . . . . . . . . . . . . . . . . | (a) | $66,000 | $81,000 |
| Shares of common stock outstanding, during the year . . . . . . . . . . . | (b) | 5,000 | 4,000 |
| Earnings per share of common stock (a ÷ b) . . . . . . . . . . . . . . . . . |  | $ 13.20 | $ 20.25 |

Notice that earnings per share have decreased by *$7.05* in 2011, representing a decline of nearly *35 percent* from their level in 2010 ($7.05 ÷ $20.25 = 34.8%). Common stockholders consider a decline in earnings per share to be an unfavorable development. A decline in earnings per share generally represents a decline in the profitability of the company and creates uncertainty as to the company's prospects for future growth.

With such a significant decline in earnings per share, we should expect to see a decline in the market value of Seacliff's common stock during 2011. [For purposes of our illustration, we assume the common stock had a market value of *$160* at December 31, 2010, and of *$132* at the end of 2011. This drop of $28 per share represents a *17½ percent* decline in the market value of every common stockholder's investment ($28 decline ÷ $160 = 17.5%).]

### Price-Earnings Ratio

As we mentioned earlier in this chapter, the relationship between the market price of common stock and earnings per share is widely recognized and is expressed as a ratio, called the *price-earnings ratio* (or *p/e ratio*). The p/e ratio is determined by dividing the market price per share by the annual earnings per share.

The outlook for future earnings is the major factor influencing a company's p/e ratio. Companies with track records of rapid growth may sell at p/e ratios of perhaps 30 to 1, or even higher. Companies with "flat" earnings or earnings expected to decline in future years often sell at price-earnings ratios below 10 to 1.

At the end of 2010, Seacliff's p/e ratio was approximately *8 to 1* ($160 ÷ $20.25 = 7.9), suggesting that investors *were expecting* earnings to decline in 2011. At December 31, 2011, the price-earnings ratio was *10 to 1* ($132 ÷ $13.20 = 10.0). A p/e ratio in this range suggests that investors expect future earnings to stabilize around the current level.

### Dividend Yield

Dividends are of prime importance to some stockholders, but a secondary factor to others. Some stockholders invest primarily to receive regular cash income, while others invest in stocks principally with the expectation of rising market prices. If a corporation is profitable and retains its earnings for expansion of the business, the expanded operations should produce an increase in the net income of the company and thus tend to make each share of stock more valuable.

In comparing the merits of alternative investment opportunities, we should relate earnings and dividends per share to the *market value* of the stock at a particular date. Dividends per share divided by market price per share determine the *yield* rate of a company's stock. Dividend yield is especially important to those investors whose objective is to maximize the dividend revenue from their investments. For Seacliff, the dividend yield on its common stock was 3.1 percent in 2010 ($5 ÷ $150) and 3.6 percent in 2011 ($4.80 ÷ $132).

Comprehensive Illustration: Seacliff Company

**643**

## Summary of Earnings and Dividend Data for Seacliff    The relationships of Seacliff's per-share earnings and dividends to its year-end stock prices are summarized in Exhibit 14–12.

| Date | Market Value per Share | Earnings per Share | Price-Earnings Ratio | Dividends per Share | Dividend Yield, % |
|------|------|------|------|------|------|
| Dec. 31, 2010 . . . . . . . . . . | $160 | $20.25 | 8 | $5.00 | 3.1 |
| Dec. 31, 2011 . . . . . . . . . . | 132 | 13.20 | 10 | 4.80 | 3.6 |

**Exhibit 14–12**

**EARNINGS AND DIVIDENDS PER SHARE OF COMMON STOCK**

Earnings and dividends related to market price of common stock

The decline in market value during 2011 presumably reflects the decreases in both earnings and dividends per share. Investors appraising this stock at December 31, 2011, should consider whether a price-earnings ratio of 10 and a dividend yield of 3.6 percent meet their expectations in light of alternative investment opportunities. These investors will also place considerable weight on estimates of the company's prospective future earnings and the probable effect of such estimated earnings on the market price of the stock and on dividend payments.

## Revenue and Expense Analysis    The trend of earnings of Seacliff Company is unfavorable, and stockholders will want to know the reasons for the decline in net income. The comparative income statements in Exhibit 14–6 show that despite a 20 percent increase in net sales, net income fell from $90,000 in 2010 to $75,000 in 2011, a decline of 16.7 percent. As a percentage of net sales, net income fell from 12 percent to only 8.3 percent. The primary causes of this decline were the increases in selling expenses (56.0 percent), general and administrative expenses (32.6 percent), and the cost of goods sold (26.2 percent), all of which exceeded the 20 percent increase in net sales.

Let us assume that further investigation reveals Seacliff Company decided in 2011 to reduce its sales prices in an effort to generate greater sales volume. This would explain the decrease in the gross profit rate from 44 percent to 41.1 percent of net sales. Since the dollar amount of gross profit increased $40,000 in 2011, the strategy of reducing sales prices to increase volume would have been successful if there had been little or no increase in operating expenses. However, operating expenses rose by $73,000, resulting in a $33,000 decrease in operating income.

The next step is to find which expenses increased and why. An investor may be limited here, because detailed operating expenses are not usually shown in published financial statements. Some conclusions, however, can be reached on the basis of even the condensed information available in the comparative income statements for Seacliff Company shown in Exhibit 14–6.

The substantial increase in selling expenses presumably reflects greater selling effort during 2011 in an attempt to improve sales volume. However, the fact that selling expenses increased $42,000 while gross profit increased only $40,000 indicates that the cost of this increased sales effort was not justified in terms of results. Even more bothersome is the increase in general and administrative expenses. Some growth in administrative expenses might be expected to accompany increased sales volume, but because some of the expenses are fixed, the growth generally should be *less than proportional* to any increase in sales. The increase in general and administrative expenses from 12.7 percent to 14 percent of sales should be of concern to informed investors.

Management generally has greater control over operating expenses than over revenue. The *operating expense ratio* is often used as a measure of management's ability to control its operating expenses. We show the unfavorable trend in this ratio for Seacliff Company in Exhibit 14–13.

| | 2011 | 2010 |
|------|------|------|
| Operating expenses . . . . . . . . . . . . . . . . . . . . . . . . . . . . . . . . . . . . . | (a) $243,000 | $170,000 |
| Net sales . . . . . . . . . . . . . . . . . . . . . . . . . . . . . . . . . . . . . . . . . . . | (b) $900,000 | $750,000 |
| Operating expense ratio (a ÷ b) . . . . . . . . . . . . . . . . . . . . . . . . | 27.0% | 22.7% |

**Exhibit 14–13**

**OPERATING EXPENSE RATIO**

Does a higher operating expense ratio indicate higher net income?

If management were able to increase the sales volume while at the same time increasing the gross profit rate and decreasing the operating expense ratio, the effect on net income could be dramatic. For example, if in the year 2012 Seacliff Company can increase its sales by approximately 11 percent, to $1,000,000, increase its gross profit rate from 41.1 to 44 percent, and reduce the operating expense ratio from 27 to 24 percent, its operating income will increase from $127,000 to $200,000 ($1,000,000 − $560,000 − $240,000), an increase of over 57 percent.

## RETURN ON INVESTMENT (ROI)

The rate of return on investment (often called ROI) is a measure of management's efficiency in using available resources. Regardless of the size of the organization, capital is a scarce resource and must be used efficiently. In judging the performance of branch managers or of companywide management, it is reasonable to raise the question: What rate of return have you earned on the resources under your control?

**Return on Assets**    An important test of management's ability to earn a return on funds supplied from all sources is the rate of return on total assets.

As noted previously, the income figure used in computing this ratio should be *operating income,* since interest expense and income taxes are determined by factors other than the efficient use of resources. Operating income is earned throughout the year and therefore should be related to the *average* investment in assets during the year. In Exhibit 14–14, the computation of this ratio of Seacliff Company assumes total assets at the beginning of 2010 were $820,000.

**Exhibit 14–14**

**PERCENTAGE RETURN ON ASSETS**

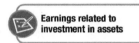

Earnings related to investment in assets

|  |  | 2011 | 2010 |
|---|---|---|---|
| Operating income | (a) | $127,000 | $160,000 |
| Total assets, beginning of year | (b) | $860,000 | $820,000 |
| Total assets, end of year | (c) | $950,000 | $860,000 |
| Average investment in assets [(b + c) ÷ 2] | (d) | $905,000 | $840,000 |
| Return on assets (a ÷ d) |  | 14% | 19% |

This ratio shows that the rate of return earned on the company's assets fell in 2011. Before drawing conclusions as to the effectiveness of Seacliff's management, however, we should consider the trend in the return on assets earned by other companies of similar kind and size.

**Return on Common Stockholders' Equity**    We introduced the concept of return on equity using a company that had only one class of capital stock. Therefore, the return on equity was simply net income divided by average stockholders' equity. But Seacliff has issued both preferred stock *and* common stock. The preferred stock does not participate fully in the company's earnings; rather, the return to preferred stockholders is limited to their dividend. Thus, we must adjust the return on equity computation to reflect the return on *common* stockholders' equity.

The return to common stockholders is equal to net income *less* any preferred dividends. Thus, the return on common stockholders' equity, assuming common stockholders' equity at the beginning of 2010 was $355,000, is computed in Exhibit 14–15.

**Exhibit 14–15**

**RETURN ON COMMON STOCKHOLDERS' EQUITY**

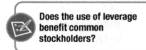

Does the use of leverage benefit common stockholders?

|  |  | 2011 | 2010 |
|---|---|---|---|
| Net income |  | $ 75,000 | $ 90,000 |
| Less: Preferred dividend requirements |  | 9,000 | 9,000 |
| Net income applicable to common stock | (a) | $ 66,000 | $ 81,000 |
| Common stockholders' equity, beginning of year | (b) | $416,000 | $355,000 |
| Common stockholders' equity, end of year | (c) | $538,000 | $416,000 |
| Average common stockholders' equity [(b + c) ÷ 2] | (d) | $477,000 | $385,500 |
| Return on common stockholders' equity (a ÷ d) |  | 13.8% | 21.0% |

In both years, the rate of return on common stockholders' equity was higher than the 12 percent rate of interest paid to long-term creditors or the 9 percent dividend rate paid to preferred stockholders. This result was achieved through the favorable use of leverage.

## LEVERAGE

Applying leverage means using borrowed money to earn a return *greater* than the cost of borrowing, increasing net income and the return on common stockholders' equity. In other words, if you can borrow money at 12 percent and use it to earn 20 percent, you will benefit by doing so. However, leverage can act as a double-edged sword; the effects may be favorable or unfavorable to the holders of common stock.

If the rate of return on total assets should fall *below* the average rate of interest on borrowed capital, leverage will *reduce* the return on common stockholders' equity. In this situation, paying off the loans that carry high interest rates would appear to be a logical move. However, many companies do not have enough cash to retire long-term debt on short notice. Therefore, the common stockholders may become locked in to the unfavorable effects of leverage.

In deciding how much leverage is appropriate, the common stockholders should consider the *stability* of the company's return on assets as well as the relationship of this return to the average cost of borrowed capital. If a business incurs so much debt that it becomes unable to meet the required interest and principal payments, the creditors may force liquidation or reorganization of the business.

**Debt Ratio**    One indicator of the amount of leverage used by a business is the debt ratio. This ratio measures the proportion of the total assets financed by creditors, as distinguished from stockholders. It is computed by dividing total liabilities by total assets. A *high* debt ratio indicates an extensive use of leverage, that is, a large proportion of financing provided by creditors. A low debt ratio, on the other hand, indicates that the business is making little use of leverage.

The debt ratio at year-end for Seacliff is determined as shown in Exhibit 14–16.

| | 2011 | 2010 |
|---|---|---|
| Total liabilities . . . . . . . . . . . . . . . . . . . . . . . . . . . . . . . . . . . . . . . . | (a) $312,000 | $344,000 |
| Total assets (or total liabilities & stockholders' equity) . . . . . . . . . . | (b) $950,000 | $860,000 |
| Debt ratio (a ÷ b) . . . . . . . . . . . . . . . . . . . . . . . . . . . . . . . . . . . . | 32.8% | 40.0% |

**Exhibit 14–16**

**DEBT RATIO**

Proportion of assets financed by creditors

Seacliff Company has a lower debt ratio in 2011 than in 2010. Is this favorable or unfavorable?

From the viewpoint of the common stockholder, a high debt ratio produces maximum benefits if management is able to earn a rate of return on assets greater than the rate of interest paid to creditors. However, a high debt ratio can be *unfavorable* if the return on assets falls *below* the rate of interest paid to creditors. Since the return on total assets earned by Seacliff Company has declined from 19 percent in 2010 to a relatively low 14 percent in 2011, the common stockholders probably would *not* want to risk a high debt ratio. The action by management in 2011 of retiring $50,000 in long-term liabilities will help to protect the common stockholders from the unfavorable effects of leverage if the rate of return on assets continues to decline.

---

**CASE IN POINT**

A historical example from Dell Inc. provides an interesting case study in how financial leverage can be used to greatly increase the returns earned by common stockholders without appreciably increasing the company's risk profile. Dell's 2004 return on assets was an impressive 20 percent, and its return on common equity was an eye-popping 47 percent. Clearly Dell benefited from favorable financial leverage.

Moreover, Dell benefited from favorable financial leverage without increasing its risk profile. That is, most of Dell's leverage was in the form of *non-interest*-bearing liabilities. Although liabilities comprised 67.5 percent of Dell's assets, *interest-bearing* liabilities represented only 2.6 percent of assets. Approximately 84 percent of Dell's liabilities were current, representing either trade credit (accounts payable) or accrued liabilities (e.g., unpaid salaries and benefits). In essence, much of Dell's financing was being provided by its trade creditors and employees, which are essentially free sources of financing.

## ANALYSIS BY LONG-TERM CREDITORS

Bondholders and other long-term creditors are primarily interested in three factors: (1) the rate of return on their investment, (2) the firm's ability to meet its interest requirements, and (3) the firm's ability to repay the principal of the debt when it falls due.

### Yield Rate on Bonds

The yield rate on bonds or other long-term indebtedness cannot be computed in the same manner as the yield rate on shares of stock, because bonds, unlike stocks, have a definite maturity date and amount. The ownership of a 12 percent, 10-year, $1,000 bond represents the right to receive $120 each year for 10 years plus the right to receive $1,000 at the end of 10 years. If the market price of this bond is $950, the yield rate on an investment in the bond is the rate of interest that will make the *present value* of these two contractual rights equal to the $950 market price.

When bonds sell at maturity value, the yield rate is equal to the bond interest rate. *The yield rate varies inversely with changes in the market price of the bond.* If interest rates rise, the market price of existing bonds will fall; if interest rates decline, the price of bonds will rise. If the price of a bond is above maturity value, the yield rate is less than the bond interest rate; if the price of a bond is below maturity value, the yield rate is higher than the bond interest rate.

### Interest Coverage Ratio

Bondholders feel that their investments are relatively safe if the issuing company earns enough income to cover its annual interest obligations by a comfortable margin.

A common measure of creditors' safety is the ratio of operating income available for the payment of interest to the annual interest expense, called the *interest coverage ratio* or *times interest earned*. See this computation for Seacliff Company in Exhibit 14–17.

**Exhibit 14–17**

**INTEREST COVERAGE RATIO**

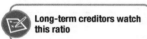

Long-term creditors watch this ratio

|  | | 2011 | 2010 |
|---|---|---|---|
| Operating income (before interest and income taxes) . . . . . . . . . . | (a) | $127,000 | $160,000 |
| Annual interest expense . . . . . . . . . . . . . . . . . . . . . . . . . . . . . . . . . | (b) | $ 24,000 | $ 30,000 |
| Interest coverage (a ÷ b) . . . . . . . . . . . . . . . . . . . . . . . . . . . . . . . . . |  | 5.3 times | 5.3 times |

The ratio remained unchanged at a satisfactory level during 2011. Generally an interest coverage ratio above 2.0 is considered strong.

### Debt Ratio

Long-term creditors are interested in the percentage of total assets financed by debt, as distinguished from the percentage financed by stockholders. The percentage of total assets financed by debt is measured by the debt ratio, which was computed in Exhibit 14–16.

From a creditor's viewpoint, the lower the debt ratio, the better, since this means that stockholders have contributed a higher percentage of the funds to the business, and therefore the margin of protection to creditors against a shrinkage of the assets is high.

As shown in Exhibit 14–16, the debt ratio, or the percentage of assets financed by debt, decreased from 2010 to 2011 from 40 percent to 32.8 percent. This would generally be considered by long-term creditors to be a favorable change because the debt burden, including required interest payments, is less in 2011 than in 2010, thereby making the claim of each creditor more secure.

### Secured Claims

Sometimes the claims of long-term creditors are secured with specific collateral, such as the land and buildings owned by the borrower. In these situations, the secured creditors may look primarily to the *value of the collateral* in assessing the safety of their claims.

Assets pledged as collateral to secure specific liabilities are disclosed in notes to the financial statements. As Seacliff makes no such disclosures, we may assume that none of its assets have been pledged as collateral to secure specific liabilities.

## ANALYSIS BY SHORT-TERM CREDITORS

Bankers and other short-term creditors share the interest of stockholders and bondholders in the profitability and long-run stability of a business. Their primary interest, however, is in the current position of the company—its ability to generate sufficient funds (working capital) to meet current operating needs and to pay current debts promptly. Thus, the analysis of financial statements by a banker considering a short-term loan, or by a trade creditor investigating the credit status of a customer, is likely to center on the working capital position of the prospective debtor.

**Amount of Working Capital** Working capital is the excess of current assets over current liabilities. It represents the cash and near-cash assets that provide a "cushion" of liquidity over the amount expected to be needed in the near future to satisfy maturing obligations. The details of the working capital of Seacliff Company are shown in Exhibit 14–18.

**Exhibit 14–18 SEACLIFF SCHEDULE OF WORKING CAPITAL**

| | | | | | | | |
|---|---|---|---|---|---|---|---|
| **SEACLIFF COMPANY** COMPARATIVE SCHEDULE OF WORKING CAPITAL AS OF DECEMBER 31, 2011, AND DECEMBER 31, 2010 | | | | | | | |
| | | | **Increase or (Decrease)** | | **Percentage of Total Current Items** | | |
| | **2011** | **2010** | **Dollars** | **%** | **2011** | **2010** | |
| Current assets: | | | | | | | |
| Cash ......................................... | $ 38,000 | $ 40,000 | $ (2,000) | (5.0) | 9.7 | 13.9 | |
| Accounts receivable (net) ............................ | 117,000 | 86,000 | 31,000 | 36.0 | 30.0 | 29.9 | |
| Inventories ...................................... | 180,000 | 120,000 | 60,000 | 50.0 | 46.2 | 41.6* | |
| Prepaid expenses ................................ | 55,000 | 42,000 | 13,000 | 31.0 | 14.1 | 14.6 | |
| Total current assets .................................... | $390,000 | $288,000 | $102,000 | 35.4 | 100.0 | 100.0 | |
| Current liabilities: | | | | | | | |
| Notes payable to creditors ................................. | $ 14,600 | $ 10,000 | $ 4,600 | 46.0 | 13.1* | 10.7* | |
| Accounts payable ................................ | 66,000 | 30,000 | 36,000 | 120.0 | 58.9 | 31.9 | |
| Accrued liabilities ............................... | 31,400 | 54,000 | (22,600) | (41.9) | 28.0 | 57.4 | |
| Total current liabilities .................................. | $112,000 | $ 94,000 | $ 18,000 | 19.1 | 100.0 | 100.0 | |
| Working capital ..................................... | $278,000 | $194,000 | $ 84,000 | 43.3 | | | |

*Amounts adjusted so that totals equal 100.0.

This schedule shows that current assets increased $102,000, while current liabilities rose by only $18,000. As a result, working capital increased $84,000.

**Quality of Working Capital** In evaluating the debt-paying ability of a business, short-term creditors should consider the quality of working capital as well as the total dollar amount. The principal factors affecting the quality of working capital are (1) the nature of the current assets and (2) the length of time required to convert those assets into cash.

The schedule in Exhibit 14–18 shows an unfavorable shift in the composition of Seacliff Company's working capital during 2011: cash decreased from 13.9 percent to 9.7 percent of current assets, while inventory rose from 41.6 percent to 46.2 percent. Inventory is a less liquid resource than cash. Therefore, the quality of working capital is not as liquid as in 2010. *Turnover rates* (or *ratios*) may be used to assist short-term creditors in estimating the time required to turn assets such as receivables and inventory into cash.

**Accounts Receivable Turnover Rate** As explained in Chapter 7, the accounts receivable turnover rate indicates how quickly a company converts its accounts receivable into cash. The accounts receivable turnover *rate* is determined by dividing net sales by the average balance of accounts receivable.[5] The number of *days* required (on average) to collect accounts receivable then may be determined by dividing the number of days in a year (365) by the turnover rate. The computations in Exhibit 14–19 use the data in our Seacliff example, assuming accounts receivable at the beginning of 2010 were $80,000.

**Exhibit 14–19**

**ACCOUNTS RECEIVABLE TURNOVER**

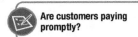
Are customers paying promptly?

| | 2011 | 2010 |
|---|---|---|
| Net sales . . . . . . . . . . . . . . . . . . . . . . . . . . . . . . . . . . . . . . . . . . . . . | (a) $900,000 | $750,000 |
| Accounts receivable, beginning of year . . . . . . . . . . . . . . . . . . . | $ 86,000 | $ 80,000 |
| Accounts receivable, end of year . . . . . . . . . . . . . . . . . . . . . . . . | $117,000 | $ 86,000 |
| Average accounts receivable . . . . . . . . . . . . . . . . . . . . . . . . . . . . | (b) $101,500 | $ 83,000 |
| Accounts receivable turnover per year (a ÷ b) . . . . . . . . . . . . . . . | 8.9 times | 9.0 times |
| Average number of days to collect accounts receivable (divide 365 days by accounts receivable turnover). . . . . . . . . . . . . . . | 41 days | 41 days |

There has been no change in the average time required to collect receivables. The interpretation of the average age of receivables depends upon the company's credit terms and the seasonal activity immediately before year-end. For example, if the company grants 30-day credit terms to its customers, the analysis in Exhibit 14–19 indicates that accounts receivable collections are lagging. If the terms are for 60 days, however, collections are being made ahead of schedule.

**Inventory Turnover Rate** The inventory turnover rate indicates how many times during the year the company is able to sell a quantity of goods equal to its average inventory. Mechanically, this rate is determined by dividing the cost of goods sold for the year by the average amount of inventory on hand during the year. The number of days required to sell this amount of inventory may be determined by dividing 365 days by the turnover rate. These computations were explained in Chapter 8 and are demonstrated in Exhibit 14–20 using the information for Seacliff Company, assuming inventory at the beginning of 2010 was $100,000. The trend indicated by this analysis is unfavorable, since the length of time required for Seacliff to turn over (sell) its inventory is increasing.

**Exhibit 14–20**

**INVENTORY TURNOVER**

| | 2011 | 2010 |
|---|---|---|
| Cost of goods sold . . . . . . . . . . . . . . . . . . . . . . . . . . . . . . . . . . . . | (a) $530,000 | $420,000 |
| Inventory, beginning of year . . . . . . . . . . . . . . . . . . . . . . . . . . . . | $120,000 | $100,000 |
| Inventory, end of year. . . . . . . . . . . . . . . . . . . . . . . . . . . . . . . . . . | $180,000 | $120,000 |
| Average inventory. . . . . . . . . . . . . . . . . . . . . . . . . . . . . . . . . . . . . | (b) $150,000 | $110,000 |
| Average inventory turnover per year (a ÷ b) . . . . . . . . . . . . . . . . | 3.5 times | 3.8 times |
| Average number of days to sell inventory (divide 365 days by inventory turnover). . . . . . . . . . . . . . . . . . . . . . . . | 104 days | 96 days |

Companies that have low gross profit rates often need high inventory turnover rates in order to operate profitably. This is another way of saying that if the gross profit rate is low, a high volume of transactions is necessary to produce a satisfactory amount of profits. Companies that sell high markup items, such as jewelry stores and art galleries, can operate successfully with much lower inventory turnover rates.

**Operating Cycle** The inventory turnover rate indicates how quickly inventory *sells,* but not how quickly this asset converts into *cash.* Short-term creditors, of course, are interested primarily in the company's ability to generate cash.

The period of time required for a merchandising company to convert its inventory into cash is called the *operating cycle.* The illustration appeared in Chapter 6 and is repeated in Exhibit 14–21 for your convenience.

[5] Ideally, the accounts receivable turnover is computed by dividing net *credit* sales by the *monthly* average of receivables. Such detailed information, however, generally is not provided in annual financial statements.

Comprehensive Illustration: Seacliff Company

**649**

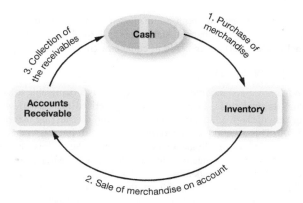

## Exhibit 14–21
**OPERATING CYCLE**

The operating cycle repeats continuously

Seacliff's operating cycle in 2011 was approximately 145 days, computed by adding the 104 days required to turn over inventory and the average 41 days required to collect receivables. This compares with an operating cycle of only 137 days in 2010, computed as 96 days to dispose of the inventory plus 41 days to collect the resulting receivables. From the viewpoint of short-term creditors, the *shorter* the operating cycle, the *higher the quality* of the borrower's working capital. Therefore, these creditors would regard the lengthening of Seacliff Company's operating cycle as an unfavorable trend.

**Current Ratio** The current ratio expresses the relationship between current assets and current liabilities. A strong current ratio provides considerable evidence that a company will be able to meet its obligations coming due in the near future. The current ratio for Seacliff Company is computed in Exhibit 14–22.

| | 2011 | 2010 |
|---|---|---|
| Total current assets | (a) $390,000 | $288,000 |
| Total current liabilities | (b) $112,000 | $ 94,000 |
| Current ratio (a ÷ b) | 3.5 | 3.1 |

## Exhibit 14–22
**CURRENT RATIO**

Does this indicate satisfactory debt-paying ability?

**Quick Ratio** Because inventories and prepaid expenses are further removed from conversion into cash than other current assets, the *quick ratio* is sometimes computed as a supplement to the current ratio. The quick ratio compares the most liquid current assets (cash, marketable securities, and receivables) with current liabilities. Seacliff Company has no marketable securities; its quick ratio is computed in Exhibit 14–23.

| | 2011 | 2010 |
|---|---|---|
| Quick assets (cash and accounts receivable) | (a) $155,000 | $126,000 |
| Current liabilities | (b) $112,000 | $ 94,000 |
| Quick ratio (a ÷ b) | 1.4 | 1.3 |

## Exhibit 14–23
**QUICK RATIO**

A measure of liquidity

Here again the analysis reveals a favorable trend and a strong position. If the credit periods extended to customers and granted by creditors are roughly equal, a quick ratio of 1.0 or better is considered satisfactory.

**Unused Lines of Credit** From the viewpoint of a short-term creditor, a company's unused lines of credit represent a resource almost as liquid as cash. An unused line of credit means that a bank has agreed in advance to lend the company any amount, up to the specified limit. As long as this line of credit remains available, creditors know that the business can borrow cash quickly and easily for any purpose, including payments of creditors' claims.

Existing unused lines of credit are *disclosed* in notes accompanying the financial statements. See Note 2 to the financial statements in Exhibit 14–10. Short-term creditors would view Seacliff's $35,000 line of credit as enhancing the company's liquidity.

## CASH FLOW ANALYSIS

We often have stressed the importance of a company's being able to generate sufficient cash flows from its operations. In 2010, Seacliff generated net cash flows of $95,000 from its operating activities—a relatively "normal" amount, considering that net income for the year was $90,000. This $95,000 remained *after* payment of interest to creditors and amounted to more than three times the dividends paid to stockholders. Thus, in 2010 the net cash flows from operating activities appeared quite sufficient to ensure that Seacliff could pay its interest obligations and also pay dividends.

In 2011, however, net cash flows from operating activities declined to $19,000, an amount far below the company's $75,000 net income and only approximately 58 percent of the amount of dividends paid. Stockholders and creditors would view this dramatic decline in cash flows as a negative and potentially dangerous development.

A reconciliation of Seacliff's net income in 2011 with its net cash flows from operating activities is shown in Exhibit 14–24. For purposes of this analysis, we assume that the notes payable to creditors resulted from purchases from suppliers rather than loans from a financial institution. Therefore, the increase in notes payable is treated in the same way as the increase in accounts payable as part of the reconciliation of net income to net cash from operating activities. Had the notes payable resulted from borrowing activities, the change would be classified as a financing activity and not as an adjustment to net income in determining net cash from operating activities.

**Exhibit 14–24**

**SEACLIFF RECONCILIATION OF NET INCOME TO NET CASH FROM OPERATING ACTIVITIES**

| | | |
|---|---:|---:|
| Net income . . . . . . . . . . . . . . . . . . . . . . . . . . . . . . . . . . . . . . . . | | $ 75,000 |
| Add: | | |
| Depreciation expense . . . . . . . . . . . . . . . . . . . . . . . . . . . . . . . . | $30,000 | |
| Increase in notes payable to creditors . . . . . . . . . . . . . . . . . . . . . . | 4,600 | |
| Increase in accounts payable . . . . . . . . . . . . . . . . . . . . . . . . . . . . | 36,000 | 70,600 |
| | | $145,600 |
| Less: | | |
| Increase in accounts receivable . . . . . . . . . . . . . . . . . . . . . . . . . . | $31,000 | |
| Increase in inventories . . . . . . . . . . . . . . . . . . . . . . . . . . . . . . . . | 60,000 | |
| Increase in prepaid expenses . . . . . . . . . . . . . . . . . . . . . . . . . . . . | 13,000 | |
| Decrease in accrued liabilities . . . . . . . . . . . . . . . . . . . . . . . . . . . . | 22,600 | 126,600 |
| Net cash flows from operating activities . . . . . . . . . . . . . . . . . . . . . . | | $ 19,000 |

As explained in Chapter 13, the FASB requires companies to provide this reconciliation either in the body of the statement of cash flows or in a supplemental schedule.

The primary reasons for Seacliff's low net operating cash flows appear to be the growth in uncollected accounts receivable and inventories, combined with the substantial reduction in accrued liabilities. Given the significant increase in sales during 2011, the increase in accounts receivable is to be expected. The large reduction in accrued liabilities may be a one-time event that will not necessarily recur next year. The large increase in inventory, however, may have reduced Seacliff's liquidity unnecessarily.

Seacliff's financial position, particularly its short-term liquidity, would appear considerably stronger if its increased sales volume were supported by a higher *inventory turnover rate,* instead of a larger inventory.

### Cash Flows from Operations to Current Liabilities    An additional measure of liquidity that is sometimes computed, based in part on information from the statement of cash flows, is the ratio of cash flows from operations to current liabilities. This measure provides evidence of the company's ability to cover its currently maturing liabilities from

normal operations. For 2010 and 2011, the ratio is computed for Seacliff Corporation in Exhibit 14–25.

|  | 2011 | 2010 |
| --- | --- | --- |
| Cash flows from operations .............................. | (a) $ 19,000 | $95,000 |
| Current liabilities ....................................... | (b) $112,000 | $94,000 |
| Cash flows from operations to current liabilities (a ÷ b) ......... | 0.17 | 1.01 |

**Exhibit 14–25**

**CASH FLOWS FROM OPERATIONS TO CURRENT LIABILITIES**

As you can see from this measure, Seacliff was much stronger in 2010 than in 2011. In 2010, operating cash flows were slightly more than current liabilities at year-end, indicating an ability to cover current obligations from normal operations without regard to the amount of existing current assets. In 2011, however, operations provided only 17 percent as much cash as needed to meet current obligations, implying a need to rely more heavily on existing current assets than in 2010. Some analysts consider a ratio of cash flows from operations to current liabilities of 0.40 or higher to be strong.

## USEFULNESS OF NOTES TO FINANCIAL STATEMENTS

A set of financial statements normally is accompanied by several *notes,* disclosing information useful in *interpreting* the statements. Users should view these notes as an *integral part* of the financial statements.

In preceding chapters we have identified many items that are disclosed in notes accompanying the financial statements. Among the most useful are the following:

- Accounting policies and methods
- Unused lines of credit
- Significant commitments and loss contingencies
- Current values of financial instruments (if different from the carrying values shown in the statements)
- Dividends in arrears
- Concentrations of credit risk
- Assets pledged to secure specific liabilities

In Exhibit 14–10 the notes accompanying Seacliff's financial statements are quite clean—that is, they contain no surprises or cause for concern. Of course, the unused line of credit disclosed in Note 2 would be of interest to anyone evaluating the company's short-term debt-paying ability.

**YOUR TURN**    **You as a Financial Analyst**

Assume that you are a financial analyst and that two of your clients are requesting your advice on certain companies as potential investments. Both clients are interested in purchasing common stock. One is primarily interested in the dividends to be received from the investment. The second is primarily interested in the growth of the market value of the stock. What information would you advise your clients to focus on in their respective analyses?

(See our comments on the Online Learning Center Web site.)

## INTERNATIONAL FINANCIAL REPORTING STANDARDS

As you have learned throughout this text, an effort is currently under way to standardize financial reporting practices worldwide. During this period of transition, which is expected to require several years, analyzing financial statements that originate in different countries poses a significant challenge due to differences in reporting practices. There exist many different local standards, as in the United States, and there are emerging international standards which are rapidly being accepted in various countries.

Two areas of particular interest in analyzing financial statements are consolidated statements and segment reporting. Earlier in this chapter, we briefly covered consolidated financial statements; where there are strong financial connections (e.g., overlapping ownership) between or among two or more companies, those companies typically present consolidated financial statements. This means that they report as a single entity rather than as separate entities, although legally they may be recognized as separate entities. At the present time, there is no single agreed-upon criterion for when consolidated financial statements should be prepared. This makes comparisons difficult because of the significant impact preparing consolidated statements has on the information provided when compared with presenting information about each separate entity.

Segment reporting refers to the presentation of information about parts of a business, usually along industry or product lines and geographic areas. Because risks that companies take vary considerably by industry and location, accounting standards require companies to provide supplemental information that informs investors and creditors of the extent of contribution a company's operations in different industries and in different geographic areas to the totals found in the primary financial statements. Some of the differences that exist around the world among individual country standards and between those standards and international standards deal with the definitions used in presenting segment information, the criteria used to identify segments for which disclosure is required, and the specific information that must be presented when disclosure is required.

Policies regarding consolidated financial statements and segment reporting are only two of the many areas the financial statement analyst must be aware of in approaching financial statements from different parts of the world. The authors are confident that, over time, we will move toward greater standardization for these and other aspects of financial reporting so that, in the future, we will be able to place even greater reliance than today on the comparability of financial statements worldwide.

## SUMMARY OF ANALYTICAL MEASUREMENTS

The financial ratios and other measurements introduced in this textbook thus far, including this chapter—and their significance—are summarized in Exhibit 14–26.

### Exhibit 14-26 SUMMARY OF ANALYTICAL MEASURES

| Ratios or Other Measurements | Method of Computation | Significance |
|---|---|---|
| **Measures of short-term liquidity** | | |
| Current ratio | $\dfrac{\text{Current Assets}}{\text{Current Liabilities}}$ | A measure of short-term debt-paying ability |
| Quick ratio | $\dfrac{\text{Quick Assets}}{\text{Current Liabilities}}$ | A measure of short-term debt-paying ability |
| Working capital | Current Assets − Current Liabilities | A measure of short-term debt-paying ability |
| Net cash provided by operating activities | Appears in the statement of cash flows | Indicates the cash generated by operations after allowing for cash payment of expenses and operating liabilities |
| Cash flow from operations to current liabilities | $\dfrac{\text{Cash Flows from Operating Activities}}{\text{Current Liabilities}}$ | Indicates ability to cover currently maturing obligations from recurring operations |
| Accounts receivable turnover rate | $\dfrac{\text{Net Sales}}{\text{Average Accounts Receivable}}$ | Indicates how quickly receivables are collected |
| Days to collect average accounts receivable | $\dfrac{\text{365 Days}}{\text{Accounts Receivable Turnover Rate}}$ | Indicates in days how quickly receivables are collected |
| Inventory turnover rate | $\dfrac{\text{Cost of Goods Sold}}{\text{Average Inventory}}$ | Indicates how quickly inventory sells |

(continued on next page)

Comprehensive Illustration: Seacliff Company

## Exhibit 14–26  continued

| Ratios or Other Measurements | Method of Computation | Significance |
|---|---|---|
| Days to sell the average inventory | $$\frac{365 \text{ Days}}{\text{Inventory Turnover Rate}}$$ | Indicates in days how quickly inventory sells |
| Operating cycle | Days to Sell Inventory + Days to Collect Receivables | Indicates in days how quickly cash invested in inventory converts back into cash |
| Free cash flow | Net Cash from Operating Activities − Cash Used for Investing Activities and Dividends | Excess of operating cash flow over basic needs |
| **Measures of long-term credit risk** | | |
| Debt ratio | $$\frac{\text{Total Liabilities}}{\text{Total Assets}}$$ | Percentage of assets financed by creditors; indicates relative size of the equity position |
| Trend in net cash provided by operating activities | Appears in comparative statements of cash flows | Indicator of a company's ability to generate the cash necessary to meet its obligations |
| Interest coverage ratio | $$\frac{\text{Income before Interest and Taxes}}{\text{Annual Interest Expense}}$$ | Indicator of a company's ability to meet its interest payment obligations |
| **Measures of profitability** | | |
| Percentage changes; that is, in net sales and net income | $$\frac{\text{Dollar Amount of Change}}{\text{Financial Statement Amount in the Earlier Year}}$$ | The rate at which a key measure is increasing or decreasing; the "growth rate" |
| Gross profit rate | $$\frac{\text{Gross Profit}}{\text{Net Sales}}$$ | A measure of the profitability of the company's products |
| Operating expense ratio | $$\frac{\text{Operating Expenses}}{\text{Net Sales}}$$ | A measure of management's ability to control expenses |
| Operating income | Gross Profit − Operating Expenses | The profitability of a company's basic business activities |
| Net income as a percentage of net sales | $$\frac{\text{Net Income}}{\text{Net Sales}}$$ | An indicator of management's ability to control costs |
| Earnings per share | $$\frac{\text{Net Income} - \text{Preferred Dividends}}{\text{Average Number of Common Shares Outstanding}}$$ | Net income applicable to each share of common stock |
| Return on assets | $$\frac{\text{Operating Income}}{\text{Average Total Assets}}$$ | A measure of the productivity of assets, regardless of how the assets are financed |
| Return on equity | $$\frac{\text{Net Income}}{\text{Average Total Equity}}$$ | The rate of return earned on the stockholders' equity in the business |
| Return on common stockholders' equity | $$\frac{\text{Net Income} - \text{Preferred Dividends}}{\text{Average Common Stockholders' Equity}}$$ | The rate of return earned on the common stockholders' equity; appropriate when company has both common and preferred stock |
| **Measures for evaluating the current market price of common stock** | | |
| Market value of financial instruments | Quoted in financial press or disclosed in financial statements | Reflects both investors' expectations and current market conditions |
| Price-earnings ratio | $$\frac{\text{Current Stock Price}}{\text{Earnings per Share}}$$ | A measure of investors' expectations about the company's future prospects |
| Dividend yield | $$\frac{\text{Annual Dividend}}{\text{Current Stock Price}}$$ | Dividends expressed as a rate of return on the market price of the stock |
| Book value per share | $$\frac{\text{Common Stockholders' Equity}}{\text{Shares of Common Stock Outstanding}}$$ | The recorded value of net assets underlying each share of common stock |

## Ethics, Fraud & Corporate Governance

The tools discussed in this chapter involve using financial statement numbers to help make investment and credit decisions. Given the high-profile accounting frauds of the early 2000s and the resulting focus on corporate governance, a new type of tool has arisen to help investors and creditors make investment decisions. This new tool involves ratings of the quality of a company's corporate governance. Many investors and creditors believe that better-governed firms are better managed, and that these firms will either offer superior performance (returns) over time and/or will offer returns comparable to less well governed firms but with less risk.

A number of organizations provide ratings of corporate governance quality for public companies. Two of the most prominent of these organizations are ISS Governance Services, a unit of Risk Metrics Group, and The Corporate Library (TCL) (Portland, Maine).

ISS Governance Services describes itself as "a leader in proxy voting and corporate governance matters." ISS provides coverage of over 38,000 shareholder meetings across 100 markets, serving institutional and corporate clients. These clients hire ISS to analyze corporate proxy statements and to make recommendations on the manner in which these institutional and corporate clients should vote on matters subject to shareholder ratification.

ISS rates the quality of a company's corporate governance by computing a Corporate Governance Quotient (CGQ). ISS computes CGQs for more than 7,500 companies worldwide. A company's CGQ is based on its ratings in these eight core categories: (1) board structure and composition, (2) audit issues, (3) charter and bylaw provisions, (4) laws of the state of incorporation, (5) executive and director compensation, (6) progressive practices, (7) D&O stock ownership, and (8) director education.

The Corporate Library (TCL) is a more recent entrant into the market for rating governance effectiveness. Unlike ISS, TCL claims that its proprietary dynamic indicators go beyond conventional benchmarks for good corporate governance. Many rating systems are based on a company's compliance with governance practices perceived as best practices; TCL attempts to differentiate its rating system by focusing only on those board characteristics that its proprietary research has found to be associated with preserving and enhancing shareholder wealth. TCL considers a company's governance in four key areas: (1) board composition and succession planning, (2) CEO compensation practices, (3) takeover defenses, and (4) board level accounting concerns.

## Concluding Remarks

For the most part, our discussion in this chapter has been limited to the kinds of analysis that can be performed by external users who do not have access to the company's accounting records. Investors and creditors must rely to a considerable extent on the financial statements published in annual and quarterly reports. In the case of publicly owned corporations, additional information is filed with the Securities and Exchange Commission (SEC) and is available to the public in hard copy, as well as on the Internet. In fact, the Internet is the fastest growing source of *free* information available to decision makers in this information age.

Many financial analysts who evaluate the financial statements and future prospects of publicly owned companies sell their conclusions and investment recommendations for a fee. For example, detailed financial analyses of most large companies are available from Standard & Poor's, Moody's Investors Service, and The Value Line Investment Survey. Anyone may subscribe to these investment services.

Bankers and major creditors usually are able to obtain detailed financial information from borrowers simply by requesting it as a condition for granting a loan. Suppliers and other trade creditors may obtain some financial information about almost any business from credit-rating agencies, such as Dun & Bradstreet.

Stock prices, like p/e ratios, are a *measure of investors' expectations*. A company may be highly profitable and growing fast. But if investors had expected even better performance, the market price of its stock may decline. Similarly, if a troubled company's losses are smaller than expected, the price of its stock may rise.

In financial circles, evaluating stock price by looking at the underlying profitability of the company is termed **fundamental analysis.** This approach to investing works better in the long run than in the short run. In the short run, stock prices can be significantly affected by many factors, including short-term interest rates, current events, political events, fads, and rumors. But in the long run, good companies increase in value.

# END-OF-CHAPTER REVIEW

## SUMMARY OF LEARNING OBJECTIVES

**L01** Explain the uses of dollar and percentage changes, trend percentages, component percentages, and ratios. An important aspect of financial statement analysis is determining relevant relationships among specific items of information. Companies typically present financial information for more than one time period, which permits users of the information to make comparisons that help them understand changes over time. Dollar and percentage changes and trend percentages are tools for comparing information from successive time periods. Component percentages and ratios, on the other hand, are tools for establishing relationships and making comparisons within an accounting period. Both types of comparisons are important in understanding an enterprise's financial position, results of operations, and cash flows.

**L02** Discuss the quality of a company's earnings, assets, and working capital. Assessing the quality of information is an important aspect of financial statement analysis. Enterprises have significant latitude in the selection of financial reporting methods within generally accepted accounting principles. Assessing the quality of a company's earnings, assets, and working capital is done by evaluating the accounting methods selected for use in preparing financial statements. Management's choice of accounting principles and methods that are in the best long-term interests of the company, even though they may currently result in lower net income, reported total assets, or working capital, leads to a conclusion of high quality in reported accounting information.

**L03** Explain the nature and purpose of classifications in financial statements. In classified financial statements, items with certain common characteristics are placed together in a group, or classification. The purpose of these classifications is to develop subtotals that will assist users in analyzing the financial statements.

**L04** Prepare a classified balance sheet and compute widely used measures of liquidity and credit risk. In a classified balance sheet, assets are subdivided into the categories of current assets, plant and equipment, and other assets. Liabilities are classified either as current or long-term.

The liquidity measures derived from the balance sheet are as follows:

**Working capital.** Current assets minus current liabilities.

**Current ratio.** Current assets divided by current liabilities.

**Quick ratio.** Quick assets divided by current liabilities.

A measure of long-term credit risk is the debt ratio, which is total liabilities expressed as a percentage of (divided by) total assets.

**L05** Prepare a multiple-step and a single-step income statement and compute widely used measures of profitability. In a multiple-step income statement, the cost of goods sold is deducted from net sales to provide the subtotal, gross profit. Operating expenses then are deducted to arrive at income from operations. As a final step, nonoperating items are added together and subtracted from income from operations to arrive at net income. In a single-step income statement, all revenue items are listed first, and then all expenses are combined and deducted from total revenue.

The profitability measures discussed in this chapter are as follows:

**Percentage change.** The dollar amount of change in a financial statement item from one period to the next, expressed as a percentage of (divided by) the item value in the earlier of the two periods being compared.

**Gross profit rate.** Dollar amount of gross profit divided by net sales. A measure of the profitability of a company's products.

**Net income as a percentage of sales.** Net income divided by net sales. A measure of management's ability to control expenses.

**Earnings per share.** In the simplest case, net income divided by shares of capital stock outstanding. Indicates the earnings applicable to each share of stock.

**Price-earnings ratio.** Market price of the stock divided by earnings per share. A measure of investors' expectations regarding future profitability.

**Return on assets.** Operating income divided by average total assets. Measures the return generated by assets, regardless of how the assets are financed.

**Return on equity.** Net income divided by average total equity. Indicates the rate of return earned on owners' equity.

**L06** Put a company's net income into perspective by relating it to sales, assets, and stockholders' equity. Financial accounting information is most useful if viewed in comparison with other relevant information. Net income is an important measure of the financial success of an enterprise. To make the amount of net income even more useful than if it were viewed simply in isolation, it is often compared with the sales from which net income results, the assets used to generate the income, and the amount of stockholders' equity invested by owners to earn the net income.

**L07** Compute the ratios widely used in financial statement analysis and explain the significance of each. Ratios are mathematical calculations that compare one financial statement item with another financial statement item. The two items may come from the same financial statement, such as the current ratio, which compares the amount of current assets with the amount of current liabilities, both of which appear in the statement of financial position (balance sheet). On the other hand, the items may come from two different financial statements, such as the return on stockholders' equity, which compares net income from the income statement with the amount of stockholders' equity from the statement of financial position (balance sheet). Accountants and financial analysts have developed many ratios that place information from a company's financial statements in a context to permit better understanding to support decision making.

 **Analyze financial statements from the viewpoints of common stockholders, creditors, and others.** Different groups of users of financial statements are interested in different aspects of a company's financial activities. Short-term creditors are interested primarily in the company's ability to make cash payments in the short term; they focus their attention on operating cash flows and current assets and liabilities. Long-term creditors, on the other hand, are more interested in the company's long-term ability to pay interest and principal and would not limit their analysis to the company's ability to make cash payments in the immediate future. The focus of common stockholders can vary from one investor to another, but generally stockholders are interested in the company's ability to pay dividends and increase the market value of the stock of the company. Each group may focus on different information in the financial statements to meet its unique objectives.

## Key Terms Introduced or Emphasized In Chapter 14

**annual report** (p. 631)   A document issued annually by publicly owned companies to their stockholders. Includes audited comparative financial statements, management's discussion and analysis of performance and liquidity, and other information about the company.

**classified financial statements** (p. 622)   Financial statements in which similar items are arranged in groups, and subtotals are shown to assist users in analyzing the statements.

**comparative financial statements** (p. 622)   Financial statements of one company for two or more years presented in a side-by-side format to facilitate comparison.

**consolidated financial statements** (p. 622)   Financial statements that show the combined activities of a parent company and its subsidiaries.

**current assets** (p. 627)   Cash and other assets that can be converted into cash or used up within one year or the operating cycle (whichever is longer) without interfering with normal business operations.

**current liabilities** (p. 629)   Existing liabilities that are expected to be satisfied by using the enterprise's current assets.

**current ratio** (p. 629)   Current assets divided by current liabilities. A measure of short-term debt-paying ability.

**debt ratio** (p. 630)   Total liabilities divided by total assets. Represents the portion of total assets financed by debt, rather than by equity capital.

**earnings per share** (p. 636)   Net income expressed on a per-share basis.

**fundamental analysis** (p. 655)   Evaluating the reasonableness of a company's stock price by evaluating the performance and financial strength of the company.

**management's discussion and analysis** (p. 631)   A discussion by management of the company's performance during the current year and its financial position at year-end. These discussions are included in the annual reports of publicly owned companies.

**market share** (p. 634)   A company's percentage share of total dollar sales within its industry.

**operating cycle** (p. 627)   The time required to invest cash in inventory, sell the inventory, and collect the receivable, resulting in an increase in cash.

**operating income** (p. 634)   A subtotal in a multiple-step income statement representing the income resulting from the company's principal business activities.

**parent company** (p. 622)   A corporation that does portions of its business through other companies that it owns (termed *subsidiaries*).

**percentage change** (p. 634)   The change in a dollar amount between two accounting periods, expressed as a percentage of the amount in an earlier period. Used in evaluating rates of growth (or decline).

**price-earnings (p/e) ratio** (p. 636)   The current market price of a company's capital stock, expressed as a multiple of earnings per share. Reflects investors' expectations regarding future earnings.

**quick assets** (p. 630)   The most liquid current assets, which include only cash, marketable securities, and receivables.

**quick ratio** (p. 630)   Quick assets (cash, marketable securities, and receivables) divided by current liabilities. A measure of short-term debt-paying ability. (Sometimes referred to as the acid-test ratio.)

**return on assets** (p. 638)   Operating income expressed as a percentage of average total assets. A measure of the efficiency with which management utilizes the assets of a business.

**return on equity** (p. 638)   Net income expressed as a percentage of average total stockholders' equity. A measure of the rate of return earned on the stockholders' equity in the business.

**subsidiary** (p. 622)   A company that is owned and operated by a parent company. In essence, the subsidiary is a part of the parent organization.

**window dressing** (p. 631)   Measures taken by management to make a business look as strong as possible at the balance sheet date.

**working capital** (p. 629)   Current assets less current liabilities. A measure of short-term debt-paying ability.

## Demonstration Problem

The following data are adapted from a recent annual report of Walgreen Drug Stores (dollar amounts are stated in millions):

|  | 2009 | 2008 |
|---|---|---|
| **Balance sheet data:** | | |
| Quick assets | $ 5,083 | $ 2,970 |
| Current assets | 12,049 | 10,433 |
| Current liabilities | 6,769 | 6,644 |
| Stockholders' equity | 14,376 | 12,869 |
| Total assets | 25,142 | 22,410 |
| **Income statement data:** | | |
| Net sales | $63,335 | $59,034 |
| Gross profit | 17,613 | 16,643 |
| Operating income | 3,247 | 3,441 |
| Net earnings | 2,006 | 2,157 |

### Instructions

**a.** Compute the following for 2009 and 2008. (Round to one decimal place.)

1. Working capital
2. Current ratio
3. Quick ratio

**b.** Comment on the trends in the liquidity measures and state whether Walgreen appears to be able to satisfy its liabilities at the end of 2009.

**c.** Compute the percentage changes for 2009 in the amounts of net sales and net income. (Round to one-tenth of 1 percent.)

**d.** Compute the following for 2009 and 2008. (Round to one-tenth of 1 percent. For items **3** and **4,** use the year-end amounts stated above as substitutes for average assets and average stockholders' equity.)

1. Gross profit rate
2. Net income as a percentage of sales
3. Return on assets
4. Return on stockholders' equity

**e.** Comment on the trends in the profitability measures computed in parts **c** and **d**.

### Solution to the Demonstration Problem

**a.**

|  |  | 2009 | 2008 |
|---|---|---|---|
| 1. | **Working capital:** | | |
|  | $12,049 − $6,769 | $5,280 | |
|  | $10,433 − $6,644 | | $3,789 |
| 2. | **Current ratio:** | | |
|  | $12,049 ÷ $6,769 | 1.78 to 1 | |
|  | $10,433 ÷ $6,644 | | 1.57 to 1 |
| 3. | **Quick ratio:** | | |
|  | $5,083 ÷ $6,769 | 0.75 to 1 | |
|  | $2,970 ÷ $6,644 | | 0.45 to 1 |

**b.** Working capital during 2009 increased by $1,491 million, from $3,789 million to $5,280 million. The current ratio increased from 1.57 to 1.78. The quick ratio increased from 0.45 to 0.75. The relatively low quick ratio may be of some concern in terms of the company's ability to satisfy its future obligations.

**c.** Percentage change from 2008:

| | 2009 |
|---|---|
| Net sales: [($63,335 − $59,034) ÷ $59,034] . . . . . . . . . . . . . . . . . . . . . . . . . . . | +7.3% |
| Net income: [($2,006 − $2,157) ÷ $2,157] . . . . . . . . . . . . . . . . . . . . . . . . . . . . . | −7.0% |

**d.**

| | | 2009 | 2008 |
|---|---|---|---|
| **1.** | **Gross profit rate:** | | |
| | $17,613 ÷ $63,335 . . . . . . . . . . . . . . . . . . . . . . . . . . . . . . . . . . | 27.8% | |
| | $16,643 ÷ $59,034 . . . . . . . . . . . . . . . . . . . . . . . . . . . . . . . . . . | | 28.2% |
| **2.** | **Net income as a percentage of sales:** | | |
| | $2,006 ÷ $63,335 . . . . . . . . . . . . . . . . . . . . . . . . . . . . . . . . . . . | 3.2% | |
| | $2,157 ÷ $59,034 . . . . . . . . . . . . . . . . . . . . . . . . . . . . . . . . . . . | | 3.7% |
| **3.** | **Return on assets:** | | |
| | $2,006 ÷ $25,142 . . . . . . . . . . . . . . . . . . . . . . . . . . . . . . . . . . . | 8.0% | |
| | $2,157 ÷ $22,410 . . . . . . . . . . . . . . . . . . . . . . . . . . . . . . . . . . . | | 9.6% |
| **4.** | **Return on equity:** | | |
| | $2,006 ÷ $14,376 . . . . . . . . . . . . . . . . . . . . . . . . . . . . . . . . . . . | 14.0% | |
| | $2,157 ÷ $12,869 . . . . . . . . . . . . . . . . . . . . . . . . . . . . . . . . . . . | | 16.8% |

**e.** Profitability indicators are generally negative.
- Net sales increased, but net earnings decreased.
- The gross profit rate decreased by 0.4% (28.2% to 27.8%).
- Net income as a percentage of sales decreased by 0.5% (3.7% to 3.2%).
- Return on assets decreased by 1.6% (9.6% to 8.0%).
- Return on equity decreased by 2.8% (16.8% to 14.0%).

While the percentage changes are relatively small, they are applied to very large dollar amounts, resulting in relatively large dollar changes. Small percentage improvements in these key financial statement numbers can render significant improvements in the company's financial performance.

# Self-Test Questions

*The answers to these questions appear on page 679.*

**1.** Which of the following usually is *least* important as a measure of short-term liquidity?

   **a.** Quick ratio.

   **b.** Debt ratio.

   **c.** Current ratio.

   **d.** Cash flows from operating activities.

**2.** In each of the past five years, the net sales of Plaza Co. have increased at about half the rate of inflation, but net income has increased at approximately *twice* the rate of inflation. During this period, the company's total assets, liabilities, and equity have remained almost unchanged; dividends are approximately equal to net income. These relationships suggest (indicate all correct answers):

   **a.** Management is successfully controlling costs and expenses.

   **b.** The company is selling more merchandise every year.

   **c.** The annual return on assets has been increasing.

   **d.** Financing activities are likely to result in a net use of cash.

3. From the viewpoint of a stockholder, which of the following relationships do you consider of *least* significance?

   a. The return on assets consistently is higher than the industry average.

   b. The return on equity has increased in each of the past five years.

   c. Net income is greater than the amount of working capital.

   d. The return on assets is greater than the rate of interest being paid to creditors.

4. The following information is available from the annual report of Frixell, Inc.:

| | | | |
|---|---|---|---|
| Current assets .... | $ 480,000 | Current liabilities .... | $300,000 |
| Average total assets .... | 2,000,000 | Operating income ..... | 240,000 |
| Average total equity .... | 800,000 | Net income .... | 80,000 |

   Which of the following statements are correct? (More than one statement may be correct.)

   a. The return on equity exceeds the return on assets.

   b. The current ratio is 0.625 to 1.

   c. Working capital is $1,200,000.

   d. None of the above answers is correct.

5. Hart Corporation's net income was $400,000 in 2010 and $160,000 in 2011. What percentage increase in net income must Hart achieve in 2012 to offset the decline in profits in 2011?

   a. 60%.

   b. 150%.

   c. 600%.

   d. 67%.

6. If a company's current ratio declined in a year during which its quick ratio improved, which of the following is the most likely explanation?

   a. Inventory is increasing.

   b. Inventory is declining.

   c. Receivables are being collected more rapidly than in the past.

   d. Receivables are being collected more slowly than in the past.

7. In financial statement analysis, the most difficult of the following items to predict is whether:

   a. The company will be liquid in six months.

   b. The company's market share is increasing or declining.

   c. Profits have increased since the previous year.

   d. The market price of capital stock will rise or fall over the next two months.

---

**ASSIGNMENT MATERIAL** **Discussion Questions**

1. In financial statement analysis, what is the basic objective of observing trends in data and ratios? Suggest some other standards of comparison.

2. In financial statement analysis, what information is produced by computing a ratio that is not available in a simple observation of the underlying data?

3. Distinguish between *trend percentages* and *component percentages*. Which would be better suited for analyzing the change in sales over a term of several years?

4. Differentiate between *horizontal* and *vertical* analysis.

5. What is the basic purpose of *classifications* in financial statements? Identify the classifications widely used in a balance sheet, a multiple-step income statement, and a statement of cash flows.

6. Distinguish between the terms *classified, comparative,* and *consolidated* as they apply to financial statements. May a given set of financial statements have more than one of these characteristics?

7. What is the characteristic common to all *current assets*? Many retail stores regularly sell merchandise on installment plans, calling for payments over a period of 24 or 36 months. Do such receivables qualify as current assets? Explain.

8. Identify four ratios or other analytical tools used to evaluate profitability. Explain briefly how each is computed.

9. Distinguish between *operating income* and *net income.*

10. Why might earnings per share be more significant to a stockholder in a large corporation than the total amount of net income?

11. Assume that Congress announces its intention to limit the prices and profits of pharmaceutical companies as part of an effort to control health care costs. What effect would you expect this announcement to have on the p/e ratios and stock prices of pharmaceutical companies such as Merck and Bristol-Myers Squibb? Explain.

12. Under what circumstances might a company have a high p/e ratio even when investors are *not* optimistic about the company's future prospects?

13. Spencer Company earned a 16 percent return on its total assets. Current liabilities are 10 percent of total assets.

Long-term bonds carrying an 11 percent coupon rate are equal to 30 percent of total assets. There is no preferred stock. Is this application of leverage favorable or unfavorable from the viewpoint of Spencer's stockholders?

**14.** Ahi Co. has a current ratio of 3 to 1. Ono Corp. has a current ratio of 2 to 1. Does this mean that Ahi's operating cycle is longer than Ono's? Why?

**15.** An investor states, "I bought this stock for $50 several years ago and it now sells for $100. It paid $5 per share in dividends last year so I'm earning 10 percent on my investment." Evaluate this statement.

# Brief Exercises

<table>
<tr><td>L01</td><td>**BRIEF EXERCISE 14.1**<br>Dollar and Percentage Change</td><td>Wofford Company had net sales of $150,000 in its first year and $187,500 in its second year. Calculate the amount of change in terms of both dollars and percentage.</td></tr>
<tr><td>L01</td><td>**BRIEF EXERCISE 14.2**<br>Trend Percentages</td><td>White, Inc., had depreciation expenses on its plant assets as follows for 2009, 2010, and 2011, respectively: $267,000, $289,000, and $357,000. Compute the trend percentages for these years, assuming 2009 is the base year.</td></tr>
<tr><td>L01</td><td>**BRIEF EXERCISE 14.3**<br>Component Percentages</td><td>Yankee Doodle, Inc., had the following income statement figures:</td></tr>
</table>

| | |
|---|---|
| Sales | $560,000 |
| Cost of sales | (340,000) |
| Gross margin | $220,000 |
| Operating expenses | (150,000) |
| Net income | $ 70,000 |

Calculate component percentages for this information.

<table>
<tr><td>L04</td><td>**BRIEF EXERCISE 14.4**<br>Working Capital and Current Ratio</td><td>Harrisonburg Company had current and total assets of $450,000 and $1,000,000, respectively. The company's current and total liabilities were $267,000 and $600,000, respectively. Calculate the amount of working capital and the current ratio using this information.</td></tr>
<tr><td>L04</td><td>**BRIEF EXERCISE 14.5**<br>Current and Quick Ratio</td><td>Garrett Company had current assets and current liabilities as follows:</td></tr>
</table>

| | |
|---|---|
| **Current assets:** | |
| Cash | $ 50,000 |
| Accounts receivable | 75,000 |
| Inventory | 125,000 |
| **Current liabilities:** | |
| Accrued expenses | $ 25,000 |
| Accounts payable | 110,000 |
| Current portion of long-term debt | 45,000 |

Calculate the current and quick ratios using the information provided.

**662**    **Chapter 14** Financial Statement Analysis

**LO4 BRIEF EXERCISE 14.6**
Debt Ratio

Maxey Company had current and noncurrent liabilities of $50,000 and $150,000, respectively. The company's current assets were $76,000, out of a total asset figure of $424,000. Calculate the company's debt ratio.

**LO6 BRIEF EXERCISE 14.7**
Net Income as Percentage of Sales

Lone Star, Inc., reported sales of $560,000, cost of sales of $240,000, and operating expenses of $130,000 for the current year. Using this information, calculate the amount of net income and net income as a percentage of sales.

**LO6 BRIEF EXERCISE 14.8**
Earnings Per Share

Multi-Star, Inc., had sales of $890,000, cost of sales and operating expenses of $450,000 and $200,000, respectively, and 10,000 shares of common stock outstanding. Calculate the amount of earnings per share.

**LO7 BRIEF EXERCISE 14.9**
Return on Assets

Walland Company's operating income for the current year was $450,000. The company's average total assets for the same period were $3,500,000, and its total liabilities were $1,000,000. Calculate the company's return on assets.

**LO7 BRIEF EXERCISE 14.10**
Return on Equity

Fillips Company had net income of $36,700 in a year when its stockholders' equity averaged $450,000 and its total assets averaged $2,500,000. Calculate the company's return on equity for the period.

## Exercises

**LO1 EXERCISE 14.1**
Percentage Changes

Selected information taken from the financial statements of Maxum Company for two successive years follows. You are to compute the percentage change from 2010 to 2011 whenever possible. Round all calculations to the nearest whole percentage.

|     |                          | 2011      | 2010      |
|-----|--------------------------|-----------|-----------|
| a.  | Accounts receivable      | $126,000  | $160,000  |
| b.  | Marketable securities    | –0–       | 250,000   |
| c.  | Retained earnings        | 80,000    | (80,000)  |
| d.  | Notes receivable         | 120,000   | –0–       |
| e.  | Notes payable            | 870,000   | 800,000   |
| f.  | Cash                     | 84,000    | 80,000    |
| g.  | Sales                    | 970,000   | 910,000   |

**LO1 EXERCISE 14.2**
Trend Percentages

Compute *trend percentages* for the following items taken from the financial statements of Lopez Plumbing over a five-year period. Treat 2007 as the base year. State whether the trends are favorable or unfavorable. (Dollar amounts are stated in thousands.)

|                    | 2011     | 2010     | 2009     | 2008     | 2007     |
|--------------------|----------|----------|----------|----------|----------|
| Sales              | $81,400  | $74,000  | $61,500  | $59,000  | $50,000  |
| Cost of goods sold | 58,500   | 48,000   | 40,500   | 37,000   | 30,000   |

**LO1 EXERCISE 14.3**
Common Size Income Statements

Prepare *common size* income statements for Pellum Company, a sole proprietorship, for the two years shown below by converting the dollar amounts into percentages. For each year, sales will appear as 100 percent and other items will be expressed as a percentage of sales. (Income taxes are not involved as the business is not incorporated.) Comment on whether the changes from 2010 to 2011 are favorable or unfavorable.

|  | 2011 | 2010 |
|---|---|---|
| Sales . . . . . . . . . . . . . . . . . . . . . . . . . . . . . . . . . . . . . . . . . . . . . . . . . . . . . . . . . . | $500,000 | $400,000 |
| Cost of goods sold . . . . . . . . . . . . . . . . . . . . . . . . . . . . . . . . . . . . . . . . . . . | 330,000 | 268,000 |
| Gross profit . . . . . . . . . . . . . . . . . . . . . . . . . . . . . . . . . . . . . . . . . . . . . . . . . . | $170,000 | $132,000 |
| Operating expenses. . . . . . . . . . . . . . . . . . . . . . . . . . . . . . . . . . . . . . . . . . | 130,000 | 116,000 |
| Net income. . . . . . . . . . . . . . . . . . . . . . . . . . . . . . . . . . . . . . . . . . . . . . . . . . . | $ 40,000 | $ 16,000 |

**L03** **EXERCISE 14.4**

Measures of Liquidity

**L04**

Roy's Toys is a manufacturer of toys and children's products. The following are selected items appearing in a recent balance sheet (dollar amounts are in millions):

| | |
|---|---|
| Cash and short-term investments . . . . . . . . . . . . . . . . . . . . . . . . . . . . . . . . . . . | $ 47.3 |
| Receivables . . . . . . . . . . . . . . . . . . . . . . . . . . . . . . . . . . . . . . . . . . . . . . . . . . . . . | 159.7 |
| Inventories . . . . . . . . . . . . . . . . . . . . . . . . . . . . . . . . . . . . . . . . . . . . . . . . . . . . . | 72.3 |
| Prepaid expenses and other current assets . . . . . . . . . . . . . . . . . . . . . . . . . . . | 32.0 |
| Total current liabilities. . . . . . . . . . . . . . . . . . . . . . . . . . . . . . . . . . . . . . . . . . . . | 130.1 |
| Total liabilities . . . . . . . . . . . . . . . . . . . . . . . . . . . . . . . . . . . . . . . . . . . . . . . . . . . | 279.4 |
| Total stockholders' equity . . . . . . . . . . . . . . . . . . . . . . . . . . . . . . . . . . . . . . . . . | 344.0 |

**a.** Using the information above, compute the amounts of Roy's Toys (**1**) quick assets and (**2**) total current assets.

**b.** Compute for Roy's Toys the (**1**) quick ratio, (**2**) current ratio, and (**3**) dollar amount of working capital. (Round ratios to one decimal place.)

**c.** Discuss whether Roy's Toys appears liquid from the viewpoint of a short-term creditor.

**L05** **EXERCISE 14.5**

Multiple-Step Income Statements

| LINK, INC. STATEMENT OF EARNINGS FOR THE YEAR ENDED DECEMBER 31, 2011 | |
|---|---|
| Net sales. . . . . . . . . . . . . . . . . . . . . . . . . . . . . . . . . . . . . . . . . . . . . . . . . . . . . . . | $4,395,253 |
| Costs and expenses: | |
| Cost of goods sold . . . . . . . . . . . . . . . . . . . . . . . . . . . . . . . . . . . . . . . . . . . . . | (2,821,455) |
| Operating expenses . . . . . . . . . . . . . . . . . . . . . . . . . . . . . . . . . . . . . . . . . . . . | (1,004,396) |
| Interest revenue . . . . . . . . . . . . . . . . . . . . . . . . . . . . . . . . . . . . . . . . . . . . . . | 15,797 |
| Earnings before income tax . . . . . . . . . . . . . . . . . . . . . . . . . . . . . . . . . . . . . . | $ 585,199 |
| Income tax expense . . . . . . . . . . . . . . . . . . . . . . . . . . . . . . . . . . . . . . . . . . . . . | (204,820) |
| Net earnings . . . . . . . . . . . . . . . . . . . . . . . . . . . . . . . . . . . . . . . . . . . . . . . . . . . | $ 380,379 |
| Earnings per share . . . . . . . . . . . . . . . . . . . . . . . . . . . . . . . . . . . . . . . . . . . . . . | $1.70 |

Comparative balance sheets report average total assets for the year of *$2,450,000* and average total equity of *$1,825,000* (dollar amounts in thousands, except earnings per share).

**a.** Prepare an income statement for the year in a multiple-step format.

**b.** Compute the (**1**) gross profit rate, (**2**) net income as a percentage of net sales, (**3**) return on assets, and (**4**) return on equity for the year. (Round computations to the nearest one-tenth of 1 percent.)

**c.** Explain why interest revenue is not included in the company's gross profit computation.

**LO6**  **EXERCISE 14.6**
ROI

Shown below are selected data from a recent annual report of Kimberly-Clark Corporation, a large consumer products provider. (Dollar amounts are in millions.)

| | Beginning of the Year | End of the Year |
|---|---|---|
| Total assets . . . . . . . . . . . . . . . . . . . . . . . . . . . . . . . . . . . . . . . . . | $17,660 | $18,840 |
| Total stockholders' equity . . . . . . . . . . . . . . . . . . . . . . . . . . . . . | 4,280 | 5,690 |
| Operating income . . . . . . . . . . . . . . . . . . . . . . . . . . . . . . . . . . . | | 3,210 |
| Net income . . . . . . . . . . . . . . . . . . . . . . . . . . . . . . . . . . . . . . . . | | 1,880 |

a.   Compute for the year Kimberly-Clark's return on average total assets. (Round computations to the nearest two-tenths of 1 percent.)

b.   Compute for the year Kimberly-Clark's return on average total stockholders' equity. (Round computations to the nearest two-tenths of 1 percent.)

c.   What is the most likely explanation why Kimberly-Clark's total stockholders' equity for the year increased?

**LO1**  **EXERCISE 14.7**
Computing and
Interpreting Rates
**LO6**  of Change

Selected information from the financial statements of Rochet, Inc., includes the following:

| | 2011 | 2010 |
|---|---|---|
| Net sales. . . . . . . . . . . . . . . . . . . . . . . . . . . . . . . . . . . . . . . . . | $2,200,000 | $2,000,000 |
| Total expenses . . . . . . . . . . . . . . . . . . . . . . . . . . . . . . . . . . . . | 1,998,000 | 1,800,000 |

a.   Compute the percentage change in 2011 for the amounts of (1) net sales and (2) total expenses.

b.   Using the information developed in part a, express your opinion as to whether the company's *net income* for 2011:

1.   Increased at a greater or lower percentage rate than did net sales.

2.   Represented a larger or smaller percentage of net sales revenue than in 2010. For each answer, explain your reasoning *without* making any computations or references to dollar amounts.

**LO6**  **EXERCISE 14.8**
Research Problem

Obtain from your library, the Internet, or other source the most recent annual report of a publicly owned company.

a.   Using the annual report data, compute the basic measures of liquidity, long-term credit risk, and profitability summarized in Exhibit 14–26. Compare these measures with the appropriate industry norms available in your library. Briefly comment on your findings.

b.   Using the financial pages of a daily newspaper (such as *The Wall Street Journal*), determine (1) the current market price of your company's common stock, (2) its 52-week high and low market prices, and (3) its p/e ratio. Briefly comment on your findings.

c.   On the basis of your analysis in parts a and b, make a recommendation as to whether investors should buy shares of the stock, hold the shares they currently own, or sell the shares they currently own. Defend your position.

**LO3**  **EXERCISE 14.9**
Home Depot, Inc.,
Management's
**LO4**  Discussion and
Analysis

**LO6**

The financial statements of large public companies are often accompanied by a multiple-year summary of key financial and other information that is helpful in understanding the company. Appendix A of this text includes the financial statements of Home Depot, Inc., and selected other information from the company's annual report. Included is a ten-year Summary of Financial and Operating Results for the period 2000–2009. Locate this summary in Appendix A and respond to the following.

a.   Considering the "store data" section of the ten-year summary, what conclusions can you draw about the change in size of Home Depot, Inc., during the ten-year period?

b.   Comment on the ten-year trend in net earnings as a percentage of sales and what this trend means to you as an investor in the company.

c.   Has the company's liquidity improved or diminished over the 10-year period? Justify your answer.

**L04** **EXERCISE 14.10**
Evaluating
**L08** Employment
Opportunities

Assume that you will soon graduate from college and that you have job offers with two pharmaceutical firms. The first offer is with Alpha Research, a relatively new and aggressive company. The second is with Omega Scientific, a very well established and conservative company.

Financial information pertaining to each firm, and to the pharmaceutical industry as a whole, is as follows:

| Financial Measure | Alpha | Omega | Industry Average |
|---|---|---|---|
| Current ratio . . . . . . . . . . . . . . . . . . . . . . . . . . . . . . . . . . . . | 2.2 to 1 | 4.5 to 1 | 2.5 to 1 |
| Quick ratio. . . . . . . . . . . . . . . . . . . . . . . . . . . . . . . . . . . . . | 1.2 to 1 | 2.8 to 1 | 1.5 to 1 |
| Return on assets. . . . . . . . . . . . . . . . . . . . . . . . . . . . . . . | 17% | 8% | 10% |
| Return on equity . . . . . . . . . . . . . . . . . . . . . . . . . . . . . . . | 28% | 14% | 16% |
| P/e ratio . . . . . . . . . . . . . . . . . . . . . . . . . . . . . . . . . . . . | 20 to 1 | 10 to 1 | 12 to 1 |

The Omega offer is for $36,000 per year. The Alpha offer is for $32,000. However, unlike Omega, Alpha awards its employees a stock option bonus based on profitability for the year. Each option enables the employee to purchase shares of Alpha's common stock at a significantly reduced price. The more profitable this company is, the more stock each employee can buy at a discount.

Show how the above information may help you justify accepting the Alpha Research offer, even though the starting salary is $4,000 lower than the Omega Scientific offer.

**L07** **EXERCISE 14.11**
Ratios for a Retail
Store

Selected financial data for SellFast, Inc., a retail store, appear as follows:

| | 2011 | 2010 |
|---|---|---|
| Sales (all on account). . . . . . . . . . . . . . . . . . . . . . . . . . . . . . . . . . . | $750,000 | $610,000 |
| Cost of goods sold . . . . . . . . . . . . . . . . . . . . . . . . . . . . . . . . . . . | 495,000 | 408,000 |
| Average inventory during the year . . . . . . . . . . . . . . . . . . . . . . . | 110,000 | 102,000 |
| Average receivables during the year . . . . . . . . . . . . . . . . . . . . . | 150,000 | 100,000 |

a. Compute the following for both years:
  1. Gross profit percentage
  2. Inventory turnover
  3. Accounts receivable turnover
b. Comment on favorable and unfavorable trends.

**L07** **EXERCISE 14.12**
Computing Ratios

A condensed balance sheet for Bradford Corporation prepared at the end of the year appears as follows:

| Assets | | Liabilities & Stockholders' Equity | |
|---|---|---|---|
| Cash. . . . . . . . . . . . . . . . . . . | $ 95,000 | Notes payable (due in 6 months) . . . . . . . . . . . . . . | $ 40,000 |
| Accounts receivable . . . . . . . . | 155,000 | Accounts payable. . . . . . . . . . | 110,000 |
| Inventory. . . . . . . . . . . . . . . . | 270,000 | Long-term liabilities . . . . . . . . | 360,000 |
| Prepaid expenses. . . . . . . . . . | 60,000 | Capital stock, $5 par. . . . . . . . | 300,000 |
| Plant & equipment (net) . . . . . | 570,000 | Retained earnings . . . . . . . . . | 430,000 |
| Other assets . . . . . . . . . . . . . | 90,000 | | |
| Total . . . . . . . . . . . . . . . . . . | $1,240,000 | Total . . . . . . . . . . . . . . . . . . | $1,240,000 |

During the year the company earned a gross profit of $1,116,000 on sales of $2,950,000. Accounts receivable, inventory, and plant assets remained almost constant in amount throughout the year.

**666**   **Chapter 14** Financial Statement Analysis

Compute the following:

**a.** Current ratio.

**b.** Quick ratio.

**c.** Working capital.

**d.** Debt ratio.

**e.** Accounts receivable turnover (all sales were on credit).

**f.** Inventory turnover.

**g.** Book value per share of capital stock.

 **EXERCISE 14.13**
Current Ratio, Debt
Ratio, and Earnings
per Share

Selected items from successive annual reports of Carey, Inc., appear as follows:

|  | 2011 | 2010 |
|---|---|---|
| Total assets (40% of which are current) .......................... | $400,000 | $325,000 |
| Current liabilities ........................................ | $ 80,000 | $100,000 |
| Bonds payable, 12%.................................... | 100,000 | 50,000 |
| Capital stock, $5 par value .............................. | 100,000 | 100,000 |
| Retained earnings.................................... | 120,000 | 75,000 |
| Total liabilities & stockholders' equity ........................ | $400,000 | $325,000 |

Dividends of $16,000 were declared and paid in 2011.

Compute the following:

**a.** Current ratio for 2011 and 2010.

**b.** Debt ratio for 2011 and 2010.

**c.** Earnings per share for 2011.

 **EXERCISE 14.14**
Ratio Analysis for Two
Similar Companies

Selected data from the financial statements of Italian Marble Co. and Brazil Stone Products for the year just ended follow. Assume that for both companies dividends declared were equal in amount to net earnings during the year and therefore stockholders' equity did not change. The two companies are in the same line of business.

|  | Italian Marble Co. | Brazil Stone Products |
|---|---|---|
| Total liabilities...................................... | $ 200,000 | $ 100,000 |
| Total assets ...................................... | 800,000 | 400,000 |
| Sales (all on credit).................................... | 1,800,000 | 1,200,000 |
| Average inventory.................................... | 240,000 | 140,000 |
| Average receivables.................................... | 200,000 | 100,000 |
| Gross profit as a percentage of sales.................... | 40% | 30% |
| Operating expenses as a percentage of sales.............. | 36% | 25% |
| Net income as a percentage of sales.................... | 3% | 5% |

Compute the following for each company and state a brief conclusion about which company is in the stronger financial position.

**a.** Net income.

**b.** Net income as a percentage of stockholders' equity.

**c.** Accounts receivable turnover.

**d.** Inventory turnover.

Problem Set A                                                                                                      **667**

<table>
<tr><td>L08<br>L07</td><td>**EXERCISE 14.15**<br>Ratio Analysis for<br>Feature Company</td><td>Johnson & Johnson's 2009 financial statements include the following items (all dollars in millions):</td></tr>
</table>

|  | 2009 | 2008 |
|---|---|---|
| Balance sheet |  |  |
| Current assets | $39,541 | $34,377 |
| Current liabilities | 21,731 | 20,852 |
| Total assets | 94,682 | 84,912 |
| Income statement |  |  |
| Sales | $61,897 | $63,747 |
| Gross profit | 43,450 | 45,231 |
| Net earnings (income) | 12,266 | 12,949 |

Compute the following ratios and comment on the trend you can observe from the limited two years of data you have available.

**a.** Gross profit rate

**b.** Net income as a percentage of sales

**c.** Current ratio

## Problem Set A

| L01<br>L05 | **PROBLEM 14.1A**<br>Comparing Operating<br>Results with Average<br>Performance in the<br>Industry | Campers, Inc., manufactures camping equipment. Shown below for the current year are the income statement for the company and a common size summary for the industry in which the company operates. (Notice that the percentages in the right-hand column are *not* for Campers, Inc., but are average percentages for the industry.) |
|---|---|---|

|  | Campers,<br>Inc. | Industry<br>Average |
|---|---|---|
| Sales (net) | $20,000,000 | 100% |
| Cost of goods sold | 9,800,000 | 57 |
| Gross profit on sales | $10,200,000 | 43% |
| Operating expenses: |  |  |
| Selling | $ 4,200,000 | 16% |
| General and administrative | 3,400,000 | 20 |
| Total operating expenses | $ 7,600,000 | 36% |
| Operating income | $ 2,600,000 | 7% |
| Income tax expense | 1,200,000 | 3 |
| Net income | $ 1,400,000 | 4% |
| Return on assets | 23% | 14% |

**Instructions**

**a.** Prepare a two-column common size income statement. The first column should show for Campers, Inc., all items expressed as a percentage of net sales. The second column should show the equivalent industry average for the data given in the problem. The purpose of this common size statement is to compare the operating results of Campers, Inc., with the average for the industry.

**b.** Comment specifically on differences between Campers, Inc., and the industry average with respect to gross profit on sales, selling expenses, general and administrative expenses, operating income, net income, and return on assets. Suggest possible reasons for the more important disparities.

**PROBLEM 14.2A**

Analysis to Identify
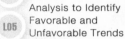 Favorable and
Unfavorable Trends

The following information was developed from the financial statements of Darwin, Inc. At the beginning of 2011, the company's former supplier went bankrupt, and the company began buying merchandise from another supplier.

|  | 2011 | 2010 |
| --- | --- | --- |
| Gross profit on sales | $1,008,000 | $1,134,000 |
| Income before income tax | 230,400 | 252,000 |
| Net income | 172,800 | 189,000 |
| Net income as a percentage of net sales | 6.0% | 7.5% |

### Instructions

a.   Compute the net sales for each year.

b.   Compute the cost of goods sold in dollars and as a percentage of net sales for each year.

c.   Compute operating expenses in dollars and as a percentage of net sales for each year. (Income taxes expense is not an operating expense.)

d.   Prepare a condensed comparative income statement for 2010 and 2011. Include the following items: net sales, cost of goods sold, gross profit, operating expenses, income before income tax, income taxes expense, and net income. Omit earnings per share statistics.

e.   Identify the significant favorable and unfavorable trends in the performance of Darwin, Inc. Comment on any unusual changes.

**PROBLEM 14.3A**

Measures of Liquidity

Some of the accounts appearing in the year-end financial statements of Roger Grocery, Inc., appear below. This list includes all of the company's current assets and current liabilities.

| | |
| --- | --- |
| Sales | $1,880,000 |
| Accumulated depreciation: equipment | 370,000 |
| Notes payable (due in 90 days) | 70,000 |
| Retained earnings | 241,320 |
| Cash | 67,600 |
| Capital stock | 150,000 |
| Marketable securities | 175,040 |
| Accounts payable | 127,500 |
| Mortgage payable (due in 15 years) | 320,000 |
| Salaries payable | 7,570 |
| Dividends | 25,000 |
| Income taxes payable | 14,600 |
| Accounts receivable | 230,540 |
| Inventory | 179,600 |
| Unearned revenue | 10,000 |
| Unexpired insurance | 4,500 |

### Instructions

a.   Prepare a schedule of the company's current assets and current liabilities. Select the appropriate items from the preceding list.

b.   Compute the current ratio and the amount of working capital. Explain how each of these measurements is computed. State, with reasons, whether you consider the company to be in a strong or weak current position.

**PROBLEM 14.4A**
Liquidity of Kroger

L04

L07

The Kroger Company is one of the world's largest supermarket chains. These selected items were adapted from a recent Kroger balance sheet. (Dollar amounts are in millions.)

| | |
|---|---:|
| Cash (including deposit-in-transit) | $1,078 |
| Receivables | 909 |
| Merchandise inventories | 4,902 |
| Other current assets | 561 |
| Property, plant and equipment (net of depreciation) | 13,929 |
| Retained earnings | 7,344 |
| Total current liabilities | 7,714 |

**Instructions**

a. Using the information above, compute the amounts of Kroger's total current assets and total quick assets.

b. Compute the company's (1) current ratio, (2) quick ratio, and (3) working capital. (Round to two decimal points.)

c. From these computations, are you able to conclude whether Kroger is a good credit risk for short-term creditors or on the brink of bankruptcy? Explain.

d. Is there anything unusual about the operating cycle of supermarkets that would make you think that they normally would have lower current ratios than, say, large department stores?

e. What *other types of information* could you utilize in performing a more complete analysis of Kroger's liquidity?

 **PROBLEM 14.5A**
Balance Sheet
Measures of Liquidity
and Credit Risk

L04

L07

A recent balance sheet of Sweet Tooth, Inc., included the following items, among others. (Dollar amounts are stated in thousands.)

| | |
|---|---:|
| Cash | $ 49,625 |
| Marketable securities (short-term) | 55,926 |
| Accounts receivable | 23,553 |
| Inventories | 32,210 |
| Prepaid expenses | 5,736 |
| Retained earnings | 121,477 |
| Notes payable to banks (due within one year) | 20,000 |
| Accounts payable | 5,912 |
| Dividends payable | 1,424 |
| Accrued liabilities (short-term) | 21,532 |
| Income taxes payable | 6,438 |

The company also reported total assets of $353,816 thousand, total liabilities of $81,630 thousand, and a return on total assets of *18.1 percent*.

**Instructions**

a. Compute Sweet Tooth's (1) quick assets, (2) current assets, and (3) current liabilities.

b. Compute Sweet Tooth's (1) quick ratio, (2) current ratio, (3) working capital, and (4) debt ratio. (Round to one decimal place.)

c. Discuss the company's liquidity from the viewpoints of (1) short-term creditors, (2) long-term creditors, and (3) stockholders.

**670**

L04

**PROBLEM 14.6A**

Financial Statement
Analysis

L05

e**X**cel

L07

Shown below is selected information from the financial statements of Downing, Inc., a retail furniture store.

**From the balance sheet:**

| | |
|---|---:|
| Cash .......................................................... | $ 30,000 |
| Accounts receivable ......................................... | 150,000 |
| Inventory .................................................... | 200,000 |
| Plant assets (net of accumulated depreciation) ............. | 500,000 |
| Current liabilities ........................................... | 150,000 |
| Total stockholders' equity .................................. | 300,000 |
| Total assets................................................. | 1,000,000 |

**From the income statement:**

| | |
|---|---:|
| Net sales.................................................... | $1,500,000 |
| Cost of goods sold ......................................... | 1,080,000 |
| Operating expenses ......................................... | 315,000 |
| Interest expense ........................................... | 84,000 |
| Income tax expense ........................................ | 6,000 |
| Net income ................................................ | 15,000 |

**From the statement of cash flows:**

| | | |
|---|---:|---:|
| Net cash provided by operating activities (including interest paid of $79,000) ............................... | | $ 40,000 |
| Net cash used in investing activities ............................. | | (46,000) |
| Financing activities: | | |
| Amounts borrowed ................................. | $ 50,000 | |
| Repayment of amounts borrowed ..................... | (14,000) | |
| Dividends paid..................................... | (20,000) | |
| Net cash provided by financing activities........................ | | 16,000 |
| Net increase in cash during the year............................. | | $ 10,000 |

**Instructions**

a.  Explain how the interest expense shown in the income statement could be $84,000, when the interest payment appearing in the statement of cash flows is only $79,000.

b. . Compute the following (round to one decimal place):

1.  Current ratio

2.  Quick ratio

3.  Working capital

4.  Debt ratio

c.  Comment on these measurements and evaluate Downing, Inc.'s short-term debt-paying ability.

d.  Compute the following ratios (assume that the year-end amounts of total assets and total stockholders' equity also represent the average amounts throughout the year):

1.  Return on assets

2.  Return on equity

e.  Comment on the company's performance under these measurements. Explain *why* the return on assets and return on equity are so different.

f.  Discuss (**1**) the apparent safety of long-term creditors' claims and (**2**) the prospects for Downing, Inc., continuing its dividend payments at the present level.

**L04** **PROBLEM 14.7A**
Basic Ratio Analysis

**L05**

**L07**

Medtronics is a world leader in medical technology. The following selected data are adapted from a recent annual report. (Dollar amounts are stated in millions.)

| | Beginning of the Year | End of the Year |
|---|---|---|
| Total current assets . . . . . . . . . . . . . . . . . . . . . . . . . . . . . . . . . . . | $ 7,322 | $ 7,460 |
| Total current liabilities. . . . . . . . . . . . . . . . . . . . . . . . . . . . . . . . . . | 3,535 | 3,147 |
| Total assets . . . . . . . . . . . . . . . . . . . . . . . . . . . . . . . . . . . . . . . . . | 22,198 | 23,661 |
| Total stockholders' equity. . . . . . . . . . . . . . . . . . . . . . . . . . . . . . . | 11,536 | 12,851 |
| Operating income. . . . . . . . . . . . . . . . . . . . . . . . . . . . . . . . . . . . . . | | 2,594 |
| Net income . . . . . . . . . . . . . . . . . . . . . . . . . . . . . . . . . . . . . . . . . . | | 2,169 |

The company has long-term liabilities that bear interest at annual rates ranging from 6 percent to 8 percent.

**Instructions**

a. Compute the company's current ratio at (**1**) the *beginning* of the year and (**2**) the *end* of the year. (Carry to two decimal places.)

b. Compute the company's working capital at (**1**) the beginning of the year and (**2**) the end of the year. (Express dollar amounts in thousands.)

c. Is the company's short-term debt-paying ability improving or deteriorating?

d. Compute the company's (**1**) return on average total assets and (**2**) return on average stockholders' equity. (Round average assets and average equity to the nearest dollar and final computations to the nearest 1 percent.)

e. As an equity investor, do you think that Medtronic's management is utilizing the company's resources in a reasonably efficient manner? Explain.

**L05** **PROBLEM 14.8A**
Ratios; Consider Advisability of Incurring Long-Term Debt

**L07**

At the end of the year, the following information was obtained from the accounting records of Zachery, Inc.

| | |
|---|---|
| Sales (all on credit). . . . . . . . . . . . . . . . . . . . . . . . . . . . . . . . . . . . . . . . . . . . . | $2,750,000 |
| Cost of goods sold . . . . . . . . . . . . . . . . . . . . . . . . . . . . . . . . . . . . . . . . . . . . . | 1,755,000 |
| Average inventory. . . . . . . . . . . . . . . . . . . . . . . . . . . . . . . . . . . . . . . . . . . . . . | 375,000 |
| Average accounts receivable . . . . . . . . . . . . . . . . . . . . . . . . . . . . . . . . . . . . . | 290,000 |
| Interest expense. . . . . . . . . . . . . . . . . . . . . . . . . . . . . . . . . . . . . . . . . . . . . . . | 45,000 |
| Income tax expense . . . . . . . . . . . . . . . . . . . . . . . . . . . . . . . . . . . . . . . . . . . . | 84,000 |
| Net income . . . . . . . . . . . . . . . . . . . . . . . . . . . . . . . . . . . . . . . . . . . . . . . . . . | 159,000 |
| Average investment in assets. . . . . . . . . . . . . . . . . . . . . . . . . . . . . . . . . . . . . | 1,800,000 |
| Average stockholders' equity . . . . . . . . . . . . . . . . . . . . . . . . . . . . . . . . . . . . . | 895,000 |

**Instructions**

a. From the information given, compute the following:

   **1.** Inventory turnover.

   **2.** Accounts receivable turnover.

   **3.** Total operating expenses.

   **4.** Gross profit percentage.

   **5.** Return on average stockholders' equity.

   **6.** Return on average assets.

**672** Chapter 14 Financial Statement Analysis

**b.** Zachery has an opportunity to obtain a long-term loan at an annual interest rate of 12 percent and could use this additional capital at the same rate of profitability as indicated by the given data. Would obtaining the loan be desirable from the viewpoint of the stockholders? Explain.

**PROBLEM 14.9A**
Ratios: Evaluation of Two Companies

Shown below are selected financial data for Another World and Imports, Inc., at the end of the current year:

| | Another World | Imports, Inc. |
|---|---|---|
| Net credit sales. . . . . . . . . . . . . . . . . . . . . . . . . . . . . . . . . . . . . . . . | $675,000 | $560,000 |
| Cost of goods sold . . . . . . . . . . . . . . . . . . . . . . . . . . . . . . . . . . . . | 504,000 | 480,000 |
| Cash. . . . . . . . . . . . . . . . . . . . . . . . . . . . . . . . . . . . . . . . . . . . . . . . | 51,000 | 20,000 |
| Accounts receivable (net). . . . . . . . . . . . . . . . . . . . . . . . . . . . . . | 75,000 | 70,000 |
| Inventory. . . . . . . . . . . . . . . . . . . . . . . . . . . . . . . . . . . . . . . . . . . . | 84,000 | 160,000 |
| Current liabilities. . . . . . . . . . . . . . . . . . . . . . . . . . . . . . . . . . . . . | 105,000 | 100,000 |

Assume that the year-end balances shown for accounts receivable and for inventory approximate the average balances of these items throughout the year.

**Instructions**

**a.** For each of the two companies, compute the following:
   1. Working capital.
   2. Current ratio.
   3. Quick ratio.
   4. Number of times inventory turned over during the year and the average number of days required to turn over inventory (round computation to the nearest day).
   5. Number of times accounts receivable turned over during the year and the average number of days required to collect accounts receivable (round computation to the nearest day).
   6. Operating cycle.

**b.** From the viewpoint of a short-term creditor, comment on the *quality* of each company's working capital. To which company would you prefer to sell $20,000 in merchandise on a 30-day open account?

## Problem Set B

**PROBLEM 14.1B**
Comparing Operating Results with Average Performance in the Industry

Bathrooms, Inc., manufactures bathroom equipment. Shown below for the current year are the income statements for the company and a common size summary for the industry in which the company operates. (Notice that the percentages in the right-hand column are *not* for Bathrooms, Inc., but are average percentages for the industry.)

| | Bathrooms, Inc. | Industry Average |
|---|---|---|
| Sales (net) . . . . . . . . . . . . . . . . . . . . . . . . . . . . . . . . . . . . . . . . . | $12,000,000 | 100% |
| Cost of goods sold . . . . . . . . . . . . . . . . . . . . . . . . . . . . . . . . . . | 7,320,000 | 70 |
| Gross profit on sales. . . . . . . . . . . . . . . . . . . . . . . . . . . . . . . . . | $ 4,680,000 | 30% |
| Operating expenses: | | |
|   Selling . . . . . . . . . . . . . . . . . . . . . . . . . . . . . . . . . . . . . . . . . | $ 1,800,000 | 10% |
|   General and administrative . . . . . . . . . . . . . . . . . . . . . . . . . . | 720,000 | 14 |
| Total operating expenses . . . . . . . . . . . . . . . . . . . . . . . . . . . . . | $ 2,520,000 | 24% |
| Operating income . . . . . . . . . . . . . . . . . . . . . . . . . . . . . . . . . . . | $ 2,160,000 | 6% |
| Income tax expense . . . . . . . . . . . . . . . . . . . . . . . . . . . . . . . . . | 120,000 | 2 |
| Net income . . . . . . . . . . . . . . . . . . . . . . . . . . . . . . . . . . . . . . . . | $ 2,040,000 | 4% |
| Return on assets. . . . . . . . . . . . . . . . . . . . . . . . . . . . . . . . . . . . | 20% | 12% |

## Instructions

**a.** Prepare a two-column common size income statement for Bathrooms, Inc. The first column should show for Bathrooms, Inc., all items expressed as a percentage of net sales. The second column should show the equivalent industry average for the data given in the problem. The purpose of this common size statement is to compare the operating results of Bathrooms, Inc., with the average for the industry. (Round to the nearest percent.)

**b.** Comment specifically on differences between Bathrooms, Inc., and the industry average with respect to gross profit on sales, selling expenses, general and administrative expenses, operating income, net income, and return on assets. Suggest possible reasons for the more important disparities.

**L03**
**PROBLEM 14.2B**
Analysis to Identify
**L05** Favorable and
Unfavorable Trends

The following information was developed from the financial statements of Slow Time, Inc. At the beginning of 2011, the company's former supplier went bankrupt, and the company began buying merchandise from another supplier.

|                                           | 2011      | 2010      |
|-------------------------------------------|-----------|-----------|
| Gross profit on sales.....................................| $720,000  | $800,000  |
| Income before income tax ...............................| 200,000   | 220,000   |
| Net income ..............................................| 150,000   | 170,000   |
| Net income as a percentage of net sales....................| 8%        | 10%       |

## Instructions

**a.** Compute the net sales for each year.

**b.** Compute the cost of goods sold in dollars and as a percentage of net sales for each year.

**c.** Compute operating expenses in dollars and as a percentage of net sales for each year. (Income taxes expense is not an operating expense.)

**d.** Prepare a condensed comparative income statement for 2010 and 2011. Include the following items: net sales, cost of goods sold, gross profit, operating expenses, income before income tax, income tax expense, and net income. Omit earnings per share statistics.

**e.** Identify the significant favorable and unfavorable trends in the performance of Slow Time, Inc. Comment on any unusual changes.

**L03**
**PROBLEM 14.3B**
Measures of Liquidity
**L04**

Some of the accounts appearing in the year-end financial statements of Gino, Inc., appear below. This list includes all of the company's current assets and current liabilities.

| | |
|---|---:|
| Sales..................................................... | $2,500,000 |
| Accumulated depreciation: equipment ............................ | 180,000 |
| Notes payable (due in 120 days) ............................... | 85,000 |
| Retained earnings............................................ | 240,000 |
| Cash....................................................... | 61,000 |
| Capital stock............................................... | 250,000 |
| Marketable securities ........................................ | 160,000 |
| Accounts payable ........................................... | 105,000 |
| Mortgage payable (due in 20 years)............................. | 650,000 |
| Salaries payable............................................ | 5,800 |
| Dividends ................................................. | 20,000 |
| Income taxes payable......................................... | 14,400 |
| Accounts receivable ......................................... | 217,000 |
| Inventory.................................................. | 195,000 |
| Unearned revenue ........................................... | 15,000 |
| Unexpired insurance.......................................... | 8,000 |

**Instructions**

a.  Prepare a schedule of the company's current assets and current liabilities. Select the appropriate items from the above list.

b.  Compute the current ratio and the amount of working capital. Explain how each of these measurements is computed. State, with reasons, whether you consider the company to be in a strong or weak current position.

**L03**  **PROBLEM 14.4B**

Liquidity of Cheese, Inc.

**L04**

**L07**

Cheese, Inc., is one of the world's largest cheese store chains. Shown below are selected items adapted from a recent Cheese, Inc., balance sheet. (Dollar amounts are in the millions.)

| | |
|---|---:|
| Cash . . . . . . . . . . . . . . . . . . . . . . . . . . . . . . . . . . . . . . . . . . . . . . . . . . . . . . . . . . . . . . . . . . . . . . . | $   72.4 |
| Receivables . . . . . . . . . . . . . . . . . . . . . . . . . . . . . . . . . . . . . . . . . . . . . . . . . . . . . . . . . . . . . . | 150.4 |
| Merchandise inventories. . . . . . . . . . . . . . . . . . . . . . . . . . . . . . . . . . . . . . . . . . . . . . . . . . . . . | 1,400.0 |
| Prepaid expenses. . . . . . . . . . . . . . . . . . . . . . . . . . . . . . . . . . . . . . . . . . . . . . . . . . . . . . . . . . . | 91.0 |
| Fixtures and equipment . . . . . . . . . . . . . . . . . . . . . . . . . . . . . . . . . . . . . . . . . . . . . . . . . . . . . . | 3,150.0 |
| Retained earnings. . . . . . . . . . . . . . . . . . . . . . . . . . . . . . . . . . . . . . . . . . . . . . . . . . . . . . . . . . . | 295.0 |
| Total current liabilities. . . . . . . . . . . . . . . . . . . . . . . . . . . . . . . . . . . . . . . . . . . . . . . . . . . . . . . | 2,500.0 |

**Instructions**

a.  Using the information above, compute the amounts of Cheese's total current assets and total quick assets.

b.  Compute the company's (**1**) current ratio, (**2**) quick ratio, and (**3**) working capital. (Round to two decimal places.)

c.  From these computations, are you able to conclude whether Cheese is a good credit risk for short-term creditors or on the brink of bankruptcy? Explain.

d.  Is there anything unusual about the operating cycle of cheese stores that would make you think that they normally would have lower current ratios than, say, large department stores?

e.  What *other types of information* could you utilize in performing a more complete analysis of Cheese's liquidity?

**L03**  **PROBLEM 14.5B**

Balance Sheet Measures of Liquidity and Credit Risk

**L04**

**L07**

A recent balance sheet of Sweet as Sugar included the following items, among others. (Dollar amounts are stated in thousands.)

| | |
|---|---:|
| Cash. . . . . . . . . . . . . . . . . . . . . . . . . . . . . . . . . . . . . . . . . . . . . . . . . . . . . . . . . . . . . . . . . . . . . . . . | $ 49,630 |
| Marketable securities (short-term) . . . . . . . . . . . . . . . . . . . . . . . . . . . . . . . . . . . . . . . . . . . . | 65,910 |
| Accounts receivable . . . . . . . . . . . . . . . . . . . . . . . . . . . . . . . . . . . . . . . . . . . . . . . . . . . . . . . . | 25,330 |
| Inventories . . . . . . . . . . . . . . . . . . . . . . . . . . . . . . . . . . . . . . . . . . . . . . . . . . . . . . . . . . . . . . . . | 44,000 |
| Prepaid expenses. . . . . . . . . . . . . . . . . . . . . . . . . . . . . . . . . . . . . . . . . . . . . . . . . . . . . . . . . . . | 5,850 |
| Retained earnings. . . . . . . . . . . . . . . . . . . . . . . . . . . . . . . . . . . . . . . . . . . . . . . . . . . . . . . . . . . | 350,000 |
| Notes payable to banks (due within one year) . . . . . . . . . . . . . . . . . . . . . . . . . . . . . . . . . . | 28,000 |
| Accounts payable . . . . . . . . . . . . . . . . . . . . . . . . . . . . . . . . . . . . . . . . . . . . . . . . . . . . . . . . . . . | 4,900 |
| Dividends payable . . . . . . . . . . . . . . . . . . . . . . . . . . . . . . . . . . . . . . . . . . . . . . . . . . . . . . . . . . | 1,800 |
| Accrued liabilities (short-term) . . . . . . . . . . . . . . . . . . . . . . . . . . . . . . . . . . . . . . . . . . . . . . . | 21,500 |
| Income taxes payable. . . . . . . . . . . . . . . . . . . . . . . . . . . . . . . . . . . . . . . . . . . . . . . . . . . . . . . | 8,500 |

The company also reported total assets of $600,000, total liabilities of $90,000, and a return on total assets of 20 percent.

**Instructions**

a.  Compute Sweet as Sugar's: (**1**) quick assets, (**2**) current assets, and (**3**) current liabilities.

b.  Compute Sweet as Sugar's: (**1**) quick ratio, (**2**) current ratio, (**3**) working capital, and (**4**) debt ratio. (Round to one decimal place.)

c.  Discuss the company's liquidity from the viewpoints of (**1**) short-term creditors, (**2**) long-term creditors, and (**3**) stockholders.

Problem Set B

**675**

L04 **PROBLEM 14.6B**
Financial Statement
L05 Analysis

L07

Shown below are selected data from the financial statements of Hamilton Stores, a retail lighting store.

**From the balance sheet:**

| | |
|---|---:|
| Cash | $ 35,000 |
| Accounts receivable | 175,000 |
| Inventory | 225,000 |
| Plant assets (net of accumulated depreciation) | 550,000 |
| Current liabilities | 190,000 |
| Total stockholders' equity | 500,000 |
| Total assets | 1,300,000 |

**From the income statement:**

| | |
|---|---:|
| Net sales | $2,400,000 |
| Cost of goods sold | 1,800,000 |
| Operating expenses | 495,000 |
| Interest expense | 80,000 |
| Income tax expense | 4,000 |
| Net income | 21,000 |

**From the statement of cash flows:**

| | | |
|---|---:|---:|
| Net cash provided by operating activities (including interest paid of $72,000) | | $ 50,000 |
| Net cash used in investing activities | | (54,000) |
| Financing activities: | | |
| Amounts borrowed | $ 56,000 | |
| Repayment of amounts borrowed | (25,000) | |
| Dividends paid | (24,000) | |
| Net cash provided by financing activities | | 7,000 |
| Net increase in cash during the year | | $ 3,000 |

**Instructions**

a. Explain how the interest expense shown in the income statement could be $80,000, when the interest payment appearing in the statement of cash flows is only $72,000.

b. Compute the following (round to one decimal place):

   **1.** Current ratio      **3.** Working capital

   **2.** Quick ratio       **4.** Debt ratio

c. Comment on these measurements and evaluate Hamilton's short-term debt-paying ability.

d. Compute the following ratios (assume that the year-end amounts of total assets and total stockholders' equity also represent the average amounts throughout the year):

   **1.** Return on assets

   **2.** Return on equity

e. Comment on the company's performance under these measurements. Explain *why* the return on assets and return on equity are so different.

f. Discuss (**1**) the apparent safety of long-term creditors' claims and (**2**) the prospects for Hamilton Stores continuing its dividend payments at the present level.

L04 **PROBLEM 14.7B**
Basic Ratio Analysis
L05

L07

Balsum Corporation is engaged primarily in the business of manufacturing raincoats. Shown below are selected information from a recent annual report. (Dollar amounts are stated in thousands.)

| | Beginning of the Year | End of the Year |
|---|---:|---:|
| Total current assets | $ 43,000 | $ 82,000 |
| Total current liabilities | 54,000 | 75,000 |
| Total assets | 230,000 | 390,000 |
| Total stockholders' equity | 120,000 | 205,000 |
| Operating income | | 74,000 |
| Net income | | 51,000 |

**676** Chapter 14 Financial Statement Analysis

The company has long-term liabilities that bear interest at annual rates ranging from 8 percent to 12 percent.

### Instructions

**a.** Compute the company's current ratio at (**1**) the beginning of the year and (**2**) the end of the year. (Carry to two decimal places.)

**b.** Compute the company's working capital at (**1**) the beginning of the year and (**2**) the end of the year. (Express dollar amounts in thousands.)

**c.** Is the company's short-term debt-paying ability improving or deteriorating?

**d.** Compute the company's (**1**) return on average total assets and (**2**) return on average stockholders' equity. (Round average assets and average equity to the nearest dollar and final computations to the nearest 1 percent.)

**e.** As an equity investor, do you think that Balsum's management is utilizing the company's resources in a reasonably efficient manner? Explain.

---

**L05** **PROBLEM 14.8B**

**L07** Ratios: Consider Advisability of Incurring Long-Term Debt

At the end of the year, the following information was obtained from the accounting records of Clips Systems, Inc.:

| | |
|---|---:|
| Sales (all on credit) | $4,800,000 |
| Cost of goods sold | 3,000,000 |
| Average inventory | 420,000 |
| Average accounts receivable | 380,000 |
| Interest expense | 50,000 |
| Income tax expense | 80,000 |
| Net income | 280,000 |
| Average investment in assets | 2,600,000 |
| Average stockholders' equity | 1,000,000 |

### Instructions

**a.** From the information given, compute the following:

| | |
|---|---|
| **1.** Inventory turnover. | **4.** Gross profit percentage. |
| **2.** Accounts receivable turnover. | **5.** Return on average stockholders' equity. |
| **3.** Total operating expenses. | **6.** Return on average assets. |

**b.** Clips Systems has an opportunity to obtain a long-term loan at an annual interest rate of 8 percent and could use this additional capital at the same rate of profitability as indicated by the given data. Would obtaining the loan be desirable from the viewpoint of the stockholders? Explain.

---

**L05** **PROBLEM 14.9B**

**L07** Ratios: Evaluation of Two Companies

**L08**

Shown below are selected financial data for THIS Star, Inc., and THAT Star, Inc., at the end of the current year:

| | THIS Star, Inc. | THAT Star, Inc. |
|---|---:|---:|
| Net credit sales | $900,000 | $840,000 |
| Cost of goods sold | 700,000 | 640,000 |
| Cash | 90,000 | 40,000 |
| Accounts receivable (net) | 100,000 | 90,000 |
| Inventory | 50,000 | 160,000 |
| Current liabilities | 120,000 | 110,000 |

Assume that the year-end balances shown for accounts receivable and for inventory also represent the average balances of these items throughout the year.

### Instructions

**a.** For each of the two companies, compute the following:

1. Working capital.
2. Current ratio.

3. Quick ratio.

4. Number of times inventory turned over during the year and the average number of days required to turn over inventory (round computation to the nearest day).

5. Number of times accounts receivable turned over during the year and the average number of days required to collect accounts receivable (round computation to the nearest day).

6. Operating cycle.

b. From the viewpoint of a short-term creditor, comment on the *quality* of each company's working capital. To which company would you prefer to sell $50,000 in merchandise on a 30-day open account?

## Critical Thinking Cases

**L01** **CASE 14.1**
Season's Greetings

Holiday Greeting Cards is a local company organized late in July of 2010. The company's net income for each of its first six calendar quarters of operations is summarized below. (Amounts are stated in thousands of dollars.)

|  | 2011 | 2010 |
|---|---|---|
| First quarter (Jan. through Mar.) | $ 253 | –0– |
| Second quarter (Apr. through June) | 308 | –0– |
| Third quarter (July through Sept.) | 100 | $ 50 |
| Fourth quarter (Oct. through Dec.) | 450 | 500 |
| Total for the calendar year | $1,111 | $550 |

Glen Wallace reports the business and economic news for a local radio station. On the day that Holiday Greeting Cards released the above financial information, you heard Wallace make the following statement during his broadcast: "Holiday Greeting Cards enjoyed a 350 percent increase in its profits for the fourth quarter, and profits for the entire year were up by over 100 percent."

### Instructions

a. Show the computations that Wallace probably made in arriving at his statistics. (Hint: Wallace did not make his computations in the manner recommended in this chapter. His figures, however, can be developed from these financial data.)

b. Do you believe that Wallace's percentage changes present a realistic impression of Holiday Greeting Cards's rate of growth in 2011? Explain.

c. What figure would you use to express the percentage change in Holiday's fourth-quarter profits in 2011? Explain why you would compute the change in this manner.

**L03** **CASE 14.2**
through Evaluating
**L05** Debt-Paying Ability

You are a loan officer with Third Texas Bank. Dan Scott owns two successful restaurants, each of which has applied to your bank for a $250,000 one-year loan for the purpose of opening a second location. Condensed balance sheets for the two business entities are shown below.

### TEXAS STEAK RANCH
### BALANCE SHEET
### DECEMBER 31, 2011

| Assets | | Liabilities & Stockholders' Equity | |
|---|---|---|---|
| Current assets | $ 75,000 | Current liabilities | $ 30,000 |
| Plant and equipment | 300,000 | Long-term liabilities | 200,000 |
| | | Capital stock | 100,000 |
| | | Retained earnings | 45,000 |
| Total assets | $375,000 | Total liabilities & stockholders' equity | $375,000 |

| THE STOCKYARDS BALANCE SHEET DECEMBER 31, 2011 | | | |
|---|---|---|---|
| **Assets** | | **Liabilities & Owners' Equity** | |
| Current assets . . . . . . . . . . . . . | $ 24,000 | Current liabilities . . . . . . . . . . . . | $ 30,000 |
| Plant and equipment . . . . . . . . | 301,000 | Long-term liabilities . . . . . . . . . . . | 200,000 |
| | | Capital, Dan Scott . . . . . . . . . . . | 95,000 |
| | | Total liabilities & | |
| Total assets . . . . . . . . . . . . . . . | $325,000 | owners' equity . . . . . . . . . . . . | $325,000 |

Both restaurants are popular and have been successful over the past several years. Texas Steak Ranch has been slightly more profitable, but the operating results for the two businesses have been quite similar. You think that either restaurant's second location should be successful. On the other hand, you know that restaurants are a very "faddish" type of business and that their popularity and profitability can change very quickly.

Dan Scott is one of the wealthiest people in Texas. He made a fortune—estimated at more than $2 billion—as the founder of Micro Time, a highly successful manufacturer of computer software. Scott now is retired and spends most of his time at Second Life, his 50,000-acre cattle ranch. Both of his restaurants are run by experienced professional managers.

**Instructions**

**a.** Compute the current ratio and working capital of each business entity.

**b.** On the basis of the information provided in this case, which of these businesses do you consider to be the better credit risk? Explain fully.

**c.** What simple measure might you insist upon that would make the other business as good a credit risk as the one you identified in part **b?** Explain.

**L05**   **CASE 14.3**

Strategies to Improve the Current Ratio

Nashville Do-It-Yourself owns a chain of nine retail stores that sell building materials, hardware, and garden supplies. In early October, the company's current ratio is 1.7 to 1. This is about normal for the company, but it is lower than the current ratios of several large competitors. Management feels that, to qualify for the best credit terms from its suppliers, the company's year-end balance sheet should indicate a current ratio of at least 2 to 1.

**Instructions**

**a.** Indicate whether taking each of the following actions would increase or decrease the company's current ratio. Explain your reasoning.

  **1.** Pay some of the company's current liabilities.

  **2.** Purchase large amounts of inventory on account.

  **3.** Offer credit customers a special discount if they pay their account balance prior to year-end.

**b.** Propose several other ethical steps that management might take to increase the company's current ratio prior to year-end.

**L05**   **CASE 14.4**

Evaluating Corporate Governance Quality

Assume that you are an intern working for the California Public Employees Retirement System (CALPERS) in its investments office and you have been asked to evaluate a number of companies for possible investment by CALPERS. You prepare an analysis of each company's prospects using the tools of financial statement analysis (e.g., trend analysis, common size statements, ratio analysis). Thinking you are done, you present your analysis to your boss. She tells you that, although your analysis of each company's financial information is fine, she is also interested in the quality of each company's corporate governance. Pick a public company, download their most recent proxy statement in support of the annual meeting of shareholders, and write a brief report on the quality of each company's board of directors in terms of board composition and structure, size, committees, and expertise.

Critical Thinking Cases

**INTERNET CASE 14.5**

Evaluating Liquidity and Profitability

Use the Internet search engine of your choice and do a general search on the name of a company of interest to you (e.g., General Motors, Johnson & Johnson, Coca-Cola, etc.). Explore the Web site of the company you choose and locate that company's most recent financial statements. You may need to look under a category that provides general information about the company and/or investor information.

**Instructions**

a. Find and read the description of the company, including the type of business it is in. Why is gaining an understanding of the industry and type of business an important starting point for financial statement analysis?

b. Locate the company's primary financial statements. Find the summary table of ratios in this chapter in Exhibit 14–26. Calculate three of the listed ratios under each of the following categories: "Measures of short-term liquidity" and "Measures of profitability." Show your work in calculating these ratios. Write a brief statement describing what you have learned about your company's liquidity and profitability.

c. Why do you think the Internet has become such a widely used source of financial information by investors and creditors?

*Internet sites are time and date sensitive. It is the purpose of these exercises to have you explore the Internet. You may need to use the Yahoo! search engine* http://www.yahoo.com *(or another favorite search engine) to find a company's current Web address.*

## Answers to Self-Test Questions

**1.** b  **2.** a, c, d  **3.** c  **4.** d (see below)  **5.** b (see below)  **6.** b  **7.** d

Why answers a, b, and c in question **4** are incorrect:

a. The return on assets, 12 percent ($240,000 ÷ $2,000,000), exceeds the return on equity, which is 10 percent ($80,000 ÷ $800,000).

b. The current ratio is 1.6 to 1 ($480,000 ÷ $300,000).

c. Working capital amounts to $180,000 ($480,000 − $300,000).

Increase in net income required in question **5** : ($400,000 − $160,000) ÷ $160,000 = 150%

# CHAPTER 16

# Management Accounting
## A Business Partner

© Imagestate Media Partners Limited-Impact Photos/Alamy

**AFTER STUDYING THIS CHAPTER, YOU SHOULD BE ABLE TO:**

**LO1** Explain the three principles guiding the design of management accounting systems.

**LO2** Describe the three basic types of manufacturing costs.

**LO3** Distinguish between product costs and period costs.

**LO4** Describe how manufacturing costs flow through perpetual inventory accounts.

**LO5** Distinguish between direct and indirect costs.

**LO6** Prepare a schedule of the cost of finished goods manufactured.

Learning Objective

## COCA-COLA COMPANY

The secret syrup formula for Coca-Cola® was created in 1886 by Dr. John S. Pemberton, a pharmacist in Atlanta, Georgia.[1] Dr. Pemberton's partner, Frank Robinson, a management accountant, penned the famous trademark symbol *Coca-Cola.*® In 1891, when Asa Candler purchased the Coca-Cola business from Pemberton for $2,300, he also recognized the value of the management accounting skills of Frank Robinson. In 1892, Candler and Robinson, along with three other associates, formed the Georgia corporation now known as the Coca-Cola Company.

Today, the Coca-Cola Company produces more than 3,300 products in over 200 countries. Seventy-four percent of Coca-Cola's income is derived from sales outside the United States. To help manage its global business, the Coca-Cola Company employs thousands of management accountants in hundreds of countries. ▪

---

[1] For more details, see www.thecoca-colacompany.com/heritage/chronicle_birth_refreshing_idea.html.

## Management Accounting: Basic Framework

Because accounting information is critical for assessing an organization's output, performance measurement and reporting are key activities frequently coordinated through accounting. In this chapter, you will learn how management accounting becomes an important business partner. Management accounting information links decision-making authority with the information necessary to make decisions. It also provides a means to assess decision performance. This chapter introduces the foundations of management accounting.

The opening story describes a management accountant at Coca-Cola Company. **Management accounting** is the design and use of accounting information systems inside the company to achieve the company's objectives. Three principles govern how management accounting systems are designed. First, management accounting systems help to decide who has decision-making authority over company assets. Second, accounting information produced by or created from the management accounting system supports planning and decision making. Finally, management accounting reports provide a means of monitoring, evaluating, and rewarding performance.

### MANAGEMENT ACCOUNTING'S ROLE IN ASSIGNING DECISION-MAKING AUTHORITY

**Learning Objective**

**LO1** Explain the three principles guiding the design of management accounting systems.

To achieve organizational goals, managers are assigned decision-making authority for some of the firm's assets. For example, plant managers typically are responsible for decisions about equipment in the plant, employees at the plant, the physical plant layout, and sources of raw materials, among other things. Within the plant, the materials inventory manager may be delegated decision-making responsibility for reordering materials, and the production supervisor may be delegated decision-making responsibility for assigning employees to jobs on the production line. The point is that all members of an organization have some decision-making authority.

Employees within a corporation know their decision-making responsibilities because they are outlined in a variety of ways, such as in job descriptions, verbal instructions from their supervisors, and management accounting system documents and reports. Just as you have received a course syllabus that outlines your instructor's standards for you to follow to earn an A or B in this course, managers receive management accounting reports that outline expected outcomes to help achieve the organization's goals. Just as you have decision-making responsibility over the "assets" necessary to achieve an A or B (the time you allocate to studying), managers have decision-making responsibility over the assets included in their management accounting reports.

### MANAGEMENT ACCOUNTING'S ROLE IN DECISION MAKING

Managers need reliable and timely information on which to base their decisions. For example, the plant manager needs information to help assess if equipment is inefficient or if certain work arrangements and plant layouts are more productive than others. Thus, managers need both historical information (for example, the current equipment's cost and productivity) and projected information (for example, the productivity and cost of other available equipment). They need information oriented both toward their specific operations and toward other parts of the organization's value chain. A **value chain** is the linked set of activities and resources necessary to create and deliver the product or service to the customer. Therefore, plant managers will require information from other parts of the value chain such as engineering or sales. They need information from both internal operations and externally oriented benchmark sources.

More and more organizations are sharing information. It is very common for organizations to participate in and undertake **benchmark studies.** Independent consulting companies often create benchmark reports by collecting information from companies in the same industry. These studies show an organization how its costs and processes compare with others in its industry. Organizations also share information with customers and suppliers in their value chain. For example, in order for shipments from suppliers to arrive at the exact time they are needed for use in production, buyers and suppliers share their production information. Customers often require or are voluntarily provided quality information. As shown in Exhibit 16–1, the management accounting system provides past-, current-, and future-oriented information for users both inside and outside the firm.

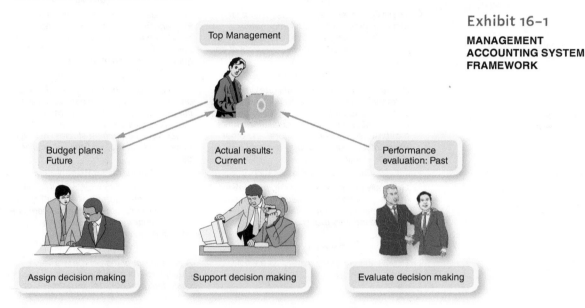

**Exhibit 16–1**

**MANAGEMENT ACCOUNTING SYSTEM FRAMEWORK**

Top Management

Budget plans: Future

Actual results: Current

Performance evaluation: Past

Assign decision making

Support decision making

Evaluate decision making

## MANAGEMENT ACCOUNTING'S ROLE IN PERFORMANCE EVALUATION AND REWARDS

The assets over which managers have decision-making authority do not belong to these managers. The corporation owns these assets, and the returns from these assets belong to the corporation. To make sure the assets are earning a good return, the corporation monitors the outcomes of the decisions made by the managers. When the corporation is owned by shareholders, the external financial statements discussed in previous chapters serve this monitoring role for the corporation as a whole. Parallel monitoring systems are designed to serve similar functions inside corporations. For example, many companies prepare plant-level income statements. Headquarters' executives compare these plant-level financial statements with budgets to monitor the decisions made by plant managers. Frequently, managerial rewards and bonuses are related to the outcomes of these internally prepared financial statements.

Exhibit 16–1 shows that the accounting system must be designed to fulfill all of the three roles described above simultaneously. The system must clearly allocate decision-making authority, provide information for decision making, and furnish information for evaluating and rewarding performance. The accounting system must be constantly monitored and adjusted to make sure all three roles are being supported.

## ACCOUNTING SYSTEMS: A BUSINESS PARTNER

Creating accounting information systems that can satisfy the demands of both external users (shareholders, creditors, IRS, SEC) and internal users (plant managers, marketing managers, human resource personnel, CFO, CEO) is very challenging. Exhibit 16–2 outlines the demands placed on accounting information systems. Users want accounting information for different, sometimes conflicting, reasons. Information necessary for planning and decision making is likely to be future oriented, and information for monitoring is likely to be historical. Shareholders, creditors, and the IRS do not expect information that is as timely, or at the same level of detail, as the information needed by a plant manager. Yet, the same accounting information system usually serves multiple sets of users. Employees use it across a multitude

**Exhibit 16–2**

**DEMAND FOR ACCOUNTING INFORMATION**

| THE ACCOUNTING SYSTEM | |
|---|---|
| **Financial Accounting** | **Management Accounting** |
| Purpose | Purpose |
| *To provide investors, creditors, and other external parties with useful information about the financial position, financial performance, and cash flow prospects of an enterprise.* | *To provide managers with information useful for planning, evaluating and rewarding performance, and sharing with other outside parties. To apportion decision-making authority over firm resources.* |
| Types of Reports | Types of Reports |
| *Primarily financial statements (statement of financial position or balance sheet, income statement, statement of cash flows) and related notes and supplemental disclosures that provide investors, creditors, and other users information to support external decision-making processes.* | *Many different types of reports, depending on the nature of the business and the specific information needs of management. Examples include budgets, financial projections, benchmark studies, activity-based cost reports, and cost-of-quality assessment.* |
| Standards for Presentation | Standards for Presentation |
| *Generally accepted accounting principles, including those formally established in the authoritative accounting literature and standard industry practice.* | *Rules are set within each organization to produce information most relevant to the needs of management. Management needs include reporting to both external constituents and internal users.* |
| Reporting Entity | Reporting Entity |
| *Usually the company viewed as a whole.* | *A component of the company's value chain, such as a business segment, supplier, customer, product line, department, or product.* |
| Time Periods Covered | Time Periods Covered |
| *Usually a year, quarter, or month. Most reports focus on completed periods. Emphasis is placed on the current (latest) period, with prior periods often shown for comparison.* | *Any period—year, quarter, month, week, day, even a work shift. Some reports are historical in nature; others focus on estimates of results expected in future periods.* |

| Users of Information | Users of Information |
|---|---|
| *Outsiders as well as managers. For financial statements, these outsiders include stockholders, creditors, prospective investors, regulatory authorities, and the general public.* | *Management (different reports to different managers), customers, auditors, suppliers, and others involved in an organization's value chain.* |

of organizational levels and job responsibilities, and it spreads over numerous geographic areas with different cultures, languages, currencies, and economic environments. Companies such as Coca-Cola Company are much better than they were 15 years ago at designing cost-efficient accounting information systems to serve multiple users. One of the primary reasons for better accounting information systems is the advance in these systems' technological capabilities.

Due to rapidly evolving changes in technology and information needs, business managers study management accounting throughout their professional careers. In fact, many companies require employees to complete training in a variety of accounting techniques. Professional certification is available to individuals who plan to make their career in management accounting. The Institute of Certified Management Accountants sponsors two certification exams, the Certified Management Accountant (CMA) exam and the Certified Financial Manager (CFM) exam. To become either a CMA or a CFM, an individual must meet educational and experience requirements as well as pass a rigorous examination.

---

**CASE IN POINT**

As the tech industry shifted from the PC to the Internet, the company Michael Dell started in his college dorm to efficiently build and sell personal computers fell on hard times. For example, in 2005 Dell was valued at $100 billion, but by 2009 its value fell to $30 billion.[2] It seems clear that Dell had stayed with its old playbook of cranking out PCs as efficiently as possible for too long.

© Keith Eng 2007/DAL

Michael Dell returned to the chief executive roll in 2007 with the objective of remaking the company. However, lack of structure at the massive company including a lack of management accounting processes, tools, and culture didn't support a new way of doing business. To get executives to seize new business opportunities and take more risks, Dell needed to change the company's management structure and culture.

He arranged for leaders of each division to be *responsible for meeting financial targets and have broad authority to figure out how to reach them.* Dell thought that by focusing outward and giving top managers more responsibility and more flexibility, the company would be more responsive to clients. Results are supporting his claims. By late 2009, Dell was beginning to show improvement in its financial results.

---

As you progress through the remaining chapters, keep in mind the three principles of management accounting systems: assigning decision-making authority, making and supporting decisions, and evaluating and rewarding performance. The procedures and techniques discussed in the remaining chapters are aimed at one or more of these principles. In addition, you will encounter many familiar terms and concepts because of the overlap of management and financial accounting. After all, a single accounting system serves both sets of users. It is common for managers to use information about revenue, expenses, and assets in their daily decision making. Managers receive customized accounting information (for example, by product line or customer) as needed to make decisions.

## Accounting for Manufacturing Operations

A merchandising company buys its inventory in a ready-to-sell condition. Therefore, its cost of goods is mostly composed of the purchase price of the products it sells. A *manufacturing* company, however, *produces* the goods that it sells. As a consequence, its cost of goods sold consists of various **manufacturing costs,** including the cost of materials, wages earned by production workers, and a variety of other costs relating to the operation of a production facility.[3]

Manufacturing operations are an excellent example of how managerial and financial accounting overlap because manufacturing costs are of vital importance to both financial and managerial accountants. Financial accountants use manufacturing costs to determine the cost of goods sold and inventory values reported in financial statements. Management accountants also rely on prompt and reliable information about manufacturing costs to help answer such questions as:

---

[2] "Dell's Do-Over," *BusinessWeek,* Iss. 4152, October 26, 2009, p. 36.

[3] Manufacturing costs are the cost of producing inventory, which is an asset. Therefore, these expenditures are termed *costs* rather than *expenses.* Unexpired costs are assets; expired costs are expenses.

- What sales price must we charge for our products to earn a reasonable profit?
- Is it possible to lower the cost of producing a particular product line in order to be more price competitive?
- Is it less expensive to buy certain parts used in our products or to manufacture these parts ourselves?
- Should we automate our production process with a robotic assembly line?

## CLASSIFICATIONS OF MANUFACTURING COSTS

A typical manufacturing company purchases raw materials and converts these materials into finished goods through the process of production. The costs of converting raw materials into finished goods, specifically the direct labor and overhead costs, are called **conversion costs.** In contrast, the direct materials and direct labor that are consumed in production are referred to as **prime costs.** Thus, direct labor is both a prime cost and a conversion cost. These cost classifications are illustrated in Exhibit 16–3 and described below. The manufacturing costs are often divided into three broad categories:

1. **Direct materials**—the raw materials and component parts used in production whose costs are directly traceable to the products manufactured.
2. **Direct labor**—wages and other payroll costs of employees whose efforts are directly traceable to the products they manufacture.
3. **Manufacturing overhead**—a catchall classification, which includes all manufacturing costs *other than* the costs of direct materials and direct labor. Examples include factory utilities, supervisor salaries, equipment repairs, and depreciation on production machinery.

**Exhibit 16–3**    **FLOW OF PHYSICAL GOODS IN PRODUCTION**

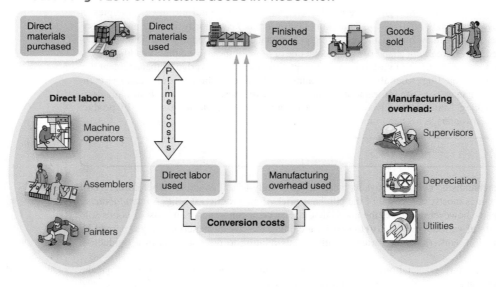

Note that manufacturing costs are *not* immediately recorded as current period expenses. Rather, they are costs of *creating inventory,* and they remain on the balance sheet until the inventory is sold. For this reason, manufacturing costs are often called *product costs* (or inventoriable costs).

## PRODUCT COSTS VERSUS PERIOD COSTS

The terms *product costs* and *period costs* are helpful in explaining the difference between manufacturing costs and operating expenses. In a manufacturing environment, **product costs** are those costs incurred to manufacture inventory. Thus, until the related goods are sold, product costs *represent inventory.* As such, they are reported in the balance sheet as an asset. When the goods are ultimately sold, product costs are transferred from the balance sheet to the income statement, where they are deducted from revenue as the cost of goods sold.

Operating expenses associated with *time periods,* rather than with the production of inventory, are referred to as **period costs.** Period costs are charged directly to expense accounts on the assumption that their benefit is recognized entirely in the period when the cost is incurred. Period costs include all selling expenses, general and administrative expenses, interest expense, and income tax expense. In short, period costs are classified in the income statement separately from cost of goods sold, as deductions from a company's gross profit.

The flow of product costs and period costs through the financial statements is shown in Exhibit 16–4.

### Exhibit 16–4 "FLOW" OF COSTS THROUGH FINANCIAL STATEMENTS

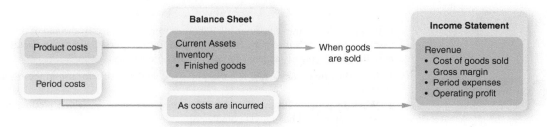

To further illustrate the distinction between product and period costs, consider two costs that, on the surface, appear quite similar: the depreciation of a warehouse used to store raw materials versus depreciation of a warehouse used to store finished goods. Depreciation of the raw materials warehouse is considered a *product cost* (a component of manufacturing overhead) because the building is part of the manufacturing process. Once the manufacturing process is complete and the finished goods are available for sale, all costs associated with their storage are considered selling expenses. Thus, the depreciation of the finished goods warehouse is a *period cost.*

## Ethics, Fraud & Corporate Governance

A company can artificially inflate reported income by improperly capitalizing period costs. Capitalizing period costs violates GAAP. For example, the Securities and Exchange Commission (SEC) brought an enforcement action against Winners Internet Network, Inc. (Winners), its former chairman/CEO/president, and its former auditing firm for filing materially misleading financial statements with the SEC, due at least in part to the improper capitalization of period costs.

Winners capitalized wages, payroll taxes, rent, travel, marketing, and consulting costs—all period costs that were related to the employment of Winners's chairman/CEO/

president. These costs were unrelated to the development of Winners's software asset. As such, these costs should have been expensed as incurred. Winners's improper capitalization of period costs resulted in an overstatement of its total assets by 416 percent.

The SEC sought and received a permanent injunction barring American Television and Film Company (the successor company to Winners) from further violations of the securities laws, in addition to issuing other sanctions against Winners's former chairman/CEO/president and Winners's former accounting firm.

## PRODUCT COSTS AND THE MATCHING PRINCIPLE

Underlying the distinction between product costs and period costs is a familiar accounting concept—the *matching principle*. In short, product costs should be reported in the income statement only when they can be matched against product revenue. To illustrate, consider a real estate developer who starts a tract of 10 homes in May of the current year. During the year, the developer incurs material, labor, and overhead costs amounting to $1 million (assume $100,000 per house). By the end of December, none of the houses has been sold. How much of the $1 million in construction costs should appear in the developer's income statement for the current year?

The answer is *none*. These costs are not related to any revenue earned by the developer during the current year. Instead, they are related to future revenue the developer will earn when the houses are eventually sold. Therefore, at the end of the current year, the $1 million of product costs should appear in the developer's balance sheet as *inventory*. As each house is sold, $100,000 will be deducted from sales revenue as cost of goods sold. This way, the developer's income statements in future periods will properly match sales revenue with the cost of each sale.

## INVENTORIES OF A MANUFACTURING BUSINESS

In the preceding example, assume all 10 houses were completed by the end of the year. In this case, the developer's inventory consists only of finished goods. Most manufacturing companies, however, typically account for *three types* of inventory:

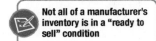

**Not all of a manufacturer's inventory is in a "ready to sell" condition**

1. **Materials inventory**—raw materials on hand and available for use in the manufacturing process.
2. **Work in process inventory**—partially completed goods on which production activities have been started but not yet completed.
3. **Finished goods inventory**—unsold finished products available for sale to customers.

All three of these inventories are classified on the balance sheet as current assets. The cost of the materials inventory is based in its purchase price. The work in process and finished goods inventories are based on the costs of direct material, direct labor, and manufacturing overhead assigned to them.

**INTERNATIONAL** CASE IN POINT

In many countries such as Argentina and Greece, inventory valuation does not conform to the lower of cost or market value rules used in the United States. In addition, many countries, including Korea, Mexico, Nigeria, Poland, and Taiwan, allow upward revaluation of property and equipment. These differences in accounting methods make comparing inventory values of companies from different parts of the world very difficult.

Manufacturing companies may use either a perpetual or a periodic inventory system. Perpetual systems have many advantages, however, such as providing managers with up-to-date information about the amounts of inventory on hand and the per-unit costs of manufacturing products. For these reasons, virtually all large manufacturing companies use *perpetual inventory systems*. Also, the flow of manufacturing costs through the inventory accounts and into the cost of goods sold is most easily illustrated in a perpetual inventory system. Therefore, we will assume the use of a perpetual inventory system in our discussion of manufacturing activities.

## THE FLOW OF COSTS PARALLELS THE FLOW OF PHYSICAL GOODS

When a perpetual inventory system is in use, the flow of manufacturing costs through the company's general ledger accounts closely parallels the physical flow of goods through the production process. This relationship is illustrated in Exhibit 16–5. The numbered boxes in the exhibit represent six *general ledger accounts* used by manufacturing companies to account for their production activities: (1) Materials Inventory, (2) Direct Labor, (3) Manufacturing Overhead, (4) Work in Process Inventory, (5) Finished Goods Inventory, and (6) Cost of Goods Sold.

**Learning Objective**
**Describe how manufacturing costs flow through perpetual inventory accounts.**   LO4

## Exhibit 16–5   FLOW OF COST ASSOCIATED WITH PRODUCTION

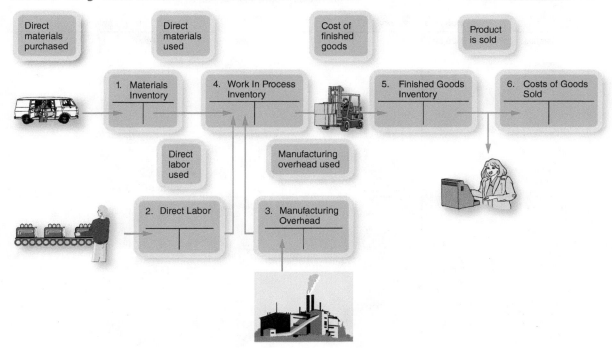

## ACCOUNTING FOR MANUFACTURING COSTS: AN ILLUSTRATION

To illustrate accounting for manufacturing costs, we will assume that Conquest, Inc., manufactures high-quality mountain bikes in Bend, Oregon. The company relies on cost information to monitor its production efficiency, set prices, and maintain control over its inventories.

Conquest carefully tracks the flow of manufacturing costs through its general ledger accounts as illustrated in Exhibit 16–6 on the following page. The figures shown represent all of Conquest's manufacturing costs for the current year. The debit and credit entries summarize the numerous transactions recorded by the company throughout the year.

Our use of several colors in this illustration will help you follow the flow of manufacturing costs through these accounts. The beginning balances in the three inventory accounts are shown in black. Manufacturing costs, and the arrows showing the transfer of these costs from one account to another, are shown in red. Account balances at year-end, which will appear in the company's financial statements, are shown in blue.

Let us now look more closely at exactly how the company's manufacturing costs flow through these general ledger accounts.

## DIRECT MATERIALS

*Direct materials* are the raw materials and component parts that become an integral part of finished products and can be traced directly and conveniently to products manufactured. Conquest's direct materials include lightweight alloy tubing for cycle frames, brakes, shifting levers, pedals, sprockets, tires, and so on. The mountain bikes assembled from these components are Conquest's *finished goods.*

The terms *direct materials* and *finished goods* are defined from the viewpoint of individual manufacturing companies. For example, Conquest views brake components as a direct

Exhibit 16–6  **ACCOUNTING FOR MANUFACTURING COSTS**

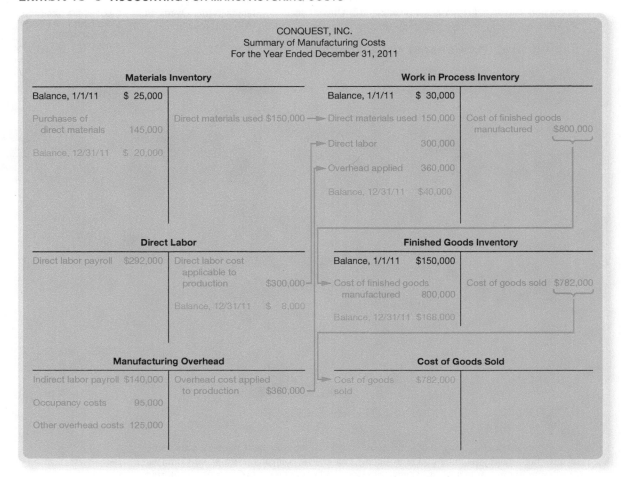

material. However, the Shimano Company (a brake manufacturer) views the brake components it sells to Conquest as finished goods.

Conquest uses a perpetual inventory system. Accordingly, the costs of direct materials purchased are debited directly to the Materials Inventory account. As these materials are placed into production, their costs are transferred from the Materials Inventory account to the Work in Process Inventory account by debiting Work in Process Inventory and crediting Materials Inventory. The balance remaining in the Materials Inventory account at year-end represents the cost of direct materials on hand and ready for use.

Some materials used in the production process cannot be traced conveniently or directly to the finished goods manufactured. For Conquest, examples include bearing grease, welding materials, and material used in factory maintenance such as cleaning compounds. These items are referred to as **indirect materials** and are classified as part of manufacturing overhead.

## DIRECT LABOR

The Direct Labor account is used to record the payroll cost of direct workers and assign this cost to the goods they help manufacture.[4] Direct workers are those employees who work directly on the bicycles being manufactured, either by hand or by using machines.

---

[4] As explained in Chapter 10, payroll costs include such factors as payroll taxes and "fringe benefits" as well as the wages earned by employees. Some companies classify fringe benefits as overhead because they are not proportionally related to hourly wages.

Conquest employs five classifications of direct laborers. Each classification and its corresponding job description are as follows:

| Classification | Job Description |
| --- | --- |
| Cutters | Cut alloy tubing into appropriate lengths. |
| Welders | Transform the cut pieces of alloy tubing into bicycle frames. |
| Painters | Prime and paint each frame. |
| Assemblers | Partially assemble each bicycle in preparation for packing. |
| Packers | Pack the partially assembled bicycles in boxes. |

There are two separate and distinct aspects of accounting for direct labor costs. The first involves the *payment* of cash made to the direct workers at the end of each pay period. At each payroll date, the Direct Labor account is debited for the total direct labor payroll, and an offsetting credit is made to Cash. The second aspect involves the *application* of direct labor costs to the goods being produced. As direct labor employees contribute to the production process during the period, the cost of their labor is *applied* to production by debiting the Work in Process Inventory account and crediting the Direct Labor account.

In our T accounts in Exhibit 16–6, the flow of direct labor costs looks similar to the flow of direct materials costs. There is, however, one significant difference. Materials are purchased *before* they are used; therefore, the Materials Inventory account has a *debit* balance equal to the cost of unused materials on hand. The services of employees, however, are used before the employees are paid. Thus, the credits to the Direct Labor account are recorded *throughout* the payroll period, but the debits are not recorded until the *end* of the payroll period. If the balance sheet date falls between payroll dates and before adjusting entries are made, the Direct Labor account will have a *credit* balance representing the amount owed to employees for work already performed. This credit balance should be listed in the balance sheet as *wages payable,* a current liability.

Many employees in a manufacturing plant do not work directly on the goods being manufactured. Examples at Conquest include factory supervisors, maintenance personnel, forklift drivers, and security guards. These **indirect labor** costs, which are handled in a fashion similar to that used for indirect materials costs, are considered part of Conquest's manufacturing overhead.

## MANUFACTURING OVERHEAD

All manufacturing costs, *other than* direct materials and direct labor, are classified as *manufacturing overhead.* The Manufacturing Overhead account is used to (1) record all costs classified as "overhead" and (2) assign these costs to products being manufactured.

There are many types of overhead costs. Consequently, Manufacturing Overhead is treated as a *control account* for which subsidiary records are typically maintained to keep track of various overhead classifications.

Because of the diverse nature of manufacturing companies, it simply isn't possible to prepare a complete list of all overhead cost types. However, specific examples at Conquest include the following:

1. *Indirect materials costs*
   a. Factory supplies that do not become an integral part of finished goods, such as oil used to lubricate the cutting machines and solvents used to clean the painting machines.
   b. Materials that become an integral part of finished goods but whose cost would require great effort to actually trace to finished goods. These items include grease used in each bike's bearing assembly and the nuts and bolts used to attach shift levers and other component parts.

2. *Indirect labor costs*
   a. Supervisors' salaries.
   b. Salaries of factory maintenance workers, forklift drivers, receiving clerks in the materials warehouse, and factory security personnel.

3. *Plant occupancy costs*
   a. Depreciation of the factory and the materials warehouse.
   b. Insurance and property taxes on land and buildings.
   c. Maintenance and repairs on buildings.
   d. Utilities and telephone costs.
4. *Machinery and equipment costs*
   a. Depreciation of machinery.
   b. Maintenance of machinery.
5. *Cost of regulatory compliance*
   a. Meeting factory safety requirements.
   b. Disposal of waste materials such as empty paint canisters.
   c. Control over factory emissions (meeting clean air standards).

Selling expenses and general and administrative expenses do *not* relate to the manufacturing process and are *not* included in manufacturing overhead. Certain costs, such as insurance, property taxes, and utilities, sometimes apply in part to manufacturing operations and in part to selling and administrative functions. In such cases, these costs are *apportioned* among manufacturing overhead, general and administrative expenses, and selling expenses.

**Recording Overhead Costs**   The Manufacturing Overhead account is debited to record any cost classified as overhead. Examples of costs debited to this account include the payment of indirect labor payrolls, the payment of factory utilities, the recording of depreciation on factory assets, and the purchase of indirect materials.[5] The account credited will vary depending on the nature of the overhead cost. For example, in recording the purchase of indirect materials, the account credited is usually Accounts Payable. In recording depreciation on machinery, however, the account credited is Accumulated Depreciation.

As the items included in total overhead costs are consumed by production activities, the related costs are transferred from the Manufacturing Overhead account into the Work in Process Inventory account (debit Work in Process Inventory, credit Manufacturing Overhead). In the course of the year, all the overhead costs incurred should be assigned to units of product manufactured. Thus, at year-end, the Manufacturing Overhead account should have a zero balance.

## DIRECT AND INDIRECT MANUFACTURING COSTS

**Learning Objective**

**L05**  **Distinguish between direct and indirect costs.**

The costs of direct materials and direct labor may be traced conveniently and directly to specific units of product. At Conquest, for example, it is relatively easy to determine the cost of the metal tubing and the cost of the direct labor that go into making a particular bicycle. For this reason, accountants call these items **direct manufacturing costs.**

Overhead, however, is an **indirect manufacturing cost.** Consider, for example, the types of costs that Conquest classifies as overhead. These costs include property taxes on the factory, depreciation on tools and equipment, supervisors' salaries, and repairs to equipment. How much of these indirect costs should be assigned to each bicycle?

There is no easy answer to this question. By definition, indirect costs *cannot* be traced easily and directly to specific units of production. While these costs are often easier to view *as a whole* than on a per-unit basis, we will see that both financial and management accountants require unit cost information. Therefore, manufacturing companies must develop methods of allocating an appropriate portion of total manufacturing overhead to each product manufactured. These methods will be discussed in detail in Chapter 17.

## WORK IN PROCESS INVENTORY, FINISHED GOODS INVENTORY, AND THE COST OF GOODS SOLD

We have devoted much of this chapter to discussing the three types of manufacturing costs—direct materials, direct labor, and manufacturing overhead. We will now shift our attention to

---

[5] Some companies record the purchase of indirect materials in the Materials Inventory account or in a separate inventory account. Our approach is commonly used when the quantity of indirect materials purchased does not differ significantly from the quantity of indirect materials used during each period.

the three accounts that provide the structure for the flow of these costs—the Work in Process Inventory account, the Finished Goods Inventory account, and the Cost of Goods Sold account.

The Work in Process Inventory account is used (1) to record the accumulation of manufacturing costs associated with the units of product worked on during the period and (2) to allocate these costs between those units completed during the period and those that are only partially completed.

Because direct materials, direct labor, and manufacturing overhead are consumed in production, their related costs are debited to the Work in Process Inventory account. The flow of costs into this inventory account (rather than into a corresponding expense account) is consistent with the idea that manufacturing costs are *product costs,* not period costs.

As specific units are completed, the cost of manufacturing them is transferred from the Work in Process Inventory account to the Finished Goods Inventory account. Thus, the balance in the Work in Process account represents only the manufacturing costs associated with units still "in process."

It is important to realize that once products are classified as finished goods, *no additional costs are allocated to them.* Therefore, the costs of storing, marketing, or delivering finished goods are regarded as *selling expenses,* not manufacturing costs. When units of finished goods are sold, their related costs must "flow" from the balance sheet through the income statement in compliance with the matching principle. Accordingly, as products are sold, their costs are transferred from the Finished Goods Inventory account to the Cost of Goods Sold account.

**YOUR TURN**          **You as a Chief Financial Officer**

Assume that you are CFO of Conquest, Inc., and that you have just received an income statement and balance sheet from plant accountant Jim Sway in Bend, Oregon. In your conversations with Jim you learn that, in the recent reporting period, plant manager Darlene Cosky asked that inventory transportation cost, the cost of repairing the plant parking lot, and the newly installed plant landscaping costs all be allocated to cost of production. In addition, when these allocations took place, the plant produced many more bicycles than were sold, creating significant increases in the amount of inventory on hand. As a result, most of the costs described by Jim have been assigned to the inventory on hand (included as part of inventory costs in the balance sheet) but have not been assigned to cost of goods sold expenses (included on the income statement). Furthermore, during the recent reporting period both Darlene and Jim earned significant bonuses based on plant profitability. What, if anything, would you do as the CFO?

(See our comments on the Online Learning Center Web site.)

## THE NEED FOR PER-UNIT COST DATA

Transferring the cost of specific units from one account to another requires knowledge of each unit's *per-unit cost*—that is, the total manufacturing costs assigned to specific units. The determination of unit cost is one of the primary goals of every cost accounting system and will be explained and illustrated more completely in Chapter 17.

Unit costs are of importance to both financial and management accountants. Financial accountants use unit costs in recording the transfer of completed goods from Work in Process to Finished Goods and from Finished Goods to Cost of Goods Sold. Management accountants use the same information to make pricing decisions, evaluate the efficiency of current operations, and plan for future operations.

## DETERMINING THE COST OF FINISHED GOODS MANUFACTURED

**Learning Objective**

Prepare a schedule of the cost of finished goods manufactured.

**LO6**

Most manufacturing companies prepare a **schedule of the cost of finished goods manufactured** to provide managers with an overview of manufacturing activities during the period.

Using the information from Exhibit 16–6, a schedule of Conquest's cost of finished goods manufactured is shown in Exhibit 16–7.

**Exhibit 16-7**

**SCHEDULE OF MANUFACTURING ACTIVITIES AT CONQUEST, INC., FOR 2011**

| CONQUEST, INC. SCHEDULE OF THE COST OF FINISHED GOODS MANUFACTURED FOR THE YEAR ENDED DECEMBER 31, 2011 | | |
|---|---|---|
| Work in process inventory, beginning of the year | | $ 30,000 |
| Manufacturing cost assigned to production: | | |
| Direct materials used | $150,000 | |
| Direct labor | 300,000 | |
| Manufacturing overhead | 360,000 | |
| Total manufacturing costs | | 810,000 |
| Total cost of all work in process during the year | | $840,000 |
| Less: Work in process inventory, end of the year | | (40,000) |
| Cost of finished goods manufactured | | $800,000 |

Notice that all of the figures in this schedule were obtained from Conquest's Work in Process Inventory account illustrated in Exhibit 16–6. In short, Exhibit 16–7 summarizes the flow of manufacturing costs into and out of the Work in Process Inventory account.

**Purpose of the Schedule** A schedule of the cost of finished goods manufactured is *not* a formal financial statement and generally does not appear in the company's annual report. Rather, it is intended primarily to assist managers in understanding and evaluating the overall cost of manufacturing products. By comparing these schedules for successive periods, for example, managers can determine whether direct labor or manufacturing overhead is rising or falling as a percentage of total manufacturing costs. In addition, the schedule is helpful in developing information about unit costs.

If a company manufactures only a single product line, its cost per unit simply equals its *cost of finished goods manufactured* divided by the *number of units produced.* For example, if Conquest produces only one line of mountain bikes, its average cost per unit would be *$80* had it produced *10,000* finished units during 2011 ($800,000 divided by 10,000 units). If Conquest produced multiple lines of mountain bikes, it would prepare a separate schedule of the cost of finished goods manufactured for each product line.

## FINANCIAL STATEMENTS OF A MANUFACTURING COMPANY

Let us now illustrate how the information used in our example will be reported in the 2011 income statement and balance sheet of Conquest, Inc.

The company's 2011 income statement is presented in Exhibit 16–8.

Notice that no manufacturing costs appear among the company's operating expenses. In fact, manufacturing costs appear in only two places in a manufacturer's financial statements. First, costs associated with units *sold* during the period appear in the income statement as the *cost of goods sold.* The $782,000 cost of goods sold figure reported in Conquest's income statement was taken directly from the company's perpetual inventory records. However, this amount may be verified as follows:

| | |
|---|---|
| Beginning finished goods inventory (1/1/11) | $150,000 |
| Add: Cost of finished goods manufactured during the year | 800,000 |
| Cost of finished goods available for sale | $950,000 |
| Less: Ending finished goods inventory (12/31/11) | 168,000 |
| Cost of goods sold | $782,000 |

| CONQUEST, INC. INCOME STATEMENT FOR THE YEAR ENDED DECEMBER 31, 2011 | | |
|---|---:|---:|
| Sales | | $1,300,000 |
| Cost of goods sold | | 782,000 |
| Gross profit on sales | | $ 518,000 |
| Operating expenses: | | |
| Selling expenses | $135,000 | |
| General and administrative expenses | 265,000 | |
| Total operating expenses | | 400,000 |
| Income from operations | | $ 118,000 |
| Less: Interest expense | | 18,000 |
| Income before income taxes | | $ 100,000 |
| Income taxes expense | | 30,000 |
| Net income | | $ 70,000 |

**Exhibit 16–8**

**REPORTED INCOME AT CONQUEST, INC., FOR 2011**

Second, all manufacturing costs associated with goods *still on hand* are classified as *inventory* and appear in the balance sheet. The balance sheet presentation of Conquest's three types of inventory is illustrated in Exhibit 16–9.

| CONQUEST, INC. PARTIAL BALANCE SHEET DECEMBER 31, 2011 | | |
|---|---:|---:|
| **Current assets:** | | |
| Cash and Cash Equivalents | | $ 60,000 |
| Accounts Receivable (net of allowance for doubtful accounts) | | 190,000 |
| Inventories: | | |
| Materials | $ 20,000 | |
| Work in Process | 40,000 | |
| Finished Goods | 168,000 | |
| Total Inventories | | 228,000 |
| Total current assets | | $478,000 |

**Exhibit 16–9**

**CONQUEST, INC.'S CURRENT ASSET BALANCE AT THE END OF 2011**

Notice the three types of inventory

As previously mentioned, Conquest's balance sheet includes a current liability for wages payable equal to the unadjusted $8,000 credit balance in the Direct Labor account.

## INTERNATIONAL FINANCIAL REPORTING STANDARDS AND INVENTORIES

U.S. generally accepted accounting principles (GAAP) allows a variety of inventory methods for financial statement presentation including the average cost approach discussed in this chapter (others are specific identification, LIFO, FIFO, or average cost). However, international accounting standards are not consistent with several U.S. GAAP methods. For example, as discussed in Chapter 8, LIFO methods are allowed by U.S. GAAP, but not allowed under IFRS. Further, when impairment of inventory occurs then both U.S. GAAP and IFRS require companies to write inventories down. However, IFRS requires revaluation under certain circumstances, but U.S. GAAP does not allow such a revaluation. As the members of the FASB and the IASB work to reconcile differences and converge their financial reporting standards, consideration of internal management accounting activities are brought to their attention from such organizations as the Institute of Management Accountants, mentioned earlier in this chapter.

## Concluding Remarks

This chapter provides a framework to help you think about the role of management accounting in business. The framework says management accounting information, tools, and techniques help (1) assign decision-making responsibility, (2) support the decision-making process, and (3) evaluate decision outcomes. Past, current, and future information is collected by the management accounting system to support various decisions. Much of what you will learn in later chapters is based on this initial framework and on the management accounting terminology introduced in this chapter. These ideas will be useful to you whether you currently (or in the future will) work for a business or if you someday (or now) own your own business.

# END-OF-CHAPTER REVIEW

## SUMMARY OF LEARNING OBJECTIVES

**LO1 Explain the three principles guiding the design of management accounting systems.** First, management accounting systems help to decide who has the decision-making authority over company assets. Second, accounting information produced or created from the management accounting system supports planning and decision making. Finally, management accounting reports provide a means of monitoring, evaluating, and rewarding performance.

**LO2 Describe the three basic types of manufacturing costs.** Direct materials used consist of the parts and materials that become part of the finished products. Direct labor cost consists of the wages paid to factory employees who work directly on the products being manufactured. Manufacturing overhead includes all manufacturing costs other than the cost of materials used and direct labor. Examples of manufacturing overhead include depreciation of machinery and the plant security service.

**LO3 Distinguish between product costs and period costs.** Product costs are the costs of creating inventory. They are treated as assets until the related goods are sold, at which time the product costs are deducted from revenue as the cost of goods sold. Thus, goods manufactured this year but not sold until next year are deducted from next year's revenue.

Period costs are charged to expense in the accounting period in which they are incurred. Period costs are not related to production of goods; consequently, they are deducted from revenue on the assumption that the benefits obtained from the expenditures are received in the same period as the costs are incurred. Period costs include general and administrative expense, selling expense, and income taxes expense.

**LO4 Describe how manufacturing costs flow through perpetual inventory accounts.** Manufacturing costs originally are recorded in three controlling accounts: Materials Inventory, Direct Labor, and Manufacturing Overhead. As these costs become applicable to goods placed into production, they are transferred from these manufacturing cost accounts to the Work in Process Inventory account. As units are completed, their cost is transferred from the Work in Process account to Finished Goods Inventory. Then, when units are sold, their costs are transferred from Finished Goods Inventory to the Cost of Goods Sold account.

**LO5 Distinguish between direct and indirect costs.** Direct manufacturing costs (direct materials and direct labor) can be identified with specific products. Indirect manufacturing costs are the many elements of manufacturing overhead that apply to factory operations as a whole and cannot be traced to specific products.

**LO6 Prepare a schedule of the cost of finished goods manufactured.** This schedule summarizes the flow of manufacturing costs into and out of the Work in Process Inventory account. Its purpose is to assist management in understanding and evaluating manufacturing costs incurred in the period.

To prepare this schedule, start by listing the work in process inventory at the beginning of the year. To this amount, add the materials used, direct labor costs, and overhead for the period. Combining these four items indicates the total cost of all work in process during the period. A final step is deducting the cost of work still in process at the end of the period. This gives us the cost of finished goods manufactured during the period.

## Key Terms Introduced or Emphasized in Chapter 16

**benchmark study** (p. 722)   A study designed to show an organization how its costs and processes compare to others in the industry.

**conversion costs** (p. 726)   The direct labor and overhead costs required to convert raw materials into finished goods.

**direct labor** (p. 726)   Payroll costs for employees who work directly on the products being manufactured, either by hand or with machines.

**direct manufacturing cost** (p. 732)   A manufacturing cost that can be traced conveniently and directly into the quantity of finished goods manufactured. Examples include direct materials and direct labor.

**direct materials** (p. 726)   Materials and component parts that become an integral part of the manufactured goods and can be traced directly to the finished products.

**finished goods inventory** (p. 728)   The completed units that have emerged from the manufacturing process and are on hand available for sale.

**indirect labor** (p. 731)   Payroll costs relating to factory employees who do not work directly on the goods being manufactured. Examples are wages of security guards and maintenance personnel. Indirect labor costs are classified as manufacturing overhead.

**indirect manufacturing cost** (p. 732)   A manufacturing cost that cannot be conveniently traced to the specific products being manufactured. Examples include property taxes, depreciation on machinery, and other types of manufacturing overhead.

**indirect materials** (p. 730)   Materials used in the manufacturing process that cannot be traced conveniently to specific units of production. Examples include lubricating oil, maintenance supplies, and glue. Indirect materials are accounted for as part of manufacturing overhead.

**management accounting** (p. 722)   The design and use of accounting information systems inside the firm to achieve the firm's objectives.

**manufacturing costs** (p. 725)   The cost of manufacturing the goods that will be sold to customers. The basic types of manufacturing costs are direct materials, direct labor, and manufacturing overhead.

**manufacturing overhead** (p. 726)   A "catchall" category including all manufacturing costs other than the costs of direct materials used and direct labor.

**materials inventory** (p. 728)   The cost of direct materials on hand and available for use in the manufacturing process.

**period costs** (p. 727)   Costs that are charged to expense accounts in the period that the costs are incurred. Includes all items classified as "expense."

**prime costs** (p. 726)   The direct materials and direct labor consumed in the production of goods and services.

**product costs** (p. 726)   The costs of purchasing or manufacturing inventory. Until the related goods are sold, these product costs represent an asset—inventory. Once the goods are sold, these costs are deducted from revenue as the cost of goods sold.

**schedule of the cost of finished goods manufactured** (p. 733)   A schedule summarizing the flow of manufacturing costs into and out of the Work in Process Inventory account. Intended to assist managers in evaluating manufacturing costs.

**value chain** (p. 722)   The linked set of activities and resources necessary to create and deliver a product or service to customers.

**work in process inventory** (p. 728)   Goods at any stage of the manufacturing process short of completion. As these units are completed, they become finished goods.

## Demonstration Problem

The following T accounts summarize the flow of manufacturing costs during the current year through the ledger accounts of Marston Manufacturing Company:

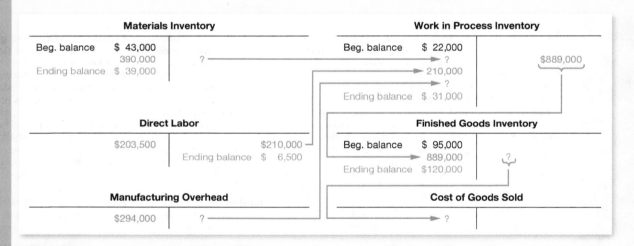

### Instructions

Using the data above, determine the following amounts. Some amounts already appear in the T accounts; others require short computations.

**a.** Purchases of direct materials.

**b.** Direct materials used during the year.

**c.** Direct labor costs assigned to production.

**d.** The year-end liability to direct workers for wages payable.

**e.** The overhead costs assigned to production during the year.

**f.** Total manufacturing costs charged to production during the year.

**g.** The cost of finished goods manufactured.

**h.** The cost of goods sold.

**i.** The total costs classified as inventory in the year-end balance sheet.

### Solution to the Demonstration Problem

| | | |
|---|---|---:|
| **a.** | Purchases of direct materials | <u>$390,000</u> |
| **b.** | Computation of direct materials used: | |
| |     Materials inventory, beginning of year | $ 43,000 |
| |     Purchases of direct materials | 390,000 |
| |     Direct materials available for use | $433,000 |
| |     Less: Materials inventory, end of year | 39,000 |
| |     Direct materials used | <u>$394,000</u> |
| **c.** | Direct labor costs assigned to production | <u>$210,000</u> |
| **d.** | Year-end liability for direct wages payable | <u>$ 6,500</u> |
| **e.** | Overhead costs during the year: | |
| |     Cost transferred out of work in process | $889,000 |
| |     Ending work in process | 31,000 |
| |     Total cost to account for | $920,000 |
| |     Less: Direct materials used (part **b**) | 394,000 |
| |         Direct labor used | 210,000 |
| |         Beginning work in process | 22,000 |
| |     Overhead assigned | <u>$294,000</u> |
| **f.** | Total manufacturing costs charged to production: | |
| |     Direct materials used (part **b**) | $394,000 |
| |     Direct labor costs assigned to production | 210,000 |
| |     Manufacturing overhead assigned (part **e**) | 294,000 |
| |         Total manufacturing costs charged to production | <u>$898,000</u> |
| **g.** | Cost of finished goods manufactured | <u>$889,000</u> |
| **h.** | Computation of cost of goods sold: | |
| |     Beginning inventory of finished goods | $ 95,000 |
| |     Cost of finished goods manufactured | 889,000 |
| |     Cost of goods available for sale | $984,000 |
| |     Less: Ending inventory of finished goods | 120,000 |
| |     Cost of goods sold | <u>$864,000</u> |
| **i.** | Total year-end inventory: | |
| |     Materials | $ 39,000 |
| |     Work in process | 31,000 |
| |     Finished goods | 120,000 |
| |         Total inventory | <u>$190,000</u> |

## Self-Test Questions

*The answers to these questions appear on page 757.*

1. Indicate which of the following statements are more descriptive of management accounting than of financial accounting. (More than one answer may be appropriate.)

   a. Recognized standards are used for presentation.

   b. Information is tailored to the needs of individual decision makers.

   c. Information is more widely distributed.

   d. Emphasis is on expected future results.

2. In a manufacturing company, the costs debited to the Work in Process Inventory account represent:

   a. Direct materials used, direct labor, and manufacturing overhead.

   b. Cost of finished goods manufactured.

c. Period costs and product costs.

d. None of the above; the types of costs debited to this account will depend on the type of products being manufactured.

3. The Work in Process Inventory account had a beginning balance of $4,200 on February 1. During February, the cost of direct materials used was $29,000 and direct labor cost assigned to production was $3,000. $3,600 of overhead was assigned. If the cost of finished goods manufactured was $34,100, compute the balance in the Work in Process Inventory account at the *end* of February.

   a. $9,900.     c. $2,100.

   b. $1,500.     d. $5,700.

4. Manufacturing overhead costs would include:

   a. Marketing costs related to selling the product.

   b. The salary of the production line supervisor.

   c. The chief executive officer's salary.

   d. Research and development costs for a new product.

5. The accounting records of Newport Mfg. Co. include the following information for the most recent year ended December 31:

| | Dec. 31 | Jan. 1 |
|---|---|---|
| Inventory of work in process . . . . | $ 20,000 | $10,000 |
| Inventory of finished goods . . . . . | 80,000 | 60,000 |
| Direct materials used . . . . . . . . | 200,000 | |
| Direct labor . . . . . . . . . . . . . . . . | 120,000 | |
| Manufacturing overhead . . . . . . . | 180,000 | |
| Selling expenses . . . . . . . . . . . | 150,000 | |

Indicate which of the following are correct. (More than one answer may be correct.)

   a. Amount debited to the Work in Process Inventory account during the year, $500,000.

   b. Cost of finished goods manufactured, $490,000.

   c. Cost of goods sold, $470,000.

   d. Total manufacturing costs for the year, $650,000.

---

**ASSIGNMENT MATERIAL** | # Discussion Questions

1. Briefly distinguish between management and financial accounting information in terms of (**a**) the intended users of the information and (**b**) the purpose of the information.

2. Describe the three principles guiding the design of management accounting systems.

3. Is management accounting information developed in conformity with generally accepted accounting principles or some other set of prescribed standards? Explain.

4. A manufacturing firm has three inventory control accounts. Name each of the accounts, and describe briefly what the balance in each at the end of any accounting period represents.

5. Is the cost of disposing of hazardous waste materials resulting from factory operations a product cost or a period cost? Explain.

6. An important focus of management accounting is decision-making authority. Everyone within an organization has some decision-making authority. How do employees and managers know what decision-making authority they have regarding firm assets?

7. What amounts are *debited* to the Materials Inventory account? What amounts are *credited* to this account? What type of balance (debit or credit) is this account likely to have at year-end? Explain.

8. Briefly explain what accounting benchmark studies are and why they are important for an organization's management accounting system.

9. What amounts are debited to the Direct Labor account during the year? What amounts are credited to this account? What type of balance (debit or credit) is this account likely to have at year-end? Explain.

10. Exhibit 16–6 includes six ledger accounts. Which of these six accounts often have balances at year-end that appear in the company's formal financial statements? Briefly explain how these balances will be classified in the financial statements.

11. Argo Mfg. Co. uses approximately $1,200 in janitorial supplies to clean the work area and factory equipment each month. Should this $1,200 be included in the cost of direct materials used? Explain.

12. What amounts are *debited* to the Work in Process Inventory account during the year? What amounts are *credited* to this account? What does the year-end balance in this account represent?

13. What amounts are *debited* to the Finished Goods Inventory account during the year? What amounts are *credited* to this account? What type of balance (debit or credit) is this account likely to have at year-end?

14. Briefly describe the computation of the cost of finished goods manufactured as it appears in a schedule of the cost of finished goods manufactured.

15. A schedule of the cost of finished goods manufactured is a helpful tool in determining the per-unit cost of manufactured products. Explain several ways in which information about per-unit manufacturing costs is used by (**a**) management accountants and (**b**) financial accountants.

# Brief Exercises

**L03**   **BRIEF EXERCISE 16.1**
Product vs. Period Costs

During the year, Coronado Boat Yard has incurred manufacturing costs of $420,000 in building three large sailboats. At year-end, each boat is about 70 percent complete. How much of these manufacturing costs should be recognized as expense in Coronado Boat Yard's income statement for the current year? Explain.

**L04**   **BRIEF EXERCISE 16.2**
Direct Materials Used

During the current year, the cost of direct materials purchased by a manufacturing firm was $510,000, and the direct materials inventory increased by $40,000. What was the cost of direct materials used during the year?

**L03**   **BRIEF EXERCISE 16.3**
**L04**   Cost of Goods Sold

A company that assembles trucks produces 60 trucks during the current year and incurs $3 million of material, labor, and overhead costs. Fifty-three trucks were sold during the year and each is allocated the same amount of costs. How much of the $3 million assembly costs should appear on the company's income statement for the current year?

**L04**   **BRIEF EXERCISE 16.4**
Materials Inventory

Hula's Heavyweights, Inc., is a company that manufactures forklifts. During the year, Hula's purchased $1,450,000 of direct materials and placed $1,525,000 worth of direct materials into production. Hula's beginning balance in the Materials Inventory account was $320,000. What is the ending balance in Hula's Materials Inventory account?

**L02**   **BRIEF EXERCISE 16.5**
**L04**   Direct Labor Journal Entries

A.J.'s Cooling Systems, Inc., assigns $230,000 of direct labor costs to production during the current period. A.J.'s also pays employees $200,000 during the period. What are the two journal entries used to record these transactions?

**L04**   **BRIEF EXERCISE 16.6**
**L05**   Manufacturing Overhead Assigned

During the current year, CF Manufacturing Co. incurred $370,000 of indirect labor costs, $15,000 of indirect materials costs, $125,000 of rent costs, and $163,000 of other overhead costs. How much did CF Manufacturing assign to the Work in Process Inventory account from the Manufacturing Overhead account?

**L04**   **BRIEF EXERCISE 16.7**
Inventory Balances

Ardvark Pets, Inc., has three stores in the state. The owner, Ms. Perkins, is having trouble tracking inventory costs in the three pet stores. Ms. Perkins knows about your skill in tracking and understanding cost flows and asks you to find the following missing items for the three stores:

|  | Midwest Ardvark | Northern Ardvark | Eastern Ardvark |
|---|---|---|---|
| Beginning inventory | $ 30,000 | ? | ? |
| Transferred in | 100,000 | $200,000 | $160,000 |
| Transferred out | 110,000 | 180,000 | 150,000 |
| Ending Inventory | ? | 60,000 | 40,000 |

**L04**   **BRIEF EXERCISE 16.8**
Work in Process Balances

The Work in Process Inventory account had a beginning balance of $16,200 on April 1. During April, the cost of direct materials used was $408,000 and direct labor cost assigned to production was $56,000. A total of $72,000 of overhead was assigned to production in April. If the cost of finished goods manufactured was $523,500, what was the balance in the Work in Process Inventory account on April 30?

**L03**   **BRIEF EXERCISE 16.9**
through
**L05**   Prime vs. Conversion Costs

Hapless Repairs Co. does all the repair work for a medium-sized manufacturer of handheld computer games. The games are sent directly to Hapless, and after the games are repaired, Hapless bills the game manufacturer for cost plus a 30 percent markup. In the month of February, purchases of parts (replacement parts) by Hapless amounted to $90,000, the beginning inventory of parts was $40,500, and the ending inventory of parts was $15,250. Payments to repair technicians during the month of February totaled $63,000. Overhead incurred was $113,000.

a. What was the cost of materials used for repair work during the month of February?

b. What was the prime cost for February?

c. What was the conversion cost for February?

d. What was the total repair cost for February?

**BRIEF EXERCISE 16.10**

Partial Balance Sheet

At the end of the year, Kyler Electronic Corporation had the following balances:

| | |
|---|---|
| Work in process ................................................. | $ 43,600 |
| Cash and cash equivalents................................... | 532,000 |
| Finished goods ................................................. | 85,700 |
| Raw materials.................................................. | 25,400 |
| Accounts receivable ........................................... | 237,000 |

Prepare a partial balance sheet for Kyler's showing the above accounts.

# Exercises

 **EXERCISE 16.1**

Accounting

**through** Terminology

**L05**

Listed below are eight technical accounting terms introduced or emphasized in this chapter:

| | |
|---|---|
| Work in Process Inventory | Cost of finished goods manufactured |
| Conversion costs | Cost of Goods Sold |
| Period costs | Management accounting |
| Product costs | Manufacturing overhead |

Each of the following statements may (or may not) describe one of these technical terms. For each statement, indicate the accounting term described, or answer "None" if the statement does not correctly describe any of the terms.

**a.** The preparation and use of accounting information designed to assist managers in planning and controlling the operations of a business.

**b.** All manufacturing costs other than direct materials used and direct labor.

**c.** Direct materials and direct labor used in manufacturing a product.

**d.** A manufacturing cost that can be traced conveniently and directly to manufactured units of product.

**e.** The account debited at the time that the Manufacturing Overhead account is credited.

**f.** The amount transferred from the Work in Process Inventory account to the Finished Goods Inventory account.

**g.** Costs that are debited directly to expense accounts when the costs are incurred.

**L02** **EXERCISE 16.2**

Basic Types of Manufacturing Costs

Into which of the three elements of manufacturing cost would each of the following be classified?

**a.** Tubing used in manufacturing bicycles.

**b.** Wages paid by an automobile manufacturer to employees who test-drive completed automobiles.

**c.** Property taxes on machinery.

**d.** Gold bullion used by a jewelry manufacturer.

**e.** Wages of assembly-line workers who package frozen food.

**f.** Salary of plant superintendent.

**g.** Electricity used in factory operations.

**h.** Salary of a nurse in a factory first-aid station.

 **EXERCISE 16.3**

Product Costs and Period Costs

**L05**

Indicate whether each of the following should be considered a *product cost* or a *period cost*. If you identify the item as a product cost, also indicate whether it is a *direct* or an *indirect* cost. For example, the answer to item **0** is "indirect product cost." Begin with item **a.**

**0.** Property taxes on factory building.

**a.** Cost of disposal of hazardous waste materials to a chemical plant.

**b.** Amounts paid by a mobile home manufacturer to a subcontractor who installs plumbing in each mobile home.

**c.** Depreciation on sales showroom fixtures.

**d.** Salaries of security guards in an administrative office building.

e.  Salaries of factory security guards.

f.  Salaries of office workers in the credit department.

g.  Depreciation on the raw materials warehouse.

h.  Income taxes on a profitable manufacturing company.

**L04** **EXERCISE 16.4**

Flow of Costs through Manufacturing Accounts

The following information was taken from the accounting records of Reliable Tool Corporation:

| | |
|---|---|
| Work in process inventory, beginning of the year . . . . . . . . . . . . . . . . . . . . . . . . . . | $ 35,000 |
| Cost of direct materials used . . . . . . . . . . . . . . . . . . . . . . . . . . . . . . . . . . . . . . . | 245,000 |
| Direct labor cost applied to production . . . . . . . . . . . . . . . . . . . . . . . . . . . . . . . | 120,000 |
| Cost of finished goods manufactured . . . . . . . . . . . . . . . . . . . . . . . . . . . . . . . . . | 675,000 |

Overhead is assigned to production at $300,000. Compute the amount of the work in process inventory on hand at year-end.

**L06** **EXERCISE 16.5**

Preparing a Schedule of the Cost of Finished Goods Manufactured

The accounting records of NuTronics, Inc., include the following information for the year ended December 31, 2011.

| | Dec. 31 | Jan. 1 |
|---|---|---|
| Inventory of materials . . . . . . . . . . . . . . . . . . . . . . . . . . . . . . . . . . . . | $ 24,000 | $20,000 |
| Inventory of work in process . . . . . . . . . . . . . . . . . . . . . . . . . . . . . . | 8,000 | 12,000 |
| Inventory of finished goods . . . . . . . . . . . . . . . . . . . . . . . . . . . . . . . | 90,000 | 80,000 |
| Direct materials used . . . . . . . . . . . . . . . . . . . . . . . . . . . . . . . . . . . | 210,000 | |
| Direct labor . . . . . . . . . . . . . . . . . . . . . . . . . . . . . . . . . . . . . . . . . | 120,000 | |
| Selling expenses . . . . . . . . . . . . . . . . . . . . . . . . . . . . . . . . . . . . . | 170,000 | |
| General and administrative expenses . . . . . . . . . . . . . . . . . . . . . . . | 140,000 | |

Overhead is assigned to production at $192,000.

a.  Prepare a schedule of the cost of finished goods manufactured. (Not all of the data given above are used in this schedule.)

b.  Assume that the company manufactures a single product and that 20,000 units were completed during the year. What is the average per-unit cost of manufacturing this product?

**L03** **through** **L05** **EXERCISE 16.6**

Flow of Costs through Manufacturing Accounts

The Bags and Luggage Company had the following account balances as of January 1:

| | |
|---|---|
| Direct Materials Inventory . . . . . . . . . . . . . . . . . . . . . . . . . . . . . . . . . . . . . . . . . . | $ 9,200 |
| Work in Process Inventory . . . . . . . . . . . . . . . . . . . . . . . . . . . . . . . . . . . . . . . . . . | 78,400 |
| Finished Goods Inventory . . . . . . . . . . . . . . . . . . . . . . . . . . . . . . . . . . . . . . . . . . | 53,600 |
| Manufacturing Overhead . . . . . . . . . . . . . . . . . . . . . . . . . . . . . . . . . . . . . . . . . . | –0– |

During the month of January, all of the following occurred:

1.  Direct labor costs were $42,000 for 1,800 hours worked.

2.  Direct materials costing $35,750 and indirect materials costing $3,500 were purchased.

3.  Sales commissions of $16,500 were earned by the sales force.

4.  $26,000 worth of direct materials were used in production.

5.  Advertising costs of $6,300 were incurred.

6.  Factory supervisors earned salaries of $12,000.

7.  Indirect labor costs for the month were $3,000.

8.  Monthly depreciation on factory equipment was $4,500.

9.  Utilities expense of $7,800 was incurred in the factory.
10. Luggage with manufacturing costs of $70,100 were transferred to finished goods.
11. Monthly insurance costs for the factory were $4,200.
12. $5,000 in property taxes on the factory were incurred and paid.
13. Luggage with manufacturing costs of $89,000 were sold for $145,000.

**Instructions**

a.  If Bags and Luggage assigns manufacturing overhead of $34,400, what will be the balances in the Direct Materials, Work in Process, and Finished Goods Inventory accounts at the end of January?

b.  As of January 31, what will be the balance in the Manufacturing Overhead account?

c.  What was Bags and Luggage's operating income for January?

---

**L01**    **EXERCISE 16.7**
Manipulating Accounting Figures

Joe Felan is the production manager at Utex Corporation. He was recently quoted as saying, "Since management reports aren't subject to generally accepted accounting principles, and they aren't directly used by outside investors and creditors, it's really okay for managers to manipulate the reports as they see fit." Do you agree with Felan's statement? Defend your answer.

---

**L01**    **EXERCISE 16.8**
Design of Management Accounting Systems

Sheila Lufty manages the plant that produces dining room furniture for Bastile Furniture Company. Sheila's annual performance is evaluated based on how well she manages all the costs incurred to run the plant and produce the furniture. For her annual evaluation, the costs incurred for the year are compared to the budgeted costs that were established at the beginning of the year. Sheila receives a large bonus if the total costs are less than those budgeted at the beginning of the year.

Recently, Sheila provided the following end-of-year explanation to her boss, the division head, Rose Pantle:

> Rose, I know that the plant costs were over budget again this year. However, during the year I only receive four reports from accounting about the plant costs. These quarterly reports from accounting tell me what the actual plant costs are each quarter. Because the budget is based on yearly totals, it is difficult to tell from the accounting reports if we are falling behind budget. In addition, the sales department decides how many sets of dining room furniture we will produce during the year. This year, sales demanded 1,000 more dining room sets than budgeted at the beginning of the year. These extra sets increased the plant costs significantly.

On the basis of the three principles of management accounting system design discussed in this chapter, identify three problems with Bastile Furniture Company's management accounting system. What would you recommend that Bastile do to fix the problems?

---

**L04**    **EXERCISE 16.9**
**L06**    Preparing an Income Statement Using the Cost of Finished Goods Manufactured

The Anthony Company, a sole proprietorship, reports the following information pertaining to its operating activities:

|  | Ending Balance | Beginning Balance |
| --- | --- | --- |
| Materials Inventory | $10,000 | $40,000 |
| Work in Process Inventory | 29,000 | 60,000 |
| Finished Goods Inventory | 52,000 | 42,000 |

During the year, the company purchased $40,000 of direct materials and incurred $21,000 of direct labor costs. Total manufacturing overhead costs for the year amounted to $18,000. Selling and administrative expenses amounted to $60,000, and the company's annual sales amounted to $250,000.

a.  Prepare Anthony's schedule of the cost of finished goods manufactured.

b.  Prepare Anthony's income statement (ignore income taxes).

**L04**

 **L06**

**EXERCISE 16.10**

Preparing an Income
Statement Using
the Cost of Finished
Goods Manufactured

Ridgeway Company reports the following information pertaining to its operating activities:

|  | Ending Balance | Beginning Balance |
|---|---|---|
| Materials Inventory | $70,000 | $60,000 |
| Work in Process Inventory | 41,000 | 29,000 |
| Finished Goods Inventory | 16,000 | 21,000 |

During the year, the company purchased $35,000 of direct materials and incurred $22,000 of direct labor costs. Total manufacturing overhead costs for the year amounted to $19,000. Selling and administrative expenses amounted to $30,000, and the company's annual sales amounted to $80,000.

**a.** Prepare Ridgeway's schedule of the cost of finished goods manufactured.

**b.** Prepare Ridgeway's income statement (ignore income taxes).

**L01**

**EXERCISE 16.11**

Management
Accounting Systems
Design

Boeing Company has had its financial ups and downs. Recently, the CFO for Boeing helped turn its problems around by analyzing the amount of value each product was providing to the company's bottom line. The analysis ultimately determined which programs were making or losing money for Boeing. Based on the analysis, key operational metrics were established and reported to managers on a regular basis. These performance metrics detailed the company's progress toward reducing inventory, reducing costs, and streamlining operations. Managers were evaluated based on these metrics.

Explain how the above description of activities at Boeing Company is consistent with the three principles that govern how management accounting systems are designed and used in companies.

 **L03**

**L04**

 **L06**

**EXERCISE 16.12**

Costs at Hobart
Industries

The accounting records of Hobart Industries show the following information for the most recent year ended December 31:

|  | Dec. 31 | Jan. 1 |
|---|---|---|
| Inventory of work in process | $ 40,000 | $18,000 |
| Inventory of finished goods | 60,000 | 68,000 |
| Direct materials used | 250,000 | |
| Direct labor | 120,000 | |
| Manufacturing overhead | 145,000 | |
| Selling expenses | 135,000 | |

**a.** Find the amount debited to the Work In Process Inventory account during the year.

**b.** What is the cost of goods manufactured for the year?

**c.** What is the cost of goods sold for the year?

**d.** What are the total manufacturing costs for the year?

**L02**

**L03**

**L05**

**EXERCISE 16.13**

Classifying Costs

Classify each of the following costs as a *product cost* or *period cost*. If it is a product cost, classify it as *direct* (or *indirect*) *materials, direct* (or *indirect*) *labor,* or *overhead.*

**a.** Wheat used to make flour at General Mills.

**b.** Sales commissions paid to sales personnel at Gap retail stores.

**c.** Costs incurred by General Motors to ship automobile seats purchased from the Lear Corporation to GM assembly plants.

**d.** Insurance paid on the Target retail stores in Michigan.

**e.** Insurance paid on the Target warehouse holding merchandise inventory.

**f.** Bonus paid to all production employees of General Motors at the end of a profitable fiscal year.

**g.** Health care costs for the office workers at the headquarters of Johnson & Johnson Company.

**h.** Bolts used by Trek Bicycle Corporation to secure the bike parts to the frame.

**746**   Chapter 16   Management Accounting: A Business Partner

**LO2**   **EXERCISE 16.14**
Manufacturing Costs
**LO5**   at Coca-Cola

Go to the following Web site for the Coca-Cola Company:
   http://www.worldofcoca-cola.com
Select the "Virtual Tour" from the list of activities on the left-hand side of the screen. Choose "Bottle work" to see the bottling operation.

**a.**   Determine five direct materials that are used to create Coca-Cola.®

**b.**   Identify at least three types of labor. For each type of labor, identify it as *direct* or *indirect*.

**c.**   Identify at least three types of overhead costs.

**LO3**   **EXERCISE 16.15**

Home Depot Product
vs. Period Costs

Use the Home Depot 2009 financial statements in Appendix A at the end of this textbook. Read note 1 to the financial statements that summarizes significant accounting policies for Home Depot. Read the section titled "Cost of Sales" on page A-9. Explain how Home Depot classifies some transportation, shipping, and handling costs as period expenses and others as product costs. On what basis does it distinguish between shipping or transportation costs that are period expenses and those that are product costs?

## Problem Set A   ⊟connect
ACCOUNTING

**LO3**   **PROBLEM 16.1A**
An Introduction to
**LO4**   Product Costs

Aqua-Marine manufactures fiberglass fishing boats. The manufacturing costs incurred during its first year of operations are shown as follows:

| | |
|---|---:|
| Direct materials purchased | $225,000 |
| Direct materials used | 216,000 |
| Direct labor | 200,000 |
| Manufacturing overhead | 350,000 |
| Cost of finished goods manufactured (112 boats) | 728,000 |

During the year, 112 completed boats were manufactured, of which 100 were sold. (Assume that the amount of the ending inventory of finished goods and the cost of goods sold are determined using the average per-unit cost of manufacturing a completed boat.)

**Instructions**

**a.**   Compute each of the following and show all computations:

   **1.**   The average per-unit cost of manufacturing a completed boat during the current year.

   **2.**   The year-end balances of the inventories of materials, work in process, and finished goods.

   **3.**   The cost of goods sold during the year.

**b.**   For the current year, the costs of direct materials purchased, direct labor assigned to production, and actual manufacturing overhead total $775,000. Is this the amount of manufacturing costs deducted from revenue in the current year? Explain fully.

**LO2**   **PROBLEM 16.2A**
An Introduction to
through   Product Costs
**LO4**

Road Warrior Corporation began operations early in the current year, building luxury motor homes. During the year, the company started and completed 45 motor homes at a cost of $55,000 per unit. Of these, 43 were sold for $105,000 each and two remain in finished goods inventory. In addition, the company had six partially completed units in its factory at year-end. Total costs for the year (summarized alphabetically) were as follows:

| | |
|---|---:|
| Direct materials used | $ 750,000 |
| Direct labor | 800,000 |
| Income tax expense | 100,000 |
| General and administrative expenses | 500,000 |
| Manufacturing overhead | 1,200,000 |
| Selling expenses | 500,000 |

**Instructions**

Compute the following for the current year:

a.  Total manufacturing costs charged to work in process during the period.

b.  Cost of finished goods manufactured.

c.  Cost of goods sold.

d.  Gross profit on sales.

e.  Ending inventories of (**1**) work in process and (**2**) finished goods.

**L04    PROBLEM 16.3A**

The Flow of
Manufacturing Costs
through Ledger
Accounts

The flow of manufacturing costs through the ledger accounts of Superior Locks, Inc., in the current year is illustrated below in summarized form.

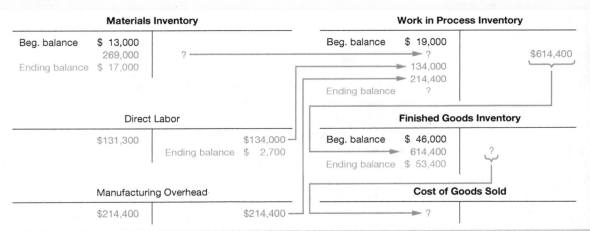

**Instructions**

Indicate the amounts requested below. Some amounts are shown in the illustrated T accounts; others require short computations. (Show all computations.)

a.  Purchases of direct materials.

b.  The cost of direct materials used.

c.  Direct labor costs assigned to production.

d.  The year-end liability for direct wages payable.

e.  Total manufacturing costs charged to the Work in Process Inventory account during the current year.

f.  The cost of finished goods manufactured.

g.  The year-end balance in the Work in Process Inventory account.

h.  The cost of goods sold.

i.  The total amount of inventory listed in the year-end balance sheet.

**L04    PROBLEM 16.4A**

The Flow of
Manufacturing Costs
through Perpetual
Inventory Records

The following T accounts summarize the flow of manufacturing costs during the current year through the ledger accounts of Double Bar Corporation:

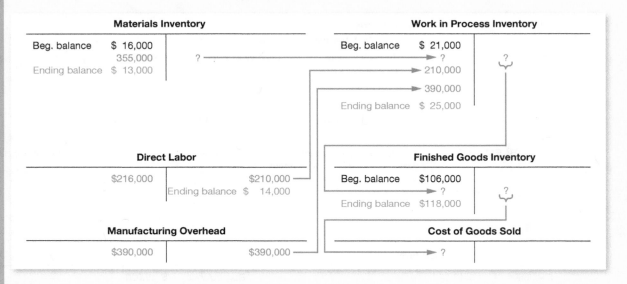

## Instructions

From the data supplied above, indicate the following amounts. Some amounts are shown in the T accounts; others require short computations. (Show all computations.)

**a.**  Purchases of direct materials during the year.

**b.**  The cost of direct materials used.

**c.**  Direct labor payrolls paid during the year.

**d.**  Direct labor costs assigned to production.

**e.**  Total manufacturing costs charged to the Work in Process Inventory account during the year.

**f.**  The cost of finished goods manufactured.

**g.**  The cost of goods sold.

**h.**  The total costs to be classified as inventory in the year-end balance sheet.

**L03**

**L04**

**L06**

**PROBLEM 16.5A**
The Flow of
Manufacturing Costs:
A Comprehensive
Problem

The balances in the perpetual inventory accounts of Hillsdale Manufacturing Corporation at the beginning and end of the current year are as follows:

|  | End of Year | Beginning of Year |
| --- | --- | --- |
| Inventory accounts: |  |  |
| Materials | $26,000 | $22,000 |
| Work in Process | 9,000 | 5,000 |
| Finished Goods Inventory | 25,000 | 38,000 |

The total dollar amounts debited and credited during the year to the accounts used in recording manufacturing activities are as follows:

|  | Debit Entries | Credit Entries |
| --- | --- | --- |
| Account: |  |  |
| Materials Inventory | $410,000 | $   ? |
| Direct Labor Payable | 189,000 | 192,000 |
| Manufacturing Overhead | 393,600 | 393,600 |
| Work in Process Inventory | ? | ? |
| Finished Goods Inventory | ? | ? |

**Instructions**

a.  Using these data, state or compute for the year the following amounts:

   1.  Direct materials purchased.

   2.  Direct materials used.

   3.  Payments of direct labor payrolls.

   4.  Direct labor cost assigned to production.

   5.  Total manufacturing costs charged to the Work in Process Inventory account during the year.

   6.  The cost of finished goods manufactured.

   7.  Cost of goods sold.

   8.  The total amount to be classified as inventory in the year-end balance sheet.

b.  Prepare a schedule of the cost of finished goods manufactured.

---

**LO4**  **PROBLEM 16.6A**

Determining and
Reporting Product
**LO6**  Cost Information

*eXcel*

The following are data regarding last year's production of Dicer Ricer, one of the major products of Kitchen Gadget Company:

| | |
|---|---:|
| Purchases of direct materials | $332,000 |
| Direct materials used | 333,600 |
| Direct labor payrolls (paid during the year) | 176,700 |
| Direct labor costs assigned to production | 180,000 |
| Manufacturing overhead | 288,000 |

During the year, 61,000 units of this product were manufactured and 62,100 units were sold. Selected information concerning inventories during the year follows:

| | End of Year | Beginning of Year |
|---|---:|---:|
| Materials | $   ? | $12,800 |
| Work in Process | 4,700 | 3,000 |
| Finished Goods, Jan. 1 (3,000 units @ $13) | ? | 39,000 |

**Instructions**

a.  Prepare a schedule of the cost of finished goods manufactured for the Dicer Ricer product.

b.  Compute the average cost of a Dicer Ricer per finished unit for last year.

c.  Compute the cost of goods sold associated with the sale of Dicer Ricer. Assume that there is a first-in, first-out (FIFO) flow through the Finished Goods Inventory account and that all units completed during the year are assigned the per-unit costs determined in part **b.**

d.  Compute the amount of inventory relating to Dicer Ricer that will be listed in the company's balance sheet at December 31. Show supporting computations for the year-end amounts of materials inventory and finished goods inventory.

e.  Explain how the $180,000 in direct labor costs assigned to production affect the company's income statement and balance sheet.

---

**LO4**  **PROBLEM 16.7A**

Determining Unit
Costs Using the Cost
**LO6**  of Finished Goods
Manufactured

The accounting records of Idaho Paper Company include the following information relating to the current year:

| | Dec. 31 | Jan. 1 |
|---|---:|---:|
| Materials inventory | $ 20,000 | $ 25,000 |
| Work in process inventory | 37,500 | 40,000 |
| Finished goods inventory, Jan. 1 (10,000 units @ $21 per unit) | ? | 210,000 |
| Purchases of direct materials during year | 330,000 | |
| Direct labor costs assigned to production | 375,000 | |
| Manufacturing overhead | 637,500 | |

750    Chapter 16  Management Accounting: A Business Partner

The company manufactures a single product; during the current year, *45,000* units were manufactured and *40,000* units were sold.

### Instructions

a.  Prepare a schedule of the cost of finished goods manufactured for the current year. (Show a supporting computation of the cost of direct materials *used* during the year.)

b.  Compute the average per-unit cost of production during the current year.

c.  Compute the cost of goods sold during the year, assuming that the FIFO (first-in, first-out) method of inventory costing is used.

d.  Compute the cost of the inventory of finished goods at December 31 of the current year, assuming that the FIFO (first-in, first-out) method of inventory costing is used.

 **PROBLEM 16.8A**
Measuring Unit Cost

Early in the year, John Raymond founded Raymond Engineering Co. for the purpose of manufacturing a special flow control valve that he had designed. Shortly after year-end, the company's accountant was injured in a skiing accident, and no year-end financial statements were prepared. However, the accountant had correctly determined the year-end inventories at the following amounts:

| | |
|---|---:|
| Materials | $46,000 |
| Work in process | 31,500 |
| Finished goods (3,000 units) | 88,500 |

As this was the first year of operations, there were no beginning inventories.

While the accountant was in the hospital, Raymond improperly prepared the following income statement from the company's accounting records:

| | | |
|---|---:|---:|
| Net sales | | $610,600 |
| Cost of goods sold: | | |
| Purchases of direct materials | $181,000 | |
| Direct labor costs | 110,000 | |
| Manufacturing overhead | 170,000 | |
| Selling expenses | 70,600 | |
| Administrative expenses | 132,000 | |
| Total costs | | 663,600 |
| Net loss for year | | $ (53,000) |

Raymond was very disappointed in these operating results. He stated, "Not only did we lose more than $50,000 this year, but look at our unit production costs. We sold 10,000 units this year at a cost of $663,600; that amounts to a cost of $66.36 per unit. I know some of our competitors are able to manufacture similar valves for about $35 per unit. I don't need an accountant to know that this business is a failure."

### Instructions

a.  Prepare a schedule of the cost of finished goods manufactured for the year. (As there were no beginning inventories, your schedule will start with "Manufacturing costs assigned to production:".) Show a supporting computation for the cost of direct materials used during the year.

b.  Compute the average cost per unit manufactured.

c.  Prepare a corrected income statement for the year, using the multiple-step format. If the company has earned any operating income, assume an income tax rate of 30 percent. (Omit earnings per share figures.)

d.  Explain whether you agree or disagree with Raymond's remarks that the business is unprofitable and that its unit cost of production ($66.36, according to Raymond) is much higher than that of competitors (around $35). If you disagree with Raymond, explain any errors or shortcomings in his analysis.

## Problem Set B

**PROBLEM 16.1B**

An Introduction to Product Costs

Pinning, Inc., manufactures dowhats. The manufacturing costs incurred during its first year of operations are as follows:

| | |
|---|---:|
| Direct materials purchased | $415,000 |
| Direct materials used | 385,000 |
| Direct labor | 335,000 |
| Manufacturing overhead | 430,000 |
| Cost of finished goods manufactured (100 dowhats) | 880,000 |

During the year, 110 completed dowhats were manufactured, of which 90 were sold. (Assume that the amount of the ending inventory of finished goods and the cost of goods sold are determined using the average per-unit cost of manufacturing a completed dowhat.)

**Instructions**

a. Compute each of the following and show all computations:

   **1.** The average per-unit cost of manufacturing a completed dowhat during the current year.

   **2.** The year-end balances of the following inventories: materials, work in progress, and finished goods.

   **3.** The cost of goods sold during the year.

b. For the current year, the costs of direct materials purchased, direct labor, and manufacturing overhead total $1,180,000. Is this the amount of manufacturing costs deducted from revenue in the current year? Explain fully.

**PROBLEM 16.2B**

An Introduction to Product Costs

River Queen Corporation began operations early in the current year, building luxury boats. During the year, the company started and completed 40 boats at a cost of $80,000 per unit. Of these, 30 were sold for $130,000 each and 10 remain in finished goods inventory. In addition, the company had five partially completed units in its factory at year-end. Total costs for the year (summarized alphabetically) were as follows:

| | |
|---|---:|
| Direct materials used | $ 800,000 |
| Direct labor | 1,000,000 |
| Income tax expense | 80,000 |
| General and administrative expenses | 600,000 |
| Manufacturing overhead | 2,000,000 |
| Selling expenses | 400,000 |

**Instructions**

Compute the following for the current year:

a. Total manufacturing costs charged to work in process during the period.

b. Cost of finished goods manufactured.

c. Cost of goods sold.

d. Gross profit on sales.

e. Ending inventories of (**1**) work in process and (**2**) finished goods.

**PROBLEM 16.3B**

The Flow of Manufacturing Costs through Ledger Accounts

The flow of manufacturing costs through the ledger accounts of ISP, Inc., in the current year is illustrated below in summarized form:

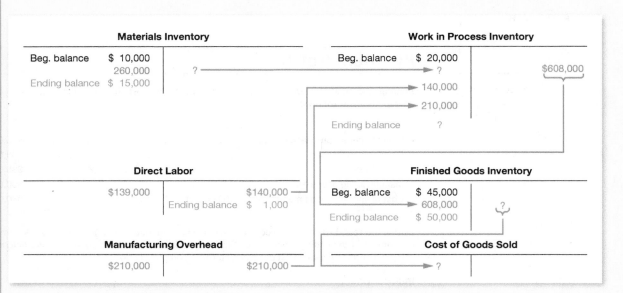

### Instructions

Indicate the amounts requested below. Some amounts are shown in the T accounts above; others require short computations. (Show all computations.)

a.   Purchases of direct materials.
b.   The cost of direct materials used.
c.   Direct labor costs assigned to production.
d.   The year-end liability for direct wages payable.
e.   The overhead as a percentage of direct labor costs.
f.   Total manufacturing costs charged to the Work in Process Inventory account during the current year.
g.   The cost of finished goods manufactured.
h.   The year-end balance in the Work in Process Inventory account.
i.   The cost of goods sold.
j.   The total amount of inventory listed in the year-end balance sheet.

**L04**   **PROBLEM 16.4B**
The Flow of Manufacturing Costs through Perpetual Inventory Records

The following T accounts summarize the flow of manufacturing costs during the current year through the ledger accounts of Payback Corporation:

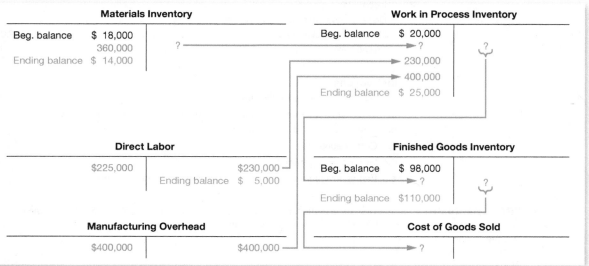

## Instructions

From the data supplied above, indicate the following amounts. Some amounts are shown in the T accounts above; others require short computations. (Show all computations.)

**a.** Purchases of direct materials during the year.

**b.** The cost of direct materials used.

**c.** Direct labor payrolls paid during the year.

**d.** Direct labor costs assigned to production.

**e.** The overhead assigned to production as a percentage of direct labor costs.

**f.** Total manufacturing costs charged to the Work in Process Inventory account during the current year.

**g.** The cost of finished goods manufactured.

**h.** The cost of goods sold.

**i.** The total costs to be classified as inventory in the year-end balance sheet.

**L03**
**L04**
**L06**

**PROBLEM 16.5B**

The Flow of Manufacturing Costs: A Comprehensive Problem

The balances in the perpetual inventory accounts of Valleyview Manufacturing Corporation at the beginning and end of the current year are as follows:

|  | End of Year | Beginning of Year |
| --- | --- | --- |
| Inventory accounts: |  |  |
| Materials . . . . . . . . . . . . . . . . . . . . . . . . . . . . . . . . . . . . . . . . . . . . . . . . | $15,000 | $25,000 |
| Work in Process . . . . . . . . . . . . . . . . . . . . . . . . . . . . . . . . . . . . . . . . . . | 10,000 | 8,000 |
| Finished Goods Inventory . . . . . . . . . . . . . . . . . . . . . . . . . . . . . . . . | 24,000 | 30,000 |

Total dollar amounts debited and credited during the year to the accounts used in recording manufacturing activities are as follows:

|  | Debit Entries | Credit Entries |
| --- | --- | --- |
| Account: |  |  |
| Materials Inventory . . . . . . . . . . . . . . . . . . . . . . . . . . . . . . . . . . . . . . . | $225,000 | $  ? |
| Direct Labor . . . . . . . . . . . . . . . . . . . . . . . . . . . . . . . . . . . . . . . . . . . . | 200,000 | 210,000 |
| Manufacturing Overhead . . . . . . . . . . . . . . . . . . . . . . . . . . . . . . . . | 420,000 | 420,000 |
| Work in Process Inventory . . . . . . . . . . . . . . . . . . . . . . . . . . . . . . . | ? | ? |
| Finished Goods Inventory . . . . . . . . . . . . . . . . . . . . . . . . . . . . . . . . | ? | ? |

## Instructions

**a.** Using these data, state or compute for the year the following amounts:

1. Direct materials purchased.

2. Direct materials used.

3. Payments of direct labor payrolls.

4. Direct labor cost assigned to production.

5. The overhead assigned to production stated as a percentage of direct labor costs.

6. Total manufacturing costs charged to the Work in Process Inventory account during the year.

7. The cost of finished goods manufactured.

8. The cost of goods sold.

9. The total amount to be classified as inventory in the year-end balance sheet.

**b.** Prepare a schedule of the cost of finished goods manufactured.

L04 **PROBLEM 16.6B**

Determining and
Reporting Product
L06 Cost Information

The following are data regarding last year's production of Old Joe, one of the major products of Columbus Toy Company:

| | |
|---|---:|
| Purchases of direct materials | $400,000 |
| Direct materials used | 402,000 |
| Direct labor payrolls (paid during the year) | 180,000 |
| Direct labor costs assigned to production | 220,000 |
| Manufacturing overhead (incurred and applied) | 330,000 |

During the year, 50,000 units of this product were manufactured and 51,500 units were sold. Selected information concerning inventories during the year follows:

| | End of Year | Beginning of Year |
|---|---:|---:|
| Materials | $ ? | $15,000 |
| Work in Process | 6,000 | 5,000 |
| Finished Goods, Jan. 1 (4,000 units @ $19) | ? | 76,000 |

**Instructions**

a. Prepare a schedule of the cost of finished goods manufactured for the Old Joe product.

b. Compute the average cost of Old Joe per finished unit.

c. Compute the cost of goods sold associated with the sale of Old Joe. Assume that there is a first-in, first-out (FIFO) flow through the Finished Goods Inventory account and that all units completed are assigned the per-unit costs determined in part **b**.

d. Compute the amount of inventory relating to Old Joe that will be listed in the company's balance sheet at December 31. Show supporting computations for the year-end amounts of materials inventory and finished goods inventory.

e. Explain how the $220,000 in direct labor costs assigned to production affect the company's income statement and balance sheet.

L04 **PROBLEM 16.7B**

Determining Unit
Costs Using the Cost
L06 of Finished Goods
Manufactured

The accounting records of Maine Products Company include the following information relating to the current year:

| | Dec. 31 | Jan. 1 |
|---|---:|---:|
| Materials inventory | $ 22,000 | $ 30,000 |
| Work in process inventory | 39,000 | 39,000 |
| Finished goods inventory, Jan. 1 (8,000 units @ $22 per unit) | ? | 176,000 |
| Purchases of direct materials during year | 290,000 | |
| Direct labor costs assigned to production | 350,000 | |
| Manufacturing overhead assigned to production | 552,000 | |

The company manufactures a single product; during the current year, *60,000* units were manufactured and *50,000* units were sold.

**Instructions**

a. Prepare a schedule of the cost of finished goods manufactured for the current year. (Show a supporting computation of the cost of direct materials *used* during the year.)

b. Compute the average per-unit cost of production during the current year.

c. Compute the cost of goods sold during the year, assuming that the FIFO (first-in, first-out) method of inventory costing is used.

d. Compute the cost of the inventory of finished goods at December 31 of the current year, assuming that the FIFO (first-in, first-out) method of inventory costing is used.

**PROBLEM 16.8B**
Measuring Unit Cost

L04

L06

Early in the year, Jane Jackson founded Jackson Engineering Co. for the purpose of manufacturing a special plumbing device that she had designed. Shortly after year-end, the company's accountant was injured in an auto accident, and no year-end financial statements were prepared. However, the accountant had correctly determined the year-end inventories at the following amounts:

| | |
|---|---:|
| Materials . . . . . . . . . . . . . . . . . . . . . . . . . . . . . . . . . . . . . . . . . . . . . . . | $51,000 |
| Work in process . . . . . . . . . . . . . . . . . . . . . . . . . . . . . . . . . . . . . . . . . . . | 32,000 |
| Finished goods (4,000 units) . . . . . . . . . . . . . . . . . . . . . . . . . . . . . . . . . | 108,000 |

As this was the first year of operations, there were no beginning inventories.

While the accountant was in the hospital, Jackson improperly prepared the following income statement from the company's accounting records:

| | | |
|---|---:|---:|
| Net sales . . . . . . . . . . . . . . . . . . . . . . . . . . . . . . . . . . . . . . . . | | $625,000 |
| Cost of goods sold: | | |
|    Purchases of direct materials . . . . . . . . . . . . . . . . . . . . . . . . . . . | $188,000 | |
|    Direct labor costs assigned to production . . . . . . . . . . . . . . . . . . | 113,000 | |
|    Manufacturing overhead applied to production . . . . . . . . . . . . . . | 160,000 | |
|    Selling expenses . . . . . . . . . . . . . . . . . . . . . . . . . . . . . . . . . . . | 75,000 | |
|    Administrative expenses . . . . . . . . . . . . . . . . . . . . . . . . . . . . . . | 135,000 | |
|      Total costs . . . . . . . . . . . . . . . . . . . . . . . . . . . . . . . . . . . . . | | 671,000 |
| Net loss for year . . . . . . . . . . . . . . . . . . . . . . . . . . . . . . . . . . . . | | $ (46,000) |

Jackson was very disappointed in these operating results. She stated, "Not only did we lose more than $40,000 this year, but look at our unit production costs. We sold 10,000 units this year at a cost of $671,000; that amounts to a cost of $67.10 per unit. I know some of our competitors are able to manufacture similar plumbing devices for about $30 per unit. I don't need an accountant to know that this business is a failure."

### Instructions

a.  Prepare a schedule of the cost of finished goods manufactured for the year. (As there were no beginning inventories, your schedule will start with "Manufacturing costs assigned to production:".) Show a supporting computation for the cost of direct materials used during the year.

b.  Compute the average cost per-unit manufactured. (Round your answer to two decimal places.)

c.  Prepare a corrected income statement for the year, using the multiple-step format. If the company has earned any operating income, assume an income tax rate of 20 percent. (Omit earnings per share figures.)

d.  Explain whether you agree or disagree with Jackson's remarks that the business is unprofitable and that its unit cost of production ($67.10, according to Jackson) is much higher than that of competitors (around $30). If you disagree with Jackson, explain any errors or shortcomings in her analysis.

## Critical Thinking Cases

L03 **CASE 16.1**

Effect on Income
Statement of
L04 Errors in Handling
Manufacturing Costs

L06

William Nelson, the chief accountant of West Texas Guitar Company, was injured in an automobile accident shortly before the end of the company's first year of operations. At year-end, a clerk with a very limited understanding of accounting prepared the following income statement, which is unsatisfactory in several respects:

| WEST TEXAS GUITAR COMPANY<br>INCOME STATEMENT<br>FOR THE YEAR ENDED DECEMBER 31, 20— | | |
|---|---|---|
| Net sales | | $ 1,300,000 |
| Cost of goods sold: | | |
| Purchases of direct materials | $460,000 | |
| Direct labor | 225,000 | |
| Indirect labor | 90,000 | |
| Depreciation on machinery—factory | 50,000 | |
| Rent | 144,000 | |
| Insurance | 16,000 | |
| Utilities | 28,000 | |
| Miscellaneous manufacturing overhead | 34,600 | |
| Other operating expenses | 273,800 | |
| Dividends declared on capital stock | 46,000 | |
| Cost of goods sold | | $(1,367,400) |
| Loss for year | | $    (67,400) |

You are asked to help management prepare a corrected income statement for the first year of operations. Management informs you that 60 percent of the rent, insurance, and utilities applies to factory operations, and that the remaining 40 percent should be classified as period expenses. Also, the correct ending inventories are as follows:

| Material | $ 38,000 |
|---|---|
| Work in process | 10,000 |
| Finished goods | 110,400 |

As this is the first year of operations, there were no beginning inventories.

**Instructions**

a.  Identify the shortcomings and errors in the above income statement. On the basis of the short-comings you have identified, explain whether you would expect the company's actual net income for the first year of operations to be higher or lower than the amount shown.

b.  Prepare schedules to determine:
  1.  The cost of direct materials used.
  2.  Total manufacturing overhead.

c.  Prepare a schedule of cost of finished goods manufactured during the year. (Use the amounts computed in part **b** as the costs of direct materials used and manufacturing overhead.)

d.  Prepare a corrected income statement for the year, using a multiple-step format. Assume that income tax expense amounts to 30 percent of income before income taxes.

  **CASE 16.2**
 The Meadowbrooke
**through** Miracle

Prescott Manufacturing operates several plants, each of which produces a different product. Early in the current year, John Walker was hired as the new manager of the Meadowbrooke Plant. At year-end, all the plant managers are asked to summarize the operations of their plants at a meeting of the company's board of directors. John Walker displayed the following information on a chart as he made his presentation:

| | Current<br>Year | Last<br>Year |
|---|---|---|
| Inventories of finished goods: | | |
| Beginning of the year (30,000 units in the current year and 10,000 units last year) | $255,000 | $  85,000 |
| End of the year (20,000 units in the current year and 30,000 units last year) | 202,000 | 255,000 |
| Cost of finished goods manufactured | 909,000 | 1,020,000 |

Walker made the following statements to the board: "As you know, sales volume has remained constant for the Meadowbrooke Plant. Both this year and last, our sales amounted to 100,000 units. We have made real gains, however, in controlling our manufacturing costs. Through efficient plant operations, we have reduced our cost of finished goods manufactured by over $100,000. These economies are reflected in a reduction of the manufacturing cost per unit sold from $10.20 last year ($1,020,000 ÷ 100,000 units) to $9.09 in the current year ($909,000 ÷ 100,000 units)."

Father Alan Carter is president of St. Mary's University and is a member of Prescott Manufacturing's board of directors. However, Father Carter has little background in the accounting practices of manufacturing companies, and he asks you for assistance in evaluating Walker's statements.

### Instructions

**a.** As a preliminary step to your analysis, compute the following for the Meadowbrooke Plant in each of the two years:

1. Cost of goods sold.

2. Number of finished units manufactured.

3. Average cost per unit manufactured.

4. Average cost per unit sold.

**b.** Evaluate the statements made by Walker. Comment specifically on Walker's computation of the manufacturing cost of units sold and on whether it appears that the reduction in the cost of finished goods sold was in fact achieved through more efficient operations.

 **INTERNET CASE 16.3**

 Calculating Cost of Goods Manufactured

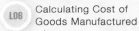

**Pfizer, Inc.**, develops and manufactures various pharmaceutical products. Visit its home page at the following address:

www.pfizer.com

From the home page, access the most recent annual report by clicking on the investors' tab.

### Instructions

**a.** What categories of inventory does Pfizer show in its inventories footnote under "Notes to Consolidated Financial Statements"?

**b.** Using the income statement and inventory information from the footnote, calculate the cost of finished goods manufactured for the most recent year.

**c.** What elements of manufacturing overhead can you identify using the annual report?

 **INTERNET CASE 16.4**

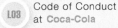 Code of Conduct at Coca-Cola

Many companies have established business codes of conduct that outline procedures for employees, suppliers, and customers to alert management about suspected accounting, internal control, or auditing problems. As discussed in this chapter, one potential violation of GAAP would be to capitalize period costs, inflating the value of inventory and understating the expenses on the income statement for the period. Coca-Cola Company provides a "Code of Business Conduct" at http://www.thecoca-colacompany.com/ourcompany/pdf/COBC_English.pdf that identifies the code and what constitutes a violation. Also provided are examples of what employees and others can do if they suspect ethics or fraud violations at Coca-Cola. Go to the above Web site and find the following information:

**a.** Identify the accounting-related components of the code.

**b.** Review the section titled "Administration of the Code." Identify the steps that an employee would take if he or she wanted to report capitalization of period costs by a bottling plant manager.

**c.** Identify the types of disciplinary actions the company can impose on employees who are found to be in violation of the company's code of conduct.

**d.** Identify how the violation might be recorded and who would be notified about the violation.

*Internet sites are time and date sensitive. It is the purpose of these exercises to have you explore the Internet. You may need to use the Yahoo! search engine http://www.yahoo.com (or another favorite search engine) to find a company's current Web address.*

## Answers to Self-Test Questions

1. b, d    2. a    3. d (4,200 + 29,000 + 3,000 + 3,600 − 34,100)
4. b    5. a, b, c

## CHAPTER 17

# Job Order Cost Systems and Overhead Allocations

© Lon C. Diehl/PhotoEdit

## GM GOODWRENCH

Either because of general wear and tear or because of an accident, almost every driver, sooner or later, visits a vehicle service garage. With over 7,000 locations nationwide, the GM Goodwrench network is the industry's largest service provider. GM Goodwrench has been able to maintain its extensive service network because it provides GM Goodwrench dealers with the latest GM vehicle technical information, the most advanced equipment, and GM parts, and because dealers service all types of GM vehicles.

GM Goodwrench service providers use a system called job order costing to track repairs and maintenance costs to specific automobiles or trucks. Because each repair or maintenance job on a vehicle is unique, service providers must have a costing system that is able to trace the specific work and cost of that work to the associated vehicle. When customers arrive to pay for the service work on their vehicles, the service provider can give them an accurate record of the actual work performed, including the cost of parts, labor, and overhead for their vehicles. ■

## Cost Accounting Systems

An organization's accounting system must provide a good "map" that links costs to the processes used in creating goods and/or services. An effective cost accounting system matches processes that consume resources with associated costs so that managers can decide how to best provide products or services to customers. Moreover, cost accounting systems are essential for maintaining competitive advantage.

**Learning Objective**

**L01**   Explain the purpose of cost accounting systems.

**Cost accounting systems** are the methods and techniques used by enterprises to track resources consumed in creating and delivering products and services to customers. Management uses the information produced by cost accounting systems to monitor resource consumption and to evaluate and reward employee performance. In addition, the information produced by cost accounting systems is used for external reporting requirements. Inventories, cost of goods sold, and period costs are tracked by cost accounting systems and are reported in the balance sheet and income statement.

In manufacturing and service companies, cost accounting systems help attain two important management objectives: (1) to determine unit manufacturing costs and (2) to provide managers with useful information for planning and cost control functions. As we saw in Chapter 16, *unit costs* are determined by tracing direct materials, direct labor, and overhead to specific units of production.

A unit of product is defined differently in different industries. It is easy to think of units as individual products, such as automobiles or television sets. In some industries, however, units of production may be stated in tons, gallons, kilowatt hours, board-feet, passenger miles flown, or any other appropriate unit of output. Regardless of how they are stated, unit costs provide a basis for inventory valuation and determination of the cost of goods sold. They also provide managers with information for setting prices, deciding what products to manufacture or services to provide, evaluating the efficiency of operations, and controlling costs.

*Cost control* refers to keeping costs at reasonable levels. When cost accounting systems provide timely information about unit costs, managers can react quickly should costs begin to rise to unacceptable levels. By comparing current unit costs with budgeted costs and other target measures, managers are able to identify those areas in which corrective actions are most needed.

### JOB ORDER COST SYSTEMS AND THE CREATION OF GOODS AND SERVICES

Cost accounting systems are typically designed to accommodate the specific needs of individual companies. In this chapter, we demonstrate a widely used accounting system for measuring and tracking resource consumption: job order costing.

**Learning Objective**

**L02**   Identify the processes for creating goods and services that are suited to job order costing.

**Job order costing** is typically used by companies that tailor their goods or services to the specific needs of individual customers. In job order costing, the costs of direct materials, direct labor, and overhead are accumulated separately for each job. A "job" represents the goods manufactured or services provided to fill a particular order, or the production of a batch of a particular product. If a job contains multiple units of a product, unit costs are determined by dividing the total cost charged to the job by the number of units manufactured.

Construction companies use job order cost systems because each construction project is unique. Job order cost systems are also used by shipbuilders, motion picture studios, defense contractors, print shops, and custom furniture makers. In addition, these systems are widely used in service organizations, such as automotive repair shops, accounting firms, law firms, doctors' offices, and hospitals.

To summarize, job order costing is appropriate for environments characterized by customized jobs that require differing amounts and types of direct labor, direct materials, and overhead. Other costing methods are used for production processes that produce mass quantities of identical units that use the same amounts and types of direct labor, direct materials, and overhead. The type of cost accounting system best suited to a particular company *depends on the nature of the company's operations*. In fact, a company that is involved in diverse activities may use many cost accounting methods concurrently. In the following sections of this chapter, we will illustrate and explain job order cost accounting systems.

## OVERHEAD APPLICATION RATES

Before we begin the discussion of job order costing in detail, it is important to have a clear understanding of how and why overhead costs are allocated to products and services using an estimated overhead application rate. There are at least three reasons why overhead isn't applied to products by simply dividing the company's annual actual overhead cost by the actual number of units produced or services provided during the year. First, total overhead costs and total units produced are not known until the end of the year. Because the amount of overhead assigned to a unit of service or product is important information for setting prices to charge customers at the time of sale, an estimated amount is necessary. Second, not all products and services consume an equal amount of overhead. Third, an expected amount of overhead per product or service helps managers make decisions about whether too much overhead is being used in production.

**Learning Objective**
Explain the purpose and computation of overhead application rates for job order costing.    LO3

Thus, estimated overhead application rates are used to assign overhead costs to specific units of production as services are being provided or as units are being produced throughout the accounting period. The rate expresses an expected relationship between overhead costs and some *activity base* related to the production process (direct labor hours, machine hours, and so forth). Overhead is then assigned to products *in proportion* to this activity base. For example, a company using direct labor hours as an activity base would allocate the greatest proportion of its overhead costs to those products or services requiring the most direct labor hours.

The **overhead application rate** is determined at the *beginning* of the period and is based on *estimated* amounts. The rate is typically computed as follows:

$$\text{Overhead Application Rate} = \frac{\text{Estimated Overhead Costs}}{\text{Estimated Units in the Activity Base}}$$

The mechanics of computing and using an overhead application rate are quite simple. The challenging problems for accountants are (1) selecting an appropriate activity base and (2) making reliable estimates at the beginning of the accounting period regarding the total of the overhead costs to be incurred and the total units in the activity base that will be required.

**Computation and Use of Overhead Application Rates**    Consider, for example, Compuline Corporation, a company that creates individualized software programs for other companies. Assume that, at the beginning of 2011, Compuline's management makes the following estimates relating to software development for the coming year:

| | |
|---|---|
| Estimated total overhead costs for the year . . . . . . . . . . . . . . . . . . . . . . . . | $360,000 |
| Estimated total direct labor hours for the year . . . . . . . . . . . . . . . . . . . . . . | 30,000 hours |
| Estimated total lines of code for the year . . . . . . . . . . . . . . . . . . . . . . . . . . | 1,000,000 lines |

Using the above estimates, we will illustrate the use of an overhead application rate using two independent assumptions.

**Assumption 1: Compuline Uses Direct Labor Hours as Its Activity Base**    If Compuline uses direct labor hours to apply overhead costs, the application rate will be *$12 per direct labor hour* ($360,000 of estimated overhead costs, divided by 30,000 estimated direct labor hours). Throughout the year, manufacturing overhead costs will be assigned in direct proportion to the *actual* direct labor hours required to create a software product for a company. For example, if creating a particular piece of software uses 200 direct labor hours, then $2,400 of manufacturing overhead will be assigned as a part of that software's costs (200 direct labor hours used, multiplied by the $12 application rate). The assignment will be made by debiting the Work in Process Inventory account and crediting the Manufacturing Overhead account for $2,400.

### Assumption 2: Compuline Uses Lines of Code as Its Activity Base   If Compuline chooses to use lines of code to apply overhead costs, its application rate will be $0.36 per line of code ($360,000 of estimated overhead costs divided by 1,000,000 estimated lines of code). Using this approach, overhead costs will be assigned to software jobs based on the number of lines of code required to create the software package. If 1,000 lines were required for a particular piece of software, that software would be assigned $360 of overhead costs (1,000 lines times $0.36 per line). Again, the assignment is made by debiting the Work in Process Inventory account and crediting the Overhead account for $360.

**YOUR TURN**   **You as a Manager**

Assume you are the manager of the engineering group at Compuline that creates the software code. Also assume that Compuline is using lines of code as the activity base to apply overhead costs to the software packages created. One of the engineers in your group has just approached you suggesting that if the lines of code used for software packages could be reduced by 10 percent in general, the company could reduce overhead costs by $36,000 per year (10% × $360,000). How would you respond?

(See our comments on the Online Learning Center Web site.)

## WHAT "DRIVES" OVERHEAD COSTS?

For overhead application rates to provide reliable results, any activity base chosen to compute an application rate must be a significant "driver" of overhead costs. To be a **cost driver,** an activity base must be a *causal factor* in the incurrence of overhead costs. In other words, an increase in the number of activity base units (for example, direct labor hours worked) must cause a proportional increase in the actual overhead costs incurred.

Historically, direct labor hours (or direct labor costs) were viewed as the primary driver of overhead costs—and for good reason. Products that required more direct labor often required more indirect labor (supervision), resulted in more wear and tear on machinery (maintenance costs), and consumed a greater amount of supplies. Therefore, manufacturing companies often followed the practice of applying all manufacturing overhead costs in proportion to direct labor hours or direct labor costs.

As factories have become more highly automated, direct labor has become much less of a causal factor in driving many overhead costs. Today, many manufacturing companies find that activity bases such as machine hours, computer time, or the time required to set up a production run result in a better matching of overhead costs and activities.

### The Use of Multiple Overhead Application Rates   In an attempt to gain a better understanding of what it costs to manufacture different types of products, many companies have begun to implement techniques that rely on the use of *multiple* allocation bases. One such approach, **activity-based costing,** is illustrated later in this chapter.

In essence, activity-based costing uses multiple allocation bases that represent different types of manufacturing overhead costs. For instance, machine maintenance costs may be allocated using machine hours as an activity base, whereas supervision costs may be allocated using direct labor hours. Different application rates may also be used in each production department and in applying overhead costs to different types of products.

The key point is that each manufactured product should be charged with the overhead costs *generated by* the creation of that product. If the activity base used to apply overhead costs is *not* a primary cost driver, the relative production cost of different products and services may become *significantly distorted.*

### The Increasing Importance of Proper Overhead Allocation   In today's global economy, competition among companies is greater than ever before. If a company is to determine whether it can compete effectively in the marketplace, it must first know with some

degree of precision its costs on a per-unit basis. In highly automated factories, overhead is often the largest of the three basic categories of manufacturing costs. Therefore, the allocation of overhead costs is one of the major challenges facing management accountants.

## Job Order Costing

Overhead allocations are particularly important for job order costing because the distinguishing characteristic of job order costing is that costs are accumulated separately for each job. Thus, overhead must be assigned separately to each job. As explained in Chapter 16, all product or service costs are charged (debited) to the Work in Process Inventory account as incurred. In job costing, Work in Process Inventory is a control (or summary) account, supported by **job cost sheets** for each job. Collectively, the job cost sheets serve as a subsidiary ledger showing the details of costs charged to each job.

If a company is using an accounting software package, job cost information is recorded in computer-based files. However, the form and content of most job cost records are basically the same, regardless of whether they are maintained manually or by computer.

### THE JOB COST SHEET

Job cost sheets are the heart of job order costing. A separate job cost sheet is prepared for each job and is used to accumulate a record of all manufacturing costs charged to the job. Once the job is finished, the job cost sheet indicates the cost of the finished goods and provides the information necessary to compute the unit costs of production.

Direct manufacturing costs (direct materials used and direct labor) are recorded on the job cost sheet as quickly as these costs can be traced to the job. Simultaneously, overhead costs are applied using an overhead application rate. Exhibit 17–1 is a completed job cost sheet of Oak & Glass Furniture Co. Job no. 831. This job involved the manufacture of 100 dining tables of a particular style.

**Learning Objective**
Describe the purpose and the content of a job cost sheet.          L04

**OAK & GLASS FURNITURE CO.**
**JOB COST SHEET**                                831

Product __French Court dining tables__          Date started __1/03/11__

Number of units manufactured __100__          Date completed __1/21/11__

**COSTS CHARGED TO THIS JOB**

| MANUFACTURING DEPARTMENT | DIRECT MATERIALS | DIRECT LABOR | | MANUFACTURING OVERHEAD | |
|---|---|---|---|---|---|
| | | HOURS | COST | RATE | COST APPLIED |
| Milling & Carving | $10,000 | 70 | $14,000 | 150% | $21,000 |
| Finishing | 15,000 | 300 | 6,000 | 150% | 9,000 |

**COST SUMMARY AND UNIT COSTS**

| | Total Costs | Unit Costs |
|---|---|---|
| Direct materials used | $25,000 | $250 |
| Direct labor | 20,000 | 200 |
| Manufacturing overhead applied | 30,000 | 300 |
| Cost of finished goods manufactured (100 tables) | $75,000 | $750 |

**Exhibit 17–1**

**COMPLETED JOB COST SHEET**

Throughout the production process, manufacturing costs traceable to the job were accumulated in the "Costs Charged to This Job" section of the job cost sheet. The "Cost Summary" section was filled in when the job was completed.

The total cost of completing job no. 831 was *$75,000*. Upon completion, this amount should be transferred from the Work in Process Inventory account to the Finished Goods Inventory account. The unit cost figures shown in the job cost sheet were determined by dividing the total manufacturing costs by the 100 units manufactured.

## FLOW OF COSTS IN JOB COSTING: AN ILLUSTRATION

Chris Kerrigan/DAL

**Learning Objective**

**L05**  **Account for the flow of costs when using job order costing.**

Exhibit 17–2a and b on pages 766 and 767 illustrates the flow of costs for Oak & Glass Furniture Co. This flowchart summarizes the company's manufacturing operations during the month of January. Notice that each of the inventory accounts (Materials, Work in Process, and Finished Goods) is supported by a subsidiary ledger.

In our flowchart, all subsidiary ledger accounts are shown in T account form to conserve space. In practice, the individual job cost sheets serve as the subsidiary ledger for the Work in Process Inventory account. Also, the subsidiary ledger accounts for direct materials and finished goods would have additional columns providing detailed information as to quantities on hand and unit costs.

We will now use Oak & Glass Furniture Co. to explain the flow of manufacturing costs when using job order costing.

## ACCOUNTING FOR DIRECT MATERIALS

In a perpetual inventory system, purchases of direct materials are posted from the purchases journal to the accounts in the materials subsidiary ledger. The entries in the subsidiary ledger indicate the type, quantity, and cost of the material purchased. As shown in Exhibit 17–2a, at the end of each month, a summary entry is made debiting the Materials Inventory account for the total cost of direct materials *purchased* during the period. (The offsetting credit normally is to Accounts Payable.)

Likewise, at month-end, all the materials used during the month are totaled, and the following summary entry is made in the accounts:

**Recording materials used during the month**

| | | |
|---|---|---|
| Work in Process Inventory .................................... | 50,000 | |
|    Materials Inventory ........................................ | | 50,000 |

To record the cost of all direct materials placed into production during Jan.

**INTERNATIONAL** CASE IN POINT

Multinational companies frequently source their direct materials from many countries. Because suppliers of direct materials are located in different countries, the costs of those materials are affected by international differences that do not affect direct materials sourced from domestic suppliers. Such factors as import duties, exchange rate fluctuations, and foreign taxes have an impact on the cost of direct materials, making the purchasing function more complex for companies sourcing internationally.

## ACCOUNTING FOR DIRECT LABOR COSTS

Debits to the Direct Labor account arise from making payments to direct factory workers; the offsetting credit is to the Cash account.[1] Payments to *indirect* factory workers (such as supervisors and security guards) are debited to Manufacturing Overhead, not to the Direct Labor account.

The Direct Labor account is credited as direct labor is *used*—that is, as employees work on specific jobs. A number of mechanical and computerized means have been developed for determining the direct labor cost applicable to each job. One common method is to prepare *time cards* for each employee, showing the number of hours worked on each job, the employee's rate of pay, and the direct labor cost chargeable to each job.

As shown in Exhibit 17–2a and b, at the end of each month, a summary entry is made debiting Work in Process Inventory and crediting the Direct Labor account for all direct labor costs assigned to jobs during the month. For Oak & Glass, this entry is as follows:

| | | |
|---|---|---|
| Work in Process Inventory . . . . . . . . . . . . . . . . . . . . . . . . . . . . . . . . . . . . . | 60,000 | |
| Direct Labor . . . . . . . . . . . . . . . . . . . . . . . . . . . . . . . . . . . . . . . . . . | | 60,000 |
| To record in the general ledger all direct labor costs charged to jobs during Jan. | | |

**Recording direct labor costs**

Notice that the Direct Labor account is debited (with an offsetting credit to Cash) when employees are *paid,* but it is credited for the cost of work *performed* on jobs. Work is performed on a daily basis, but employees are paid only at periodic intervals, such as every two weeks. Thus, the direct labor cost charged to jobs does not necessarily equal the amount paid to employees during the month. In our example, $60,000 of direct labor was assigned to the three jobs in process, but payments to employees totaled only $52,000. Thus, the unadjusted $8,000 credit balance of the Direct Labor account at month-end represents a *liability for accrued wages payable* and is reported in the balance sheet.

## ACCOUNTING FOR OVERHEAD COSTS

Manufacturing overhead includes all manufacturing costs *other than* the costs of direct materials and direct labor. Manufacturing Overhead is a control account; the details of the many different types of overhead costs are kept in a subsidiary ledger.

The Manufacturing Overhead account is debited for the *actual* amount of overhead costs incurred during the period. As shown in Exhibit 17–2a, actual overhead costs in January total $93,000. These costs are posted to the overhead account from several sources. Indirect labor costs, for example, come from payroll records; purchases of indirect materials and payments of utility bills come from invoices and receipts; and depreciation of plant assets comes from end-of-period adjusting entries in the general journal.

**Application of Overhead Costs to Jobs**  Overhead is an *indirect* cost and cannot be traced conveniently to specific jobs or units. As discussed previously, a predetermined overhead application rate is used to assign overhead costs to work in process. Oak & Glass uses an overhead application rate equal to *150 percent of direct labor cost.* Therefore, each job cost sheet is charged with overhead costs equal to 150 percent of the direct labor cost relating to the job.

On the bottom of the page 766 is the summary entry made in the general ledger to record all overhead costs applied to jobs during the period.

---

[1] To the extent that amounts are withheld from employees' pay for such purposes as income taxes and Social Security taxes, the offsetting credits are to various current liability accounts. Accounting for payrolls was discussed in Chapter 10.

Exhibit 17–2a  **FLOW OF COSTS FOR OAK & GLASS FURNITURE CO.**

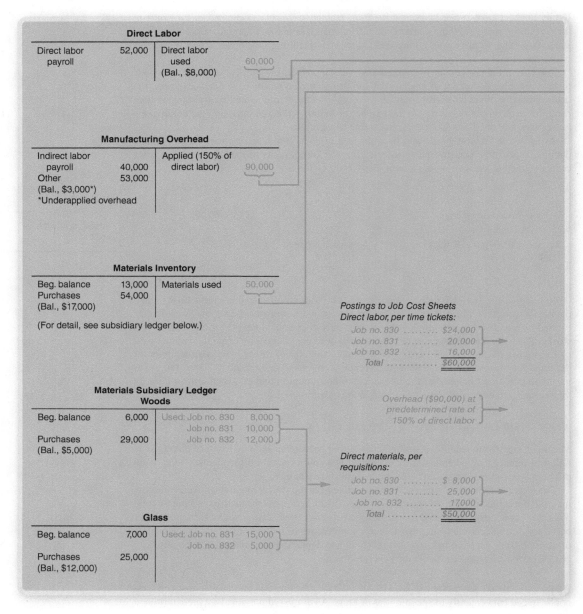

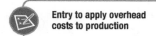

**Entry to apply overhead costs to production**

| | | |
|---|---|---|
| Work in Process Inventory . . . . . . . . . . . . . . . . . . . . . . . . . . . . . . . . . . . . . . . | 90,000 | |
|    Manufacturing Overhead . . . . . . . . . . . . . . . . . . . . . . . . . . . . . . . . . . | | 90,000 |

To charge the Work in Process account with
overhead costs applied to jobs during the month (150% of
direct labor costs for the month; $60,000 × 150% = $90,000).

**Over- or Underapplied Overhead**    In our example, actual overhead costs incurred during January amounted to $93,000, while the overhead applied to jobs using the overhead application rate totaled only $90,000. We should not expect that applied overhead will

Job Order Costing                                   **767**

## Exhibit 17–2b   FLOW OF COSTS FOR OAK & GLASS FURNITURE CO. (CONTINUED)

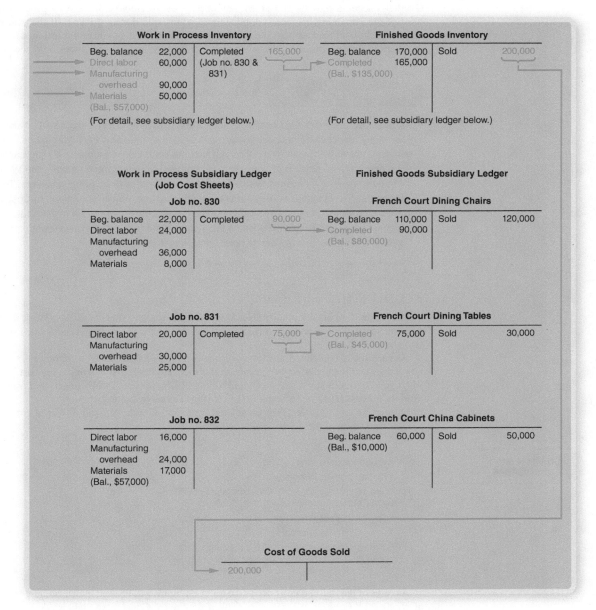

exactly equal actual overhead because the predetermined overhead application rate is based on *estimates*.

A debit balance in the Manufacturing Overhead account at month-end indicates that overhead applied to jobs was *less* than the actual overhead costs incurred during the month. Therefore, a debit balance remains in the Manufacturing Overhead account and it is called **underapplied overhead.** A credit balance remaining in the account indicates that overhead applied to jobs *exceeded* actual overhead costs; thus a credit balance is termed **overapplied overhead.**

The month-end balances remaining in the Manufacturing Overhead account normally are allowed to accumulate throughout the year. These amounts tend to balance out from month to month, and the amount of overapplied or underapplied overhead at year-end usually *is not material* in dollar amount. In this case, the year-end balance in the Manufacturing Overhead account may be closed *directly to the Cost of Goods Sold,* on the grounds that most of the remaining balance is applicable to goods sold during the year. If the year-end balance in the overhead account *is material* in dollar amount, it should be apportioned among the Work in Process Inventory, Finished Goods Inventory, and Cost of Goods Sold accounts.

| YOUR TURN | **You as a Treasurer** |
|---|---|

Assume you are the treasurer of ABI, Inc., a manufacturer of industrial lasers. Among your many responsibilities is supervising preparation of the company's tax returns. The assistant treasurer has pointed out to you that the controller is allocating a significantly large and material amount of underapplied overhead from last period among the Work in Process Inventory, Finished Goods Inventory, and Cost of Goods Sold accounts. The assistant suggests that assigning the entire amount of underapplied overhead to Cost of Goods Sold would have advantageous tax consequences. She says the result would be a higher cost of goods sold expense on the income statement and resulting lower profits. Lower profits would, in turn, reduce taxes. How should you respond?

(See our comments on the Online Learning Center Web site.)

## ACCOUNTING FOR COMPLETED JOBS

We have now explained how manufacturing costs are charged (debited) to the Work in Process Inventory account and how the costs of specific jobs are separately accumulated on job cost sheets.

As each job is completed, the job cost sheet is removed from the work in process subsidiary ledger and the manufacturing costs on the sheet are totaled to determine the cost of finished goods manufactured. As shown in Exhibit 17–2b, this cost then is transferred from the Work in Process Inventory account to the Finished Goods Inventory account.

During January, Oak & Glass completed work on job nos. 830 and 831. The entries to record completion of these jobs appear as follows:

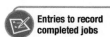
**Entries to record completed jobs**

| | | |
|---|---|---|
| Finished Goods Inventory. . . . . . . . . . . . . . . . . . . . . . . . . . . . . . . . . . . . . . . . . . . | 90,000 | |
|     Work in Process Inventory . . . . . . . . . . . . . . . . . . . . . . . . . . . . . . . . . . . . . . | | 90,000 |
| To record completion of job no. 830, consisting of 600 French Court dining chairs (unit cost, $150). | | |
| Finished Goods Inventory. . . . . . . . . . . . . . . . . . . . . . . . . . . . . . . . . . . . . . . . . . . | 75,000 | |
|     Work in Process Inventory . . . . . . . . . . . . . . . . . . . . . . . . . . . . . . . . . . . . . . | | 75,000 |
| To record completion of job no. 831, consisting of 100 French Court dining tables (unit cost, $750). | | |

As sales of the finished units occur, the unit cost figure will be used in determining the cost of goods sold. For example, the sale of 40 of the French Court dining tables at a total sales price of $48,000 is recorded as follows:

| | | |
|---|---|---|
| Accounts Receivable (Anthony's Fine Furniture) . . . . . . . . . . . . . . . . . . . . . | 48,000 | |
|     Sales. . . . . . . . . . . . . . . . . . . . . . . . . . . . . . . . . . . . . . . . . . . . . . . . . . . . . . | | 48,000 |
| Sold 40 French Court dining tables on account. | | |
| Cost of Goods Sold . . . . . . . . . . . . . . . . . . . . . . . . . . . . . . . . . . . . . . . . . . | 30,000 | |
|     Finished Goods Inventory . . . . . . . . . . . . . . . . . . . . . . . . . . . . . . . . . . . . . | | 30,000 |
| To record the cost of the 40 French Court dining tables sold to Anthony's Fine Furniture (40 × $750 cost per unit = $30,000). | | |

## JOB ORDER COSTING IN SERVICE INDUSTRIES

In the preceding example, we have emphasized the use of job order costing in a manufacturing company. However, many service industries also use this method to accumulate the costs of servicing a particular customer.

In a hospital, for example, each patient represents a separate "job," and the costs of caring for the patient are accumulated on a job cost sheet. Costs of such items as medicine, blood transfusions, and x-rays represent the usage of direct materials; services rendered by doctors are direct labor. The costs of nursing, meals, linen service, and depreciation of the hospital building and equipment all are part of the hospital's overhead. In a hospital, overhead often is applied to each patient's account at a predetermined daily rate.

## Activity-Based Costing (ABC)

For Oak & Glass Furniture Co. discussed above, we illustrated how manufacturing overhead costs may be applied to production using an overhead application rate based on a single cost driver (such as direct labor hours). This approach works well for many companies, especially if all products are manufactured in a similar manner.

But now consider a company that uses *very different processes* in manufacturing different products. The factors that drive overhead costs may vary greatly among different product lines. Such companies may benefit from *activity-based costing*. Activity-based costing (ABC) is an overhead allocation method that uses multiple overhead rates to track indirect costs by the *activities* that consume those costs. Examples of activities that consume overhead resources include purchasing and storing materials for production, supervising direct labor, number of machine runs, consuming electricity, or maintenance work on equipment.

In ABC, *many different* activity bases (or cost drivers) are used in applying overhead costs to products. Thus, ABC recognizes the special overhead considerations of each product line. As a result, overhead allocations tend to be more useful. In addition, ABC provides management with information about the cost of performing various overhead activities.

**CASE IN POINT**

**Ford Motor Company** used ABC techniques to cut costs by 20 percent in its accounts payable department. The process was so successful that it led to a wholesale reworking of Ford's procurement system. Previously, when a supplier shipped an ordered part, a clerk attempted to reconcile three documents—the purchase order, the receiving document, and the vendor's invoice. When all three agreed, payment was issued. Now orders are entered into a database. When the part arrives, the receiving department checks the database for agreement and approves payment. The payment is automatically issued to the supplier upon approval.

© AP Photo/David Zalubowki

**How ABC Works**    Activity-based costing consists of two stages. The first stage in ABC is to subdivide overhead costs into a number of **activity cost pools.** Each cost pool represents a type of overhead activity, such as building maintenance, purchasing materials, heating of the factory, and machinery repairs. In the second ABC stage, the overhead costs in each pool are applied to production separately. In short, ABC separately identifies and makes use of the most appropriate cost driver for applying each category of overhead costs.

**The Benefits of ABC**    Measurement of unit costs may assist managers in several ways. For example, it helps them in setting sales prices and in evaluating the profitability of each product line. ABC also helps managers to better understand what activities drive overhead costs. This understanding may inspire them to develop new operating procedures that may reduce overhead costs.

### ABC VERSUS A SINGLE APPLICATION RATE: A COMPARISON

Assume that Master File, Inc., makes two lines of file cabinets: (1) metal file cabinets, sold through office supply outlets for commercial use, and (2) wooden file cabinets, sold through fine furniture stores for home use.

In a typical year, the company produces and sells approximately 42,000 metal cabinets and 9,000 wooden cabinets. Total manufacturing overhead at this level of production is expected to average *$249,600 per year* and is currently allocated to products at a rate of *$1.60 per direct labor hour (DLH)*, as computed below.

*Step 1: Compute total direct labor hours at normal levels of production.*

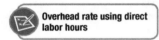
Overhead rate using direct labor hours

| | |
|---|---|
| Metal cabinets (42,000 units per year × 2 DLH per unit) | 84,000 DLH |
| Wooden cabinets (9,000 units per year × 8 DLH per unit) | 72,000 DLH |
| Total DLH at normal production levels | 156,000 DLH |

*Step 2: Compute the overhead application rate per DLH.*

| | |
|---|---|
| Overhead application rate ($249,600 ÷ 156,000 DLH) | $1.60 per DLH |

Using direct labor hours as a single activity base, the company's total manufacturing costs per unit average *$38.20* for metal cabinets and *$117.80* for wooden cabinets, as shown below.

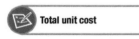
Total unit cost

| | Metal Cabinets | Wooden Cabinets |
|---|---|---|
| Direct materials | $15.00 | $ 25.00 |
| Direct labor (at $10.00 per hour) | 20.00 | 80.00 |
| Manufacturing overhead (at $1.60 per DLH) | 3.20 | 12.80 |
| Total manufacturing costs per unit | $38.20 | $117.80 |

Master File sets its selling prices at *160 percent* of total manufacturing costs. Thus, the company sells its metal cabinets for *$61.12* (total unit cost of $38.20 × 160%) and its wooden cabinets for *$188.48* (total unit cost of $117.80 × 160%). At these prices, the metal cabinets sell for about *$3 less* per unit than comparable cabinets sold by Master File's competitors. However, the price of wooden cabinets averages *$10 more* per unit than comparable products available on the market.

Glen Brown, Master File's marketing director, believes that sales of the wooden cabinets have suffered as a result of the company's pricing policy. He recently hired a consultant, Lisa Scott, to evaluate how prices are set. Scott drafted the memo in Exhibit 17–3 summarizing her findings:

Exhibit 17–3

**MEMO ABOUT OVERHEAD ALLOCATIONS**

**MEMO**

**DATE:** January 16

**TO:** Glen Brown, Marketing Director, Master File, Inc.

**FROM:** Lisa Scott, Consultant, Scott & Associates

Having carefully examined Master File's pricing policy, I find it consistent with pricing policies used throughout the office furniture industry. Therefore, I recommend that you continue setting prices at 160% of total manufacturing costs.

I do, however, strongly encourage management to change the method currently used to allocate manufacturing overhead to products. The use of direct labor hours as an activity base is causing an excessive share of total overhead costs to be allocated to the wooden cabinet line. Let me explain what is happening.

The wooden product line is very labor intensive in comparison to the metal cabinet line (that is, it takes an average of eight direct labor hours to manufacture a wooden cabinet, compared to an average of two direct labor hours to manufacture a metal cabinet). Because manufacturing overhead is allocated on the basis of direct labor hours, each wooden cabinet receives a far greater cost allocation than each metal cabinet. This would be appropriate if direct labor hours were the primary overhead *cost driver.* The fact is, however, that direct labor hours are not a significant driver of your overhead costs.

My analysis of manufacturing overhead at Master File, Inc., reveals that the most significant cost drivers are activities most closely associated with the metal cabinet line. Thus, it would make sense if your company selected activity bases that allocate more overhead costs to the metal cabinets. This would indicate a lower cost for the wooden cabinets and provide justification for lowering their selling prices, making them more in line with the competition.

I suggest that we make an appointment to discuss using *activity-based costing* at Master File, Inc.

Assume that Master File decides to implement ABC as suggested by the consultant. Remember that the company's expected *total overhead costs* at normal levels of production average *$249,600 per year*. Let us assume that these overhead costs fall into two broad categories: (1) Maintenance Department costs and (2) utilities costs. Recall that ABC is typically undertaken in two stages—first, identify separate activity cost pools and, second, allocate each cost pool to the product with an appropriate cost driver. We will create an ABC system for Master File, Inc., by using these two stages. Exhibit 17–4 illustrates stage 1 of the ABC system for Master File.

## STAGE 1: SEPARATE ACTIVITY COST POOLS

**Maintenance Department Costs**    The Maintenance Department incurs approximately *$180,000* of Master File's total overhead costs. The department has five full-time employees. Three employees are responsible for repair work, such as fixing the large cutting and bending machines used to manufacture metal file cabinets. The other two employees are responsible for set-up activities, such as adjusting machinery prior to each production run.

Using ABC, Master File identifies repair activities and set-up activities as separate *activity cost pools.* Thus each pool is assigned a portion of the department's $180,000 in total costs. Management believes that the *number of employees* engaged in each activity is the most significant *cost driver* of the Maintenance Department's total costs. As shown in Exhibit 17–4, by using the number of employees as an *activity base, $108,000* is assigned to the *repair cost pool,* and *$72,000* is assigned to the *set-up cost pool.* These computations are shown beneath Exhibit 17–4 on the following page.

Exhibit 17–4    **STAGE 1: CREATING ACTIVITY COST POOLS**
### ACTIVITY COST POOLS
### MASTER FILE, INC.

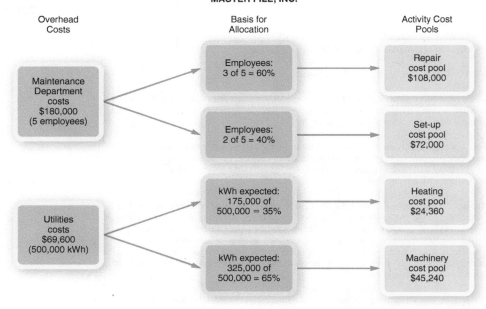

## Assigning Maintenance Department Costs to Activity Pools
*Step 1: Establish the percentage of total Maintenance Department costs to be assigned to each activity cost pool using the number of employees as an activity base.*

|  |  | % of total |
| --- | --- | --- |
| Employees engaged in repair activities | 3 | 60% |
| Employees engaged in set-up activities | 2 | 40% |
| Employees in the Maintenance Department | 5 | 100% |

*Step 2: Assign total Maintenance Department costs of $180,000 to each activity cost pool based on the percentages computed in step 1.*

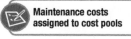
**Maintenance costs assigned to cost pools**

| Costs assigned to the repair cost pool ($180,000 × 60%) | $108,000 |
| --- | --- |
| Costs assigned to the set-up cost pool ($180,000 × 40%) | 72,000 |
| Total Maintenance Department costs assigned | $180,000 |

**Utilities Costs**    Utilities costs account for nearly $69,600 of Master File's total manufacturing overhead costs. A large portion of this amount is incurred to heat the factory and supply power to the large machines used in manufacturing the metal cabinet line.

Thus, using ABC, Master File identifies heating demands and machinery power demands as separate *activity cost pools.* As shown in Exhibit 17–4, each of these pools is assigned a portion of the $69,600 utilities costs. Management believes that the *number of kilowatt hours (kWh)* required for each activity is the most significant driver of utilities costs. With kilowatt hours as an *activity base,* $24,360 is assigned to the *heating cost pool,* whereas $45,240 is assigned to the *machinery cost pool,* as computed at the top of the following page.

## Assigning Utilities Costs to Activity Pools
*Step 1: Establish the percentage of total utilities costs to be assigned to each activity cost pool using the number of kilowatt hours as an activity base.*

| | | % of total |
|---|---|---|
| kWh per year for heating requirements . . . . . . . . . . . . . . . . . . . . . . . . | 175,000 | 35% |
| kWh per year for machinery requirements . . . . . . . . . . . . . . . . . . . . | 325,000 | 65% |
| kWh required per year . . . . . . . . . . . . . . . . . . . . . . . . . . . . . . . . . . . . | 500,000 | 100% |

*Step 2: Assign total utilities costs of $69,600 to each activity cost pool based on the percentages computed in step 1.*

| | |
|---|---|
| Costs assigned to the heating cost pool ($69,600 × 35%) . . . . . . . . . . . . . . . . . . . | $24,360 |
| Costs assigned to the machinery cost pool ($69,600 × 65%) . . . . . . . . . . . . . . . . . | 45,240 |
| Total utilities costs assigned . . . . . . . . . . . . . . . . . . . . . . . . . . . . . . . . . . . . . . . . | $69,600 |

 **Utilities costs assigned to cost pools**

## STAGE 2: ALLOCATE ACTIVITY COST POOLS TO THE PRODUCTS

The costs assigned to each cost pool must now be allocated to Master File's two product lines. Exhibit 17–5 shows that management has determined that the *number of repair work orders* is the most appropriate activity base for allocating the *repair cost pool* to each product line. The Maintenance Department receives approximately *250* repair work orders each year. Of these, about *200* are related to the metal cabinet line, and *50* are related to the wooden cabinet line. In a typical year, the metal cabinets are allocated approximately *$86,400* from the repair costs pool, whereas wooden cabinets are allocated approximately *$21,600,* as computed below.

### Allocation of Repair Cost Pool to Each Product Line
*Step 1: Establish the percentage of repair cost pool to be allocated to each product line using the number of work orders as an activity base.*

| | | % of total |
|---|---|---|
| Work orders related to metal cabinet line per year. . . . . . . . . . . . . . . . . . . | 200 | 80% |
| Work orders related to wooden cabinet line per year. . . . . . . . . . . . . . . . . | 50 | 20% |
| Total work orders per year . . . . . . . . . . . . . . . . . . . . . . . . . . . . . . . . . . . . . | 250 | 100% |

*Step 2: Allocate $108,000 from the repair cost pool to each product line based on the percentages computed in step 1.*

| | |
|---|---|
| Costs allocated to the metal cabinet line ($108,000 × 80%) . . . . . . . . . . . . . . . . . | $ 86,400 |
| Costs allocated to the wooden cabinet line ($108,000 × 20%) . . . . . . . . . . . . . . . | 21,600 |
| Total repair costs allocated to both product lines . . . . . . . . . . . . . . . . . . . . . . . . | $108,000 |

**Repair cost pool allocated to each product line**

The *number of production runs* is determined to be the most significant driver of set-up costs. Thus, production runs will serve as the activity base for allocating the *set-up cost pool* to each product line. Master File schedules approximately *200* production runs each year. Of these, about *150* are for metal cabinets, and *50* are for wooden cabinets. Thus, in a typical year, the metal cabinets are allocated approximately *$54,000* from the set-up cost pool, whereas wooden cabinets are allocated about *$18,000,* as shown in Exhibit 17–5 and computed beneath Exhibit 17–5 on the following page.

### Allocation of Set-up Cost Pool to Each Product Line
*Step 1: Establish the percentage of set-up cost pool to be allocated to each product line using the number of production runs as an activity base.*

| | | % of total |
|---|---|---|
| Production runs of metal cabinets per year . . . . . . . . . . . . . . . . . . . . . . . . | 150 | 75% |
| Production runs of wooden cabinets per year . . . . . . . . . . . . . . . . . . . . . . . | 50 | 25% |
| Total production runs per year. . . . . . . . . . . . . . . . . . . . . . . . . . . . . . . . . . | 200 | 100% |

Exhibit 17–5    **STAGE 2: ALLOCATION OF COST POOLS TO EACH PRODUCT**
OVERHEAD COST ALLOCATIONS
MASTER FILE, INC.

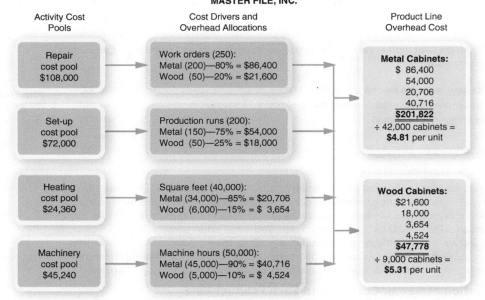

***Step 2: Allocate $72,000 from the set-up cost pool to each product line based on the percentages computed in step 1.***

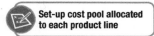
**Set-up cost pool allocated
to each product line**

| | |
|---|---|
| Costs allocated to the metal cabinet line ($72,000 × 75%) . . . . . . . . . . . . . . . . . . . . . | $54,000 |
| Costs allocated to the wooden cabinet line ($72,000 × 25%) . . . . . . . . . . . . . . . . . | 18,000 |
| Total set-up costs allocated to both product lines. . . . . . . . . . . . . . . . . . . . . . . . . . . | $72,000 |

   In summary, the Maintenance Department averages $108,000 in repair-related costs and $72,000 in set-up costs each year (or total costs of $180,000). Thus, at normal levels of production, ABC allocates $86,400 in repair costs to the metal cabinet line and $21,600 in repair costs to the wooden cabinet line. In addition, ABC allocates $54,000 in set-up costs to the metal cabinet line and $18,000 in set-up costs to the wooden cabinet line.

   The costs assigned to each heating and machinery cost pool must now be allocated to the metal and wooden product lines. Management believes that *square feet* of production space occupied by each product line is the most appropriate activity base for allocating the *heating cost pool*. Of the company's 40,000 square feet of production space, about *34,000* is dedicated to the metal cabinet line, and *6,000* is dedicated to the wooden cabinet line. Thus, in a typical year, the metal cabinets are allocated *$20,706* of heating pool costs, whereas wooden cabinets are allocated only *$3,654,* as computed at the top of the following page.

### Allocation of Heating Cost Pool to Each Product Line
***Step 1: Establish the percentage of heating cost pool to be allocated to each product line using square feet of production space as an activity base.***

| | | % of total |
|---|---|---|
| Square feet occupied by the metal cabinet line . . . . . . . . . . . . . . . . . . | 34,000 | 85% |
| Square feet occupied by the wooden cabinet line . . . . . . . . . . . . . . . . | 6,000 | 15% |
| Square feet of total production space occupied . . . . . . . . . . . . . . . . . . | 40,000 | 100% |

***Step 2: Allocate $24,360 in the heating cost pool to each product line based on the percentages computed in step 1.***

| | |
|---|---|
| Costs allocated to the metal cabinet line ($24,360 × 85%) ................... | $20,706 |
| Costs allocated to the wooden cabinet line ($24,360 × 15%) ................. | 3,654 |
| Total heating costs allocated to both product lines........................ | $24,360 |

Heating cost pool allocated to each product line

The *number of machine hours* is determined to be the most significant driver of machinery power costs. Thus, machine hours will serve as the activity base for allocating the *machinery cost pool* to each product line. The company utilizes approximately *50,000* machine hours each year. Of these, about *45,000* pertain to machinery used to manufacture metal cabinets, and *5,000* pertain to machines used for making wooden cabinets. Thus, in a typical year, the metal cabinets are allocated approximately *$40,716* of machinery pool costs, whereas wooden cabinets are allocated approximately *$4,524*, as shown in Exhibit 17–5 and computed below.

## Allocation of Machinery Cost Pool to Each Product Line
***Step 1: Establish the percentage of machinery cost pool to be allocated to each product line using the number of machine hours as an activity base.***

| | | % of total |
|---|---|---|
| Machine hours used for metal cabinets per year ................. | 45,000 | 90% |
| Machine hours used for wooden cabinets per year ............... | 5,000 | 10% |
| Total machine hours per year.................................. | 50,000 | 100% |

***Step 2: Allocate $45,240 in the machinery cost pool to each product line based on the percentages computed in step 1.***

| | |
|---|---|
| Costs allocated to the metal cabinet line ($45,240 × 90%) ................... | $40,716 |
| Costs allocated to the wooden cabinet line ($45,240 × 10%) ................. | 4,524 |
| Total machinery costs allocated to both product lines ...................... | $45,240 |

Machinery cost pool allocated to each product line

In summary, annual utilities costs average $24,360 for heating and $45,240 for powering machinery (for a total of $69,600). At normal levels of production, ABC allocates approximately $20,706 of heating costs to the metal cabinet line and $3,654 of heating costs to the wooden cabinet line. In addition, it allocates $40,716 of machinery power costs to the metal cabinet line and $4,524 to the wooden cabinet line.

## DETERMINING UNIT COSTS USING ABC

We may now compute Master File's overhead costs on a *per-unit* basis. At normal levels of activity, the company produces and sells 42,000 metal file cabinets and 9,000 wooden file cabinets per year. Thus, the unit manufacturing overhead cost of each metal cabinet is *$4.81*, compared to *$5.31* for each wooden cabinet. These unit costs are computed below.

Unit costs using ABC

| | Metal Cabinets | Wooden Cabinets |
|---|---|---|
| Maintenance Department costs: | | |
| Allocated from the repair cost pool .......................... | $ 86,400 | $21,600 |
| Allocated from the set-up cost pool.......................... | 54,000 | 18,000 |
| Utilities costs: | | |
| Allocated from the heating cost pool ........................ | 20,706 | 3,654 |
| Allocated from the machinery cost pool ...................... | 40,716 | 4,524 |
| Total manufacturing costs allocated to each line ............... | $201,822 | $47,778 |
| Total units produced and sold per year ...................... | 42,000 | 9,000 |
| Manufacturing overhead costs per unit ...................... | $ 4.81 | $ 5.31 |

Two observations should be made regarding these figures. First, at normal levels of activity, Master File's ABC process allocates the entire $249,600 in annual overhead costs to each product line ($201,822 to the metal cabinet line and $47,778 to the wooden cabinet line). Second, the amount of manufacturing overhead allocated to each product is significantly *different* than what was allocated using a single activity base, as shown below.

**Comparing methods**

|  | Metal Cabinets | Wooden Cabinets |
|---|---|---|
| Manufacturing overhead allocated using ABC .................... | $4.81 | $ 5.31 |
| Manufacturing overhead applied using direct labor hours (DLH): |  |  |
| Metal cabinets (2 DLH × $1.60 per DLH) ..................... | 3.20 |  |
| Wooden cabinets (8 DLH × $1.60 per DLH) .................. |  | 12.80 |
| Differences in overhead application per unit .................... | $1.61 | $(7.49) |

As indicated, manufacturing overhead applied to the metal file cabinets using ABC is *$1.61 more* than it was when a single activity base of direct labor hours was used. However, the amount applied to the wooden cabinets using ABC is *$7.49 less* than it was previously. As a consequence, Master File is likely to *raise* the selling price of its metal file cabinets and *lower* the selling price of its wooden file cabinets, as shown below.

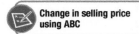
**Change in selling price using ABC**

|  | Metal Cabinets | Wooden Cabinets |
|---|---|---|
| Direct materials ......................................... | $15.00 | $ 25.00 |
| Direct labor (at $10.00 per hour) .......................... | 20.00 | 80.00 |
| Manufacturing overhead (using the ABC system) .............. | 4.81 | 5.31 |
| Total manufacturing costs per unit .......................... | $39.81 | $110.31 |
| Sales price as a percentage of total manufacturing cost .......... | 160% | 160% |
| Selling prices indicated by the ABC system ................... | $63.70 | $176.50 |
| Selling prices indicated by the single activity base system ......... | 61.12 | 188.48 |
| Price increase (reduction) indicated by the ABC system .......... | $ 2.58 | $ (11.98) |

If Master File maintains its current pricing policy, it will raise the price of metal file cabinets by *$2.58* per unit and lower the price of its wooden file cabinets by *$11.98* per unit.[2]

You will recall that Master File currently is selling its metal filing cabinets for about *$3 less* than competitive products. Therefore, the metal cabinet prices will remain competitive even if their sales price is raised by $2.58 per unit. However, the company's wooden file cabinets have been priced at *$10.00 more* than competitive products. Thus, by the lowering of the unit selling price by $11.98, Master File's wooden cabinets can now be priced competitively *without sacrificing product quality.*

## The Trend toward More Informative Cost Accounting Systems

Today's global economy is fiercely competitive. To a large extent, competitive means cost-efficient. If you cannot produce quality products efficiently, you may lose out to Japanese, German, or Korean companies, or a company down the street.

Up to this point, we have discussed job order and activity-based costing methods. Job order costing has two advantages: (1) it measures the costs of products produced in "batches," and

---

[2] To keep our illustration short, we assumed that maintenance and utilities costs were Master File's *only* manufacturing overhead costs. Consequently, overhead costs are relatively low in comparison to the cost of direct materials and direct labor. In many companies, overhead represents a much larger component of total manufacturing costs. Thus, cost distortions often are significantly greater than those shown here.

(2) unit costs are determined as soon as the job is complete. In an ABC system, the allocation of manufacturing overhead is based on the specific activities that drive overhead costs. Thus, ABC should provide a more useful measure of each product's cost. Many companies today have "hybrid" cost systems, designed to realize the advantages of many costing approaches.

## Ethics, Fraud & Corporate Governance

In addition to allocating manufacturing overhead costs to products (as discussed in this chapter), many companies allocate general corporate overhead charges to their segments or divisions. However, failure to do so properly can result in misleading financial statement information and potentially jeopardize the careers of those responsible.

The Securities and Exchange Commission (SEC) brought an enforcement action against the former chief accounting officer (CAO) and controller of Vivendi Universal, S.A. Vivendi is a French entertainment conglomerate, and its stock was cross-listed in Paris and New York. Vivendi's shares were traded on the New York Stock Exchange.

The former CAO and controller was involved in making improper allocations of corporate overhead to Vivendi's music division, Universal Music Group (UMG). Vivendi's senior management had established a €250 million target number for UMG's earnings before interest, taxes, depreciation, and amortization (EBITDA) for the third quarter of operations. In October, Vivendi's CAO and controller temporarily reduced the amount of corporate overhead charged to UMG by €7 million, exactly the reduction needed for UMG to report €250 million in EBITDA for the third quarter.

The change in the allocation of corporate overhead to UMG was made without proper supporting documentation and was not in conformity with U.S. GAAP. GAAP requires that accounting allocations be distributed according to a plan or a formula, and that allocated amounts affecting the reporting of a segment's performance be allocated in a reasonable manner. Vivendi's former CAO and controller did not reasonably allocate corporate overhead in accordance with a plan or formula; rather, the allocation was based on a desire to report a predetermined EBITDA amount.

The SEC permanently barred Vivendi's CAO and controller from appearing or practicing before the SEC as an accountant. Even if a reinstatement request is granted, the SEC will require this individual's work to be reviewed by the independent audit committee of any future employer or in some other manner acceptable to the SEC for as long as this individual works for a public company.

There are three important takeaways from this case. First, metrics other than net income are often important to investors and creditors; therefore, misstatements of other metrics valued by the capital markets can attract SEC scrutiny. Second, investors and creditors often are interested in the performance of different parts of the business (i.e., segments). As a result, GAAP requires the disclosure of segment information in the notes to the financial statements. Misstatement of the financial statement notes can attract regulatory scrutiny. Third, sanctions against individuals for violations of the securities laws can be severe. Although the SEC does not have criminal enforcement power, the ability to bar an individual from practicing before it as an accountant, as well as the SEC's ability to bar an individual from serving as an officer or director of a public company, can have severe economic consequences for individuals subject to these sanctions.

## Concluding Remarks

Job order costing is ideal for companies that create unique products or services. Many professional service firms such as medical, law, or accounting firms rely on job order costing techniques to determine the price to charge for their services. However, job order costing alone does not provide the detail that many companies need to sufficiently track overhead to jobs. Activity-based costing, used simultaneously with job order costing, gives managers and their customers a clearer understanding of how a particular service or product uses up indirect overhead costs. In coming chapters, we will see how understanding the significant activities that cause costs to vary can provide a basis for planning future activities and managing the costs of current activities.

# END-OF-CHAPTER REVIEW

**LO1 Explain the purposes of cost accounting systems.** Cost accounting systems provide information useful for managing the activities that consume resources. Managers use the information to evaluate and reward employee performance. In addition, the cost information is reported on external financial statements as, for example, inventories, cost of goods sold, and period expenses.

**LO2 Identify the processes for creating goods and services that are suited to job order costing.** Job order costing methods are appropriate for businesses and companies producing customized jobs that require differing amounts and types of direct labor, direct materials, and overhead.

**LO3 Explain the purpose and computation of overhead application rates for job order costing.** An overhead application rate is a device used to assign appropriate amounts of overhead costs to specific services, products, or jobs that are in progress. The overhead application rate expresses the relationship between the overhead costs and some activity base that can be used to trace costs directly to each specific job. An overhead application rate is computed by dividing the expected or estimated overhead costs for the period by the expected amount of activity (for example, machine hours, labor hours, etc.) related to the activity base.

**LO4 Describe the purpose and the content of a job cost sheet.** The purpose of a job cost sheet is to keep track of all manufacturing costs relating to a particular job. Each job cost sheet shows the cost of all the materials, direct labor, and factory overhead charged to the job. The job cost sheets of all jobs in process serve as a subsidiary ledger supporting the balance of the Work in Process Inventory account.

**LO5 Account for the flow of costs when using job order costing.** Costs flow from the Direct Labor account, the Direct Materials Inventory account, and the Manufacturing Overhead account into the Work in Process Inventory account. As jobs are completed, the accumulated costs are transferred to the Finished Goods Inventory account. As units are sold, their costs flow from the Finished Goods Inventory account to the Cost of Goods Sold account.

**LO6 Define overhead-related *activity cost pools* and provide several examples.** Activity cost pools are the costs of resources consumed by an activity that is necessary to produce a good or service. Types of overhead activity cost pools include building maintenance, utilities, purchasing activities, and machinery repairs, among others.

**LO7 Demonstrate how activity bases are used to assign activity cost pools to units produced.** Activity bases are the measures of the activity that consumes the associated resource cost pool. Thus, for the purchasing activities cost pool, the activity base is the number of purchase orders processed. Dividing the activity cost pool by the activity base provides the cost per unit of activity. Activity costs are assigned to the product by tracking the activity base associated with the product and multiplying it by the appropriate cost per unit of activity.

---

## Key Terms Introduced or Emphasized in Chapter 17

**activity-based costing** (p. 762)   Cost accounting method that tracks indirect costs to the activities that consume resources.

**activity cost pools** (p. 769)   Overhead categories that represent the costs associated with an activity that consumes overhead resources.

**cost accounting systems** (p. 760)   The methods and techniques used by enterprises to track resources consumed in creating and delivering products and services to customers.

**cost driver** (p. 762)   An activity base that can be traced directly to units produced and that serves as a causal factor in the incurrence of overhead costs. Serves as an activity base in an overhead application rate.

**job cost sheet** (p. 763)   A record used in job order costing to summarize the manufacturing costs (materials, labor, and overhead) applicable to each job or batch of production. Job cost sheets may be viewed as a subsidiary ledger supporting the balance of the Work in Process Inventory control account.

**job order costing** (p. 760)   A cost accounting method under which the focal point of costing is a quantity of product known as a *job* or *lot*. Costs of direct materials, direct labor, and manufacturing overhead applicable to each job are compiled to arrive at average unit cost.

**over- or underapplied overhead** (p. 767)   The difference between the actual manufacturing overhead incurred during the period and the amount applied to work in process by use of a predetermined overhead application rate.

**overhead application rate** (p. 761)   A device used to apply a normal amount of overhead costs to work in process. The rate is predetermined at the beginning of the year and expresses the percentage relationship between estimated total overhead for the year and the estimated total of some cost driver, such as direct labor hours, direct labor costs, or machine hours. Use of the overhead application rate causes overhead to be charged to work in process in proportion to the amount of "cost driver" traceable to those units.

# Demonstration Problem

Oceanview Enterprises is a print shop that uses job order costing. Overhead is applied to individual jobs at a predetermined rate based on direct labor costs. The job cost sheet for job no. 21 appears below.

**JOB COST SHEET**

JOB NUMBER: __21__    DATE STARTED: __Feb. 1__

PRODUCT: __Income Tax Handbook__    DATE COMPLETED: __Feb. 6__

UNITS COMPLETED: __2,500__

| | |
|---|---:|
| Direct materials used . . . . . . . . . . . . . . . . . . . . . . . . . . . . . . . . . . . . . . . . . . . . . . . . | $3,200 |
| Direct labor. . . . . . . . . . . . . . . . . . . . . . . . . . . . . . . . . . . . . . . . . . . . . . . . . . . . . . . . . | 400 |
| Manufacturing overhead applied . . . . . . . . . . . . . . . . . . . . . . . . . . . . . . . . . . . . . . | 1,200 |
| Total cost of job no. 21 . . . . . . . . . . . . . . . . . . . . . . . . . . . . . . . . . . . . . . . . . . . . . . . | $4,800 |
| Unit cost ($4,800 ÷ 2,500 units) . . . . . . . . . . . . . . . . . . . . . . . . . . . . . . . . . . . . . . . . | $ 1.92 |

## Instructions

Prepare general journal entries to:

**a.** Summarize the manufacturing costs charged to job no. 21. (Use one compound entry.)

**b.** Record the completion of job no. 21.

**c.** Record the credit sale of 2,000 units from job no. 21 at a unit sales price of $4. Record in a separate entry the related cost of goods sold.

## Solution to the Demonstration Problem

| GENERAL JOURNAL | | |
|---|---:|---:|
| **a.** Work in Process Inventory . . . . . . . . . . . . . . . . . . . . . . . . . . . . . . . . . . . . . | 4,800 | |
|     Materials Inventory . . . . . . . . . . . . . . . . . . . . . . . . . . . . . . . . . . . . . . . | | 3,200 |
|     Direct Labor. . . . . . . . . . . . . . . . . . . . . . . . . . . . . . . . . . . . . . . . . . . . . | | 400 |
|     Manufacturing Overhead . . . . . . . . . . . . . . . . . . . . . . . . . . . . . . . . | | 1,200 |
|   Manufacturing costs incurred on job no. 21. | | |
| **b.** Finished Goods Inventory . . . . . . . . . . . . . . . . . . . . . . . . . . . . . . . . . . . . | 4,800 | |
|     Work in Process Inventory . . . . . . . . . . . . . . . . . . . . . . . . . . . . . . . | | 4,800 |
|   To record completion of job no. 21. | | |
| **c.** Accounts Receivable . . . . . . . . . . . . . . . . . . . . . . . . . . . . . . . . . . . . . . . . | 8,000 | |
|     Sales . . . . . . . . . . . . . . . . . . . . . . . . . . . . . . . . . . . . . . . . . . . . . . . . . . | | 8,000 |
|   To record credit sale of 2,000 units from job no. 21 | | |
|     @ $4 per unit. | | |
| Cost of Goods Sold . . . . . . . . . . . . . . . . . . . . . . . . . . . . . . . . . . . . . . . . . | 3,840 | |
|     Finished Goods Inventory . . . . . . . . . . . . . . . . . . . . . . . . . . . . . . . . | | 3,840 |
|   To record cost of sales for 2,000 units from job no. 21 | | |
|     (2,000 × $1.92 per unit). | | |

## Self-Test Questions

*The answers to these questions appear on page 801.*

1. If CustomCraft uses *job order* costing, each of the following is true, *except:*

   a. Individual job cost sheets accumulate all manufacturing costs applicable to each job and together constitute a subsidiary ledger for the Work in Process Inventory account.

   b. Direct labor cost applicable to individual jobs is recorded when paid by a debit to Work in Process Inventory and a credit to Cash, as well as by entering the amount on the job cost sheets.

   c. The amount of direct materials used in individual jobs is recorded by debiting the Work in Process Inventory account and crediting the Materials Inventory account, as well as by entering the amount used on job cost sheets.

   d. The manufacturing overhead applied to each job is transferred from the Manufacturing Overhead account to the Work in Process Inventory account, as well as entered on the individual job cost sheets.

2. When job costing is in use, *underapplied* overhead:

   a. Represents the cost of manufacturing overhead that relates to unfinished jobs.

   b. Is indicated by a credit balance remaining at year-end in the Manufacturing Overhead account.

   c. Is closed out at year-end into the Cost of Goods Sold account if the amount is not material.

   d. Results when actual overhead costs incurred during a year are less than the amounts applied to individual jobs.

3. Which of the following businesses would most likely use *job order* costing?

   a. A print shop that specializes in wedding invitations.

   b. A company that makes frozen pizzas.

   c. A brewery.

   d. An oil refinery.

4. The purpose of an overhead application rate is to:

   a. Assign a portion of indirect manufacturing costs to each product manufactured.

   b. Determine the type and amount of costs to be debited to the Manufacturing Overhead account.

   c. Charge the Work in Process Inventory account with the appropriate amount of direct manufacturing costs.

   d. Allocate manufacturing overhead to expense in proportion to the number of units manufactured during the period.

5. Which of the following are *true* regarding activity-based costing?

   a. A primary goal of using ABC is a more useful allocation of manufacturing overhead to product lines.

   b. Under ABC, direct labor hours are never used to allocate overhead costs to activity pools or product lines.

   c. The use of ABC is indicated when it is suspected that each of a firm's product lines consumes approximately the same amount of overhead resources but the current allocation scheme assigns each line a substantially different amount.

   d. ABC can be used in conjunction with job order costing.

6. Which of the following would be the most appropriate basis for allocating the costs of plant insurance that covers equipment theft and damage?

   a. Direct labor hours.

   b. Value of equipment.

   c. Machine hours.

   d. Square feet of plant space.

7. Using ABC to allocate manufacturing overhead can help managers to:

   a. Identify what activities drive overhead costs.

   b. Set product prices.

   c. Locate inefficiencies in the production process.

   d. Do all of the above.

---

**ASSIGNMENT MATERIAL**    ## Discussion Questions

1. What is a cost accounting system?

2. What are the major objectives of a cost accounting system in a manufacturing company?

3. What factors should be taken into account in deciding whether to use job order costing in any given manufacturing situation?

4. What is meant by the term *overhead application rate*?

5. What is meant by the term *overhead cost driver*? How does the cost driver enter into the computation of an overhead application rate?

6. What is meant by underapplied overhead? By overapplied overhead?

7. Gerox Company applies manufacturing overhead on the basis of machine-hours, using a predetermined overhead rate. At the end of the current year, the Manufacturing Overhead account has a credit balance. What are the possible explanations for this? What disposition should be made of this balance?

8. Taylor & Malone is a law firm. Would the concepts of job order costing be appropriate for this type of service business? Explain.

9. Define the term *activity base*.

10. Define the term *cost driver*.

11. Why is the use of a single activity base inappropriate for some companies?

12. Describe how activity-based costing can improve overhead cost allocations in companies that produce a diverse line of products.

13. What is an *activity cost pool*?

14. Why is the use of direct labor hours as an activity base likely to be inappropriate in a highly mechanized production facility?

15. Discuss the potential benefits associated with using activity-based costing.

## Brief Exercises

### L05 | BRIEF EXERCISE 17.1
Accounting for Overhead

Newton Corporation uses a job order costing system and allocates manufacturing overhead at a rate of $25 per machine hour. During the period, the company used 600 machine hours and actually incurred manufacturing overhead costs of $14,500.

a. Prepare a summary journal entry to record total manufacturing overhead allocated to jobs during the period.

b. Prepare a summary journal entry to record actual overhead costs incurred during the period (make the credit portion of the entry to "Various Accounts").

c. Prepare the journal entry to close the Manufacturing Overhead account directly to Cost of Goods Sold at the end of the period.

### L05 | BRIEF EXERCISE 17.2
Transferring Costs in a Job Order System

Mayfield Corporation finished job no. 314 on June 1. On June 10, the company sold job no. 314 for $10,000, cash. Total manufacturing costs allocated to this job at the time of the sale amounted to $6,500.

a. Record the transfer of job no. 314 from Work in Process to Finished Goods on June 1.

b. Record the sale of job no. 314, and the transfer of its costs from Finished Goods, on June 10.

### L03 | BRIEF EXERCISE 17.3
Overhead Application Rates

Munson Manufacturing applies manufacturing overhead at a rate of $30 per direct labor hour.

a. When during the year was this rate computed?

b. Describe briefly how this rate was computed.

c. Identify the shortcomings of this rate that will cause overhead applied during the period to differ from the actual overhead costs incurred during the period.

### L03 | BRIEF EXERCISE 17.4
L05 | Actual Overhead versus Applied Overhead

Swanson Corporation applies manufacturing overhead to jobs at a rate of $30 per direct labor hour. During the current period, actual overhead costs totaled $175,000, and 6,000 direct labor hours were worked by the company's employees.

a. Record the journal entry to close the Manufacturing Overhead account directly to Cost of Goods Sold at the end of the period.

b. Was manufacturing overhead overapplied, or was it underapplied?

### L01 | BRIEF EXERCISE 17.5
L02 | Types of Cost Accounting Systems

Indicate whether job order costing is appropriate for each of the following businesses. Explain why.

a. Old Home Bakery, Inc. (a bakery that produces to order).

b. Baxter, Claxter, and Stone, CPAs.

c. Thompson Construction Company.

d. Satin Wall Paints, Inc.

e. Apache Oil and Gas Refinery.

f. Dr. Carr's Auto Body Shoppe.

g. Health-Rite Vitamins.

h. Shampoo Products International.

782    **Chapter 17** Job Order Cost Systems and Overhead Allocations

**L05** **BRIEF EXERCISE 17.6**

Applying Direct Labor Costs

Willoughby Manufacturing pays its direct labor employees $20 per hour. During the current period, 300 direct labor hours were recorded on employee time cards, and the company actually paid its direct labor employees $5,400.

a.   Record the summary journal entry to apply direct labor costs to all jobs during the period.

b.   Prepare the summary journal entry to record direct labor wages paid during the period.

c.   What is the balance of the Direct Labor account at the end of the period? How is it reported in the company's financial statements?

**L05** **BRIEF EXERCISE 17.7**

Applying Direct Materials Costs

Zappe Industries purchased direct materials costing $500,000 during the current period. It actually used only $350,000 of direct materials on jobs during the period.

a.   Prepare the summary journal entry to record direct materials purchased during the period. Assume that all purchases are made on account.

b.   Prepare the summary journal entry to record all direct materials used during the period.

**L05** **BRIEF EXERCISE 17.8**

Recording Manufacturing Costs

For each of the accounts listed below, prepare *two* summary journal entries. In the first entry, illustrate a transaction that would cause the account to be *debited*. In the second entry, illustrate a transaction that would cause the account to be *credited*. Assume that perpetual inventory records are maintained. Include a brief written explanation with each journal entry and use "XXX" in place of dollar amounts.

a.   Materials Inventory

b.   Direct Labor

c.   Manufacturing Overhead

d.   Finished Goods Inventory

**L06** **BRIEF EXERCISE 17.9**

Selecting Activity Bases

Listed below are the eight activity cost pools used by Charvez Corporation.

| | |
|---|---|
| Production set-up costs | Maintenance costs |
| Heating costs | Design and engineering costs |
| Machinery power costs | Materials warehouse costs |
| Purchasing department costs | Product inspection costs |

Suggest an appropriate activity base for allocating each of the above activity cost pools to products. (Consider each cost pool independently.)

**L06** **BRIEF EXERCISE 17.10**

Allocations in an ABC System

Leah, Inc., applies manufacturing overhead to production using an activity-based costing system. The company's utilities cost pool has accumulated $150,000, its maintenance cost pool has accumulated $200,000, and its set-up cost pool has accumulated $50,000. The company has two product lines, Deluxe and Basic. The utilities cost pool is allocated to these product lines on the basis of machine hours. The maintenance pool is allocated on the basis of work orders. The set-up pool is allocated on the basis of production runs.

a.   Allocate the utilities cost pool to each product line assuming the Deluxe model used 4,000 machine hours and the Basic model used 1,000 machine hours.

b.   Allocate the maintenance pool to each product line assuming the Deluxe model required 25 work orders and the Basic model required 75 work orders.

c.   Allocate the set-up pool to each product line assuming the Deluxe model required 9 production runs and the Basic model required 21 production runs.

## Exercises

**L01 through L04 L06 L07** **EXERCISE 17.1**

Accounting Terminology

Listed below are seven technical accounting terms introduced or emphasized in this chapter.

| | |
|---|---|
| Job order costing | Cost driver |
| Overhead application rate | Cost of finished goods manufactured |
| Overapplied overhead | Job cost sheet |
| Activity-based costing | |

Each of the following statements may (or may not) describe these technical terms. For each statement, indicate the term described, or answer "None" if the statement does not correctly describe any of the terms.

**a.** An activity base that can be traced directly to units produced and can be used as a denominator in computing an overhead application rate.

**b.** The total of all direct labor, direct materials, and manufacturing overhead transferred from work in process to finished goods.

**c.** A means of assigning indirect product costs to work in process during the period.

**d.** A debit balance remaining in the Manufacturing Overhead account at the end of the period.

**e.** The type of cost accounting system likely to be used by a construction company.

**f.** The type of cost accounting method likely to be used for overhead costs.

| L01 | **EXERCISE 17.2** |
|---|---|
| through | Flow of Costs in Job |
| L05 | Order Costing |

The information below was taken from the job cost sheets of Bates Company.

| Job Number | Manufacturing Costs as of June 30 | Manufacturing Costs in July |
|---|---|---|
| 101 | $4,200 | |
| 102 | 3,240 | |
| 103 | 900 | $2,000 |
| 104 | 2,250 | 4,000 |
| 105 | | 6,000 |
| 106 | | 3,700 |

During July, jobs no. 103 and 104 were completed, and jobs no. 101, 102, and 104 were delivered to customers. Jobs no. 105 and 106 are still in process at July 31. From this information, compute the following:

**a.** The work in process inventory at June 30.

**b.** The finished goods inventory at June 30.

**c.** The cost of goods sold during July.

**d.** The work in process inventory at July 31.

**e.** The finished goods inventory at July 31.

| L01 | **EXERCISE 17.3** |
|---|---|
| through | Journal Entries in Job |
| L05 | Order Costing |

Riverside Engineering is a machine shop that uses job order costing. Overhead is applied to individual jobs at a predetermined rate based on direct labor costs. The job cost sheet for job no. 321 appears below.

---

**JOB COST SHEET**

JOB NUMBER: __321__                                        DATE STARTED: __May 10__

PRODUCT: __2" Brass Check Valves__                          DATE COMPLETED: __May 21__

UNITS COMPLETED: __4,000__

Direct materials used . . . . . . . . . . . . . . . . . . . . . . . . . . . . . . . . . . . . . . . . . . $ 7,720
Direct labor. . . . . . . . . . . . . . . . . . . . . . . . . . . . . . . . . . . . . . . . . . . . . . . . . .   1,400
Manufacturing overhead applied . . . . . . . . . . . . . . . . . . . . . . . . . . . . . . . . .   3,080
Total cost of job no. 321 . . . . . . . . . . . . . . . . . . . . . . . . . . . . . . . . . . . . . . . $12,200
Unit cost ($12,200 ÷ 4,000 units) . . . . . . . . . . . . . . . . . . . . . . . . . . . . . . . . $  3.05

Prepare general journal entries to:

a. Summarize the manufacturing costs charged to job no. 321. (Use one compound entry.)

b. Record the completion of job no. 321.

c. Record the credit sale of 2,100 units from job no. 321 at a unit sales price of $5. Record in a separate entry the related cost of goods sold.

**EXERCISE 17.4**

Overhead Cost Drivers; Determination and Use of Unit Cost

During June, Assembly Department no. 4 of Riverview Electronics produced 12,000 model 201 computer keyboards. Assembly of these units required 1,476 hours of direct labor at a cost of $26,400, direct materials costing $318,960, and 2,880 hours of machine time. Based on an analysis of overhead costs at the beginning of the year, overhead is applied to keyboards using the following formula:

$$\text{Overhead} = 75\% \text{ of Direct Labour Cost} + \$32 \text{ per Machine Hour}$$

a. Compute the total amount of overhead cost applied to the 12,000 keyboards.

b. Compute the *per-unit cost* of manufacturing these keyboards.

c. Briefly explain *why* the department might use *two separate activity bases* in applying overhead costs to one type of product.

d. Identify at least two types of overhead cost pools that might be "driven" by each of the two cost drivers indicated in this situation.

e. What appears to be the *primary* driver of overhead costs in the manufacture of keyboards?

f. Compute the gross profit that will result from the sale of 2,000 of these keyboards at a sales price of $75 each.

**EXERCISE 17.5**

Cost Classifications

Identify whether each of the following costs of Granite Construction, Inc., would be classified as direct labor, direct materials, manufacturing overhead, or as selling, general, and administrative costs.

a. Hourly wages paid to backhoe operators.

b. Crankcase oil used in construction machinery.

c. PVC pipes used in a municipal sewer construction project.

d. Depreciation of bulldozers and other construction equipment.

e. Advertising costs.

f. Steel beams used in the construction of an office building.

g. Salaries paid to foremen responsible for supervising multiple construction projects.

h. Legal costs.

i. Gasoline used in trucks that haul construction equipment to various job sites.

j. Hourly wages paid to masons and carpenters.

k. Costs for accounting and tax services.

l. The CEO's salary.

m. Rivets, screws, nuts, and bolts.

**EXERCISE 17.6**

Cost Flows and Financial Statements

Conklin Corporation recorded the following activities during its first month of operations:

• Purchased materials costing $250,000.

• Used direct materials in production costing $230,000.

• Incurred direct labor costs of $300,000, of which $275,000 had actually been paid at the end of the month.

• Applied manufacturing overhead at a rate of $15 per direct labor hour. (Direct labor workers earn $25 per hour.)

• Incurred actual manufacturing overhead costs of $175,000.

• Transferred completed jobs costing $520,000 to finished goods.

• Sold completed jobs for $700,000. The cost applied to the jobs sold totaled $480,000.

- Closed the Manufacturing Overhead account directly to Cost of Goods Sold at the end of the month.

- Incurred selling and administrative costs of $100,000 during the month.

**a.** Prepare Conklin Corporation's income statement for its first month of operations. Ignore income taxes.

**b.** Determine the company's inventory balances at the end of its first month of operations.

---

**L03**  **through** **L05**

**EXERCISE 17.7**

Journal Entries, Cost Flows, and Determining Account Balances

Zelda Manufacturing organized in June and recorded the following transactions during June, its first month of operations:

1. Purchased materials costing $800,000.
2. Used direct materials in production costing $485,000.
3. Applied direct labor costs of $500,000 to various jobs.
4. Applied manufacturing overhead at a rate of $10 per direct labor hour. (Direct labor workers earn $20 per hour.)
5. Incurred actual manufacturing overhead costs of $245,000 (credit "Various Accounts").
6. Transferred completed jobs costing $745,000 to finished goods.
7. Sold completed jobs for $1,000,000 on account. The cost applied to the jobs sold totaled $615,000.
8. Closed the Manufacturing Overhead account directly to Cost of Goods Sold on June 30.

**a.** Prepare a journal entry for each of the eight transactions listed above.

**b.** Compute the balance of the Cost of Goods Sold account at June 30.

**c.** Determine the company's inventory balances at the end of June.

---

**L03** **through** **L05**

**EXERCISE 17.8**

Journal Entries, Cost Flows, and Financial Reporting

Blue Plate Construction organized in December and recorded the following transactions during its first month of operations:

| | |
|---|---|
| **Dec. 2** | Purchased materials on account for $400,000. |
| **Dec. 3** | Used direct materials costing $100,000 on job no. 100. |
| **Dec. 9** | Used direct materials costing $150,000 on job no. 101. |
| **Dec. 15** | Used direct materials costing $30,000 on job no. 102. |
| **Dec. 28** | Applied the following direct labor costs to jobs: job no. 100, $9,000; job no. 101, $11,000; job no. 102, $5,000. |
| **Dec. 28** | Applied manufacturing overhead to all jobs at a rate of 300% of direct labor dollars. |
| **Dec. 29** | Completed and transferred job no. 100 and job no. 101 to the finished goods warehouse. |
| **Dec. 30** | Sold job no. 100 on account for $200,000. |
| **Dec. 31** | Recorded and paid actual December manufacturing overhead costs of $78,000, cash. |
| **Dec. 31** | Closed the Manufacturing Overhead account directly to Cost of Goods Sold. |

**a.** Record each of the above transactions as illustrated on pages 764–768.

**b.** Compute the amount at which Cost of Goods Sold is reported in the company's income statement for the month ended December 31.

**c.** Determine the inventory balances reported in the company's balance sheet dated December 31.

**d.** Was manufacturing overhead in December overapplied, or was it underapplied? Explain.

---

**L03** **through** **L05**

**EXERCISE 17.9**

Journal Entries, Cost Flows, and Financial Reporting

Schmeltz Industries organized in January and recorded the following transactions during its first month of operations:

| | |
|---|---|
| **Jan. 5** | Purchased materials on account for $800,000. |
| **Jan. 9** | Used materials costing $450,000 on job no. 1001. |
| **Jan. 14** | Used materials costing $200,000 on job no. 1002. |
| **Jan. 18** | Used materials costing $100,000 on job no. 1003. |

**Jan. 25**    Applied the following direct labor costs to jobs: job no. 1001, $3,600; job no. 1002, $5,400; job no. 1003, $1,350. (Direct labor workers earn $18 per hour.)

**Jan. 27**    Applied manufacturing overhead to all jobs at a rate of $450 per direct labor hour.

**Jan. 28**    Completed and transferred job no. 1001 and job no. 1002 to the finished goods warehouse.

**Jan. 29**    Sold job no. 1001 on account for $725,000.

**Jan. 31**    Recorded and paid actual January manufacturing overhead costs of $250,000, cash.

**Jan. 31**    Closed the Manufacturing Overhead account directly to Cost of Goods Sold.

**a.**    Prepare journal entries for each of the above transactions.

**b.**    Compute the balance of the Cost of Goods Sold account at January 31.

**c.**    Determine the company's inventory balances at January 31.

**d.**    Was manufacturing overhead in January overapplied, or was it underapplied? Explain.

---

**L03**  **EXERCISE 17.10**
through
**L05**  Journal Entries, Cost Flows, and Financial Reporting

Crenshaw uses a job order costing system to account for projects. It applies manufacturing overhead to jobs on the basis of direct labor hours and pays its direct labor workers $25 per hour. The following relates to activity for the month of December:

| | |
|---|---:|
| Manufacturing overhead budgeted (estimated on December 1) | $133,000 |
| Budgeted driver activity (DLH) (estimated on December 1) | 1,900 DLH |
| Direct materials purchased in December | $125,000 |
| Direct materials used in December | 100,000 |
| Actual direct labor costs in December | 50,000 |
| Actual manufacturing overhead in December | 150,000 |
| Cost of jobs completed in December | 275,000 |
| Revenue earned in December | 600,000 |
| Cost of goods sold in December (prior to adjusting for overhead) | 325,000 |
| Selling and administrative costs in December | 250,000 |
| Materials Inventory, December 1 | 20,000 |
| Work in Process Inventory, December 1 | 75,000 |
| Finished Goods Inventory, December 1 | 105,000 |

**a.**    Record the purchase of direct materials in December. Assume all purchases are made on account.

**b.**    Record the cost of direct materials applied to jobs in December.

**c.**    Record the cost of direct labor applied to jobs in December.

**d.**    Record the *actual* cost of manufacturing overhead incurred in December. Assume all overhead costs were paid in cash.

**e.**    Record the cost of manufacturing overhead *applied* to jobs in December.

**f.**    Record revenue and the related cost of jobs sold in December. Assume all sales are made on account.

**g.**    Record December selling and administrative costs. Assume all selling and administrative costs were paid in cash.

**h.**    Close the Manufacturing Overhead account directly to Cost of Goods Sold on December 31.

**i.**    Compute the company's December income. Ignore taxes.

---

**L03**  **EXERCISE 17.11**
through
**L05**  Solving for Missing Amounts in a Job Costing System

Rush Company budgeted that it would incur $180,000 of manufacturing overhead costs in the upcoming period. By the end of the period, Rush had actually incurred manufacturing overhead costs totaling $192,000. Other information from the company's accounting records is provided below:

- Beginning Work in Process Inventory was $30,000, whereas ending Work in Process Inventory was $25,000.

- Total manufacturing costs of $470,000 were charged to Work in Process Inventory during the period. This amount included direct materials costs of $200,000.

- Workers logged 5,400 direct labor hours during the period.

- Beginning Finished Goods Inventory was $50,000.
- The Manufacturing Overhead account had a $30,000 debit balance immediately prior to closing at the end of the period. Manufacturing overhead was applied to jobs throughout the period on the basis of direct labor hours.
- Prior to any adjustment to account for overapplied or underapplied manufacturing overhead, Cost of Goods Sold had a $520,000 debit balance.
- Sales for the period totaled $1,050,000, whereas selling and administrative expenses totaled $400,000.

a. Determine how much manufacturing overhead was *applied* to jobs during the period.

b. Determine the company's manufacturing overhead *application rate* per direct labor hour.

c. How many direct labor hours were *budgeted* at the beginning of the period?

d. What was the average hourly wage rate earned by direct labor workers?

e. What was the company's ending Finished Goods Inventory balance?

f. What was the company's net income for the period? Ignore taxes.

 **EXERCISE 17.12**

 Solving for Missing Amounts in a Job Costing System

Fenwick Corporation's manufacturing and finished goods warehouse facilities burned to the ground on January 31. The loss was fully covered by insurance. The insurance company wanted to know the cost of the inventories destroyed in the fire. The company's accountants gathered the following information:

| | |
|---|---:|
| Direct materials purchased in January | $160,000 |
| Work in Process Inventory, January 1 | 34,000 |
| Materials Inventory, January 1 | 16,000 |
| Finished Goods Inventory, January 1 | 30,000 |
| Direct labor costs incurred in January | 190,000 |
| Prime costs charged to jobs in January | 294,000 |
| Cost of finished goods available for sale in January | 450,000 |
| Sales revenue earned in January | 500,000 |
| Gross profit as a percentage of January sales | 25% |
| Manufacturing overhead applied to jobs in January as a percentage of total conversion costs | 60% |

Assume that actual manufacturing overhead was exactly equal to the amount applied to production at the time of the fire.

On the basis of the information shown above, compute the cost of the following inventories lost in the fire. (Hint: Prime costs and conversion costs were discussed in Chapter 16.)

a. Materials inventory (assume materials inventory is comprised entirely of direct materials).

b. Work in process inventory.

c. Finished goods inventory.

 **EXERCISE 17.13**

Determining Balance Sheet Amounts from Job Sheets

Robinson International began operations in early February. The company has provided the following summary of total manufacturing costs assigned to the job sheets of its entire client base during its first three months of operations:

| Job Number | February | March | April | Total Costs Assigned |
|---|---|---|---|---|
| 1000 | $12,400 | $ 6,800 | | $19,200 |
| 1001 | 15,000 | 7,400 | $1,400 | 23,800 |
| 1002 | 2,000 | | | 2,000 |
| 1003 | | 16,000 | 4,000 | 20,000 |
| 1004 | | 9,000 | 6,000 | 15,000 |

Job no. 1002 was completed in February and sold in March. Job no. 1000 was completed and sold in March. Job no. 1001 was completed and sold in April. Job no.1003 was completed in April, but won't be delivered until early May. Only job no. 1004 remains in process at April 30. The selling prices are set at 175 percent of the manufacturing costs assigned to each job.

**a.** Determine the Work in Process Inventory balance at the end of February, March, and April.

**b.** Determine the Finished Goods Inventory balance at the end of February, March, and April.

**c.** Compute the company's *total gross profit* for the three months ended April 30.

**LO6**
**LO7**

### EXERCISE 17.14
Allocating Activity Cost Pool

Costume Kings has two product lines: machine-made costumes and hand-made costumes. The company assigns $80,000 in manufacturing overhead costs to two cost pools: power costs and inspection costs. Of this amount, the power cost pool has been assigned $32,000 and the inspection cost pool has been assigned $48,000. Additional information about each product line is shown below.

|  | Machine-Made | Hand-Made |
|---|---|---|
| Sales revenue | $240,000 | $160,000 |
| Direct labor and materials costs | $120,000 | $ 96,000 |
| Units produced and sold | 48,000 | 16,000 |
| Machine hours | 96,000 | 4,000 |
| Square feet of production space | 1,200 | 800 |
| Material orders received | 150 | 100 |
| Quality control inspection hours | 2,000 | 500 |

**a.** Allocate the manufacturing overhead from the activity cost pools to each product line. Use what you believe are the most significant cost drivers from the information provided.

**b.** Compute the cost per unit of machine-made costumes and hand-made costumes.

**c.** On a per-unit basis, which product line appears to be the most profitable? Explain.

**LO6**
**LO7**

### EXERCISE 17.15
Using ABC to Determine a Bid Price

Spear Custom Furniture uses an activity-based cost accounting system to apply overhead to production. The company maintains four overhead cost pools. The four cost pools, and their budgeted amounts for the upcoming period, are as follows:

| | |
|---|---|
| Maintenance | $40,000 |
| Materials handling | 20,000 |
| Set-ups | 10,000 |
| Quality control | 45,000 |

Four cost drivers are used by Spear to allocate its overhead cost pools to production. The four cost drivers, and their budgeted total levels of activity for the upcoming period, are shown below:

| | |
|---|---|
| Machine hours (to allocate maintenance costs) | 600 hours |
| Material moves (to allocate materials handling costs) | 400 moves |
| Set-ups (to allocate set-up costs) | 100 set-ups |
| Number of inspections (to allocate quality control costs) | 300 inspections |

The company has been asked by Cosmopolitan University to submit a bid for tables to be used in a new computer lab. The plant manager feels that obtaining this job would result in new business in future years. Estimates for the Cosmopolitan University project are as follows:

| | |
|---|---|
| Direct materials | $14,000 |
| Direct labor (500 hours) | $15,000 |
| Number of machine hours | 60 |
| Number of material moves | 20 |
| Number of set-ups | 4 |
| Number of inspections | 2 |

a. Estimate the *total cost* of manufacturing the tables for Cosmopolitan University.

b. Determine the company's bid price if bids are based upon the total estimated manufacturing cost of a particular project, plus 75 percent.

## Problem Set A

 **PROBLEM 17.1A**

through

Job Order Costing: Computations and

**L05** Journal Entries

Chesapeake Sailmakers uses job order costing. Manufacturing overhead is charged to individual jobs through the use of a predetermined overhead rate based on direct labor costs. The following information appears in the company's Work in Process Inventory account for the month of June:

| | |
|---|---:|
| Debits to account: | |
|   Balance, June 1 .......................................... | $ 7,200 |
|   Direct materials ......................................... | 12,000 |
|   Direct labor ............................................. | 9,000 |
|   Manufacturing overhead (applied to jobs as 150% of direct labor cost) ....... | 13,500 |
|     Total debits to account ................................ | $41,700 |
| Credits to account: | |
|   Transferred to Finished Goods Inventory account ..................... | 33,200 |
| Balance, June 30 ........................................... | $ 8,500 |

### Instructions

a. Assuming that the direct labor charged to the jobs still in process at June 30 amounts to $2,100, compute the amount of manufacturing overhead and the amount of direct materials that have been charged to these jobs as of June 30.

b. Prepare general journal entries to summarize:

1. The manufacturing costs (direct materials, direct labor, and overhead) charged to production during June.

2. The transfer of production completed during June to the Finished Goods Inventory account.

3. The cash sale of 90 percent of the merchandise completed during June at a total sales price of $46,500. Show the related cost of goods sold in a separate journal entry.

 **PROBLEM 17.2A**

through

Job Order Costing: Journal Entries and

**L05** Cost Flows

The following information relates to the manufacturing operations of O'Shaughnessy Mfg. Co. during the month of March. The company uses job order costing.

a. Purchases of direct materials during the month amount to $59,700. (All purchases were made on account.)

b. Materials requisitions issued by the Production Department during the month total $56,200.

c. Time cards of direct workers show 2,000 hours worked on various jobs during the month, for a total direct labor cost of $30,000.

d. Direct workers were paid $26,300 in March.

e. Actual overhead costs for the month amount to $34,900 (for simplicity, you may credit Accounts Payable).

f. Overhead is applied to jobs at a rate of $18 per direct labor hour.

g. Jobs with total accumulated costs of $116,000 were completed during the month.

h. During March, units costing $128,000 were sold for $210,000. (All sales were made on account.)

### Instructions

Prepare general journal entries to summarize each of these transactions in the company's general ledger accounts.

**L01**
**through**
**L05**

**PROBLEM 17.3A**
Job Order Costing:
A Comprehensive
Problem

Georgia Woods, Inc., manufactures furniture to customers' specifications and uses job order cost-ing. A predetermined overhead rate is used in applying manufacturing overhead to individual jobs. In Department One, overhead is applied on the basis of machine-hours, and in Department Two, on the basis of direct labor hours. At the beginning of the current year, management made the follow-ing budget estimates to assist in determining the overhead application rate:

|  | Department One | Department Two |
|---|---|---|
| Direct labor cost . . . . . . . . . . . . . . . . . . . . . . . . . . . . . . . . . . . | $300,000 | $225,000 |
| Direct labor hours . . . . . . . . . . . . . . . . . . . . . . . . . . . . . . . . . . | 20,000 | 15,000 |
| Manufacturing overhead. . . . . . . . . . . . . . . . . . . . . . . . . . . . . | $420,000 | $337,500 |
| Machine-hours . . . . . . . . . . . . . . . . . . . . . . . . . . . . . . . . . . . . | 12,000 | 7,500 |

Production of a batch of custom furniture ordered by City Furniture (job no. 58) was started early in the year and completed three weeks later on January 29. The records for this job show the following cost information:

|  | Department One | Department Two |
|---|---|---|
| Job order for City Furniture (job no. 58): |  |  |
| Direct materials cost . . . . . . . . . . . . . . . . . . . . . . . . . . . . . . . | $10,100 | $ 7,600 |
| Direct labor cost . . . . . . . . . . . . . . . . . . . . . . . . . . . . . . . . . . | $16,500 | $11,100 |
| Direct labor hours . . . . . . . . . . . . . . . . . . . . . . . . . . . . . . . . . | 1,100 | 740 |
| Machine-hours . . . . . . . . . . . . . . . . . . . . . . . . . . . . . . . . . . . | 750 | 500 |

Selected additional information for January is as follows:

|  | Department One | Department Two |
|---|---|---|
| Direct labor hours—month of January . . . . . . . . . . . . . . . . . . . | 1,600 | 1,200 |
| Machine-hours—month of January . . . . . . . . . . . . . . . . . . . . . | 1,100 | 600 |
| Manufacturing overhead incurred in January. . . . . . . . . . . . . . | $39,010 | $26,540 |

**Instructions**

a. Compute the predetermined overhead rate for each department.

b. What is the total cost of the furniture produced for City Furniture?

c. Prepare the entries required to record the sale (on account) of the furniture to City Furniture. The sales price of the order was $147,000.

d. Determine the over- or underapplied overhead for each department at the end of January.

**L01**
**through**
**L05**

**PROBLEM 17.4A**
Job Order Costing:
A Comprehensive
Problem

Precision Instruments, Inc., uses job order costing and applies manufacturing overhead to indi-vidual jobs by using predetermined overhead rates. In Department A, overhead is applied on the basis of machine-hours, and in Department B, on the basis of direct labor hours. At the beginning of the current year, management made the following budget estimates as a step toward determining the overhead application rates:

|  | Department A | Department B |
|---|---|---|
| Direct labor . . . . . . . . . . . . . . . . . . . . . . . . . . . . . . . . . . . . . . | $420,000 | $300,000 |
| Manufacturing overhead. . . . . . . . . . . . . . . . . . . . . . . . . . . . . | $540,000 | $412,500 |
| Machine-hours . . . . . . . . . . . . . . . . . . . . . . . . . . . . . . . . . . . | 18,000 | 1,900 |
| Direct labor hours . . . . . . . . . . . . . . . . . . . . . . . . . . . . . . . . . | 28,000 | 25,000 |

Production of 4,000 tachometers (job no. 399) was started in the middle of January and completed two weeks later. The cost records for this job show the following information:

|  | Department A | Department B |
|---|---|---|
| Job no. 399 (4,000 units of product): |  |  |
| Cost of materials used on job . . . . . . . . . . . . . . . . . . . . | $6,800 | $4,500 |
| Direct labor cost . . . . . . . . . . . . . . . . . . . . . . . . . . . . . | $8,100 | $7,200 |
| Direct labor hours . . . . . . . . . . . . . . . . . . . . . . . . . . . . | 540 | 600 |
| Machine-hours . . . . . . . . . . . . . . . . . . . . . . . . . . . . . . . | 250 | 100 |

**Instructions**

a.  Determine the overhead rate that should be used for each department in applying overhead costs to job no. 399.

b.  What is the total cost of job no. 399, and what is the unit cost of the product manufactured on this production order?

c.  Prepare the journal entries required to record the sale (on account) of 1,000 of the tachometers to SkiCraft Boats. The total sales price was $19,500.

d.  Assume that actual overhead costs for the year were $517,000 in Department A and $424,400 in Department B. Actual machine-hours in Department A were 17,000, and actual direct labor hours in Department B were 26,000 during the year. On the basis of this information, determine the over- or underapplied overhead in each department for the year.

**L01**
through
**L05**

**PROBLEM 17.5A**

Poor Drivers Are
Cost Drivers

Ye Olde Bump & Grind, Inc., is an automobile body and fender repair shop. Repair work is done by hand and with the use of small tools. Customers are billed based on time (direct labor hours) and materials used in each repair job.

The shop's overhead costs consist primarily of indirect materials (welding materials, metal putty, and sandpaper), rent, indirect labor, and utilities. Rent is equal to a percentage of the shop's gross revenue for each month. The indirect labor relates primarily to ordering parts and processing insurance claims. The amount of indirect labor, therefore, tends to vary with the size of each job.

Henry Lee, manager of the business, is considering using either direct labor hours or number of repair jobs as the basis for allocating overhead costs. He has estimated the following amounts for the coming year:

| | |
|---|---|
| Estimated total overhead. . . . . . . . . . . . . . . . . . . . . . . . . . . . . . . . . . . . . . . . . . . . . . | $123,000 |
| Estimated direct labor hours . . . . . . . . . . . . . . . . . . . . . . . . . . . . . . . . . . . . . . . . . | 10,000 |
| Estimated number of repair jobs . . . . . . . . . . . . . . . . . . . . . . . . . . . . . . . . . . . . . . | 300 |

**Instructions**

a.  Compute the overhead application rate based on (**1**) direct labor hours and (**2**) number of repair jobs.

b.  Shown below is information for two repair jobs:

   **Job 1**   Repair a dented fender. Direct material used, $25; direct labor hours, 5; direct labor cost, $75.

   **Job 2**   Repair an automobile involved in a serious collision. Direct materials used, $3,800; direct labor hours, 200; direct labor cost, $3,000.

Determine the *total cost* of each repair job, assuming that overhead costs are applied to each job based on:

   **1.**   Direct labor hours.

   **2.**   Number of repair jobs.

c.  Discuss the results obtained in part **b.** Which overhead application method appears to provide the more realistic results? Explain the reasoning behind your answer, addressing the issue of what "drives" overhead costs in this business.

**PROBLEM 17.6A**

Applying Overhead
Costs Using ABC

e**X**cel

Norton Chemical Company produces two products: Amithol and Bitrite. The company uses activity-based costing (ABC) to allocate manufacturing overhead to these products. The costs incurred by Norton's Purchasing Department average $80,000 per year and constitute a major portion of the company's total manufacturing overhead.

Purchasing Department costs are assigned to two activity cost pools: (1) the order cost pool and (2) the inspection cost pool. Costs are assigned to the pools based on the number of employees engaged in each activity. Of the department's five full-time employees, one is responsible for ordering raw materials, and four are responsible for inspecting incoming shipments of materials.

Costs assigned to the order pool are allocated to products based on the total number of purchase orders generated by each product line. Costs assigned to the inspection pool are allocated to products based on the number of inspections related to each product line.

For the upcoming year, Norton estimates the following activity levels:

| | Total | Amithol | Bitrite |
|---|---|---|---|
| Purchase orders generated . . . . . . . . . . . . . . . . . . . . . . . . . . . | 10,000 | 2,000 | 8,000 |
| Inspections conducted . . . . . . . . . . . . . . . . . . . . . . . . . . . . . . | 2,400 | 1,800 | 600 |

In a normal year, the company conducts 2,400 inspections to sample the quality of raw materials. The large number of Amithol-related inspections is due to quality problems experienced in the past. The quality of Bitrite materials has been consistently good.

### Instructions

**a.** Assign the Purchasing Department's costs to the individual cost pools.

**b.** Allocate the order cost pool to the individual product lines.

**c.** Allocate the inspection cost pool to the individual product lines.

**d.** Suggest how Norton might reduce manufacturing costs incurred by the Purchasing Department.

**PROBLEM 17.7A**

ABC versus Use of a
Single Activity Base

e**X**cel

Dixon Robotics manufactures three robot models: the A3B4, the BC11, and the C3PO. Dixon allocates manufacturing overhead to each model based on machine hours. A large portion of the company's manufacturing overhead costs is incurred by the Maintenance Department. This year, the department anticipates that it will incur $100,000 in total costs. The following estimates pertain to the upcoming year:

| Model | Estimated Machine-Hours | Estimated Units of Production |
|---|---|---|
| A3B4 | 20,000 | 6,250 |
| BC11 | 15,000 | 5,000 |
| C3PO | 5,000 | 2,500 |

Ed Smith, Dixon's cost accountant, suspects that unit costs are being distorted by using a single activity base to allocate Maintenance Department costs to products. Thus, he is considering the implementation of activity-based costing (ABC).

Under the proposed ABC method, the costs of the Maintenance Department would be allocated to the following activity cost pools using the number of work orders as an activity base: (1) the repairs pool and (2) the janitorial pool. Of the 2,000 work orders filed with the Maintenance Department each year, approximately 400 relate to repair activities, and 1,600 relate to janitorial activities.

Machinery repairs correlate with the number of production runs of each robot model. Thus, the repairs pool would be allocated to robots based on each model's corresponding number of production runs. Janitorial services correlate with square feet of production space. Thus, the janitorial pool would be allocated to products based on the square feet of production space devoted to each robot model. The following table provides a summary of annual production run activity and square footage requirements:

| Model | Estimated Number of Production Runs | Estimated Square Feet of Production Space Used |
|---|---|---|
| A3B4 | 50 | 5,000 |
| BC11 | 150 | 10,000 |
| C3PO | 200 | 25,000 |

## Instructions

**a.** Calculate the amount of Maintenance Department costs that would be allocated to each robot model (on a per-unit basis) using machine-hours as a single activity base.

**b.** Calculate the amount of Maintenance Department costs that would be allocated to each robot model (on a per-unit basis) using the proposed ABC method.

**c.** Are cost allocations distorted using machine-hours as a single activity base? Explain your answer.

**L06**
**L07**
**PROBLEM 17.8A**
ABC versus Use of a Single Activity Base

Healthy Hound, Inc., makes two lines of dog food: (1) Basic Chunks, and (2) Custom Cuts. The Basic Chunks line is a dry food that is processed almost entirely by an automated process. Custom Cuts is a canned food made with real horsemeat. The slabs of meat are cut and trimmed by hand before being shoveled into a automated canning machine. Basic Chunks sells very well and is priced significantly below competitive brands. Sales of Custom Cuts have been on the decline, as the company has failed to keep the brand price competitive. Other information concerning each product line is provided below.

| | Basic Chunks | Custom Cuts |
|---|---|---|
| Number of units* produced and sold per month . . . . . . . . . | 50,000 | 20,000 |
| Direct materials cost per unit . . . . . . . . . . . . . . . . . . . . . . | $2 | $4 |
| Direct labor cost per hour . . . . . . . . . . . . . . . . . . . . . . . . . | $12 | $12 |
| Direct labor hours per unit . . . . . . . . . . . . . . . . . . . . . . . . | 0.01 | 0.10 |

*Units for Basic Chunks refer to *bags*; units for Custom Cuts refer to *cases*.

The company currently allocates manufacturing overhead to each product line on the basis of direct labor hours. Budgeted manufacturing overhead per month is $24,600, whereas budgeted direct labor hours amount to 2,500 per month.

Healthy Hound recently hired a consultant to examine its cost accounting system. The consultant recommends that the company adopt activity-based costing to allocate manufacturing overhead. She proposes that the following cost pools and cost drivers be used:

| Cost Pool | Amount Allocated | Cost Driver | Total Driver Volume |
|---|---|---|---|
| Utilities | $ 8,000 | Kilowatt-hours | 100,000 kWh |
| Maintenance | 1,000 | Machine-hours | 200 mh |
| Depreciation of plant and equipment | 15,000 | Square feet occupied | 80,000 sq. ft. |
| Miscellaneous | 600 | Direct labor hours | 2,500 DLH |
| Total allocation | $24,600 | | |

The amount of driver activity corresponding to each product line is as follows:

| Cost Driver | Basic Chunks | Custom Cuts |
|---|---|---|
| Kilowatt-hours. . . . . . . . . . . . . . . . . . . . . . . . . . . . . . . . . . | 90,000 kWh | 10,000 kWh |
| Machine-hours . . . . . . . . . . . . . . . . . . . . . . . . . . . . . . . . . . | 160 mh | 40 mh |
| Square feet occupied . . . . . . . . . . . . . . . . . . . . . . . . . . . . . | 60,000 sq. ft. | 20,000 sq. ft. |
| Direct labor hours. . . . . . . . . . . . . . . . . . . . . . . . . . . . . . . . | 500 DLH | 2,000 DLH |

**Instructions**

a.  Allocate *manufacturing overhead* costs to each product line using direct labor hours as a single cost driver.

b.  Allocate *manufacturing overhead* costs to each product line using the activity-based costing approach recommended by the consultant.

c.  Compute the *total monthly manufacturing costs* assigned to each product line when activity-based costing is used to allocate manufacturing overhead.

d.  Assume that the company sets selling prices as a fixed percentage above the total manufacturing costs allocated to each product line. On the basis of your results from parts **a** and **b,** discuss a possible reason why sales of the Custom Cuts product line are currently experiencing a decline.

e.  Discuss reasons why the company should adopt the recommendation of the consultant and implement an activity-based costing system.

## Problem Set B

**L01**  
**through**  
**L05**

**PROBLEM 17.1B**

Job Order Costing: Computations and Journal Entries

Hastings International uses job order costing. Manufacturing overhead is charged to individual jobs through the use of a predetermined overhead rate based on direct labor costs. The following information appears in the company's Work in Process Inventory account for the month of April:

| | |
|---|---|
| Debits to account: | |
| Balance, April 1 . . . . . . . . . . . . . . . . . . . . . . . . . . . . . . . . . . . . . . . . . . . . . . | $12,000 |
| Direct materials . . . . . . . . . . . . . . . . . . . . . . . . . . . . . . . . . . . . . . . . . . . . . . | 18,000 |
| Direct labor . . . . . . . . . . . . . . . . . . . . . . . . . . . . . . . . . . . . . . . . . . . . . . . . . . | 15,000 |
| Manufacturing overhead (applied to jobs as 160% of direct labor cost) . . . . . . . . | 24,000 |
| Total debits to account . . . . . . . . . . . . . . . . . . . . . . . . . . . . . . . . . . . . . . . | $69,000 |
| Credits to account: | |
| Transferred to Finished Goods Inventory account . . . . . . . . . . . . . . . . . . . . . . . | 55,000 |
| Balance, April 30 . . . . . . . . . . . . . . . . . . . . . . . . . . . . . . . . . . . . . . . . . . . . . . | $14,000 |

**Instructions**

a.  Assuming that the direct labor charged to the jobs still in process at April 30 amounts to $3,750, compute the amount of manufacturing overhead and the amount of direct materials that have been charged to these jobs as of April 30.

b.  Prepare general journal entries to summarize:

1.  The manufacturing costs (direct materials, direct labor, and overhead) charged to production during April.

2.  The transfer of production completed during April to the Finished Goods Inventory account.

3.  The cash sale of 90 percent of the merchandise completed during April at a total sales price of $77,000. Show the related cost of goods sold in a separate journal entry.

**L01**  
**through**  
**L05**

**PROBLEM 17.2B**

Job Order Costing: Journal Entries and Cost Flows

The following information relates to the manufacturing operations of Fargo Development Co. during the month of July. The company uses job order costing.

a.  Purchases of direct materials during the month amount to $100,000. (All purchases were made on account.)

b.  Materials issued for various jobs in process during the month total $98,000.

c.  Time cards of direct workers show 1,800 hours worked on various jobs during the month, for a total direct labor cost of $54,000.

d.  Direct workers were paid $50,000 in July.

e.  Actual overhead costs for the month amount to $110,000 (for simplicity, you may credit Accounts Payable).

f.  Overhead is applied to jobs at a rate of $60 per direct labor hour.

**g.** Jobs with total accumulated costs of $222,000 were completed during the month.

**h.** During July, units costing $180,000 were sold for $288,000. (All sales were made on account.)

### Instructions

Prepare general journal entries to summarize each of these transactions in the company's general ledger accounts.

**L01**
**through**
**L05**

### PROBLEM 17.3B

Job Order Costing: A Comprehensive Problem

Lincoln Estates manufactures log homes to customers' specifications and uses job order costing. A predetermined overhead rate is used in applying manufacturing overhead to individual jobs. In the Cutting Department, overhead is applied on the basis of machine-hours. In the Assembly Department, overhead is applied on the basis of direct labor hours. At the beginning of the current year, management made the following estimates to assist in determining the overhead application rates:

| Annual Estimates | Cutting Department | Assembly Department |
|---|---|---|
| Direct labor cost . . . . . . . . . . . . . . . . . . . . . . . . . . . . . . . . . . . . | $800,000 | $960,000 |
| Direct labor hours . . . . . . . . . . . . . . . . . . . . . . . . . . . . . . . . . . | 40,000 | 32,000 |
| Manufacturing overhead . . . . . . . . . . . . . . . . . . . . . . . . . . . . . . | $600,000 | $480,000 |
| Machine-hours . . . . . . . . . . . . . . . . . . . . . . . . . . . . . . . . . . . . . | 30,000 | 15,000 |

Production of a home ordered by Cliff Newton (job no. 80) was started early in the year and completed at the end of the first quarter, on March 31. The records for this job show the following cost information:

| | Cutting Department | Assembly Department |
|---|---|---|
| Job order for Cliff Newton (job no. 80): | | |
| Direct materials cost . . . . . . . . . . . . . . . . . . . . . . . . . . . . . . :. . | $100,000 | $150,000 |
| Direct labor cost . . . . . . . . . . . . . . . . . . . . . . . . . . . . . . . . . . | $10,000 | $108,000 |
| Direct labor hours . . . . . . . . . . . . . . . . . . . . . . . . . . . . . . . . . . | 500 | 3,600 |
| Machine-hours . . . . . . . . . . . . . . . . . . . . . . . . . . . . . . . . . . . . | 400 | 300 |

Selected additional information for the first quarter is as follows:

| | Cutting Department | Assembly Department |
|---|---|---|
| Direct labor hours—first quarter . . . . . . . . . . . . . . . . . . . . . . . | 8,000 | 6,000 |
| Machine-hours—first quarter . . . . . . . . . . . . . . . . . . . . . . . . . . | 7,000 | 3,000 |
| Manufacturing overhead incurred in first quarter . . . . . . . . . . . | $142,000 | $87,000 |

### Instructions

**a.** Compute the predetermined overhead rate for each department.

**b.** What is the total cost of the home produced for Cliff Newton?

**c.** Prepare the entries required to record the sale (on account) of the home to Cliff Newton. The sales price of the order was $602,000.

**d.** Determine the over- or underapplied overhead for each department at the end of the first quarter.

**L01**
**through**
**L05**

### PROBLEM 17.4B

Job Order Costing: A Comprehensive Problem

Monark Electronics uses job order costing and applies manufacturing overhead to individual jobs by using predetermined overhead rates. In Department A, overhead is applied on the basis of machine hours, and in Department B, on the basis of direct labor hours. At the beginning of the current year, management made the following budget estimates as a step toward determining the overhead application rates:

| Annual Estimates | Department A | Department B |
|---|---|---|
| Direct labor . . . . . . . . . . . . . . . . . . . . . . . . . . . . . . . . . . . . . . . | $630,000 | $450,000 |
| Manufacturing overhead. . . . . . . . . . . . . . . . . . . . . . . . . | $810,000 | $620,000 |
| Machine-hours . . . . . . . . . . . . . . . . . . . . . . . . . . . . . . . . . | 16,200 | 3,000 |
| Direct labor hours . . . . . . . . . . . . . . . . . . . . . . . . . . . . . . | 25,200 | 24,800 |

Production of 1,000 circuit boards (job no. 652) was started in the middle of January and completed two weeks later. The cost records for this job show the following information:

| | Department A | Department B |
|---|---|---|
| Job no. 652 (1,000 units of product): | | |
| Cost of materials used on job . . . . . . . . . . . . . . . . . . . . | $19,000 | $1,750 |
| Direct labor cost . . . . . . . . . . . . . . . . . . . . . . . . . . . . . | $1,500 | $750 |
| Direct labor hours . . . . . . . . . . . . . . . . . . . . . . . . . . . . | 60 | 40 |
| Machine-hours . . . . . . . . . . . . . . . . . . . . . . . . . . . . . . | 180 | 120 |

### Instructions

**a.** Determine the overhead rate that should be used for each department in applying overhead costs to job no. 652.

**b.** What is the total cost of job no. 652, and what is the unit cost of the product manufactured on this production order?

**c.** Prepare the journal entries required to record the sale (on account) of all 1,000 circuit boards to Computex Computers. The total sales price was $50,000.

**d.** Assume that actual overhead costs for the year were $800,000 in Department A and $615,000 in Department B. Actual machine-hours in Department A were 16,500, and actual direct labor hours in Department B were 24,000 during the year. On the basis of this information, determine the over- or underapplied overhead in each department for the year.

**PROBLEM 17.5B**

L01 through L05

Drivers for Drivers

Big Boomers makes custom clubs for golfers. The company also provides repair services for golfers with broken clubs. Most of the work is done by hand and with small tools used by craftsmen. Customers are quoted a price in advance of their clubs being manufactured or repaired. To produce and repair clubs at a profit, management must have a thorough understanding of product costs.

Jeff Ranck, manager of the business, is considering using either direct labor hours or the number of jobs as the basis for allocating overhead costs. He has estimated the following amounts for the coming year:

| | |
|---|---|
| Estimated total overhead. . . . . . . . . . . . . . . . . . . . . . . . . . . . . . . . . . . . . . . . . . . . . . | $180,000 |
| Estimated direct labor hours . . . . . . . . . . . . . . . . . . . . . . . . . . . . . . . . . . . . . . . . . . | 15,000 |
| Estimated number of jobs . . . . . . . . . . . . . . . . . . . . . . . . . . . . . . . . . . . . . . . . . . . . | 2,500 |

### Instructions

**a.** Compute the overhead application rate based on (**1**) direct labor hours and (**2**) the number of jobs.

**b.** Shown below is information for two customer orders:

**Job 1**  Manufacture a full set of custom clubs. Direct materials used, $300; direct labor hours, 12; direct labor cost, $276.

**Job 2**  Repair broken putter and replace grips on a full set of irons. Direct materials used, $100; direct labor hours, 3; direct labor cost, $60.

Determine the *total cost* of each job assuming that overhead costs are applied on the basis of:

**1.** Direct labor hours

**2.** Number of jobs

**c.** Discuss the results obtained in part **b**. Which overhead application method appears to provide more realistic results? Explain the reasoning behind your answer.

**PROBLEM 17.6B**

Applying Overhead Costs Using ABC

Logan Pharmaceutical produces two products: Caltrate and Dorkamine. The company uses activity-based costing (ABC) to allocate manufacturing costs to each product line. The costs incurred by the Quality Control Department average $5 million per year and constitute one of the largest components of the company's total manufacturing overhead.

The Quality Control Department conducts routine inspections at two critical points. First, all raw materials are inspected before they are entered into the production process. Second, all completed batches of product are inspected before being shipped to the finished goods warehouse. The department's costs are assigned to two activity cost pools: (1) preproduction inspections, and (2) postproduction inspections. Costs are assigned to the pools based on the number of employees engaged in each activity. Of the department's 16 full-time employees, 4 are responsible for preproduction inspections and 12 are responsible for postproduction inspections.

Costs assigned to the preproduction pool are allocated to products based on the number of materials shipments received for each product line. Costs assigned to the postproduction pool are allocated to products based on the number of batches of each product produced.

For the upcoming year, Logan Pharmaceutical estimates the following activity levels:

|  | Total | Caltrate | Dorkamine |
|---|---|---|---|
| Shipments received | 1,200 | 900 | 300 |
| Batches produced | 2,000 | 400 | 1,600 |

The materials used to produce Caltrate can be ordered only in small quantities and therefore must be ordered frequently. The company's four preproduction inspectors devote a disproportionate amount of their time inspecting the 900 shipments of Caltrate materials. Dorkamine can be produced only in small batches and therefore must be produced frequently. Most of the problems associated with completed batches of Dorkamine can be traced to poor-quality materials. Very few problems are associated with the quality of Caltrate materials.

**Instructions**

**a.** Assign the Quality Control Department's costs to the individual cost pools.

**b.** Allocate the preproduction cost pool to each product line.

**c.** Allocate the inspection cost pool to each product line.

**d.** Suggest how Logan Pharmaceutical might reassign responsibilities to make better use of its quality control inspectors.

**PROBLEM 17.7B**

ABC versus Use of a Single Activity Base

Downhill Fast manufactures three ski products: boots, poles, and helmets. The company allocates manufacturing costs to each product line based on machine-hours. A large portion of its manufacturing overhead cost is incurred by the Maintenance Department. This year, the department anticipates that it will incur $250,000 in total costs. The following estimates pertain to the upcoming year:

| Product | Estimated Machine-Hours | Estimated Units of Production |
|---|---|---|
| Boots | 5,000 | 50,000 |
| Poles | 10,000 | 200,000 |
| Helmets | 35,000 | 20,000 |

Carol Safooma, the company's cost accountant, suspects that unit costs are being distorted by using a single activity base to allocate Maintenance Department costs to products. She is considering the implementation of an activity-based costing system (ABC).

Under the proposed ABC system, the maintenance costs would be allocated to the following activity cost pools using the number of work orders as an activity base: (1) the equipment set-up pool, and (2) the custodial pool. Of the 2,400 work orders filed with the Maintenance Department each year, approximately 600 relate to equipment set-up activities, whereas 1,800 relate to custodial functions.

Equipment set-ups correlate with the number of production runs associated with each product line. Thus, the equipment set-up pool would be allocated based on the number of production runs required for each product. Custodial services correlate with square feet of production space and would be allocated based on the space required to produce each product line. The following table provides a summary of annual production activity and square footage requirements:

| Product | Estimated Production Runs | Estimated Square Feet of Production Space |
|---------|--------------------------|-------------------------------------------|
| Boots ............................ | 500 | 9,000 |
| Poles ............................ | 300 | 15,000 |
| Helmets .......................... | 200 | 6,000 |

### Instructions

a. Calculate the amount of Maintenance Department costs that would be allocated to each product line (on a per-unit basis) using machine-hours as a single activity base.

b. Calculate the amount of Maintenance Department costs that would be allocated to each product line (on a per-unit basis) using the proposed ABC system.

c. Are cost allocations currently being distorted using machine-hours as a single activity base? Defend your answer.

**PROBLEM 17.8B**

ABC versus Use of a Single Activity Base

Happy Cat, Inc., makes two lines of cat food: (1) Tabby Treat, and (2) Fresh n' Fishy. The Tabby Treat line is a dry food that is processed almost entirely by an automated process. Fresh n' Fishy is a canned food made with real carp from the Mississippi River. Each carp is filleted by hand before being tossed into an automated grinding and canning machine. Tabby Treat sells very well and is priced significantly below competitive brands. Sales of Fresh n' Fishy have been on the decline, as the company has failed to keep the brand price competitive. Other information concerning each product line is provided below.

| | Tabby Treat | Fresh n' Fishy |
|---|---|---|
| Number of units* produced and sold per month...................... | 75,000 | 48,000 |
| Direct materials cost per unit ..................................... | $1 | $3 |
| Direct labor cost per hour ........................................ | $16 | $16 |
| Direct labor hours per unit........................................ | 0.04 | 0.25 |

*Units for Tabby Treat refer to *bags*. Units for Fresh n' Fishy refer to *cases*.

The company currently allocates manufacturing overhead to each product line on the basis of direct labor hours. Budgeted manufacturing overhead per month is $60,000, whereas budgeted direct labor hours amount to 15,000 per month.

Happy Cat recently hired a consultant to examine its cost accounting system. The consultant recommends that the company adopt activity-based costing to allocate manufacturing overhead. He proposes that the following cost pools and cost drivers be used:

| Cost Pool | Amount Allocated | Cost Driver | Total Driver Volume |
|-----------|------------------|-------------|---------------------|
| Utilities | $26,000 | Kilowatt-hours | 250,000 kWh |
| Maintenance | 19,000 | Machine set-ups | 100 set-ups |
| Depreciation of plant and equipment | 12,000 | Square feet occupied | 50,000 sq. ft. |
| Miscellaneous | 3,000 | Direct labor hours | 15,000 DLH |
| Total allocation | $60,000 | | |

The amount of driver activity corresponding to each product line is as follows:

| Cost Driver | Tabby Treat | Fresh n' Fishy |
|-------------|-------------|----------------|
| Kilowatt-hours.................................... | 200,000 kWh | 50,000 kWh |
| Machine set-ups.................................. | 70 mh | 30 mh |
| Square feet occupied ............................ | 42,000 sq. ft. | 8,000 sq. ft. |
| Direct labor hours................................ | 3,000 DLH | 12,000 DLH |

## Instructions

**a.** Allocate *manufacturing overhead* costs to each product line using direct labor hours as a single cost driver.

**b.** Allocate *manufacturing overhead* costs to each product line using the activity-based costing approach recommended by the consultant.

**c.** Compute the *total monthly manufacturing costs* assigned to each product line when activity-based costing is used to allocate manufacturing overhead.

**d.** Assume that the company sets selling prices as a fixed percentage above the total manufacturing costs allocated to each product line. On the basis of your results from parts **a** and **b,** discuss a possible reason why sales of the Fresh n' Fishy product line are currently experiencing a decline.

**e.** Discuss reasons why the company should adopt the recommendation of the consultant to implement an activity-based costing system.

# Critical Thinking Cases

L01
L03
L06
L07

**CASE 17.1**

Effect of Overhead Application on Performance Evaluation

Classic Cabinets has one factory in which it produces two product lines. Walter manages the Wood Division, which produces wood cabinets, and Mary manages the Metal Division, which produces metal cabinets. Estimated unit production costs for the two types of cabinets are as follows:

|  | Wood | Metal |
|---|---|---|
| Direct materials. | $50.00 | $35.00 |
| Direct labor cost | 20.00 | 30.00 |
| Manufacturing overhead | 16.30 | 24.45 |
| Total production cost per unit | $86.30 | $89.45 |
| | | |
| Selling price per unit | $180 | $160 |
| Direct labor hours required per unit | 2 | 3 |
| Direct labor cost per hour | $10 | $10 |

At the end of the year, total overhead costs are allocated to each division based on direct labor hours used. A breakdown of estimated yearly overhead costs is as follows:

| | |
|---|---|
| Salaries: | |
| Walter. | $ 50,000 |
| Mary. | 50,000 |
| Maintenance | 20,000 |
| Utilities. | 16,000 |
| Property taxes | 10,000 |
| Annual straight-line depreciation: | |
| Equipment, Wood Division. | 80,000 |
| Equipment, Metal Division | 120,000 |
| Total overhead | $346,000 |

Demand for cabinets over the past several years has been steady and is not expected to change. The Marketing Department estimates that approximately 10,000 wood cabinets and 7,500 metal cabinets will be sold each year for the foreseeable future. Each manager's performance evaluation is based on the total production cost per unit for his or her product line. The manager that succeeds in reducing unit costs by the greatest amount from those estimated will earn a bonus.

Mary is considering purchasing a new machine for $500,000 that will last approximately 10 years and have no salvage value. If the machine is purchased, the direct labor hours required to produce a metal cabinet will be reduced to 2.5 hours.

**Instructions**

**a.** If the machine is purchased, what will be the total unit costs of production for each type of cabinet, assuming all other cost and production estimates are correct?

**b.** From Mary's point of view, should the machine be purchased? Discuss whether Mary and Walter should be given sole authority over which equipment to purchase for their respective divisions.

**c.** What information do you think is necessary to decide whether to purchase the machine?

**d.** If the machine is purchased, do you think the performance evaluation of Walter and Mary will be accurate and fair under the current system?

**LO6**
**LO7**

**CASE 17.2**

Implementing ABC

Dave Miller is the controller of Mica Corporation. Mica produces five industrial cleaning products. Miller recently decided to implement activity-based costing at Mica. In designing the system, he decided to identify heating costs as a separate cost pool. These costs will be allocated to products using the square feet of production space as a cost driver. Thus, the more square footage a particular product line requires, the greater its allocation of heating costs will be.

Miller has asked each production manager to submit an estimate of the production space occupied by their respective product lines. The figures he receives will be used to allocate the heating cost pool. The five production managers at Mica are paid an annual bonus based on their ability to control production costs traceable to their respective product lines.

**Instructions**

**a.** What ethical concern do you have regarding the method used to gather information about space utilization at Mica?

**b.** What suggestions do you have regarding how this information should be gathered?

**LO1**
**LO2**
**LO4**

**CASE 17.3**

The Bidding Wars

Kendahl Plastics Corporation contracts with NASA to manufacture component parts used in communications satellites. NASA reimburses Kendahl on the basis of the actual manufacturing costs it incurs, plus a fixed percentage. Prior to being awarded a contract, Kendahl must submit a bid that details the estimated costs associated with each project. An examination of Kendahl's job cost sheets reveals that actual costs consistently exceed cost estimates quoted during the bidding process. As a consequence, NASA ends up paying considerably more than the bids Kendahl submits.

A Kendahl representative was recently quoted as saying, "We really aren't overcharging NASA for the work that we do. The actual costs shown on our job cost sheets seem high only because we are forced to understate our bid estimates in order to be awarded contracts. It's a common practice, and everybody does it. The truth of the matter is companies that quote realistic bid prices are not awarded contracts."

**Instructions**

Let us assume that it is common practice to purposely underestimate bids in order to win NASA contracts. Is it wrong for Kendahl to take part in this activity as long as it does not overstate the actual costs it incurs?

**LO1**
**LO2**
**LO4**
**LO7**

**INTERNET CASE 17.4**

Costing Construction Work

C. Erickson and Sons, Inc., is a Philadelphia-based construction company. Visit its home page at the following address:

www.cerickson.com

**Instructions**

**a.** Identify three projects and/or services provided by the company.

**b.** For each project or service identified, explain how cost accounting information would be useful to the company in providing the service or creating the project.

**c.** Which projects or services that you have identified would be most likely to benefit from job order costing and/or activity-based costing? Explain why.

*Internet sites are time and date sensitive. It is the purpose of these exercises to have you explore the Internet. You may need to use the Yahoo! search engine http://www.yahoo.com (or another favorite search engine) to find a company's current Web address.*

## Answers to Self-Test Questions

**1.** b  **2.** c  **3.** a  **4.** a  **5.** a, c, d  **6.** b  **7.** d

# CHAPTER 18

# Process Costing

AFTER STUDYING THIS CHAPTER, YOU SHOULD BE ABLE TO:

**LO1** Distinguish production procedures that match with process costing from those that correspond with job order costing.

**LO2** Account for the physical flows and related cost flows when using process costing.

**LO3** Demonstrate how to calculate equivalent units.

**LO4** Use the costs of resources consumed to calculate the cost per equivalent unit of production.

**LO5** Use the cost per equivalent unit to assign costs to the work completed during the period.

**LO6** Create a process costing production report and use the report for decision making.

Learning Objectives

# KELLOGG COMPANY

Located in Battle Creek, Michigan, Kellogg Company uses production methods that are ideal for process costing. William Kellogg's accidental discovery of cereal in 1894 illustrates these methods. While experimenting with different food production techniques at the Battle Creek Sanatorium in Michigan, William and his brother, Dr. John Kellogg, decided to run boiled wheat dough through rollers, which enabled them to produce thin sheets of wheat. After a sudden interruption in their laboratory activities left cooked wheat exposed to the air for more than a day, the Kellogg brothers decided to run the wheat through the rollers despite the fact it was no longer fresh. To their amazement, instead of a single, large sheet of wheat, the rollers discharged a single flake for each wheat berry—and cereal flakes were born.

With net sales in excess of $12.5 billion, Kellogg Company is the world's leading producer of cereal and a leading producer of convenience foods, including cookies, crackers, toaster pastries, cereal bars, frozen waffles, meat alternatives, pie crusts, and ice cream cones. Kellogg products are manufactured in 19 countries and marketed in more than 160 countries around the world. ∎

# Production of Goods and Services and Costing Systems

Business owners and managers rely heavily upon information provided by **cost accounting systems.** Costing systems provide information that is used for a large variety of business decisions, including planning production of goods and services, pricing products, and controlling associated costs of production. Thus, the choice of an appropriate costing system is a key underlying foundation for good decision making. In choosing the appropriate cost systems, managers carefully consider how products and services are created. The production procedures for goods and services are matched to the appropriate costing system.

A production procedure that results in a large number of identical products, such as described for Kellogg's cornflakes in the chapter opener, is a candidate for process costing procedures. **Process costing** is a method for accumulating the direct and indirect costs of a production process and averaging those costs over the identical units produced by that process. Process costing differs from **job order costing** because job order costing traces specific direct costs, that is, direct labor and direct materials, to the specific job being created. In addition, job order costing applies overhead to jobs using an activity base representing resources consumed by the job. However, process costing averages direct and indirect costs across mass-produced identical units.

As we discussed in the previous chapter, processes that result in unique services, products, or batches are well suited to job order costing. Thus, automobile repair, furniture creation, lawn services, and accounting services are examples of production processes consistent with job order costing. Alternatively, packaged food products, oil and gas, paint, compact disks, television sets, textiles, and hand tools are examples of products that are created by production procedures suited for process costing. Exhibit 18–1 compares the production characteristics that help managers decide if job order or process costing is appropriate for their businesses.

**Learning Objective**

**L01**

**Learning Objective**

Distinguish production procedures that match with process costing from those that correspond with job order costing.

**Exhibit 18–1**

**DISTINGUISHING JOB ORDER AND PROCESS COSTING OPERATIONS**

| Job Order Costing | Process Costing |
|---|---|
| Product characteristics: | Product characteristics: |
| • Use different amounts of direct materials | • Are high volume |
| • Use different amounts of direct labor | • Are identical |
| • Tend to be unique | • Use identical amounts of direct materials |
| • Are typically low volume | • Use identical amounts of direct labor |
| • Are often custom-ordered | • Are created with repetitive operations |

Of course, we know that many businesses have multiple operations associated with creating goods and services. Some of these operations may be consistent with a job order costing system and some of these operations may be better suited to process costing procedures. For example, consider Dell Computer's goal of custom designing computer systems to customer-ordered specifications. Customer specifications differ widely and create unique products delivered to the customer's door. However, most of the system components, such as monitors and keyboards, are the product of mass production processes. Process costing systems are useful to track costs associated with the manufacture of the keyboard, but job order costing procedures are useful to track the specific combination of components ordered by individual customers. Thus, it is not uncommon to find companies that use both types of costing systems simultaneously. Surveys show that job order costing is more widely used than process costing, but that a majority of companies use both types of systems.

INTERNATIONAL CASE IN POINT

A survey* of 141 manufacturers shows that 51 percent use job order costing, 14 percent use process costing, and another 11 percent use combinations of costing methods. The same survey shows that direct materials costs are 47 percent of the total manufacturing costs, followed by overhead costs (38 percent) and direct labor (15 percent). As companies become more automated, and as labor is continually outsourced to countries with lower wage rates, overhead costs will increase as direct labor costs decrease. Such trends in overhead and automation frequently require the use of process costing procedures.

*See E. Shim and J. Larkin, "A Survey of Current Managerial Accounting Practices: Where Do We Stand?" *Ohio CPA Journal* 53(1), pp. 21–27.

## Process Costing

Many companies produce a *continuous stream of identical units,* such as bottles of beer, gallons of gasoline, or kilowatt-hours of electricity. When identical products are produced in a continuous stream, there are no distinct "jobs." Therefore, companies engaging in mass production often use *process costing* rather than job order costing.

Mass production usually involves a series of specific steps, or manufacturing *processes.* Process costing measures separately the cost of performing *each process* and then allocates these costs to the units processed during the month.

Process costing serves two related purposes. First, it measures the cost of goods manufactured on both a total and per-unit basis. This information is used in valuing inventories and in recording the cost of goods sold. But process costing also provides management with information about the *per-unit cost of performing each step* in the production process. This information is useful in evaluating the *efficiency* of production departments and often draws attention to potential cost savings.

CASE IN POINT

Large bottles of Heinz ketchup used to have two labels—one in front and one on the back. Through a careful analysis of manufacturing costs, production managers found that Heinz could save several hundred thousand dollars per year by applying only one label.

## TRACKING THE PHYSICAL FLOW AND RELATED PRODUCTION COSTS

**Understanding Physical Flows**    Because process costing involves averaging costs across products produced, it is very important to know the actual units worked on and those transferred out during the period. Therefore, one of the first steps in process costing is to make sure there is a clear understanding of the physical flow of products during the period in which costs are being assigned to products.

We use the company Metal Products, Inc., to illustrate the steps in process costing. Metal Products produces small metal souvenir products such as key rings and bottle openers. Production of these souvenirs occurs in three sequential departments, the Cutting Department, the Assembly Department, and the Packaging Department. Each department is considered to be a separate process in the production of the final product. Exhibit 18–2 describes the processes that occur in each department.

Exhibit 18–2 **PRODUCTION PROCESS FOR METAL PRODUCTS, INC.**

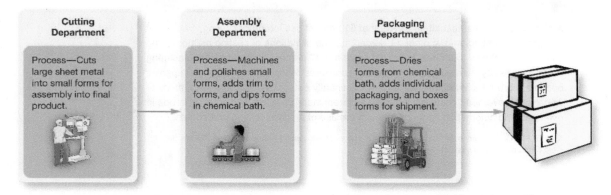

**Learning Objective**

**L02** Account for the physical flows and related cost flows when using process costing.

Production begins at Metal Products when rolled sheet metal is shipped into the Cutting Department and put into production. The Cutting Department tracks usage of the sheet metal by pounds until cutting produces the souvenir form (for example, a key chain or bottle opener). When the forms are transferred to the Assembly Department they become units. Throughout the remainder of the production process, units are used to track and assign costs of production. Exhibit 18–3 shows the typical physical flow of units and costs associated with Metal Products, Inc., for one month. Notice in the exhibit that it is important to know the number of units that are in four categories: (1) beginning work in process, (2) the number of units started during the period, (3) the number of units transferred to the next department during the period, and (4) the number of units in ending work in process. When you know where all units are during a period, then you know the physical flow.

Exhibit 18–3 **PHYSICAL FLOWS AND COST FLOWS FOR PROCESS COSTING**

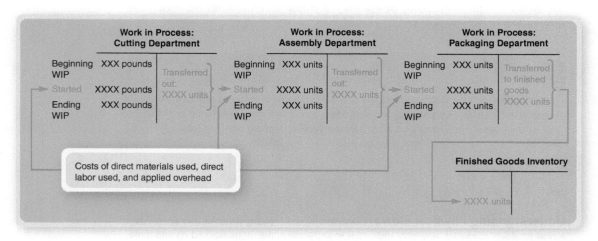

**Understanding Cost Flows**   Process costing uses a separate Work in Process Inventory account to measure the costs incurred in *each production process.* Costs flow through these accounts *in sequence,* just as the units on an assembly line move from one production process to the next. Only when the units complete the *final* production process are their costs transferred to the Finished Goods Inventory account.

**Accounting for Material, Labor, and Applied Overhead**   Each Work in Process account is charged (debited) for the materials used, direct labor, and overhead that relate to *that specific process.* For example, only those materials that require cutting are charged to the Cutting Department. Component parts sent directly to the Assembly Department are charged to the Assembly Department's Work in Process account. Direct labor and overhead costs related to the work done in that department also are applied separately to each Work in Process account.

### Costs Flow from One Process to the Next

Units in production pass from one process to the next. Process costing parallels this physical flow of units by transferring their *cost* from one Work in Process account to the next.

Assume that during the current month, $200,000 in manufacturing costs (including direct materials, direct labor, and overhead) were charged to the Cutting Department. Assume also that this department cut enough material to manufacture 10,000 units of product, and that the cut materials were transferred to the Assembly Department. At month-end, the following journal entry would be made to summarize the transfer of cut materials during the month:

| | | |
|---|---|---|
| Work in Process: Assembly Department ......................... | 200,000 | |
|     Work in Process: Cutting Department ..................... | | 200,000 |
| To transfer cost of processed units from the Cutting Department to the Assembly Department. Cutting cost per unit, $20 ($200,000 ÷ 10,000 units). | | |

**Transferring work from one department to the next**

In essence, the output of the Cutting Department is a form of "direct materials" charged to the Assembly Department.

Notice that we transferred *all $200,000* of the Cutting Department's production costs to the Assembly Department. In effect, we assumed that all of the Cutting Department's costs are applicable to the *units completed and transferred during the month.*

## PROCESS COSTING AND EQUIVALENT UNITS

Although some companies do not have significant ending work in process inventories, others that do must assign production costs to unfinished units. Consider the Assembly Department of Metal Products, Inc. As illustrated previously in Exhibit 18–2, the Assembly Department receives cut materials from the Cutting Department and processes them further by consuming additional direct labor, direct materials, and overhead.

Assume that the cut materials transferred in from the Cutting Department are first machined and polished. Let's say that this step represents 30 percent of the assembly process. Next, additional trim material is added to the polished cut units. Assume that this step represents 50 percent of the assembly process. Finally, before being transferred to the Packaging Department, the nearly completed units must be washed in a chemical bath. This step represents the final 20 percent of the assembly process. Because direct labor and overhead costs are incurred uniformly throughout the period, they are lumped together for convenience and referred to as **conversion costs.** Exhibit 18–4 illustrates the three steps of the production process in the Assembly Department.

Assume that, at the end of March, the Assembly Department has 3,000 units in process that are 80 percent finished (that is, they have not yet undergone step 3, the chemical bath). As discussed in previous chapters, any significant costs incurred in creating partially finished units should be assigned to work in process inventories.

In process costing systems, unfinished units are restated in terms of **equivalent units.** An equivalent unit is a percentage measure of a completed unit's resource requirements present in a partially finished unit. Thus, the Assembly Department's work in process that is 80 percent complete on March 31 is considered *100 percent* complete with respect to the cut material transferred in from the Cutting Department and the trim material added in the Assembly Department. In other words, the materials used to partially complete these units are *equivalent* to the materials needed to produce 3,000 *finished* units. These same units are only 80 percent complete with respect to their conversion requirements (direct labor and overhead). The conversion required to make 3,000 units 80 percent complete is *equivalent* to the conversion required to make 2,400 units 100 percent complete (3,000 units × 80%). Thus, we can say

Exhibit 18–4

**STEPS IN THE PRODUCTION PROCESS AT METAL PRODUCTS, INC.**

**ASSEMBLY DEPARTMENT PRODUCTION PROCESS**

Add cut
materials from
Cutting Department

Add other
direct materials
(trim pieces)

Finish and
send to Packaging
Department

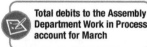

Step 1:
Machining and polishing
(30% of assembly process)

Step 2:
Trim added
(50% of assembly process)

Step 3:
Chemical bath
(20% of assembly process)

Direct labor and overhead added over the entire process

that ending inventory in the Assembly Department is comprised of 1,000 equivalent units of cut material transferred in from the Cutting Department, 1,000 equivalent units of trim material added in step 2, and 2,400 equivalent units of conversion added throughout the period. We will see that expressing resources consumed in terms of equivalent units enables companies to better understand the costs of production.

To illustrate process costing more fully, consider a typical month in the Assembly Department. Let's assume that on March 1, 1,000 units were in process. These units were 30 percent complete (they had not yet been through step 2 or step 3). During March, 10,000 units of cut materials were transferred from the Cutting Department to the Assembly Department. On March 31, there were 3,000 units in process. These units were 80 percent complete with respect to their conversion (they had not yet been through step 3). Exhibit 18–5 summarizes the costs accounted for by the Assembly Department in March.

Exhibit 18–5

**MARCH COSTS IN THE ASSEMBLY DEPARTMENT**

Total debits to the Assembly Department Work in Process account for March

| | |
|---|---:|
| Beginning work in process (March 1) | $ 29,500 |
| Cut materials transferred from Cutting Department in March | 200,000 |
| Trim materials added in March | 44,000 |
| Direct labor incurred in March | 105,000 |
| Overhead incurred in March | 147,500 |
| Total costs to account for in March | $526,000 |

During March, the Assembly Department transferred 8,000 completed units to the Packaging Department. Of the units transferred, 1,000 were the units of beginning inventory carried forward from February, and 7,000 were units *started and completed* in March. Assuming a first-in, first-out (FIFO) physical flow of units, these amounts can be computed as follows:

Computing started and completed units is an important step in tracking equivalent units of production

| | |
|---|---:|
| Beginning inventory, March 1 | 1,000 |
| Add: Units started in March (units transferred in from the Cutting Department) | 10,000 |
| Total units in process | 11,000 |
| Less: Ending inventory, March 31 | 3,000 |
| Units transferred to the Packaging Department in March | 8,000 |
| Less: Beginning inventory | 1,000 |
| Units started and completed in March | 7,000 |

Given the physical flow of units shown above, Exhibit 18–6 summarizes the equivalent units of resource inputs consumed by the Assembly Department in March.

| Resources Used to: | Equivalent Units of Resource Inputs in March | | |
| --- | --- | --- | --- |
| | Cut Materials Transferred in | Trim Materials | Conversion |
| Finish beginning work in process, 1,000 units . . . | –0– | 1,000 | 700 |
| Start and complete 7,000 new units . . . . . . . . . . . | 7,000 | 7,000 | 7,000 |
| Start (but not complete) 3,000 new units . . . . . . . | 3,000 | 3,000 | 2,400 |
| Total equivalent units of input in March. . . . . . . | 10,000 | 11,000 | 10,100 |

**Exhibit 18–6**

EQUIVALENT UNITS OF RESOURCE INPUTS IN MARCH

**Learning Objective**
Demonstrate how to calculate equivalent units. **L03**

The first row of figures in Exhibit 18–6 represents the equivalent units of resource inputs required to *finish* the 1,000 units of beginning inventory carried forward from February. Zero equivalent units of cut materials were required in March to complete these units because all of their cut material was transferred to the Assembly Department in February. These 1,000 units had only gone through step 1 of the assembly process (machining and polishing), so to finish them required 100 percent of their trim materials, or 1,000 equivalent units. Having completed step 1 of the assembly process, the units in beginning inventory had received 30 percent of their conversion requirements in February. Thus, they required an additional 70 percent of their conversion resource inputs, or 700 equivalent units to complete them in March (1,000 units × 70 percent conversion added in March).

The second row of figures in Exhibit 18–6 reveals that the 7,000 units started and completed in March required 100 percent of each resource input, or 7,000 equivalent units of cut materials, 7,000 units of trim materials, and 7,000 units of conversion.

The third row of figures in Exhibit 18–6 indicates the equivalent units of resource inputs required to *start but not finish* the 3,000 units in ending inventory on March 31. These units were fully processed through step 1 and step 2 of the assembly process. Thus, they had received 100 percent of their cut materials and trim materials in March, or 3,000 equivalent units of each. However, because these units had not undergone step 3 of the assembly process (the chemical bath), they had received only 80 percent of their conversion resource inputs, or 2,400 equivalent units (3,000 units × 80 percent conversion added in March).

## COST PER EQUIVALENT UNIT

To determine the amount of cost to assign to the four types of work completed—beginning work in process, ending work in process, started and completed, and transferred out—managers compute the cost per equivalent unit. This simple averaging technique divides the cost accumulated for each resource in a given time frame by the associated total equivalent units for each resource. For example, divide the total trim materials cost for March, $44,000, by the total equivalent units for trim, 11,000 (shown in Exhibit 18–6), to get $4 of trim cost per equivalent unit. Exhibit 18–7 provides the details of the computation of the cost per equivalent unit of each resource input used in March by the Assembly Department.

**Learning Objective**
Use the costs of resources consumed to calculate the cost per equivalent unit of production. **L04**

**Exhibit 18–7**   COST PER EQUIVALENT UNIT OF RESOURCE INPUTS IN MARCH

| | Cut Materials Transferred in | Trim Materials | Conversion |
| --- | --- | --- | --- |
| Total cost of resources used in March (from Exhibit 18–5) . . . . . . . . . . . . . . . . . . | $200,000 | $44,000 | $252,500 |
| Equivalent units of resource inputs in March (from Exhibit 18–6) . . . . . . . . . . . . . | 10,000 | 11,000 | 10,100 |
| Cost per equivalent unit of resource inputs in March . . . . . . . . . . . . . . . . . . . . . . | $ 20 | $ 4 | $ 25 |

The total per-unit cost of the started and completed units in March is $49 ($20 + $4 + $25). The costs of the resource inputs and the associated units transferred in March for the Assembly Department are shown in the Work in Process T account in Exhibit 18–8.

Exhibit 18–8

**ASSIGN COST TO
PRODUCTION**

| Details for the Assembly Department Work in Process Inventory for March | | | |
|---|---|---|---|
| Beg. balance | | Cost transferred to Packaging: | |
| (1,000 units) | $ 29,500 | (8,000 units) | |
| | | (1) From beg. work in process: | |
| Direct labor | 105,000 | Beg. balance | $ 29,500 |
| | | Work in March | |
| Direct materials: | | Trim (1,000 × $4) | 4,000 |
| From Cutting Dept. | 200,000 | Conversion | |
| Trim | 44,000 | (700 × $25) | 17,500 |
| | | (2) Started and completed | |
| Overhead | 147,500 | (7,000 × $49) | 343,000 |
| Total to account for: | $526,000 | Total transferred out (8,000 units) | $394,000 |
| Ending balance | | | |
| Direct materials: | | | |
| Cut (3,000 equivalent units × $20) | $ 60,000 | | |
| Trim (3,000 equivalent units × $4) | 12,000 | | |
| Conversion (2,400 equivalent units × $25) | 60,000 | | |
| Total ending work in process (3,000 units) | $132,000 | | |

**Learning Objective**

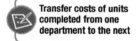

**L05**  Use the cost per equivalent unit to assign costs to the work completed during the period

The 3,000 units in ending work in process are assigned $132,000, which will be the April beginning Work in Process balance. During the month of March, $394,000 of costs are transferred from Assembly to Packaging. The following journal entry would be made to summarize the transfer of costs from Assembly to Packaging:

**Transfer costs of units completed from one department to the next**

| | | |
|---|---|---|
| Work in Process: Packaging. . . . . . . . . . . . . . . . . . . . . . . . . . . . . . . . . . . | 394,000 | |
| Work in Process: Assembly. . . . . . . . . . . . . . . . . . . . . . . . . . . . . . | | 394,000 |
| To transfer cost of completely processed units from the Assembly Department to the Packaging Department. | | |

Notice that the $394,000 transferred from Assembly to Packaging includes a portion of the $200,000 previously transferred from Cutting to Assembly. Eventually, all of the company's manufacturing costs will be transferred to Cost of Goods Sold in the income statement.

**YOUR TURN**    **You as a Cost Accountant**

Assume that you have been hired as the cost accountant of a large candy manufacturer. The company currently uses a process costing system to assign costs to several work in process accounts. You observe that units of production pass very quickly through the various phases of production, often in a matter of hours. To simplify the accounting system, you propose that all manufacturing costs be charged directly to Finished Goods Inventory, thereby eliminating the need to report any work in process in the company's balance sheet. Is this practice ethical? Defend your answer.

(See our comments on the Online Learning Center Web site.)

## TRACKING COSTS USING A PROCESS COSTING PRODUCTION REPORT

In this section we will illustrate how a production cost report is used in a process costing system to help managers track costs. Assume that RainTree Cola produces a bottled soft drink. The company has two production departments: the Syrup Department, which mixes the cola syrup; and the Bottling Department, which bottles a mixture of the syrup and carbonated water.

Assume that on June 1, there were 1,000 gallons of syrup mix in the Syrup Department inventory. Costs associated with the mix carried forward from May 31 totaled $4,400. The mix was 100 percent complete with respect to its direct materials, but only 40 percent complete with respect to its conversion requirements. During June, the Syrup Department started 76,000 new gallons of mix and transferred 75,000 gallons of finished mix to the Bottling Department. June production costs in the Syrup Department were comprised of $304,000 of direct materials and $75,000 of conversion (of which $32,000 was direct labor and $43,000 was manufacturing overhead). At June 30, there were 2,000 gallons of partially processed syrup mix remaining in inventory. The mix was 100 percent complete with respect to its direct materials, but only 20 percent complete with respect to conversion.

© Neil Beer/Getty Images/DAL

Exhibit 18–9 provides a summary of the activity in the Syrup Department for the month of June. This information will later be used to complete the department's production cost report for the month of June.

### Exhibit 18-9
**SUMMARY OF SYRUP DEPARTMENT ACTIVITY IN JUNE**

| Physical Goods Flow in Units (gallons) | | |
|---|---|---|
| Beginning work in process, June 1 | 1,000 | |
| Units (gallons) started in June | 76,000 | |
| Total units in production | 77,000 | |
| Less: Ending work in process, June 30 | 2,000 | |
| Gallons of mix transferred to the Bottling Department | 75,000 | |
| Less: Beginning work in process, June 1 | 1,000 | |
| Units (gallons) started and completed in June | 74,000 | |

| Equivalent Units of Resource Inputs (gallons) | Direct Materials | Conversion |
|---|---|---|
| Finish 1,000 units of beginning work in process inventory: | | |
|   Direct materials (100% complete; require 0%) | 0 | |
|   Conversion (40% complete; requires 60%) | | 600 |
| Units started and completed in June: | 74,000 | 74,000 |
| Start 2,000 units of ending work in process inventory: | | |
|   Direct materials (100% complete) | 2,000 | |
|   Conversion (20% complete) | | 400 |
| Total equivalent units of resource inputs in June | 76,000 | 75,000 |

| Cost per Equivalent Unit of Resource Input in June | Direct Materials | Conversion |
|---|---|---|
| Costs incurred in June | $304,000 | $ 75,000 |
| Total equivalent units of resource inputs in June | ÷ 76,000 | ÷ 75,000 |
| Cost per equivalent unit of input in June | $   4 | $   1 |

The flow of manufacturing costs through RainTree's entire process costing system is illustrated in Exhibit 18–10. The entries in red represent the costs of materials, direct labor, and manufacturing overhead charged to production in June. The entries made to record materials used and direct labor were made *throughout the period,* based on materials requisitions and employee time cards. Overhead was applied at month-end, using a separate overhead application rate for each department. The entries shown in *green* and in *blue* are the entries made at month-end to transfer the cost of units processed during the period from one department to the next.

**Exhibit 18–10**

**PROCESS COSTING UNIT COST FLOWS**

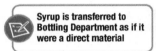

Syrup is transferred to Bottling Department as if it were a direct material

Finished bottles transferred to Finished Goods

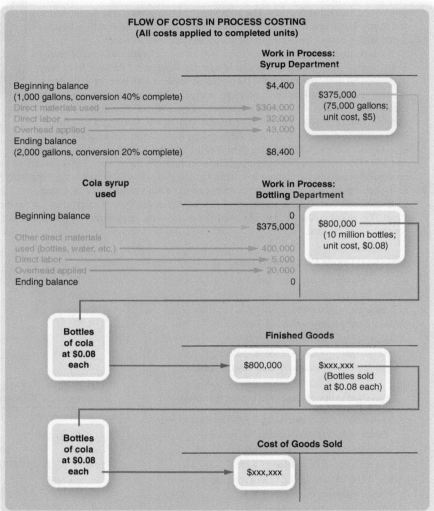

Per-unit processing costs are easily computed using process costing methods—not just for the finished products but also for the output of each department. For example, the cost of finished goods emerging from the Bottling Department this month was *$0.08 per bottle* ($800,000 ÷ 10 million bottles produced); the cost of syrup produced in the Syrup Department was *$5 per gallon* ($375,000 ÷ 75,000 gallons).[1]

**Learning Objective**

**LO6** Create a process costing production report and use the report for decision making

**Production Cost Report for Process Costing**    Companies frequently present the results of operations for a period, typically a month, with a production cost report. The **production cost report** is a summary of the work completed during the period and of the related cost, both per-unit and total costs. Exhibit 18–11 displays the June production cost report for RainTree

---

[1] Notice that, in each of our two departments, "units" of output are defined differently. In the Syrup Department, units are expressed in *gallons of syrup,* whereas in the Bottling Department, units are defined as *bottles of cola.*

Cola's Syrup Department. Because companies design their cost reports to help manage each individual production process, these reports can look different from company to company. However, several common pieces of information are typically contained in these reports.[2]

Exhibit 18–11

**JUNE PRODUCTION COST REPORT FOR RAINTREE COLA SYRUP DEPARTMENT**

| Part I.  Physical Flow | Total Units | | |
|---|---|---|---|
| Inputs: | | | |
| • Beginning WIP | 1,000 | | |
| • Started | 76,000 | | |
| Gallons to account for | 77,000 | | |
| Outputs: | | | |
| • Gallons completed | 75,000 | | |
| • Ending WIP | 2,000 | | |
| Gallons accounted for | 77,000 | | |

| Part II.  Equivalent Units | | Direct Materials | Conversion |
|---|---|---|---|
| Based on monthly input: | | | |
| • Finish beginning WIP | | –0– | 600 |
| • Start new units in June | | 76,000 | 74,400 |
| Equivalent units of input | | 76,000 | 75,000 |
| Based on monthly output: | | | |
| • Units transferred | | 74,000 | 74,600 |
| • Ending WIP | | 2,000 | 400 |
| Equivalent units of output | | 76,000 | 75,000 |

| Part III.  Cost per Equivalent Unit | Total Unit Cost | Direct Materials | Conversion Costs |
|---|---|---|---|
| Cost of input resources, June | | $304,000 | $75,000 |
| Equivalent units, June | | ÷76,000 | ÷75,000 |
| Cost per equivalent unit, June | $5.00 | $4.00 | $1.00 |

| Part IV.  Total Cost Assignment | Total Costs | Direct Materials | Conversion Costs |
|---|---|---|---|
| Costs to account for: | | | |
| • Cost of beginning WIP, June 1 | $    4,400 | | |
| • Cost added in June | 379,000 | | |
| Total cost to account for, June | $383,400 | | |
| Costs accounted for: | | | |
| • Cost of goods transferred in June: | | | |
| Beginning WIP costs, June 1 | $    4,400 | $    4,000[a] | $      400[b] |
| Cost to complete beginning WIP | 600 | –0– | 600[c] |
| Cost of units started and completed | 370,000 | 296,000[d] | 74,000[e] |
| Total cost transferred in June | $375,000 | $300,000 | $75,000 |
| • Add ending WIP, June 30 | 8,400 | 8,000[f] | 400[g] |
| Total cost accounted for in June | $383,400 | $308,000 | $75,400 |

Supporting calculations (figures taken from Exhibit 18–9):
[a] 1,000 equivalent units × $4 = $4,000.
[b] 1,000 equivalent units × 40% complete × $1 = $400.
[c] 1,000 equivalent units × 60% required × $1 = $600.
[d] 74,000 equivalent units × $4 = $296,000.
[e] 74,000 equivalent units × $1 = $74,000.
[f] 2,000 equivalent units × $4 = $8,000.
[g] 2,000 equivalent units × 20% complete × $1 = $400.

---

[2] The production cost report shown in Exhibit 18–11 is typically referred to as a FIFO-based report. That is, physical units and costs are traced on a first-in, first-out basis. Another widely used method is referred to as the weighted-average process costing method. This method averages costs each period over the units transferred out and the ending work in process. The weighted-average method assumes that the difference between beginning and ending work in process is not material in any given month. More advanced accounting courses provide details on both methods.

One function of the production cost report is to trace the physical flow of equivalent units during the period. Notice that the arrows on the side of column 1 in Exhibit 18–11 show that the physical flow is accounted for by identifying both the physical inputs and outputs during the period. This tells management that all inflows during the period are accounted for by matching outflows. Another function of the production cost report is to match cost flows in and out during the period. For example, use the third set of arrows outside column 1 from Exhibit 18–11 to find *Total cost to account for, June,* and *Total cost accounted for in June.* Observe that all costs, including beginning work in process costs and costs added during the period, must be accounted for by assigning those costs to either the units transferred out or the ending work in process.

The production cost report in Exhibit 18–11 also shows that the equivalent unit outcomes are identical when focusing either on the resources consumed by the inputs or the work needed to complete the outputs during the month (second set of arrows). The inputs to the Syrup Department during the current month are direct materials and conversion. For the direct materials resources, all 76,000 gallons started during the month consumed materials (sugar, corn syrup, water, etc.) and are counted as equivalent units of work. On the other hand, for the beginning work in process units, direct materials were added in the previous month and thus, no equivalent units are used for materials.

However, beginning work in process gallons are in need of additional conversion. In fact, 600 equivalent units were needed to finish beginning work in process units. Finally, 74,400 equivalent units of conversion work were completed on the units started during the month including (1) 74,000 started and completed and (2) another 400 equivalent units from 2,000 ending work in process units that were 20 percent complete at the end of the month.

The existence of beginning and ending work in process makes equivalent unit computations one of the more difficult concepts for students. It is helpful, when considering the equivalent units associated with the physical flow of outputs, to remember that the 75,000 gallons transferred from the Syrup Department to the Bottling Department includes 1,000 gallons from beginning work in process and 74,000 gallons out of the 76,000 gallons started during the month.

Exhibit 18–12 provides a more detailed illustration of the equivalent units computations for RainTree Cola's Syrup Department. As shown in the last column of Exhibit 18–12, 600 equivalent units of conversion were needed to finish the beginning work in process gallons and 74,000 conversion equivalent units were needed to finish the remaining gallons transferred out. As shown in column 3 of Exhibit 18–12, 74,000 direct materials equivalent units were needed to finish the gallons started and completed during the month. Because direct materials were added to the beginning work in process in the previous month, no equivalent units of direct materials were used for beginning work in process during the current month. Finally, as shown in the fourth row of Exhibit 18–12, resources were consumed to create the ending work in process gallons. Those resources include 2,000 equivalent units of direct materials added in the current month, but only 400 equivalent units of conversion because ending work in process gallons are only 20 percent processed at month-end.

## Exhibit 18–12

**RAINTREE COLA SYRUP DEPARTMENT ACCOUNTING FOR EQUIVALENT UNITS**

| | Matching Physical Flow | Direct Materials Equivalent Units | Conversion Equivalent Units |
|---|---|---|---|
| Beginning WIP, June 1 | 1,000 gallons (40% complete) | –0– | 600 |
| Started and completed in June: | 74,000 gallons (100% complete) | 74,000 | 74,000 |
| Total equivalent units transferred out: | 75,000 gallons | 74,000 | 74,600 |
| Add ending WIP, June 30 | 2,000 gallons (20% complete) | 2,000 | 400 |
| Total equivalent units during June | | 76,000 | 75,000 |

In summary, a typical production cost report contains the four parts that are shown in bold print in Exhibit 18–11: (1) accounting for the physical flow, (2) determining equivalent units, (3) finding the cost per equivalent unit, and (4) assigning costs to the production for the period. These four parts help management make several decisions related to the production process.

RainTree's management will use the unit cost data provided by process costing for many purposes, including the following:

- Setting sales prices.
- Evaluating the efficiency of manufacturing departments.
- Forecasting future manufacturing costs.
- Valuing inventories and measuring the cost of goods sold, in both financial statements and income tax returns.

| YOUR TURN | **You as a Product-Line Manager** |
|---|---|

Assume you are the manager of the RainTree Cola product line. As one of your responsibilities, you must motivate, evaluate, and reward the performance of the managers of the Syrup Department and the Bottling Department. How could you use process costing information to help with these management responsibilities?

(See our comments on the Online Learning Center Web site.)

## EVALUATING DEPARTMENTAL EFFICIENCY

One of management's key concerns is whether the costs of resource inputs consumed in the current period have risen, fallen, or stayed the same as in prior months. For instance, June unit costs in the Syrup Department were $4 per gallon for direct labor and $1 per gallon for conversion (see Exhibit 18–9 and Exhibit 18–11). These amounts are *exactly the same* as those carried forward from May in the Syrup Department's beginning inventory (1,000 equivalent units of direct materials × $4, plus 400 equivalent units of conversion × $1, equals the Syrup Department's $4,400 beginning inventory balance on June 1). Thus, management may conclude that unit costs in the Syrup Department have held steady from May through June.

In evaluating the efficiency of a production department, management should consider only those costs incurred as a result of *that department's activities.* Costs transferred in from other processing departments should not be allowed to "cloud the picture." To illustrate, consider the Bottling Department in our example. As shown in Exhibit 18–10, a total of $800,000 was charged to the Bottling Department during June. But $375,000 of this cost was 75,000 gallons transferred in from the Syrup Department at $5 per gallon. This amount represents the cost of *making syrup,* not the cost of bottling cola.

Manufacturing costs resulting from *bottling activities* include only the direct materials, direct labor, and overhead charged to the Bottling Department. For RainTree's Bottling Department, these costs total *$425,000,* or *$0.0425 per unit* ($425,000 ÷ 10 million bottles produced).

In summary, total unit costs *accumulate* as the product passes from one processing department to the next. These total unit costs are used in valuing inventory, measuring the cost of goods sold, and evaluating the overall efficiency of manufacturing operations. But in evaluating the efficiency of a particular processing department, management should look primarily at the costs incurred *within that department.*

Of course, managers can also compute the per-unit costs of the materials, direct labor, and overhead incurred within each department. This detailed cost information should assist them in quickly identifying the *cause of any change* in a product's total unit cost.

## Ethics, Fraud & Corporate Governance

Using a process costing system requires ethics and judgment in computing equivalent units of production. By deliberately overstating equivalent units of resources in ending inventory, managers can understate cost of goods sold and thereby overstate net income. Equivalent units of production can easily be overstated by inflating the application of direct labor and overhead to work in process. Given the complexity of many manufacturing processes, company employees are often in the best position to know if management has overstated the equivalent units of production. The Sarbanes-Oxley Act (SOX) contains provisions to increase the likelihood that employees will come forward with concerns they may have about possible fraudulent financial reporting.

SOX requires publicly traded companies to develop procedures to encourage employees to report questionable accounting or auditing matters. The audit committees of these companies must establish procedures to ensure that employees have a confidential, anonymous mechanism by which they can report concerns regarding questionable practices (often referred to as a whistleblower hotline). In addition, employees who make allegations in good faith are granted certain protections. The protections apply if the allegations are made to criminal investigators, federal regulators, Congress, or an employee's supervisor (or other appropriate individuals within the company). When good faith allegations are made through these appropriate channels, the company is prohibited from discharging, demoting, suspending, threatening, harassing, or in any other manner discriminating against the employee. Employers who violate this provision can be held liable to reinstate the employee with back pay (including interest), and to pay for all litigation costs.

Although SOX provides protection from retaliation, employees still take some risks when making allegations. In short, the protections provided under SOX are only as effective as their enforcement. Employees who believe that they have been retaliated against because they expressed a concern about the company's potential violation of securities law can file a complaint with the U.S. Department of Labor (DOL). One criticism of this well-intentioned provision is that the DOL lacks the resources and expertise to effectively investigate potential retaliation by an employer against an employee for alleging securities law violations. Notwithstanding this possible concern, employees now have a better means by which to expose questionable accounting and auditing practices and better protection against potential retaliation.

## Concluding Remarks

In this chapter and the previous chapter, we have emphasized the measurement of unit costs. In upcoming chapters we will see how managers identify, measure, and employ related cost information for allocating decision-making authority, planning, and controlling costs. Unit cost information is ever present in business settings. We will see that having a thorough understanding of how unit costs are created provides a sturdy foundation for running a profitable business.

# END-OF-CHAPTER REVIEW

## SUMMARY OF LEARNING OBJECTIVES

**LO1** **Distinguish production procedures that match with process costing from those that correspond with job order costing.** Job order costing methods are appropriate for businesses and companies producing customized jobs that require differing amounts and types of direct labor, direct materials, and overhead. Process costing is used for production processes that produce mass quantities of identical units that use the same amounts and types of direct labor, direct materials, and overhead.

**LO2** **Account for the physical flows and related cost flows when using process costing.** The physical flow associated with a production process includes the beginning work in process, the units started during the period, the ending work in process, and the units transferred out during the period. Costs in process costing flow through the accounts in a manner similar to job order costing. Throughout the period, the costs of direct labor, direct materials, and overhead are charged to the appropriate work in process accounts. At the end of each period, costs in each Work in Process account are transferred to the next Work in Process account (or to a Finished Goods account).

**LO3** **Demonstrate how to calculate equivalent units.** Equivalent units are measures of productive activity that include work performed on partially completed units. The basic idea is that performing, say, 50 percent of the processing on 500 units is equivalent to performing all of the processing on 250 units.

**LO4** **Use the costs of resources consumed to calculate the cost per equivalent unit of production.** Costs associated with work done in the current period and added to work in process for the current period are pooled for each significant input. Dividing total costs by total equivalent units provides cost per equivalent unit for each input.

**LO5** **Use the cost per equivalent unit to assign costs to the work completed during the period.** The equivalent units associated with the units transferred out are multiplied by the cost per equivalent unit for each input. The units transferred out will typically contain some units in process at the start of the period. The remaining transferred units will be started and completed during the current period. Beginning work in process units will have some cost attached to them from the previous period and some costs added during the current period. Both costs must be transferred out with the completed units.

**LO6** **Create a process costing production report and use the report for decision making.** The process costing production report is a summary of the work completed during the period and the related cost, both per-unit and total costs. A typical production cost report contains four parts: (1) accounting for the physical flow, (2) determining equivalent units, (3) finding the cost per equivalent unit, and (4) assigning costs to the production for the period. The report is used to help management make several decisions related to the production process.

## Key Terms Introduced or Emphasized in Chapter 18

**conversion costs** (p. 807)   The direct labor and overhead costs associated with converting direct materials into the units transferred out.

**cost accounting systems** (p. 804)   The method and techniques used by enterprises to track resources consumed in creating and delivering products and services to customers.

**equivalent units** (p. 807)   A measure of the work done during an accounting period. Includes work done on beginning and ending inventories of work in process as well as work on units completely processed during the period.

**job order costing** (p. 804)   A cost accounting method under which the focal point of costing is a quantity of product known as a job or a lot. Costs of direct materials, direct labor, and overhead applicable to each job are compiled to arrive at average unit costs.

**process costing** (p. 804)   A cost accounting method used in enterprises with processes characterized by continuous mass production. Costs are assigned to a manufacturing process or department before being averaged over units produced.

**production cost report** (p. 812)   A detailed production report for a specified process and time period that details (1) the physical flow, (2) equivalent units, (3) cost per equivalent unit, and (4) total costs assigned.

## Demonstration Problem

Magna Bin, Inc., manufactures large metal waste containers that are purchased by local sanitation departments. Containers are produced in two processing departments, Fabricating and Painting. In the Fabricating Department, all of the direct materials are added at the beginning of the process, overhead is applied evenly throughout the entire process, and labor is added evenly only during the last 50 percent of the process. In the Painting Department, materials and labor are added evenly throughout the first half of the process, while overhead is applied evenly throughout the entire process. Magna Bin uses process costing and had the following cost and production information available for the month of January:

| | Fabricating Department | Painting Department |
|---|---|---|
| Direct materials costs . . . . . . . . . . . . . . . . . . . . . . . . . . . . . . . . . | $ 7,740 | $13,752 |
| Direct labor costs . . . . . . . . . . . . . . . . . . . . . . . . . . . . . . . . . . . | 18,060 | 8,022 |
| Manufacturing overhead applied . . . . . . . . . . . . . . . . . . . . . . . | 27,090 | 12,033 |
| Units in beginning work in process . . . . . . . . . . . . . . . . . . . . . | 0 | 0 |
| Units started during Jan. . . . . . . . . . . . . . . . . . . . . . . . . . . . . . | 750 | 600 |
| Units completed and transferred out . . . . . . . . . . . . . . . . . . . . | 600 | 510 |

At the end of January, units remaining in work in process in the Fabricating Department were 30 percent complete, while units in ending work in process in the Painting Department were 70 percent complete. During the month, 450 containers were sold at an average selling price of $180 each.

### Instructions

a. Calculate the number of equivalent units produced for each cost category in each of the two departments during January.

b. Based on equivalent units, what were the fabricating cost, painting cost, and total cost of producing a container in January?

c. Prepare the journal entries summarizing the manufacturing costs charged to the Fabricating Department and the Painting Department.

d. Prepare the month-end journal entries to transfer the costs of containers moved from the Fabricating Department to the Painting Department and from the Painting Department to Finished Goods Inventory.

e. Prepare the entries to record the sales made in January and the corresponding reduction of Finished Goods Inventory.

f. Using T accounts, calculate the ending balances in the Work in Process accounts and Finished Goods Inventory.

### Solution to Demonstration Problem

**a.**    **Equivalent Units of Production—Fabricating Department**

| | Direct Materials | Labor | Overhead |
|---|---|---|---|
| Beginning work in process . . . . . . . . . . . . . . . | 0 | 0 | 0 |
| Started and completed . . . . . . . . . . . . . . . . . . | 600 | 600 | 600 |
| Ending work in process . . . . . . . . . . . . . . . . | 150 | 0 | 45 (150 × 0.3) |
| Total equivalent units . . . . . . . . . . . . . . . . . . | 750 | 600 | 645 |

*Note:* Since the units in ending work in process are 30 percent complete, all direct materials have been added, no direct labor has been used, and 30 percent of the overhead has been applied.

**Equivalent Units of Production—Painting Department**

| | Direct Materials | Labor | Overhead |
|---|---|---|---|
| Beginning work in process . . . . . . . . . . . . . . . | 0 | 0 | 0 |
| Started and completed . . . . . . . . . . . . . . . . . . | 510 | 510 | 510 |
| Ending work in process . . . . . . . . . . . . . . . . | 90 | 90 | 63 (90 × 0.7) |
| Total equivalent units . . . . . . . . . . . . . . . . . . | 600 | 600 | 573 |

*Note:* Since the units in ending work in process are 70 percent complete, all direct materials and labor have been added, while only 70 percent of the overhead has been applied.

**b.** Fabricating costs per container produced during January:

| | |
|---|---|
| Direct materials costs ($7,740 ÷ 750 equivalent units) . . . . . . . . . . . . . . . . . . . . . . . | $10.32 |
| Direct labor costs ($18,060 ÷ 600 equivalent units) . . . . . . . . . . . . . . . . . . . . . . . . | 30.10 |
| Manufacturing overhead ($27,090 ÷ 645 equivalent units) . . . . . . . . . . . . . . . . . . . | 42.00 |
| Fabricating costs per container. . . . . . . . . . . . . . . . . . . . . . . . . . . . . . . . . . . . . . | $82.42 |

Painting costs per container produced during January:

| | |
|---|---|
| Direct materials costs ($13,752 ÷ 600 equivalent units) . . . . . . . . . . . . . . . . . . . . . . | $ 22.92 |
| Direct labor costs ($8,022 ÷ 600 equivalent units) . . . . . . . . . . . . . . . . . . . . . . . . . | 13.37 |
| Manufacturing overhead ($12,033 ÷ 573 equivalent units) . . . . . . . . . . . . . . . . . . . | 21.00 |
| Painting costs per container . . . . . . . . . . . . . . . . . . . . . . . . . . . . . . . . . . . . . . . . | $ 57.29 |
| Total cost per container ($82.42 + $57.29) . . . . . . . . . . . . . . . . . . . . . . . . . . . . . . | $139.71 |

**c.**

| | | |
|---|---|---|
| Work in Process—Fabricating . . . . . . . . . . . . . . . . . . . . . . . . . . . . | 52,890.00 | |
| Direct Materials Inventory . . . . . . . . . . . . . . . . . . . . . . . . . . . . | | 7,740.00 |
| Direct Labor . . . . . . . . . . . . . . . . . . . . . . . . . . . . . . . . . . . . . . | | 18,060.00 |
| Manufacturing Overhead Applied . . . . . . . . . . . . . . . . . . . . . . | | 27,090.00 |
| Summary of costs incurred during January by the Fabricating Department. | | |
| Work in Process—Painting . . . . . . . . . . . . . . . . . . . . . . . . . . . . . | 33,807.00 | |
| Direct Materials Inventory . . . . . . . . . . . . . . . . . . . . . . . . . . . . | | 13,752.00 |
| Direct Labor . . . . . . . . . . . . . . . . . . . . . . . . . . . . . . . . . . . . . . | | 8,022.00 |
| Manufacturing Overhead Applied . . . . . . . . . . . . . . . . . . . . . . | | 12,033.00 |
| Summary of costs incurred during January by the Painting Department. | | |

**d.**

| | | |
|---|---|---|
| Work in Process—Painting. . . . . . . . . . . . . . . . . . . . . . . . . . . . . . | 49,452.00 | |
| (600 units transferred × $82.42 cost/unit) | | |
| Work in Process—Fabricating. . . . . . . . . . . . . . . . . . . . . . . . . | | 49,452.00 |
| To transfer the cost of completely processed units from the Fabricating Department to the Painting Department. | | |
| Finished Goods Inventory. . . . . . . . . . . . . . . . . . . . . . . . . . . . . . | 71,252.10 | |
| (510 units transferred × $139.71 cost/unit) | | |
| Work in Process—Painting . . . . . . . . . . . . . . . . . . . . . . . . . . . | | 71,252.10 |
| To transfer the cost of completely processed units from the Painting Department to Finished Goods Inventory. | | |

**e.**

| | | |
|---|---|---|
| Cash, Accounts Receivable. . . . . . . . . . . . . . . . . . . . . . . . . . . . . . | 81,000.00 | |
| Sales Revenue . . . . . . . . . . . . . . . . . . . . . . . . . . . . . . . . . . . . | | 81,000.00 |
| (450 units sold × $180/unit) | | |
| To record sales made during Jan. | | |
| Cost of Goods Sold. . . . . . . . . . . . . . . . . . . . . . . . . . . . . . . . . . . | 62,869.50 | |
| (450 units sold × $139.71 cost/unit) | | |
| Finished Goods Inventory . . . . . . . . . . . . . . . . . . . . . . . . . . . . | | 62,869.50 |
| To record the cost of goods sold during Jan. | | |

**f.**

| Work in Process—Fabricating | | | |
|---|---|---|---|
| Direct materials | 7,740.00 | | |
| Direct labor | 18,060.00 | | |
| Manufacturing overhead applied | 27,090.00 | 49,452.00 | Transferred to Painting |
| Ending balance | 3,438.00 | | |

| Work in Process—Painting | | | |
|---|---|---|---|
| From Fabricating | 49,452.00 | | |
| Direct materials | 13,752.00 | | |
| Direct labor | 8,022.00 | | |
| Manufacturing overhead applied | 12,033.00 | 71,252.10 | Transferred to Finished Goods Inventory |
| Ending balance | 12,006.90 | | |

| Finished Goods Inventory | | | |
|---|---|---|---|
| From Painting | 71,252.10 | | |
| | | 62,869.50 | Transferred to Cost of Goods Sold |
| Ending balance | 8,382.60 | | |

# Self-Test Questions

*The answers to these questions appear on page 838.*

1. If Power Products uses *process costing,* which of the following are likely to be true:

   **a.** The production processes are high volume.

   **b.** The products use different amounts of direct labor.

   **c.** The products are created with repetitive processes.

   **d.** The products are created to customer specifications.

2. Which of the following businesses would most likely use *process* costing?

   **a.** A law firm.

   **b.** A maker of frozen orange juice.

   **c.** A hospital.

   **d.** An auto repair shop.

3. Nut House manufactures and sells jars of peanut butter. All of the company's output passes through five production processes, which are performed in sequential order. Identify all correct answers, assuming that process costing is in use.

   **a.** The processing departments may define "units of output" differently.

   **b.** Costs transferred from one processing department are charged to the next processing department (or to finished goods).

   **c.** The cost accounting system separately measures the per-unit cost of each manufacturing process.

   **d.** No manufacturing overhead is charged to each processing department.

4. Indicate which of the following phrases correctly completes this sentence: "Equivalent units of production . . ." (Indicate all correct answers.)

   **a.** Are a measure of productive activity.

   **b.** Represent work done on units still in process, as well as those completed during the period.

   **c.** Are used as the basis for computing per-unit costs in most process cost accounting systems.

   **d.** Are computed separately for each significant input consumed in the production process.

5. A production cost report contains which of the following parts? (Identify all correct answers.)

   **a.** Equivalent units for each significant category of resources consumed in making the product.

   **b.** The total cost to account for.

   **c.** The physical flow of production.

   **d.** The overhead costs applied to each completed job.

   **e.** The total costs accounted for.

## ASSIGNMENT MATERIAL    Discussion Questions

1. Why would a company use multiple cost accounting systems?

2. What factors should be taken into account in deciding whether to use job order costing or process costing in any given production situation?

3. Rodeo Drive Jewelers makes custom jewelry for celebrities. Would you expect the company to use job order or process costing? Explain.

4. Describe at least two products or production processes that might use both process and job order costing methods to determine the cost of a finished unit.

5. What are the four significant parts of the production cost report for process costing?

6. Taylor & Malone is a law firm. Would the concepts of job order or process costing be more appropriate for this type of service business? Explain.

7. Briefly explain the operation of process costing, including the manner in which the unit costs of finished goods are determined.

8. Some companies that use process costing simply assign the entire cost of production to those units completed and transferred during the month, even if some units remain in process at the end of the period. Is this practice reasonable?

9. Discuss how managers use information they obtain from process costing.

10. Explain the term *equivalent units*. In a fast-moving, assembly-line operation, are the equivalent units likely to differ significantly from the number of units completed during a month? Explain.

11. Identify various product characteristics that distinguish job costing systems from process costing systems.

12. In a process costing system, what condition must be present in order for accountants to combine direct labor and manufacturing overhead costs and treat them simply as conversion costs?

13. Why is the combination of direct labor and manufacturing overhead referred to as a conversion cost?

14. Why might the unit cost of those items started and completed during the period differ from the unit cost of all items completed and transferred during the period?

15. In a process costing system that uses a FIFO cost flow assumption, how is the number of units started and completed during the period computed?

## Brief Exercises

 **L01**

**BRIEF EXERCISE 18.1**

Selecting Cost Accounting Systems

Determine whether each of the following companies is best suited for a job order cost system, a process costing system, or both.

a. C. Erickson & Sons, Inc. (a construction company with multiple job sites).

b. Apple Computer (a manufacturer of computers for individual and institutional clients).

c. PlayWorld Systems, Inc. (a provider of custom-designed playground equipment for city parks and schools districts).

d. Strong Industries (a manufacturer of injection-molded plastic doghouses).

e. Nature Made Nutritional Products (a maker of vitamins and nutritional supplements).

 **L01**

**BRIEF EXERCISE 18.2**

Matching Cost Systems and Business Activities

Match the business with the appropriate cost system(s) for that business using the number of the cost system where 1 = job order costing, 2 = process costing, and 3 = activity-based costing.

a. Ketcher, Tryer, and Friar, attorneys-at-law

b. Walmart Inc.

c. Johnson & Johnson Company

d. Handyman Special, Inc.

e. Carpet Makers Corporation

**L02**

**BRIEF EXERCISE 18.3**

Flow of Costs in a Cost Accounting System

For each of the four accounts listed below, prepare an example of a journal entry that would cause the account to be (1) debited and (2) credited using a process costing system. Assume perpetual inventory records are maintained. Include written explanations with your journal entries and use "XXX" in place of dollar amounts.

a. Materials Inventory

b. Direct Labor

c. Manufacturing Overhead

d. Finished Goods Inventory

**BRIEF
EXERCISE 18.4**

Journal Entries in
Process Costing
Systems

Morning Glow Corporation uses a process costing system for its two production departments: Mixing and Packaging. The company provided the following manufacturing cost information for the month of May:

|  | Mixing | Packaging |
|---|---|---|
| Beginning work in process | $ 500 | $ 900 |
| Costs transferred in | ? | ? |
| Costs incurred in May | 3,000 | 5,000 |
| Ending work in process | 1,200 | 1,500 |

a. Record the transfer of costs from the Mixing Department to the Packaging Department in May.

b. Record the transfer of costs from the Packaging Department to Finished Goods Inventory in May.

**BRIEF
EXERCISE 18.5**

Computing Equivalent
Units of Resource
Inputs

Dittmar Products has provided the following information pertaining to equivalent units of production in its Cutting Department for the month of September:

|  | Direct Materials | Conversion |
|---|---|---|
| Units in beginning work in process, September 1 | 5,000 | ? |
| Units started and completed in September | ? | 15,000 |
| Units in ending work in process, September 30 | 2,000 | ? |

All of the direct materials used in the Cutting Department are added at the beginning of the process. On September 1, beginning inventory was 20 percent complete with respect to conversion. On September 30, ending inventory was 60 percent complete with respect to conversion.

Compute equivalent units of direct materials and conversion used by the Cutting Department in September.

**BRIEF
EXERCISE 18.6**

Determining the Cost
per Equivalent Unit of
Input Resource

On March 1, Lesher Manufacturing had 2,000 units in its Molding Department. These units were 90 percent complete with respect to direct materials requirements and 30 percent complete with respect to their conversion requirements. During March, the Molding Department started and completed 20,800 units. Direct materials costs in March incurred in the Molding Department totaled $152,600, whereas March conversion costs totaled $203,400. On March 31, there remained 1,000 units in ending inventory that were 80 percent complete with respect to direct materials, and 40 percent complete with respect to conversion.

a. Compute the Molding Department's cost per equivalent unit of direct materials in March.

b. Compute the Molding Department's cost per equivalent unit of conversion in March.

**BRIEF
EXERCISE 18.7**

Solving for Missing
Information

Green Dragon Corporation had 5,000 units of beginning inventory in its Forming Department on July 1. The units were 100 percent complete with respect to direct materials requirements but only 30 percent complete with respect to conversion requirements. On July 31, the company had 4,000 units of inventory remaining in its Forming Department. These units were 100 percent complete with respect to their direct materials requirements but only 40 percent complete with respect to conversion. The Forming Department's direct materials cost for July totaled $380,000, or $20 per equivalent unit consumed. Its conversion costs for July totaled $603,000, or $30 per equivalent unit.

Determine how many units were started and completed in the Forming Department during July.

**BRIEF
EXERCISE 18.8**

Determining
Departmental
Manufacturing Costs

On September 1, the Blending Department of Jordan Bakery had costs carried forward from August totaling $30,000. Resources consumed to complete the beginning inventory totaled $20,000. The total cost of units started in the Blending Department during September was $400,000. On September 30, costs assigned to the department's ending inventory totaled $40,000.

Compute the costs transferred out of the Blending Department during September.

**BRIEF
EXERCISE 18.9**

Interpreting a
Production Cost Report

The following equivalent unit figures were taken from the December production cost report of the Distillation Department of Meadow Brook Lubricants:

| Equivalent Units | Direct Materials | Conversion |
|---|---|---|
| Equivalent units to finish beginning inventory . . . . . . . . . . . . . . . . | 0 | 800 |
| Equivalent units to start new units in December . . . . . . . . . . . . . . | 48,000 | 47,000 |
| Equivalent units of input in December . . . . . . . . . . . . . . . . . . . . | 48,000 | 47,800 |

**a.** At what point in the production process are direct materials added in the company's Distillation Department? Explain your answer.

**b.** If the Distillation Department's ending inventory on December 31 is comprised of 5,000 equivalent units of direct materials and 4,000 equivalent units of conversion, how many units were started and completed by the department during December?

 **BRIEF EXERCISE 18.10**

Interpreting a Production Cost Report

Iverson Industrial's production cost report for its Packaging Department reveals that the cost per equivalent unit started and completed in November was $148. The same report reveals that the cost per equivalent unit transferred out of the Packaging Department in November was $150.

Were November manufacturing costs per equivalent unit higher than, lower than, or the same as October costs per equivalent unit? Explain your answer.

## Exercises

 **EXERCISE 18.1**

Accounting Terminology

**through**

Listed below are six technical accounting terms introduced or emphasized in this chapter.

| | |
|---|---|
| Job order costing | Equivalent units |
| Process costing | Cost of finished goods manufactured |
| Conversion costs | Production cost report |

Each of the following statements may (or may not) describe these technical terms. For each statement, indicate the term described, or answer "None" if the statement does not correctly describe any of the terms.

**a.** The type of cost accounting method likely to be used in a Coca-Cola bottling plant.

**b.** Direct labor and overhead consumed in a production process.

**c.** A measure of the *quantity* of production work done during a time period, including work on partially completed units.

**d.** Process cost information for the period, including physical flow and total cost to account for.

**e.** The type of cost accounting method likely to be used by a construction company.

 **EXERCISE 18.2**

Calculating Equivalent Units

Starr Scopes, Inc., produces telescopes for use by high school students. All direct materials used in the production of telescopes are added at the beginning of the manufacturing process. Labor and overhead are added evenly thereafter, as each unit is assembled, adjusted, and tested. Starr Scopes uses process costing and had the following unit production information available for the months of January and February:

| | Jan. | Feb. |
|---|---|---|
| Number of units in beginning work in process inventory . . . . . . . . . . . . . . . . . | 0 | 50 |
| Number of units started during the month . . . . . . . . . . . . . . . . . . . . . . . . . | 200 | 300 |
| Total number of units transferred to finished goods . . . . . . . . . . . . . . . . . . . . | 150 | 250 |

The units remaining in work in process at the end of January were approximately 40 percent complete. During the month of February, all of the beginning work in process units was completed and the units remaining in work in process at the end of the month were approximately 75 percent complete.

**a.** For the month of January, calculate the equivalent units produced for each of the two cost categories—direct materials *and* labor and overhead.

**b.** For the month of February, calculate the equivalent units produced for each of the two cost categories—direct materials *and* labor and overhead.

**824** Chapter 18 Process Costing

**EXERCISE 18.3**

Process Costing

Shamrock Industries uses process costing. All of the company's manufacturing activities take place in a single processing department. The following information was available for the month of June:

| | |
|---|---|
| Direct materials . . . . . . . . . . . . . . . . . . . . . . . . . . . . . . . . . . . . . . . . . . . . | $ 89,750 |
| Direct labor . . . . . . . . . . . . . . . . . . . . . . . . . . . . . . . . . . . . . . . . . . . . . . . | 28,975 |
| Manufacturing overhead applied . . . . . . . . . . . . . . . . . . . . . . . . . . . . . . . | 40,275 |
| Total costs to account for in June . . . . . . . . . . . . . . . . . . . . . . . . . . . . . . | $159,000 |

The amounts of work in process at the beginning and end of the month were immaterial and assigned no dollar value. During June, 13,250 units were completed, of which 10,000 were sold on account at $25 per unit.

**a.** Prepare a journal entry to summarize the total manufacturing costs applied to production in June.

**b.** Prepare the journal entry to transfer completed units from work in process to the finished goods warehouse in June.

**c.** Prepare the journal entries to record the sale of 10,000 units manufactured during the period and the related cost of goods sold.

**EXERCISE 18.4**

Production Cost Report

Use the information from Exercise 18.3 to complete a production cost report for Shamrock Industries for the month of June.

**EXERCISE 18.5**

Computing Costs per Equivalent Unit

Old Victrola, Inc., produces top-quality stereos and uses process costing. The manufacture of stereos is such that direct materials, labor, and overhead are all added evenly throughout the production process. Due to the smooth production process, only one cost category—manufacturing costs—is used for equivalent unit calculations. Old Victrola had the following cost and production information available for the months of March and April:

| | March | April |
|---|---|---|
| Direct materials costs . . . . . . . . . . . . . . . . . . . . . . . . . . . . . | $ 978,460 | $1,168,310 |
| Direct labor costs . . . . . . . . . . . . . . . . . . . . . . . . . . . . . . . . | 2,562,260 | 3,041,940 |
| Manufacturing overhead applied . . . . . . . . . . . . . . . . . . . . . . | 3,438,640 | 3,571,030 |
| Total manufacturing costs . . . . . . . . . . . . . . . . . . . . . . . . . . | $6,979,360 | $7,781,280 |
| Units in beginning work in process . . . . . . . . . . . . . . . . . . . . . | 7,000 | 4,800 |
| Units transferred to finished goods . . . . . . . . . . . . . . . . . . . . . | 18,500 | 23,000 |
| Units in ending work in process . . . . . . . . . . . . . . . . . . . . . . . | 4,800 | 6,400 |

Beginning work in process was 30 percent complete in March and 60 percent complete in April. Ending work in process was 60 percent complete in March and 35 percent complete in April.

**a.** For each of the two months, calculate the equivalent units of production.

**b.** Based on equivalent units produced, did total manufacturing costs per unit increase or decrease between March and April?

**c.** Did the direct materials cost per equivalent unit increase or decrease between March and April?

**EXERCISE 18.6**

Process Costing with No Beginning Inventories: Part I

Ogden Office Outfitters began making high-quality office furniture in January. The company's executive desks are produced in two departments: Cutting and Finishing. Component kits are produced in the Cutting Department and then transferred to the Finishing Department for trimming and assembly. During its first month of operations, the Cutting Department started 10,000 executive desk kits. January direct materials costs in the Cutting Department totaled $200,000, and conversion costs totaled $258,000. Ending inventory on January 31 consisted of 2,000 partially processed component kits. These units were 100 percent complete with respect to direct materials, but only 30 percent complete with respect to conversion.

**a.** Compute the number of component kits transferred from the Cutting Department to the Finishing Department in January.

**b.** Compute the equivalent units of input resources for the Cutting Department in January.

c.  Compute the cost per equivalent unit of input resource for the Cutting Department in January.

d.  Prepare the summary journal entry required to transfer finished component kits from the Cutting Department to the Finishing Department in January.

e.  Compute the total cost assigned to the Cutting Department's ending inventory on January 31.

## L02 through L05 — EXERCISE 18.7

Process Costing with No Beginning Inventories: Part II

Exercise 18.7 is an extension of Exercise 18.6.

Assume that on January 31 the Finishing Department of Ogden Office Outfitters had 1,000 partially trimmed and assembled executive desks in ending inventory. These units were, of course, 100 percent complete with respect to components transferred in from the Cutting Department, but only 20 percent complete with respect to direct trim materials, and 40 percent complete with respect to conversion. During January, the Finishing Department incurred direct materials costs (for trim) of $43,200, and conversion costs of $81,400.

a.  Compute how many units were started in the Finishing Department during January.

b.  Compute the number of executive desks transferred out of the Finishing Department in January.

c.  Compute the equivalent units of input resources for the Finishing Department in January.

d.  Compute the cost per equivalent unit of input resource for the Finishing Department in January.

e.  Prepare the summary journal entry required to transfer the cost of executive desks from the Finishing Department's Work in Process Inventory to the company's Finished Goods Inventory in January.

f.  Compute the total cost assigned to the Finishing Department's ending inventory in process on January 31.

## L02 through L05 — EXERCISE 18.8

Process Costing with Beginning Inventories: Part I

Dahl's Treats makes institutional cakes. Finished cakes must pass through two departments: Mixing and Baking. Vats of cake batter are processed in the Mixing Department and then transferred to the Baking Department, where individual cakes are baked, cooled, and frosted. There were 200 gallons of partially mixed batter in the Mixing Department's inventory on August 1. The batter was 100 percent complete with respect to direct materials, but only 20 percent complete with respect to conversion. Manufacturing costs assigned to the inventory carried forward from July totaled $440. During August, the Mixing Department started 8,000 new gallons of batter. August direct materials costs in the Mixing Department totaled $16,000, and conversion costs totaled $8,120. Ending inventory on August 31 consisted of 100 partially mixed gallons of batter. These units were 100 percent complete with respect to direct materials, but only 60 percent complete with respect to conversion.

a.  Prepare a schedule showing: (1) gallons of mix transferred from the Mixing Department to the Baking Department in August, and (2) gallons of mix started and completed by the Mixing Department in August.

b.  Compute the equivalent units of input resources for the Mixing Department in August.

c.  Compute the cost per equivalent unit of input resource for the Mixing Department in August.

d.  Prepare the summary journal entry required to transfer the cost of fully mixed batter from the Mixing Department to the Baking Department in August.

e.  Compute the total cost assigned to the Mixing Department's ending inventory on August 31.

## L02 through L05 — EXERCISE 18.9

Process Costing with Beginning Inventories: Part II

Exercise 18.9 is an extension of Exercise 18.8.

Dahl's Treats uses one gallon of mix for each cake produced by the Baking Department. On August 1, the Baking Department had 500 cakes in process. These units were 100 percent complete with respect to batter transferred in from the Mixing Department during July, but only 70 percent complete with respect to direct (frosting) materials, and 80 percent complete with respect to conversion. Costs applied to these units carried forward from July totaled $2,600. Costs incurred by the Baking Department during August included $8,040 of direct materials and $31,900 of conversion. The ending inventory in the Baking Department on August 31 consisted of 300 cakes in process. These units were 100 percent complete with respect to batter transferred in from the Mixing Department, but only 30 percent complete with respect to direct (frosting) materials, and 25 percent complete with respect to conversion.

a.  Compute how many cakes were started in the Baking Department during August.

b.  Prepare a schedule showing: (1) cakes transferred out of the Baking Department in August, and (2) cakes *started and completed* by the Baking Department in August.

c.  Compute the equivalent units of input resources for the Baking Department in August.

d.  Compute the cost per equivalent unit of input resource for the Baking Department in August.

826    **Chapter 18**  Process Costing

e. Prepare the summary journal entry required to transfer the cost of baked cakes from the Baking Department's Work in Process Inventory to the company's Finished Goods Inventory in August.

f. Compute the total cost assigned to the Baking Department's ending inventory in process on August 31.

**L02**
through
**L05**

**EXERCISE 18.10**

Process Costing through Two Departments: Department I

Accessory World makes floor mats for the automobile industry. Finished sets of mats must pass through two departments: Cutting and Coating. Large sheets of synthetic material are cut to size in the Cutting Department and then transferred to the Coating Department, where each set is sprayed with a chemical coating for improved durability. The following information pertains to May activity in the Cutting Department:

**Cost data:**

| | |
|---|---|
| Total cost of beginning inventory on May 1 . . . . . . . . . . . . . . . . . . . . . . . . . . . | $ 44,800 |
| Direct materials costs incurred in May . . . . . . . . . . . . . . . . . . . . . . . . . . . . . | 200,000 |
| Conversion costs incurred in May . . . . . . . . . . . . . . . . . . . . . . . . . . . . . . . | 87,200 |

**Physical units data:**

| | |
|---|---|
| Units in process, May 1 . . . . . . . . . . . . . . . . . . . . . . . . . . . . . . . . . . . . . | 8,000 sets |
| Units started in May . . . . . . . . . . . . . . . . . . . . . . . . . . . . . . . . . . . . . . . | 50,000 sets |
| Units in process, May 31 . . . . . . . . . . . . . . . . . . . . . . . . . . . . . . . . . . . . | 10,000 sets |

**Percentage of completion data:**

| | |
|---|---|
| Direct materials, May 1 . . . . . . . . . . . . . . . . . . . . . . . . . . . . . . . . . . . . . . | 100% |
| Conversion, May 1 . . . . . . . . . . . . . . . . . . . . . . . . . . . . . . . . . . . . . . . . | 80 |
| Direct materials, May 31 . . . . . . . . . . . . . . . . . . . . . . . . . . . . . . . . . . . . . | 100% |
| Conversion, May 31 . . . . . . . . . . . . . . . . . . . . . . . . . . . . . . . . . . . . . . . | 20 |

a. Prepare a schedule showing: (1) the number of mat sets transferred from the Cutting Department to the Coating Department in May, and (2) the number of mat sets *started and completed* by the Cutting Department in May.

b. Compute the equivalent units of input resources for the Cutting Department in May.

c. Compute the cost per equivalent unit of input resource for the Cutting Department in May.

d. Prepare the summary journal entry required to transfer the cost of completed mat sets from the Cutting Department to the Coating Department in May.

e. Compute the total cost assigned to the Cutting Department's ending inventory on May 31.

**L02**
through
**L05**

**EXERCISE 18.11**

Process Costing through Two Departments: Department II

Exercise 18.11 is an extension of Exercise 18.10.

The following information pertains to May activity in Accessory World's Coating Department:

**Cost data:**

| | |
|---|---|
| Total cost of beginning inventory on May 1 . . . . . . . . . . . . . . . . . . . . . . . . . . . | $45,300 |
| Direct materials costs incurred in May . . . . . . . . . . . . . . . . . . . . . . . . . . . . . | 11,925 |
| Conversion costs incurred in May . . . . . . . . . . . . . . . . . . . . . . . . . . . . . . . . | 84,525 |
| Cut sets transferred in during May . . . . . . . . . . . . . . . . . . . . . . . . . . . . . . . | ? |

**Physical units data:**

| | |
|---|---|
| Units in process, May 1 . . . . . . . . . . . . . . . . . . . . . . . . . . . . . . . . . . . . . | 6,000 sets |
| Units started in May . . . . . . . . . . . . . . . . . . . . . . . . . . . . . . . . . . . . . . . | ?    sets |
| Units in process, May 31 . . . . . . . . . . . . . . . . . . . . . . . . . . . . . . . . . . . . | 9,000 sets |

**Percentage of completion data:**

| | |
|---|---|
| Direct materials, May 1 . . . . . . . . . . . . . . . . . . . . . . . . . . . . . . . . . . . . . | 60% |
| Conversion, May 1 . . . . . . . . . . . . . . . . . . . . . . . . . . . . . . . . . . . . . . . . | 80 |
| Cut sets transferred in, May 1 . . . . . . . . . . . . . . . . . . . . . . . . . . . . . . . . . | ? |
| Direct materials, May 31 . . . . . . . . . . . . . . . . . . . . . . . . . . . . . . . . . . . . | 70% |
| Conversion, May 31 . . . . . . . . . . . . . . . . . . . . . . . . . . . . . . . . . . . . . . . | 90 |
| Cut sets transferred in, May 31 . . . . . . . . . . . . . . . . . . . . . . . . . . . . . . . . | ? |

a.  Compute how many cut mat sets were started in the Coating Department during May.

b.  Prepare a schedule showing: (1) the number of mat sets transferred out of the Coating Department in May, and (2) the number of mat sets *started and completed* by the Coating Department in May.

c.  Compute the equivalent units of input resources for the Coating Department in May.

d.  Compute the cost per equivalent unit of input resource for the Coating Department in May.

e.  Prepare the summary journal entry required to transfer the cost of finished mat sets from the Coating Department's Work in Process Inventory to the company's Finished Goods Inventory in May.

f.  Compute the total cost assigned to the Coating Department's ending inventory in process on May 31.

**L02**
through
**L05**

**EXERCISE 18.12**

Solving for Missing Account Information

Comas Corporation manufactures metal roofing in two departments: Pressing and Painting. Sheets of metal material are formed in the Pressing Department before being transferred to the Painting Department. The following information was taken from the company's general ledger and cost accounting records on June 30:

| Work in Process: Pressing Department | | | | | |
|---|---|---|---|---|---|
| 6/1 | Beginning balance | $ 6,000 | 6/30 | Transferred to Painting | ? |
| 6/30 | Direct materials | 25,500 | | | |
| 6/30 | Direct labor | 8,200 | | | |
| 6/30 | Manufacturing overhead | 32,800 | | | |
| 6/30 | Ending balance | ? | | | |

**Physical Units: Pressing Department**

| | |
|---|---|
| Units in process, June 1 .......................................... | 300 sheets |
| Units transferred to Painting Department in June ...................... | 1,500 sheets |
| Units in process, June 30 ......................................... | 500 sheets |

**Percentages of Completion: Pressing Department**

| | |
|---|---|
| Direct materials, June 1 .......................................... | 100% |
| Conversion, June 1 .............................................. | 20 |
| Direct materials, June 30 ......................................... | 100% |
| Conversion, June 30 ............................................. | 40 |

a.  Compute the number of sheets *started* by the Pressing Department in June.

b.  Compute the number of units *started and completed* by the Pressing Department in June.

c.  Compute the equivalent units of input resources for the Pressing Department in June.

d.  Compute the cost per equivalent unit of input resource for the Pressing Department in June.

e.  Prepare the summary journal entry required to transfer pressed sheets from the Pressing Department to the Painting Department in June.

f.  Compute the total cost assigned to the Pressing Department's ending inventory on June 30.

**L01**
through
**L06**

**EXERCISE 18.13**

Assessing the Need for Process Costing

Goodwater Corporation mass-produces pencils through several processing departments. The company currently uses a process costing system and traces manufacturing costs from one process department to the next. The company produces over 90 million pencils per year. The number of pencils in production at any single point in time never exceeds 40,000.

Rick Brintnall has just been hired as the company's cost accountant. Given the company's annual output relative to production activity at any single point in time, Brintnall suspects that the cost of maintaining a process costing system outweighs the benefit. Therefore, Brintnall recommends that the company's current work in process inventory accounts be eliminated, and that all manufacturing costs be charged directly to the Finished Goods Inventory account.

Defend Brintnall's recommendation.

Chapter 18  Process Costing

 **LO2**
through
 **LO6**

**EXERCISE 18.14**

Interpreting Information from a Production Cost Report

Lavalear Corporation uses a process costing system and traces costs through several processing departments, starting with the Bonding Department. Shown below is information taken from the Bonding Department's September production cost report:

**Cost Data: Bonding Department**

| | |
|---|---|
| Direct materials costs in beginning inventory, September 1 | $ 50,400 |
| Conversion costs in beginning inventory, September 1 | 36,000 |
| Direct materials costs incurred in September | 789,750 |
| Conversion costs incurred in September | 787,500 |

**Physical Units: Bonding Department**

| | |
|---|---|
| Units in process, September 1 | 300 |
| Units transferred out during September | 1,500 |
| Units in process, September 30 | 500 |

**Percentages of Completion: Bonding Department**

| | |
|---|---|
| Direct materials, September 1 | 40% |
| Conversion, September 1 | 25 |
| Direct materials, September 30 | 75% |
| Conversion, September 30 | 30 |

a. Compute the cost per equivalent unit of direct materials and conversion carried forward from *August* and assigned to the Bonding Department's beginning inventory on September 1.

b. Compute the cost per equivalent unit of direct materials and conversion incurred by the Bonding Department in *September*.

c. Discuss how the cost figures computed in parts **a** and **b** would be useful to the company's management.

**LO2**
through
**LO6**

**EXERCISE 18.15**

Finding Missing Information for a Production Cost Report

Newton Corporation uses a process costing system to trace costs through several phases of production, starting with the Blending Department and ending with the Packaging Department. Recent computer problems have caused some of the company's accounting records to be destroyed. Shown below is a partial summary of information retrieved by accountants from the Blending Department's February production cost report:

**Cost Data: Blending Department**

| | |
|---|---|
| Direct materials costs in beginning inventory, February 1 | $ 12,000 |
| Conversion costs in beginning inventory, February 1 | 25,200 |
| Direct materials costs incurred in February | 162,000 |
| Conversion costs incurred in February | 271,000 |
| Cost per equivalent unit of conversion in February | 5 |

**Physical Units: Blending Department**

| | |
|---|---|
| Units in process, February 1 | ? |
| Units transferred out during February | 58,000 |
| Units started in February | 54,000 |
| Units in process, February 28 | 2,000 |

**Percentage of Completion: Blending Department**

| | |
|---|---|
| Direct materials, February 1 | 100% |
| Conversion, February 1 | ? |
| Direct materials, February 28 | 100% |
| Conversion, February 28 | 20 |

a. Compute the number of units that were in the Blending Department's beginning inventory on February 1.

b. Compute the number of units that were *started and completed* by the Blending Department in February.

c.  Compute the cost per equivalent unit of direct materials and conversion carried forward from *January* and assigned to the Blending Department's beginning inventory on February 1.

d.  Compute the Blending Department's cost per equivalent unit of *direct materials* consumed in *February*.

---

## Problem Set A

  **PROBLEM 18.1A**
Calculating Equivalent
Units

 **eXcel**

Superior Lighting, Inc., mass-produces reading lamps. Materials used in constructing the body of the lamp are added at the start of the process, while the materials used in wiring the lamps are added at the halfway point. All labor and overhead are added evenly throughout the manufacturing process. Superior uses process costing and had the following unit production information available for the months of June and July:

|  | June | July |
|---|---|---|
| Number of lamps in beginning work in process ....................... | 850 | 1,200 |
| Lamps transferred to finished goods ................................ | 3,500 | 3,300 |
| Number of lamps in ending work in process ......................... | 1,200 | 900 |

In June, the lamps in beginning work in process were approximately 80 percent complete, while those in ending work in process were only 30 percent complete. In July, the units remaining in ending work in process were 60 percent complete. All lamps in ending work in process are finished during the next month.

### Instructions

a.  For the month of June, calculate the equivalent units of production for the three major cost categories—body materials, wiring materials, and labor and overhead.

b.  For the month of July, calculate the equivalent units of production for the three major cost categories—body materials, wiring materials, and labor and overhead.

  **PROBLEM 18.2A**
through **Computing and Using**
Unit Costs

 **eXcel**

One of Sun Appliance's products is a dishwasher. Two processing departments are involved in the dishwasher's manufacture. The tub is assembled in one department, and a second department assembles and installs the motor. There is no beginning or ending work in process in either department. During March, the company incurred the following costs in the manufacture of 4,000 dishwashers.

|  | Tub Department | Motor Department |
|---|---|---|
| Direct materials ..................................... | $150,000 | $96,000 |
| Direct labor ........................................ | 12,000 | 18,000 |
| Manufacturing overhead ........................... | 18,000 | 6,000 |

### Instructions

a.  Compute the following *per-unit* costs for the month of March:

   1.  A tub assembly transferred to the Motor Department.

   2.  Assembling a motor and installing it.

   3.  A completed dishwasher.

   4.  Materials used in assembling a tub.

   5.  Direct labor cost of assembling and installing a motor.

b.  Which of these unit costs would be most useful to management in evaluating the overall monthly efficiency of the Motor Department? Explain your reasoning.

 **PROBLEM 18.3A**
Production Cost
Report

Refer to the information from Problem 18.2A.

### Instructions

Complete a production cost report for the Motor Department of Sun Appliance for March.

**830**

L02
through
L05

**PROBLEM 18.4A**

Process Costing
with No Beginning or
Ending Inventories

Toll House makes chocolate chip cookies. The cookies pass through three production processes: mixing the cookie dough, baking, and packaging. Toll House uses process costing.

The following are data concerning the costs incurred in each process during May, along with the number of units processed:

|  | Mixing | Baking | Packaging |
|---|---|---|---|
| Direct materials | $3,600 | $    0 | $1,020 |
| Direct labor | 3,000 | 1,800 | 2,100 |
| Manufacturing overhead | 6,000 | 12,000 | 1,200 |
| Output | 14,000 lbs. | 4,000 gross* | 48,000 boxes |

*A gross is 12 dozen.

To ensure freshness, cookies are baked and packaged on the same day that the dough is mixed. Thus, the company has no inventory still in process at the end of a business day.

**Instructions**

a. Prepare a separate journal entry summarizing the costs incurred by the Mixing Department in preparing 14,000 pounds of cookie dough in May. In the explanation of your entry, indicate the department's unit cost.

b. Prepare the month-end entry recording the transfer of cookie dough to the Baking Department during May.

c. Prepare a journal entry summarizing the costs incurred by the Baking Department in May (excluding the costs transferred from the Mixing Department). In the explanation, indicate the *cost per gross* of the baking process.

d. Prepare the month-end entry recording the transfer of cookies from the Baking Department to the Packaging Department in May.

e. Prepare a journal entry summarizing the costs incurred by the Packaging Department in May. In the explanation, indicate the packaging cost per box.

f. Prepare the month-end entry to record the transfers in May of boxes of cookies from the Packaging Department to the finished goods warehouse. In the explanation, indicate the total cost per box transferred.

g. Briefly explain how management will use the unit cost information appearing in entries **a, c, e,** and **f.**

L02
through
L04

**PROBLEM 18.5A**

Calculate Cost per
Equivalent Unit

Badgersize Company has the following information for its Forming Department for the month of August:

| Work in Process Inventory, August 1: 20,000 units | |
|---|---|
| Direct materials: 100% complete | $ 80,000 |
| Conversion: 20% complete | 24,000 |
| Balance in work in process, August 1 | $104,000 |
| Units started during August | 50,000 |
| Units completed and transferred in August | 60,000 |
| Work in process (70% complete), August 31 | ? |
| Costs charged to Work in Process in August | |
| Direct materials | $150,000 |
| Conversion costs: | |
| Direct labor | $120,000 |
| Overhead applied | 132,000 |
| Total conversion | $252,000 |

Assume materials are added at the start of processing.

**Instructions**

a. Calculate the equivalent units for the Forming Department for the month of August.

b. Find the cost per equivalent unit of the transferred units.

**PROBLEM 18.6A**

Production Cost
Report

Refer to the information in Problem 18.5A.

**Instructions**

a. Complete a production cost report for the Badgersize Company Forming Department for the month of August.

b. Discuss how management might use the production cost report to help manage costs.

**PROBLEM 18.7A**

Process Costing
through Two
Departments

Hound Havens produces plastic doghouses as part of a continuous process through two departments: Molding and Finishing. Direct materials and conversion are added throughout the month in both departments, but at different rates. The information presented below was compiled at the end of April:

| | Molding Department | Finishing Department |
|---|---|---|
| **Beginning Inventories (on April 1):** | | |
| Physical units in production carried forward from March 31 ... | 2,800 | 5,000 |
| Costs: | | |
|    Transferred Molding costs carried forward from March 31 .. | | $125,000 |
|    Direct materials costs carried forward from March 31 ...... | $ 33,340 | 15,000 |
|    Conversion costs carried forward from March 31 ......... | 11,180 | 6,000 |
| **Current Production (in April):** | | |
| Units started during April ............................. | 48,200 | ? |
| Units in ending inventories as of April 30 ................. | 3,400 | 2,000 |
| Costs: | | |
|    Molding costs transferred to Finishing during April ........ | | ? |
|    Direct materials costs incurred in April ................. | $669,200 | $496,000 |
|    Conversion costs incurred in April .................... | 521,840 | 147,600 |
| **Percentage of Completion:** | | |
| Inventories with respect to direct materials on April 1 ........ | 90% | 30% |
| Inventories with respect to conversion on April 1 ........... | 30 | 40 |
| Inventories with respect to direct materials on April 30 ....... | 80% | 25% |
| Inventories with respect to conversion on April 30 .......... | 20 | 30 |

**Instructions**

a. Complete the following requirements for the *Molding Department:*

  1. Prepare a schedule showing units *started and completed* in the Molding Department during April.

  2. Compute the equivalent units of direct materials and conversion for the Molding Department in April.

  3. Determine the cost per equivalent unit of input resource for the Molding Department during April.

  4. Prepare the summary journal entry required to transfer units from the Molding Department to the Finishing Department during April.

  5. Compute the costs assigned to ending inventory in the Molding Department on April 30.

b. Complete the following requirements for the *Finishing Department:*

  1. Prepare a schedule showing units *started and completed* in the Finishing Department during April.

  2. Compute the equivalent units of direct materials and conversion for the Finishing Department in April. Direct materials include both those transferred in from the Molding Department and those added by the Finishing Department.

  3. Determine the cost per equivalent unit of input resource for the Finishing Department during April.

4. Prepare the summary journal entry required to transfer units from the Finishing Department to Finished Goods Inventory during April.

5. Compute the costs assigned to ending inventory in the Finishing Department on April 30.

 **PROBLEM 18.8A**

Process Costing
through Two
Departments

Wilson Dynamics makes flanges in a continuous process through two departments: Forging and Assembly. All direct materials are added at the *beginning* of the process in the Forging Department, whereas all direct materials are added at the *end* of the process in the Assembly Department. Conversion costs are incurred uniformly over time in both departments. As units are completed in the Forging Department they are transferred to the Assembly Department. The costs associated with the transferred units are included in the computation of the Assembly Department's total costs. The information presented below was compiled at the end of July:

| | Forging Department | Assembly Department |
|---|---|---|
| **Beginning Inventories (on July 1):** | | |
| Physical units in production carried forward from June 30 .... | 5,000 | 4,000 |
| Costs: | | |
| Transferred Forging costs carried forward from June 30 .... | | $ 68,000 |
| Direct materials costs carried forward from June 30 ....... | $ 45,000 | ? |
| Conversion costs carried forward from June 30 ........... | 16,000 | 3,000 |
| **Current Production (in July):** | | |
| Units started during July............................... | 75,000 | ? |
| Units in ending inventories as of July 31 ................. | 8,000 | 16,000 |
| Costs: | | |
| Forging costs transferred to Assembly during July......... | | ? |
| Direct materials costs incurred in July .................. | $675,000 | $720,000 |
| Conversion costs incurred in July ...................... | 608,000 | 191,400 |
| **Percentage of Completion:** | | |
| Inventories with respect to conversion on July 1 ............ | 40% | 25% |
| Inventories with respect to conversion on July 31 ........... | 75 | 30 |

**Instructions**

a. Complete the following requirements for the *Forging Department:*

   1. Prepare a schedule showing units *started and completed* in the Forging Department during July.

   2. Compute the equivalent units of direct materials and conversion for the Forging Department in July.

   3. Determine the cost per equivalent unit of input resource for the Forging Department during July.

   4. Prepare the summary journal entry required to transfer units from the Forging Department to the Assembly Department during July.

   5. Compute the costs assigned to ending inventory in the Forging Department on July 31.

b. Complete the following requirements for the *Assembly Department:*

   1. Prepare a schedule showing units *started and completed* in the Assembly Department during July.

   2. Compute the equivalent units of direct materials and conversion for the Assembly Department in July. Direct materials include both those transferred in from the Forging Department and those added by the Assembly Department.

   3. Determine the cost per equivalent unit of input resource for the Assembly Department during July.

   4. Prepare the summary journal entry required to transfer units from the Assembly Department to Finished Goods Inventory during July.

   5. Compute the costs assigned to ending inventory in the Assembly Department on July 31.

# Problem Set B

 **PROBLEM 18.1B**

Calculating Equivalent Units

Morgan Industries, Inc., mass-produces street lights. Materials used in constructing the body of the lights are added at the start of the process, while the materials used in wiring the lights are added at the halfway point. All labor and overhead are added evenly throughout the manufacturing process. Morgan uses process costing and had the following unit production information available for the months of March and April:

|  | March | April |
|---|---|---|
| Number of lights in beginning work in process ...................... | 600 | 1,600 |
| Lights transferred to finished goods ............................... | 4,200 | 4,000 |
| Number of lights in ending work in process ........................ | 1,600 | 700 |

In March, the lights in beginning work in process were approximately 60 percent complete, while those in ending work in process were only 20 percent complete. In April, the units remaining in ending work in process were 70 percent complete. All lights in ending work in process are finished during the next month.

**Instructions**

a. For the month of March, calculate the equivalent units of production for the three major cost categories—body materials, wiring materials, and labor and overhead.

b. For the month of April, calculate the equivalent units of production for the three major cost categories—body materials, wiring materials, and labor and overhead.

**PROBLEM 18.2B**

Computing and Using Unit Costs

One of MowTown Manufacturing's products is a small lawnmower. Two processing departments are involved in the mower's production. The deck is assembled in one department, and a second department assembles and installs the engine. There is no beginning or ending work in process in either department. During May, the company incurred the following costs in the manufacture of 6,000 lawnmowers:

|  | Deck Department | Engine Department |
|---|---|---|
| Direct materials ...................................... | $192,000 | $480,000 |
| Direct labor........................................ | 48,000 | 108,000 |
| Manufacturing overhead............................. | 54,000 | 66,000 |

**Instructions**

a. Compute the following *per-unit* costs for the month of May.
   1. A deck assembly transferred to the Engine Department.
   2. Assembling an engine and installing it.
   3. A completed lawnmower.
   4. Materials used in assembling a deck.
   5. Direct labor cost of assembling and installing an engine.

b. Which of these unit costs would be most useful to management in evaluating the overall monthly efficiency of the Engine Department? Explain your reasoning.

 **PROBLEM 18.3B**

Production Cost Report

Refer to the information from Problem 18.2B.

**Instructions**

Complete a production cost report for the Engine Department of MowTown Manufacturing for May.

**834**     Chapter 18 Process Costing

L02
through
L05
**PROBLEM 18.4B**

Process Costing with No Beginning or Ending Inventories

Snack Happy makes chocolate brownies. The brownies pass through three production processes: mixing the batter, baking, and packaging. The company uses process costing.

The following are data concerning the costs incurred in each process during August, along with the number of units processed:

|  | Mixing | Baking | Packaging |
|---|---|---|---|
| Direct materials | $25,000 | $ 0 | $ 3,000 |
| Direct labor | 60,000 | 40,000 | 14,000 |
| Manufacturing overhead | 35,000 | 50,000 | 7,000 |
| Output | 20,000 lbs. | 5,000 gross* | 12,000 cases |

*A gross is 12 dozen.

To ensure freshness, brownies are baked and packaged on the same day that the batter is mixed. Thus, the company has no inventory still in process at the end of a business day.

**Instructions**

a. Prepare a separate journal entry summarizing the costs incurred by the Mixing Department in preparing 20,000 pounds of batter in August. In the explanation of your entry, indicate the department's unit cost.

b. Prepare the month-end entry recording the transfer of batter to the Baking Department during August.

c. Prepare a journal entry summarizing the costs incurred by the Baking Department in August (excluding the costs transferred from the Mixing Department). In the explanation, indicate the *cost per gross* of the baking process.

d. Prepare the month-end entry recording the transfer of brownies from the Baking Department to the Packaging Department in August.

e. Prepare a journal entry summarizing the costs incurred by the Packaging Department in August. In the explanation, indicate the packaging cost per case.

f. Prepare the month-end entry to record the transfers in August of cases of brownies from the Packaging Department to the finished goods warehouse. In the explanation, indicate the total cost per case transferred.

g. Briefly explain how management will use the unit cost information appearing in entries **a, c, e,** and **f.**

**PROBLEM 18.5B**

Calculate Cost per Equivalent Unit

Balfanz Company has the following information for its Finishing Department for the month of September:

| Work in Process Inventory, September 1: 50,000 units | |
|---|---|
| Direct materials: 100% complete | $ 150,000 |
| Conversion: 40% complete | 120,000 |
| Balance in work in process, September 1 | $ 270,000 |
| Units started during September | 300,000 |
| Units completed and transferred in September | 280,000 |
| Work in process (80% complete), September 30 | ? |
| Costs charged to Work in Process in September | |
| Direct materials | $1,200,000 |
| Conversion costs: | |
| Direct labor | $1,000,000 |
| Overhead applied | $1,212,000 |
| Total conversion | $2,212,000 |

Assume materials are added at the start of processing.

**Instructions**

**a.** Calculate the equivalent units for the Finishing Department for the month of September.

**b.** Find the cost per equivalent unit of the transferred units.

 **PROBLEM 18.6B**
Production Cost
 Report

Refer to the information in Problem 18.5B.

**Instructions**

**a.** Complete a production cost report for the Balfanz Company Finishing Department for the month of September.

**b.** Discuss how management might use the production cost report to help manage costs.

**PROBLEM 18.7B**

Process Costing
through Two
Departments

Delray Industries manufactures plastic wading pools as part of a continuous process through two departments: Molding and Finishing. Direct materials and conversion are added throughout the month in both departments, but at different rates. The information presented below was compiled at the end of June:

| | Molding Department | Finishing Department |
|---|---|---|
| **Beginning Inventories (on June 1):** | | |
| Physical units in production carried forward from May 31 . . . . . | 3,000 | 5,000 |
| Costs: | | |
|    Transferred Molding costs carried forward from May 31. . . . . | | $150,000 |
|    Direct materials costs carried forward from May 31 . . . . . . . . | $ 37,800 | 4,000 |
|    Conversion costs carried forward from May 31. . . . . . . . . . . | 14,400 | 24,000 |
| **Current Production (in June):** | | |
| Units started during June . . . . . . . . . . . . . . . . . . . . . . . . . . . | 50,000 | ? |
| Units in ending inventories as of June 30. . . . . . . . . . . . . . . . | 1,000 | 2,000 |
| Costs: | | |
|    Molding costs transferred to Finishing during June. . . . . . . . | | ? |
|    Direct materials costs incurred in June . . . . . . . . . . . . . . . . . | $912,600 | $222,000 |
|    Conversion costs incurred in June . . . . . . . . . . . . . . . . . . . . | 612,000 | 430,400 |
| **Percentage of Completion:** | | |
| Inventories with respect to direct materials on June 1 . . . . . . . . | 70% | 20% |
| Inventories with respect to conversion on June 1. . . . . . . . . . . . | 40 | 60 |
| Inventories with respect to direct materials on June 30 . . . . . . . | 80% | 75% |
| Inventories with respect to conversion on June 30. . . . . . . . . . . | 20 | 90 |

**Instructions**

**a.** Complete the following requirements for the *Molding Department:*

   **1.** Prepare a schedule showing units *started and completed* in the Molding Department during June.

   **2.** Compute the equivalent units of direct materials and conversion for the Molding Department in June.

   **3.** Determine the cost per equivalent unit of input resource for the Molding Department during June.

   **4.** Prepare the summary journal entry required to transfer units from the Molding Department to the Finishing Department during June.

   **5.** Compute the costs assigned to ending inventory in the Molding Department on June 30.

**b.** Complete the following requirements for the *Finishing Department:*

1. Prepare a schedule showing units *started and completed* in the Finishing Department during June.

2. Compute the equivalent units of direct materials and conversion for the Finishing Department in June. Direct materials include both those transferred in from the Molding Department and those added by the Finishing Department.

3. Determine the cost per equivalent unit of input resource for the Finishing Department during June.

4. Prepare the summary journal entry required to transfer units from the Finishing Department to Finished Goods Inventory during June.

5. Compute the costs assigned to ending inventory in the Finishing Department on June 30.

**PROBLEM 18.8B**

Process Costing through Two Departments

Thompson Tools produces dampers in a continuous process through two departments: Assembly and Packaging. All direct materials are added at the *beginning* of the process in the Assembly Department, whereas all direct materials are added at the *end* of the process in the Packaging Department. Conversion costs are incurred uniformly over time in both departments. As units are completed in the Assembly Department, they are transferred to the Packaging Department. The costs associated with the transferred units are included in the computation of the Packaging Department's total costs. The information presented below was compiled at the end of March:

| | Assembly Department | Packaging Department |
|---|---|---|
| **Beginning Inventories (on March 1):** | | |
| Physical units in production carried forward from February 28 . . . . . . . . . . . . . . . . . . . . . . . . . . . | 5,000 | 4,000 |
| Costs: | | |
| Transferred Assembly costs carried forward from February 28 . . . . . . . . . . . . . . . . . . . . . . . . . . . | | $ 60,000 |
| Direct materials costs carried forward from February 28 . . . . . . . . . . . . . . . . . . . . . . . . . . . . . . | $ 45,000 | ? |
| Conversion costs carried forward from February 28 . . . . . . . . . . . . . . . . . . . . . . . . . . . . . . . . . | 9,000 | 3,200 |
| **Current Production (in March):** | | |
| Units started during March . . . . . . . . . . . . . . . . . . . . . . . . . . . . . . . . . . . . . . . . . . . . . . . . . . . | 80,000 | ? |
| Units in ending inventories as of March 31 . . . . . . . . . . . . . . . . . . . . . . . . . . . . . . . . . . . . . . . . | 9,000 | 20,000 |
| Costs: | | |
| Assembly costs transferred to Packaging during March . . . . . . . . . . . . . . . . . . . . . . . . . . . . . . . | | ? |
| Direct materials costs incurred in March . . . . . . . . . . . . . . . . . . . . . . . . . . . . . . . . . . . . . . . . . . | $720,000 | $840,000 |
| Conversion costs incurred in March . . . . . . . . . . . . . . . . . . . . . . . . . . . . . . . . . . . . . . . . . . . . . . | 490,200 | 260,800 |
| **Percentage of Completion:** | | |
| Inventories with respect to conversion on March 1 . . . . . . . . . . . . . . . . . . . . . . . . . . . . . . . . . . | 30% | 20% |
| Inventories with respect to conversion on March 31 . . . . . . . . . . . . . . . . . . . . . . . . . . . . . . . . . | 80 | 30 |

**Instructions**

**a.** Complete the following requirements for the *Assembly Department:*

1. Prepare a schedule showing units *started and completed* in the Assembly Department during March.

2. Compute the equivalent units of direct materials and conversion for the Assembly Department in March.

3. Determine the cost per equivalent unit of input resource for the Assembly Department during March.

4. Prepare the summary journal entry required to transfer units from the Assembly Department to the Packaging Department during March.

5. Compute the costs assigned to ending inventory in the Assembly Department on March 31.

**b.** Complete the following requirements for the *Packaging Department:*

1. Prepare a schedule showing units *started and completed* in the Packaging Department during March.

2. Compute the equivalent units of direct materials and conversion for the Packaging Department in March. Direct materials include both those transferred in from the Assembly Department and those added by the Packaging Department.

3. Determine the cost per equivalent unit of input resource for the Packaging Department during March.

4. Prepare the summary journal entry required to transfer units from the Packaging Department to Finished Goods Inventory during March.

5. Compute the costs assigned to ending inventory in the Packaging Department on March 31.

# Critical Thinking Cases

**L01**
through
**L03**

**CASE 18.1**

Evaluation of a Cost System: Does It Meet the Company's Needs?

Viking Beer is a microbrewery that produces one type of beer. The production level is 18,000 gallons per month, which is bottled in 192,000 twelve-ounce bottles. The beer is brewed in batches of 3,600 gallons, which is the capacity of the fermenting tanks. Each batch requires six days of processing, during which it passes through six separate production processes.

Viking uses process costing. All manufacturing costs incurred during the month are assigned to the 192,000 bottles produced; no valuation is assigned to the 3,600 gallons currently sitting in the fermenting tanks.

Viking has hired Matt Brown, a recent college graduate, as a cost analyst. After learning about the company's cost accounting system, Brown sent the following memo to Viking's controller:

> I have two suggestions as to how we might improve our cost accounting system. First, our beer is processed in identifiable batches; so we could use *job order*, rather than process, costing. This would enable us to determine separately the cost of each batch.
>
> Second, we always have 3,600 gallons of beer in the fermenting tanks. But our cost accounting system assigns all manufacturing costs during the period to the finished goods produced. Some of these costs should be assigned to the beer in the fermenting tanks and identified as "work in process inventory." This can be done by computing the *equivalent units* that these 3,600 gallons represent.

**Instructions**

As Viking's controller, draft a memo responding to Brown's suggestions.

**L02**
through
**L06**

**CASE 18.2**

Interpreting and Using Process Costing Information

Assume that you are the production manager of the Assembly Department illustrated on pages 807–810 of this chapter (Metal Products, Inc.). One of your responsibilities is to determine whether costs are remaining relatively stable from month to month. Assume that the $29,500 associated with the 1,000 units in process on *March 1* (see Exhibit 18–5, page 808) is comprised of the following:

| | |
|---|---|
| Cut materials transferred from the Cutting Department in *February* . . . . . . . . . . . . . | $25,000 |
| Direct materials added in the Assembly Department in *February* . . . . . . . . . . . . . . . | 0 |
| Conversion added in the Assembly Department in *February* . . . . . . . . . . . . . . . . . | 4,500 |
| Total cost associated with beginning inventory on *March 1* . . . . . . . . . . . . . . . . . | $29,500 |

The *cost per equivalent unit* of input resource used by the Assembly Department in March is as follows (see Exhibit 18–7, page 809):

| | |
|---|---|
| Cut materials transferred from the Cutting Department in *March* . . . . . . . . . . . . . . . . . . . | $20 |
| Direct materials added in the Assembly Department in *March* . . . . . . . . . . . . . . . . . . . . | 4 |
| Conversion added in the Assembly Department in *March* . . . . . . . . . . . . . . . . . . . . . . . | 25 |
| Cost per equivalent unit of input resource used in *March* . . . . . . . . . . . . . . . . . . . . . . | $49 |

## Instructions

**a.** By how much did the cost per equivalent unit of cut material transferred in from the Cutting Department in *February* differ from the cost per equivalent unit of cut material transferred to the Assembly Department in *March*?

**b.** By how much did the cost per equivalent unit of conversion for the Assembly Department in *February* differ from the cost per equivalent unit of conversion for the Assembly Department in *March*?

**c.** Speculate as to why the cost per equivalent unit of input resource (cut materials and conversion) may have changed from February to March.

**L01**  
**L02**  
**CASE 18.3**  
Processes and Product Costs at PepsiCo

Visit the PepsiCo Web site at:

http://www.pepsiusa.com/faqs.php/

Follow the link to "How Pepsi is Made" (under "Product Information") for parts **a.**, **b.**, and **c.** Follow the links under "Community Information" for part **d.**

## Instructions

**a.** Identify and discuss briefly the processes involved in manufacturing Pepsi.

**b.** What are Pepsi's direct materials?

**c.** Of the company's conversion costs, does labor or manufacturing overhead comprise the larger component of manufacturing costs? Defend your answer.

**d.** View the PepsiCo's charitable, educational, and environmental initiatives. Would it be improper for PepsiCo to report these initiatives as product costs? Do you believe that it is ethical for PepsiCo to report only the positive impacts of its community-oriented efforts throughout the world? Defend your answer.

**L01**  
**L02**  
**INTERNET CASE 18.4**  
Manufacturing Processes

Wrigley Company manufactures chewing gum. Visit its home page at the following address:

www.wrigley.com

From the home page, click on the choices labeled "About Us," then "About Gum,"and then "How Gum Is Made."

## Instructions

**a.** Prepare a simple flowchart that illustrates the major steps in the manufacture of chewing gum.

**b.** If Wrigley uses process costing, how many separate processing departments might be used and what would you label them?

**c.** What do you think are the major types of manufacturing overhead at Wrigley? What activity bases could be used to assign each type of overhead to the processing departments you listed in part **b?**

*Internet sites are time and date sensitive. It is the purpose of these exercises to have you explore the Internet. You may need to use the Yahoo! search engine* http://www.yahoo.com *(or another favorite search engine) to look for a company's current Web address.*

## Answers To Self-Test Questions

**1.** a, c    **2.** b    **3.** a, b, c    **4.** a, b, c, d    **5.** a, b, c, e

# CHAPTER 19

# Costing and the Value Chain

## AFTER STUDYING THIS CHAPTER, YOU SHOULD BE ABLE TO:

**Learning Objectives**

**LO1**  Define the value chain and describe its basic components.

**LO2**  Distinguish between non-value-added and value-added activities.

**LO3**  Explain how activity-based management is related to activity-based costing (ABC).

**LO4**  Describe the target costing process and list its components.

**LO5**  Identify the relationship between target costing and the value chain.

**LO6**  Explain the nature and goals of a just-in-time (JIT) manufacturing system.

**LO7**  Identify the components of the cost of quality.

**LO8**  Describe the characteristics of quality measures.

# KIMBERLY-CLARK CORPORATION

For nearly 140 years, Kimberly-Clark has helped improve the quality of life for millions of people by developing some of the world's most trusted and recognized health and hygiene brands. Kimberly-Clark is a recognized leader in sustainable resource initiatives. In its annual sustainability report,[1] Kimberly-Clark shares its vision to reduce product packaging by 5 percent by 2013, while continuing to work toward recycling 100 percent of nonhazardous solid waste from operations. In a recent sustainability report, Kimberly-Clark reports that they produced 1.48 million tons of total waste, of which 293,000 tons were sent to landfills. . . . Approximately 423,000 tons were recycled, composted, or incinerated and 762,000 tons were reused directly or in other products or processes.

By identifying non-value-added activities in its value chain, like sending waste to a landfill rather than recycling or reusing that waste, Kimberly-Clark was able to save more than $10 million. ■

---

[1] http://www.kimberly-clark.com/aboutus/sus_2010/sustainability_pg41.aspx.

## The Value Chain

To focus on core operations, management begins by identifying components of the organization's value chain. In Chapter 16, we defined the **value chain** as the set of activities and resources necessary to create and deliver the product or service valued by customers.

Obviously, the details of each organization's value chain will look different. Further, the value chain for each particular product or service within an organization can be very different. Consider Kimberly-Clark Corporation, the company discussed in the chapter opener. On its Web site, Kimberly-Clark lists some of its products and services for the consumer, health care, and professional markets. These categories represent different markets with different types of suppliers and customers. For example, product characteristics that are valued by a typical consumer will differ significantly from those valued by a health care customer. In addition, the suppliers for health care and consumer products differ significantly. Creating a value chain to satisfy diverse customer needs is a major challenge for most businesses.

For each of a company's products and services, the following components of the value chain (as also shown in Exhibit 19–1) are active:

- *Research and development (R&D) and design activities* include the creation of ideas and the development of prototype products, processes, and services.
- *Suppliers and production-related activities* include the procurement of raw materials and supplies and the activities needed to convert them into finished goods and services.
- *Marketing and distribution activities* are designed to provide information to potential customers and make the products and services accessible to customers.
- *Customer service activities* are those resources consumed by supporting the product or service after it is sold to the customer.

### INTERNATIONAL FINANCIAL REPORTING STANDARDS AND THE VALUE CHAIN

Several reporting differences between U.S. generally accepted accounting principles (GAAP) and IFRS are value chain related. Two examples are accounting for R&D and creating multiple sets of financial statements. First, IFRS requires some research and development activities to be capitalized while U.S. GAAP requires them to be expensed. This difference may affect R&D investment decision making.

Second, companies with operations in countries where IFRS is the accepted standard may need to file financial reports that meet both local GAAP and IFRS standards. They may also need to reconcile to U.S. GAAP to meet reporting requirements of the U.S. parent company. Similarly, a U.S. company that's a subsidiary of a publicly traded international firm headquartered in an IFRS reporting country must prepare IFRS financial statements. Or it must be able to reconcile its U.S. GAAP statement to IFRS for inclusion in the parent company's consolidated financial statement. These additional reporting requirements add costs to the value chain.

### VALUE- AND NON-VALUE-ADDED ACTIVITIES

Organizations attempt to identify and eliminate the **non-value-added activities** in their value chains. **Value-added activities** add to the product's or service's desirability in the eyes of the consumer. Non-value-added activities do not add to the product's desirability. Thus, an organization can decrease its costs if a non-value-added activity that consumes resources can be eliminated without changing the product's desirability. Examples of value-added and non-value-added activities are included in Exhibit 19–1. One example of a non-value-added activity is having large amounts of raw materials, work in process, or finished goods inventory. Kimberly-Clark's management recognizes the non-value-added cost associated with holding inventories because a part of its operating plan is to focus on tight inventory control. Just-in-time inventory management processes, discussed later in this chapter, have been developed to reduce the consumption of non-value-added resources associated with large amounts of inventories.

**YOUR TURN**    **You as a Raw Materials Inventory Manager**

Assume you are the manager of raw materials for a lumber mill. What types of resources are being consumed when a large amount of redwood logs sits idle, waiting to be put through the mill?

(See our comments on the Online Learning Center Web site.)

**Exhibit 19–1**  **VALUE-ADDED AND NON-VALUE-ADDED ACTIVITIES IN THE VALUE CHAIN**

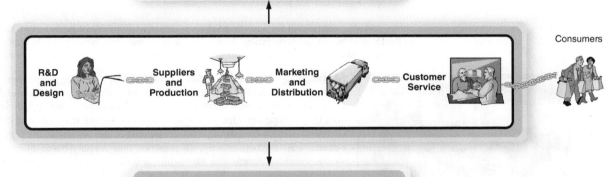

**Value-added activities in the value chain:**
- Designs that meet customer specifications
- Use of suppliers that provide timely high-quality inputs
- Production process that provides just-in-time output for customer
- Timely distribution and easy access to customer
- Clear and truthful marketing
- Competent and timely after-sales customer help

R&D and Design → Suppliers and Production → Marketing and Distribution → Customer Service → Consumers

**Non-value-added activities in the value chain:**
- Designs that meet engineering specifications but not customer needs
- Supplier deliveries that are poor quality or not timely, causing delays in production
- Production processes that create rework, scrap, and significant work in process inventories
- Delayed distribution to customer
- Deceptive or misleading marketing
- After-sales customer help that is not valued by customers

In the previous three chapters, we concentrated our cost analysis only on the production phase of the value chain. However, resources are consumed across the value chain. Organizations attempt to minimize resource consumption at all points on the value chain while simultaneously providing the products and services desired by consumers at competitive prices. In this chapter, we will consider other cost accounting procedures and techniques that have been developed to assess resource use and costs in all parts of the value chain. These procedures include *activity-based management,* which is effective over the entire value chain; *target costing,* designed for the R&D and design phase of the value chain; *just-in-time manufacturing procedures;* and, finally, *total quality management,* which is also relevant over the entire value chain.

## Activity-Based Management

Previously, when we introduced activity-based costing (ABC), we provided an ABC example focused on production overhead. You may remember that the basic procedures related to ABC include the following:

1. Identify the *activity.*
2. Create an associated *activity cost pool.*
3. Identify an *activity measure.*
4. Create the *cost per unit of activity.*

Our earlier focus was on using ABC to assign cost to units of the product. However, activity-based cost information is also important in management decision making. Remember that management is trying to eliminate non-value-added activities from the value chain. For example, if the downtime needed for equipment repair can be eliminated from the value chain *without increasing the cost associated with the total value chain,* then it is a non-value-added activity. The process of using activity-based costs to help reduce and eliminate non-value-added activities is **activity-based management.** Redesigning equipment layout, acquiring higher-quality materials as inputs, buying new equipment, outsourcing repair work, or some combination of these management decisions may reduce or eliminate activity cost and associated resource use.

### ACTIVITY-BASED MANAGEMENT ACROSS THE VALUE CHAIN

While activity-based cost information is very important in the production portion of the value chain, it is also very useful for assessing activities associated with most period expenses such as R&D, distribution, administration, finance, marketing, and customer service. In many organizations, period expenses are more significant to overall profitability than product expenses.

© Ryan McVay/Getty Images/DAL

**Managing Activities: An Illustration**  Management uses ABC information to identify activities and processes that are non-value-added or where the added costs of those activities and processes outweigh their benefits to the customer. One way that managers compare the costs and benefits of activities is by contrasting the internal cost of the activity to the purchased external cost for that activity. To illustrate how activity-based management works, consider Boards and More, Inc., a company that sells lumber, paper, and packaging products. Boards and More's chief financial officer (CFO) has been approached by a software vendor selling software called "Transaction Reduction." The software is designed to reduce the cost of processing transactions. In order to determine the cost savings for Boards and More, the CFO decides to undertake an ABC study of the activities of his Accounting and Finance (A&F) Department.

The activities performed by the A&F Department include:

1. Transaction-related activities.
2. External financial reporting.
3. Annual planning and budgeting.
4. Specially requested analyses.

In addition, the labor cost pool and associated wages are:

1. Twelve clerks at $20 per hour.
2. Five finance analysts at a salary of $45,000 each.
3. Six budget analysts at a salary of $39,000 each.
4. Three senior analysts at $75,000 each and the CFO at $185,000.

The CFO, with the help of the employees, completes an extensive activity analysis of the labor time consumed for the four identified activities. The CFO then determines the percentage of time devoted to each of the four activities by each of the four labor categories. Please study Exhibit 19–2 carefully. It shows the related percentages, cost pools, and activities for the A&F Department.

Remember that the objective of the ABC analysis is to compare the internal cost of processing transactions with the external cost of the proposed software. Thus, the next step in the activity analysis is to calculate the detailed cost for each activity. Exhibit 19–3 breaks out the cost of each activity by using the percentages from Exhibit 19–2 and the cost of each type of labor. The ABC analysis in Exhibit 19–2 will help the CFO manage his own activities and those of the 26 employees in the A&F Department. In particular, the CFO can consider whether the internal transaction-related activity costs are non-value-added in comparison to the external cost of the Transaction Reduction software.

**Exhibit 19–2** **IDENTIFYING COST POOLS AND ACTIVITIES**

**Boards and More, Inc.**
**Department of Accounting and Finance**

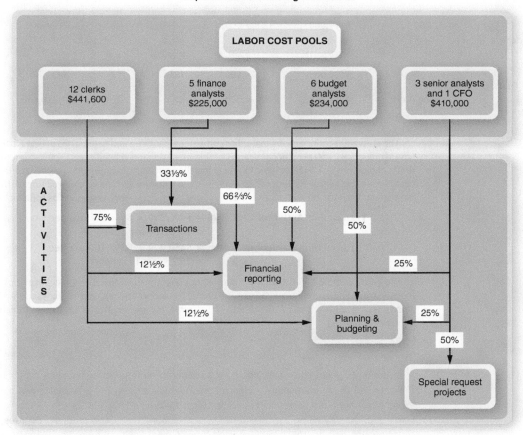

Examine the transaction-related activity costs in the first column in Exhibit 19–3. These costs are required to make sure basic journal entries are properly recorded and monitored throughout the firm to safeguard the firm's assets. Account clerks complete much of the detailed work. However, financial analysts are also involved in assessing transactions and undertaking analysis in order to complete their financial reporting responsibilities. As a result of the ABC analysis, the CFO estimates $406,200 of the total labor cost pool of $1,310,600 is associated with transaction-related activities.

## Exhibit 19–3   ACTIVITY COST ANALYSES

| Labor Category | Transaction-Related | Financial Reporting | Planning and Budgeting | Special Analyses | Total Labor Resources |
|---|---|---|---|---|---|
| | **Activity Category** | | | | |
| Clerks | ¾ (75%) | ⅛ (12.5%) | ⅛ (12.5%) | 0 | 22,080 hours = (12 clerks, 46 weeks @ 40 hrs. per week @ $20/hr) = |
| | $331,200 | $55,200 | $55,200 | $0 | $441,600 |
| Finance analysts | ⅓ (33.33%) | ⅔ (66.67%) | 0 | 0 | 5 salaried analysts @$45,000 each = |
| | $75,000 | $150,000 | $0 | $0 | $225,000 |
| Budget analysts | 0 | ½ (50%) | ½ (50%) | 0 | 6 salaried analysts @ $39,000 = |
| | $0 | $117,000 | $117,000 | $0 | $234,000 |
| Senior analysts and CFO | 0 | ¼ (25%) | ¼ (25%) | ½ (50%) | 3 seniors @$75,000 each and 1 CFO @$185,000 = |
| | $0 | $102,500 | $102,500 | $205,000 | $410,000 |
| **Total activity resources** | $406,200 | $424,700 | $274,700 | $205,000 | **$1,310,600** |

The software vendor affirms that other companies installing and using Transaction Reduction have experienced a 50 percent per year reduction in transaction-related costs. Transaction Reduction's quoted price is $450,000 for the fully installed package, including employee training and customer support services. If the CFO purchases the software and the vendor's savings estimates are correct, the software will recover its initial cost after 2.22 years, computed as follows:

$$\text{Transaction Activities Cost Pool} = \$406,200 \times 50\% \text{ savings per year}$$
$$= \$203,100 \text{ per year}$$
$$\text{"Transaction Reduction" Costs} = \$450,000 \div \$203,100 \text{ per year}$$
$$= 2.22 \text{ years to recover}$$

We know that the CFO will have many other concerns in addition to the cost savings from the software. For example, since ¾ of the clerks (9 clerks) are engaged in transaction-related activities, would 4½ need to be fired? If so, what are the legal and human implications?

### INTERNATIONAL CASE IN POINT

These days, value chain activities such as drawing up detailed architectural blueprints, slicing and dicing a company's financial disclosures, or designing a revolutionary microprocessor are often outsourced overseas. That's why Intel Inc. and Texas Instruments Inc. are furiously hiring Indian and Chinese engineers, many with graduate degrees, to design chip circuits. Dutch consumer electronics giant Philips has shifted research and development on most televisions, cell phones, and audio products to Shanghai. Procter & Gamble Co. has employees in Manila, most of whom have business and finance degrees, to help prepare P&G 's tax returns around the world.

One of the biggest trends reshaping the global economy is in process. The driving forces are digitization, the Internet, and high-speed data networks that girdle the globe. Now, all kinds of knowledge work can be done almost anywhere. Predictions are that at least 3.3 million white-collar jobs and $136 billion in wages will be added to low-cost countries by 2015.

The CFO may also be concerned that a longer time to recover the initial investment would be undesirable given rapid change in software technology. In order to determine the exact resources (clerks versus analysts) that might be affected by the new software, a more detailed analysis than that just displayed must be undertaken.

## ABC: A SUBSET OF ACTIVITY-BASED MANAGEMENT

ABC information must be created before management of the activity can occur. To see this, consider the ABC data from Boards and More, Inc. Suppose the external auditors for Boards and More proposed to the CFO that an independent consulting firm could perform the financial analysts' function for $190,000. At the simplest level, this might be considered a cost reduction because the five financial analysts consume $225,000 in resources and the proposed outsourcing consumes $190,000 in resources. This suggests that a savings of $35,000 per year ($225,000 − $190,000) would result from hiring the outside firm. Closer inspection of the external auditors' proposal, however, reveals that the activities under consideration are restricted to those in the financial reporting area. The ABC data, however, tell the CFO that these activities comprise only two-thirds of the total financial analysts' activities ($\frac{2}{3} \times$ $225,000 = $150,000). Thus, the true resource cost from the external auditors' proposal would be a loss of $40,000 ($150,000 − $190,000), rather than the $35,000 yearly savings. Thus, the CFO should reject the external auditors' proposal.

Managing the activities at Boards and More requires a clear understanding of what consumes resources *and* the costs associated with these resources. In addition, having benchmark information about competitive practices can help the company identify non-value-added activities. This benchmark information can be in the form of industry studies, competitive outside bids, or internal prototyping. Thus, ABC is a critical component of activity-based management, but managing the activities also requires benchmark information. Exhibit 19–4 captures the details of activity-based management.

**Learning Objective**
**Explain how activity-based management is related to activity-based costing (ABC).**    L03

**Exhibit 19–4**  **ABC IS A SUBSET OF ACTIVITY-BASED MANAGEMENT**

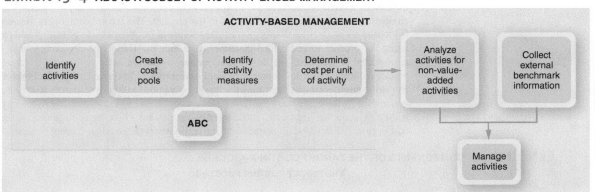

## The Target Costing Process

The previous example based on Boards and More, Inc., is aimed at considering activities of existing, established processes. **Target costing** is a business process aimed at the earliest stages of new product and service development, before creation and design of production methods. It is a process driven by the customer, focused on design, and encompassing the entire life of the product. The objective is to create a production process that provides adequate profits. By focusing simultaneously on profit and cost planning over the entire value chain, organizations are able to tap synergies among the various value chain parts. Consideration of the entire value chain at the product development phase is critical because research demonstrates that 80 percent of production-related expenses are committed once the production process begins. These committed resources cannot be changed later without great cost to the company.

The target costing process begins with the customer. Customer desires about functionality, quality, and, most important, price drive the analysis. Having a clear understanding of customer needs is critical. There are likely to be functional requirements that must be present to meet customer needs. Further, the customer may be unwilling to trade off functional requirements for lower price or lower quality. Knowing customer requirements also means understanding competitor offerings. Consumers do not operate in a vacuum. They demand product characteristics based on what is available in the marketplace. If a competitor offers a higher-quality product with a similar functionality at a lower price, then companies attempt to reengineer their processes to meet that competition.

## COMPONENTS OF THE TARGET COSTING PROCESS

At the most basic level, the *desired* target cost is the cost of resources that should be consumed to create a product that can be sold at a target price. The target costing process begins with identifying the target price. The target price is determined through interaction with consumers. However, management must determine an acceptable profit margin for the product to compute the desired target cost. That profit margin, although not considered in detail here, is a function of the type of business and the demands of the marketplace. The basic target cost formula is as follows:

$$\textbf{Target Cost} = \textbf{Target Price} - \textbf{Profit Margin}$$

Target costing can be best understood by considering its four components:

- Planning and market analysis.
- Concept development.
- Production design and value engineering.
- Production and continuous improvement.

First, significant resources are consumed in *planning and market analysis.* During planning, the customer niche is identified and thoroughly documented. Market analysts carefully consider competitors and their potential reactions to the product. The second component, *development,* is focused on product feasibility studies. Development involves a cycle of testing and reformulating the product to understand customer requirements. These first two components lead to an expected target price. The third phase, *production design,* follows the establishment of the product concept in the development phase. Engineering and experienced production personnel use **value engineering** to determine the least costly combination of resources to create a product desired by the customer. Finally, *production* begins and a continuous improvement process is used to attain the target cost. These latter two stages are where the achievement of the target cost occurs. Exhibit 19–5 illustrates how the components of the target costing process interact.

## Exhibit 19-5 COMPONENTS OF THE TARGET COSTING PROCESS
### THE TARGET COSTING PROCESS

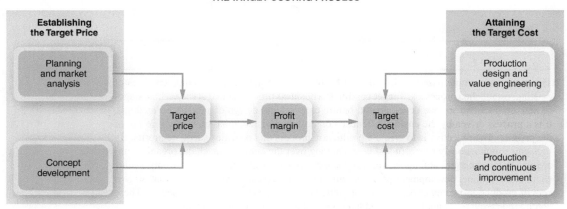

## TARGET COSTING: AN ILLUSTRATION

To illustrate the target costing process, we will use Boards and More, Inc., the company previously discussed. One of Boards and More's product lines is creating paper packaging for various products. The company bids on packaging jobs for such products as laundry soap, cereal boxes, and pancake mix. The typical value chain for the cardboard boxes is shown in Exhibit 19–6. The value chain for these packaging materials includes the research and development objective of creating cardboard with superior quality and strength at the lowest possible weight. Boards and More produces the cardboard in large rolls that are shipped to suppliers for printing and box formation before the boxes are shipped to, in this example, the soap manufacturer.

**Exhibit 19–6  TARGET COSTING ACROSS THE VALUE CHAIN**

**VALUE CHAIN FOR CARDBOARD PACKAGING**

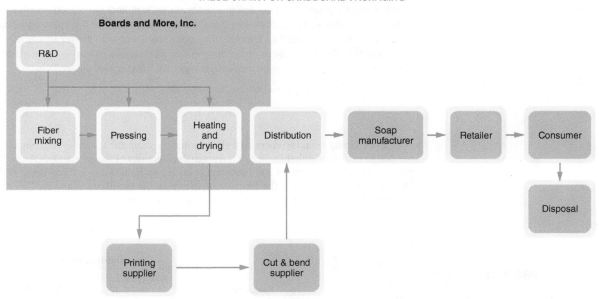

In a recent survey of the soap box market by Boards and More's Marketing and Planning Department, customers expressed dissatisfaction with currently available packaging. Further analysis reveals soap manufacturers believe the packaging is too heavy, increasing their shipping costs. Soap consumers are also unhappy with the ink used because, when the boxes get wet, the printing bleeds or rubs off.

A cross-functional, cross-organizational team is assembled to create a product to satisfy customer needs. Notice that two sets of customers, both in the value chain, are important: the soap manufacturer and the soap consumer. The product creation team consists of marketing, design engineering, accounting, and production engineering personnel from Boards and More and similar personnel from the printing firm and the soap company. The charge to the team is to create new paperboard for the cardboard soap boxes that satisfies customers' needs.

Observe that, although Boards and More leads the new product team, all members of the value chain should participate in new product creation. If the new cardboard created by Boards and More is of a lighter weight but cannot properly absorb ink, then the solution is not

**The customer affects target costs**

**The entire value chain affects target costs**

viable. Similarly, if the cardboard is lightweight but its strength does not allow proper filling by the machinery at the soap manufacturer, then the solution is not feasible. Finally, in addition to the design changes that Boards and More considers undertaking, other team members from the printing or soap companies may want to modify or change their processes to satisfy the ultimate customer, the soap consumer.

**YOUR TURN**   **You as a Team Leader**

Assume you are the leader of the Boards and More product creation team for the new soap box design. At the initial meeting of the cross-organizational team, a serious reservation is raised by the team members from the printing firm about the confidentiality and intellectual properties of any new designs created by the overall team. The printing firm has a policy of keeping all printing formulas and processes secret to protect its competitive advantage in the marketplace. The printing firm team members point out that five years ago Boards and More engineers used an idea that they got while talking with the engineers from the printing firm. The reservations of the printing firm representatives are so serious that the viability of the soap box design project is threatened. What should you do?

(See our comments on the Online Learning Center Web site.)

The marketing team members provide information about the customer requirements, and the design engineers link those requirements to the functions of the paperboard. A small sample of relevant requirements and functions is shown in Exhibit 19–7. The "high" or "low" indicates the importance of the function in satisfying the requirement and the "+" or "−" indicates if the function and requirement are positively or negatively associated.

**Exhibit 19–7**

**PRODUCT FUNCTION ANALYSIS**

|  | Requirements | Cardboard Function | |
|---|---|---|---|
|  |  | Ability to Bend and Cut | Absorption Rate |
| Soap consumer requirements | Box is easy to pour | High (+) | Low |
|  | Ink does not bleed when wet | Low | High (+) |
| Soap manufacturer requirements | Box is lightweight for shipping | High (+) | High (+) |
|  | Box is strong for filling | High (−) | Low |

The requirements/functions table helps the design engineers to focus on product functions that can best meet the needs of the customers. In this case, the ability to bend and cut the cardboard is very important for how easy the box is to pour, its weight, and its strength. Unfortunately, the current technology in paperboard implies that, although lightweight cardboard is easier to bend and cut and is easier for the consumer to pour, it is not strong enough to meet the soap manufacturer's requirements. It seems clear from Exhibit 19–7 that if the box could be made stronger while simultaneously maintaining light weight and high absorption, several consumer requirements could be met. Of course, the problem of the additional cost associated with the lighter weight paperboard must be considered.

The Target Costing Process

The marketing members of the team must determine the target price consumers are willing to pay to gain the desired requirements. After market surveys, it becomes clear that soap consumers are unwilling to pay more than the current price of $4.50 per box for the desired requirements. The soap manufacturer is thus unwilling to increase the amount it pays to Boards and More, $2.30, for the printed soap boxes.

Additional investigation reveals competitors are about to release new packaging designed to solve some of these problems—plastic bottles. The plastic bottles are lightweight and strong and have labels that eliminate the printing problems. Although this new packaging approach does not require a price increase, the head marketing and engineering managers at Boards and More are skeptical of its acceptance by soap consumers because of pouring problems. The narrow neck of the plastic jug causes the powdered soap to clump together as it pours, creating problems for the consumer. It is clear, however, that competitors are working to solve these problems.

The design engineers, working with the accountants who have gathered ABC information, have come up with a potential solution to meet customer requirements as illustrated in Exhibit 19–8.

The design engineers propose an initial target cost of $1.77. Lowering the wood fiber content of the paperboard and using microscopic plastic fibers that reduce weight and increase strength generates this initial target cost. The new mixture would require fewer pounds of pressure when being rolled but would require longer drying time and higher heat during drying. The paperboard would then be ready for printing. However, the printing company determines the new paperboard would require new printing technology because of absorption problems created by the plastic fibers. The new paperboard would increase printing costs by $0.03 and the total cost by $0.05 per box ($1.72 to $1.77).

> **Competitors' actions affect target costs**

| Solutions | Cardboard—Cost per Box | | |
| --- | --- | --- | --- |
| | Current ABC-Based Cost | Initial Target Cost | Value Engineered Target Cost |
| Fiber mix | $0.52 | $0.55 | $0.55 |
| Pressing requirements | 0.08 | 0.05 | 0.05 |
| Drying time | 0.04 | 0.06 | 0.05 |
| Bend and cut—outsourced | 0.33 | 0.33 | 0.30 |
| Printing—outsourced | 0.75 | 0.78 | 0.77 |
| **Total** | **$1.72** | **$1.77** | **$1.72** |

**Exhibit 19–8**

**VALUE ENGINEERING TO MEET TARGET COST**

Because the initial target cost of $1.77 is too high to maintain previous margins, value engineering becomes critical. Cost must be driven out of the value chain or the proposed solution will not be acceptable. One piece of the value chain not yet considered is the bending and cutting used to create the box. Boards and More approaches the supplier that bends and cuts the boxes before they are shipped to the soap manufacturer. Boards and More asks for a price cut of $0.03 from the current price because the bending and cutting process should be easier and less costly, and the supplier agrees. Then Boards and More suggests splitting the remaining $0.02 of the total cost increase with the printer to achieve the target of $1.72, the price the soap producer is willing to pay. The printer agrees to the $0.01 reduction and Boards and More finds a way to cut $0.01 out of its heating and drying costs. Through value engineering across the value chain, suppliers and producers are able to arrive at the desired target cost.

One aspect of target costing not yet discussed is consideration of product costs over the life of the product. **Life-cycle costing** is the consideration of all potential resources consumed by the product over its entire life. These costs stretch from product development and R&D costs through warranty and disposal costs. In the Boards and More case, if the new paperboard mix for the soap boxes creates additional disposal costs for the soap consumer, these costs must be

> **Suppliers affect target costs**

considered. For example, Boards and More needs to understand the impact of the new paper-board mix that contains plastic fibers on the ability of consumers to recycle the soap boxes and on their own potential environmental costs. These additional product life-cycle considerations are a formal part of the target costing process.

## CHARACTERISTICS OF THE TARGET COSTING PROCESS

Notice several characteristics in our illustration of the target costing process. First, the entire value chain is involved in driving cost out while satisfying customer needs. Second, process understanding is the cornerstone of target costing. A clear understanding of the connection between the key components of the process and the associated costs is critical for focusing value engineering efforts. Third, target costing requires an emphasis on the product's functional characteristics and their importance to the customer. Fourth, a primary objective of the target costing process is to reduce development time. The cross-functional, cross-organizational team approach allows for simultaneous, rather than sequential, consideration of possible solutions, speeding up new product development time. Finally, ABC information is very useful in determining which process changes will drive costs out of the activities necessary to achieve the target cost.

## Just-in-Time Inventory Procedures

One approach used to drive cost out of the production process is a **just-in-time (JIT) manufacturing system.** The phrase "just in time" refers to acquiring materials and manufacturing goods only as needed to fill customer orders. JIT systems are sometimes described as *demand pull* manufacturing because production is totally driven by customer demand. This contrasts with more traditional *supply push* systems in which manufacturers simply produce as many goods as possible.

A JIT system is characterized by extremely small or nonexistent inventories of materials, work in process, and finished goods. As shown in Exhibit 19–9 materials are scheduled to

Exhibit 19–9

**JIT CHARACTERISTICS ACROSS THE VALUE CHAIN**

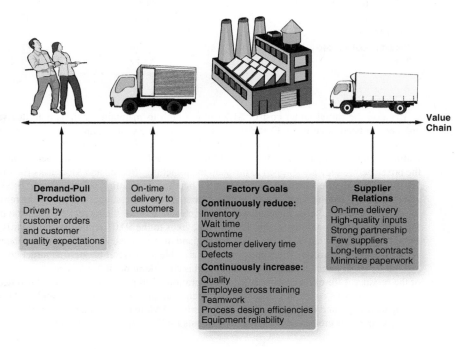

arrive only as needed, and products flow quickly from one production process to the next without wait time or downtime. Finished goods in excess of existing customer orders are not produced. One goal of a JIT system is to reduce or eliminate costs associated with storing inventory, most of which *do not add value* to the product.[2]

JIT is part of a philosophy of *eliminating non-value-added activities* and *increasing product quality* throughout the manufacturing process. As discussed previously, the term *non-value-added activities* refers to those functions that *do not* directly increase the worth of a product to a customer. Examples of non-value-added activities include storing direct materials, setting up machinery, and time during which machinery or employees stand idle.

> **Just-in-time strives to eliminate non-value-added activities**

## JIT, SUPPLIER RELATIONSHIPS, AND PRODUCT QUALITY

Perhaps the most important goal of a successful JIT system is to control product costs without sacrificing product quality. This goal is achieved, in part, by cultivating strong and lasting relationships with a limited number of select suppliers. Reliable vendor relationships are essential for achieving long-term quality, even if vendor prices are not the lowest available. In fact, slightly higher prices related to higher quality may actually result in *quality improvement and cost savings* in the long run because a JIT manufacturer can then reduce the time devoted to inspecting and testing materials received.

> **Learning Objective**
> Explain the nature and goals of a just-in-time (JIT) manufacturing system.    **LO6**

Exhibit 19–9 shows that implementing a successful JIT system involves much more than reliable vendor relationships. The workers in a JIT system must be extremely versatile. Since products are produced only as needed, workers must be able to shift quickly from the production of one product to another. To do so, they must learn to perform various tasks and operate different machines. Many companies have found that this concept of *flexible manufacturing* improves employee morale, skill, and productivity.

In order to accommodate the demands of flexible manufacturing within a JIT system, an efficient plant layout is critical. Machines used in sequential order must be close to each other to achieve a smooth and rapid flow of work in process. Since machinery downtime can interrupt the entire production process, *equipment reliability* is also a vital concern. To help ensure reliability, workers in JIT systems are often trained to perform *preventive maintenance* on the machinery they use and make many routine repairs themselves.

## MEASURES OF EFFICIENCY IN A JIT SYSTEM

Timing is of critical importance in a JIT system. Therefore, time measurements are essential for scheduling production activities in a manner that avoids bottlenecks and ensures that jobs are completed "just in time."

The length of time required for a product to pass completely through a manufacturing process is called the **cycle time.** The cycle time is often viewed as containing four separate elements: (1) processing time, (2) storage and waiting time, (3) movement time, and (4) inspection time. *Only during processing time, however, is value added to the product.* Ideally, the other elements of a product's cycle time should be reduced as much as possible.

A widely used measure of efficiency in a JIT system is the **manufacturing efficiency ratio** (or throughput ratio). This measure expresses the time spent in value-added activities (processing activities) as a percentage of total cycle time. The ratio is calculated as follows:

$$\text{Manufacturing Efficiency Ratio} = \frac{\text{Value-Added Time}}{\text{Cycle Time}}$$

The optimal efficiency ratio is *100 percent,* which indicates that *no* time is being spent on non-value-added activities. In practice, however, this ratio is always considerably less than 100 percent. But in many cases, this ratio should provide managers with a wake-up call. Companies that have not made concerted efforts to improve efficiency sometimes have manufacturing efficiency ratios *less than 10 percent.* Improvements in efficiency often translate directly into cost savings for a company.

---

[2] Factors considered in determining the optimal size of inventories were discussed in Chapter 8.

**Measuring Quality**    Accounting systems in JIT companies measure *quality,* as well as costs and cycle times. One widely used measure of production quality is *defects per million* units produced. In some companies, defect rates have been reduced to less than one defective part per million units of production. Other measures of quality include merchandise returns, number of warranty claims, customer complaints, and the results of customer satisfaction surveys.

A JIT system does not, in itself, ensure quality. Rather, it establishes *striving for quality* as a basic goal of the organization.

## Total Quality Management and the Value Chain

The widespread adoption of JIT techniques demonstrates that current global competitive market conditions require firms to compete on quality and costs. The cost of ignoring quality is very high, most notably from lost sales. Companies that are able to compete globally on quality and cost inevitably have well-developed **total quality management** (**TQM**) processes. Total quality management includes assigning responsibility for managing quality, providing good quality measures for decision making, and evaluating and rewarding quality performance. Accountants participate in this measurement and reporting process by designing systems that can track quality and assign cost to quality failures.

**Learning Objective**
**Identify the components**
**LO7  of the cost of quality.**

## COMPONENTS OF THE COST OF QUALITY

Four components of quality are typically considered when designing a measurement system to track quality costs:

- *Prevention costs* refer to the cost of resources consumed in activities that prevent defects from occurring. Examples include employee training, quality process audits, quality concern issues embedded in target costing processes for new products, and supplier quality evaluations.
- *Appraisal costs* are incurred to determine whether products conform to quality standards. Examples include inspection of incoming supplies and materials, in-process inventories, and finished goods; inspection and monitoring of production processes; and inspection of testing equipment to ensure quality.
- *Internal failure costs* include additional production-related costs incurred to correct low-quality output. Examples include rework, downtime, engineering change orders, scrap, retesting, and reinspection.
- *External failure costs* are the largest and most difficult to measure. These costs are incurred because quality failures are allowed to enter the market. They include lost sales, costs due to returns and allowances, warranty costs, product liability costs, and lost goodwill.

These four types of quality costs are not independent. Obviously, if more time and effort are spent ensuring that defective goods do not leave the firm, lower external failure costs are likely. In fact, these quality cost trade-offs have been identified and are represented by the graph in Exhibit 19–10.

The graph demonstrates that, as more resources are consumed in the prevention and appraisal categories, the costs associated with external and internal failures will decline. Designing processes to produce high-quality units through prevention of failures pays off in lower rework, higher customer satisfaction, more repeat business, and lower warranty costs, among other benefits. A focus on prevention occurs during the target costing process described earlier. But prevention also includes identifying high-quality suppliers, as discussed in the section about just-in-time inventory procedures.

The arrows in Exhibit 19–10 show a phenomenon that has been occurring over the past 20 years. Prior to computerized equipment becoming commonplace in manufacturing plants and offices, quality had to be inspected into the product through the consumption of labor resources. Using labor to inspect all incoming raw materials, work in process on the shop floor, and finished goods is very expensive and not as reliable as might be desired. The use of computerized technology to perform quality inspections has reduced appraisal costs and improved appraisal reliability. The reduction in appraisal and prevention costs has shifted the cost curves, making high quality a less costly option.

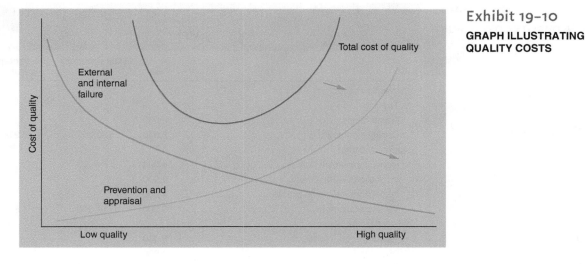

Exhibit 19–10

**GRAPH ILLUSTRATING
QUALITY COSTS**

A second, important development leading to the prominence of TQM is the recognition of the interconnectedness of the value chain. If quality is low in one part of the value chain, quality costs can increase for all components in that chain. A supplier providing low-quality inputs can cause the buyer to incur rework and warranty expenses. A retailer that provides low-quality access for the consumer will hurt sales and affect the entire value chain. Therefore, the entire value chain must participate in a total quality management approach.

---

**CASE IN POINT**

**Six Sigma** is a complementary process many companies use with total quality management. Six Sigma, a business management strategy originally developed by Motorola, has been described as TQM on steroids. The central idea behind Six Sigma is that if you can measure how many "defects" you have in a process, you can systematically figure out how to eliminate defects getting as close to "zero defects" as possible. In Six Sigma, a defect is defined as any process output that does not meet customer specifications, or that could lead to creating an output that does not meet customer specifications. To achieve Six Sigma quality, a process must produce no more than 3.4 defects per million opportunities (i.e., 99.99966% error-free).

Many companies use Six Sigma techniques to improve business and manufacturing processes. For example, General Electric Company has made Six Sigma part of its corporate culture because they believe their competitive environment leaves no room for error. However, critics of the approach suggest that it can stifle creativity by focusing too many resources on existing processes rather than on new business opportunities.

## MEASURING THE COST OF QUALITY

Quality is a multidimensional concept. Multiple measures are necessary to capture the varied aspects of quality. Most firms begin by creating a cost of quality report based on the four components of quality discussed previously. Exhibit 19–11 shows an example of such a quarterly report for Boards and More, Inc.

Simply reporting quality costs is only the first step in managing the associated activities. Twenty thousand dollars in lost sales is a significant non-value-added cost that Boards and More would like to eliminate. In order to eliminate these costs, management must understand and track the activities that created them. In other words, management must determine the

Learning Objective
**Describe the characteristics
of quality measures.**

LO8

**Exhibit 19–11**

**A QUALITY COST REPORT**

**BOARDS AND MORE, INC.**
**QUALITY COST REPORT**
**FOR QUARTER ENDED SEPTEMBER 30, 2011**

| | Cost | TQM Category Cost | Percentage of Sales |
|---|---|---|---|
| Prevention costs: | | | |
| Training. . . . . . . . . . . . . . . . . . . . . . . . . . . | $12,000 | | |
| Maintenance . . . . . . . . . . . . . . . . . . . . . . . | 10,000 | | |
| Quality planning . . . . . . . . . . . . . . . . . . . . . | 8,000 | $30,000 | 3.2% |
| Appraisal costs: | | | |
| Inspections—Materials . . . . . . . . . . . . . . . . . | 6,000 | | |
| Inspections—Equipment. . . . . . . . . . . . . . . . . | 2,000 | | |
| Inspections—Work in process. . . . . . . . . . . . . | 4,000 | | |
| Testing equipment . . . . . . . . . . . . . . . . . . . . | 5,000 | 17,000 | 1.8 |
| Internal failure costs: | | | |
| Rework . . . . . . . . . . . . . . . . . . . . . . . . . . . . | 5,000 | | |
| Downtime . . . . . . . . . . . . . . . . . . . . . . . . . . | 7,000 | | |
| Scrap. . . . . . . . . . . . . . . . . . . . . . . . . . . . . | 8,000 | 20,000 | 2.1 |
| External failure costs: | | | |
| Warranty . . . . . . . . . . . . . . . . . . . . . . . . . . . | 4,500 | | |
| Lost sales . . . . . . . . . . . . . . . . . . . . . . . . . . | 20,000 | | |
| Repairs . . . . . . . . . . . . . . . . . . . . . . . . . . . . | 6,500 | 31,000 | 3.3 |
| Totals . . . . . . . . . . . . . . . . . . . . . . . . . . . . . | | $98,000 | 10.4% |

cost drivers of lost sales, rework, warranty costs, and so on. Measuring and managing quality requires multiple measures of these cost drivers. Customer satisfaction surveys, vendor rating systems, measures of manufacturing defect rates, downtime, on-time deliveries, and so on are tracked and measured by companies using total quality management approaches.

## PRODUCTIVITY AND QUALITY

Measuring quality without simultaneous concern for productivity can be a recipe for bankruptcy. Quality and productivity are ultimately linked, and managers prefer to undertake activities that reduce the costs associated with low quality *and* increase productivity. Fortunately, this is often possible. Managers frequently find that activities that reduce scrap and rework also increase productivity.

## Ethics, Fraud & Corporate Governance

In order to increase the likelihood that public companies prepare accurate and reliable financial statements, the Sarbanes-Oxley Act requires public companies and their auditors to issue separate reports on the effectiveness of their internal control structures. The internal control structure includes all measures used by an organization to guard against errors, waste, and fraud (non-value-added activities), with the objective of ensuring the quality and reliability of accounting information. Because a company's value chain typically includes transactions recorded in accounting records, the internal control structure must take into account the reliability of the entire value chain.

The requirement that companies issue audited reports on the effectiveness of their internal control structures has been expensive. As a result, it has been very unpopular with some segments of the business community, who question whether these audited reports are value-added. In particular, smaller public companies have complained that the costs of internal control reporting place a disproportionate burden on them given their smaller size.

Productivity is usually measured by comparing inputs and outputs. Quality improvements are evident when the amount of input is reduced for a given, fixed level of output. In the quality cost report, the column labeled "Percentage of Sales" is a productivity measure. The outputs are sales dollars and the inputs are the resources consumed by quality-related activities. Increases in quality for Boards and More are signaled by a decrease in the total quality cost as a percentage of sales dollars. Earlier in this chapter, we discussed another productivity measure—the JIT manufacturing efficiency ratio. It compares the input, value-added time, and the output, cycle time, to obtain a measure of productivity throughput.

## Concluding Remarks

We have identified four techniques commonly used by organizations to manage costs over their value chain. The underlying objective of these four techniques—activity-based management, the target costing process, just-in-time procedures, and total quality management—is to eliminate non-value-added activities from the value chain. This objective is achieved by assigning employees the responsibility for managing these non-value-added activities, providing information about the cost of these activities, and rewarding managers who eliminate these activities. The customer ultimately defines non-value-added activities. It is true that, in determining the shape and structure of the value chain, the customer is king.

# END-OF-CHAPTER REVIEW

**LO1** Define the value chain and describe its basic components. We define the value chain as the set of activities and resources necessary to create and deliver the product or service valued by customers. Its basic components include research and development, production and supplier relations, marketing and distribution, and customer service activities.

**LO2** Distinguish between non-value-added and value-added activities. Value-added activities add to the product's or service's desirability in the eyes of the consumer. Non-value-added activities do not add to the product's desirability.

**LO3** Explain how activity-based management is related to activity-based costing (ABC). Activity-based management requires an understanding of the link between activities that consume resources and the costs associated with those resources. The objective of ABC is to create the cost per unit of a measured cost driver. The objective of activity-based management is to manage the activities that drive those costs.

**LO4** Describe the target costing process and list its components. Target costing is a business process aimed at the earliest stages of new product and service development. The components of target costing consist of concept development through planning and market analysis; product development using value engineering; and production with continuous improvement goals.

**LO5** Identify the relationship between target costing and the value chain. The entire value chain is involved in the target costing process to identify activities that

drive cost out while satisfying customer needs. A primary objective of the target costing process is to reduce development time. The cross-functional, cross-organizational value chain approach allows for simultaneous, rather than sequential, consideration of possible solutions, speeding up new product development time.

**LO6** Explain the nature and goals of a just-in-time (JIT) manufacturing system. In a JIT system, materials are acquired and goods are produced just in time to meet sales requirements. Thus, production is pulled by customer demand, rather than pushed by an effort to produce inventory. The goals of a JIT system are to eliminate (minimize) non-value-added activities and to increase the focus on product quality throughout the production process.

**LO7** Identify the components of the cost of quality. Quality costs are classified into four groups: (1) costs associated with preventing poor quality from occurring, (2) costs of appraising and inspecting quality into the product, (3) internal failure costs that are incurred to correct quality problems before the customer receives the good or service, and (4) external failure costs that happen when an unsatisfactory good or service is delivered to a customer.

**LO8** Describe the characteristics of quality measures. Quality measures must be customer focused because quality failures can be identified only by customers. These measures should be multidimensional, including both financial and nonfinancial components, to help management focus on activities that drive quality costs.

## Key Terms Introduced or Emphasized in Chapter 19

**activity-based management** (p. 844)   The process of using activity-based costs to help reduce and eliminate non-value-added activities.

**cycle time** (p. 853)   The length of time for a product to pass completely through a specific manufacturing process or the manufacturing process viewed as a whole. Used as a measure of efficiency in JIT systems.

**just-in-time (JIT) manufacturing system** (p. 852)   An approach to manufacturing that reduces or eliminates non-value-added activities, such as maintenance of inventories. Focuses on both efficiency and product quality.

**life-cycle costing** (p. 851)   The consideration of all potential resources consumed by the product over its entire life. It is an important part of the target costing process where target

costing teams estimate all potential costs to the consumer over the product's life.

**manufacturing efficiency ratio** (p. 853)   Processing time stated as a percentage of cycle time. Used as a measure of efficiency in JIT systems.

**non-value-added activity** (p. 842)   An activity within the value chain that does not make the product or service more valuable to the customer.

**Six Sigma** (p. 855)   A process used by companies to eliminate defects in a process with a goal of as close to zero defects as possible.

**target costing** (p. 847)   A business process aimed at the earliest stages of new product and service development, before creation and design of production methods. It is a process driven by the customer, focused on design, and encompassing the entire life of the product.

**total quality management (TQM)** (p. 854)   An approach to eliminating wasteful activities and improving quality throughout the value chain by assigning quality management responsibility, monitoring quality costs, and rewarding low-cost, high-quality results.

**value-added activity** (p. 842)   An activity within the value chain that makes the product or service more valuable to the customer.

**value chain** (p. 842)   The set of activities necessary to create and distribute a desirable product or service to a customer.

**value engineering** (p. 848)   The methods used by engineers and production personnel to determine the least costly combination of resources to create a product desired by the customer.

## Demonstration Problem

At the beginning of 2011, Suskin, Inc., initiated a quality improvement program. Considerable effort was expended to reduce the number of defective units produced. By the end of 2012, reports from the production manager revealed that scrap and rework had both decreased. The CFO was pleased to hear of the success but wanted some assessment of the financial impact of the improvements. To make this assessment, the following financial data were collected for the current and preceding two years:

|  | 2010 | 2011 | 2012 |
|---|---|---|---|
| Sales | $10,000,000 | $10,000,000 | $10,000,000 |
| Scrap | 450,000 | 400,000 | 300,000 |
| Rework | 625,000 | 600,000 | 400,000 |
| Product inspection | 100,000 | 120,000 | 125,000 |
| Product warranty | 875,000 | 800,000 | 600,000 |
| Quality training | 20,000 | 40,000 | 80,000 |
| Materials inspection | 80,000 | 40,000 | 40,000 |

### Instructions

**a.** Classify the costs as prevention, appraisal, internal failure, and external failure.

**b.** Compute total quality cost as a percentage of sales for each of the three years. By how much has profit increased because of quality improvements between 2010, 2011, and 2012?

**c.** Graph the prevention and appraisal costs versus the internal and external failure costs for 2010, 2011, and 2012. Extrapolate the curves to show the optimal quality point.

**d.** Consider the quality costs as non-value-added activities. Describe how these activities might be eliminated.

### Solution to the Demonstration Problem

**a.**

|  | Prevention | Appraisal | Internal Failure | External Failure |  |
|---|---|---|---|---|---|
|  | Quality Training | Product and Materials Inspection | Scrap and Rework | Product Warranty | Totals |
| 2010 | $20,000 | $180,000 | $1,075,000 | $875,000 | $2,150,000 |
| 2011 | 40,000 | 160,000 | 1,000,000 | 800,000 | 2,000,000 |
| 2012 | 80,000 | 165,000 | 700,000 | 600,000 | 1,545,000 |
| Change in cost 2010–2011 | +20,000 | −20,000 | −75,000 | −75,000 | −150,000 |
| Change in cost 2011–2012 | +40,000 | +5,000 | −300,000 | −200,000 | −455,000 |

**b.**

| Year | Total Quality Cost ÷ Sales | Profit Increase = Cost Decrease |
|---|---|---|
| 2010 | $2,150,000 ÷ $10,000,000 = 21.5% |  |
| 2011 | $2,000,000 ÷ $10,000,000 = 20.00% | $2,150,000 − 2,000,000 = $150,000 |
| 2012 | $1,545,000 ÷ $10,000,000 = 15.45% | $2,000,000 − 1,545,000 = $455,000 |

**860**    Chapter 19  Costing and the Value Chain

c.

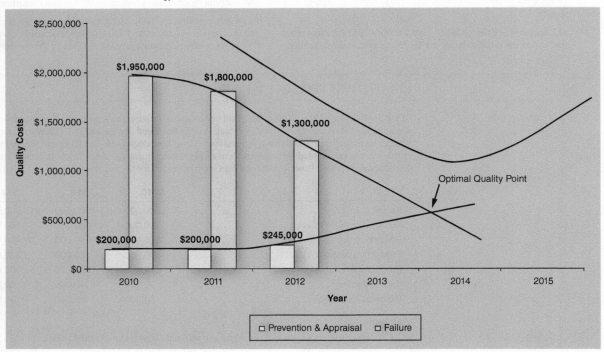

d. Non-value-added activities are those that can be eliminated without reducing the value (that is, increasing the cost or lowering the quality) of the product to the customer. The following example solutions assume that costs to the customer will not increase and quality will be maintained. Many other activities may drive these costs, and other solutions are viable.

| Quality Category | Activity | Example Solution |
| --- | --- | --- |
| Scrap | Machine problem | New equipment/better maintenance |
|  | Labor problem | Quality training and/or incentives |
| Rework | Too many parts | Value engineering |
|  | Employee carelessness | Quality training and/or incentives |
| Product inspection | Poor-quality raw materials | Supplier quality certification programs |
|  | Poor testing equipment | New testing equipment |
| Product warranty | Inspection failures | Buy more reliable equipment |
|  | Too many parts | Value engineering |
| Materials inspections | Transportation-in problem | Quality certification for shippers |
|  | Supplier ships poor-quality goods | Quality certification for suppliers |

## Self-Test Questions

*The answers to these questions appear on page 877.*

1. Which of the following would be considered non-value-added activities by a bakery's bread customers?

   a. The mixing of flour, eggs, milk, and other ingredients into bread dough.

   b. Baking the bread.

   c. Shipping the loaves to a warehouse to await distribution to local stores.

   d. Delivering loaves to local stores.

   e. Rotating bread stock in the stores so that older loaves are sold first.

Brief Exercises    **861**

2. Premo Pens, Inc., is in the process of developing a new pen to replace its existing top-of-the-line Executive Model. Market research has identified the critical features the pen must have, and it is estimated that customers would be willing to pay $30 for a pen with these features. Premo's production manager estimates that with existing equipment it will cost $26 to produce the proposed model. The current Executive Model sells for $24 and has a total production cost of $20. A competitor sells a pen similar to the proposed model, but without Premo's patented easy retract feature, for $28. It is estimated to cost the competitor $25 to produce. If Premo seeks to earn a 20 percent return on sales on the new model, which of the following represents the target cost for the new pen?

  **a.** $26.00.

  **b.** $22.40.

  **c.** $24.00.

  **d.** $19.80.

3. JIT inventory systems strive to:

  **a.** Cultivate long-term relationships with a select group of reliable suppliers.

  **b.** Keep inventories at minimal levels.

  **c.** Improve overall product quality.

  **d.** All of the above.

4. Which of the following would *not* be considered a cost of quality?

  **a.** Lost sales due to bad publicity generated by product failures.

  **b.** The cost of repairing merchandise that was dropped by a forklift in the factory.

  **c.** The amount of a bonus paid to the work team producing the fewest defective units.

  **d.** The cost of the external audit.

5. Which of the following would *not* be classified as an external failure cost?

  **a.** Extra shipping charges incurred to rush a customer an order that was delayed for rework.

  **b.** Costs incurred for a product recall.

  **c.** The cost of product liability insurance.

  **d.** The cost of maintaining a customer complaint hotline.

---

**ASSIGNMENT MATERIAL**  ## Discussion Questions

1. What are three important criteria for successful business process management?

2. Suppose you are interested in opening up a new restaurant in your area. What specific activities would you undertake in the research and development and design stage of the value chain for the restaurant?

3. What activities would make up the marketing and distribution component of the value chain of a local fire department?

4. Distinguish between value-added and non-value-added activities and provide an example of each.

5. Assume you are the manager of the finished goods warehouse of a stereo manufacturer. What costs are being incurred as stereos are stored while awaiting shipment to retail stores?

6. Why is target costing most effectively applied at the research and development and production process design stage of the value chain?

7. What is the objective of activity-based management and how does it differ from activity-based costing?

8. Why is the output of a JIT system likely to contain fewer defective units than the output of a traditional manufacturing system?

9. Why is JIT often described as a "philosophy," rather than as an inventory management technique?

10. List and describe the four components of the cost of quality and provide examples of each.

11. What is life-cycle costing and why should it be used in the target costing process?

12. Explain why the selection of cost drivers is an important part of identifying non-value-added activities.

13. Some managers believe machine performance is more important in a JIT environment than in a non-JIT environment. Do you agree or disagree? Explain your answer.

14. Why is it so important that target costing procedures focus on the customer?

15. What are the four components of target costing? Why are each of these components important for target costing?

---

## Brief Exercises

 **BRIEF EXERCISE 19.1**

Value Chain Components

SailRight Boat Company builds and sells small sailboats. Identify at least four specific components of SailRight's value chain. For each component describe what activities might take place in that part of the value chain.

**L04  BRIEF EXERCISE 19.2**

Capturing Market Share with Target Prices

Assume Bracy's, a retail establishment, wants to capture a 30 percent share of the evening gown market. In order to capture that share, it has determined that the average price of an evening gown should be $450.00. Bracy's requires a 25 percent markup on all clothing lines. What is the target cost for the average evening gown?

**L07  BRIEF EXERCISE 19.3**

Cost of Quality

Identify a restaurant where you have dined. Identify some of the types of costs that the restaurant incurs in each of the four cost-of-quality categories. Consider how those costs are related to each other.

**L02  BRIEF EXERCISE 19.4**

Cost Reduction Non-Value-Added Activities

Identify a non-value-added activity at a grocery store, a bank, and a hotel. Explain how each organization might be able to eliminate the non-value-added activity identified.

**L06  BRIEF EXERCISE 19.5**

Manufacturing Efficiency in a JIT System

Bronigan's, a maker of handheld video games, recently analyzed its manufacturing process to identify value-added and non-value-added activities. Bronigan's found that the total non-value-added manufacturing time associated with producing the average game was 12 hours and the total time to produce the average game was 16 hours. What is the manufacturing efficiency ratio for game production at Bronigan's?

**L02  BRIEF EXERCISE 19.6**

**L03**

Activity-Based Management Cost Savings

**L07**

An activity analysis at Loaf's End Bread Company found the following activities for its bread makers: 10 percent of time, adding ingredients; 60 percent of time, mixing and kneading dough; 10 percent of time, shaping into loaves; and 10 percent of time, cleaning up. The total salary and benefits cost pool for bread makers is $850,000 per year. Loaf's End is considering buying new equipment that would reduce the time required to mix and knead by 80 percent. What is the potential savings to Loaf's End per year if it acquires the new equipment? What other value chain and quality issues, besides cost savings, should be considered?

**L04  BRIEF EXERCISE 19.7**

Target Costing

Assume you've just started a new business to manufacture Weed Be-Gone, a new electronic gizmo that zaps weeds. Your business analyst tells you that in the long run Weed Be-Gone will sell for $12.50 because, after a few years pass, similar products will be introduced by your competitors. Assume that, in the long run, you want to earn $2.50 on each unit of Weed Be-Gone sold. What is the target price? What is the target profit? What is the target cost?

**L07  BRIEF EXERCISE 19.8**

Cost of Quality

Mark each of the following as true or false:

a. Total quality costs are covered by external failure and appraisal costs.

b. Traditional job order costing systems identify and account for quality costs.

c. A rise in internal failures means higher appraisal costs.

d. Quality can pay for itself.

e. As the amount of rework rises, the internal failure costs rise, but external failure costs should fall.

f. Higher quality often leads to higher productivity.

g. Just-in-time manufacturing typically requires tracking of quality costs.

h. Internal and external failure costs are independent.

**L08  BRIEF EXERCISE 19.9**

Characteristics of Quality

Acme International hired a consulting firm to determine if it had any quality-related problems. The consulting firm spent two months reviewing all processes at Acme and suggested that Acme buy new equipment to reduce throughput time. Then the consulting firm billed Acme $50,000 for services rendered. Should Acme be happy with the consulting firm's work related to product quality? Why or why not?

**L05  BRIEF EXERCISE 19.10**

Target Costing Cash Flows

Team members involved in the target costing process should consider the current and *future* effects of their proposed solutions to arrive at the proposed target cost. Assume in the Boards and More example illustrated in Exhibit 19–8 that one proposed solution is to acquire new heating and drying equipment for the new paperboard mix. Assume the new equipment has a purchase price of $500,000 and is expected to increase the annual depreciation expense from $100,000 to $150,000 per year. What are the cash flow consequences to paperboard in the current year? In future years?

# Exercises

**L02**
**through**
**L06**

**EXERCISE 19.1**
Accounting
Terminology

The following are eight technical accounting terms introduced or emphasized in this chapter:

| | |
|---|---|
| Activity-based management | Total quality management |
| Just-in-time manufacturing system | Target costing |
| Life-cycle costing | Value-added activity |
| Non-value-added activity | Value engineering |

Each of the following statements may (or may not) describe one of these terms. For each statement, indicate the accounting term described, or answer "none" if the statement does not correctly describe any of these terms.

**a.** Can be eliminated without changing a product's desirability in the eyes of consumers.

**b.** The focus of this costing method is to assign manufacturing costs to final products.

**c.** The process of determining the least costly combination of resources needed to create a product desired by customers.

**d.** This method considers all costs borne by the consumer from purchase to disposal of a product.

**e.** If eliminated, the product's desirability to consumers is decreased.

**f.** The process of using activity-based costs to help reduce and eliminate non-value-added activities.

**g.** A method in which a product's selling price is determined by adding a fixed amount to the product's current production cost.

**h.** An approach that explicitly monitors quality costs and rewards quality-enhancing behavior.

**i.** An important aspect of this method is the reduction of unnecessary inventories.

**L01**

**EXERCISE 19.2**
Value-Chain Activities

Assume you have just been hired as the management accountant in charge of providing your firm's managers with product cost information. Identify the activities you might undertake for the following four value chain components:

**a.** Research and development

**b.** Production

**c.** Marketing

**d.** Customer service

**L02**

**L03**

**EXERCISE 19.3**
Value-Added versus
Non-Value-Added
Activities

Dainty Diners, Inc., produces various types of bird feeders. The following is a detailed description of the steps involved in the production of wooden bird feeders:

**1.** Raw materials, such as wood, nails, and clear plastic are purchased.

**2.** The raw materials are unloaded from the delivery truck into a raw materials storage area.

**3.** The purchase order is checked for accuracy by an employee doing a visual count of the items.

**4.** The materials are inspected for defects such as rotting, excessive knots, and scratches.

**5.** The Cutting Department orders raw materials by sending a requisition form to the raw materials storage area.

**6.** When a requisition is received, raw materials are moved from the storage area to the Cutting Department.

**7.** The wood and plastic are cut into properly sized pieces.

**8.** The cut pieces are stacked and moved to a work in process warehouse.

**9.** The Assembly Department orders cut pieces when they are needed by sending a requisition form to the work in process warehouse.

**10.** When a requisition is received, cut pieces are moved from the work in process warehouse to the Assembly Department.

**11.** The cut pieces are assembled into a bird feeder.

**a.** For each of the above steps, indicate whether it is a value-added or non-value-added activity.

**b.** For each of the non-value-added activities, determine whether it can be eliminated; if it cannot be eliminated, suggest ways in which the costs could be minimized or productive efficiency increased.

**864** Chapter 19 Costing and the Value Chain

**EXERCISE 19.4**

Activity-Based Management

Blake Furniture, Inc., maintains an Accounts Receivable Department that currently employs eight people. Blake is interested in doing an activity analysis because an outside firm has offered to take over a portion of the activities currently handled by the Accounts Receivable Department. The four main activities handled by the department are (1) billing and recording payments, (2) customer service activities, (3) financial reporting and analysis, and (4) collecting delinquent accounts.

The salaries paid to the department's employees are as follows:

| | |
|---|---|
| Manager, 1 @ $65,000 per year | $ 65,000 |
| Clerks, 5 @ $30,000 per year | 150,000 |
| Account specialists, 2 @ $38,000 per year | 76,000 |
| Total | $291,000 |

It is estimated that the manager of the Accounts Receivable Department spends an equal amount of her time supervising the four main activities. The clerks spend approximately half of their time on billing and recording payments. Their remaining time is divided equally between reporting activities and customer service. The two account specialists spend half of their time on delinquent account activities, and the rest of their time is split equally between financial analysis activities and customer service activities that the clerks are not qualified to perform.

Paypro, Inc., has proposed that it can perform all the activities related to collecting delinquent accounts for a fee of $50,000 per year. The manager of Paypro argues that Blake can save $26,000 because the $76,000 in salaries paid to the specialists who currently handle all delinquent accounts can be eliminated. If the contract is accepted, it is estimated that the manager of the Accounts Receivable Department would need to devote a quarter of her time to dealing with Paypro employees.

a. Using the information given, prepare an activity table such as that in Exhibit 19–3 on page 846 to calculate the labor cost for personnel devoted to each of the four main activities of the Accounts Receivable Department.

b. Should Blake accept Paypro's offer to take over its delinquent account activities?

**EXERCISE 19.5**

Target Costing

On Point, Inc., is interested in producing and selling a deluxe electric pencil sharpener. Market research indicates that customers are willing to pay $40 for such a sharpener and that 20,000 units could be sold each year at this price. The cost to produce the sharpener is currently estimated to be $34.

a. If On Point requires a 20 percent return on sales to undertake production of a product, what is the target cost for the new pencil sharpener?

b. If a competitor sells basically the same sharpener for $36, what would On Point's target cost be to maintain a 20 percent return on sales?

c. At a price of $36, On Point estimates that it can sell 21,000 sharpeners per year. Assuming target costs are reached, would On Point earn more or less profit per year at the $36 selling price compared to the original estimated selling price of $40?

**EXERCISE 19.6**

Just-in-Time Manufacturing

Nanner Corporation is trying to determine how long it takes for one product to pass through the production process. The following information was gathered regarding how many days the product spent in various production activities:

| Activity | Number of Days |
|---|---|
| Inspection | 5 |
| Storage | 6 |
| Assembly | 3 |
| Handling | 2 |
| Painting | 3 |
| Packaging | 1 |

a.   Which of the above activities are value-added?

b.   What is Nanner's total cycle time?

c.   Determine Nanner's manufacturing efficiency ratio.

d.   If Nanner implements a total quality management program and a just-in-time inventory system, which of the above activities could be eliminated? What would be the change in Nanner's manufacturing efficiency ratio?

**L07**  **EXERCISE 19.7**
Cost of Quality

**L08**

Chris Hines is the manager of Lumble Manufacturing and is interested in doing a cost of quality analysis. The following cost and revenue data are available for the most recent year ended December 31:

| | |
|---|---|
| Sales revenue . . . . . . . . . . . . . . . . . . . . . . . . . . . . . . . . . . . . . . . . . . . . . . . . . . . . . | $250,000 |
| Cost of goods sold . . . . . . . . . . . . . . . . . . . . . . . . . . . . . . . . . . . . . . . . . . . . . . . . | 140,000 |
| Warranty expense . . . . . . . . . . . . . . . . . . . . . . . . . . . . . . . . . . . . . . . . . . . . . . . . | 22,000 |
| Inspection costs . . . . . . . . . . . . . . . . . . . . . . . . . . . . . . . . . . . . . . . . . . . . . . . . . | 12,000 |
| Scrap and rework . . . . . . . . . . . . . . . . . . . . . . . . . . . . . . . . . . . . . . . . . . . . . . . . | 8,000 |
| Product returns due to defects . . . . . . . . . . . . . . . . . . . . . . . . . . . . . . . . . . . . . | 6,000 |
| Depreciation expense . . . . . . . . . . . . . . . . . . . . . . . . . . . . . . . . . . . . . . . . . . . . | 10,000 |
| Machine maintenance expense . . . . . . . . . . . . . . . . . . . . . . . . . . . . . . . . . . . . . | 2,000 |
| Wage expense . . . . . . . . . . . . . . . . . . . . . . . . . . . . . . . . . . . . . . . . . . . . . . . . . . . | 35,000 |
| Machine breakdown costs . . . . . . . . . . . . . . . . . . . . . . . . . . . . . . . . . . . . . . . . . | 4,000 |
| Estimated lost sales due to poor quality . . . . . . . . . . . . . . . . . . . . . . . . . . . . . . | 5,000 |

a.   Classify each of the above costs into the four quality cost categories and prepare a cost of quality report for Lumble.

b.   What percentage of sales revenue is being spent on prevention and appraisal activities?

c.   What percentage of sales revenue is being spent on internal and external failure costs?

**L02**  **EXERCISE 19.8**
Value-Added and
Non-Value-Added
Activity Costs

**L07**

The three activities described below were part of the production process in November at Foundry & Bellows, Inc. Describe how each activity creates additional costs and whether it is value-added or non-value-added. If it is non-value-added, identify the associated cost of quality category.

a.   The Purchasing Department acquired cheaper materials at a big discount but, in order to get the discount, it had to accept delivery of a six-month supply.

b.   When materials were issued to production, they were found to be of low quality and products required extensive rework. As a result, overtime pay was required for 50 employees.

c.   The production schedule fell behind because of the additional rework. To meet the production schedule for November, workers were transferred from inspection to direct labor and inspection activities were curtailed.

**L03**  **EXERCISE 19.9**
Activity-Based
Management at
First Bank

First Bank Corporation is using activity-based cost information to determine whether it can save money by reassigning activities in its bank branches. The following information has been gathered:

| | Annual Salary | % Time on Checking Account Customers | % Time on Loan Applicants | % Time Idle |
|---|---|---|---|---|
| Tellers—8 | $25,000 | 80 | 5 | 10 |
| Loan officers—5 | $32,000 | 20 | 60 | 15 |

In its activity analysis, First Bank found that tellers have about 10 percent idle time while they wait for customers to enter the bank. The analysis also showed that tellers are able to help loan applicants complete initial paperwork. Furthermore, the analysis suggested that about 5 percent of loan officers' time is spent helping loan applicants complete initial paperwork.

Could First Bank reduce the number of loan officers at the bank branches if the loan application activity were transferred to the tellers? What other considerations should the bank investigate before assigning the loan application task to the tellers?

**LO1**
**LO2**
**LO7**

**EXERCISE 19.10**
Quality Costs and
Value Chain Decisions

Dust Buster's Inc. manufactures two types of small hand-operated vacuum cleaners. Dust Busters is concerned about quality issues and has compiled the following information for the past year associated with the two vacuums.

| | Heavy Duty | Regular | Activity Costs |
|---|---|---|---|
| Units produced . . . . . . . . . . . . . . . . . . . . . . . . . | 160,000 | 320,000 | |
| Warranty work (units) . . . . . . . . . . . . . . . . . . . . | 1,200 | 620 | $118,300 |
| Recalled units. . . . . . . . . . . . . . . . . . . . . . . . . . | 1,600 | 450 | 112,750 |
| Reworked units. . . . . . . . . . . . . . . . . . . . . . . . . | 1,900 | 520 | 55,660 |
| Inspection hrs. (incoming materials). . . . . . . . . . | 1,530 | 680 | 30,940 |
| Inspection hrs. (completed units) . . . . . . . . . . . . | 1,720 | 820 | 40,640 |
| Quality training hrs.. . . . . . . . . . . . . . . . . . . . . . | 110 | 100 | 31,500 |
| **Total Activity Costs.** . . . . . . . . . . . . . . . . . . . | | | **$389,790** |

Find the quality cost per unit for each product. (Round your answer to two decimal places.) Which product has higher quality costs? How might a manager use this quality information to make decisions (e.g., about the production process or about suppliers) related to the value chain?

**LO6**

**EXERCISE 19.11**
Just-in-Time
Efficiency Measures

The following information is related to manufacturing office furniture at Outreach, Inc.:

**a.** Accept and arrange raw materials in inventory—1 day.

**b.** Store raw materials in inventory—5 days.

**c.** Issue raw materials to various points in the production process—1 day.

**d.** Use raw materials to manufacture finished goods—3 days.

**e.** Store finished goods—8 days.

**f.** Prepare finished goods for shipping—1 day.

Compute the manufacturing efficiency ratio at Outreach.

**LO4**
**LO5**

**EXERCISE 19.12**
Target Costing at
Pizza Pies Limited

Pizza Pies Limited has the following value chain for its pizzas. Boxes are designed by Shala Designers Inc. and printed and delivered by Rodoes Printing Co. for $.95 per box. The pizzas are made in the stores with fresh ingredients and baked in the ovens for a total cost of $3.80, including labor, ingredients, and overhead. The pizza delivery costs $1.35. Pizza Pies needs to reduce the price of its pizza to $6.50 to meet local demand. However, it desires a 10 percent markup for profit.

**a.** What is the target cost? By how much will Pizza Pies need to cut costs in order to achieve the target cost?

**b.** Identify places in the Pizza Pies Limited value chain where possible savings could be achieved to meet the target cost.

**LO2**
**LO7**

**EXERCISE 19.13**
Classifying Activities

Classify each of the following activities into one of the four cost of quality categories and/or identify it as a value-added or a non-value-added activity.

**a.** Rework, due to poor materials, on bicycles at Trek.

**b.** Inspection costs incurred by Walmart on merchandise purchased from Mattel, Inc.

**c.** Costs incurred by Walmart when merchandise, purchased from Grocers, Inc., spoils in its warehouse before shipping to its stores.

**d.** Work in process inventory wait-and-move time between the lathing and finishing stages in a furniture manufacturing facility.

**e.** Training for line workers on proper operation of equipment.

**f.** Recording the number of defects produced each month.

**g.** Offering customer refunds due to defective products.

**h.** Waste disposal costs at Kimberly-Clark.

**EXERCISE 19.14**
Quality Cost
Trade-offs

Flip Flop's To Go has gathered the following data on its quality costs for the past two years:

|                              | Year 1   | Year 2   |
|------------------------------|----------|----------|
| **Prevention costs:**        |          |          |
| Quality training             | $ 8,000  | $10,500  |
| Quality technology           | 7,500    | 9,000    |
| Quality production design    | 4,000    | 9,000    |
| **Failure costs:**           |          |          |
| Warranty handling            | $15,000  | $10,000  |
| Customer reimbursements      | 11,000   | 7,200    |
| Customer returns handling    | 7,000    | 4,000    |

**a.** Compute the percentage change in the total quality costs from year 1 to year 2.

**b.** Explain what you think caused the change.

 **EXERCISE 19.15**
Home Depot Non-
Value-Added Costs

In the Home Depot 2009 financial statements in Appendix A at the end of this textbook, find note 1 to the financial statements. Note 1 summarizes significant accounting policies for Home Depot. Read the section in Note 1 titled " Merchandise Inventories."

**a.** Identify Home Depot's definition of "shrink."

**b.** What are the causes of inventory shrink mentioned by Home Depot? Classify those causes as value-added or non-value-added.

**c.** What methods does Home Depot use to measure shrink?

**d.** How does Home Depot account for shrink?

## Problem Set A

 **PROBLEM 19.1A**
Identifying Value-
Added and Non-
 Value-Added Activities

Castner Corporation is considering implementation of a JIT inventory system. The company's industrial engineer recently conducted a study to determine the average number of days spent in each activity of the production process. The following table summarizes her findings:

| Production Activity                   | Number of Days |
|---------------------------------------|----------------|
| Inspecting materials                  | 3              |
| Storing materials                     | 17             |
| Moving materials into production      | 3              |
| Setting up production equipment       | 2              |
| Cutting materials                     | 6              |
| Bending materials                     | 5              |
| Assembling finished products          | 9              |
| Painting finished products            | 5              |

**Instructions**

**a.** Identify Castner's value-added production activities.

**b.** Identify Castner's non-value-added production activities.

**c.** Calculate Castner's total cycle time.

**d.** Determine Castner's manufacturing efficiency ratio.

**e.** Which of the above activities might be reduced or eliminated if Castner implemented a JIT system?

**f.** What ethical issues might be related to eliminating some of the non-value-added activities?

**L02** **PROBLEM 19.2A**

Activity-Based
**through** Management and
Target Costing

**L05**

e**X**cel

Kallapur Company manufactures two products: KAP1, which sells for $120; and QUIN, which sells for $220. Estimated cost and production data for the current year are as follows:

|  | KAP1 | QUIN |
| --- | --- | --- |
| Direct materials cost . . . . . . . . . . . . . . . . . . . . . . . . . . . . . . . . . . . . . . . . . . | $30 | $45 |
| Direct labor cost (@ $12/hr) . . . . . . . . . . . . . . . . . . . . . . . . . . . . . . . . . . . . | $24 | $60 |
| Estimated production (units) . . . . . . . . . . . . . . . . . . . . . . . . . . . . . . . . . . . | 25,000 | 15,000 |

In addition, fixed manufacturing overhead is estimated to be $2,000,000 and variable overhead is estimated to equal $3 per direct labor hour. Kallapur desires a 15 percent return on sales for all of its products.

**Instructions**

a. Calculate the target cost for both KAP1 and QUIN.

b. Estimate the total manufacturing cost per unit of each product if fixed overhead costs are assigned to products on the basis of estimated production in units. Which of the products is earning the desired return?

c. Recalculate the total manufacturing cost per unit if fixed overhead costs are assigned to products on the basis of direct labor hours. Which of the products is earning the desired return?

d. On the basis of the confusing results of parts **b** and **c,** Kallapur's manager decides to perform an activity analysis of fixed overhead. The results of the analysis are as follows:

| Activity | Costs | Driver | Demands KAP1 | QUIN |
| --- | --- | --- | --- | --- |
| Machine set-ups . . . . . . . . . . . . . | $  400,000 | # of set-ups | 100 | 400 |
| Purchase orders . . . . . . . . . . . . . | 600,000 | # of orders | 200 | 100 |
| Machining . . . . . . . . . . . . . . . . . . | 500,000 | # of machine-hours | 2,000 | 6,000 |
| Inspection . . . . . . . . . . . . . . . . . . | 200,000 | # of batches | 50 | 30 |
| Shipping to customers . . . . . . . . . | 300,000 | # of shipments | 300 | 200 |
| Total fixed overhead . . . . . . . . | $2,000,000 | | | |

Estimate the total manufacturing cost per unit of each product if activity-based costing is used for assigning fixed overhead costs. Under this method, which product is earning the desired return?

e. What proportion of fixed overhead is value-added? In attempting to reach the target cost for QUIN, which activity would you look to improving first and why?

f. Kallapur's production manager believes that design changes would reduce the number of set-ups required for QUIN to 25. Fixed overhead costs for set-ups would remain unchanged. What will be the impact of the design changes on the manufacturing costs of both products? Which of the products will earn the desired return?

g. An alternative to the design change is to purchase a new machine that will reduce the number of set-ups for KAP1 to 20 and the number of set-ups for QUIN to 80. The machine will also reduce fixed set-up costs to $200,000. Calculate the manufacturing costs for each product if the machine is purchased. Should QUIN be redesigned or should the machine be purchased? Why?

**L04** **PROBLEM 19.3A**

Target Costing

**L05**

Meiger Mining, Inc., has just discovered two new mining sites for iron ore. Geologists and engineers have come up with the estimates on the following page regarding costs and ore yields if the mines are opened:

|  | Site A | Site B |
|---|---|---|
| Variable extraction costs per ton ........................... | $3.80 | $4.00 |
| Fixed costs over the life of the mine: |  |  |
| Blasting ........................................... | $150,000 | $185,000 |
| Construction ....................................... | 225,000 | 240,000 |
| Maintenance ....................................... | 25,000 | 20,000 |
| Restoration costs .................................. | 40,000 | 35,000 |
| Total fixed costs .................................. | $440,000 | $480,000 |
| Total tons of ore that can be extracted over the life of the mine: ..... | 200,000 | 160,000 |

Meiger's owners currently demand a return of 20 percent of the market price of iron ore.

### Instructions

**a.** If the current market price of iron ore is $8 per ton, what is Meiger's target cost per ton?

**b.** Given the $8 market price, should either of the mines be opened?

**c.** The engineer working on Site B believes that if a custom conveyor system is installed, the variable extraction cost could be reduced to $3 per ton. The purchase price of the system is $25,000, but the costs to restore the site will increase to $45,000 if it is installed. Given the current $8 market price, should Meiger install the conveyor and open Site B?

L07 **PROBLEM 19.4A**

Cost of Quality

L08

Arusetta Inc. produces a popular brand of air conditioner that is backed by a five-year warranty. In Year 1, Arusetta began implementing a total quality management program that has resulted in significant changes in its cost of quality. Listed below is Arusetta's financial information relating to sales and quality for Years 1 and 2.

|  | Year 1 | Year 2 |
|---|---|---|
| Sales revenue....................................... | $500,000 | $500,000 |
| Warranty expense..................................... | 22,000 | 18,500 |
| Product design ....................................... | 5,000 | 15,000 |
| Scrap ............................................... | 2,000 | 1,200 |
| Process reengineering ................................ | 8,000 | 12,000 |
| Raw materials inspections ............................ | 4,800 | 2,300 |
| Product liability claims .............................. | 5,000 | 8,500 |
| Rework............................................. | 3,100 | 2,800 |
| Returns resulting from defects ......................... | 7,000 | 4,500 |
| Supplier certification costs ........................... | 500 | 2,500 |
| Preventive maintenance on equipment .................. | 1,300 | 2,600 |
| Final inspection costs................................ | 10,000 | 7,000 |
| Employee quality training ............................ | 1,200 | 4,000 |
| Equipment breakdown repair costs ..................... | 8,500 | 3,000 |
| Estimate of lost sales due to quality problems .......... | 10,000 | 10,000 |

### Instructions

**a.** Prepare a cost of quality report for Arusetta covering Year 1 and Year 2. Your report should divide the above costs into the four categories of quality costs and include total dollar amounts for each category.

**b.** How have the total amounts of prevention and external failure costs changed over the two years? What are some possible explanations for these changes?

**870**

c. At Arusetta, preventive maintenance has a direct effect on the repair costs associated with equipment breakdowns. Did the decrease in repair costs justify the increase in maintenance costs?

d. Why might Arusetta's estimate of lost sales remain the same despite the adoption of the total quality management program?

**PROBLEM 19.5A**

Home Depot's Value
through Chain

Read note 1 in Home Depot's 2009 financial statements in Appendix A at the end of this textbook. With a group of students identified by your instructor, list answers to the following.

**Instructions**

a. List the specific categories in note 1 (cite the page and section) that discuss parts of its value chain. Use the value chain categories discussed at the beginning of the chapter to organize your answer.

b. Identify information in note 1 that shows management cares about the cost categories discussed in this chapter: non-value-added costs, ABC and ABM, JIT, quality cost, and/or target costing.

**PROBLEM 19.6A**

Kare Company's
Quality Improvement
Program

At the beginning of Year 1, Kare Company initiated a quality improvement program. Considerable effort was expended over two years to reduce the number of defective units produced. By the end of the second year, reports from the production manager revealed that scrap and rework had both decreased. The president of the company was pleased to hear of the success but wanted some assessment of the financial impact of the improvements. To make this assessment, the following financial data were collected for the two years.

| | Year 1 | Year 2 |
|---|---|---|
| Sales | $10,000,000 | $10,000,000 |
| Scrap | 400,000 | 300,000 |
| Rework | 600,000 | 400,000 |
| Product inspection | 100,000 | 125,000 |
| Product warranty | 800,000 | 600,000 |
| Quality training | 40,000 | 80,000 |
| Materials inspection | 60,000 | 40,000 |

**Instructions**

a. Classify the costs as prevention, appraisal, internal failure, and external failure.

b. Compute total quality cost as a percentage of sales for each of the two years. By how much has profit increased because of quality improvements between Year 1 and Year 2?

c. Graph the prevention and appraisal costs versus the internal and external failure costs for Year 1 and Year 2.

d. Several individuals are critical of the cost–benefit quality model. Identify and explain at least two criticisms. Identify measures, other than cost numbers, that companies can use to track quality.

**PROBLEM 19.7A**

Activity-Based
Management at
BookWeb, Inc.

BookWeb, Inc., sells books and software over the Internet. A recent article in a trade journal has caught the attention of management because the company has experienced soaring inventory handling costs. The article notes that similar firms have purchasing, warehousing, and distribution costs that average 13 percent of sales. Thirteen percent is attractive to BookWeb management when compared to its results for the past year, shown in the following table:

| Activity (cost) | Cost Driver | Cost Driver Quantity | % of Cost Driver for Books | % of Cost Driver for Software |
|---|---|---|---|---|
| Incoming receipts ($300,000) | Number of purchase orders | 2,000 | 70% | 30% |
| Warehousing ($360,000) | Number of inventory moves | 9,000 | 80 | 20 |
| Shipments ($225,000) | Number of shipments | 15,000 | 25 | 75 |

Book sales revenue totaled $3,900,000 and software sales revenue totaled $2,600,000. A review of the company's activities found various inefficiencies with respect to the warehousing of books and the outgoing shipments of software. In particular, book misplacements resulted in an extra 550 moves and software had 250 incorrect shipments.

**a.** What is activity-based management (as opposed to cost-based management, for example) and under what circumstances is it useful? What is a non-value-added activity?

**b.** How much did non-value-added activities cost BookWeb this past year?

**c.** Cite at least two examples of situations that may have given rise to non-value-added activities at BookWeb.

**d.** Will the elimination of non-value-added activities allow BookWeb to achieve 13 percent as a cost percentage of sales for each of the product lines? (Show all calculations to support your answer.)

**e.** Do either of the product lines require additional cost cutting to achieve the target percentages? How much additional cost cutting is needed and what tools (or methods) might the company use to achieve the cuts? Briefly describe them.

**L01** **PROBLEM 19.8A**
**through**
**L08**
Value Chain, Quality, and Efficiency at Kimberly-Clark

In a recent annual report the chief executive officer of Kimberly-Clark outlined his plans as follows:

We continue to address the elements under our control, focusing on areas critical to delivering long-term, sustainable growth and returns to our shareholders. Specifically we:

- . . . placed our near-term emphasis on realizing higher selling prices in order to improve margins.

- . . . took advantage of growth opportunities in developing and emerging (D&E) markets. We also concentrated on further extending our portfolio in higher margin segments such as the workplace and safety gear in our K-C Professional business and medical devices in Health Care.

- . . . make substantial investments in our brands and in the key capabilities—innovation, marketing and customer development—that support long-term growth.

- . . . kept our attention firmly fixed on the needs of shoppers and users of all ages worldwide. . . .

_____
*See http://rkconline.net/AR/KimberlyClark08/.

**Instructions**

For each critical area identified by Kimberly-Clark, match the area with one or more of the concepts documented in the learning objectives for this chapter. Use every learning objective at least once. Explain how each concept highlighted in the learning objectives would help Kimberly-Clark with their critical area.

## Problem Set B

**L02** **PROBLEM 19.1B**
**L06**
Identifying Value-Added and Non-Value-Added Activities

Smit Corporation is considering implementation of a JIT inventory system. The company's industrial engineer recently conducted a study to determine the average number of days spent in each activity of the production process. The following table summarizes her findings:

| Production Activity | Number of Days |
|---|---|
| Cutting materials | 13 |
| Rework | 5 |
| Warranty repairs | 7 |
| Quality training | 14 |
| Painting finished goods | 15 |
| Bending materials | 10 |
| Purchasing raw materials | 3 |
| Assembling finished products | 19 |

872    **Chapter 19** Costing and the Value Chain

### Instructions

**a.** Identify Smit's value-added production activities.

**b.** Identify Smit's non-value-added production activities.

**c.** Calculate Smit's total cycle time.

**d.** Determine Smit's manufacturing efficiency ratio.

**e.** Which of the above activities might be reduced or eliminated if Smit implemented a JIT system?

**f.** List some of the positive and negative consequences of eliminating some of the non-value-added activities.

 **PROBLEM 19.2B**

through Activity-Based
 Management and
Target Costing

Parvee Company manufactures two products: PAR, which sells for $100; and VEE, which sells for $200. Estimated cost and production data for the current year are as follows:

|                             | PAR    | VEE    |
| --------------------------- | ------ | ------ |
| Direct materials cost ........................................... | $25    | $40    |
| Direct labor cost (@ $10/hr.) .................................... | $20    | $50    |
| Estimated production (units) .................................... | 30,000 | 10,000 |

In addition, fixed manufacturing overhead is estimated to be $2,500,000 and variable overhead is estimated to equal $2.50 per direct labor hour. Parvee desires a 10 percent return on sales for all of its products.

### Instructions

**a.** Calculate the target cost for both PAR and VEE.

**b.** Estimate the total manufacturing cost per unit of each product if fixed overhead costs are assigned to products on the basis of estimated production in units. Which of the products is earning the desired return?

**c.** Recalculate the total manufacturing cost per unit if fixed overhead costs are assigned to products on the basis of direct labor hours. Which of the products is earning the desired return? (Round to the nearest penny.)

**d.** Given the confusing results of parts **b** and **c**, Parvee's production manager decides to perform an activity analysis of fixed overhead. The results of the analysis are as follows:

|                        |             |                    | Demands |       |
| ---------------------- | ----------- | ------------------ | ------- | ----- |
| **Activity**           | **Costs**   | **Driver**         | **PAR** | **VEE** |
| Machine set-ups............... | $ 350,000  | # of set-ups       | 100     | 300   |
| Purchase orders............... | 650,000    | # of orders        | 300     | 100   |
| Machining.................... | 500,000     | # of machine-hours | 3,000   | 4,000 |
| Inspection.................... | 300,000    | # of batches       | 40      | 20    |
| Shipping to customers .......... | 200,000   | # of shipments     | 400     | 100   |
| Total fixed overhead.......... | $2,000,000  |                    |         |       |

Estimate the total manufacturing cost per unit of each product if activity-based costing is used for assigning fixed overhead costs. Under this method, which product is earning the desired return?

**e.** What proportion of fixed overhead is value-added? In attempting to reach the target cost for VEE, which activity would you look to improving first and why?

**f.** Parvee's production manager believes that design changes would reduce the number of set-ups required for VEE to 75. Fixed overhead costs for set-up would remain unchanged. What will be the impact of the design changes on the manufacturing costs of both products? Which of the products will earn the desired return?

**g.** An alternative to the design change is to purchase a new machine that will reduce the number of set-ups for PAR to 50 and the number of set-ups for VEE to 140. The machine also will reduce fixed set-up costs to $275,500. Calculate the manufacturing costs for each product if the machine is purchased. Should VEE be redesigned or should the machine be purchased? Why?

L04 **PROBLEM 19.3B**

Target Costing

L05

Oro Mining, Inc., has just discovered two new mining sites for copper. Geologists and engineers have come up with the following estimates regarding costs and copper yields if the mines are opened:

| | Site A | Site Z |
|---|---|---|
| Variable extraction costs per ton | $4.20 | $4.50 |
| Fixed costs over the life of the mine: | | |
| Blasting | $160,000 | $200,000 |
| Construction | 240,000 | 260,000 |
| Maintenance | 30,000 | 30,000 |
| Restoration costs | 50,000 | 10,000 |
| Total fixed costs | $480,000 | $500,000 |
| Total tons of copper that can be extracted over the life of the mine: | 240,000 | 200,000 |

Oro's owners currently demand a return of 18 percent of the market price of copper.

**Instructions**

**a.** If the current market price of copper is $10 per ton, what is Oro's target cost per ton?

**b.** Given the $10 market price, should either of the mines be opened?

**c.** The engineer working on Site Z believes that if a custom conveyor system is installed, the variable extraction cost could be reduced to $3.50 per ton. The purchase price of the system is $20,000, but the costs to restore the site will increase to $30,000 if it is installed. Given the current $10 market price, should Oro install the conveyor and open Site Z?

L07 **PROBLEM 19.4B**

Cost of Quality

L08

Nazu, Inc., produces a popular brand of humidifier that is backed by a five-year warranty. In Year 1, Nazu began implementing a total quality management program that has resulted in significant changes in its cost of quality. Listed below is Nazu's financial information relating to sales and quality for the past two years.

| | Year 1 | Year 2 |
|---|---|---|
| Sales revenue | $600,000 | $600,000 |
| Warranty expense | 25,000 | 23,000 |
| Product design | 4,000 | 16,000 |
| Scrap | 3,000 | 1,000 |
| Process reengineering | 7,000 | 15,000 |
| Raw materials inspections | 5,200 | 2,000 |
| Product liability claims | 6,200 | 7,000 |
| Rework | 3,000 | 2,800 |
| Returns resulting from defects | 6,400 | 5,000 |
| Supplier certification costs | 600 | 2,000 |
| Preventive maintenance on equipment | 1,200 | 2,000 |
| Final inspection costs | 12,000 | 8,000 |
| Employee quality training | 1,400 | 3,000 |
| Equipment breakdown repair costs | 9,000 | 6,000 |
| Estimate of lost sales due to quality problems | 12,000 | 12,000 |

### Instructions

**a.** Prepare a cost of quality report for Nazu covering Year 1 and Year 2. Your report should divide the above costs into the four categories of quality costs and include total dollar amounts for each category.

**b.** How have the total amounts of prevention and external failure costs changed over the two years? What are some possible explanations for these changes?

**c.** At Nazu, preventive maintenance has a direct effect on the repair costs associated with equipment breakdowns. Did the decrease in repair costs justify the increase in maintenance costs?

**d.** Why might Nazu's estimate of lost sales remain the same despite the adoption of the total quality management program?

# Critical Thinking Cases

 **LO2**
**CASE 19.1**
Activity-Based
**through** Management and
**LO7** Target Costing

Dana Martin, president of Mays Electronics, is concerned about the end-of-the-year marketing report. According to Mary O'Brien, marketing manager, a price decrease for the coming year is again needed to maintain the company's market share of integrated circuit boards (CBs). The current selling price of $18 per unit is producing a $2 per-unit profit—half the customary $4 per-unit profit. Foreign competitors keep reducing their prices, and to match their latest reduction, the price must drop from $18 to $14. This price drop would put Mays's price below the cost to produce and sell a CB. How could other firms sell for such a low price?

Determined to find out if there are problems with the company's operations, Dana has decided to hire a consultant to evaluate the way in which the CBs are produced and sold. After two weeks, the consultant has identified the following activities and costs associated with producing 120,000 CBs:

| Activity | Cost |
|---|---|
| Set-ups | $ 125,000 |
| Materials handling | 180,000 |
| Inspection | 122,000 |
| Customer support | 120,000 |
| Customer complaints | 100,000 |
| Warranty expense | 170,000 |
| Storage | 80,000 |
| Rework | 75,000 |
| Direct materials | 500,000 |
| Utilities | 48,000 |
| Manual insertion labor* | 250,000 |
| Other direct labor | 150,000 |
| Total costs | $1,920,000 |

*Diodes, resistors, and integrated circuits are inserted manually into the circuit board.

The consultant indicates that some preliminary activity analysis shows that per-unit costs can be reduced by at least $7. The marketing manager indicates that the market share for the CBs could be increased by 50 percent if the price could be reduced to $12.

### Instructions

**a.** For each activity, determine whether it is value-added or non-value-added.

**b.** If all the non-value-added activities could be eliminated, by how much would the cost per CB decrease? Was the consultant correct in her preliminary cost reduction assessment?

**c.** Compute the target cost required to maintain Mays's current market share while earning the usual profit of $4 per unit. Also compute the target cost required to expand sales by 50 percent. By how much would the cost per unit need to be reduced to achieve each target?

**d.** The consultant also revealed the following: switching to automated insertion would save $90,000 of direct labor, $20,000 in rework, and $40,000 in warranty costs. The yearly cost of the necessary machinery would be $50,000. With this additional information, what is the potential cost reduction per unit available? Can Mays achieve the target cost to maintain its current market share?

**e.** In an effort to reach the target cost, Mays solicited suggestions from customers, suppliers, employees, and other consultants. The following were found to be feasible:

- Mays's production manager believes that the factory can be redesigned so that materials handling costs can be reduced by $100,000—which would in turn result in a $10,000 savings in rework costs. The cost to redesign the factory would be $20,000.

- A supplier suggests leasing a machine that would reduce set-up costs by $80,000. The yearly cost to lease the machine is $15,000.

- A customer, KD, Inc., proposes setting up a just-in-time delivery system between Mays, KD, and Mays's largest raw materials supplier. This would reduce Mays's storage costs by $45,000, while increasing shipping costs by only $5,000.

- An employee suggests that Mays train all its employees in quality control measures and then offer a bonus for meeting quality targets. An outside consultant estimates that the cost of the training and bonus would be $35,000. In return, inspections could be eliminated and rework, customer complaint costs, and warranty work could be reduced by $120,000.

If all of the above suggestions are implemented, including the automation of the insertion process, would Mays reach the target cost needed to maintain its current market share?

LO1 **CASE 19.2**

Just-in-Time Frozen
LO2 Dinners

LO6

Healthy Times produces four types of frozen TV dinners that it sells to supermarkets and independent grocery stores. The company operates from two locations: a manufacturing plant and a refrigerated warehouse located a few blocks away. (Administrative offices are located in the manufacturing plant.)

The types of dinners to be produced each week are scheduled a week in advance, based on customer orders. The *number* of dinners produced, however, is always the same. The company runs its production facilities at full capacity—20,000 units per day—to minimize fixed manufacturing costs per unit.

Every Friday, local suppliers deliver to Healthy Times's factory the fresh vegetables, chicken, fish, and other ingredients required for the following week's production. (Materials are abundant in the region.) These ingredients then are cut into meal-sized portions, "fresh frozen" using special equipment, and transported by truck to the refrigerated warehouse. The company maintains an inventory of frozen ingredients equal to approximately two weeks' production.

Every day, ingredients for 20,000 dinners are brought by truck from the warehouse to the factory. All dinners produced in a given production run must be of the same type. However, production workers can make the machinery "set-up" changes necessary to produce a different type of frozen dinner in about 10 minutes.

Monday through Thursday, Healthy Times produces one type of dinner each day. On Friday, it manufactures whatever types of dinners are needed to balance its inventories. Completed frozen dinners are transported back to the refrigerated warehouse on a daily basis.

Frozen dinners are shipped daily from the warehouse to customers. All shipments are sent by independent carriers. Healthy Times usually maintains about a 10-day inventory of frozen dinners in the warehouse. Recently, however, daily sales have been averaging about 2,000 units less than the level of production, and the finished goods inventory has swelled to a 25-day supply.

Marsha Osaka, the controller of Healthy Times, recently read about the JIT inventory system used by Toyota in its Japanese production facilities. She is wondering whether a JIT system might benefit Healthy Times.

**876** Chapter 19 Costing and the Value Chain

### Instructions

With a group of students write a report to Marsha Osaka that covers the following issues:

**a.** In *general terms,* describe a JIT manufacturing system. Identify the basic goals of a JIT manufacturing system and any basic conditions that must exist for the system to operate efficiently.

**b.** Identify any non-value-added activities in Healthy Times's operations that might be reduced or eliminated in a JIT system. Also identify specific types of costs that might be reduced or eliminated.

**c.** Assume that Healthy Times *does* adopt a JIT manufacturing system. Prepare a description of the company's operations under such a system. (Your description should be consistent with the details provided above.)

**d.** Explain whether or not you think that a JIT system would work for Healthy Times. Identify any ethical concerns that Osaka should consider and provide specific reasons supporting your conclusion.

 **CASE 19.3**

 JIT and Economywide Impacts

A book called *End of the Line: The Rise and Coming Fall of the Global Corporation,* by Barry C. Lynn suggests that global corporations have become globally lean by using JIT, identifying and eliminating non-value-added activities through outsourcing, and taking advantage of deregulation by countries around the world. However, Lynn contends that the systems are so specialized that a relatively small glitch in production on the far side of the world has the potential to be devastating to the American economy. He suggests that laws are needed that would require companies to triple-source supplies and services from two or more nations.

### Instructions

Write a paragraph that explains whether you agree or disagree with the premise of the book and provide at least three reasons why or why not.

 **INTERNET CASE 19.4**

through Lean Manufacturing Solutions

Manufacturing Engineering, Inc., is a leading provider of lean manufacturing solutions. Its Web site is at the following address:

www.mfgeng.com

On its Web site, Manufacturing Engineering lists several categories of projects. With a team of students choose a category from the list and answer the following questions:

### Instructions

**a.** What part of the value chain is targeted by the category?

**b.** What benefits can be identified from the category?

**c.** Do you believe target costing, activity-based management, cost of quality management, or just-in-time inventory was useful in the category your team looked at? Why?

*Internet sites are time and date sensitive. It is the purpose of these exercises to have you explore the Internet. You may need to use the Yahoo! search engine* http://www.yahoo.com *(or another favorite search engine) to find a company's current Web address.*

 **CASE 19.5**

 Internal Controls and through through Non-Value-Added Activities

Section 404 of the Sarbanes-Oxley Act (SOX) is designed to nip accounting problems in the bud, before they can blossom into fraud, by focusing on internal controls. Many companies, in complying with Section 404, have discovered—to their surprise—that reviewing internal controls can in fact result in benefits beyond unmasking accounting problems. For example, Pitney Bowes used the internal audit review process to consolidate four accounts receivable offices into one, saving more than $500,000 in one year alone. Cisco Systems, Inc., which spent $50 million and 240,000 hours complying with SOX, found opportunities to streamline steps for ordering products and services, making it easier for customers to do business with Cisco.

**877**

Despite reports suggesting that individual companies benefited by eliminating non-value-added costs as a result of SOX Section 404, many CFOs believe the costs are not worth the benefits to their individual companies.

**a.** Discuss with your classmates the cost–benefit outcomes of Section 404 of the Sarbanes-Oxley Act. What types of societywide benefits are being overlooked by CFOs?

**b.** Would those societywide benefits ultimately provide benefits to each individual firm? How?

## Answers to Self-Test Questions

**1.** c, e    **2.** c [$30 − (.2 × $30)]    **3.** d    **4.** d    **5.** a (rework is an internal failure)

© Chris McGrath/Getty Images

## CHAPTER 20

# Cost-Volume-Profit Analysis

**AFTER STUDYING THIS CHAPTER, YOU SHOULD BE ABLE TO:**

**L01** Explain how fixed, variable, and semivariable costs respond to changes in the volume of business activity.

**L02** Explain how economies of scale can reduce unit costs.

**L03** Prepare a cost-volume-profit graph.

**L04** Compute contribution margin and explain its usefulness.

**L05** Determine the sales volume required to earn a desired level of operating income.

**L06** Use the contribution margin ratio to estimate the change in operating income caused by a change in sales volume.

**L07** Use CVP relationships to evaluate a new marketing strategy.

**L08** Use CVP when a company sells multiple products.

**L09** Determine semivariable cost elements.

Learning Objectives

# PUMA AG

Many companies have gotten very serious about controlling costs. At Puma AG, executives are also keenly aware of the strategic importance of product mix management. By gathering information about market demand and combining it with a marketing strategy that focuses on higher margin products, Puma has been able to survive in a crowded marketplace by reinventing itself.

Puma executives understand the economic consequences of cost structure, contribution margin, and break-even sensitivity on the company's profitability and strategic decision making. Moreover, they realize that Puma's continued success depends, in large part, on their handling of resource constraints, production bottlenecks, and an array of complex nonfinancial issues. ■

Companies like **Puma** can maintain and improve their profitability by understanding the profitability of each product line. A clear understanding of the link between product costs, volume, and profitability can help managers build strategies that improve corporate earnings. This chapter will help you understand cost-volume-profit (CVP) relationships and how they can be useful for business decisions.

CVP analysis is a means of learning how costs and profits behave in response to changes in the level of business activity. An understanding of these relationships is essential in developing plans and budgets for future business operations.

Cost-volume-profit analysis may be used by managers to answer questions such as the following:

- What level of sales must be reached to cover all expenses, that is, to break even?
- How many units of a product must be sold to earn a specific operating income?
- What will happen to our profitability if we expand capacity?
- What will be the effect of changing salespeople's compensation from fixed monthly salaries to a commission of 10 percent on sales?
- If we increase our spending on advertising to $100,000 per month, what increase in sales volume will be required to maintain our current level of income from operations?

The concepts of cost-volume-profit analysis may be applied to the business as a whole; to individual segments of the business such as a division, a branch, or a department; or to a particular product line.

## Cost-Volume Relationships

To illustrate the relationships between costs and activity levels, we examine the operation of McKinley Airlines, a small charter service based in Fairbanks, Alaska. Assume that the *average* monthly cost of operating the airline is $66,000. Obviously, in any given month, it would be mere coincidence if the company's *actual* total cost exactly equaled $66,000. Indeed, many factors may cause its actual expenses to be more or less than the average. Throughout this chapter, we will discover the importance of determining which factors drive costs and how managers can use this information to improve their planning and control activities.

Managers using CVP analysis begin by identifying the activities that cause costs to vary. For each activity the manager seeks some measurable base that allows increases or decreases in that activity to be matched with increases or decreases in costs. For example, one activity that causes costs to vary is the use of machines. Machine-hours is a measurable base that can be used to match the use of machines with the costs of electricity and maintenance associated with the machines.

An activity base may be expressed in a variety of ways, depending on the nature of the company's operations. For example, in retail environments, an activity base may be defined in terms of *output,* such as units sold or dollars of sales revenue. In manufacturing operations, it is sometimes more appropriate to select key elements of production *input* as an activity base, such as direct labor hours or machine-hours. Airlines often consider *passenger miles flown* to be their most significant cost driver. Accordingly, we will use this measurement for studying the behavior of costs at McKinley Airlines.

Having identified passenger miles as an appropriate activity base, we will next classify each of the airline's operating costs into one of three broad categories: fixed costs, variable costs, and semivariable costs.

### FIXED COSTS (AND FIXED EXPENSES)

**Learning Objective**

**L01** Explain how fixed, variable, and semivariable costs respond to changes in the volume of business activity.

**Fixed costs** are those costs and expenses that *do not change* significantly in response to changes in an activity base. McKinley's depreciation expense is an example of a fixed cost, as the monthly depreciation expense does not vary with the number of passenger miles flown. Depending on the nature of a particular business, fixed costs can also include administrative and executive salaries, property taxes, rents and leases, and many types of insurance protection.

**Variable Costs (and Variable Expenses)**   A **variable cost** is one whose total rises or falls in approximate proportion to changes in an activity base. McKinley's fuel expense is an example of a variable cost, as it changes in approximate proportion to the number of passenger miles flown. For instance, if total passenger miles were to increase by 10 percent in a given month, we would expect to see a similar increase in fuel expense.

**Semivariable Costs (and Semivariable Expenses)**   **Semivariable costs** are sometimes called *mixed costs* because they contain both a *fixed* and a *variable* component. The monthly fee McKinley pays to the Fairbanks airport is a good example of a semivariable cost, since it contains both a fixed base rate and an added charge for each passenger mile flown. The fixed portion pertains to the rental of hangar space for McKinley's aircraft, which remains constant regardless of its flight activity. The variable portion pertains to the airline's use of the passenger terminal. The more passenger miles McKinley flies during a given month, the higher the terminal usage fee charged by the airport.

The concept of semivariable costs often applies when a variety of different costs are combined in one broad category. In manufacturing, for example, overhead includes a variety of fixed and variable costs. The fixed costs may include property taxes, supervisor salaries, and depreciation expense. The variable costs may include supplies, electricity, and machinery repairs.

---

**INTERNATIONAL** CASE IN POINT

Identifying and separating fixed and variable costs is not easy. This task is significantly more complicated when products are manufactured in and transferred between international locations. For example, in Jordan, because of cultural and legal differences, some costs that might be classified as fixed costs in the United States are classified as variable costs in Jordanian accounts or vice versa. Examples of the costs impacted are product warranty, freight expenses, interest expenses, and wages. Culturally acceptable methods for delaying payments, bargaining for lower sales prices, and bureaucratic delays may transform a cost thought of as variable in the United States into a fixed recurring expense in an international location. In Jordan, for instance, clearing items through customs takes inordinate numbers of repeat visits to airports or seaports and is frequently mentioned as an additional cost of doing business in Jordan.

---

## COST-VOLUME RELATIONSHIPS: A GRAPHIC ANALYSIS

To illustrate cost-volume behavior, we shall examine the somewhat simplified data pertaining to McKinley's fixed, variable, and semivariable costs given in Exhibit 20–1.

**Exhibit 20–1**

**COST INFORMATION FOR MCKINLEY AIRLINES**

| Type of Cost | Amount |
| --- | --- |
| Fixed costs | |
| Insurance | $11,000 per month |
| Depreciation | $ 8,000 per month |
| Salaries | $20,000 per month |
| Variable costs | |
| Fuel and maintenance | 8 cents per mile |
| Semivariable costs | |
| Airport usage fees | $3,000 per month + 2 cents per passenger mile |

We have expressed these cost-volume relationships graphically in Exhibit 20–2 (for each cost type and in total). Carefully note the relationship between volume (monthly passenger miles flown) and cost in each diagram.

**Exhibit 20-2** **COST BEHAVIOR AT MCKINLEY AIRLINES**

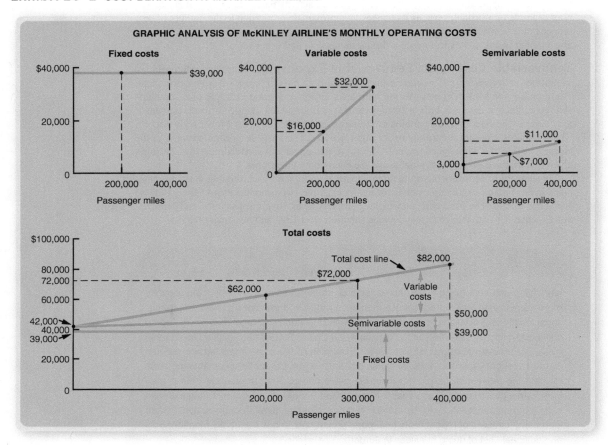

We can read from the total cost graph in Exhibit 20–2 the estimated monthly cost for any assumed volume of passenger miles. As shown, if McKinley anticipates a volume of 300,000 passenger miles in any given month, its estimated total cost is $72,000, or 24 cents per passenger mile. By separating all fixed and variable cost elements, we can generalize McKinley's cost-volume relationship and simply state that the monthly cost of operating the airline, for any given number of passenger miles, is approximately *$42,000 plus 10 cents for each passenger mile flown.*

The effect of volume on McKinley's *total unit cost* (its cost per passenger mile) can be observed by converting its total cost figures to average cost figures, as shown in Exhibit 20–3. Note that the average total cost per passenger mile decreases as passenger miles increase.

**Exhibit 20-3**

**AVERAGE COST PER PASSENGER MILE AT MCKINLEY AIRLINES**

| McKinley Airlines's Cost per Passenger Mile | | | |
|---|---|---|---|
| Total passenger miles ............................ | 200,000 | 300,000 | 400,000 |
| Costs | | | |
| Variable (8 cents per passenger mile) ............... | $16,000 | $24,000 | $32,000 |
| Fixed ($11,000 + $8,000 + $20,000) ............... | 39,000 | 39,000 | 39,000 |
| Semivariable: | | | |
| Variable portion (2 cents per passenger mile) ........ | 4,000 | 6,000 | 8,000 |
| Fixed portion ............................. | 3,000 | 3,000 | 3,000 |
| Total operating costs .......................... | $62,000 | $72,000 | $82,000 |
| Cost per passenger mile ......................... | $0.31 | $0.24 | $0.205 |

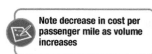
Note decrease in cost per passenger mile as volume increases

McKinley's unit cost behavior is presented graphically in Exhibit 20–4 for both total cost and fixed cost. You can see that the distance between the two cost curves (representing variable costs of 10 cents per passenger mile) *remains constant* across a range of activity base volumes.

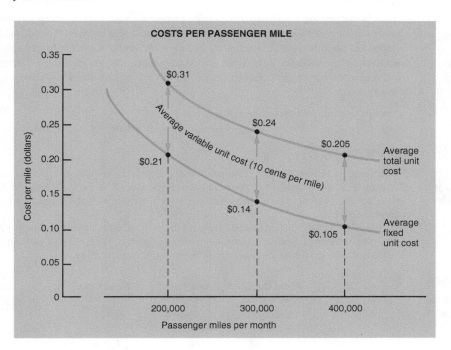

**Exhibit 20–4**

**AVERAGE COST PER PASSENGER MILE OF OPERATING MCKINLEY AIRLINES**

## THE BEHAVIOR OF PER-UNIT COSTS

In our example, note that the *variable cost per passenger mile* remains constant at 10 cents, regardless of the number of passenger miles flown. However, on a *per-passenger mile basis,* the fixed cost component gets smaller as passenger miles increase and larger as passenger miles decrease. This is because total fixed costs do not vary with changes in the activity base. As illustrated in Exhibit 20–4, fixed costs per unit decrease when volume increases. For McKinley Airlines, fixed per-unit costs decrease from 21 cents per passenger mile to 10.5 cents per passenger mile as monthly activity increases from 200,000 passenger miles to 400,000 passenger miles. Study Exhibit 20–5 to make sure you understand how costs change when volume increases or decreases.

| As Volume Increases (Decreases): | | |
|---|---|---|
| | **Variable Costs** | **Fixed Costs** |
| **Per-Unit Costs** | Stay the same | Decrease |
| | Stay the same | Increase |
| **Total Costs** | Increase | Stay the same |
| | Decrease | Stay the same |

**Exhibit 20–5**

**VOLUME VARIATION AND CHANGES IN FIXED AND VARIABLE COSTS**

## ECONOMIES OF SCALE

**Learning Objective**

**LO2** Explain how economies of scale can reduce unit costs.

The decrease in McKinley's fixed cost per unit at higher levels of activity represents a more efficient use of the company's productive assets—its aircraft. In general, *most businesses can reduce unit costs by using their facilities more intensively.*[1] These savings are called **economies of scale.**

To illustrate, assume that an automobile plant incurs fixed costs of $8.4 million per month and has the capacity to produce 7,000 automobiles per month. The fixed cost per unit manufactured is shown in Exhibit 20–6 at three different levels of production.

**Exhibit 20–6**

**FIXED COSTS AT AN AUTOMOBILE PLANT**

| Fixed Costs per Month | Level of Production | Fixed Cost per Unit |
|---|---|---|
| $8,400,000 | 4,000 cars | $2,100 |
| 8,400,000 | 6,000 cars | 1,400 |
| 8,400,000 | 7,000 cars | 1,200 |

Notice that by producing 7,000 cars per month the automaker's manufacturing costs are *$900 less* per automobile than if the automaker produces only 4,000 cars each month ($2,100 − $1,200 = $900). This cost advantage results from fully utilizing the company's production facilities and, therefore, spreading the company's fixed costs over as many units as possible.

Economies of scale are most apparent in businesses with *high fixed costs*, such as airlines, oil refineries, steel mills, and utility companies. Most large companies automatically realize some economies of scale. This is one of the reasons why it is difficult for a small company to compete with a much larger one. But smaller companies also can realize their own economies of scale by *using their facilities as intensively as possible.*

---

[1] Increasing the level of activity can increase certain per-unit costs, such as direct labor—especially if overtime rates must be paid. Seldom, however, do such cost increases fully offset the economies achieved from a higher level of output.

## ADDITIONAL COST BEHAVIOR PATTERNS

Cost relationships are seldom as simple as those in our example involving the operation of McKinley Airlines. However, the operating costs of all businesses exhibit variable, semivariable, and fixed characteristics.

In addition to the cost behaviors we have described thus far, some business costs increase in lump-sum steps as shown in graph (**a**) in Exhibit 20–7. For example, when production reaches a point where another supervisor and crew must be added, a lump-sum addition to labor costs occurs. Other costs may vary along a curve rather than a straight line, as shown in graph (**b**). For example, when a production schedule requires employees to work overtime, labor costs per unit may rise more rapidly than volume because of the overtime premium.

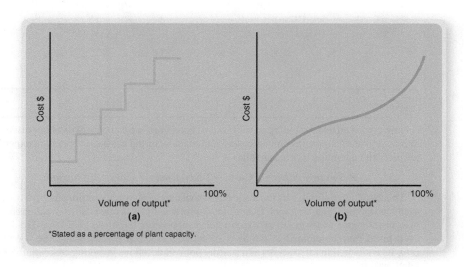

**(a)**

*Stated as a percentage of plant capacity.*

**(b)**

**Exhibit 20–7**

**SEMIVARIABLE COSTS**

 Stair-step and curvilinear costs

Taking all the possible variations of cost behavior into account would add greatly to the complexity of cost-volume analysis. How far from reality are the assumed straight-line relationships shown at the beginning of this chapter in Exhibit 20–2? Fortunately, there are two factors that make straight-line approximations of cost behavior useful for analytical purposes.

First, unusual patterns of cost behavior tend to offset one another. If we were to plot actual total costs incurred by a business over a time period in which volume changes occurred, the result might appear as in the cost-volume graph (**a**) in Exhibit 20–8. Notice that the cost pattern approximates a straight line, even though the actual points do not fall on the line itself.

Second, unusual patterns of cost behavior are most likely to occur at extremely high or extremely low levels of volume. For example, if output were increased to near 100 percent of plant capacity, variable costs would curve sharply upward because of payments for overtime. An extreme decline in volume, on the other hand, might require shutting down plants and extensive layoffs, thereby reducing some expenditures that are usually considered fixed costs. Most businesses, however, operate somewhere between perhaps 45 percent and 80 percent of capacity and try to avoid large fluctuations in volume. For a given business, the probability that volume will vary outside of a fairly narrow range is usually remote. The range over which output may be expected to vary is called the **relevant range,** as shown in graph (**b**) in Exhibit 20–8. Within this relevant range, the assumption that total costs vary in straight-line relation to changes in volume is reasonably realistic for most companies.

**Exhibit 20–8**

**IDENTIFYING THE RELEVANT RANGE**

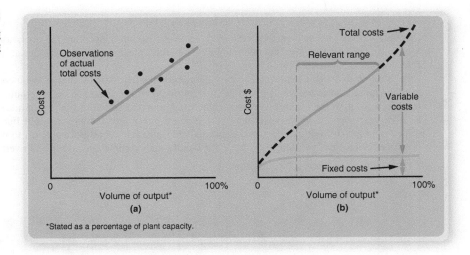

*Stated as a percentage of plant capacity.

## Cost Behavior and Operating Income

Having gained an understanding of various cost behaviors, we can now expand our discussion to include the relationships among costs (both manufacturing costs *and* operating expenses), revenue, and operating income as follows:

**Revenue − Variable Costs − Fixed Costs = Operating Income**

This basic relationship sets the stage for introducing cost-volume-profit analysis, a widely used management planning tool. Cost-volume-profit analysis is often called *break-even analysis,* in reference to the point at which total revenue exactly equals total cost. The **break-even point** may be defined as the level of activity at which operating income is equal to *zero.* Its computation often serves as a starting point in decisions involving cost-volume-profit relationships.

Before we proceed with an illustration, two final points must be emphasized. First, the term *profit* in cost-volume-profit analysis refers to *operating income,* not *net income.* This is because income taxes and nonoperating gains and losses do not possess the characteristics of variable or fixed costs. Second, cost-volume-profit analysis conveys very little information about *cash flows.* Revenue, for example, often results from both cash and credit sales, whereas expenses often result from both cash payments and charges made on account. Thus, if sales of a particular product are expected to result in long-term holdings of accounts receivable, managers may decide to include in their cost-volume-profit analysis the lost opportunity to earn a return on the cash tied up in accounts receivable.

### COST-VOLUME-PROFIT ANALYSIS: AN ILLUSTRATION

Assume that SnowGlide Company manufactures entry-level snowboards. The company currently sells its product to wholesale distributors in Colorado, Washington, and Oregon. Because of the popularity of snowboarding, the company is considering distributing to several East Coast wholesalers as well. Although wholesale prices vary depending on the quantity of boards purchased by a distributor, revenue consistently *averages* $90 per board sold. SnowGlide's monthly operating statistics are shown in Exhibit 20–9.

| | Dollars | Percentage of Sales Price |
|---|---|---|
| Average selling price per board | $90.00 | 100% |
| Variable expenses per board | | |
|    Direct labor cost | 2.25 | 2.5 |
|    Direct materials cost | 28.25 | 31.4 |
|    Variable manufacturing overhead | 3.10 | 3.4 |
|    Variable administrative expenses | 2.40 | 2.7 |
| Total variable cost per board | 36.00 | 40.0% |
| Unit contribution margin and contribution margin ratio | | |
|    (discussed on following pages) | $54.00 | 60.0% |
| Fixed costs | | |
|    Administrative salaries | $23,000 | |
|    Insurance | 1,300 | |
|    Depreciation | 5,000 | |
|    Advertising | 8,500 | |
| Total fixed cost per month | $37,800 | |

**Exhibit 20-9**

**SNOWGLIDE'S OPERATING INFORMATION**

Note variable and fixed cost elements

Notice that income taxes are not included among the monthly operating expenses. Income taxes are neither fixed nor variable because they depend on the amount of taxable income, rather than sales volume.

CVP analysis may be performed either by stating the cost-volume-profit relationships in the form of mathematical formulas or by illustrating them visually in a graph. Let us begin with a graph.

## PREPARING AND USING A COST-VOLUME-PROFIT GRAPH

The *cost-volume-profit* (or *break-even*) graph in Exhibit 20–10 is based on SnowGlide's cost and revenue statistics. The graph shows the reader, at a glance, the break-even point in units and in dollars.

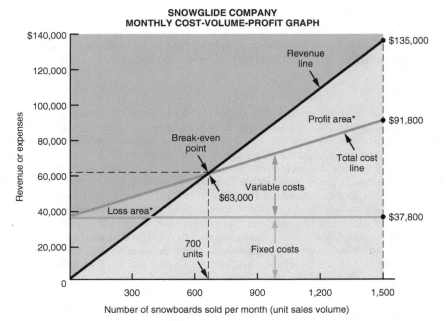

**Exhibit 20-10**

**GRAPHING PROFITS AT SNOWGLIDE**

*Profit and loss represent income or loss before income taxes.

Learning Objective

**Prepare a cost-volume-profit graph.**

L03

The horizontal axis represents the activity base, which for SnowGlide is boards sold per month. Since the company is not equipped to manufacture more than 1,500 units per month, this is assumed to be the upper limit of the relevant range. The vertical axis of the graph represents dollars of revenue and costs corresponding to various levels of unit sales activity. The steps in drawing this graph are as follows:

1. Draw the total revenue line. This line runs from $0 to $135,000 in total revenue, which is the maximum revenue that the company can currently generate, given its monthly production capacity of 1,500 units. Note that the slope of the total revenue line equals the average selling price per unit of $90.

2. Draw the fixed cost line. This is a horizontal line representing a constant $37,800 monthly fixed cost at all volumes within the company's relevant range of activity.

3. Draw the total cost line. Starting where the fixed cost line intercepts the vertical axis at $37,800, the total cost line will rise by $54,000 to a total cost of $91,800. This is the maximum total cost the company expects to incur, given its monthly production capacity of 1,500 units. Note that, for any level of activity, the distance from the fixed cost line to the total cost line represents the company's *total variable cost* and that the slope of the total cost line equals the company's *variable cost per unit* of $36. Thus, for each additional snowboard that the company sells, its total cost will increase by $36.

4. Label the point at which the revenue line intersects the total cost line as the *break-even point*. Note that SnowGlide's break-even point is at 700 units, which corresponds to $63,000 in total revenue.

The operating profit or loss expected at any sales volume equals the distance between the total revenue line and the total cost line. Since this distance is zero at the break-even point, operating income at the break-even point must be zero, verified as follows:

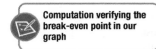

Computation verifying the break-even point in our graph

| | | |
|---|---|---|
| Revenue (700 boards × $90 per board) | | $63,000 |
| Costs and expenses: | | |
| Fixed | $37,800 | |
| Variable (700 boards × $36 per board) | 25,200 | 63,000 |
| Operating income | | $ –0– |

If SnowGlide is able to operate at its monthly capacity of 1,500 units, its monthly operating income will amount to $43,200 ($135,000 in revenue, less $91,800 in total costs).

## CONTRIBUTION MARGIN: A KEY RELATIONSHIP

Learning Objective

**Compute contribution margin and explain its usefulness.**

L04

We have shown that variable costs change in direct proportion to revenue. Thus, the generation of an additional dollar of revenue will result in an additional amount of variable cost. The operating data for SnowGlide (Exhibit 20–9) indicate that variable costs account for 40 percent of every sales dollar. In other words, for every $1 in revenue that the company earns, it can expect to incur 40 cents in variable costs. The remaining 60 cents is called the **contribution margin.**

The contribution margin is simply the *amount by which revenue exceeds variable costs.* Prior to reaching the break-even point, every $1 of SnowGlide's revenue generates 60 cents in contribution margin to help cover *fixed costs.* Once sales pass the break-even point, every $1 in additional revenue contributes 60 cents toward *operating income.* The allocation of every revenue dollar between SnowGlide's variable costs and contribution margin is illustrated in Exhibit 20–11.

Contribution margin may be expressed as a percentage of revenue, as a total dollar amount for the period (total revenue less total variable expenses), or as the **contribution margin per unit** (unit sales price less the variable cost per unit). For example, the average contribution margin *per snow board* sold by SnowGlide is *$54,* computed as follows:

**Unit Contribution Margin = Unit Selling Price − Variable Cost per Unit**

$$\underset{\$54}{} \quad = \quad \underset{\$90}{} \quad - \quad \underset{\$36}{}$$

Cost Behavior and Operating Income      **889**

Exhibit 20–11

**CONTRIBUTION MARGIN
AT SNOWGLIDE**

40¢ of each revenue dollar is consumed by variable expenses relating to the sale.

60¢ of each revenue dollar is available to cover fixed expenses up to the break-even point and contributes 60¢ to operating income thereafter. This is called the **contribution margin**.

**Contribution Margin Ratio**    When contribution margin is expressed as a *percentage of revenue,* it is termed **contribution margin ratio.** This ratio may be computed either by dividing the total contribution margin for the period by total revenue, or on a per-unit basis as follows:

$$\text{Contribution Margin Ratio} = \frac{\text{Contribution Margin per Unit}}{\text{Unit Sales Price}}$$

Using SnowGlide's per-unit data from Exhibit 20–9, we can compute the contribution margin ratio as follows:

$$\text{Contribution Margin Ratio} = \frac{\$54}{\$90} = 60\%$$

Once again, prior to breaking even, a contribution margin ratio of 60 percent means that 60 cents of every sales dollar helps to cover fixed costs. Once the break-even point is reached, every additional sales dollar provides a 60-cent increase in operating profit.

We will now examine how the important concept of contribution margin can be used to answer some fundamental questions about a company's operations.

## HOW MANY UNITS MUST WE SELL?

The concept of contribution margin provides a quick means of determining the *unit sales volume* required for a business to break even or earn any desired level of operating income. Knowing the break-even sales volume can be of vital importance, especially to companies deciding whether to introduce a new product line, build a new plant or, in some cases, remain in business.

To illustrate the relationship between sales volume and contribution margin, assume that we want to compute how many snowboards SnowGlide must sell in a month to break even. From the cost-volume-profit graph in Exhibit 20–10, we can see that the answer is 700 units. We will now prove that this is so. At the break-even point, the company must generate a total contribution exactly equal to its fixed costs. The data from Exhibit 20–9 show that monthly fixed costs amount to *$37,800.* Given a contribution margin of *$54* from each board, the company must sell 700 pairs per month to break even, as follows:

$$\text{Sales Volume (in units)} = \frac{\$37,800}{\$54} = 700 \text{ units per month}$$

This reasoning can be taken one step further to find not only the unit sales volume needed to break even but also the unit sales volume needed to achieve *any desired level of operating income.* The following formula enables us to do this:

$$\text{Sales Volume (in units)} = \frac{\text{Fixed Costs} + \text{Target Operating Income}}{\text{Contribution Margin per Unit}}$$

For example, how many snowboards must SnowGlide sell to earn a monthly operating income of *$5,400*?

$$\text{Sales Volume (in units)} = \frac{\$37,800 + \$5,400}{\$54} = 800 \text{ units per month}$$

**Learning Objective**
Determine the sales volume required to earn a desired level of operating income.   L05

## HOW MANY DOLLARS IN SALES MUST WE GENERATE?

To find the *dollar sales volume* a company must generate for a given target of operating income, we could first compute the required sales volume in units and then multiply our answer by the average selling price per unit. Thus, SnowGlide would have to generate approximately *$72,000* in revenue (800 snowboards $\times$ $90) to earn a monthly operating income of $5,400.

Taking a more direct approach to compute the required sales volume, we can simply substitute the *contribution margin ratio* for the contribution margin per unit in our CVP formula, as follows:

$$\text{Sales Volume (in dollars)} = \frac{\text{Fixed Costs} + \text{Target Operating Income}}{\text{Contribution Margin Ratio}}$$

To illustrate, let us again compute the sales volume required for SnowGlide to earn a monthly operating income of $5,400:

$$\text{Sales Volume (in dollars)} = \frac{\$37,800 + \$5,400}{60\%} = \$72,000 \text{ per month}$$

## WHAT IS OUR MARGIN OF SAFETY?

The dollar amount by which actual sales volume *exceeds* the break-even sales volume is called the **margin of safety.** It also represents the dollar amount by which sales can *decline* before an operating loss is incurred. In today's volatile economy, it is important for managers to understand the extent to which their companies can endure a downturn in sales. SnowGlide's monthly sales volume required to break even is:

$$\text{Sales Volume (in dollars)} = \frac{\$37,800}{60\%} = \$63,000 \text{ per month}$$

Thus, if monthly sales total *$73,000,* the margin of safety for that month is *$10,000* ($73,000 − $63,000).

The margin of safety can provide a quick means of estimating operating income at any projected sales level. This relationship is summarized as follows:

**Operating Income = Margin of Safety $\times$ Contribution Margin Ratio**

The rationale for this formula stems from the fact that the margin of safety represents sales dollars *in excess* of the break-even point. Therefore, if fixed costs have already been covered, the *entire contribution margin of these sales increases operating income.*

To illustrate, let us assume that we estimate SnowGlide's sales to be $72,000 next month. Given that its break-even sales volume is $63,000, its estimated margin of safety is $9,000. Thus, the projected operating income is *$5,400* ($9,000 $\times$ 60%).

## WHAT CHANGE IN OPERATING INCOME DO WE ANTICIPATE?

As stated, the contribution margin ratio in our example is 60 percent. Thus, once break-even is reached, every additional dollar of sales increases SnowGlide's operating income by 60 cents. Conversely, a $1 sales decline lowers profitability by 60 cents. This relationship may be summarized as follows:

$$\begin{array}{ccc} \text{Change in} & = & \text{Change in} & \times & \text{Contribution} \\ \text{Operating Income} & & \text{Sales Volume} & & \text{Margin Ratio} \end{array}$$

Therefore, if SnowGlide estimates a $5,000 increase in monthly sales, it would anticipate a corresponding increase in operating income of $3,000 ($5,000 $\times$ 60%).

## BUSINESS APPLICATIONS OF CVP

The use of cost-volume-profit analysis is not limited to accountants. On the contrary, it provides valuable information to many individuals throughout an organization. Cost-volume-profit

**Learning Objective**

LO6  Use the contribution margin ratio to estimate the change in operating income caused by a change in sales volume.

relationships are widely used during the budget process to set sales targets, estimate costs, and provide information for a variety of decisions.

To illustrate, let us consider several ways in which cost-volume-profit relationships might be used by the management of SnowGlide Company. As previously mentioned, the popularity of snowboarding has prompted SnowGlide to consider distribution to East Coast wholesalers. Different managers within the company will naturally have different, yet interrelated, planning concerns regarding the implementation of this new market strategy.

We now will examine the concerns of three SnowGlide executives.

### Director of Advertising
Assume that SnowGlide is currently selling approximately *900 snowboards* each month. In response to the new market strategy, the company's director of advertising is asking for an increase of $1,500 in her monthly budget. She plans to use these funds to advertise in several East Coast trade publications. From her experience, she is confident that the advertisements will result in monthly orders from East Coast distributors for 500 boards. She wishes to emphasize the impact of her request on the company's *operating income.*

### Analysis
We begin by calculating the company's current monthly income based on current sales of 900 units. We will then compute estimated monthly income based on 1,400 units, taking into account the additional advertising costs of $1,500 (an increase in total fixed costs from $37,800 to $39,300 per month). This will enable us to estimate the impact of the proposed advertising expenditures on monthly operating income.

Using the company's operating statistics shown in Exhibit 20–9 (page 887), its current operating income is computed in Exhibit 20–12.

| | |
|---|---:|
| Sales (900 units @ $90) | $81,000 |
| Variable costs (40% of sales) | (32,400) |
| Contribution margin (60% of sales) | 48,600 |
| Current monthly fixed costs | (37,800) |
| Current monthly operating income | $10,800 |

**Exhibit 20–12**

**OPERATING INCOME AT SNOWGLIDE**

As the proposed advertising is viewed as a fixed cost, this expenditure does not affect SnowGlide's contribution margin ratio of *60 percent.* Based on projected monthly sales of *$126,000* (1,400 units × $90), the projected monthly operating income can be determined as follows:

$$\text{Projected Sales} = \frac{\text{Fixed Costs} + \text{Projected Operating Income}}{\text{Contribution Margin Ratio}}$$

$$\$126,000 = \frac{\$39,300 + \text{Projected Operating Income}}{60\%}$$

$$\text{Projected Operating Income} = 60\% \ (\$126,000) - \$39,300$$
$$= \$36,300 \text{ per month}$$

The target income figure is $25,500 higher than the present monthly figure of $10,800 ($36,300 − $10,800 = $25,500). Thus, the director of advertising believes that her request for an additional $1,500 is well justified.

### Plant Manager
SnowGlide's plant manager does not completely agree with the advertising director's projections. He believes that the increased demand for the company's product will initially put pressure on the plant's production capabilities. To cope with the pressure, he asserts that many factory workers will be required to work excessive overtime hours, causing an increase in direct labor costs of approximately *$1.80 per unit.* Assuming that he is correct, he wants to know the *sales volume in units* required to achieve the advertising director's projected monthly income figure of $36,300.

**Analysis**   Holding the selling price at $90 per unit, the $1.80 overtime premium will reduce SnowGlide's current contribution margin from $54 per unit to $52.20 per unit as follows:

$$\text{Unit Contribution Margin} = \text{Selling Price} - \text{Unit Variable Cost}$$
$$= \$90.00 - (\$36.00 + \$1.80)$$
$$= \$52.20$$

If the director of advertising receives a monthly increase of $1,500 in her budget, and if a $36,300 income target is established, the number of units that must be sold is computed as follows:

$$\text{Projected Unit Sales} = \frac{\text{Fixed Costs} + \text{Target Operating Income}}{\text{Unit Contribution Margin}}$$
$$= \frac{\$39,300 + \$36,300}{\$52.20}$$
$$= 1,448 \text{ units per month}$$

Given that 1,448 units is approaching the upper limit of SnowGlide's 1,500 unit production capacity, the plant manager remains cautiously optimistic regarding the company's ability to market its product through East Coast distributors. Accordingly, he recommends that the company begin planning to increase plant capacity as soon as possible.

> **YOUR TURN**        **You as a Plant Accountant**
>
> Assume you are the plant accountant and that you have a budgeted fixed overhead of $20,800 per month for a production level at normal capacity of 1,000 units per month. Thus, your overhead application rate has been set at $20,800/1,000 units, or $20.80 per unit. You realize that a production increase to 1,500 units per month will result in over applying fixed overhead to the tune of $10,400 per month (500 units × $20.80). You are hesitant to bring up the problem of the overhead application rate with the plant manager because both of you receive a yearly bonus based on plant profitability. If overhead is being overapplied because production is at 1,500 units, the application rate is too high ($20.80 versus $20,800/1,500 = $13.87 per unit). If the projected sales volume of 1,500 units does not occur, significant fixed overhead costs will be assigned to the unsold inventories. As a result, plant income will be larger and your bonus—as well as the plant manager's—will be larger. What should you do?
>
> (See our comments on the Online Learning Center Web site.)

**Vice President of Sales**   The vice president of sales isn't convinced that an increase in the monthly advertising budget of $1,500 will yield sales of 500 units per month in the East Coast region. Her estimate is more conservative, at 350 units per month (for total monthly sales of *1,250 units*). Assume that the monthly advertising budget is increased by $1,500, and that direct labor costs actually do increase by $1.80 per unit because of the overtime premium required to meet increased production demands. If the vice president of sales is correct regarding her 1,250 unit projection, she wants to know the extent to which the company would have to *raise its selling prices* (above the current price of $90 per unit) to achieve a target monthly income figure of $36,300.

**Analysis**   If 1,250 units are sold each month instead of 1,400 units, the contribution margin per unit must increase in order for the company to achieve the same target income (taking the increases in advertising and direct labor costs into consideration). Once again, we use the following formula:

$$\text{Projected Unit Sales} = \frac{\text{Fixed Costs} + \text{Target Operating Income}}{\text{Contribution Margin per Unit}}$$

$$1{,}250 \text{ units} = \frac{\$39{,}300 + \$36{,}300}{\text{Contribution Margin per Unit}}$$

$$\text{Contribution Margin per Unit} = \frac{\$39{,}300 + \$36{,}300}{1{,}250 \text{ units}}$$

$$= \$60.48$$

Recall that the unit contribution margin is computed as follows:

**Unit Contribution Margin = Unit Selling Price − Unit Variable Cost**

Thus, given a required unit contribution margin of $60.48 and a variable cost per unit of $37.80, we can easily solve for the required unit selling price as follows:

$$\$60.48 = \text{Unit Selling Price} - \$37.80$$

$$\text{Unit Selling Price} = \$60.48 + \$37.80$$

$$= \$98.28$$

Faced with an extremely competitive wholesale sporting goods market, the vice president of sales is worried that a 9.2 percent price increase (from $90.00 per unit to $98.28 per unit) is likely to have an adverse effect on the company's total sales. Therefore, she recommends that the price remain at $90 per unit and that the company's target monthly income figure be lowered accordingly.

## ADDITIONAL CONSIDERATIONS IN CVP

In practice, the application of cost-volume-profit analysis is often complicated by various operating factors, including (1) different products with different contribution margins, (2) determining semivariable cost elements, and (3) complying with the assumptions of cost-volume-profit analysis. Let us address such considerations.

© Robert Michael/Corbis/DAL

## CVP ANALYSIS WHEN A COMPANY SELLS MANY PRODUCTS

SnowGlide sells only a single product. Most companies, however, sell a mix of many different products. In fact, the term **sales mix** often is used to describe the relative percentages of total sales provided by different products.

Different products usually have different contribution margin ratios. In many cases, decisions are based on the contribution margin of a particular product. But often managers apply cost-volume relationships to the business *viewed as a whole*. For this purpose, they use the *average* contribution margin ratio, reflecting the company's current sales mix.

The average contribution margin ratio may be computed by *weighting* the contribution margin ratios of each product line by the *percentage of total sales* which that product represents.

To illustrate, assume that, in addition to snowboards, SnowGlide sells goggles. Contribution margin ratios for the two product lines are snowboards, 60 percent, and goggles, 80 percent. Snowboards account for 90 percent of total sales, and goggles, the other 10 percent. The *average* contribution margin ratio for SnowGlide's sales "mix" is computed in Exhibit 20–13.

**Learning Objective**
Use CVP when a company sells multiple products. **LO8**

| | Product CM Ratio | | Percentage of Sales | |
|---|---|---|---|---|
| Snowboards | 60% | × | 90% | = 54% |
| Goggles | 80% | × | 10% | = 8% |
| Average contribution margin ratio | | | | 62% |

**Exhibit 20–13**

**COMPUTING THE AVERAGE CONTRIBUTION MARGIN RATIO**

**Improving the "Quality" of the Sales Mix** Notice that goggles have a higher contribution margin ratio than snowboards. A business can improve its average contribution ratio, and its overall profitability, by shifting its sales mix to include more products with *high contribution margin ratios*. This is the strategy used by Puma and described in the chapter opener.

Sales of products with the high contribution margins often are described as *quality sales* because they contribute so greatly to the company's profitability. SnowGlide management should be thinking of ways to *sell more goggles*. Almost every business encourages its salespeople to aggressively market the high-margin products.

## DETERMINING SEMIVARIABLE COST ELEMENTS: THE HIGH-LOW METHOD

**Learning Objective**
**Determine semivariable cost elements.**
LO8

As previously discussed, semivariable costs have both a fixed portion and a variable portion. Throughout this chapter we have simplified the handling of semivariable costs by providing the fixed and variable components for you. In practice, you must estimate the fixed and variable elements of semivariable costs. Several mathematical techniques may be used to accomplish this task. We will focus on one approach called the **high-low method.**[2]

To illustrate the high-low method, assume that some portion of SnowGlide's total administrative cost is fixed and that some portion varies with the level of production. Information pertaining to production and administrative costs for the first six months of the year is shown in Exhibit 20–14.

**Exhibit 20-14**

**PRODUCTION AND ADMINISTRATION COSTS AT SNOWGLIDE**

| | Total Units Produced | Total Administrative Costs |
|---|---|---|
| Jan. | 900 | $25,060 |
| Feb. | 850 | 25,040 |
| Mar. | 925 | 25,183 |
| Apr. | 950 | 25,280 |
| May | 875 | 25,140 |
| June | 910 | 25,194 |

To find the *variable portion* of total administrative costs, we relate the change in cost to the change in *the activity base* between the highest and the lowest months of production activity as shown in Exhibit 20–15.

**Exhibit 20-15**

**USING HIGHEST AND LOWEST PRODUCTION TO FIND VARIABLE ADMINISTRATION COSTS**

| | Total Units Produced | Total Administrative Costs |
|---|---|---|
| Apr. (highest) | 950 | $25,280 |
| Feb. (lowest) | 850 | 25,040 |
| Changes | 100 | $ 240 |

Notice that a 100-unit increase in production results in a $240 increase in administrative costs. Therefore, the variable element of this cost may be estimated at $240 per 100 units, or *$2.40 per unit.*

To determine the fixed portion of the monthly administrative cost, we take the *total monthly cost* at either the high point or the low point, and deduct the *variable* administrative cost from that amount. The following computation uses the highest level of activity to determine the fixed cost portion:

$$\text{Fixed Cost} = \text{Total Cost} - \text{Variable Cost}$$
$$= \$25{,}280 - (\$2.40 \text{ per unit} \times 950 \text{ units})$$
$$= \$25{,}280 - \$2{,}280$$
$$= \$23{,}000 \text{ per month}$$

---

[2] Other approaches to determining the fixed and variable elements of semivariable costs include the least squares method and regression analysis. These techniques are typically discussed in a cost accounting course.

Note that the variable and fixed administrative costs correspond to those reported in Snow-Glide's monthly summary of average operating statistics in Exhibit 20–9.

We have now developed a **cost formula** for monthly administrative costs: *$23,000 + $2.40 per unit.* In addition to helping the company evaluate the reasonableness of administrative costs incurred in a given month, this formula is also valuable in forecasting administrative costs likely to be incurred in the future. For example, what amount of administrative cost should SnowGlide expect in a month in which it has scheduled 930 units of production? The answer is approximately *$25,232*, determined as follows:

| | |
|---|---:|
| Monthly fixed administrative cost | $23,000 |
| Variable costs ($2.40 × 930 units) | 2,232 |
| Total estimated administrative cost | $25,232 |

**Calculating semivariable administrative costs**

## ASSUMPTIONS UNDERLYING COST-VOLUME-PROFIT ANALYSIS

Throughout the chapter we have relied on certain assumptions that have simplified the application of cost-volume-profit analysis. In practice, however, some of these assumptions may not always hold true. These assumptions include:

1. Sales price per unit is assumed to remain constant.
2. If more than one product is sold, the proportion of the various products sold (the sales mix) is assumed to remain constant.
3. Fixed costs (expenses) are assumed to remain constant at all levels of sales within a relevant range of activity.
4. Variable costs (expenses) are assumed to remain constant as a percentage of sales revenue.
5. For manufacturing companies, the number of units produced is assumed to equal the number of units sold each period.

Even if some of these assumptions are violated, cost-volume-profit analysis can still be a useful planning tool for management. As changes take place in selling prices, sales mix, expenses, and production levels, management should update and revise its analysis.

## SUMMARY OF BASIC COST-VOLUME-PROFIT RELATIONSHIPS

In this chapter, we have demonstrated a number of ratios and mathematical relationships that are useful in cost-volume-profit analysis. For your convenience, these relationships are summarized in Exhibit 20–16.

| Measurement | Method of Computation |
|---|---|
| Contribution Margin | Sales Revenue − Total Variable Costs |
| Unit Contribution Margin | Unit Sales Price − Variable Costs per Unit |
| Contribution Margin Ratio | $\dfrac{\text{Unit Sales Price} - \text{Variable Costs per Unit}}{\text{Unit Sales Price}}$ <br> or <br> $\dfrac{\text{Sales} - \text{Total Variable Costs}}{\text{Sales}}$ |
| Sales Volume (in units) | $\dfrac{\text{Fixed Costs} + \text{Target Operating Income}}{\text{Unit Contribution Margin}}$ |
| Sales Volume (in dollars) | $\dfrac{\text{Fixed Costs} + \text{Target Operating Income}}{\text{Contribution Margin Ratio}}$ |
| Margin of Safety | Actual Sales Volume − Break-Even Sales Volume |
| Operating Income | Margin of Safety × Contribution Margin Ratio |
| Change in Operating Income | Change in Sales Volume × Contribution Margin Ratio |

**Exhibit 20–16**

**COST-VOLUME-PROFIT MATHEMATICAL RELATIONSHIPS**

## Ethics, Fraud & Corporate Governance

As discussed in this chapter, some industries are characterized by high fixed costs. Examples of industries characterized by high fixed costs include airlines, automobile manufacturers, and telecommunications companies. Companies in these industries purchase or self-construct different types of fixed assets—for example, airplanes, production equipment, fiber optic cable, and so on. A company's heavy reliance on fixed assets may result in: (1) an airline contracting with Boeing or Airbus to purchase or lease new planes, (2) an automobile manufacturer's decision to close a production facility and lay off workers covered by its pension plan, or (3) a telecommunications company investing in a technology that later becomes obsolete or unproductive and thereby makes the investment impaired. All of these events are potentially of interest to investors and creditors. And although these events (or the effects thereof) would be reflected in quarterly and annual financial statements filed with the Securities and Exchange Commission (SEC), the Sarbanes-Oxley Act (SOX) requires a more rapid disclosure of these events to the capital markets.

Section 409 of SOX requires public companies to disclose, by filing a Form 8-K, certain material events within four business days after they occur. Such events include entering into, or terminating, material agreements. For example, if an airline enters into an agreement to purchase or lease additional planes, the airline must disclose the date of the agreement, the parties to the agreement, any relationship between the company and the parties, and the terms and conditions of the agreement. Companies must also file a Form 8-K if management is committed to disposing of long-lived assets or terminating employees covered under a pension plan. These disclosures must include all relevant dates and costs associated with these actions. Finally, a Form 8-K must be filed if a fixed asset or intangible asset has become materially impaired.

Section 409 of SOX identifies other events that require disclosure on a Form 8-K on a rapid and current basis. Examples of these events include: (1) company bankruptcy or receivership, (2) buying another business or disposing of the company's own assets, (3) delisting from a stock exchange, (4) a change in the company's audit firm, (5) the departure/election/appointment of board members or principal officers, and (6) amendments to the company's code of ethics or waivers of provisions of the code of ethics. The goal of requiring disclosure of certain material events on a rapid and current basis is to provide more timely information to market participants of material information.

## Concluding Remarks

An understanding of cost behavior—the manner in which costs normally respond to changes in the level of activity—is required in each remaining chapter of this textbook. In these chapters, we will explore the use of accounting information in evaluating the performance of managers and departments, in planning future business operations, and in making numerous types of management decisions. The concepts and terminology introduced in Chapter 20 will be used extensively in these discussions.

# END-OF-CHAPTER REVIEW

## SUMMARY OF LEARNING OBJECTIVES

**L01** Explain how fixed, variable, and semivariable costs respond to changes in the volume of business activity. Fixed costs (fixed expenses) remain unchanged despite changes in sales volume, while variable costs (or expenses) change in direct proportion to changes in sales volume. With a semivariable cost, part of the cost is fixed and part is variable. Semivariable costs change in response to a change in the level of activity, but they change by less than a proportionate amount.

**L02** Explain how economies of scale can reduce unit costs. Economies of scale are reductions in unit cost that can be achieved through a higher volume of activity. One economy of scale is fixed costs that are spread over a larger number of units, thus reducing unit cost.

**L03** Prepare a cost-volume-profit graph. The vertical axis on a break-even graph is dollars of revenue or costs, and the horizontal axis is unit sales. Lines are plotted on the graph showing revenue and total costs at different sales volumes. The vertical distance between these lines represents the amount of operating income (or loss). The lines intersect at the break-even point.

**L04** Compute contribution margin and explain its usefulness. Contribution margin is the excess of revenue over variable costs. Thus, it represents the amount of revenue available to cover fixed costs and to provide an operating profit. Contribution margin is useful in estimating the sales volume needed to achieve earnings targets, or the income likely to result from a given sales volume.

**L05** Determine the sales volume required to earn a desired level of operating income. The sales volume (in units) required to earn a target profit is equal to the sum of the fixed costs plus the target profit, divided by the unit contribution margin. To determine the sales volume in dollars, the sum of the fixed costs plus the target profit is divided by the contribution margin ratio.

**L06** Use the contribution margin ratio to estimate the change in operating income caused by a change in sales volume. Multiplying the expected dollar change in sales volume by the contribution margin ratio indicates the expected change in operating income.

**L07** Use CVP relationships to evaluate a new marketing strategy. An understanding of CVP relationships assists managers in estimating the changes in revenue and costs which are likely to accompany a change in sales volume. Thus, they are able to estimate the likely effects of marketing strategies on overall profitability.

**L08** Use CVP when a company sells multiple products. For companies that sell multiple products, CVP analysis is performed using a *weighted-average* contribution margin. The weighted-average contribution margin is based on each product's individual contribution margin and the percentage it comprises of the company's overall sales mix.

**L09** Determine semivariable cost elements. Semivariable costs have both a fixed component and a variable component. Separating semivariable costs into their fixed and variable components is a constant challenge faced by managers. The high-low method is a simple approach used by managers to better understand the structure of semivariable costs.

## Key Terms Introduced or Emphasized In Chapter 20

**break-even point** (p. 886)  The level of sales at which a company neither earns an operating profit nor incurs a loss. Revenue exactly covers costs and expenses.

**contribution margin** (p. 888)  Sales minus variable costs. The portion of sales revenue that is not consumed by variable costs and, therefore, is available to cover fixed costs and contribute to operating income.

**contribution margin per unit** (p. 888)  The excess of unit sales price over variable cost per unit; the dollar amount contributed by the sale of each unit toward covering fixed costs and generating operating income.

**contribution margin ratio** (p. 889)  The contribution margin expressed as a percentage of sales price. Represents the percentage of each revenue dollar that is available to cover fixed costs or to provide an operating profit.

**cost formula** (p. 895)  A mathematical statement expressing the expected amount of a cost in terms of the fixed element of the cost and/or the portion of the cost that varies in response to changes in some activity base. For example, the cost formula for a semivariable cost might be $2,500 per month, plus 5 percent of net sales.

**economies of scale** (p. 884)  A reduction in unit cost achieved through a higher volume of output.

**fixed costs** (p. 880)  Costs and expenses that remain unchanged despite changes in the level of the activity base.

**high-low method** (p. 894)  A method of dividing a semivariable (or mixed) cost into its fixed and variable elements by relating the change in the cost to the change in the activity base between the highest and lowest levels of observed activity.

**margin of safety** (p. 890)  Amount by which actual sales exceed the break-even point.

**relevant range** (p. 885)   The span or range of output over which output is likely to vary and assumptions about cost behavior are generally valid. Excludes extreme volume variations.

**sales mix** (p. 893)   The relative percentages of total sales generated by each type of product that a business sells.

**semivariable costs** (p. 881)   Costs and expenses that respond to changes in the level of the activity base by less than a proportionate amount.

**variable costs** (p. 881)   Costs and expenses that vary directly and proportionately with changes in the level of the activity base.

## Demonstration Problem

The management of Fresno Processing Company has engaged you to assist in the development of information to be used for management decisions.

The company has the capacity to process 20,000 tons of cottonseed per year. This processing results in several salable products, including oil, meal, hulls, and lint.

A marketing study indicates that the company can sell its output for the coming year at $200 per ton processed.

You have determined the company's cost structure to be as follows:

| | |
|---|---|
| Cost of cottonseed . . . . . . . . . . . . . . . . . . . . . . . . . . . . . . . . . . . . . . | $80 per ton |
| Processing costs: | |
|    Variable. . . . . . . . . . . . . . . . . . . . . . . . . . . . . . . . . . . . . . . . . . . . | $26 per ton |
|    Fixed. . . . . . . . . . . . . . . . . . . . . . . . . . . . . . . . . . . . . . . . . . . . . | $340,000 per year |
| Marketing costs . . . . . . . . . . . . . . . . . . . . . . . . . . . . . . . . . . . . . . | All variable, $44 per ton |
| Administrative costs . . . . . . . . . . . . . . . . . . . . . . . . . . . . . . . . . . . . | All fixed, $300,000 per year |

### Instructions

**a.**   Compute (**1**) the contribution margin and (**2**) the contribution margin ratio per ton of cottonseed processed.

**b.**   Compute the break-even sales volume in (**1**) dollars and (**2**) tons of cottonseed.

**c.**   Assume that the company's budget calls for an operating income of $240,000. Compute the sales volume required to reach this profit objective, stated (**1**) in dollars and (**2**) in tons of cottonseed.

**d.**   Compute the maximum amount that the company can afford to pay per ton of raw cottonseed and still break even by processing and selling 16,000 tons during the current year.

### Solution to the Demonstration Problem

| | | | | |
|---|---|---|---|---|
| **a.** | (**1**) | Total revenue per ton of cottonseed . . . . . . . . . . . . . . . . . . . . . . . . . . | | $200 |
| | | Less: Variable costs: | | |
| | |    Cottonseed . . . . . . . . . . . . . . . . . . . . . . . . . . . . . . . . . . . . . . . . | $80 | |
| | |    Processing . . . . . . . . . . . . . . . . . . . . . . . . . . . . . . . . . . . . . . . . | 26 | |
| | |    Marketing . . . . . . . . . . . . . . . . . . . . . . . . . . . . . . . . . . . . . . . . | 44 | 150 |
| | | Unit contribution margin ($200 − $150) . . . . . . . . . . . . . . . . . . . . . . . | | $ 50 |
| | (**2**) | Contribution margin ratio ($50 ÷ $200) . . . . . . . . . . . . . . . . . . . . . . . | | 25% |
| **b.** | (**1**) | Break-even dollar sales volume: | | |
| | | Fixed costs ($340,000 + $300,000) . . . . . . . . . . . . . . . . . . . . . . | | $ 640,000 |
| | | Contribution margin ratio (part **a**) . . . . . . . . . . . . . . . . . . . . . . . . | | 25% |
| | | Break-even dollar sales volume ($640,000 ÷ 0.25) . . . . . . . . . . . | | $2,560,000 |
| | (**2**) | Break-even unit sales volume (in tons): | | |
| | | Fixed costs (per previous) . . . . . . . . . . . . . . . . . . . . . . . . . . . . . . | | $ 640,000 |
| | | Unit contribution margin (part **a**) . . . . . . . . . . . . . . . . . . . . . . . . | | $ 50 |
| | | Break-even unit sales volume, stated in tons of | | |
| | |    cottonseed products ($640,000 ÷ $50) . . . . . . . . . . . . . . . . . | | 12,800 |

(Alternative computation: Break-even dollar sales volume, $2,560,000, divided by unit sales price, $200, equals 12,800 tons.)

**c. (1)** Required dollar sales volume:

| | |
|---|---:|
| Fixed expenses.......................................... | $ 640,000 |
| Add: Target operating income................................ | 240,000 |
| Required contribution margin.................................. | $ 880,000 |
| Contribution margin ratio (part **a**) ............................ | 25% |
| Required dollar sales volume ($880,000 ÷ 0.25)................. | $3,520,000 |

**(2)** Required unit sales volume:

| | |
|---|---:|
| Required dollar sales volume [from (**1**)] ...................... | $3,520,000 |
| Unit sales price............................................ | $ 200 |
| Required unit sales volume, in tons<br>($3,520,000 ÷ $200)....................................... | 17,600 |

(Alternative computation: Required contribution margin to cover fixed expenses and target operating income, $880,000, [part **c(1)**], divided by unit contribution margin, $50 per ton, equals 17,600 tons.)

**d.**

| | | |
|---|---:|---:|
| Total revenue (16,000 tons × $200) ............................ | | $3,200,000 |
| Less: Costs other than cottonseed: | | |
| Processing (16,000 tons × $26) .................... | $416,000 | |
| Marketing (16,000 tons × $44)..................... | 704,000 | |
| Fixed costs...................................... | 640,000 | 1,760,000 |
| Maximum amount that can be paid for 16,000 tons of<br>cottonseed, while allowing company to break even ................ | | $1,440,000 |
| Maximum amount that can be paid per ton of cottonseed,<br>while allowing company to break even<br>($1,440,000 ÷ 16,000 tons) .................................... | | $90 |

## Self-Test Questions

*The answers to these questions appear on page 915.*

1. During the current year, the net sales of Ridgeway, Inc., were 10 percent below last year's level. You should expect Ridgeway's semivariable costs to:

   a. Decrease in total, but increase as a percentage of net sales.

   b. Increase in total and increase as a percentage of net sales.

   c. Decrease in total and decrease as a percentage of net sales.

   d. Increase in total, but decrease as a percentage of net sales.

2. Marston Company sells a single product at a sales price of $50 per unit. Fixed costs total $15,000 per month, and variable costs amount to $20 per unit. If management reduces the sales price of this product by $5 per unit, the sales volume needed for the company to break even will:

   a. Increase by $5,000.

   b. Increase by $4,500.

   c. Increase by $2,000.

   d. Remain unchanged.

3. Olsen Auto Supply typically earns a contribution margin ratio of 40 percent. The store manager estimates that by spending an additional $5,000 per month for radio advertising the store will be able to increase its operating income by $3,000 per month. The manager is expecting the radio advertising to increase monthly dollar sales volume by:

   a. $12,500.

   b. $8,000.

   c. $7,500.

   d. Some other amount.

4. Shown below are the monthly high and low levels of direct labor hours and total manufacturing overhead for Apex Mfg. Co.

| | Direct Labor Hours | Total Manufacturing Overhead |
|---|---|---|
| Highest observed level ....... | 6,000 | $17,000 |
| Lowest observed level ........ | 4,000 | 14,000 |

In a month in which 5,000 direct labor hours are used, the *fixed element* of total manufacturing overhead costs should be approximately:

   a. $15,500.

   b. $8,000.

   c. $7,500.

   d. $8,000 plus $1.50 per unit.

5. Driver Company manufactures two products. Data concerning these products are shown below:

| | Product A | Product B |
|---|---|---|
| Total monthly demand (in units).. | 1,000 | 200 |
| Sales price per unit ......... | $400 | $500 |
| Contribution margin ratio..... | 30% | 40% |
| Relative sales mix ........... | 80% | 20% |

If fixed costs are equal to $320,000, what amount of total sales revenue is needed to break even?

   a. $914,286.

   b. $457,143.

   c. $320,000.

   d. $1,000,000.

---

| ASSIGNMENT MATERIAL | ## Discussion Questions |
|---|---|

**1.** Why is it important for management to understand cost-volume-profit relationships?

**2.** What is an *activity base* and why is it important in analyzing cost behavior?

**3.** What is the effect of an increase in activity on the following items?

    **a.** Total variable costs.

    **b.** Variable costs per unit of activity.

    **c.** Total fixed costs.

    **d.** Fixed costs per unit of activity.

**4.** The simplifying assumption that costs and volume vary in straight-line relationships makes the analysis of cost behavior much easier. What factors make this a reasonable and useful assumption in many cases?

**5.** Define the *relevant range* of activity.

**6.** Explain how the high-low method determines:

    **a.** The variable portion of a semivariable cost.

    **b.** The fixed portion of a semivariable cost.

**7.** Define (**a**) *contribution margin,* (**b**) *contribution margin ratio,* and (**c**) *average contribution margin ratio.*

**8.** What important relationships are shown on a cost-volume-profit (break-even) graph?

**9.** Explain how the unit contribution margin can be used to determine the unit sales required to break even.

**10.** Define *margin of safety.*

**11.** An executive of a large American steel company put the blame for lower net income for a recent fiscal period on the "shift in product mix to a higher proportion of export sales." Sales for the period increased slightly while net income declined by 28 percent. Explain how a change in product (sales) mix to a higher proportion in export sales could result in a lower level of net income.

**12.** Explain why businesses normally can reduce unit costs by utilizing their facilities more intensively.

**13.** Why does cost-volume-profit analysis focus upon *operating income* instead of *net income*?

**14.** A regional airline and a furniture manufacturer each generate annual revenue of $120 million and earn net income of $10 million. Which company probably has the higher break-even point? Explain.

**15.** List the assumptions that underlie cost-volume-profit analysis.

## Brief Exercises

 **BRIEF EXERCISE 20.1**

Patterns of Cost Behavior

Explain the effects of an increase in the volume of activity on the following costs. (Assume volume remains within the relevant range.)

    **a.** Total variable costs     **d.** Fixed cost per unit

    **b.** Variable cost per unit     **e.** Total semivariable costs

    **c.** Total fixed cost     **f.** Semivariable cost per unit

**L01** **BRIEF EXERCISE 20.2**

Classification of Various Costs

Explain whether you regard each of the following costs or categories of costs as fixed, variable, or semivariable with respect to net sales. Briefly explain your reasoning. If you do not believe that a cost fits into any of these classifications, explain.

    **a.** The cost of goods sold.

    **b.** Salaries to salespeople (these salaries include a monthly minimum amount, plus a commission on all sales).

    **c.** Income taxes expense.

    **d.** Property taxes expense.

    **e.** Depreciation expense on a sales showroom, based on the straight-line method of depreciation.

    **f.** Depreciation expense on a sales showroom, based on the double-declining-balance method of depreciation.

**L01** **BRIEF EXERCISE 20.3**

**L08** Using a Cost Formula

City Ambulance Service estimates the monthly cost of responding to emergency calls to be $19,500, plus $110 per call.

    **a.** In a month in which the company responds to 125 emergency calls, determine the estimated:

        **1.** Total cost of responding to emergency calls.

        **2.** Average cost of responding to emergency calls.

    **b.** Assume that in a given month, the number of emergency calls was unusually low. Would you expect the average cost of responding to emergency calls during this month to be higher or lower than in other months? Explain.

| L01 | **BRIEF EXERCISE 20.4** | Through using the high-low method, Regency Hotels estimates the total costs of providing room service meals to amount to $5,950 per month, plus 30 percent of room service revenue. |

L01

**BRIEF EXERCISE 20.4**

L04

L05

L09

Using a Cost Formula

Through using the high-low method, Regency Hotels estimates the total costs of providing room service meals to amount to $5,950 per month, plus 30 percent of room service revenue.

a. What is the contribution margin ratio of providing room service meals?

b. What is the break-even point for room service operations in terms of total room service revenue?

c. What would you expect to be the total cost of providing room service in a month in which room service revenue amounts to $15,000?

L04
through
L06

**BRIEF EXERCISE 20.5**

Computing Sales Volume

Porter Corporation has fixed costs of $660,000, variable costs of $24 per unit, and a contribution margin ratio of 40 percent.

Compute the following:

a. Unit sales price and unit contribution margin for the above product.

b. The sales volume in units required for Porter Corporation to earn an operating income of $300,000.

c. The dollar sales volume required for Porter Corporation to earn an operating income of $300,000.

L04
through
L06

**BRIEF EXERCISE 20.6**

Computing Sales Volume

Jackson Company recently calculated its break-even sales revenue to be $15,000. For each dollar of sales revenue, $0.70 goes to cover variable costs.

Compute the following:

a. The contribution margin ratio.

b. Total fixed costs.

c. The sales revenue that would have to be generated to earn an operating income of $9,000.

L01

L04
·
through

L06

**BRIEF EXERCISE 20.7**

Relating Contribution Margin Ratio to Sales Price

Firebird Mfg. Co. has a contribution margin ratio of 45 percent and must sell 25,000 units at a price of $80 each in order to break even.

a. Compute total fixed costs.

b. Compute variable cost per unit.

c. Develop the company's *cost formula*.

L07

**BRIEF EXERCISE 20.8**

Evaluating a Marketing Strategy

Chaps & Saddles, a retailer of tack and Western apparel, earns an average contribution margin of 45 percent on its sales volume. Recently, the advertising manager of a local "country" radio station offered to run numerous radio advertisements for Chaps & Saddles at a monthly cost of $1,800.

Compute the amount by which the proposed radio advertising campaign must increase Chaps & Saddles's monthly sales volume to:

a. Pay for itself.

b. Increase operating income by $1,000 per month. (Round computations to the nearest dollar.)

L01

**BRIEF EXERCISE 20.9**

Selecting an Activity Base

You have been hired as a consultant to assist the following companies with cost-volume-profit analysis:

Freeman's Retail Floral Shop

Susquehanna Trails Bus Service

Wilson Pump Manufacturers

McCauley & Pratt, Attorneys-at-Law

Suggest an appropriate activity base for each of these clients.

**902**

L08  **BRIEF EXERCISE 20.10**
CVP with Multiple Products

Glow Worm Corporation makes flashlights and batteries. Its monthly fixed costs average $3,680,000. The company has provided the following information about its two product lines:

| | Contribution Margin Ratio | Percentage of Total Sales |
|---|---|---|
| Flashlights ..................................... | 40% | 15% |
| Batteries ....................................... | 20 | 85 |

a.  Determine the company's monthly break-even point in *sales dollars*.

b.  How much revenue must the company generate in the upcoming month for a monthly operating income of $1,380,000?

# Exercises

L01  **EXERCISE 20.1**
Accounting Terminology

L02

L04

Listed below are nine technical accounting terms introduced in this chapter:

| | | |
|---|---|---|
| Variable costs | Relevant range | Contribution margin |
| Break-even point | Fixed costs | Semivariable costs |
| Economies of scale | Sales mix | Unit contribution margin |

Each of the following statements may (or may not) describe one of these technical terms. For each statement, indicate the accounting term described, or answer "None" if the statement does not correctly describe any of the terms.

a.  The level of sales at which revenue exactly equals costs and expenses.

b.  Costs that remain unchanged despite changes in sales volume.

c.  The span over which output is likely to vary and assumptions about cost behavior generally remain valid.

d.  Sales revenue less variable costs and expenses.

e.  Unit sales price minus variable cost per unit.

f.  The reduction in unit cost achieved from a higher level of output.

g.  Costs that respond to changes in sales volume by less than a proportionate amount.

h.  Operating income less variable costs.

L01  **EXERCISE 20.2**
High-Low Method of Cost Analysis

L08

The following information is available regarding the total manufacturing overhead of Bursa Mfg. Co. for a recent four-month period:

| | Machine-Hours | Manufacturing Overhead |
|---|---|---|
| Jan. ......................................... | 5,500 | $311,500 |
| Feb. ......................................... | 3,200 | 224,000 |
| Mar. ......................................... | 4,900 | 263,800 |
| Apr. ......................................... | 2,800 | 184,600 |

a.  Use the high-low method to determine:

1.  The variable element of manufacturing overhead costs per machine-hour.

2.  The fixed element of monthly overhead cost.

b.  Bursa expects machine-hours in May to equal 5,300. Use the cost relationships determined in part **a** to forecast May's manufacturing overhead costs.

c.  Suppose Bursa had used the cost relationships determined in part **a** to estimate the total manufacturing overhead expected for the months of February and March. By what amounts would Bursa have over- or underestimated these costs?

**L04**
**L05**
**EXERCISE 20.3**
Computing Required
Sales Volume

The following is information concerning a product manufactured by Ames Brothers:

| | |
|---|---:|
| Sales price per unit ........................................... | $ 70 |
| Variable cost per unit .......................................... | 43 |
| Total fixed manufacturing and operating costs (per month) .................. | 405,000 |

Determine the following:

a.   The unit contribution margin.

b.   The number of units that must be sold each month to break even.

c.   The unit sales level that must be reached to earn an operating income of $270,000 per month.

**L04**
through
**L08**
**EXERCISE 20.4**
Computing the
Break-Even Point

Malibu Corporation has monthly fixed costs of $63,000. It sells two products for which it has provided the following information:

| | Sales Price | Contribution Margin |
|---|---|---|
| Product 1 .................................... | $10 | $6 |
| Product 2 .................................... | 10 | 3 |

a.   What total monthly sales revenue is required to break even if the relative sales mix is 40 percent for Product 1 and 60 percent for Product 2?

b.   What total monthly sales revenue is required to earn a monthly operating income of $12,000 if the relative sales mix is 25 percent for Product 1 and 75 percent for Product 2?

**L01**
**L04**
**EXERCISE 20.5**
Cost-Volume-Profit
Relationships

For each of the six independent situations below, compute the missing amounts.

a.   Using contribution margin per unit:

| | Sales | Variable Costs | Contribution Margin per Unit | Fixed Costs | Operating Income | Units Sold |
|---|---|---|---|---|---|---|
| (1) | $_____ | $120,000 | $20 | $_____ | $25,000 | 4,000 |
| (2) | 180,000 | _____ | ___ | 45,000 | 30,000 | 5,000 |
| (3) | 600,000 | _____ | 30 | 150,000 | 90,000 | _____ |

b.   Using the contribution margin ratio:

| | Sales | Variable Costs | Contribution Margin Ratio | Fixed Costs | Operating Income |
|---|---|---|---|---|---|
| (1) | $900,000 | $720,000 | ___% | $_____ | $95,000 |
| (2) | 600,000 | _____ | 40% | _____ | 75,000 |
| (3) | _____ | _____ | 30% | 90,000 | 60,000 |

**L05**
through
**L07**
**EXERCISE 20.6**
Ethical and Behavioral
Implications of CVP

Tom Klem is the controller of Watson Manufacturing, Inc. He estimates that the company's break-even point in sales dollars is $2 million. However, he recently told all of the regional sales managers that sales of $3 million were needed to break even. He also told them that if the company failed to break even, the sales force would be reduced in size by 40 percent. Klem believes that his tactics will motivate the sales force to generate record profits for the upcoming year.

Is his approach to motivating employees ethical? What other approaches might he use?

**L04**
through
**L08**
**EXERCISE 20.7**
Using Cost-Volume-
Profit Formulas

MURDER TO GO! writes and manufactures murder mystery parlor games that it sells to retail stores. The following is per-unit information relating to the manufacture and sale of this product:

| | |
|---|---:|
| Unit sales price ............................................. | $ 28 |
| Variable cost per unit ........................................ | 7 |
| Fixed costs per year ......................................... | 240,000 |

Determine the following, showing as part of your answer the formula that you used in your computation. For example, the formula used to determine the contribution margin ratio (part **a**) is:

$$\text{Contribution Margin Ratio} = \frac{\text{Unit Sales Price} - \text{Variable Costs per Unit}}{\text{Unit Sales Price}}$$

**a.** Contribution margin ratio.

**b.** Sales volume (in dollars) required to break even.

**c.** Sales volume (in dollars) required to earn an annual operating income of $450,000.

**d.** The margin of safety sales volume if annual sales total 40,000 units.

**e.** Operating income if annual sales total 40,000 units.

**L04** through **L08**
**EXERCISE 20.8**
Using Cost-Volume-Profit Formulas

Arrow Products typically earns a contribution margin ratio of 25 percent and has current fixed costs of $80,000. Arrow's general manager is considering spending an additional $20,000 to do one of the following:

**1.** Start a new ad campaign that is expected to increase sales revenue by 5 percent.

**2.** License a new computerized ordering system that is expected to increase Arrow's contribution margin ratio to 30 percent.

Sales revenue for the coming year was initially forecast to equal $1,200,000 (that is, without implementing either of the above options).

**a.** For each option, how much will projected operating income increase or decrease relative to initial predictions?

**b.** By what percentage would sales revenue need to increase to make the ad campaign as attractive as the ordering system?

**L01** **L02** **L04** through **L08**
**EXERCISE 20.9**
Understanding Break-Even Relationships

EasyWriter manufactures an erasable ballpoint pen, which sells for $1.75 per unit. Management recently finished analyzing the results of the company's operations for the current month. At a break-even point of 40,000 units, the company's total variable costs are $50,000 and its total fixed costs amount to $20,000.

**a.** Calculate the contribution margin per unit.

**b.** Calculate the company's margin of safety if monthly sales total 45,000 units.

**c.** Estimate the company's monthly operating loss if it sells only 38,000 units.

**d.** Compute the total cost per unit at a production level of (**1**) 40,000 pens per month and (**2**) 50,000 pens per month. Explain the reason for the change in unit costs.

**L04** **L05**
**EXERCISE 20.10**
Computing Contribution Margin Ratio and Margin of Safety

The following information relates to the only product sold by Harper Company:

| | |
|---|---:|
| Sales price per unit . . . . . . . . . . . . . . . . . . . . . . . . . . . . . . . . . . . . . . . . . . . . . . | $ 24 |
| Variable cost per unit . . . . . . . . . . . . . . . . . . . . . . . . . . . . . . . . . . . . . . . . . | 18 |
| Fixed costs per year . . . . . . . . . . . . . . . . . . . . . . . . . . . . . . . . . . . . . . . . . . . | 240,000 |

**a.** Compute the contribution margin ratio and the dollar sales volume required to break even.

**b.** Assuming that the company sells 75,000 units during the current year, compute the margin of safety sales volume (dollars).

**L01** **L02** **L04** through **L08**
**EXERCISE 20.11**
Applying CVP Concepts

Mathias Corporation manufactures and sells wire rakes. The rakes sell for $16 each. Information about the company's costs is as follows:

| | |
|---|---:|
| Variable manufacturing cost per unit . . . . . . . . . . . . . . . . . . . . . . . . . . . . . . . . | $ 8 |
| Variable selling and administrative cost per unit . . . . . . . . . . . . . . . . . . . . . . . . | 4 |
| Fixed manufacturing overhead per month . . . . . . . . . . . . . . . . . . . . . . . . . . . . . | $150,000 |
| Fixed selling and administrative cost per month . . . . . . . . . . . . . . . . . . . . . . . . | 350,000 |

**a.** Determine the company's monthly break-even point in units.

**b.** Determine the sales volume (in dollars) required for a monthly operating income of $100,000.

**c.** Compute the company's margin of safety if its current monthly sales level is $3,800,000.

**d.** Estimate the amount by which monthly operating income will increase if the company anticipates a $200,000 increase in monthly sales volume.

**L05** **EXERCISE 20.12**

**L06** Finding Missing Information

Palomus Controls currently produces and sells 20,000 regulators monthly. At this level, its variable cost per regulator is $26 and its fixed cost *per regulator* is $7. The company's monthly break-even point is 10,000 regulators.

Determine the company's current *selling price* per regulator.

**L01** **EXERCISE 20.13**

**L04** Determining a Bid Price Using CVP Relationships

through

**L06**

Douglas Company has been asked to submit a bid on supplying gas masks to the Pentagon. The company's current cost structure *per mask* is as follows:

| | |
|---|---|
| Direct materials . . . . . . . . . . . . . . . . . . . . . . . . . . . . . . . . . . . . . . . . . . . . . . . . . . . . | $9 |
| Direct labor . . . . . . . . . . . . . . . . . . . . . . . . . . . . . . . . . . . . . . . . . . . . . . . . . . . . . . . . | 8 |
| Variable manufacturing overhead . . . . . . . . . . . . . . . . . . . . . . . . . . . . . . . . . . . . . . . . | 7 |
| Variable sales commissions . . . . . . . . . . . . . . . . . . . . . . . . . . . . . . . . . . . . . . . . . . . . . | 6 |

**a.** Assume that there would be *no variable sales commission* on this special order. Determine the *lowest* unit price that Douglas can bid without reducing its current level of operating income.

**b.** Assume the company desires a 36 percent contribution margin ratio from this sale and that a special sales commission of 4 percent of the bid price will be applied to the order *instead of* its normal $6 variable sales commission. Determine the bid price per unit given these unique circumstances.

**L07** **EXERCISE 20.14**

**L08** CVP with Multiple Products

Water World sells three products: ski vests, slalom skis, and ski ropes. Information related to each product line is provided below:

| | Ski Vests | Slalom Skis | Ski Ropes |
|---|---|---|---|
| Unit selling price . . . . . . . . . . . . . . . . . . . . . . . . . . | $120 | $300 | $50 |
| Unit variable cost . . . . . . . . . . . . . . . . . . . . . . . . . | 60 | 210 | 10 |
| Sales mix percentage . . . . . . . . . . . . . . . . . . . . . . | 20% | 70% | 10% |

The company's annual fixed costs are approximately $741,000.

**a.** Compute total annual sales that the company must generate to *break even*.

**b.** Compute total annual sales that the company must generate to earn *operating income* of $234,000.

**c.** As Water World's marketing manager, what marketing strategy would you pursue to help the company maximize its profit potential?

**L09** **EXERCISE 20.15**

Estimating Semivariable Costs

Dinklemyer Corporation uses direct labor hours as its single cost driver. Actual overhead costs and actual direct labor hours for the first five months of the current year are as follows:

| Month | Actual Total Overhead | Actual Direct Labor Hours |
|---|---|---|
| January | $980,000 | 19,200 |
| February | 950,000 | 18,400 |
| March | 860,000 | 17,000 |
| April | 752,500 | 12,700 |
| May | 760,000 | 13,200 |

**a.** Compute the company's estimated *variable* manufacturing overhead cost *per direct labor hour.*

**b.** Estimate the company's total monthly *fixed* manufacturing overhead cost.

**c.** Estimate the company's *total* manufacturing overhead for *June through August* if 50,000 total direct labor hours are budgeted for that specific three-month period.

## Problem Set A

L04
through
L07
**PROBLEM 20.1A**

Setting Sales Price
and Computing the
Break-Even Point

Thermal Tent, Inc., is a newly organized manufacturing business that plans to manufacture and sell 50,000 units per year of a new product. The following estimates have been made of the company's costs and expenses (other than income taxes):

|  | Fixed | Variable per Unit |
|---|---|---|
| Manufacturing costs: |  |  |
|   Direct materials . . . . . . . . . . . . . . . . . . . . . . . . . . . . . . . . . . . . . . |  | $47 |
|   Direct labor . . . . . . . . . . . . . . . . . . . . . . . . . . . . . . . . . . . . . |  | 32 |
|   Manufacturing overhead . . . . . . . . . . . . . . . . . . . . . . . . . . . . . . | $340,000 | 4 |
| Period costs: |  |  |
|   Selling expenses . . . . . . . . . . . . . . . . . . . . . . . . . . . . . . . . . . . |  | 1 |
|   Administrative expenses . . . . . . . . . . . . . . . . . . . . . . . . . . . . . | 200,000 |  |
| Totals . . . . . . . . . . . . . . . . . . . . . . . . . . . . . . . . . . . . . . . . . . . | $540,000 | $84 |

### Instructions

**a.** What should the company establish as the sales price per unit if it sets a target of earning an operating income of $260,000 by producing and selling 50,000 units during the first year of operations? (Hint: First compute the required contribution margin per unit.)

**b.** At the unit sales price computed in part **a,** how many units must the company produce and sell to break even? (Assume all units produced are sold.)

**c.** What will be the margin of safety (in dollars) if the company produces and sells 50,000 units at the sales price computed in part **a**? Using the margin of safety, compute operating income at 50,000 units.

**d.** Assume that the marketing manager thinks that the price of this product must be no higher than $94 to ensure market penetration. Will setting the sales price at $94 enable Thermal Tent to break even, given the plans to manufacture and sell 50,000 units? Explain your answer.

L01
L04
L05
**PROBLEM 20.2A**

Estimating Costs and
Profits

Blaster Corporation manufactures hiking boots. For the coming year, the company has budgeted the following costs for the production and sale of 30,000 pairs of boots:

|  | Budgeted Costs | Budgeted Costs per Pair | Percentage of Costs Considered Variable |
|---|---|---|---|
| Direct materials . . . . . . . . . . . . . . . . . . . . . . . . . . | $ 630,000 | $21 | 100% |
| Direct labor . . . . . . . . . . . . . . . . . . . . . . . . . . . . . . . | 300,000 | 10 | 100 |
| Manufacturing overhead (fixed and variable) . . . . . | 720,000 | 24 | 25 |
| Selling and administrative expenses . . . . . . . . . . . | 600,000 | 20 | 20 |
| Totals . . . . . . . . . . . . . . . . . . . . . . . . . . . . . . . . | $2,250,000 | $75 |  |

### Instructions

**a.** Compute the sales price per unit that would result in a budgeted operating income of $900,000, assuming that the company produces and sells 30,000 pairs. (Hint: First compute the budgeted sales revenue needed to produce this operating income.)

**b.** Assuming that the company decides to sell the boots at a unit price of $121 per pair, compute the following:

  **1.** Total fixed costs budgeted for the year.

  **2.** Variable cost per unit.

  **3.** The unit contribution margin.

  **4.** The number of pairs that must be produced and sold annually to break even at a sales price of $121 per pair.

**LO3**
**through**
**LO6**
**LO9**
**PROBLEM 20.3A**
Preparing a "Break-Even" Graph

Stop-n-Shop operates a downtown parking lot containing 800 parking spaces. The lot is open 2,500 hours per year. The parking charge per car is 50 cents per hour; the average customer parks two hours. Stop-n-Shop rents the lot from a development company for $7,250 per month. The lot supervisor is paid $24,000 per year. Five employees who handle the parking of cars are paid $300 per week for 50 weeks, plus $600 each for the two-week vacation period. Employees rotate vacations during the slow months when four employees can handle the reduced load of traffic. Lot maintenance, payroll taxes, and other costs of operating the parking lot include fixed costs of $3,000 per month and variable costs of 5 cents per parking-space hour.

**Instructions**

a. Draw a cost-volume-profit graph for Stop-n-Shop on an annual basis. Use thousands of parking-space hours as the measure of volume of activity. [Stop-n-Shop has an annual capacity of 2 million parking-space hours (800 spaces × 2,500 hours per year).]

b. What is the contribution margin ratio? What is the annual break-even point in dollars of parking revenue?

c. Suppose that the five employees were taken off the hourly wage basis and paid 30 cents per car parked, with the same vacation pay as before. (**1**) How would this change the contribution margin ratio and total fixed costs? (Hint: The variable costs per parking-space hour will now include 15 cents, or one-half of the 30 cents paid to employees per car parked, because the average customer parks for two hours.) (**2**) What annual revenue would be necessary to produce operating income of $300,000 under these circumstances?

**LO3**
**PROBLEM 20.4A**
Drawing a Cost-Volume-Profit Graph
**LO4**
**LO6**
**LO9**

Rainbow Paints operates a chain of retail paint stores. Although the paint is sold under the Rainbow label, it is purchased from an independent paint manufacturer. Guy Walker, president of Rainbow Paints, is studying the advisability of opening another store. His estimates of monthly costs for the proposed location are:

| | |
|---|---|
| Fixed costs: | |
| Occupancy costs ............................................... | $3,160 |
| Salaries ...................................................... | 3,640 |
| Other ........................................................ | 1,200 |
| Variable costs (including cost of paint)........................... | $6 per gallon |

Although Rainbow stores sell several different types of paint, monthly sales revenue consistently averages $10 per gallon sold.

**Instructions**

a. Compute the contribution margin ratio and the break-even point in dollar sales and in gallons sold for the proposed store.

b. Draw a monthly cost-volume-profit graph for the proposed store, assuming 3,000 gallons per month as the maximum sales potential.

c. Walker thinks that the proposed store will sell between 2,200 and 2,600 gallons of paint per month. Compute the amount of operating income that would be earned per month at each of these sales volumes.

**LO3**
**through**
**LO7**
**LO9**
**PROBLEM 20.5A**
Cost-Volume-Profit Analysis; Preparing a Graph

Simon Teguh is considering investing in a vending machine operation involving 20 vending machines located in various plants around the city. The machine manufacturer reports that similar vending machine routes have produced a sales volume ranging from 800 to 1,000 units per machine per month. The following information is made available to Teguh in evaluating the possible profitability of the operation.

1. An investment of $45,000 will be required, $9,000 for merchandise and $36,000 for the 20 machines.

2. The machines have a service life of five years and no salvage value at the end of that period. Depreciation will be computed on the straight-line basis.

3. The merchandise (candy and soft drinks) retails for an average of 75 cents per unit and will cost Teguh an average of 25 cents per unit.

4. Owners of the buildings in which the machines are located are paid a commission of 5 cents per unit of candy and soft drinks sold.

5.  One person will be hired to service the machines. The salary will be $1,500 per month.

6.  Other expenses are estimated at $600 per month. These expenses do not vary with the number of units sold.

**Instructions**

a.  Determine the unit contribution margin and the break-even volume in units and in dollars per month.

b.  Draw a monthly cost-volume-profit graph for sales volume up to 1,000 units per machine per month.

c.  What sales volume in units and in dollars per month will be necessary to produce an operating income equal to a 30 percent annual return on Teguh's $45,000 investment? (Round to the nearest unit.)

d.  Teguh is considering offering the building owners a flat rental of $30 per machine per month in lieu of the commission of 5 cents per unit sold. What effect would this change in commission arrangement have on his *monthly* break-even volume in terms of units?

  **PROBLEM 20.6A**

Analyzing the Effects of Changes in Costs

Precision Systems manufactures CD burners and currently sells 18,500 units annually to producers of laptop computers. Jay Wilson, president of the company, anticipates a 15 percent increase in the cost per unit of direct labor on January 1 of next year. He expects all other costs and expenses to remain unchanged. Wilson has asked you to assist him in developing the information he needs to formulate a reasonable product strategy for next year.

You are satisfied that volume is the primary factor affecting costs and expenses and have separated the semivariable costs into their fixed and variable segments. Beginning and ending inventories remain at a level of 1,000 units. Current plant capacity is 20,000 units.

Below are the current-year data assembled for your analysis:

| | | |
|---|---:|---:|
| Sales price per unit | | $100 |
| Variable costs per unit: | | |
| Direct materials | $10 | |
| Direct labor | 20 | |
| Manufacturing overhead and selling and administrative expenses | 30 | 60 |
| Contribution margin per unit (40%) | | $ 40 |
| Fixed costs | | $390,000 |

**Instructions**

a.  What increase in the selling price is necessary to cover the 15 percent increase in direct labor cost and still maintain the current contribution margin ratio of 40 percent?

b.  How many units must be sold to maintain the current operating income of *$350,000* if the sales price remains at $100 and the 15 percent wage increase goes into effect? (Hint: First compute the unit contribution margin.)

c.  Wilson believes that an additional $700,000 of machinery (to be depreciated at 20 percent annually) will increase present capacity (20,000 units) by 25 percent. If all units produced can be sold at the present price of $100 per unit and the wage increase goes into effect, how would the estimated operating income before capacity is increased compare with the estimated operating income after capacity is increased? Prepare schedules of estimated operating income at full capacity *before* and *after* the expansion.

 **PROBLEM 20.7A**

Analyzing the Effects of Changes in Costs and Volume

 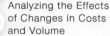

Percula Farms raises marine fish for sale in the aquarium trade. Each year, Percula obtains a batch of approximately 1 million eggs from a local supplier. Percula's manager is trying to decide whether to use the farm's facilities to raise Maroon Clownfish or Queen Angelfish. Clownfish eggs cost $5,500 per batch, while angelfish eggs cost $9,500 per batch. Due to differences in needs, only one species may be raised at a time and only one batch of fish can be raised in any 52-week period.

With current facilities, approximately 10 percent of clownfish eggs and 5 percent of angelfish eggs can be successfully raised to maturity. Clownfish take approximately 35 weeks to grow to a salable size, while angelfish take 50 weeks. Angelfish also require more care than clownfish. Each week, angelfish need two complete water changes and 20 feedings, while clownfish need only one water change and 15 feedings. Each feeding costs $150 and each water change costs $1,000. Heating and lighting costs equal $400 per week of rearing, regardless of which type of fish is being raised. Fixed overhead costs for the year amount to $80,000. Percula can sell clownfish for $4 each and angelfish for $10 each.

### Instructions

**a.** Which species should Percula raise to earn the highest operating income for the year?

**b.** Other than fixed costs, which factors or categories of costs seem to have the greatest influence on operating income?

**c.** Percula's manager is considering the following improvements, each of which will cost an additional $8,000 for the year. Due to resource limitations, only one can be implemented.

   **1.** Purchasing a higher quality filter material that will significantly improve water conditions in the rearing tanks. The higher water quality will increase the survival rates to 12 percent for clownfish and 6 percent for angelfish. The need for water changes will also be reduced to one each week for angelfish. Due to the higher yields, feeding costs will increase to $160 each.

   **2.** Installing newer, more efficient equipment that will reduce heating and lighting costs to $300 per week of rearing. The new equipment will promote more stable conditions, increasing the survival rates of clownfish to 10.5 percent and of angelfish to 5.5 percent. The slight change in survival rates is not expected to increase feeding costs.

Using your answers to part **b** above (with no calculations), which option do you think will be more beneficial?

**d.** Perform the necessary calculations to check if your answer to part **c** was correct. Should either of the investments be undertaken, and if so, which fish species should be raised?

**L04**
**through**
**L08**
**PROBLEM 20.8A**
CVP with Multiple Products

Lifefit Products sells running shoes and shorts. The following is selected per-unit information for these two products:

|                              | Shoes | Shorts |
| ---------------------------- | ----- | ------ |
| Sales price                  | $50   | $5     |
| Variable costs and expenses  | 35    | 1      |
| Contribution margin          | $15   | $4     |

Fixed costs and expenses amount to *$378,000* per month.

Lifefit has total sales of $1 million per month, of which 80 percent result from the sale of running shoes and the other 20 percent from the sale of shorts.

### Instructions

**a.** Compute separately the contribution margin ratio for each line of products.

**b.** Assuming the current sales mix, compute:

   **1.** Average contribution margin ratio of total monthly sales.

   **2.** Monthly operating income.

   **3.** The monthly break-even sales volume (stated in dollars).

**c.** Assume that through aggressive marketing Lifefit is able to *shift its sales mix* toward more sales of shorts. Total sales remain $1 million per month, but now 30 percent of this revenue stems from sales of shorts. Using this new sales mix, compute:

   **1.** Average contribution margin ratio of total monthly sales.

   **2.** Monthly operating income.

   **3.** The monthly break-even sales volume (stated in dollars).

**d.** Explain *why* the company's financial picture changes so significantly with the new sales mix.

## Problem Set B

**L04**
**through**
**L07**
**PROBLEM 20.1B**
Setting Sales Price and Computing the Break-Even Point

Satka, Inc., is a newly organized manufacturing business that plans to manufacture and sell 30,000 units per year of a new product. The following estimates have been made of the company's costs and expenses (other than income taxes):

|  | Fixed | Variable per Unit |
|---|---|---|
| Manufacturing costs: |  |  |
| Direct materials . . . . . . . . . . . . . . . . . . . . . . . . . . . . . . . . . . . . . . . |  | $ 38 |
| Direct labor . . . . . . . . . . . . . . . . . . . . . . . . . . . . . . . . . . . . . . . . . . |  | 47 |
| Manufacturing overhead . . . . . . . . . . . . . . . . . . . . . . . . . . . . . . | $440,000 | 9 |
| Period costs: |  |  |
| Selling expenses . . . . . . . . . . . . . . . . . . . . . . . . . . . . . . . . . . . . . . |  | 6 |
| Administrative expenses . . . . . . . . . . . . . . . . . . . . . . . . . . . . . . . | 360,000 |  |
| Totals . . . . . . . . . . . . . . . . . . . . . . . . . . . . . . . . . . . . . . . . . . . . . . . | $800,000 | $100 |

**Instructions**

a. What should the company establish as the sales price per unit if it sets a target of earning an operating income of $400,000 by producing and selling 30,000 units during the first year of operations? (Hint: First compute the required contribution margin per unit.)

b. At the unit sales price computed in part **a**, how many units must the company produce and sell to break even? (Assume all units produced are sold.)

c. What will be the margin of safety (in dollars) if the company produces and sells 30,000 units at the sales price computed in part **a**?

d. Assume that the marketing manager thinks that the price of this product must be no higher than $132 to ensure market penetration. Will setting the sales price at $132 enable Satka to break even, given the plans to manufacture and sell 30,000 units? Explain your answer.

**LO1** **PROBLEM 20.2B**
Estimating Costs and
**LO4** Profits

**LO5**

Snug-As-A-Bug manufactures sleeping bags. For the coming year, the company has budgeted the following costs for the production and sale of 80,000 units:

|  | Budgeted Costs | Budgeted Costs per Unit | Percentage of Costs Considered Variable |
|---|---|---|---|
| Direct materials . . . . . . . . . . . . . . . . . . . . . . . . . . | $1,440,000 | $18 | 100% |
| Direct labor . . . . . . . . . . . . . . . . . . . . . . . . . . . . . . | 160,000 | 2 | 100 |
| Manufacturing overhead (fixed and variable) . . . . . | 2,400,000 | 30 | 10 |
| Selling and administrative expenses . . . . . . . . . . . | 800,000 | 10 | 40 |
| Totals . . . . . . . . . . . . . . . . . . . . . . . . . . . . . . . . . | $4,800,000 | $60 |  |

**Instructions**

a. Compute the sales price per unit that would result in a budgeted operating income of $560,000, assuming that the company produces and sells 80,000 bags. (Hint: First compute the budgeted sales revenue needed to produce this operating income.)

b. Assuming that the company decides to sell the sleeping bags at a unit price of $71 per unit, compute the following:

1. Total fixed costs budgeted for the year.

2. Variable cost per unit.

3. The unit contribution margin.

4. The number of bags that must be produced and sold annually to break even at a sales price of $71 per unit.

**LO3** **PROBLEM 20.3B**
through Preparing a "Break-
Even" Graph
**LO6**

**LO9**

Moor-n-More operates a boat mooring service in the downtown harbor with 80 docking spaces. The business is open 3,000 hours per year. The mooring charge per boat is $5 per hour; the average boater docks for two hours. Moor-n-More rents the harbor space from the Harbor Authority for $5,000 per month. The general manager is paid $32,940 per year. Three employees assist in the operations and are paid $250 per week for 50 weeks, plus $500 each for a two-week vacation period. Employees rotate their vacations. Other costs include fixed city taxes of $1,500 per month and variable costs of 10 cents per occupied mooring-space hour (a usage tax charged by the Harbor Authority).

### Instructions

**a.** Draw a cost-volume-profit graph for Moor-n-More on an annual basis. Use thousands of mooring-space hours as the measure of volume of activity. [Moor-n-More has an annual capacity of 240,000 mooring-space hours (80 spaces × 3,000 hours per year).]

**b.** What is the contribution margin ratio? What is the annual break-even point in dollars of mooring revenue?

**c.** Suppose that the three employees were taken off the hourly wage basis and paid 40 cents per boat moored, with the same vacation pay as before. (**1**) How would this change the contribution margin ratio and total fixed costs? (Hint: The variable costs per mooring-space hour will now include 20 cents, or one-half of the 40 cents paid to employees per occupied mooring space, because the average boater stays for two hours.) (**2**) What annual revenue would be necessary to produce operating income of $112,560 under these circumstances?

### PROBLEM 20.4B

Drawing a Cost-Volume-Profit Graph

Green Thumb operates a chain of lawn fertilizer stores. Although the fertilizer is sold under the Green Thumb label, it is purchased from an independent manufacturer. Sue Smith, president of Green Thumb, is studying the advisability of opening another store. Her estimates of monthly costs for the proposed location are:

| | |
|---|---|
| Fixed costs: | |
| Occupancy costs . . . . . . . . . . . . . . . . . . . . . . . . . . . . . . . . . . . . . . . . . . . . . . . . . . . | $5,000 |
| Salaries. . . . . . . . . . . . . . . . . . . . . . . . . . . . . . . . . . . . . . . . . . . . . . . . . . . . . . . . . . | 2,400 |
| Other. . . . . . . . . . . . . . . . . . . . . . . . . . . . . . . . . . . . . . . . . . . . . . . . . . . . . . . . . . . . | 1,600 |
| Variable costs (including cost of fertilizer) . . . . . . . . . . . . . . . . . . . . . . . . . . . | $    12 per bag |

Although Green Thumb stores sell several different types of fertilizer, monthly sales revenue consistently averages $20 per bag sold.

### Instructions

**a.** Compute the contribution margin ratio and the break-even point in dollar sales and in bags sold for the proposed store.

**b.** Draw a monthly cost-volume-profit graph for the proposed store, assuming 2,000 bags per month as the maximum sales potential.

**c.** Smith thinks that the proposed store will sell between 1,500 and 1,800 bags of fertilizer per month. Compute the amount of operating income that would be earned per month at each of these sales volumes.

### PROBLEM 20.5B

Cost-Volume-Profit Analysis; Preparing a Graph

Ed Winslow is considering investing in a sandwich machine operation involving 50 sandwich machines located in various locations throughout the city. The machine manufacturer reports that similar sandwich machine routes have produced a sales volume ranging from 40 to 60 units per machine per month. The following information is made available to Winslow in evaluating the possible profitability of the operation.

**1.** An investment of $70,000 will be required, $10,000 for merchandise and $60,000 for the 50 machines.

**2.** The machines have a service life of five years and no salvage value at the end of that period. Depreciation will be computed on the straight-line basis.

**3.** Sandwiches sell for an average of $3.20 and will cost Winslow an average of $1.10 per unit to prepare.

**4.** Owners of the buildings in which the machines are located are paid a commission of 10 cents per sandwich sold.

**5.** One person will be hired to service the machines. The salary will be $1,800 per month.

**6.** Other expenses are estimated at $200 per month. These expenses do not vary with the number of units sold.

### Instructions

**a.** Determine the unit contribution margin and the break-even volume in units and in dollars per month.

**b.** Draw a monthly cost-volume-profit graph for sales volume up to 60 units per machine per month.

c. What sales volume in units and in dollars per month will be necessary to produce an operating income equal to a 12 percent annual return on Winslow's $70,000 investment? (Round to the nearest unit.)

d. Winslow is considering offering the building owners a flat rental of $45 per machine per month in lieu of the commission of 10 cents per unit sold. What effect would this change in commission arrangement have on his *monthly* break-even volume in terms of units?

**PROBLEM 20.6B**

Analyzing the Effects of Changes in Costs

Electro Systems manufactures relays and currently sells 200,000 units annually to producers of electronic equipment. Mac Scott, president of the company, anticipates a 20 percent increase in the cost per unit of direct labor on January 1 of next year. He expects all other costs and expenses to remain unchanged. Scott has asked you to assist him in developing the information he needs to formulate a reasonable product strategy for next year.

You are satisfied that volume is the primary factor affecting costs and expenses and have separated the semivariable costs into their fixed and variable segments. Beginning and ending inventories remain at a level of 3,000 units. Current plant capacity is 210,000 units.

Below are the current-year data assembled for your analysis:

| | | |
|---|---|---|
| Sales price per unit. . . . . . . . . . . . . . . . . . . . . . . . . . . . . . . . . . . . . . . . | | $15 |
| Variable costs per unit: | | |
| Direct materials. . . . . . . . . . . . . . . . . . . . . . . . . . . . . . . . . . . . . . . . . . | $3 | |
| Direct labor . . . . . . . . . . . . . . . . . . . . . . . . . . . . . . . . . . . . . . . . . . . . | 1 | |
| Manufacturing overhead and selling and administrative expenses. . . . . . . . . . . . . . . . . . . . . . . . . . . . . . . . . . . . . . . . . . | 2 | 6 |
| Contribution margin per unit (60%). . . . . . . . . . . . . . . . . . . . . . . . . . . . . | | $ 9 |
| Fixed costs . . . . . . . . . . . . . . . . . . . . . . . . . . . . . . . . . . . . . . . . . . . . . | | $1,000,000 |

**Instructions**

a. What increase in the selling price is necessary to cover the 20 percent increase in direct labor cost and still maintain the current contribution margin ratio of 60 percent?

b. Approximately how many units must be sold to maintain the current operating income of *$800,000* if the sales price remains at $15 and the 20 percent wage increase goes into effect? (Hint: First compute the unit contribution margin.)

c. Scott believes that an additional $500,000 of machinery (to be depreciated at 20 percent annually) will increase present capacity (210,000 units) by 5 percent. If all units produced can be sold at the present price of $15 per unit and the wage increase goes into effect, how would the estimated operating income before capacity is increased compare with the estimated operating income after capacity is increased? Prepare schedules of estimated operating income at full capacity *before* and *after* the expansion.

**PROBLEM 20.7B**

Analyzing the Effects of Changes in Costs and Volume

Dorsal Ranch raises fish for sale in the restaurant industry. The company can obtain batches of 2 million eggs from its supplier. Management is trying to decide whether to raise cod or salmon. Cod eggs cost $14,000 per batch, while salmon eggs cost $18,000 per batch. Due to differences in needs, only one species can be raised during a 52-week period.

With current facilities, approximately 15 percent of cod eggs and 10 percent of salmon eggs can be raised to maturity. Cod take approximately 40 weeks to grow to a marketable size, while salmon take 50 weeks. Salmon also require more care than cod. Each week, salmon require two water treatments and 35 feedings. Each feeding costs $400 and each water treatment costs $600. Cod require only 21 feedings and a single water treatment. Heat and light regulation costs average $300 per week for either species. The company can sell cod for $5 apiece and salmon for $9 a piece. Annual fixed costs, regardless of which species is raised, total $900,000.

**Instructions**

a. Which species should Dorsal Ranch raise to earn the highest operating income for the year?

b. Other than fixed costs, which factors or categories of costs seem to have the greatest influence on operating income?

c. Management is considering one of the following improvements, each of which will cost an additional $20,000 for the year. Due to resource constraints, only one can be implemented.

1. Installing a new filtration system to improve water quality. This will increase the survival rates to 20 percent for cod and 14 percent for salmon. The need for water treatments will be reduced to one per week for salmon. Due to higher yields, feeding costs will increase by $80 weekly.

2. Installing an environment regulation system that will reduce heating and lighting costs to $250 per week. The equipment will increase the survival rate for cod to 16 percent and the survival rate for salmon to 11 percent. This slight change in survival rates is not expected to increase either water changing requirements or feeding costs.

Using your answers to part **b** above (with no calculations), which option do you think will be most beneficial?

**d.** Perform the necessary calculations to check if your answer to part **c** was correct. Should either of these investments be undertaken, and if so, which species should be raised?

 **PROBLEM 20.8B**

through

CVP with Multiple Products

HomeTeam Sports sells hats and shirts licensed by the NFL and the NBA. The following is selected per-unit information for these two product lines:

|  | Hats | Shirts |
| --- | --- | --- |
| Sales price | $20 | $28 |
| Variable costs and expenses | 14 | 7 |
| Contribution margin | $ 6 | $21 |

Fixed costs and expenses amount to *$684,000* per month.

HomeTeam has total sales of $1.5 million per month, of which 60 percent result from the sale of shirts and the other 40 percent from the sale of hats.

**Instructions**

**a.** Compute separately the contribution margin ratio for each line of products.

**b.** Assuming the current sales mix, compute:

1. Average contribution margin ratio of total monthly sales.

2. Monthly operating income.

3. The monthly break-even sales volume (stated in dollars).

**c.** Assume that because of consumer trends, the company's *sales mix* shifts to a higher demand for hats. Total sales remain $1.5 million per month, but now 60 percent of this revenue stems from sales of hats. Using this new sales mix, compute:

1. Average contribution margin ratio of total monthly sales.

2. Monthly operating income.

3. The monthly break-even sales volume (stated in dollars).

**d.** Explain *why* the company's financial picture changes so significantly with the new sales mix.

## Critical Thinking Cases

 **CASE 20.1**

CVP from Different Points of View

Assume that you are preparing a seminar on cost-volume-profit analysis for nonaccountants. Several potential attendees have approached you and have asked why they should be interested in learning about your topic. The individuals include:

1. A factory worker who serves as her company's labor union representative in charge of contract negotiations.

2. A purchasing agent in charge of ordering raw materials for a large manufacturing company.

3. A vice president of sales for a large automobile company.

4. A director of research and development for a pharmaceutical company.

**Instructions**

What unique reasons would you give each of these individuals to motivate them to come to your seminar?

**914**    Chapter 20  Cost-Volume-Profit Analysis

L01

**CASE 20.2**

Evaluating Marketing

L04

Strategies

through

L07

Purple Cow operates a chain of drive-ins selling primarily ice cream products. The following information is taken from the records of a typical drive-in now operated by the company:

| | | |
|---|---:|---:|
| Average selling price of ice cream per gallon | | $14.80 |
| Number of gallons sold per month | | 3,000 |
| Variable costs per gallon: | | |
| Ice cream | $4.60 | |
| Supplies (cups, cones, toppings, etc.) | 2.20 | |
| Total variable expenses per gallon | | $6.80 |
| Fixed costs per month: | | |
| Rent on building | | $ 2,200.00 |
| Utilities and upkeep | | 760.00 |
| Wages, including payroll taxes | | 4,840.00 |
| Manager's salary, including payroll taxes but | | |
| excluding any bonus | | 2,500.00 |
| Other fixed expenses | | 1,700.00 |
| Total fixed costs per month | | $12,000.00 |

Based on these data, the monthly break-even sales volume is determined as follows:

$$\frac{\$12,000 \text{ (fixed costs)}}{\$8.00 \text{ (contribution margin per unit)}} = 1,500 \text{ gallons (or } \$22,200)$$

**Instructions**

a. Currently, all store managers have contracts calling for a bonus of 20 cents per gallon for each gallon sold *beyond* the break-even point. Compute the number of gallons of ice cream that must be sold per month in order to earn a monthly operating income of $10,000 (round to the nearest gallon).

b. To increase operating income, the company is considering the following two alternatives:

1. Reduce the selling price by an average of $2.00 per gallon. This action is expected to increase the number of gallons sold by 20 percent. (Under this plan, the manager would be paid a salary of $2,500 per month without a bonus.)

2. Spend $3,000 per month on advertising without any change in selling price. This action is expected to increase the number of gallons sold by 10 percent. (Under this plan, the manager would be paid a salary of $2,500 per month without a bonus.)

Which of these two alternatives would result in the higher monthly operating income? How many gallons must be sold per month under each alternative for a typical outlet to break even? Provide schedules in support of your answers.

c. Draft a memo to management indicating your recommendations with respect to these alternative marketing strategies.

L01

**CASE 20.3**

What They Don't

Know Won't Hurt 'Em

Floyd Christianson is the chief executive officer of Murango Pharmaceuticals. The company has been struggling in recent years to break even and its stock price has been on the decline. The company's Jacksonville plant manufactures a prescription drug that has lost significant market share to alternative drugs marketed by its competitors. On February 1, management decided that it would close the Jacksonville plant at the end of June.

On February 3, Susan Lohmar, Murango's chief financial officer, asked Christianson to review the Form 8-K she was about to file with the SEC (see this chapter's Ethics, Fraud & Corporate Governance feature on page 896). Christianson read the document and immediately instructed Lohmar not to file it, saying:

There's no need to cause alarm in the marketplace. Our stock price is depressed enough the way it is. What people don't know won't hurt 'em. Besides, the charge to income you're proposing will cause us to operate in the red, and that won't go over well with shareholders.

**Instructions**

**a.** What is a Form 8-K?

**b.** What charge to income was disclosed in the Form 8-K prepared by Susan Lohmar?

**c.** Why would filing a Form 8-K cause the company to appear unprofitable?

**d.** Do you agree with Floyd Christianson's argument against filing a Form 8-K? Defend your answer.

---

**L08** **INTERNET CASE 20.4**

Sales Mix

Visit the home page of The Securities & Exchange Commission at the following address:

www.sec.gov

Use EDGAR to locate the most recent 10-K of Ford Motor Company. Locate the tables in the 10-K that provide information about the U.S. vehicle mix of sales, and Ford's vehicle mix of sales.

**Instructions**

**a.** In the most recent year reported, which vehicle type has contributed most to Ford's sales mix?

**b.** In the most recent year reported, which vehicle type has contributed most to the U.S. automobile industry's sales mix?

**c.** Has Ford's sales mix over the past several years changed?

**d.** Has the U.S. automobile industry's sales mix, in general, changed over the past several years?

**e.** How does a company's sales mix influence its profitability?

*Internet sites are time and date sensitive. It is the purpose of these exercises to have you explore the Internet. You may need to use the Yahoo! search engine* http://www.yahoo.com *(or another favorite search engine) to find a company's current Web address.*

## Answers to Self-Test Questions

**1.** a   **2.** c (from $25,000 to $27,000)   **3.** d ($20,000)   **4.** b   **5.** d

# CHAPTER 23

# Operational Budgeting

© AP Photo/Ed Reinke

**AFTER STUDYING THIS CHAPTER, YOU SHOULD BE ABLE TO:**

Learning Objectives

**L01**    Explain how a company can be "profit rich, yet cash poor."

**L02**    Discuss the benefits that a company may derive from a formal budgeting process.

**L03**    Explain two philosophies that may be used in setting budgeted amounts.

**L04**    Describe the elements of a master budget.

**L05**    Prepare the budgets and supporting schedules included in a master budget.

**L06**    Prepare a flexible budget and explain its uses.

# HILLERICH & BRADSBY COMPANY

The family-owned company that makes the famous Louisville Slugger® baseball bat, Hillerich & Bradsby Co., began as a woodworking shop in 1856, making everything from balustrades to bedposts. By 1875, the little company was employing 20 people. According to company legend, the first pro bat was turned in 1884 for Pete Browning, a star on Louisville's professional American Association team—the Eclipse. One of Browning's nicknames was "The Louisville Slugger."

Hillerich & Bradsby increased the success of the Louisville Slugger® bat by allowing amateur baseball players to purchase the bat model of their favorite big-league player. In 1915 the Louisville Slugger first appeared in a youth-size model and in 1919 the company launched its first national advertising campaign. Just four years later, the company was producing one million bats a year.

In 1954, Hillerich & Bradsby purchased a Pennsylvania timber company to ensure an adequate supply of high-quality white ash for their bats. In 1970, the company began making aluminum baseball bats and, in 1975, they began selling baseball and softball gloves. In 2009, Hillerich & Bradsby celebrated the 125th anniversary of the Louisville Slugger®.

The above discussion shows the challenges firms face when they evolve from a small enterprise to a large company. Ensuring sources of supply and introducing new products require careful planning. The focus of this chapter, budgeting, is a key component of successful company growth. Operational budgeting is critical for long-term company viability. ∎

Companies such as Hillerich & Bradsby use the budget (1) to assign decision-making authority over the company's resources, (2) to coordinate and implement plans, and (3) to hold employees accountable for the results of their decision making.

In this chapter, we show you how to *construct* responsibility budgets and *use* those budgets to assign decision-making authority and hold employees accountable for their decisions. After describing the master budget and its many components in detail, we go on to explain how to use the master budget as a means to implement planning and control through flexible budgeting. By the time you finish studying this chapter, you should appreciate the role of budgeting as a cornerstone of successful business activity.

## Profit Rich, Yet Cash Poor

**Learning Objective**

LO1 **Explain how a company can be "profit rich, yet cash poor."**

In January 2010, Nancy Conrad founded Network Technologies, Inc. (NTI). NTI manufactures a screening device designed to safeguard personal computers against viruses transmitted through networks. Unlike disinfectant programs that remove viruses from infected hard drives, the NTI product actually screens all incoming network transmissions. If a virus is detected, it is destroyed *before* it can infect a computer's hard drive and cause damage to files.

Operating from a small manufacturing facility in Baltimore, NTI struggled through its first nine months of operations. However, the company experienced a very strong fourth quarter and managed to finish the year with total sales of $900,000 and a net income of $144,000.

The following profitability measures were taken from NTI's financial report for the year ended December 31, 2010:

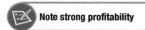 Note strong profitability

| Selected Profitability Measures | NTI | Industry Average |
| --- | --- | --- |
| Gross profit percentage (gross profit ÷ sales) | 60% | 45% |
| Net income percentage (net income ÷ sales) | 16 | 12 |
| Return on equity (net income ÷ average shareholders' equity) | 29 | 18 |
| Return on assets (net income ÷ average total assets) | 15 | 14 |

Even though NTI appears to be *profitable* relative to industry averages, it is plagued by severe *cash flow problems*. In fact, for the year ending December 31, 2010, NTI reported a *$250,000 negative cash flow from operations*. Unable to obtain additional bank credit, Conrad loaned her company $36,000 on January 1, 2011, so that payroll checks would clear.

The liquidity measures presented below were also taken from NTI's December 31, 2010, financial report. Unlike the profitability measures, these measures are all well *below* industry averages.

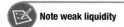 Note weak liquidity

| Selected Liquidity Measures | NTI | Industry Average |
| --- | --- | --- |
| Current ratio (current assets ÷ current liabilities) | 1.4 | 2.4 |
| Quick ratio (quick assets ÷ current liabilities) | 0.6 | 1.5 |
| Inventory turnover (cost of goods sold ÷ average inventory) | 2.2 | 7.3 |
| Accounts receivable turnover (net sales ÷ average receivables) | 4.5 | 8.0 |

What we see happening at NTI is a dilemma common to many businesses. In short, the company is *profit rich, yet cash poor*. How can a profitable business experience cash flow problems? Surprisingly, we will see that this condition often stems from *rapid growth*.

## OPERATING CASH FLOWS: THE LIFEBLOOD OF SURVIVAL

In response to a surge in demand experienced in the fourth quarter of 2010, NTI disbursed large sums of cash to manufacture goods available for sale. NTI's cash was literally *tied up* in direct materials, work in process, and finished goods inventories as units were produced. Furthermore, as these goods were sold, cash remained tied up in accounts receivable. Exhibit 23–1 shows NTI's **operating cycle** and illustrates the cause and severity of its cash flow problems.[1]

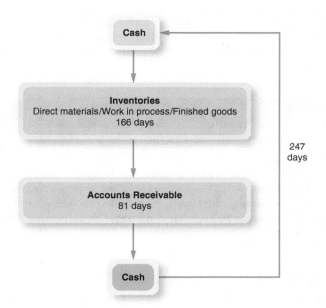

**Exhibit 23–1**

**NTI'S OPERATING CYCLE**

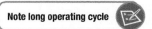

As shown, NTI's operating cycle during 2010 averaged 247 days.[2] In other words, *cash was tied up in inventory and receivables for 247 days before converting back into cash.* Throughout its operating cycle, however, payrolls, materials purchases, debt service, and overhead costs all required disbursements of cash on a timely basis (for example, 30 days). No wonder NTI's 2010 statement of cash flows reported a $250,000 negative cash flow from operations!

Fortunately, if NTI develops a comprehensive plan to control its operating activities, it may be possible to correct these cash flow problems. Such a plan is referred to as a *master budget.* In the sections that follow, we will introduce and discuss the budgeting process in detail. Then, later in the chapter, we will return to the NTI illustration and develop a master budget for its operations in 2011.

## Budgeting: The Basis for Planning and Control

A **budget** is a comprehensive *financial plan* setting forth the expected route for achieving the financial and operational goals of an organization. Budgeting is an essential step in effective financial planning. Even the smallest business will benefit from preparing a formal written plan for its future operations, including the expected levels of sales, expenses, net income, cash receipts, and cash outlays.

The use of a budget is a key element of financial planning and it assists managers in controlling costs. Managers compare actual costs with the budgeted amounts and take corrective action as necessary. Thus, controlling costs means keeping actual costs in line with the financial plan.

---

[1] The *operating cycle* of a manufacturing firm is the average time period between the purchase of direct materials and the conversion of these materials back into cash.

[2] NTI's operating cycle of 247 days is equal to the number of days required to turn over inventory (365 days ÷ 2.2 inventory turnover = 166 days) plus the number of days required to turn over accounts receivable (365 days ÷ 4.5 accounts receivable turnover = 81 days).

Virtually all economic entities—businesses, governmental agencies, universities, churches, and individuals—engage in some form of budgeting. For example, a college student with limited financial resources may prepare a list of expected monthly cash payments to see that she does not exceed expected monthly cash receipts. This list is a simple form of a cash budget.

While all businesses engage in some degree of planning, the extent to which plans are formalized in written budgets varies from one business to another. Large, well-managed companies generally have carefully developed budgets for every aspect of their operations. Inadequate or sloppy budgeting is a characteristic of companies with weak or inexperienced management.

**INTERNATIONAL** CASE IN POINT

Operational budgeting for multinational companies can be very complex. For example, Yahoo! has global operations in more than 25 worldwide locations and offerings are available in more than 30 languages. Because Yahoo! collects revenue and pays expenses in foreign currencies, Yahoo! experiences foreign exchange rate fluctuation risks. Managers try to forecast exchange rates during the budgeting period and undertake measures that manage the impact of the exchange rate changes on the revenue, assets, liabilities, and expenses incurred in these foreign currencies.

## BENEFITS DERIVED FROM BUDGETING

A budget is a forecast of future events. In fact, the process of budgeting is often called *financial forecasting.* Careful planning and preparation of a formal budget benefit a company in many ways, including the following:

**Learning Objective**

**LO2**  Discuss the benefits that a company may derive from a formal budgeting process.

1.  *Enhanced management responsibility.* On a day-to-day basis, most managers focus their attention on the routine problems of running the business. In preparing a budget, however, managers are forced to consider all aspects of a company's internal activities and to make estimates of future economic conditions, including costs, interest rates, demand for the company's products, and the level of competition. Thus, budgeting increases management's awareness of the company's external economic environment.

2.  *Assignment of decision-making responsibilities.* Because the budget shows the expected results of future operations, management is forewarned of and responsible for financial problems. If, for example, the budget shows that the company will run short of cash during the summer months, the responsible manager has advance warning to hold down expenditures or obtain additional financing.

3.  *Coordination of activities.* Preparation of a budget provides management with an opportunity to coordinate the activities of the various departments within the business. For example, the production department should be budgeted to produce approximately the same quantity of goods the sales department is budgeted to sell. A written budget shows department managers in quantitative terms exactly what is expected of their departments during the upcoming period.

4.  *Performance evaluation.* Budgets show the expected costs and expenses for each department as well as the expected output, such as revenue to be earned or units to be produced. Thus, the budgets provide a yardstick with which each department's actual performance may be measured.

## ESTABLISHING BUDGETED AMOUNTS

Comparisons of actual performance with budgeted amounts are widely used in evaluating the performance of departments and department managers. Two basic philosophies prevail today that dictate the levels at which budgeted amounts should be set. We identify these philosophies as

(1) the *behavioral* approach and (2) the *total quality management* approach. We first discuss the behavioral approach, which currently is the more widely used budgeting philosophy.

**The Behavioral Approach**   The assumption underlying the behavioral approach is that managers will be most highly motivated if they view the budget as a *fair* basis for evaluating a responsibility center's performance. Therefore, budgeted amounts are set at *reasonable and achievable levels;* that is, at levels that *can be achieved* through reasonably efficient operations. A department that operates in a highly efficient manner should be able to *exceed* the budgeted level of performance. Failure to stay within the budget, in contrast, is viewed as an unacceptable level of performance.

---

| YOUR TURN | **You as Vice President of Production and Sales** |
|---|---|

Assume that you are vice president for production and sales at NTI. Your department is a profit center and is evaluated on profits. Profit goals are set for each quarter during the year. You, your sales manager, Bob Poole, and your production manager, Joe Reco, share a $1,500 bonus each quarter you are able to meet your profit goal. Halfway through the second quarter of 2011, it becomes clear that the department will not be able to meet its profit goal for the second quarter. Bob suggests that he could "move" the booking of some sales from quarter two to quarter three to increase the likelihood of earning the quarter-three bonus. Joe also suggests using some additional resources during the second quarter to get a head start on meeting the third-quarter profit goals. Joe states, "If we use overtime labor during the second quarter to increase inventory of finished goods, then our costs in quarter three will be lower and we will be more likely to meet our profit goal and earn the quarter-three bonus." What will you say to Joe and Bob?

(See our comments on the Online Learning Center Web site.)

---

**The Total Quality Management Approach**   A basic premise of total quality management is that every individual and segment of the organization should strive for improvement constantly. The entire organization is committed to the goal of *completely eliminating* inefficiency and non-value-added activities. In short, the organization strives to achieve *perfection* across its entire value chain.

As a step toward achieving this goal, budgeted amounts may be set at levels representing *absolute efficiency.* Departments generally will fall somewhat short of achieving this level of performance. However, even small failures to achieve the budgeted performance serve to direct management's attention toward those areas in which there is room for improvement.

**Selecting and Using a Budgeting Approach**   The approach used in setting budgeted amounts reflects the philosophy and goals of top management. Under either approach, however, managers should *participate actively* in the budgeting process. Department managers generally are the best source of information about the levels of performance that can be achieved within their departments. These managers also should understand both the intended purpose of the budget and the philosophy underlying the development of budgeted amounts.

In comparing actual performance with budgeted amounts, top management should consider the philosophy used in developing the budgeted amounts. If a behavioral approach is employed, a highly efficient unit may *exceed* the budgeted level of performance. If a total quality management approach is used, a highly efficient unit should fall *slightly short* of the budget standards.

In the remainder of this chapter and in our assignment material, we will assume that budgeted amounts are set at *reasonable and achievable levels* (that is, the behavioral approach). Using this approach enables us to illustrate and discuss actual levels of performance both above and below budgeted levels.

Learning Objective
Explain two philosophies that may be used in setting budgeted amounts. L03

## Ethics, Fraud & Corporate Governance

Although we discuss budgets within the context of for-profit entities, the budgeting process is just as important for governmental and not-for-profit entities. Budgets are often included in documents given to investors when governmental or not-for-profit entities seek to obtain debt financing. Material misstatements in these budgets act as a fraud upon the purchasers of bonds issued by governmental or not-for-profit entities and expose both individuals and organizations to civil and criminal prosecution.

The Securities and Exchange Commission (SEC) brought an enforcement action against the former chief administrative officer (i.e., the city manager) of the city of Miami for including fraudulent budgetary numbers in bond offering documents provided to potential investors. In preparing its 1995 general fund budget, the city of Miami was initially facing a $15.8 million budget deficit. The city was able to reduce this preliminary deficit by $6.8 million through increases in property taxes, asset sales, and additional revenue from various licenses and permits. The city was not able to reduce the remaining $9 million deficit through additional revenue and was unwilling to reduce city operating expenses (i.e., cut services to constituents). The city ostensibly balanced its budget by including an expected payment of $9 million from the federal government under the Violent Crime Control and Law Enforcement Act of 1994.

The Violent Crime Control and Law Enforcement Act (VCCLEA), as initially drafted, would have provided lump sum grants in fiscal year 1995 to local governments for fighting crime. A report issued by a municipal lobbying group projected that the city of Miami would receive $9 million in 1995 under the VCCLEA. However, the final version of the VCCLEA reduced funding to local governments, provided for funding over five years rather than in a lump sum, and delayed the initial year of funding to fiscal year 1996. The city manager of Miami was aware of these changes to the final version of the VCCLEA. Yet he submitted his 1995 budget to Miami's city commission for approval with the $9 million still included in the budget. The city commission approved the budget, and the city's general fund budget was included in offering documents provided to potential bond investors. The general fund budget included in these debt offering documents was materially misstated, as the city of Miami did not have a balanced budget for fiscal year 1995; rather 57 percent—$9 million of the city's $15.8 million of projected revenue—was based on a source of funds that the city manager knew, or was reckless in not knowing, that the city of Miami would not receive.

The SEC settled these charges with the city manager by entering into a cease-and-desist order. The city manager of Miami agreed to cease and desist (stop) from any future violations of the securities laws. The penalty meted out in this case by the SEC was relatively mild, but future violations of the cease-and-desist order will be quite serious and will expose violators to more severe legal consequences.

## THE BUDGET PERIOD

As a general rule, the period covered by a budget should be long enough to show the effect of management policies but short enough so that estimates can be made with reasonable accuracy. This suggests that different types of budgets should be made for different time spans.

*Capital expenditures budgets,* which summarize plans for major investments in plant and equipment, might be prepared to cover plans for as long as 5 to 10 years. Projects such as building a new factory or an oil refinery require many years of planning and expenditures before the new facilities are ready for use.

Most operating budgets and financial budgets cover a period of one fiscal year. Companies often divide these annual budgets into four quarters, with budgeted figures for each quarter. The first quarter is then subdivided into budget targets for each month, while only quarterly figures are shown for the next three quarters. As the end of each quarter nears, the budget for the next quarter is reviewed, revised for any changes in economic conditions, and divided into monthly budget targets. This process assures that the budget is reviewed at least several times each year and that the budgeted figures for the months just ahead are based on current conditions and estimates. In addition, budgeted figures for relatively short periods of time enable managers to compare actual performance to the budget without waiting until year-end.

An increasing number of companies, like **IKEA**, use **rolling budgeting,** whereby a new quarter or month is added to the end of the budget as the current quarter or month draws to a close. Thus, the budget always covers the upcoming 12 months. One advantage of rolling budgeting is that it stabilizes the planning horizon at one year ahead. Under the fiscal year approach, the planning period becomes shorter as the year progresses. Also, rolling budgeting forces managers into a continuous review and reassessment of the budget estimates and the company's current progress.

## THE MASTER BUDGET: A PACKAGE OF RELATED BUDGETS

The "budget" is not a single document. Rather, the **master budget** consists of a number of interrelated budgets that collectively summarize all the planned activities of the business. The elements of a master budget vary depending on the size and nature of the business. A typical master budget for a manufacturing company would include the following:

1. Operating budgets
   a. Sales budget
   b. Production budgets including
      - Units to produce
      - Direct materials
      - Direct labor
      - Overhead
   c. Cost of goods manufactured and sold budget
   d. Selling and administrative expense budget
      - Marketing
      - Administrative expenses
      - Research and development
   e. Cash budget

2. Financial budgets
   a. Budgeted income statement
   b. Budgeted balance sheet
   c. Budgeted cash flows statement[3]
   d. Capital expenditures budget

**Learning Objective**
Describe the elements of a master budget. **LO4**

Some elements of the master budget are *organized by responsibility center.* The budgeted income statement, for example, indicates the budgeted revenue and expenses of each profit center. The cash budget shows the budgeted cash flows for each cost center as well as each revenue center. The production schedule and manufacturing cost budget indicate the unit production and manufacturing costs budgeted for each production process. The portion of the budget relating to an individual responsibility center is called a **responsibility budget.** As explained in Chapter 22, responsibility budgets are an important element of a responsibility accounting system.

The many budgets and schedules making up the master budget are closely interrelated. Some of these relationships are illustrated in Exhibit 23–2 on the following page. Our discussion relates to two categories of budgets, operating and financial. Operating budgets are internal working budgets used by employees of the company. On the other hand, financial budget information is more externally focused and more likely to be shared with creditors, investors, customers, labor unions, and so forth. Exhibit 23–2 shows that operating and financial budgets are closely linked. As we discuss NTI's 2011 budgets, you will see specifically how the operating and financial budgets link together. To help you follow our discussion in the remainder of this chapter, operating or financial budget exhibits will have either a blue or green background, respectively, the same colors shown in Exhibit 23–2.

## STEPS IN PREPARING A MASTER BUDGET

Some parts of the master budget should not be prepared until other parts have been completed. For example, the budgeted financial statements are not prepared until the sales, manufacturing, and operating expense budgets are available. This is the logical sequence of steps for preparing the annual elements of the master budget:

1. *Prepare a sales forecast.* The sales forecast is the starting point in the preparation of a master budget. This forecast is based on a business strategic plan, past experience, estimates of

---

[3] The budgeted cash flows statement and capital expenditures budget are not covered in this chapter. The focus in this chapter is on operational budgets and their relationships to the budgeted income statement and balance sheet. Capital expenditures are discussed in Chapter 26 and budgeted cash flows statements are covered in more advanced accounting courses.

Exhibit 23-2 **ORGANIZATIONAL BUDGETING**

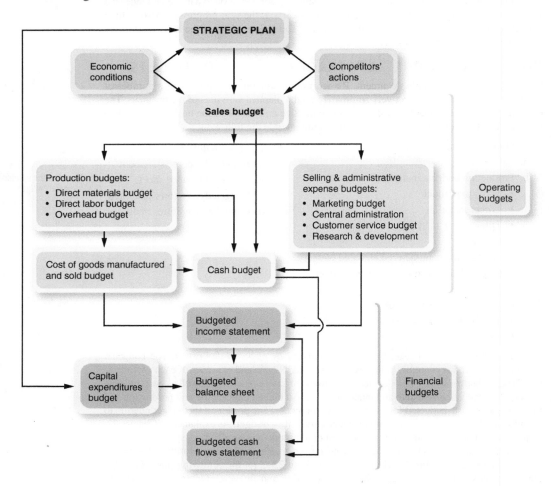

general business and economic conditions, and expected levels of competition. A forecast of the expected level of sales is a prerequisite to scheduling production and to budgeting revenue and variable costs. The arrows in Exhibit 23–2 indicate that information flows from this forecast into several other budgets.

2. *Prepare budgets for production, manufacturing costs, and operating expenses.* Once the level of sales has been forecast, production may be scheduled and estimates made of the expected manufacturing costs and operating expenses for the year. These elements of the master budget depend on both the level of sales and cost-volume relationships.

3. *Prepare a budgeted income statement.* The budgeted income statement is based on the sales forecast, the manufacturing costs comprising the cost of goods sold, and the budgeted operating expenses.

4. *Prepare a cash budget.* The cash budget is a forecast of the cash receipts and cash payments for the budget period. The cash budget is affected by many of the other budget estimates.

The budgeted level of cash receipts depends on the sales forecast, credit terms offered by the company, and the company's experience in collecting accounts receivable from customers. Budgeted cash payments depend on the forecasts of manufacturing costs, operating expenses, and capital expenditures, as well as the credit terms offered by suppliers. Anticipated borrowing, debt repayment, cash dividends, and issuance of capital stock also are reflected in the cash budget.

5. *Prepare a budgeted balance sheet.* A projected balance sheet cannot be prepared until the effects of cash transactions on various asset, liability, and owners' equity accounts have been determined. In addition, the balance sheet is affected by budgeted capital expenditures and budgeted net income.

The capital expenditures budget covers a span of many years. This budget is continuously reviewed and updated, but usually it is not prepared anew on an annual basis.

## PREPARING THE MASTER BUDGET: AN ILLUSTRATION

Let us now return to the NTI illustration introduced at the beginning of the chapter. Even though the company's first year of operations was profitable, NTI experienced significant cash flow problems due to rapid sales growth in the fourth quarter of 2010.

We will now develop NTI's master budget for 2011. A primary objective of this process is to help NTI avoid the cash flow problems experienced during 2010. Shown in Exhibit 23–3 is the company's balance sheet, dated January 1, 2011.

**Learning Objective**
Prepare the budgets and supporting schedules included in a master budget. **L05**

**Exhibit 23–3**

**NTI'S BALANCE SHEET AT THE BEGINNING OF 2011**

### NTI
### BALANCE SHEET
### JANUARY 1, 2011

#### Assets

| | | |
|---|---|---|
| Current assets: | | |
| Cash | | $ 10,000 |
| Receivables | | 225,000 |
| Inventories (FIFO method) | | |
| Direct Materials (8,000 units) | $ 60,000 | |
| Finished Goods (8,000 units) | 240,000 | 300,000 |
| Prepayments | | 5,000 |
| Total current assets | | $540,000 |
| Plant and equipment: | | |
| Buildings and Equipment | $420,000 | |
| Less: Accumulated Depreciation (straight line method) | 20,000 | |
| Total plant and equipment | | 400,000 |
| Total assets | | $940,000 |

#### Liabilities & Stockholders' Equity

| | | |
|---|---|---|
| Current liabilities: | | |
| Notes Payable, to officer (12 months @ 12%) | | $ 36,000 |
| Notes Payable, to bank (3 months @ 14%) | | 246,000 |
| Other Current Payables | | 50,000 |
| Income Taxes Payable | | 64,000 |
| Total current liabilities | | $396,000 |
| Stockholders' equity: | | |
| Capital Stock, no par, 10,000 shares outstanding | $400,000 | |
| Retained Earnings | 144,000 | 544,000 |
| Total liabilities & stockholders' equity | | $940,000 |

Sales of NTI's product are expected to increase throughout 2011. However, the company will drastically cut back production during the first quarter to liquidate some of the finished goods inventory currently on hand. As of January 1, there is no work in process inventory. No capital expenditures are planned for 2011.

## OPERATING BUDGET ESTIMATES

The first step in preparing NTI's master budget is to develop each of its operating budgets for 2011. Information from these budgets will be used to prepare budgeted quarterly income statements. All of the information needed to estimate budgeted *income from operations* comes from the operating budget estimates.

**Manufacturing Cost Estimates**    In preparation for the budget process, Lisa Scott, NTI's cost accountant, has thoroughly analyzed the company's variable and fixed manufacturing costs. Lisa determines that direct materials consist of two specially coated disks that cost $7.50 each. Variable overhead is primarily the cost of burning the programs onto the disks, packaging the disks, and insurance on the unfinished product. Direct labor is one-eighth hour per disk or one-quarter hour per finished unit. She is confident that variable manufacturing costs per unit will not increase during 2011. Lisa also analyzes fixed overhead costs and finds they consist of factory rent plus $3,500 per quarter of depreciation expense on equipment. She also believes that fixed manufacturing overhead will hold steady at approximately $15,000 per quarter. On the basis of her analysis, she compiled the following manufacturing cost estimates:

| Manufacturing Cost Estimates for 2011 | |
| --- | ---: |
| Variable costs per unit manufactured: | |
| Direct materials (2 disks @ $7.50/disk)..................................... | $    15 |
| Direct labor (¼ hour per finished unit @ $20/hour)........................ | 5 |
| Variable manufacturing overhead (per finished unit) ...................... | 7 |
| Fixed manufacturing overhead (per quarter) .............................. | $15,000 |

**The Sales Budget**    Bob Poole, NTI's marketing director, is optimistic that demand for the company's product will continue to grow in 2011. He estimates that sales will reach 8,000 units in the first quarter and 10,000 units in the second quarter. Sales estimates for the third and fourth quarters are 30,000 units and 40,000 units, respectively. To keep its product affordable to a wide range of users, NTI is committed to holding its selling price per unit at $75 throughout the year. On the basis of this information, the sales budget shown in Exhibit 23–4 is prepared.

**Production Budgets**    Upon examining performance reports for 2010, Joe Reco, NTI's production manager, concluded that he had overreacted to the rapid sales growth experienced in the fourth quarter. As a consequence, the company was carrying an excessive inventory of finished goods at the start of 2011. He immediately adopted a new policy for 2011 to increase inventory turnover and improve operating cash flows. The number of units in the finished goods inventory will be reduced and will depend on unit sales volume anticipated in the following quarter.

Joe decides that, for a given sales forecast of 10,000 units for the second quarter, the desired finished goods inventory at the end of the first quarter is 1,000 units. Likewise, given a sales forecast of 30,000 units for the third quarter, the desired finished goods inventory at the end of the second quarter is 3,000 units. Beginning in the third quarter, Joe has negotiated some delivery agreements that will allow the ending inventory to remain constant at 5,000 units in the third and fourth quarters. Based on these projections, the unit production budget shown in Exhibit 23–5, Schedule A1, is created.

**Manufacturing Cost Budgets**    Combining the production unit estimates in Exhibit 23–5, Schedule A1, with the manufacturing cost estimates prepared by Lisa Scott, the manufacturing cost budgets shown in Exhibit 23–5, Schedules A2 through A4, are created.

Notice the arrow between the sales budget and the production budget that shows the dependence between the budgets. Projected unit sales are the key element for constructing Schedule A1, which shows budgeted units of production. On the other hand, budgeted units of production provide the key information for constructing the remaining manufacturing cost budgets for direct materials, direct labor, and overhead in Schedules A2 through A4. Notice the arrows that show the flow of information between the parts of the production budget. For example, ending inventory amounts in quarter two are the beginning inventory amounts in quarter three.

### NTI
### SALES BUDGET FOR 2011

| | 1st Quarter | 2nd Quarter | 3rd Quarter | 4th Quarter |
|---|---|---|---|---|
| Projected unit sales........... | 8,000 | 10,000 | 30,000 | 40,000 |
| Sales price per unit........... | $75 | $75 | $75 | $75 |
| Projected revenue............ | $600,000 | $750,000 | $2,250,000 | $3,000,000 |

**Exhibit 23–4**

**NTI'S SALES BUDGET FOR 2011**

### NTI
### PRODUCTION BUDGETS FOR 2011

**SCHEDULE A1: Units of Production**

| | 1st Quarter | 2nd Quarter | 3rd Quarter | 4th Quarter |
|---|---|---|---|---|
| Projected unit sales .............. | 8,000 | 10,000 | 30,000 | 40,000 |
| Add desired ending inventory .................. | 1,000 | 3,000 | 5,000 | 5,000 |
| Units available for sale ............ | 9,000 | 13,000 | 35,000 | 45,000 |
| Less beginning inventory .................. | 8,000 | 1,000 | 3,000 | 5,000 |
| **Budgeted production in units** ...................... | **1,000** | **12,000** | **32,000** | **40,000** |

**SCHEDULE A2: Direct Materials Budget**

| | 1st Quarter | 2nd Quarter | 3rd Quarter | 4th Quarter |
|---|---|---|---|---|
| Disks needed for production (two disks per unit) ............. | 2,000 | 24,000 | 64,000 | 80,000 |
| Add desired ending inventory of disks............. | 8,000 | 8,000 | 8,000 | 8,000 |
| Disks available for production ................. | 10,000 | 32,000 | 72,000 | 88,000 |
| Less beginning inventory .................. | 8,000 | 8,000 | 8,000 | 8,000 |
| Budgeted unit purchases of direct materials disks ......... | **2,000** | **24,000** | **64,000** | **80,000** |
| Purchase price per unit ............ | × $7.50 | × $7.50 | × $7.50 | × $7.50 |
| Budgeted cost of purchased materials ............. | $15,000 | $180,000 | $480,000 | $600,000 |

**SCHEDULE A3: Direct Labor Budget**

| | 1st Quarter | 2nd Quarter | 3rd Quarter | 4th Quarter |
|---|---|---|---|---|
| Budgeted production ............. | 1,000 | 12,000 | 32,000 | 40,000 |
| Labor hours per unit .............. | × .25 | × .25 | × .25 | × .25 |
| Total hours needed............... | 250 | 3,000 | 8,000 | 10,000 |
| Multiply by cost per hour........... | × $20 | × $20 | × $20 | × $20 |
| Budgeted direct labor cost ......... | $5,000 | $60,000 | $160,000 | $200,000 |

**SCHEDULE A4: Overhead Budget**

| | 1st Quarter | 2nd Quarter | 3rd Quarter | 4th Quarter |
|---|---|---|---|---|
| Budgeted production ............. | 1,000 | 12,000 | 32,000 | 40,000 |
| Variable overhead cost ........... | × $7 | × $7 | × $7 | × $7 |
| Budgeted variable overhead cost .... | $7,000 | $84,000 | $224,000 | $280,000 |
| Add budgeted fixed overhead........ | $15,000 | $15,000 | $ 15,000 | $ 15,000 |
| Total budgeted overhead .......... | $22,000 | $99,000 | $239,000 | $295,000 |

**Exhibit 23–5**

**NTI'S PRODUCTION BUDGETS FOR 2011**

**Exhibit 23–6  NTI'S COST OF GOODS MANUFACTURED AND SOLD BUDGET FOR 2011**

**NTI**
**BUDGETED COST OF GOODS MANUFACTURED AND SOLD**
**FOR 2011**

|  | 1st Quarter | 2nd Quarter | 3rd Quarter | 4th Quarter |
|---|---|---|---|---|
| Finished goods, beginning inventory | $240,000 | $ 42,000 | $ 84,750 | $ 137,344 |
| Add cost of goods manufactured (from Exhibit 23–5): |  |  |  |  |
| Direct materials used | $15,000 | $180,000 | $480,000 | $600,000 |
| Direct labor used | 5,000 | 60,000 | 160,000 | 200,000 |
| Variable overhead | 7,000 | 84,000 | 224,000 | 280,000 |
| Fixed overhead | 15,000 | 15,000 | 15,000 | 15,000 |
|  | 42,000 | 339,000 | 879,000 | 1,095,000 |
| Total cost of goods available for sale | $282,000 | $381,000 | $963,750 | $1,232,344 |
| Less: Ending finished goods (see supplemental schedule below) | 42,000 | 84,750 | 137,344 | 136,875 |
| Cost of goods sold | $240,000 | $296,250 | $826,406 | $1,095,469 |

**Supplemental Schedule**
**Finished Goods Inventory**

|  | 1st Quarter | 2nd Quarter | 3rd Quarter | 4th Quarter |
|---|---|---|---|---|
| Cost of goods manufactured | $42,000 | $339,000 | $879,000 | $1,095,000 |
| Divide by: Units of production (Exhibit 23–5, Schedule A1) | ÷ 1,000 | ÷ 12,000 | ÷ 32,000 | ÷ 40,000 |
| Production cost per unit | $ 42.00 | $ 28.25 | $27.4688 | $ 27.375 |
| Multiply by ending inventory (Schedule A1) | × 1,000 | × 3,000 | × 5,000 | × 5,000 |
| Cost of ending finished goods | $42,000 | $ 84,750 | $137,344 | $ 136,875 |

### Cost of Goods Manufactured and Sold Budget

A manufacturing company's cost of goods sold is equal to its beginning finished goods inventory, plus the cost of goods manufactured during the period, less its ending finished goods inventory.

Consequently, the budget estimates for cost of goods sold in Exhibit 23–6 are computed using the beginning finished goods inventory figure from the balance sheet in Exhibit 23–3 and information from the production budgets in Exhibit 23–5. Make sure you can match up the cost of goods manufactured amounts in Exhibit 23–6 with those computed for the production budget shown in Exhibit 23–5.

### Finished Goods Inventory

As mentioned, NTI recently adopted a policy to reduce the number of units in finished goods inventory at the end of each quarter depending on the sales volume anticipated in the following quarter.

Thus, applying this policy in conjunction with the production costs shown in Exhibit 23–5, Schedules A2 to A4, ending inventory estimates are shown in the supplemental schedule in Exhibit 23–6.

© Royalty-Free/Corbis/DAL

Note that the budgeted manufacturing costs in the first quarter total *$42.00 per unit,* compared to *$28.25 per unit* in the second quarter. These amounts differ due to a *decrease in fixed manufacturing costs per unit* anticipated in the second quarter. During the first quarter, $15,000 in fixed manufacturing costs is allocated to 1,000 units produced (or *$15.00 per unit*). During the second quarter, however, $15,000 is allocated to 12,000 units produced (or *$1.25 per unit*).

### Selling and Administrative Expense Budget

NTI's variable operating expenses amount to $7.50 per unit. Most of this cost applies to sales commissions. The company's quarterly fixed operating expenses of $175,000 pertain primarily to the salaries of its officers. Based on this information, the operating expense budget in Exhibit 23–7 was prepared.

### Exhibit 23–7  NTI'S SELLING AND ADMINISTRATIVE EXPENSE BUDGET FOR 2011

| NTI SELLING AND ADMINISTRATIVE EXPENSE BUDGET FOR 2011 | | | | |
|---|---|---|---|---|
| | 1st Quarter | 2nd Quarter | 3rd Quarter | 4th Quarter |
| Variable operating expenses ($7.50 per unit sold)...... | $ 60,000 | $ 75,000 | $225,000 | $300,000 |
| Fixed operating expenses (per quarter).............. | 175,000 | 175,000 | 175,000 | 175,000 |
| Total selling and administrative expenses ......... | $235,000 | $250,000 | $400,000 | $475,000 |

## BUDGETED INCOME STATEMENT

NTI's budgeted income statements are based on estimates from Exhibits 23–4, 23–6, and 23–7. In addition, they include budgeted amounts for interest expense and income tax expense. Interest expense and income taxes are also reported in Exhibits 23–11 and 23–12, which are discussed later in the chapter. The following discussion explains how these figures were determined.

The $36,000 note payable reported in the January 1, 2011, balance sheet (Exhibit 23–3) is the loan from NTI's president, Nancy Conrad. The note is payable in four quarterly installments of $9,000, *plus* accrued interest on the outstanding balance at the end of each quarter. The note's interest rate is 12 percent (or 3 percent quarterly). Thus, interest due at the end of the first quarter is $1,080 ($36,000 × 3%), whereas interest due at the end of the second quarter is only $810 ($27,000 × 3%).

The $246,000 note payable is the remaining principal owed on a loan that originated in late December 2010. The note's interest rate is 14 percent (or 3.5 percent quarterly). The entire $246,000, plus $8,610 in accrued interest ($246,000 × 3.5%), is due at the end of the first quarter of 2011. Thus, total interest expense budgeted on notes payable for the first quarter is $9,690 ($1,080 plus $8,610).

Income tax expense is budgeted at 40 percent of income before income taxes.

On the basis of this information, we prepared the budgeted income statement shown in Exhibit 23–8.

## Exhibit 23–8  NTI'S 2011 BUDGETED INCOME STATEMENT

| NTI BUDGETED INCOME STATEMENT FOR EACH QUARTER IN 2011 | | | | | | | |
|---|---|---|---|---|---|---|---|
| | | 1st Quarter | | 2nd Quarter | | 3rd Quarter | 4th Quarter |
| Sales (Exhibit 23–4) . . . . . . . . . . . . | | $600,000 | | $750,000 | | $2,250,000 | $3,000,000 |
| Cost of goods sold (Exhibit 23–6) . . | | 240,000 | | 296,250 | | 826,406 | 1,095,469 |
| Gross profit . . . . . . . . . . . . . . . . . . | | $360,000 | | $453,750 | | $1,423,594 | $1,904,531 |
| Less operating expenses: | | | | | | | |
| Selling and administrative (Exhibit 23–7) . . . . . . . . . . . . | $235,000 | | $250,000 | | $400,000 | | $475,000 |
| Interest (Exhibit 23–11) . . . . . . | 9,690 | 244,690 | 810 | 250,810 | 540 | 400,540 | 270  475,270 |
| Operating income before tax . . . . . . | | $115,310 | | $202,940 | | $1,023,054 | $1,429,261 |
| Income tax (40%) (Exhibit 23–12) . . | | 46,124 | | 81,176 | | 409,222 | 571,704 |
| Net income . . . . . . . . . . . . . . . . . . | | $ 69,186 | | $121,764 | | $ 613,832 | $ 857,557 |

The budgeted income statement shows the effects that budgeted activities are expected to have on NTI's revenue, expenses, and net income. However, it is not indicative of the company's cash flow expectations for 2011. *Recall that during 2010 the company was profit rich, yet it remained cash poor.*

Now we must prepare *cash budget estimates* to formulate NTI's quarterly cash flow expectations. These estimates will also help us to prepare the company's budgeted balance sheets each quarter.

## CASH BUDGET ESTIMATES

The estimates and data necessary to prepare the cash budget and budgeted balance sheets are called *cash budget estimates*. These include budgeted disbursements for payables, prepayments, debt service, and taxes. In addition, NTI must budget cash receipts from collection of receivables. To avoid confusing these figures with the *operating budget estimates* used to prepare the budgeted income statement, the amounts in Exhibits 23–9 through 23–13 to be used in the preparation of NTI's cash budget are highlighted in *red*.

**Current Payables Budget**    Our preparation of a cash budget begins with estimating the portion of budgeted costs and expenses that will require *cash payment in the near future.* Certain expenses will *not* require an outlay of cash. These include (1) expenses that result from the expiration of prepaid items (such as insurance policies) and (2) the depreciation of plant assets. However, *only* those costs and expenses financed by *current payables* (which include immediate *cash* payments as well as accounts payable and accrued expenses) will require cash payments.

Exhibit 23–9 separates the costs and expenses financed by NTI's current payables from those related to the expiration of prepayments and depreciation. The last row, labeled "Cash payments for current payables," indicates the portion of current costs and expenses that requires cash disbursements in the near future. Examples of these items include purchases of direct materials (whether for cash or on account), factory payrolls, and various overhead costs. The amounts shown under the rows labeled "Prepayments for Insurance" and "Depreciation" are reported as *expenses* in the company's budgeted income statement. However, these amounts do not call for future disbursements of cash. We will assume that the expired prepayment estimates were made based on an evaluation of the company's insurance policies.

**Exhibit 23-9 NTI'S BUDGET FOR CURRENT PAYABLES AND DISBURSEMENTS FOR PAYABLES FOR 2011**

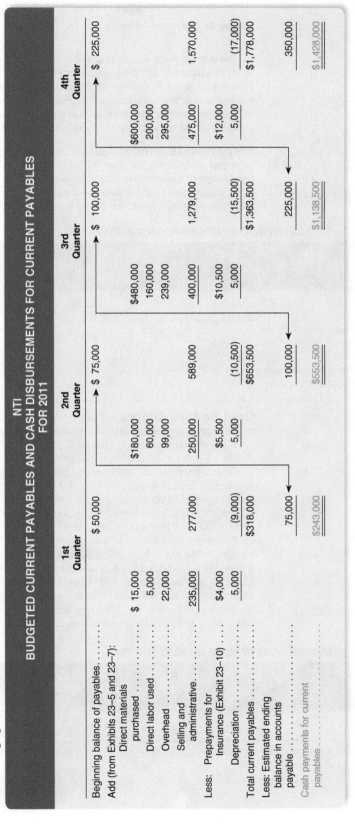

NTI
BUDGETED CURRENT PAYABLES AND CASH DISBURSEMENTS FOR CURRENT PAYABLES
FOR 2011

|  | 1st Quarter | 2nd Quarter | 3rd Quarter | 4th Quarter |
|---|---|---|---|---|
| Beginning balance of payables......... | $ 50,000 | $ 75,000 | $ 100,000 | $ 225,000 |
| Add (from Exhibits 23–5 and 23–7): |  |  |  |  |
| Direct materials purchased ............ | $ 15,000 | $180,000 | $480,000 | $600,000 |
| Direct labor used .............. | 5,000 | 60,000 | 160,000 | 200,000 |
| Overhead ............... | 22,000 | 99,000 | 239,000 | 295,000 |
| Selling and administrative........... | 235,000 | 250,000 | 400,000 | 475,000 |
|  | 277,000 | 589,000 | 1,279,000 | 1,570,000 |
| Less: Prepayments for Insurance (Exhibit 23–10) ..... | $4,000 | $5,500 | $10,500 | $12,000 |
| Depreciation ............ | 5,000 | 5,000 | 5,000 | 5,000 |
|  | (9,000) | (10,500) | (15,500) | (17,000) |
| Total current payables ....... | $318,000 | $653,500 | $1,363,500 | $1,778,000 |
| Less: Estimated ending balance in accounts payable ............ | 75,000 | 100,000 | 225,000 | 350,000 |
| Cash payments for current payables .............. | $243,000 | $553,500 | $1,138,500 | $1,428,000 |

The starting point in Exhibit 23–9 is the $50,000 beginning payables balance appearing in NTI's January 1, 2011, balance sheet (see Exhibit 23–3). To this amount, we add the total payables budgeted in Exhibits 23–5 and 23–7. The balance of current payables at the end of the first quarter was estimated by Paul Foss, NTI's treasurer, after making a thorough analysis of suppliers' credit terms. Note, as shown by the arrows, that the beginning balance of current payables for the second quarter is simply the ending balance from the first quarter.

**Prepayments Budget**   Exhibit 23–10 budgets the expected cash payments for prepayments made during the year. For NTI, these payments involve its insurance policies. Thus, preparation of the schedule called for an analysis of all policies reported on the January 1, 2011, balance sheet and the anticipated expiration of prepayments. Based on this analysis, the prepayments budget in Exhibit 23–10 was prepared.

**Exhibit 23–10** PREPAYMENTS BUDGET FOR NTI IN 2011

| NTI PREPAYMENTS BUDGET FOR 2011 | 1st Quarter | 2nd Quarter | 3rd Quarter | 4th Quarter |
|---|---|---|---|---|
| Balance at beginning of quarter | $ 5,000 | $ 7,000 | $ 8,000 | $ 9,500 |
| Estimated cash expenditure during quarter | 6,000 | 6,500 | 12,000 | 15,000 |
| Total prepayments | $11,000 | $13,500 | $20,000 | $24,500 |
| Less: Expiration of prepayments | 4,000 | 5,500 | 10,500 | 12,000 |
| Prepayments at end of quarter | $ 7,000 | $ 8,000 | $ 9,500 | $12,500 |

**Debt Service Budget**   The purpose of this schedule is to summarize the cash payments (both principal and interest) required to service NTI's debt each quarter. NTI has two notes payable outstanding on January 1, 2011.

The 12 percent, $36,000 note payable is the loan from Nancy Conrad, NTI's president. The loan agreement calls for quarterly payments of $9,000 plus interest accrued on the outstanding balance at a quarterly rate of 3 percent. The debt service on this note in the first quarter equals $9,000 in principal plus interest of $1,080 ($36,000 × 3%), or a cash outlay of *$10,080*. The note's debt service in the second quarter equals $9,000 in principal plus interest of $810 ($27,000 × 3%), or a cash outlay of *$9,810*.

The 14 percent, $246,000 note payable is to NTI's bank. The loan agreement calls for payment of the entire $246,000 at the end of the first quarter of 2011, plus interest accrued at a quarterly rate of 3.5 percent. Thus, the debt service on this note in the first quarter equals $246,000 plus interest of $8,610 ($246,000 × 3.5%), or a cash outlay of *$254,610*. There is no debt service cost associated with this note in the second quarter.

As shown in Exhibit 23–11, the total debt service cash outflow is budgeted at *$264,690* in the first quarter, *$9,810* in the second quarter, and, by the end of 2011, notes payable declines to $0.

**Exhibit 23–11** NTI'S DEBT SERVICE BUDGET FOR 2011

| NTI DEBT SERVICE BUDGET FOR 2011 | 1st Quarter | 2nd Quarter | 3rd Quarter | 4th Quarter |
|---|---|---|---|---|
| Notes payable at the beginning of the quarter | $282,000 | $27,000 | $18,000 | $9,000 |
| Interest expense for the quarter | 9,690 | 810 | 540 | 270 |
| Total principal plus accrued interest | $291,690 | $27,810 | $18,540 | $9,270 |
| Less: Cash payments (principal and interest) | 264,690 | 9,810 | 9,540 | 9,270 |
| Notes payable at the end of the quarter | $ 27,000 | $18,000 | $ 9,000 | $ 0 |

**Budgeted Income Taxes**   The budgeted cash payments for income tax expense are summarized in Exhibit 23–12. Each quarter, NTI makes income tax payments equal to its income tax liability at the beginning of that quarter. NTI's $64,000 liability at the beginning of the first quarter was taken from its January 1, 2011, balance sheet. The $46,124 liability at the beginning of the second quarter is simply the income tax liability at the end of the first quarter. These tax liabilities are shown on the budgeted income statement in Exhibit 23–8.

### Exhibit 23–12 NTI'S INCOME TAX BUDGET FOR 2011

| NTI BUDGETED INCOME TAXES FOR 2011 | | | | |
|---|---|---|---|---|
| | 1st Quarter | 2nd Quarter | 3rd Quarter | 4th Quarter |
| Income tax liability at beginning of quarter . . . . . . . . . . . . . . . . . . . . . . | $ 64,000 | $ 46,124 | $ 81,176 | $409,222 |
| Estimated income taxes for the quarter (per budgeted income statement, Exhibit 23–8) . . . . . . . . . . . . . . . . . . . . . . . . . | 46,124 | 81,176 | 409,222 | 571,704 |
| Total accrued income tax liability . . . . . . . . . . . . . . . . . . . . . . . . . | $110,124 | $127,300 | $490,398 | $980,926 |
| Cash payment of amount owed at beginning of quarter . . . . . . . . . . . | 64,000 | 46,124 | 81,176 | 409,222 |
| Income tax liability at end of quarter . . . . . . . . . . . . . . . . . . . . . . . . | $ 46,124 | $ 81,176 | $409,222 | $571,704 |

**Estimated Cash Receipts from Customers**   All of NTI's sales are made on account. As such, the sole source of cash receipts is the collection of accounts receivable. NTI's operating cycle in Exhibit 23–1 shows that NTI turned over its accounts receivable 4.5 times during 2010. Thus, the average account was outstanding for *81 days* (365 days ÷ 4.5 = 81).

In an attempt to improve cash flow performance in 2009, NTI's credit manager, Richard Baker, set the following goals for his department: (1) to collect the entire $225,000 of accounts receivable reported on the January 1, 2011, balance sheet by the end of the first quarter, and (2) to collect 75 percent of quarterly sales during the quarter in which they are made and collect the remaining 25 percent in the subsequent quarter. If successful, Baker estimates that NTI's average collection period will be reduced from 81 days to 30 days.

Exhibit 23–13 on the following page shows the budgeted cash collections under the new collection policy. Losses for uncollectible accounts are ignored in our example. As shown in Exhibit 23–13, the beginning accounts receivable balance, plus credit sales and minus collections on account, equals the estimated ending balance of accounts receivable. The arrows show that the ending balance of accounts receivable in a quarter is the beginning balance in the next quarter.

| YOUR TURN | **You as Manager of the Credit Department** |
|---|---|

Assume you are the manager of NTI's credit department. Nancy Conrad, the founder of NTI, has asked you to manage receivables and payables by leading and lagging. Leading receivables implies collecting cash from customers more quickly than previously. Lagging payables means delaying payment to creditors. You are concerned that what Conrad is suggesting is unethical. What should you do?

(See our comments on the Online Learning Center Web site.)

## THE CASH BUDGET

We use NTI's cash flow budget estimates from Exhibits 23–9 through 23–13 to create the 2011 cash budget shown in Exhibit 23–14. This cash budget demonstrates that NTI expects to have enough cash to service its debt, particularly in the first quarter.

Exhibit 23–13 NTI'S BUDGET FOR ACCOUNTS RECEIVABLE AND COLLECTIONS OF RECEIVABLES FOR 2011

**NTI**

**BUDGETED ACCOUNTS RECEIVABLE AND CASH COLLECTIONS FROM CUSTOMERS**
**FOR 2011**

|  | 1st Quarter | 2nd Quarter | 3rd Quarter | 4th Quarter |
|---|---|---|---|---|
| Beginning balance of receivables | $225,000 | $150,000 | $ 187,500 | $ 562,500 |
| Add: Sales on account from sales budget (Exhibit 23–4) | 600,000 | 750,000 | 2,250,000 | 3,000,000 |
| Total accounts receivable during the month | $825,000 | $900,000 | $2,437,500 | $3,562,500 |
| Less total cash receipts from customers: |  |  |  |  |
| Previous quarter | $225,000 | $150,000 | $ 187,500 | $ 562,500 |
| This quarter | 450,000 | 562,500 | 1,687,500 | 2,250,000 |
|  | 675,000 | 712,500 | 1,875,000 | 2,812,500 |
| Estimated ending balance in accounts receivable | $150,000 | $187,500 | $ 562,500 | $ 750,000 |

**Exhibit 23–14 NTI'S CASH BUDGET FOR 2011**

NTI
CASH BUDGET
FOR 2011

| | 1st Quarter | | 2nd Quarter | | 3rd Quarter | | 4th Quarter | |
|---|---|---|---|---|---|---|---|---|
| Cash balance at beginning of quarter . . . | | $ 10,000 | | $107,310 | | $ 203,876 | | $ 837,660 |
| Add: Cash receipts (Exhibit 23–13) . . . . . | | 675,000 | | 712,500 | | 1,875,000 | | 2,812,500 |
| Total cash available . . . . . . . . . . . . . . | | $685,000 | | $819,810 | | $2,078,876 | | $3,650,160 |
| Less: Cash payments for | | | | | | | | |
| Current payables (Exhibit 23–9) . . . . . . | $243,000 | | $553,500 | | $1,138,500 | | $1,428,000 | |
| Prepayments (Exhibit 23–10) . . . . . . . . . | 6,000 | | 6,500 | | 12,000 | | 15,000 | |
| Debt service (Exhibit 23–11) . . . . . . . . . | 264,690 | | 9,810 | | 9,540 | | 9,270 | |
| Income tax (Exhibit 23–12) . . . . . . . . . . | 64,000 | 577,690 | 46,124 | 615,934 | 81,176 | 1,241,216 | 409,222 | 1,861,492 |
| Cash balance at end of quarter . . . . . . . | | $107,310 | | $203,876 | | $ 837,660 | | $1,788,668 |

**1010** Chapter 23 Operational Budgeting

NTI's budgeted cash position at the end of 2011 is a vast improvement over its actual cash position at the end of 2010. We have discussed two primary reasons for the anticipated turnaround. First, a new policy was developed to improve control of inventory management and production scheduling. Second, ambitious goals were established to tighten credit policies. Keep in mind that these cash figures are based completely on budget *estimates*. Only if management's estimates and expectations are *realistic* will the company's cash flow problems be resolved.

## BUDGETED BALANCE SHEETS

We now have the necessary information to forecast NTI's financial position at the end of each quarter in 2011. The company's quarterly budgeted balance sheets are shown in Exhibit 23–15. The budget exhibits used to derive various figures are indicated parenthetically.

**Exhibit 23–15** NTI'S BUDGETED BALANCE SHEET FOR 2011

| NTI BUDGETED BALANCE SHEET AT THE END OF EACH QUARTER IN 2011 | 1st Quarter | 2nd Quarter | 3rd Quarter | 4th Quarter |
|---|---|---|---|---|
| Current assets: | | | | |
| Cash (Exhibit 23–14) . . . . . . . . . . . . . . . . . . . . . . | $107,310 | $203,876 | $ 837,660 | $1,788,668 |
| Receivables (Exhibit 23–13) . . . . . . . . . . . . . . | 150,000 | 187,500 | 562,500 | 750,000 |
| Inventories: | | | | |
| Direct materials (Exhibit 23–5, Schedule A2, 8,000 units @ $7.50 each) . . . . . . . . . . | 60,000 | 60,000 | 60,000 | 60,000 |
| Finished goods (Exhibit 23–6) . . . . . . . . . . . . | 42,000 | 84,750 | 137,344 | 136,875 |
| Prepayments (Exhibit 23–10). . . . . . . . . . . . . . | 7,000 | 8,000 | 9,500 | 12,500 |
| Total current assets . . . . . . . . . . . . . . . . . . . | $366,310 | $544,126 | $1,607,004 | $2,748,043 |
| Plant and equipment: | | | | |
| Buildings and equipment . . . . . . . . . . . . . . . . . . | $420,000 | $420,000 | $ 420,000 | $ 420,000 |
| Less: Accumulated depreciation . . . . . . . . . . . . | (25,000) | (30,000) | (35,000) | (40,000) |
| Total plant and equipment . . . . . . . . . . . . . . . | $395,000 | $390,000 | $ 385,000 | $ 380,000 |
| Total assets . . . . . . . . . . . . . . . . . . . . . . . . . . . . . | $761,310 | $934,126 | $1,992,004 | $3,128,043 |
| Current liabilities: | | | | |
| Notes payable to officer (Exhibit 23–11) . . . . . . | $ 27,000 | $ 18,000 | $ 9,000 | $ -0- |
| Other current payables (Exhibit 23–9) . . . . . . . . | 75,000 | 100,000 | 225,000 | 350,000 |
| Income taxes payable (Exhibit 23–12). . . . . . . . | 46,124 | 81,176 | 409,222 | 571,704 |
| Total current liabilities. . . . . . . . . . . . . . . . . . | $148,124 | $199,176 | $ 643,222 | $ 921,704 |
| Stockholders' equity: | | | | |
| Capital stock, no par, 10,000 shares . . . . . . . . . | $400,000 | $400,000 | $ 400,000 | $ 400,000 |
| Retained earnings, beginning of quarter . . . . . . | 144,000 ⟩ | 213,186 ⟩ | 334,950 ⟩ | 948,782 |
| Quarterly income (Exhibit 23–8). . . . . . . . . . . . . | 69,186 ⟩ | 121,764 ⟩ | 613,832 ⟩ | 857,557 |
| Total stockholders' equity. . . . . . . . . . . . . . . . | $613,186 | $734,950 | $1,348,782 | $2,206,339 |
| Total liabilities & stockholders' equity . . . . . . . . . | $761,310 | $934,126 | $1,992,004 | $3,128,043 |

## INTERNATIONAL FINANCIAL REPORTING: STANDARDS AND BUDGETING

For many companies, U.S. generally accepted accounting principles (GAAP) requirements are embedded in their operating budget computations. The adoption of, or convergence with, IFRS is likely to require significant revision in the budgeting processes of U.S. companies. For example, regarding revenue recognition, IFRS and U.S. GAAP generally agree at the principles level. However, U.S. GAAP contains extensive supporting literature that provides detailed and industry-specific guidance for revenue recognition. U.S. publicly traded companies are required to follow that specific guidance in creating their external financial statements. There are other areas where U.S. GAAP, with over 20,000 pages of supporting authoritative guidance, has specific and detailed recommendations that are not embodied in the 4,000 pages of authoritative IFRS guidance. Standard setters are currently considering whether the additional guidance provided with U.S. GAAP will become a part of the IFRS guidance in future years.

## USING BUDGETS EFFECTIVELY

In preparing a budget, managers are forced to consider carefully all aspects of the company's activities. This study and analysis should, in itself, enable managers to do a better job of managing.

The primary benefits of budgeting, however, result from how the budgeted information is used. Among these benefits are:

1. *Advance warning of and assignment of responsibility for conditions that require corrective action.* For example, NTI now knows that one result of the expected increase in sales between the first and fourth quarters (8,000 units to 40,000 units) is a large increase in needed direct labor hours from the 400 hours in the first quarter to 10,000 hours by the fourth quarter. Hiring additional skilled labor and training them will be assigned to human resources personnel.

2. *Coordination of activities among all departments within the organization.* The increased demand for direct labor, described above, will require significant coordination between the administration (particularly human resources, payroll, etc.) and the manufacturing department. Also, NTI might need to add one or two work shifts and/or find additional production space to accommodate the additional workers.

3. *The creation of standards for evaluating performance.* Because Lisa Scott, NTI's cost accountant, analyzed the direct labor required to produce a finished unit, the company now has an expected or standard amount of time to produce a finished unit (one-quarter hour). This standard allows for planning the number of employees to hire and allows for an evaluation of the efficiency of current employees.

Let us now consider in more detail how NTI's master budget serves these functions.

### Advance Warning of and Responsibility for Decision Making    Earlier in this chapter, we described NTI's financial condition as *profit rich, yet cash poor.* We attributed this condition to the rapid sales growth experienced in the fourth quarter of 2010. In short, a sudden surge in demand for NTI's product caused excessive amounts of cash to become *tied up* in inventories and receivables. As a result, one of management's major responsibilities at the start of 2011 is generating enough cash flow from operations to meet obligations as they become due. Had a master budget been prepared in 2010, management would have been *forewarned* of this condition, thereby making the severity of the current situation less threatening to the company's survival.

### Coordination of the Activities of Departments    The budget provides a comprehensive plan enabling all of the departments to work together in a coordinated manner. For example, the Production Department knows the quantity of goods to produce to meet the expected needs of the Sales Department. The Purchasing Department, in turn, is informed of the quantities of direct materials that must be ordered to meet the requirements of the Production Department. The budgeting process requires that managers of departments and other segments of the organization *communicate with each other.*

**A Yardstick for Evaluating Management Performance**    The comparison of actual results with budgeted amounts is a common means of evaluating performance in organizations. As discussed in Chapter 22, the evaluation of performance should be based only on the revenue and costs that are *under the control* of the person being evaluated. Therefore, for the purposes of evaluation, budgeted fixed costs should be subdivided into the categories of *controllable costs* and *committed costs.*

## FLEXIBLE BUDGETING

Performance may become difficult to evaluate if the actual level of activity (either sales or production) differs substantially from the level originally budgeted. A **flexible budget** is one that can be adjusted easily to show budgeted revenue, costs, and cash flows at *different levels* of activity. Thus, if a change in volume lessens the usefulness of the original budget, a new budget may be prepared quickly to reflect the actual level of activity for the period.

To illustrate the usefulness of a flexible budget, assume that on March 31, 2011, Joe Reco (NTI's production manager) is presented with the **performance report** shown in Exhibit 23–16. The report compares the manufacturing costs originally budgeted for the quarter (Exhibit 23–5) with his department's actual performance for the period.

**Exhibit 23–16**

NTI'S PRODUCTION
DEPARTMENT
PERFORMANCE REPORT
FOR THE FIRST
QUARTER OF 2011

### NTI
### PERFORMANCE REPORT OF THE PRODUCTION DEPARTMENT
### FOR THE 1ST QUARTER ENDED MARCH 31, 2011

|  | Amount Budgeted | Actual | Over (Under) Budget |
|---|---|---|---|
| Manufacturing costs: |  |  |  |
| Direct materials used ..................... | $15,000 | $21,000 | $ 6,000 |
| Direct labor ........................... | 5,000 | 7,000 | 2,000 |
| Variable manufacturing overhead ........................... | 7,000 | 9,500 | 2,500 |
| Fixed manufacturing overhead ........................... | 15,000 | 15,750 | 750 |
| Total manufacturing costs— first quarter ........................... | $42,000 | $53,250 | $11,250 |

At first glance, it appears that Reco's performance is quite poor, as all production costs exceed the amounts budgeted. However, we have deliberately omitted one piece of information from this performance report. To meet a higher-than-expected customer demand for NTI's product, the production department produced *1,500 units* instead of the *1,000 units* originally budgeted for the first quarter.

Under these circumstances, we should reevaluate our conclusions concerning Reco's ability to control manufacturing costs. At this higher level of production, variable manufacturing costs should naturally exceed the amounts originally budgeted. In order to evaluate his performance, the budget must be adjusted to indicate the levels of cost that would have been budgeted to manufacture 1,500 units.

Flexible budgeting may be viewed as combining the concepts of budgeting and cost-volume-profit analysis. Using the variable and fixed cost estimates prepared by Lisa Scott (page 1000), the manufacturing cost budget for NTI can be revised to reflect any level of production. For example, in Exhibit 23–17, these relationships are used to forecast quarterly manufacturing costs at three different levels of production:

| | Level of Production (in units) | | |
|---|---|---|---|
| | 500 | 1,000 | 1,500 |
| Manufacturing cost estimates: | | | |
| Variable costs: | | | |
| Direct materials ($15 per unit) . . . . . . . . . . . . . . . . . . . . . | $ 7,500 | $15,000 | $22,500 |
| Direct labor ($5 per unit). . . . . . . . . . . . . . . . . . . . . . . . . | 2,500 | 5,000 | 7,500 |
| Variable manufacturing overhead ($7 per unit) . . . . . . . . . | 3,500 | 7,000 | 10,500 |
| Fixed costs: | | | |
| Manufacturing overhead ($15,000 per quarter) . . . . . . . . . | 15,000 | 15,000 | 15,000 |
| Total manufacturing costs—first quarter . . . . . . . . . . . . . . | $28,500 | $42,000 | $55,500 |

**Exhibit 23–17**

**NTI'S BUDGETED PRODUCTION COSTS AT VARIOUS PRODUCTION VOLUMES FOR 2011**

Notice that budgeted *variable* manufacturing costs change with the level of production, whereas budgeted *fixed costs* remain the same.

We can now modify the performance report for NTI's production department to reflect the actual *1,500* unit level of production achieved during the first quarter of 2011. The modified report is presented in Exhibit 23–18.

| NTI PERFORMANCE REPORT OF THE PRODUCTION DEPARTMENT FOR THE 1ST QUARTER ENDED MARCH 31, 2011 | | | | |
|---|---|---|---|---|
| | Level of Production (in units) | | | Actual Costs Over (Under) Flexible Budget |
| | Originally Budgeted 1,000 | Flexible Budget 1,500 | Actual Cost 1,500 | |
| Manufacturing costs: | | | | |
| Direct materials used . . . . . . . | $15,000 | $22,500 | $21,000 | $(1,500) |
| Direct labor . . . . . . . . . . . . . . | 5,000 | 7,500 | 7,000 | (500) |
| Variable overhead . . . . . . . . . | 7,000 | 10,500 | 9,500 | (1,000) |
| Fixed overhead . . . . . . . . . . . | 15,000 | 15,000 | 15,750 | 750 |
| Total manufacturing costs . . . . . . . . . . . . . . . . . . | $42,000 | $55,500 | $53,250 | $(2,250) |

**Exhibit 23–18**

**FLEXIBLE BUDGET-BASED PERFORMANCE REPORT AT NTI FOR 2011**

This comparison paints quite a different picture from the report presented in Exhibit 23–16. Considering the actual level of production, the production manager has kept all manufacturing costs below budgeted amounts, with the exception of fixed overhead (most of which may be committed costs).

The techniques of flexible budgeting may also be applied to profit centers by applying cost-volume-profit relationships to the actual level of *sales* achieved.

## Computers and Flexible Budgeting
Adjusting the entire budget to reflect a different level of sales or production would be a sizable task in a manual system. In a computer-based system, however, it can be done quickly and easily. Once the cost-volume-profit relationships have been entered into a budgeting program, the computer instantly performs the computations necessary to generate a complete master budget for any level of business activity. There are numerous budgeting software programs available on the market. However, many managers choose to develop their own budgeting programs using spreadsheet packages.

Managers often use their budgeting software to generate complete budgets under many different assumptions. These managers use a standard cost system to provide the costs of resources consumed. We will discuss standard cost systems in the next chapter. For managers using standard costs, software becomes a valuable planning tool with which to assess the expected impact of changes in sales, production, and other key variables on all aspects of their operations.

## Concluding Remarks

Chapter 23 serves as a link between the preceding several chapters and the next chapters. The preparation of a master budget closely relates to the use of standard costs, covered in the next chapter, and draws heavily on concepts regarding cost flows, product costing, cost-volume-profit analysis, and responsibility accounting. In our next chapters, we will see how managers select and use budget information for controlling operations and when making decisions pertaining to investments in long-term assets.

# END-OF-CHAPTER REVIEW

## SUMMARY OF LEARNING OBJECTIVES

**LO1** Explain how a company can be "profit rich, yet cash poor." Companies must often tie up large sums of cash in direct materials, work in process, and finished goods inventories. As finished goods are sold, cash continues to remain tied up in accounts receivable. Thus, a company may be reporting record profits, yet still experience cash flow problems.

**LO2** Discuss the benefits that a company may derive from a formal budgeting process. The benefits of budgeting are the benefits that come from thinking ahead. Budgeting helps to coordinate the activities of the different departments, provides a basis for evaluating department performance, and provides managers with responsibility for future decision making. In addition, budgeting forces management to estimate future economic conditions, including costs of materials, demand for the company's products, and interest rates.

**LO3** Explain two philosophies that may be used in setting budgeted amounts. The most widely used approach is to set budgeted amounts at levels that are reasonably achievable under normal operating conditions. The goal in this case is to make the budget a fair and reasonable basis for evaluating performance.

An alternative is to budget an ideal level of performance. Under this approach, departments normally fall somewhat short of budgeted performance, but the variations may identify areas in which improvement is possible.

**LO4** Describe the elements of a master budget. A "master budget" is a group of related budgets and forecasts that together summarize all the planned activities of the business. A master budget usually includes a sales forecast, production schedule, manufacturing costs budget, operating expense budget, cash budget, capital expenditures budget, and projected financial statements. The number and type of individual budgets and schedules that make up the master budget depend on the size and nature of the business.

**LO5** Prepare the budgets and supporting schedules included in a master budget. A logical sequence of steps in preparing a master budget begins with a sales forecast. The operating budget estimates are used primarily in preparing a budgeted income statement, whereas the cash flow estimates are used in preparing the cash budget and budgeted balance sheets.

**LO6** Prepare a flexible budget and explain its uses. A flexible budget shows budgeted revenue, costs, and profits for different levels of business activity. Thus, a flexible budget can be used to evaluate the efficiency of departments throughout the business, even if the actual level of business activity differs from management's original estimates. The amounts included in a flexible budget at any given level of activity are based on cost-volume-profit relationships.

## Key Terms Introduced or Emphasized in Chapter 23

**budget** (p. 993)   A plan or forecast for a future period expressed in quantitative terms. Establishes objectives and aids in evaluating subsequent performance.

**flexible budget** (p. 1012)   A budget that can be readily revised to reflect budgeted amounts given the actual levels of activity (sales and production) achieved during the period. Makes use of cost-volume-profit relationships to restate the master budget for the achieved level of activity.

**master budget** (p. 997)   An overall financial and operating plan, including budgets for all aspects of business operations and for all responsibility centers.

**operating cycle** (p. 993)   The average time required for the cash invested in inventories to be converted into the cash ultimately collected on sales made to customers.

**performance report** (p. 1012)   A schedule comparing the actual and budgeted performance of a particular responsibility center.

**responsibility budget** (p. 997)   A portion of the master budget showing the budgeted performance of a particular responsibility center within the organization.

**rolling budgeting** (p. 996)   A technique of extending the budget period by one month as each month passes. Therefore, the budget always covers the upcoming 12 months.

## Demonstration Problem

Gertz Corporation is completing its master budget for the first two quarters of the current year. The following financial budget estimates (labeled *E1* through *E5*) have been prepared:

### Payments on Current Payables (E1)

| | 1st Quarter | 2nd Quarter |
|---|---|---|
| Balance at beginning of quarter . . . . . . . . . . . . . . . . . . . . . . . . . . . . | $244,000 | $ 80,000 |
| Budgeted increase in payables during the quarter. . . . . . . . . . . . . . . | 300,000 | 320,000 |
| Total payables during quarter . . . . . . . . . . . . . . . . . . . . . . . . . . . . | $544,000 | $400,000 |
| Less: Estimated balance at end of quarter . . . . . . . . . . . . . . . . . . . . | 80,000 | 90,000 |
| Payments on current payables during quarter . . . . . . . . . . . . . . . . . | $464,000 | $310,000 |

### Prepayments Budget (E2)

| | 1st Quarter | 2nd Quarter |
|---|---|---|
| Balance at beginning of quarter . . . . . . . . . . . . . . . . . . . . . . . . . . . | $ 5,000 | $ 7,000 |
| Estimated cash expenditure during quarter . . . . . : . . . . . . . . . . . . . | 8,000 | 9,000 |
| Total prepayments . . . . . . . . . . . . . . . . . . . . . . . . . . . . . . . . . . . | $13,000 | $16,000 |
| Less: Expiration of prepayments . . . . . . . . . . . . . . . . . . . . . . . . . . | 6,000 | 8,000 |
| Prepayments at end of quarter . . . . . . . . . . . . . . . . . . . . . . . . . . . | $ 7,000 | $ 8,000 |

### Debt Service Budget (E3)

| | 1st Quarter | 2nd Quarter |
|---|---|---|
| Notes payable at the beginning of the quarter . . . . . . . . . . . . . . . . . . | $50,000 | $49,000 |
| Interest expense for the quarter . . . . . . . . . . . . . . . . . . . . . . . . . . . | 1,500 | 1,470 |
| Total principal plus accrued interest . . . . . . . . . . . . . . . . . . . . . . . . | $51,500 | $50,470 |
| Less: Cash payments (principal and interest) . . . . . . . . . . . . . . . . . | 2,500 | 2,500 |
| Notes payable at the end of the quarter . . . . . . . . . . . . . . . . . . . . . | $49,000 | $47,970 |

### Budgeted Income Taxes (E4)

| | 1st Quarter | 2nd Quarter |
|---|---|---|
| Income tax liability at beginning of quarter . . . . . . . . . . . . . . . . . . . . | $25,000 | $30,000 |
| Estimated income taxes for the quarter (per budgeted income statement) . . . . . . . . . . . . . . . . . . . . . . . . . . . . . | 30,000 | 40,000 |
| Total accrued income tax liability. . . . . . . . . . . . . . . . . . . . . . . . . . . | $55,000 | $70,000 |
| Cash payment of amount owed at beginning of quarter . . . . . . . . . . . . | 25,000 | 30,000 |
| Income tax liability at end of quarter . . . . . . . . . . . . . . . . . . . . . . . . | $30,000 | $40,000 |

### Estimated Receipts from Customers (E5)

| | 1st Quarter | 2nd Quarter |
|---|---|---|
| Balance of receivables at beginning of year. . . . . . . . . . . . . . . . . . . . | $150,000 | |
| Collections on first quarter sales of $500,000— 60% in first quarter and 40% in the second quarter . . . . . . . . . . . . . | 300,000 | $200,000 |
| Collections on second quarter sales of $600,000— 60% in the second quarter and 40% in the third quarter . . . . . . . . . | | 360,000 |
| Cash receipts from customers . . . . . . . . . . . . . . . . . . . . . . . . . . . . | $450,000 | $560,000 |

## Instructions

**a.** Prepare a cash budget for Gertz Corporation for the first two quarters of the current year. Assume that the company's cash balance at the beginning of the first quarter is $50,000.

**b.** Discuss any cash flow problems revealed by your budget.

## Solution to the Demonstration Problem

**a.** The following cash budget can be prepared using the financial budget estimates provided:

| GERTZ CORPORATION<br>CASH BUDGET<br>FIRST TWO QUARTERS OF CURRENT YEAR | | |
| --- | --- | --- |
| | **1st Quarter** | **2nd Quarter** |
| Cash balance at beginning of quarter. . . . . . . . . . . . . . . . . . . . . . . . . | $ 50,000 | $ 500 |
| Cash receipts: | | |
| Cash received from customers (E5) . . . . . . . . . . . . . . . . . . . . . . . . . | 450,000 | 560,000 |
| Total cash available. . . . . . . . . . . . . . . . . . . . . . . . . . . . . . . . . . | $500,000 | $560,500 |
| Cash payments: | | |
| Payment of current payables (E1) . . . . . . . . . . . . . . . . . . . . . . . . . | $464,000 | $310,000 |
| Prepayments (E2). . . . . . . . . . . . . . . . . . . . . . . . . . . . . . . . . . . . | 8,000 | 9,000 |
| Debt service, including interest (E3) . . . . . . . . . . . . . . . . . . . . . . . | 2,500 | 2,500 |
| Income tax payments (E4) . . . . . . . . . . . . . . . . . . . . . . . . . . . . . | 25,000 | 30,000 |
| Total disbursements . . . . . . . . . . . . . . . . . . . . . . . . . . . . . . . . . . | $499,500 | $351,500 |
| Cash balance at end of the quarter . . . . . . . . . . . . . . . . . . . . . . . . | $ 500 | $209,000 |

**b.** The cash budget reveals that Gertz expects to disburse more cash than it will collect during the first quarter. As a result, a cash balance of only $500 is budgeted for the end of that quarter. Because these figures are estimates, it is possible that its cash balance may actually be less than the amount budgeted. Thus, Gertz should arrange for a line of credit now, in the event that a short-term loan becomes necessary. It does not appear that the company will have any cash flow problems during the second quarter.

# Self-Test Questions

*The answers to these questions appear on page 1035.*

**1.** Which of the following statements correctly describes relationships within the master budget? (More than one answer may be correct.)

**a.** The production budgets are based in large part on the sales forecast.

**b.** In many elements of the master budget, the amounts budgeted for the upcoming quarter are reviewed and subdivided into monthly budget figures.

**c.** The operating budgets affect the budgeted income statement, the cash budget, and the budgeted balance sheet.

**d.** The capital expenditures budget affects the direct materials budget.

**2.** During the first quarter of its operations, Morris Mfg. Co. expects to sell 50,000 units and create an ending inventory of 20,000 units. Variable manufacturing costs are budgeted at $10 per unit, and fixed manufacturing costs at $100,000 per quarter. The company's treasurer expects that 80 percent of the variable manufacturing costs will require cash payment during the quarter and that 20 percent will be financed through accounts payable and accrued liabilities. Only 50 percent of the fixed manufacturing costs are expected to require cash payments during the quarter. In the cash budget, payments for manufacturing costs during the quarter will total:

**a.** $800,000.

**b.** $610,000.

**c.** $600,000.

**d.** $450,000.

**3.** Rodgers Mfg. Co. prepares a flexible budget. The original budget forecasts sales of 100,000 units @ $20 and operating expenses of $300,000 fixed, plus $2 per unit. Production was budgeted at 100,000 units. Actual sales and production for the period totaled 110,000 units. When the budget is adjusted to reflect these new activity levels, which of the following budgeted amounts will increase, but by *less than* 10 percent?

**a.** Sales revenue.

**b.** Variable manufacturing costs.

**1018** **Chapter 23** Operational Budgeting

c. Fixed manufacturing costs.

d. Total operating expenses.

4. Lamberton Manufacturing Company has just completed its master budget. The budget indicates that the company's operating cycle needs to be shortened. Thus, the company will likely attempt:

   a. Stocking larger inventories.

   b. Reducing cash discounts for prompt payment.

   c. Tightening credit policies.

   d. None of the above selections is correct.

5. Which of the following is *not* an element of the master budget?

   a. The capital expenditures budget.

b. The production schedule.

c. The operating expense budget.

d. All of the above are elements of the master budget.

6. Which of the following is *not* a potential benefit of using budgets?

   a. Enhanced coordination of firm activities.

   b. More motivated managers.

   c. More accurate external financial statements.

   d. Improved interdepartmental communication.

---

**ASSIGNMENT MATERIAL** ## Discussion Questions

1. Explain the relationship between the management functions of *planning* and *controlling costs*.

2. Briefly explain at least three ways in which a business may expect to benefit from preparing a formal budget.

3. Criticize the following quotation:

   "At our company, budgeted revenue is set so high and budgeted expenses so low that no department can ever meet the budget. This way, department managers can never relax; they are motivated to keep working harder no matter how well they are already doing."

4. Why is the preparation of a sales forecast one of the earliest steps in preparing a master budget?

5. What are *responsibility budgets*? What responsibility centers would serve as the basis for preparing responsibility sales budgets in a large retail store, such as Sears or Nordstrom?

6. What is a *flexible budget*? Explain how a flexible budget increases the usefulness of budgeting as a means of evaluating performance.

7. An article in *BusinessWeek* stated that approximately one-third of the total federal budget is considered "controllable." What is meant by a budgeted expenditure being

controllable? Give two examples of government expenditures that may be considered "noncontrollable."

8. Explain why companies that undergo periods of rapid growth often experience cash flow problems.

9. Explain how to compute the average collection period and why it is a critical factor in creating the collections of receivables budget (see Exhibit 23–13).

10. List and briefly explain the two budget philosophies described in the chapter.

11. Some expenses that appear in the income statement do not require a direct cash payment during the period. List at least two such expenses.

12. Explain why it is necessary to distinguish between cash budget estimates and operating budget estimates.

13. When evaluating the performance of a manager, why should fixed costs be divided into the categories of controllable costs and committed costs?

14. What is a rolling budget? Why do some companies choose to use rolling budgets?

15. Frequently, the disadvantages of budgeting are not discussed in textbooks. Go to the Web site www.bbrt.org. Click on Beyond Budgeting to find some disadvantages to budgeting.

---

## Brief Exercises

 **BRIEF EXERCISE 23.1**

Budgeting Philosophies

Renaldo's Boutiques, Inc., has 14 stores located in a midwestern part of the United States. Renaldo, the president of the company, has set budgets for each store that do not allow for lost, stolen, or misplaced merchandise (inventory shrinkage). Research shows the disappearance of store merchandise is attributed to a combination of internal and external causes:

Customer theft—35 percent

Employee theft—40 percent

Administrative errors—18 percent

Vendor dishonesty—7 percent

This chapter discussed two types of budgeting philosophies. Which philosophy do you believe Renaldo is following? Use information in this problem to support your answer.

**LO1** **BRIEF EXERCISE 23.2**

**LO5** Cash Flow at Body Builders

Body Builders Corporation is opening a chain of five health clubs in the Minneapolis area. Body Builders's marketing manager has suggested a marketing plan designed to generate new memberships. The plan would allow new members to delay payment for the first three months' membership and pay at the end of the first quarter. Thus, the cash flow from membership fees will not occur for three months.

Discuss the implications of this marketing approach for the cash flows of Body Builders.

**LO4** **BRIEF EXERCISE 23.3**

Production Budget

Expected sales for tents at Sandy's Camping Gear are 4,200, 6,100, 2,200, 3,400, and 5,300 for the next five quarters. At the end of the current year, inventory of finished tents on hand is 500 tents. Sandy's has a desired ending inventory of 10 percent of next quarter's sales.

Create the production budget in numbers of tents for quarters one through four for the coming year.

**LO4** **BRIEF EXERCISE 23.4**

Estimating Direct Materials Inventory

On January 1, Salter Corporation determined that its direct materials inventory needs to contain 6,500 pounds of materials by March 31. To achieve this goal, Salter will have to use 10 pounds of direct materials for every pound that it purchases during the upcoming quarter. On the basis of the company's budgeted sales volume, management estimates that 10,000 pounds of direct materials need to be purchased by March 31.

Determine the number of pounds in Salter's beginning direct materials inventory on January 1.

**LO2** **BRIEF EXERCISE 23.5**

Benefits of Budgeting

Cheri Standish, the controller at Harmonics International, overheard the following conversation among two of her product line department heads, Bob, manager of Pianos and Keyboards, and Fran, manager of Horns and Stringed Instruments.

**Fran:** "This budgeting process is consuming an inordinate amount of time. Each time I prepare a budget and send it to the controller's office, it comes back for revision. This is the third time I have had to reallocate funds for my budget requests.

**Bob:** "I know what you mean. And because we are evaluated on our ability to stay in budget, it is critical to have a cushion in case the economy turns south and sales of musical instruments do not meet projections."

What comments should the controller make to these two department heads about the benefits and the importance of the budgeting process?

**LO4** **BRIEF EXERCISE 23.6**

**LO5** Elements of the Budget

Match each budget in column A with the corresponding budget(s) in column B that represent **key** elements in its construction:

| Column A | Column B |
| --- | --- |
| **1.** Budgeted income statement | **a.** Direct materials budget |
| **2.** Budgeted balance sheet | **b.** Cost of goods sold budget |
| **3.** Cash flow budget | **c.** Production budget |
| **4.** Cost of goods sold budget | **d.** Payables budget |
| **5.** Production budget | **e.** Sales budget |
|  | **f.** Budgeted income statement |

**LO8** **BRIEF EXERCISE 23.7**

Flexible Budgets

Falstags Brewery has estimated $63,375, $68,625, and $73,875 budgeted costs for the manufacture of 3,500, 4,500, and 5,500 gallons of beer, respectively, next quarter.

What are the variable and fixed manufacturing costs in the flexible budget for Falstags Brewery?

**LO4** **BRIEF EXERCISE 23.8**

**LO5** Operating Expense Budget

Last month, Widner Corporation generated sales of $800,000 and incurred selling and administrative expenses of $320,000, half of which were variable. This month, the company estimates that it will generate sales of $900,000. Management does not anticipate any changes in unit variable costs. However, it does expect fixed selling and administrative costs to increase by $5,000.

Compute Widner's total selling and administrative expense budget for the upcoming month.

**LO2** **BRIEF EXERCISE 23.9**

**LO3** Costs of Budgeting Systems

Many managers complain about the budgeting process. They claim it takes too long, requires too much management time, encourages managers to "pad the budget" because of uncertainties, and creates unnecessary tension among managers. As a result of these charges, some managers and business leaders have called for an abandonment of traditional budgeting practices. However,

1020    **Chapter 23**  Operational Budgeting

regardless of budgeting's failures, it continues to be widely used across all types of businesses and not-for-profit enterprises. One reason for the continued use of budgeting is the belief that a competent management team can plan for, manage, and control in large measure the relevant variables that dominate the life of a business. Managers must grapple with uncertainties regardless of whether or not they have a budget.

Do you think that managers' complaints about the budgeting process are realistic? Do these complaints create costs for organizations? If so, why do organizations continue to use budgets?

**LO6**

**BRIEF EXERCISE 23.10**

Evaluating Managers with Flexible Budgets

Harry Blackmun, manager of the Dry Goods Department at Goodright's Grocery, has a budget of $6,000 per month for the current year. This budget includes the allocation of $500 of storewide common costs based on the square feet occupied by Dry Goods. Recently, Dry Goods expanded its total store space to include household items that had not previously been included in the store. During the current month, Mr. Blackmun was over budget by $700. The store manager was upset with the manager of Dry Goods and asked for an explanation.

What could be causing the budget overage? What budget tool could Goodright's use to better evaluate its department managers?

# Exercises

**LO4**

**EXERCISE 23.1**

Budgeting Purchases and Cash Payments

**LO5**

The following information is from the manufacturing budget and the budgeted financial statements of Fabor Fabrication:

| | |
|---|---:|
| Direct materials inventory, Jan. 1 | $ 68,000 |
| Direct materials inventory, Dec. 31 | 80,000 |
| Direct materials budgeted for use during the year | 255,000 |
| Accounts payable to suppliers of materials, Jan. 1 | 50,000 |
| Accounts payable to suppliers of materials, Dec. 31 | 79,000 |

Compute the budgeted amounts for:

**a.**  Purchases of direct materials during the year.

**b.**  Cash payments during the year to suppliers of materials.

**LO4**

**EXERCISE 23.2**

Budgeting Labor Costs

**LO5**

Deep Valley Foods manufactures a product that is first smoked and then packed for shipment to customers. During a normal month the product's direct labor cost per pound is budgeted using the following information:

| | Direct Labor Hours (per pound) | Budgeted Direct Labor Cost (per hour) |
|---|:---:|:---:|
| Process: | | |
| Smoking | .04 | $10.00 |
| Packing | .01 | 8.00 |

The budget for March calls for the production of 500,000 pounds of product. However, March's direct labor costs for smoking are expected to be 5 percent above normal due to anticipated scheduling inefficiencies. Yet direct labor costs in the packing room are expected to be 3 percent below normal because of changes in equipment layout.

Prepare a budget for direct labor costs in March using three column headings: Total, Smoking, and Packing.

**EXERCISE 23.3**
Production Budgets

Mercury Bag Company produces cases of grocery bags. The managers at Mercury are trying to develop budgets for the upcoming quarter. The following data have been gathered:

| | |
|---|---|
| Projected sales in units . . . . . . . . . . . . . . . . . . . . . . . . . . . . . . . . . . . . . . . . . . . . . . . . . | 1,200 cases |
| Selling price per case . . . . . . . . . . . . . . . . . . . . . . . . . . . . . . . . . . . . . . . | $240 |
| Inventory at the beginning of the quarter . . . . . . . . . . . . . . . . . . . . . . . . . . . . | 150 cases |
| Target inventory at the end of the quarter . . . . . . . . . . . . . . . . . . . . . . . . . . . | 100 cases |
| Direct labor hours needed to produce one case . . . . . . . . . . . . . . . . . . . . . . . | 2 hours |
| Direct labor wages . . . . . . . . . . . . . . . . . . . . . . . . . . . . . . . . . . . . . . . . . . . . . . | $10 per hour |
| Direct materials cost per case. . . . . . . . . . . . . . . . . . . . . . . . . . . . . . . . . . . . . . | $8 |
| Variable manufacturing overhead cost per case . . . . . . . . . . . . . . . . . . . . . . . | $6 |
| Fixed overhead costs for the upcoming quarter . . . . . . . . . . . . . . . . . . . . . . . . | $220,000 |

**a.** Using the above information, develop Mercury's sales forecast in dollars and production schedule in units.

**b.** What is Mercury's budgeted variable manufacturing cost per case?

**c.** Prepare Mercury's manufacturing cost budget.

**d.** What is the projected ending value of the Inventory account?

**EXERCISE 23.4**
Production and Direct Materials Budget

Lock Tight, Inc., produces outside doors for installation on homes. The following information was gathered to prepare budgets for the upcoming year beginning January 1:

| | |
|---|---|
| Sales forecast in units . . . . . . . . . . . . . . . . . . . . . . . . . . . . . . . . . . . . . . . . . . . | 6,500 doors |
| Finished goods inventory, Jan. 1 . . . . . . . . . . . . . . . . . . . . . . . . . . . . . . . . . . . | 720 doors |
| Target finished goods inventory, Dec. 31. . . . . . . . . . . . . . . . . . . . . . . . . . . . . | 680 doors |
| Raw materials inventory—steel, Jan. 1 . . . . . . . . . . . . . . . . . . . . . . . . . . . . . | 40,000 pounds |
| Target inventory—steel, Dec. 31 . . . . . . . . . . . . . . . . . . . . . . . . . . . . . . . . . . | 80,000 pounds |
| Raw materials inventory—glass, Jan. 1. . . . . . . . . . . . . . . . . . . . . . . . . . . . . | 6,000 square feet |
| Target inventory—glass, Dec. 31 . . . . . . . . . . . . . . . . . . . . . . . . . . . . . . . . . . | 4,000 square feet |
| Budgeted purchase price—steel . . . . . . . . . . . . . . . . . . . . . . . . . . . . . . . . . . | $4 per pound |
| Budgeted purchase price—glass . . . . . . . . . . . . . . . . . . . . . . . . . . . . . . . . . . | $2 per square foot |

The manufacture of each door requires 20 pounds of steel and 6 square feet of glass.

**a.** Prepare the production schedule in units for Lock Tight.

**b.** Using the production schedule, develop the direct materials purchase budgets for steel and glass.

**c.** Why might Lock Tight's target level of steel inventory be higher than last year's ending balance and its target level of glass inventory be lower than last year's ending balance?

**EXERCISE 23.5**
Budgeting for Prepayments

Springfield Company's master budget includes estimated costs and expenses of $325,000 for its third quarter of operations. Of this amount, $300,000 is expected to be financed with current payables. Depreciation expense for the quarter is budgeted at $20,000. Springfield's prepayments balance at the end of the third quarter is expected to be twice that of its prepayments balance at the beginning of the quarter. The company estimates it will prepay expenses totaling $8,000 in the third quarter. What is Springfield's budgeted prepayments balance at the end of the third quarter?

**EXERCISE 23.6**
Budgeting for Interest Expense

On February 1, 2011, Willmar Corporation borrowed $100,000 from its bank by signing a 12 percent, 15-year note payable. The note calls for 180 monthly payments of $1,200. Each payment includes an interest and a principal component.

**a.** Compute the interest expense in February.

**b.** Compute the portion of Willmar's March 31, 2011, $1,200 payment that will be applied to the principal of the note.

**c.** Compute the carrying value of the note on April 30, 2011 (round to the nearest dollar).

**LO6**  **EXERCISE 23.7**
Preparing a Flexible
Overhead Budget

Razmon's Jewelers has accumulated the following budgeted overhead information (dollar amounts may include both fixed and variable costs):

|  | Direct Labor Hours | |
| --- | --- | --- |
|  | **1,000 hours** | **2,000 hours** |
| Maintenance . . . . . . . . . . . . . . . . . . . . . . . . . . . . . . . . . . . . . . | $10,000 | $16,000 |
| Depreciation . . . . . . . . . . . . . . . . . . . . . . . . . . . . . . . . . . . . . | 5,000 | 5,000 |
| Supervision . . . . . . . . . . . . . . . . . . . . . . . . . . . . . . . . . . . . | 15,000 | 15,000 |
| Indirect supplies . . . . . . . . . . . . . . . . . . . . . . . . . . . . . . . . | 1,400 | 2,800 |
| Utilities . . . . . . . . . . . . . . . . . . . . . . . . . . . . . . . . . . . . . . . . | 750 | 1,500 |
| Other . . . . . . . . . . . . . . . . . . . . . . . . . . . . . . . . . . . . . . . . . . | 8,100 | 8,200 |

Use this information to create the overhead budget for 1,500 direct labor employee hours.

**LO4**  **EXERCISE 23.8**
Budgeting Cash
**LO5**  Receipts

Sales on account for the first two months of the current year are budgeted as follows:

| | |
| --- | --- |
| Jan. . . . . . . . . . . . . . . . . . . . . . . . . . . . . . . . . . . . . . . . . . . . . . . . . . . . . . . . . . . . . . . . . . . . . . | $700,000 |
| Feb. . . . . . . . . . . . . . . . . . . . . . . . . . . . . . . . . . . . . . . . . . . . . . . . . . . . . . . . . . . . . . . . . . . . . . | 750,000 |

All sales are made on terms of 2/10, n/30 (2% discount if paid in 10 days, full amount by 30 days); collections on accounts receivable are typically made as follows:

| | |
| --- | --- |
| Collections within the month of sale: | |
| Within discount period . . . . . . . . . . . . . . . . . . . . . . . . . . . . . . . . . . . . . . . . . . . . . | 60% |
| After discount period . . . . . . . . . . . . . . . . . . . . . . . . . . . . . . . . . . . . . . . . . . . . . . | 15 |
| Collections within the month following sale: | |
| Within discount period . . . . . . . . . . . . . . . . . . . . . . . . . . . . . . . . . . . . . . . . . . . . . | 15 |
| After discount period . . . . . . . . . . . . . . . . . . . . . . . . . . . . . . . . . . . . . . . . . . . . . . | 7 |
| Returns, allowances, and uncollectibles . . . . . . . . . . . . . . . . . . . . . . . . . . . . . . . . | 3 |
| Total . . . . . . . . . . . . . . . . . . . . . . . . . . . . . . . . . . . . . . . . . . . . . . . . . . . . . . . . . . . | 100% |

Compute the estimated cash collections on accounts receivable for the month of *February*.

**LO4**  **EXERCISE 23.9**
Budgeting an Ending
**LO5**  Cash Balance

On March 1 of the current year, Spicer Corporation compiled information to prepare a cash budget for March, April, and May. All of the company's sales are made on account. The following information has been provided by Spicer's management:

| Month | Credit Sales |
| --- | --- |
| Jan. . . . . . . . . . . . . . . . . . . . . . . . . . . . . . . . . . . . . . . . . . . . . . . | $300,000 (actual) |
| Feb. . . . . . . . . . . . . . . . . . . . . . . . . . . . . . . . . . . . . . . . . . . . . . | 400,000 (actual) |
| Mar. . . . . . . . . . . . . . . . . . . . . . . . . . . . . . . . . . . . . . . . . . . . . | 600,000 (estimated) |
| Apr. . . . . . . . . . . . . . . . . . . . . . . . . . . . . . . . . . . . . . . . . . . . . | 700,000 (estimated) |
| May . . . . . . . . . . . . . . . . . . . . . . . . . . . . . . . . . . . . . . . . . . . . | 800,000 (estimated) |

The company's collection activity on credit sales historically has been as follows:

| | |
| --- | --- |
| Collections in the month of the sale . . . . . . . . . . . . . . . . . . . . . . . . . . . . . . . . . . . . . | 50% |
| Collections one month after the sale . . . . . . . . . . . . . . . . . . . . . . . . . . . . . . . . . . . . | 30 |
| Collections two months after the sale . . . . . . . . . . . . . . . . . . . . . . . . . . . . . . . . . . | 15 |
| Uncollectible accounts . . . . . . . . . . . . . . . . . . . . . . . . . . . . . . . . . . . . . . . . . . . . . . | 5 |

Spicer's total cash expenditures for March, April, and May have been estimated at $1,200,000 (an average of $400,000 per month). Its cash balance on March 1 of the current year is $500,000. No financing or investing activities are anticipated during the second quarter.
    Compute Spicer's budgeted cash balance at the ends of March, April, and May.

**LO6  EXERCISE 23.10**

Preparing a Flexible Budget

Outdoor Outfitters has created a flexible budget for the 70,000-unit and the 80,000-unit levels of activity as shown below.

|  | 70,000 Units | 80,000 Units | 90,000 Units |
|---|---|---|---|
| Sales ................................ | $1,400,000 | $1,600,000 | $ |
| Cost of goods sold ...................... | 840,000 | 960,000 | _____ |
| Gross profit on sales .................... | $ 560,000 | $ 640,000 | $ |
| Operating expenses ($90,000 fixed) ........ | 370,000 | 410,000 | _____ |
| Operating income...................... | $ 190,000 | $ 230,000 | $ |
| Income taxes (30% of operating income)..... | 57,000 | 69,000 | _____ |
| Net income ........................... | $ 133,000 | $ 161,000 | $ |

Complete Outdoor Outfitters's flexible budget at the 90,000-unit level of activity. Assume that the cost of goods sold and variable operating expenses vary directly with sales and that income taxes remain at 30 percent of operating income.

**LO6  EXERCISE 23.11**

More on Flexible Budgeting

The cost accountant for Upload Games Company prepared the following monthly performance report relating to the Packaging Department:

|  | Budgeted Production (10,000 units) | Actual Production (11,000 units) | Variances | |
|---|---|---|---|---|
|  |  |  | Favorable | Unfavorable |
| Direct materials used ...... | $310,000 | $320,000 |  | $10,000 |
| Direct labor............. | 110,000 | 115,000 |  | 5,000 |
| Variable manufacturing overhead............. | 20,000 | 21,500 |  | 1,500 |
| Fixed manufacturing overhead............. | 150,000 | 149,200 | $800 | |

Prepare a revised performance report in which the variances are computed by comparing the actual costs incurred with estimated costs *using a flexible budget* for 11,000 units of production.

**LO2  EXERCISE 23.12**

Budget Estimates

**LO3**

William George is the marketing manager at Crunchy Cookie Company. Each quarter, he is responsible for submitting a sales forecast to be used in the formulation of the company's master budget. George consistently understates the sales forecast because, as he puts it, "I am reprimanded if actual sales are less than I've projected, and I look like a hero if actual sales exceed my projections."

**a.** What would you do if you were the marketing manager at Crunchy Cookie Company? Would you also understate sales projections? Defend your answer.

**b.** What measures might be taken by the company to discourage the manipulation of sales forecasts?

**LO4  EXERCISE 23.13**

Budgeting Manufacturing Overhead

**LO5**

Wells Enterprises manufactures a component that is processed successively by Department I and Department II. Manufacturing overhead is applied to units produced at the following budget costs:

|  | Manufacturing Overhead per Unit | | |
|---|---|---|---|
|  | Fixed | Variable | Total |
| Department I ....................................... | $15 | $8 | $20 |
| Department II ....................................... | 12 | 6 | 15 |

These budgeted overhead costs per unit are based on the normal volume of production of 5,000 units per month. In January, variable manufacturing overhead in Department II is expected to be 25 percent above budget because of major scheduled repairs to equipment. The company plans to produce 8,000 units during January.

Prepare a budget for manufacturing overhead costs in January using three column headings: Total, Department I, and Department II.

**1024**    Chapter 23 Operational Budgeting

L02
L03

**EXERCISE 23.14**

Establishing Budget Amounts

Budgets are essential for the successful operation of an organization. Finding the resources to implement budget goals requires extensive use of human resources. How managers perceive their roles in the budgeting process is important to the successful and effective use of the budget as a tool for planning, communicating, and controlling operations.

Discuss the implications for planning and control when a company's management employs an imposed budgetary approach where managers do not actively participate in setting the budget. Contrast this approach with a participative budgetary approach. How does communication work differently when using an imposed versus a participative budgetary approach?

L02
L03

**EXERCISE 23.15**

Home Depot's Budget Goals

Locate the table titled "10-Year Summary of Financial and Operating Results" in the Home Depot 2009 Financial Information in Appendix A. Assume Home Depot identifies each store as a profit center. Identify the categories of information in the "Store Data" section of the table that would provide useful goals to be included in each store's annual budget. Explain why these categories would be useful and how each associated storewide goal could be used for performance evaluation of a store.

## Problem Set A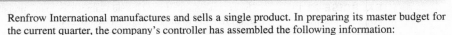

L04
L05

**PROBLEM 23.1A**

Budgeting Production, Inventories, and Cost of Sales

eXcel

Renfrow International manufactures and sells a single product. In preparing its master budget for the current quarter, the company's controller has assembled the following information:

|  | Units | Dollars |
|---|---|---|
| Sales (budgeted) | 150,000 | $7,500,000 |
| Finished goods inventory, beginning of quarter | 38,000 | 975,000 |
| Finished goods inventory, end of quarter | 28,000 | ? |
| Cost of finished goods manufactured (assume a budgeted manufacturing cost of $28 per unit) | ? | ? |

Renfrow International used the average cost method of pricing its inventory of finished goods.

### Instructions

Compute the following budgeted quantities or dollar amounts:

**a.** Planned production of finished goods (in units).

**b.** Cost of finished goods manufactured.

**c.** Ending finished goods inventory. (Remember that in using the average cost method you must first compute the average cost of units available for sale.)

**d.** Cost of goods sold.

L04
L05

**PROBLEM 23.2A**

Short Budgeting Problem

Harmony Corporation manufactures and sells a single product. In preparing the budget for the first quarter, the company's cost accountant has assembled the following information:

|  | Units | Dollars |
|---|---|---|
| Sales (budgeted) | 150,000 | $12,150,000 |
| Finished goods inventory, Jan. 1 (actual) | 30,000 | 1,080,000 |
| Finished goods inventory, Mar. 31 (budgeted) | 20,000 | ? |
| Cost of finished goods manufactured (budgeted manufacturing cost is $39 per unit) | ? | ? |

The company uses the first-in, first-out method of pricing its inventory of finished goods.

### Instructions

Compute the following budgeted quantities or dollar amounts:

**a.** Planned production of finished goods (in units).

**b.** Cost of finished goods manufactured.

**c.** Finished goods inventory, March 31. (Remember to use the first-in, first-out method in pricing the inventory.)

**d.** Cost of goods sold.

**L04**
**PROBLEM 23.3A**
Budgeting for Cash

**L05**

Barnum Distributors wants a projection of cash receipts and cash payments for the month of November. On November 28, a note will be payable in the amount of $98,500, including interest. The cash balance on November 1 is $29,600. Accounts payable to merchandise creditors at the end of October were $217,000.

The company's experience indicates that 70 percent of sales will be collected during the month of sale, 20 percent in the month following the sale, and 7 percent in the second month following the sale; 3 percent will be uncollectible. The company sells various products at an average price of $11 per unit. Selected sales figures are as follows:

|  | Units |
|---|---|
| Sept.—actual | 40,000 |
| Oct.—actual | 60,000 |
| Nov.—estimated | 80,000 |
| Dec.—estimated | 50,000 |
| Total estimated for the current year | 800,000 |

Because purchases are payable within 15 days, approximately 50 percent of the purchases in a given month are paid in the following month. The average cost of units purchased is $7 per unit. Inventories at the end of each month are maintained at a level of 2,000 units plus 10 percent of the number of units that will be sold in the following month. The inventory on October 1 amounted to 8,000 units.

Budgeted operating expenses for November are $220,000. Of this amount, $90,000 is considered fixed (including depreciation of $35,000). All operating expenses, other than depreciation, are paid in the month in which they are incurred.

The company expects to sell fully depreciated equipment in November for $8,400 cash.

**Instructions**

Prepare a cash budget for the month of November, supported by schedules of cash collections on accounts receivable and cash payments for purchases of merchandise.

**L01**
**PROBLEM 23.4A**
Estimating Borrowing Requirements

**L02**

**L04**

**L05**

Former Corporation sells office supplies to government agencies. At the beginning of the current quarter, the company reports the following selected account balances:

| | |
|---|---|
| Cash | $ 10,000 |
| Accounts receivable | 210,000 |
| Current payables | 88,000 |

Former's management has made the following budget estimates regarding operations for the current quarter:

| | |
|---|---|
| Sales (estimated) | $500,000 |
| Total costs and expenses (estimated) | 400,000 |
| Debt service payment (estimated) | 145,000 |
| Tax liability payment (estimated) | 45,000 |

Of Former's total costs and expenses, $20,000 is quarterly depreciation expense, and $20,000 represents the expiration of prepayments. The remaining $360,000 is to be financed with current payables. The company's ending prepayments balance is expected to be the same as its beginning prepayments balance. Its ending current payables balance is expected to be $22,000 more than its beginning balance.

All of Former's sales are on account. Approximately 65 percent of its sales are collected in the quarter in which they are made. The remaining 35 percent are collected in the following quarter. Because all of the company's sales are made to government agencies, it experiences virtually no uncollectible accounts.

Former's minimum cash balance requirement is $10,000. Should the balance fall below this amount, management negotiates a short-term loan with a local bank. The company's debt ratio (liabilities ÷ assets) is currently 80 percent.

**1026**

**Instructions**

a. Compute Former's budgeted cash receipts for the quarter.

b. Compute Former's payments of current payables budgeted for the quarter.

c. Compute Former's cash prepayments budgeted for the quarter.

d. Prepare Former's cash budget for the quarter.

e. Estimate Former's short-term borrowing requirements for the quarter.

f. Discuss problems Former might encounter in obtaining short-term financing.

 **L01**
 **L02**

**PROBLEM 23.5A**

Budgeted Income
Statement and Cash
Budget

**L04**

**L05**

Rizzo's has been in business since January of the current year. The company buys frozen pizza crusts and resells them to large supermarket chains in five states. The following information pertains to Rizzo's first four months of operations:

| | Purchases | Sales |
|---|---|---|
| Jan. | $40,000 | $62,000 |
| Feb. | 32,000 | 49,000 |
| Mar. | 44,000 | 65,000 |
| Apr. | 24,000 | 42,000 |

Rizzo's expects to open several new sales territories in May. In anticipation of increased volume, management forecasts May sales at $72,000. To meet this demand, purchases in May are budgeted at $42,000. The company maintains a gross profit margin of approximately 40 percent.

All of Rizzo's sales are on account. Due to strict credit policies, the company has no bad debt expense. The following collection performance is anticipated for the remainder of the year:

| | |
|---|---|
| Percent collected in month of sale | 30% |
| Percent collected in month following sale | 60 |
| Percent collected in the second month following sale | 10 |

Rizzo's normally pays for 80 percent of its purchases in the month that the purchases are made. The remaining amount is paid in the following month. The company's fixed selling and administrative expenses average $12,000 per month. Of this amount, $4,000 is depreciation expense. Variable selling and administrative expenses are budgeted at 5 percent of sales. The company pays all of its selling and administrative expenses in the month that they are incurred.

Rizzo's debt service is $5,000 per month. Of this amount, approximately $4,500 represents interest expense, and $500 is payment on the principal. The company's tax rate is approximately 35 percent. Quarterly tax payments are made at the end of March, June, September, and December.

**Instructions**

a. Prepare Rizzo's budgeted income statement for May.

b. Prepare Rizzo's cash budget for May. Assume that the company's cash balance on May 1 is $25,000.

c. Explain why Rizzo's budgeted cash flow in May differs from its budgeted net income.

**L01** **PROBLEM 23.6A**

Preparing a Cash
Budget

**L02**

**L04**

**L05**

Jake Marley, owner of Marley Wholesale, is negotiating with the bank for a $200,000, 90-day, 12 percent loan effective July 1 of the current year. If the bank grants the loan, the proceeds will be $194,000, which Marley intends to use on July 1 as follows: pay accounts payable, $150,000; purchase equipment, $16,000; add to bank balance, $28,000.

The current working capital position of Marley Wholesale, according to financial statements as of June 30, is as follows:

| | |
|---|---|
| Cash in bank | $ 20,000 |
| Receivables (net of allowance for doubtful accounts) | 160,000 |
| Merchandise inventory | 90,000 |
| Total current assets | $270,000 |
| Accounts payable (including accrued operating expenses) | 150,000 |
| Working capital | $120,000 |

The bank loan officer asks Marley to prepare a forecast of his cash receipts and cash payments for the next three months to demonstrate that the loan can be repaid at the end of September.

Marley has made the following estimates, which are to be used in preparing a three-month cash budget: Sales (all on account) for July, $300,000; August, $360,000; September, $270,000; and October, $200,000. Past experience indicates that 80 percent of the receivables generated in any month will be collected in the month following the sale, 19 percent will be collected in the second month following the sale, and 1 percent will prove uncollectible. Marley expects to collect $120,000 of the June 30 receivables in July and the remaining $40,000 in August.

Cost of goods sold consistently has averaged about 65 percent of sales. Operating expenses are budgeted at $36,000 per month plus 8 percent of sales. With the exception of $4,400 per month depreciation expense, all operating expenses and purchases are on account and are paid in the month following their incurrence.

Merchandise inventory at the end of each month should be sufficient to cover the following month's sales.

### Instructions

**a.** Prepare a monthly cash budget showing estimated cash receipts and cash payments for July, August, and September, and the cash balance at the end of each month. Supporting schedules should be prepared for estimated collections on receivables, estimated merchandise purchases, and estimated payments for operating expenses and of accounts payable for merchandise purchases.

**b.** On the basis of this cash forecast, write a brief report to Marley explaining whether he will be able to repay the $200,000 bank loan at the end of September.

 **LO2**

 **LO4**

through

**LO6**

**PROBLEM 23.7A**

Preparing and Using a Flexible Budget

Snells is a retail department store. The following cost-volume relationships were used in developing a flexible budget for the company for the current year:

| | Yearly Fixed Expenses | Variable Expenses per Sales Dollar |
|---|---|---|
| Cost of merchandise sold . . . . . . . . . . . . . . . . . . . . . . . . . . . . . . . | | $0.600 |
| Selling and promotion expense . . . . . . . . . . . . . . . . . . . . . . . . | $ 210,000 | 0.082 |
| Building occupancy expense . . . . . . . . . . . . . . . . . . . . . . . . . . | 186,000 | 0.022 |
| Buying expense . . . . . . . . . . . . . . . . . . . . . . . . . . . . . . . . . . . . . | 150,000 | 0.041 |
| Delivery expense . . . . . . . . . . . . . . . . . . . . . . . . . . . . . . . . . . . . | 111,000 | 0.008 |
| Credit and collection expense. . . . . . . . . . . . . . . . . . . . . . . . . . | 72,000 | 0.002 |
| Administrative expense. . . . . . . . . . . . . . . . . . . . . . . . . . . . . . . | 531,000 | 0.003 |
| Totals . . . . . . . . . . . . . . . . . . . . . . . . . . . . . . . . . . . . . . . . . . | $1,260,000 | $0.758 |

Management expected to attain a sales level of $12 million during the current year. At the end of the year, the actual results achieved by the company were as follows:

| | |
|---|---|
| Net sales . . . . . . . . . . . . . . . . . . . . . . . . . . . . . . . . . . . . . . . . . . . . . . . . . . | $10,500,000 |
| Cost of goods sold . . . . . . . . . . . . . . . . . . . . . . . . . . . . . . . . . . . . . . . . . . . | 6,180,000 |
| Selling and promotion expense . . . . . . . . . . . . . . . . . . . . . . . . . . . . . . . . . | 1,020,000 |
| Building occupancy expense . . . . . . . . . . . . . . . . . . . . . . . . . . . . . . . . . . . | 420,000 |
| Buying expense . . . . . . . . . . . . . . . . . . . . . . . . . . . . . . . . . . . . . . . . . . . . . . | 594,000 |
| Delivery expense . . . . . . . . . . . . . . . . . . . . . . . . . . . . . . . . . . . . . . . . . . . . | 183,000 |
| Credit and collection expense . . . . . . . . . . . . . . . . . . . . . . . . . . . . . . . . . . | 90,000 |
| Administrative expense . . . . . . . . . . . . . . . . . . . . . . . . . . . . . . . . . . . . . . . | 564,000 |

### Instructions

**a.** Prepare a schedule comparing the actual results with flexible budget amounts developed for the actual sales volume of $10,500,000. Organize your schedule as a partial multiple-step income statement, ending with operating income. Include separate columns for (1) flexible budget amounts, (2) actual amounts, and (3) any amount over (under) budget. Use the cost-volume relationships given in the problem to compute the flexible budget amounts.

**1028**

**b.** Write a statement evaluating the company's performance in relation to the plan reflected in the flexible budget.

**PROBLEM 23.8A**

Flexible Budgeting

eXcel

through

Braemar Saddlery uses department budgets and performance reports in planning and controlling its manufacturing operations. The following annual performance report for the custom saddle production department was presented to the president of the company:

| | Budgeted Costs for 5,000 Units | | Actual Costs Incurred | Over (Under) Budget |
|---|---|---|---|---|
| | Per Unit | Total | | |
| **Variable manufacturing costs:** | | | | |
| Direct materials . . . . . . . . . . . . . . . . . . . . . | $ 30.00 | $150,000 | $171,000 | $21,000 |
| Direct labor . . . . . . . . . . . . . . . . . . . . . . . | 48.00 | 240,000 | 261,500 | 21,500 |
| Indirect labor . . . . . . . . . . . . . . . . . . . . . . | 15.00 | 75,000 | 95,500 | 20,500 |
| Indirect materials, supplies, etc. . . . . . . . . . | 9.00 | 45,000 | 48,400 | 3,400 |
| Total variable manufacturing costs . . . . . . | $102.00 | $510,000 | $576,400 | $66,400 |
| **Fixed manufacturing costs:** | | | | |
| Lease rental . . . . . . . . . . . . . . . . . . . . . . | $ 9.00 | $ 45,000 | $ 45,000 | –0– |
| Salaries of foremen . . . . . . . . . . . . . . . . . | 24.00 | 120,000 | 125,000 | $ 5,000 |
| Depreciation and other . . . . . . . . . . . . . . . | 15.00 | 75,000 | 78,600 | 3,600 |
| Total fixed manufacturing costs . . . . . . . . | $ 48.00 | $240,000 | $248,600 | $ 8,600 |
| Total manufacturing costs . . . . . . . . . . . . . . | $150.00 | $750,000 | $825,000 | $75,000 |

Although a production volume of 5,000 saddles was originally budgeted for the year, the actual volume of production achieved for the year was *6,000* saddles. Direct materials and direct labor are charged to production at actual cost. Factory overhead is applied to production at the predetermined rate of 150 percent of the actual direct labor cost.

After a quick glance at the performance report showing an unfavorable manufacturing cost variance of $75,000, the president said to the accountant: "Fix this thing so it makes sense. It looks as though our production people really blew the budget. Remember that we exceeded our budgeted production schedule by a significant margin. I want this performance report to show a better picture of our ability to control costs."

**Instructions**

**a.** Prepare a revised performance report for the year on a flexible budget basis. Use the same format as the production report above, but revise the budgeted cost figures to reflect the actual production level of *6,000* saddles.

**b.** Briefly comment on Braemar's ability to control its variable manufacturing costs.

**c.** What is the amount of over- or underapplied manufacturing overhead for the year?

## Problem Set B

**PROBLEM 23.1B**

Budgeting Production, Inventories, and Cost of Sales

Frowren Domestic manufactures and sells a single product. In preparing its master budget for the current quarter, the company's controller has assembled the following information:

| | Units | Dollars |
|---|---|---|
| Sales (budgeted) . . . . . . . . . . . . . . . . . . . . . . . . . . . . . . . . . . . . . . . . | 200,000 | $8,000,000 |
| Finished goods inventory, beginning of quarter . . . . . . . . . . . . . . . | 30,000 | 750,000 |
| Finished goods inventory, end of quarter . . . . . . . . . . . . . . . . . . . . . | 25,000 | ? |
| Cost of finished goods manufactured (assume a budgeted manufacturing cost of $26 per unit) . . . . . . . . . . . . . . . . | ? | ? |

Frowren Domestic used the average cost method of pricing its inventory of finished goods.

## Instructions

Compute the following budgeted quantities or dollar amounts:

a. Planned production of finished goods (in units).

b. Cost of finished goods manufactured.

c. Ending finished goods inventory. (Remember that in using the average cost method you first must compute the average cost of units available for sale.)

d. Cost of goods sold.

**L04 PROBLEM 23.2B**
**L05** Short Budgeting Problem

Melody Corporation manufactures and sells a single product. In preparing the budget for the first quarter, the company's cost accountant has assembled the following information:

|  | Units | Dollars |
|---|---|---|
| Sales (budgeted) . . . . . . . . . . . . . . . . . . . . . . . . . . . . . . . . . . . . . | 200,000 | $15,000,000 |
| Finished goods inventory, Jan. 1 (actual) . . . . . . . . . . . . . . . . . . . . | 40,000 | 1,440,000 |
| Finished goods inventory, Mar. 31 (budgeted) . . . . . . . . . . . . . . . . | 30,000 | ? |
| Cost of finished goods manufactured (budgeted manufacturing cost is $38 per unit) . . . . . . . . . . . . . . . . . . . . . . | ? | ? |

The company uses the first-in, first-out method of pricing its inventory of finished goods.

## Instructions

Compute the following budgeted quantities or dollar amounts:

a. Planned production of finished goods (in units).

b. Cost of finished goods manufactured.

c. Finished goods inventory, March 31. (Remember to use the first-in, first-out method in pricing the inventory.)

d. Cost of goods sold.

**L04 PROBLEM 23.3B**
**L05** Budgeting for Cash

Barley, Inc., wants a projection of cash receipts and cash payments for the month of November. On November 28, a note will be payable in the amount of $102,250, including interest. The cash balance on November 1 is $37,200. Accounts payable to merchandise creditors at the end of October were $206,000.

The company's experience indicates that 70 percent of sales will be collected during the month of sale, 25 percent in the month following the sale, and 3 percent in the second month following the sale; 2 percent will be uncollectible. The company sells various products at an average price of $10 per unit. Selected sales figures are as follows:

|  | Units |
|---|---|
| Sept.—actual . . . . . . . . . . . . . . . . . . . . . . . . . . . . . . . . . . . . . . . . . . . . . . . . . . . . | 50,000 |
| Oct.—actual . . . . . . . . . . . . . . . . . . . . . . . . . . . . . . . . . . . . . . . . . . . . . . . . . . . . . . | 70,000 |
| Nov.—estimated . . . . . . . . . . . . . . . . . . . . . . . . . . . . . . . . . . . . . . . . . . . . . . . . . | 90,000 |
| Dec.—estimated . . . . . . . . . . . . . . . . . . . . . . . . . . . . . . . . . . . . . . . . . . . . . . . . . | 60,000 |
| Total estimated for the current year . . . . . . . . . . . . . . . . . . . . . . . . . . . . . . . . . . | 900,000 |

Because purchases are payable within 15 days, approximately 50 percent of the purchases in a given month are paid in the following month. The average cost of units purchased is $6 per unit. Inventories at the end of each month are maintained at a level of 2,000 units plus 10 percent of the number of units that will be sold in the following month. The inventory on October 1 amounted to 9,000 units.

Budgeted operating expenses for November are $225,000. Of this amount, $100,000 is considered fixed (including depreciation of $40,000). All operating expenses, other than depreciation, are paid in the month in which they are incurred.

The company expects to sell fully depreciated equipment in November for $9,000 cash.

## Instructions

Prepare a cash budget for the month of November, supported by schedules of cash collections on accounts receivable and cash payments for purchases of merchandise.

**1030**

**L01**  **PROBLEM 23.4B**
**L02**  Estimating Borrowing
Requirements
**L04**
**L05**

Peter Corporation sells its products to a single customer. At the beginning of the current quarter, the company reports the following selected account balances:

| | |
|---|---|
| Cash . . . . . . . . . . . . . . . . . . . . . . . . . . . . . . . . . . . . . . . . . . . . . . . . . . . . . . . . . . . . . | $ 10,000 |
| Accounts receivable . . . . . . . . . . . . . . . . . . . . . . . . . . . . . . . . . . . . . . . . . . . . . . . | 250,000 |
| Current payables . . . . . . . . . . . . . . . . . . . . . . . . . . . . . . . . . . . . . . . . . . . . . . . . . . | 90,000 |

Peter's management has made the following budget estimates regarding operations for the current quarter:

| | |
|---|---|
| Sales (estimated) . . . . . . . . . . . . . . . . . . . . . . . . . . . . . . . . . . . . . . . . . . . . . . . . . . | $700,000 |
| Total costs and expenses (estimated) . . . . . . . . . . . . . . . . . . . . . . . . . . . . . . . . . | 500,000 |
| Debt service payment (estimated) . . . . . . . . . . . . . . . . . . . . . . . . . . . . . . . . . . . . | 260,000 |
| Tax liability payment (estimated) . . . . . . . . . . . . . . . . . . . . . . . . . . . . . . . . . . . . . | 50,000 |

Of Peter's total costs and expenses, $40,000 is quarterly depreciation expense, and $18,000 represents the expiration of prepayments. The remaining $442,000 is to be financed with current payables. The company's ending prepayments balance is expected to be the same as its beginning prepayments balance. Its ending current payables balance is expected to be $15,000 more than its beginning balance.

All of Peter's sales are on account. Approximately 70 percent of its sales are collected in the quarter in which they are made. The remaining 30 percent are collected in the following quarter. Because all of the company's sales are made to a single customer, it experiences virtually no uncollectible accounts.

Peter's minimum cash balance requirement is $10,000. Should the balance fall below this amount, management negotiates a short-term loan with a local bank. The company's debt ratio (liabilities ÷ assets) is currently 90 percent.

**Instructions**

a.  Compute Peter's budgeted cash receipts for the quarter.

b.  Compute Peter's payments of current payables budgeted for the quarter.

c.  Compute Peter's cash prepayments budgeted for the quarter.

d.  Prepare Peter's cash budget for the quarter.

e.  Estimate Peter's short-term borrowing requirements for the quarter.

f.  Discuss problems Peter might encounter in obtaining short-term financing.

**L01**  **PROBLEM 23.5B**
**L02**  Budgeted Income
Statement and Cash
Budget
**L04**
**L05**

Synder's has been in business since January of the current year. The company buys fresh pasta and resells it to large supermarket chains in five states. The following information pertains to Synder's first four months of operations:

| | Purchases | Sales |
|---|---|---|
| Jan. . . . . . . . . . . . . . . . . . . . . . . . . . . . . . . . . . . . . . . . . . . . . | $50,000 | $80,000 |
| Feb. . . . . . . . . . . . . . . . . . . . . . . . . . . . . . . . . . . . . . . . . . . . . | 40,000 | 60,000 |
| Mar. . . . . . . . . . . . . . . . . . . . . . . . . . . . . . . . . . . . . . . . . . . . | 55,000 | 90,000 |
| Apr. . . . . . . . . . . . . . . . . . . . . . . . . . . . . . . . . . . . . . . . . . . . . | 25,000 | 40,000 |

Synder's expects to open several new sales territories in May. In anticipation of increased volume, management forecasts May sales at $100,000. To meet this demand, purchases in May are budgeted at $60,000. The company maintains a gross profit margin of approximately 40 percent.

All of Synder's sales are on account. Due to strict credit policies, the company has no bad debt expense. The following collection performance is anticipated for the remainder of the year:

| | |
|---|---|
| Percent collected in month of sale . . . . . . . . . . . . . . . . . . . . . . . . . . . . . . . . . . . . . | 40% |
| Percent collected in month following sale . . . . . . . . . . . . . . . . . . . . . . . . . . . . . . . . | 50 |
| Percent collected in the second month following sale . . . . . . . . . . . . . . . . . . . . . . | 10 |

Synder's normally pays for 75 percent of its purchases in the month that the purchases are made. The remaining amount is paid in the following month. The company's fixed selling and administrative expenses average $10,000 per month. Of this amount, $3,000 is depreciation expense. Variable selling and administrative expenses are budgeted at 5 percent of sales. The company pays all of its selling and administrative expenses in the month that they are incurred.

Synder's debt service is $4,000 per month. Of this amount, approximately $3,000 represents interest expense, and $1,000 is payment on the principal. The company's tax rate is approximately 25 percent. Quarterly tax payments are made at the end of March, June, September, and December.

### Instructions

a. Prepare Synder's budgeted income statement for May.

b. Prepare Synder's cash budget for May. Assume that the company's cash balance on May 1 is $30,000.

c. What are the primary benefits that Synder's will gain from preparing and using a budget?

**L01**
**L02**
**L04**
**L05**

## PROBLEM 23.6B

Preparing a Cash Budget

Ann Hoffman, owner of Hoffman Industries, is negotiating with the bank for a $250,000, 90-day, 15 percent loan effective July 1 of the current year. If the bank grants the loan, the net proceeds will be $240,000, which Hoffman intends to use on July 1 as follows: pay accounts payable, $200,000; purchase equipment, $25,000; and add to bank balance, $15,000.

The current working capital position of Hoffman Industries, according to financial statements as of June 30, is as follows:

| | |
|---|---|
| Cash in bank | $ 18,000 |
| Receivables (net of allowance for doubtful accounts) | 200,000 |
| Merchandise inventory | 80,000 |
| Total current assets | $298,000 |
| Accounts payable (including accrued operating expenses) | 160,000 |
| Working capital | $138,000 |

The bank loan officer asks Hoffman to prepare a forecast of her cash receipts and cash payments for the next three months to demonstrate that the loan can be repaid at the end of September.

Hoffman has made the following estimates, which are to be used in preparing a three-month cash budget: Sales (all on account) for July, $340,000; August, $360,000; September, $300,000; and October, $220,000. Past experience indicates that 75 percent of the receivables generated in any month will be collected in the month following the sale, 24 percent will be collected in the second month following the sale, and 1 percent will prove uncollectible. Hoffman expects to collect $160,000 of the June 30 receivables in July and the remaining $40,000 in August.

Cost of goods sold consistently has averaged about 65 percent of sales. Operating expenses are budgeted at $40,000 per month plus 10 percent of sales. With the exception of $5,000 per month depreciation expense, all operating expenses and purchases are on account and are paid in the month following their incurrence.

Merchandise inventory at the end of each month should be sufficient to cover the following month's sales.

### Instructions

a. Ann Hoffman has contacted you to prepare a cash budget showing estimated cash receipts and cash payments for July, August, and September. First, you must prepare the following schedules:

1. Estimated cash collections on receivables.

2. Estimated merchandise purchases.

3. Estimated cash payments for operating expenses.

4. Estimated cash payments on accounts payable (including operating expenses).

b. Once the schedules have been prepared, complete the cash budgets for July, August, and September showing the cash balance at the end of each month.

**LO2** **LO4** through **LO6**

**PROBLEM 23.7B**
Preparing and Using a
Flexible Budget

Eight Flags is a retail department store. The following cost-volume relationships were used in developing a flexible budget for the company for the current year:

| | Yearly Fixed Expenses | Variable Expenses per Sales Dollar |
|---|---|---|
| Cost of merchandise sold | | $0.65 |
| Selling and promotion expense | $160,000 | 0.09 |
| Building occupancy expense | 120,000 | 0.02 |
| Buying expense | 100,000 | 0.05 |
| Delivery expense | 110,000 | 0.01 |
| Credit and collection expense | 60,000 | 0.01 |
| Administrative expense | 300,000 | 0.02 |
| Totals | $850,000 | $0.85 |

Management expected to attain a sales level of $20 million during the current year. At the end of the year, the actual results achieved by the company were as follows:

| | |
|---|---|
| Net sales | $18,000,000 |
| Cost of goods sold | 11,160,000 |
| Selling and promotion expense | 800,000 |
| Building occupancy expense | 450,000 |
| Buying expense | 720,000 |
| Delivery expense | 200,000 |
| Credit and collection expense | 100,000 |
| Administrative expense | 360,000 |

**Instructions**

a. Prepare a schedule comparing the actual results with flexible budget amounts developed for the actual sales volume of $18,000,000. Organize your schedule as a partial multiple-step income statement, ending with operating income. Include separate columns for (**1**) flexible budget amounts, (**2**) actual amounts, and (**3**) any amount over (under) budget. Use the cost-volume relationships given in the problem to compute the flexible budget amounts.

b. Write a statement evaluating the company's performance in relation to the plan reflected in the flexible budget.

c. Why is a flexible budget useful in evaluating the performance of the Eight Flags store?

d. Do fixed costs and variable costs always change in a flexible budget?

**LO2** **LO4** through **LO6**

**PROBLEM 23.8B**
Flexible Budgeting

XL Industries uses department budgets and performance reports in planning and controlling its manufacturing operations. The following annual performance report for the widget production department was presented to the president of the company:

| | Budgeted Costs for 4,000 Units | | Actual Costs Incurred | Over (Under) Budget |
|---|---|---|---|---|
| | Per Unit | Total | | |
| Variable manufacturing costs: | | | | |
| Direct materials | $ 25.00 | $100,000 | $120,000 | $20,000 |
| Direct labor | 50.00 | 200,000 | 210,000 | 10,000 |
| Indirect labor | 12.00 | 48,000 | 50,000 | 2,000 |
| Indirect materials, supplies, etc. | 10.00 | 40,000 | 43,000 | 3,000 |
| Total variable manufacturing costs | $ 97.00 | $388,000 | $423,000 | $35,000 |
| Fixed manufacturing costs: | | | | |
| Lease rental | $ 10.00 | $ 40,000 | $ 40,000 | –0– |
| Salaries of foremen | 25.00 | 100,000 | 104,000 | $ 4,000 |
| Depreciation and other | 18.00 | 72,000 | 75,000 | 3,000 |
| Total fixed manufacturing costs | $ 53.00 | $212,000 | $219,000 | $ 7,000 |
| Total manufacturing costs | $150.00 | $600,000 | $642,000 | $42,000 |

Although a production volume of 4,000 widgets was originally budgeted for the year, the actual volume of production achieved for the year was *5,000* widgets. Direct materials and direct labor are charged to production at actual costs. Factory overhead is applied to production at the predetermined rate of 150 percent of the actual direct labor cost.

After a quick glance at the performance report showing an unfavorable manufacturing cost variance of $42,000, the president said to the accountant: "Fix this thing so it makes sense. It looks as though our production people really blew the budget. Remember that we exceeded our budgeted production schedule by a significant margin. I want this performance report to show a better picture of our ability to control costs."

**Instructions**

a. Prepare a revised performance report for the year on a flexible budget basis. Use the same format as the production report above, but revise the budgeted cost figures to reflect the actual production level of *5,000* widgets.

b. Briefly comment on XL's ability to control its variable manufacturing costs.

c. What is the amount of over- or underapplied manufacturing overhead for the year?

## Critical Thinking Cases

**L02**
**L05**

**CASE 23.1**

Budgeting in a Nutshell

The purpose of this problem is to demonstrate some of the interrelationships in the budgeting process. Shown below is a very simple balance sheet at January 1, along with a simple budgeted income statement for the month. (Assume dollar amounts are stated in thousands; you also may state dollar amounts in this manner.)

| NUTSHELL BALANCE SHEET JANUARY 1 | | | |
|---|---|---|---|
| **Assets** | | **Liabilities & Equity** | |
| Cash.......... | $ 40 | Accounts payable....... | $ 30 |
| Accounts receivable..... | 120 | Owners' equity ........ | 180 |
| Inventory ....... | 50 | | |
| Total.......... | $210 | Total.......... | $210 |

| NUTSHELL BUDGETED INCOME STATEMENT FOR JANUARY | |
|---|---|
| Sales ........... | $100 |
| Cost of goods sold ........... | 60 |
| Gross profit ....... | $ 40 |
| Expenses......... | 25 |
| Net income........ | $ 15 |

As Nutshell has no plant assets, there is no depreciation expense. Prepare a cash budget for January and a budgeted balance sheet as of January 31.

These budgets are to reflect *your own assumptions* as to the amounts of cash and credit sales, collections of receivables, purchases of inventory, and payments to suppliers. We require only that the cash balance be *$50* at January 31, that receivables and inventory *change* from the January 1 levels, and that the company engage in *no* "financing" or "investing" activities (as these terms are used in a statement of cash flows).

Clearly state your assumptions as part of your solution, and be prepared to explain in class how they result in the amounts shown in your budgets.

**L01**
**through**
**L03**

**CASE 23.2**

An Ethical Dilemma

Beta Computers is experiencing financial difficulties attributed to declining sales of its mainframe computer systems. Several years ago, the company obtained a large loan from Midland State Bank. The covenants of the loan agreement strictly state that if Beta is unable to maintain a current ratio of 3:1, a quick ratio of 1:1, and a return on assets of 12 percent, the bank will exercise its right to liquidate the company's assets in settlement of the loan. To monitor Beta's performance, the bank demands quarterly financial statements that have been reviewed by an independent CPA.

Nick Price, Beta's CEO, has just reviewed the company's master budget projections for the first two quarters of the current year. What he has learned is disturbing. If sales trends continue, it appears that Beta will be in violation of its loan covenants by the end of the second quarter. If

**1034** Chapter 23 Operational Budgeting

these projections are correct, the bank might foreclose on the company's assets. As a consequence, Beta's 750 employees will join the ranks of the unemployed.

In February of the current year, Rembrant International contacted Beta to inquire about purchasing a custom-configured mainframe computer system. Not only would the sale generate over a million dollars in revenue, it would put Beta back in compliance with its loan covenants. Unfortunately, Rembrant International is an extremely bad credit risk, and the likelihood of collecting on the sale is slim. Nonetheless, Nick Price approved the sale on February 1, which resulted in the recording of a $1.4 million receivable.

On March 31, Edgar Gamm, CPA, arrived at Beta's headquarters. In Gamm's opinion, the $1.4 million receivable from Rembrant International should immediately be written off as uncollectible. Of course, if the account is written off, Beta will be in violation of its loan covenants and the bank will soon foreclose. Gamm told Price that it is his professional duty to prevent any material misstatement of the company's assets.

Price reminded Gamm that if the account is written off, 750 employees will be out of work, and that Gamm's accounting firm probably could not collect its fee for this engagement. Price then showed Gamm Beta's master budget for the third and fourth quarters of the current year. The budget indicated a complete turnaround for the company. Gamm suspected, however, that most of the budget's estimates were overly optimistic.

### Instructions

With a group of students answer the following questions:

**a.** Should Gamm insist that the Rembrant International account be classified as uncollectible? Should the optimistic third and fourth quarter master budget projections influence his decision? What would you do if you were in his position? Defend your actions.

**b.** If you were the president of Midland State Bank, what would you do if you discovered that the Rembrant International account constituted a large portion of Beta's reported liquid assets and sales activity for the quarter? How would you react if Edgar Gamm's accounting firm had permitted Beta to classify the account as collectible?

**CASE 23.3**

Cash Budgeting

The importance of cash budgets for all types of businesses and individuals cannot be overemphasized. The following six steps to cash flow control are critical.

1. Create a monthly cash flow budget. Determine the amount you need to achieve your business and personal financial goals, including enough to pay taxes and fund your retirement.

2. At the end of each month compare cash inflows and outflows to make necessary adjustments to cash spending or saving.

3. Accounting software can help automate the process.

4. Set aside cash each month to pay your taxes on time.

5. Make quarterly contributions to a retirement account.

6. Establish a line of credit with a bank, or investigate other short-term financing sources, well before you think you'll need the extra cash.

### Instructions

**a.** Assume for item number 2 that a business's actual cash flows are not enough to achieve its business goals and some necessary adjustments must be made. Name at least four adjustment procedures that businesses can use to equalize cash flows.

**b.** Write a short paragraph discussing how cash budgeting can be critical for your ongoing success.

 **INTERNET CASE 23.4**

 Budgeting Shareware

**Medlin Accounting Shareware** produces accounting programs that Internet users can download and try for free. Access the Medlin Web site at:

www.medlin.com/budget.htm

Investigate the Medlin budgeting package.

### Instructions

a.  What features are provided with the budgeting software?

b.  Explain how the features can be used for (**1**) advance warning and assignment of responsibility for corrective action, (**2**) coordination of activities among all departments within the organization, or (**3**) the creation of standards for evaluating performance.

*Internet sites are time and date sensitive. It is the purpose of these exercises to have you explore the Internet. You may need to use the Yahoo! search engine* http://www.yahoo.com *(or another favorite search engine) to find a company's current Web address.*

**L04**  **CASE 23.5**

Budgeting and
Internal Controls

Under the Public Company Accounting Oversight Board (PCAOB) procedures, companies are required to disclose "material weaknesses" in their internal controls. A material weakness means a company's deficiencies are so bad that there's more than a remote chance of a material misstatement in its financial reports. An example is when a bank does not regularly check for errors in estimating loan-loss expenses. This type of undetected error, for instance, could be rooted in a formula in a computer spreadsheet that budgets how lending will be affected by interest rate changes. Fannie Mae, the mortgage finance company, reported a $1.3 billion error from its computer models prior to a large accounting scandal. Some auditors are reporting that the material weaknesses they are seeing are the result of flawed checks on formulas used to figure, for example, income tax expense.

### Instructions

Consider how errors in formulas, embedded in linked budgeting spreadsheets and used to estimate sales each quarter, can impact the budgeting process.

a.  Use Exhibit 23–2 to trace how errors can permeate the various budgets of a company. Explain how an error that causes a material overstatement of budgeted sales will affect other budgets for the organization.

b.  Explain how the PCAOB requirements to evaluate internal controls can improve the budgeting process at a company.

## Answers to Self-Test Questions

1.  a, b, c    2.   b (70,000 units $\times$ $10 per unit $\times$ 80%) + ($100,000 $\times$ 50%) = $610,000
3.  d    **4.**  c    **5.**  d    **6.**  c

# CHAPTER 26

# Capital Budgeting

AFTER STUDYING THIS CHAPTER, YOU SHOULD BE ABLE TO:

**L01** Explain the nature of capital investment decisions.

**L02** Identify nonfinancial factors in capital investment decisions.

**L03** Evaluate capital investment proposals using (a) payback period, (b) return on investment, and (c) discounted cash flows.

**L04** Discuss the relationship between net present value and an investor's required rate of return.

**L05** Explain the behavioral issues involved in capital budgeting and identify how companies try to control the capital budgeting process.

## Learning Objectives

## GENERAL ELECTRIC COMPANY

GE traces its beginnings to Thomas A. Edison, who established Edison Electric Light Company in 1878. In 1892, a manager of Edison General Electric Company and Thomson-Houston Electric Company created General Electric Company. GE currently operates in more than 100 countries, employs about 300,000 people worldwide, and is one of the most admired companies in the world for its innovativeness, sustainability leadership, and ethical reputation.

Currently, GE has new initiatives under way focused on developing countries. The idea is to take the needs of consumers in developing countries as a starting point for innovation and work backward. The initiatives have been dubbed "reverse innovation." Other terms are "frugal" or "constraint-based" innovation. Frugal innovation is not just about redesigning products; it involves rethinking entire production processes and business models. Companies need to squeeze costs so they can reach many more customers, and accept thin profit margins to gain volume. In order to bring these frugal innovations to market, companies like GE use a process of careful planning called capital budgeting. ∎

## Capital Investment Decisions

**Learning Objective**

**L01** Explain the nature of capital investment decisions.

One of the greatest challenges managers face is making capital investment decisions. The term **capital investment** refers broadly to large expenditures made to purchase plant assets, develop new product lines, or acquire subsidiary companies. Such decisions commit financial resources for large periods of time and are difficult, if not impossible, to reverse once the funds are invested. Thus, companies stand to benefit from good capital investments (or suffer from poor ones) for many years.

The process of evaluating and prioritizing capital investment opportunities is called **capital budgeting.** Capital budgeting relies heavily on *estimates of future operating results.* These estimates often involve a considerable degree of uncertainty and should be evaluated accordingly. In addition, many *nonfinancial* factors are taken into consideration.

### FINANCIAL AND NONFINANCIAL CONSIDERATIONS

**Learning Objective**

**L02** Identify nonfinancial factors in capital investment decisions.

Perhaps the most important financial consideration in capital budgeting is the expected effects on *future cash flows* and *future profitability.* But in some cases, nonfinancial considerations are the deciding factor.

Exhibit 26–1 provides a few examples of capital investment proposals in which *nonfinancial* factors may be the primary consideration.

**Exhibit 26–1**

**NONFINANCIAL FACTORS IN CAPITAL EXPENDITURES**

| Investment Proposal | Nonfinancial Considerations |
| --- | --- |
| Pollution control system | Environmental concerns<br>Corporate image |
| New factory lighting | Better working conditions<br>Product quality |
| Employee health club | Employee morale<br>Healthier employees |
| Employee child care facility | Accommodate working parents<br>Enhance scheduling flexibility |

We will now address three widely used methods of evaluating the *financial* aspects of capital investment proposals: payback period, return on average investment, and discounting future cash flows.

### EVALUATING CAPITAL INVESTMENT PROPOSALS: AN ILLUSTRATION

To illustrate the application of capital budgeting techniques, we will evaluate two investments being considered by the Maine LobStars (commonly referred to as the Stars), a minor league baseball team from Portland, Maine. The first involves the purchase of 10 vending machines for the team's Portland stadium. The second involves the purchase of a new bus to replace the one currently in use.

The Stars' stadium currently has no concession stand for preparing and selling food during games. Steve Wilson, the team's owner, has received several bids for constructing a concession stand under the stadium bleachers. The low bid of $150,000 includes a 1,000-square-foot cement block building, equipped with cash registers, deep fryers, a grill, soda machines, and a walk-in freezer and cooler. Unfortunately, the most that the struggling organization is willing to invest for this purpose is $75,000.

Wilson recently received an alternative proposal from VendiCorp International. Vendi-Corp sells vending machines that dispense hot and cold sandwiches and drinks. The company has offered to sell 10 vending machines to the Stars for $75,000 ($7,500 each). While the machines are in use, VendiCorp is responsible for keeping them stocked with sandwiches and drinks. At the end of a five-year estimated life, VendiCorp will repurchase the machines for $5,000 ($500 each). VendiCorp will also provide the Stars with an insurance and maintenance contract costing $3,000 per year.

Estimates provided by VendiCorp indicate that the 10 machines will take in $1,875 per ball game. The Stars play 45 home games each season. Thus, the machines have the potential to generate annual revenue of $84,375 ($1,875 per game × 45 games). Of this amount, Vendi-Corp is to receive $50,625, representing the cost of goods sold (60 percent of sales). The Stars are required to reimburse VendiCorp only for those items that sell. As shown in Exhibit 26–2, the machines are expected to increase the Stars's net income by $10,000 per year.

| Estimated Increases in Annual Revenue and Expenses from Vending Machines | | |
|---|---:|---:|
| Increase in annual revenue from investment | | $84,375 |
| Less: Cost of goods sold (60% of sales paid to VendiCorp) | | 50,625 |
| Increase in annual gross profit (40% of sales) | | $33,750 |
| Less: Cost of maintenance & insurance contract | $ 3,000 | |
| Depreciation [($75,000 − $5,000) ÷ 5 years] | 14,000 | |
| Increase in utilities & miscellaneous costs | 350 | 17,350 |
| Increase in annual pretax operating income from investment | | $16,400 |
| Less: Additional income taxes (approximately 39%) | | 6,400 |
| Increase in annual net income from investment | | $10,000 |

**Exhibit 26–2**

**INCREASE IN STARS' NET INCOME BECAUSE OF VENDING MACHINES**

Most capital budgeting techniques involve analysis of the *annual net cash flows* pertaining to an investment. Annual net cash flows refer to the excess of cash receipts over cash disbursements in a given year. We may assume in our example that all of the vending machine revenue is received in cash, and that all expenses (other than depreciation) are immediately paid in cash. In other words, the *only difference* between net income and net cash flows relates to depreciation expense.

The annual net cash flows expected to be generated by the vending machines are $24,000, determined as follows:

| | |
|---|---:|
| Increase in annual net income from investment | $10,000 |
| Annual depreciation expense | 14,000 |
| Annual net cash flows from investment | $24,000 |

This computation reflects the fact that depreciation is a *noncash expense*. Because depreciation expense decreases annual net income from an investment, it must be added back to annual net income to find the annual net cash flows.

In our example, the vending machines are expected to increase *both* net income and net cash flows. But the real question is whether these increases *are adequate to justify the required investment*. We will attempt to answer this question using three different capital budgeting techniques.

## PAYBACK PERIOD

The **payback period** is the length of time necessary to recover the entire cost of an investment from the resulting annual net cash flows. In our example, the payback period is computed as follows:

$$\frac{\text{Amount to Be Invested}}{\text{Estimated Annual Net Cash Flows}} = \frac{\$75,000}{\$24,000} = 3.125 \text{ years}$$

Payback calculation

In the selection among alternative investment opportunities, a short payback period is considered desirable because the more quickly an investment's cost is recovered, the sooner the funds may be put to other use. A short payback period also reduces the risk that changes in economic conditions will prevent full recovery of an investment.

However, the payback period should never be the only factor considered in a major capital budgeting decision because it ignores two important issues. First, it ignores the total profitability and cash flows anticipated over the *entire life* of an investment (in this case, five years). Second, it ignores the *timing* of the future cash flows. We will address this issue in greater depth later in the chapter.

## RETURN ON AVERAGE INVESTMENT

The **return on average investment (ROI)** is the average annual net income from an investment expressed as a percentage of the *average* amount invested.[1] The Stars will initially have to invest $75,000 to purchase 10 new vending machines. However, each year depreciation expense will reduce the carrying value of these machines by a total of $14,000. Because the annual net cash flow is expected to exceed net income by this amount, we may view depreciation expense as providing for the *recovery* of the amount originally invested. The amount that the Stars will have invested in the equipment at any given time is represented by the carrying value of the vending machines (their cost less accumulated depreciation).

When straight-line depreciation is used, the carrying value of an asset decreases uniformly over the asset's life. Thus, the average carrying value over the life of an asset is equal to the amount halfway between its original cost and its salvage value. If the salvage value is zero, the average carrying value (or average investment) is simply one-half of the asset's original cost.

Mathematically, the average amount invested over the life of an asset may be determined as follows:

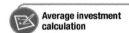
Average investment calculation

$$\text{Average Investment} = \frac{\text{Original Cost} + \text{Salvage Value}}{2}$$

Thus, over the life of the 10 new vending machines, the Stars will have an average investment of ($75,000 + $5,000) ÷ 2, or *$40,000*. We may compute the expected return on average investment as follows:

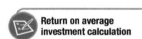
Return on average investment calculation

$$\frac{\text{Average Estimated Net Income}}{\text{Average Investment}} = \frac{\$10,000}{\$40,000} = 25\%$$

In deciding whether 25 percent is a satisfactory rate of return, Wilson should consider such factors as the reliability of VendiCorp's forecasts of income and cash flows, the return available from other investment opportunities, and the Stars' cost of capital.[2] In comparing alternative investment opportunities, managers prefer the one with the *lowest risk*, the *highest rate of return*, and the *shortest payback period*.

The concept of return on investment shares a common weakness with the payback method. It fails to consider that the **present value** of an investment depends on the *timing* of its future cash flows. Cash flows received late in the life of an investment, for example, are of *less value* to an investor today than cash flows of equal amount received early in the life of an investment. The return on investment computation simply ignores the question of whether cash receipts will occur early or late in the life of an investment. It also fails to consider whether the purchase price of the investment must be paid in advance or in installments stretching over a period of years. *Discounting* future cash flows is a technique that does take into account cash flow timing issues.

---

[1] In Chapter 25, ROI is defined as operating income divided by average investment. Operating income rather than net income is frequently used in ROI calculations designed to evaluate *historical* performance. Because interest on the investment and taxes are not controlled by the manager being evaluated, they are not included in the ROI calculations. However, when *future* investment performance is being evaluated, all related cash flows (including nonoperating interest and tax items) must be considered.

[2] A firm's cost of capital refers to the cost of financing investments. In situations where an investment is entirely financed with debt, the cost of capital is the interest rate paid by the firm on borrowed funds. For investments that are financed all or in part with equity, the computation is more complex. Approaches for determining a firm's cost of capital are addressed in a corporate finance course.

## DISCOUNTING FUTURE CASH FLOWS

As explained in earlier chapters, the present value of a future cash flow is the amount that a knowledgeable investor would pay today for the right to receive that future amount. Arriving at a present value figure depends on (1) the amount of the future cash flow, (2) the length of time that the investor must wait to receive the cash flow, and (3) the rate of return required by the investor. *Discounting* is the process by which the present value of cash flows (referred to as the **discounted cash flows**) is determined.

The use of present value tables to discount future cash flows is demonstrated in Appendix B (at the end of this text). Those who are not familiar with the concept of present value or with present value tables should read the appendix before continuing with this chapter.

For your convenience, the two present value tables presented in the appendix are repeated in this chapter. Exhibit 26–3 shows the present value of a *single lump-sum payment* of $1

**Learning Objective**

Evaluate capital investment proposals using (c) discounted cash flows.

**LO8**

### Present Value of $1 Due in *n* Periods*

| Number of Periods (n) | Discount Rate | | | | | | | | |
|---|---|---|---|---|---|---|---|---|---|
| | 1% | 1½% | 5% | 6% | 8% | 10% | 12% | 15% | 20% |
| 1 | .990 | .985 | .952 | .943 | .926 | .909 | .893 | .870 | .833 |
| 2 | .980 | .971 | .907 | .890 | .857 | .826 | .797 | .756 | .694 |
| 3 | .971 | .956 | .864 | .840 | .794 | .751 | .712 | .658 | .579 |
| 4 | .961 | .942 | .823 | .792 | .735 | .683 | .636 | .572 | .482 |
| 5 | .951 | .928 | .784 | .747 | .681 | .621 | .567 | .497 | .402 |
| 6 | .942 | .915 | .746 | .705 | .630 | .564 | .507 | .432 | .335 |
| 7 | .933 | .901 | .711 | .665 | .583 | .513 | .452 | .376 | .279 |
| 8 | .923 | .888 | .677 | .627 | .540 | .467 | .404 | .327 | .233 |
| 9 | .914 | .875 | .645 | .592 | .500 | .424 | .361 | .284 | .194 |
| 10 | .905 | .862 | .614 | .558 | .463 | .386 | .322 | .247 | .162 |
| 20 | .820 | .742 | .377 | .312 | .215 | .149 | .104 | .061 | .026 |
| 24 | .788 | .700 | .310 | .247 | .158 | .102 | .066 | .035 | .013 |
| 36 | .699 | .585 | .173 | .123 | .063 | .032 | .017 | .007 | .001 |

**Exhibit 26–3**

**PRESENT VALUE OF $1 PAYABLE IN *n* PERIODS**

*The present value of $1 is computed by the formula $p = 1/(1 + i)^n$, where $p$ is the present value of $1, $i$ is the discount rate, and $n$ is the number of periods until the future cash flow will occur. Amounts in this table have been rounded to three decimal places and are shown for a limited number of periods and discount rates. Many calculators are programmed to use this formula and can compute present values when the future amount is entered along with values for $i$ and $n$.

### Present Value of $1 to Be Received Periodically for *n* Periods

| Number of Periods (n) | Discount Rate | | | | | | | | |
|---|---|---|---|---|---|---|---|---|---|
| | 1% | 1½% | 5% | 6% | 8% | 10% | 12% | 15% | 20% |
| 1 | 0.990 | 0.985 | 0.952 | 0.943 | 0.926 | 0.909 | 0.893 | 0.870 | 0.833 |
| 2 | 1.970 | 1.956 | 1.859 | 1.833 | 1.783 | 1.736 | 1.690 | 1.626 | 1.528 |
| 3 | 2.941 | 2.912 | 2.723 | 2.673 | 2.577 | 2.487 | 2.402 | 2.283 | 2.106 |
| 4 | 3.902 | 3.854 | 3.546 | 3.465 | 3.312 | 3.170 | 3.037 | 2.855 | 2.589 |
| 5 | 4.853 | 4.783 | 4.329 | 4.212 | 3.993 | 3.791 | 3.605 | 3.352 | 2.991 |
| 6 | 5.795 | 5.697 | 5.076 | 4.917 | 4.623 | 4.355 | 4.111 | 3.784 | 3.326 |
| 7 | 6.728 | 6.598 | 5.786 | 5.582 | 5.206 | 4.868 | 4.564 | 4.160 | 3.605 |
| 8 | 7.652 | 7.486 | 6.463 | 6.210 | 5.747 | 5.335 | 4.968 | 4.487 | 3.837 |
| 9 | 8.566 | 8.361 | 7.108 | 6.802 | 6.247 | 5.759 | 5.328 | 4.772 | 4.031 |
| 10 | 9.471 | 9.222 | 7.722 | 7.360 | 6.710 | 6.145 | 5.650 | 5.019 | 4.192 |
| 20 | 18.046 | 17.169 | 12.462 | 11.470 | 9.818 | 8.514 | 7.469 | 6.259 | 4.870 |
| 24 | 21.243 | 20.030 | 13.799 | 12.550 | 10.529 | 8.985 | 7.784 | 6.434 | 4.937 |
| 36 | 30.108 | 27.661 | 16.547 | 14.621 | 11.717 | 9.677 | 8.192 | 6.623 | 4.993 |

**Exhibit 26–4**

**PRESENT VALUE OF A $1 ANNUITY RECEIVABLE EACH PERIOD FOR *n* PERIODS**

to be received in *n* periods (years) in the future. Exhibit 26–4 shows the present value of a $1 *annuity*—that is, $1 to be received *each year* for *n* consecutive years. For illustrative purposes, both tables have been kept short. They include only selected discount rates and only extend for a limited number of periods. However, they contain the appropriate rates and periods for all of the problem material in this chapter.

The **discount rate** may be viewed as an investor's *required rate of return.* The present value of an investment's future cash flows is the maximum amount that an investor should be willing to pay for the investment and still expect to earn the required rate of return. Therefore, an investment is considered desirable when its cost is less than the present value of its future cash flows. In such cases, the expected rate of return *exceeds* the rate of return required by the investor. Conversely, when the cost of an investment exceeds the present value of its future cash flows, its expected return is *less* than that required by the investor.

The higher the discount rate being used, the lower the resulting present value figure will be. It follows that, the *higher the required rate of return* for a particular investment, the *less* an investor will be willing to pay for the investment. The appropriate discount rate (or required rate of return) for determining the present value of a specific investment depends on the nature of the investment, the alternative investment opportunities available, and the investor's cost of capital.

The required rate of return is adjusted in many companies for a variety of strategic reasons. For example, management may allow a lower required rate of return when there is a strategic necessity to penetrate a new market or to acquire new technology. Also, for certain capital expenditures, such as new technology, estimating the cash flows and the timing of those cash flows can be extremely difficult. Managers know that establishing a high required rate of return will place projects with higher cash flows occurring in the more distant future at a disadvantage. Using a high discount rate for projects where high net cash flows are not received until several years in the future will result in low net present values.

Let us now apply the concept of discounting cash flows to our example. We shall assume that the Stars require a *15 percent* annual rate of return on all capital investments. As shown in Exhibit 26–5, the 10 vending machines are expected to generate annual net cash inflows of $24,000 for five years. Exhibit 26–4 shows that the present value of $1 to be received annually for five years, discounted at 15 percent, is *3.352.* Therefore, the present value of $24,000 received annually for five years is $24,000 × 3.352, or *$80,448.* Notice in Exhibit 26–5 that, even though the total annual cash inflows are $120,000, their present value is only $80,448.

In addition to these annual cash flows, Wilson expects that VendiCorp will repurchase the machines from the Stars at the end of five years for $5,000 (their salvage value). Referring to Exhibit 26–3, we see that the present value of $1 to be received in five years, discounted at 15 percent, is *.497.* Thus, the present value of $5,000 to be received at the end of five years

**Exhibit 26–5** **PRESENT VALUE OF CASH FLOWS FOR VENDICORP**

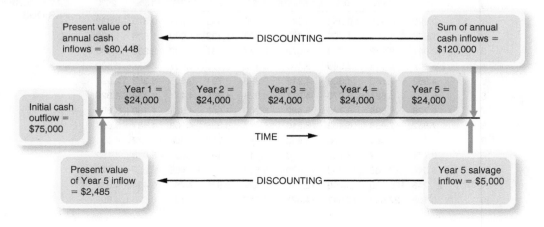

is $5,000 × .497, or *$2,485*. Using the information in Exhibit 26–5, we may now analyze the proposal to invest in the 10 vending machines in the following manner:

| | |
|---|---|
| Present value of expected annual cash flows ($24,000 × 3.352) . . . . . . . . . . . . . . | $80,448 |
| Present value of proceeds from disposal ($5,000 × .497) . . . . . . . . . . . . . . . . . . . | 2,485 |
| Total present value of investment's future cash flows . . . . . . . . . . . . . . . . . . . . . . . | $82,933 |
| Cost of investment (payable in advance) . . . . . . . . . . . . . . . . . . . . . . . . . . . . . . . | 75,000 |
| Net present value of proposed investment . . . . . . . . . . . . . . . . . . . . . . . . . . . . . . | $ 7,933 |

**Investment's net present value**

This analysis indicates that the present value of the vending machines' future cash flows, discounted at a rate of 15 percent, amounts to *$82,933*. This is the *maximum amount* that the Stars could invest in these machines and still expect to earn the required annual return of 15 percent. As the actual cost of the investment is only $75,000, the machines have the potential to earn a rate of return *in excess* of 15 percent.

The **net present value** of VendiCorp's proposal is the difference between the total present value of the net cash flows and the cost of the investment. If the net present value is equal to zero, the rate of return is equal to the discount rate. A *positive* net present value means that the investment is expected to provide a rate of return *greater* than the discount rate, whereas a *negative* net present value means that the investment is likely to yield a return *less* than the discount rate. In financial terms, proposals with a positive net present value are considered acceptable and those with a negative net present value are viewed as unacceptable. These relationships are summarized in Exhibit 26–6.

**Learning Objective**
Discuss the relationship between net present value and an investor's required rate of return.

L04

| Net Present Value (NPV) | Interpretation | Action |
|---|---|---|
| NPV > Zero | Return exceeds the discount rate. | Accept |
| NPV = Zero | Return is equal to the discount rate. | Accept |
| NPV < Zero | Return is less than the discount rate. | Reject |

**Exhibit 26–6**

**SUMMARY OF RELATIONSHIPS AMONG NPV, THE DISCOUNT RATE, AND PROJECT ACCEPTABILITY**

On the basis of our cash flow analysis, purchase of the vending machines appears to be an acceptable proposal. However, there are numerous nonfinancial issues that might be considered before making a decision based *purely on the numbers*.

For instance, all of the revenue and expense estimates used in determining these financial measures were supplied by VendiCorp. It is entirely possible that these estimates may be overly optimistic. Furthermore, Wilson knows nothing about VendiCorp's business reputation. What assurances does he have that VendiCorp will honor its agreement to stock the machines with fresh merchandise before each game, maintain the machines when they break down, and repurchase the machines for $5,000 at the end of five years? Has Wilson obtained bids from other suppliers of vending machines? Or has he considered an arrangement with an outside catering service to provide concessions at the Stars' home ball games? Finally, perhaps there are unrelated investment opportunities to consider, such as investing in a new pitching machine, team uniforms, or new stadium seats.

**YOUR TURN**     **You as a Chief Financial Officer**

You are attending your first meeting with the management team for the Maine LobStars. Your job is to discuss planned capital budgeting projects to get management's approval. Management, including the owner, Steve Wilson, is accustomed to looking at payback period and return on average assets. However, you have also prepared net present value information for management's review. Steve Wilson complains that the net present value information is redundant and unnecessary. How will you respond?

(See our comments on the Online Learning Center Web site.)

## REPLACING ASSETS

Many capital investment decisions involve the possible replacement of existing assets. Such decisions involve several decision-making techniques, including identifying *relevant information, incremental analysis,* and *discounting future cash flows.* Careful consideration also should be given to the *income tax effects* of the decision and to *nonfinancial factors.*

**Data for an Illustration**  To illustrate, assume the Maine LobStars own an old bus that transports the team from game to game. This old bus guzzles gas, frequently needs repair, has no air conditioning, and is cramped and uncomfortable. An opportunity arises to purchase another bus that, although used, is larger, in better condition, has air conditioning, and is more fuel efficient.

The financial data in Exhibit 26–7 relate to this capital investment proposal.

**Exhibit 26–7**

**DATA FOR BUS REPLACEMENT ANALYSIS AT MAINE LOBSTARS**

| | |
|---|---|
| Cost of new bus | $65,000 |
| Book value of existing bus | 25,000 |
| Current sales value of existing bus | 10,000 |
| Estimated annual operating costs (gas, repairs, insurance): | |
| New bus | 18,000 |
| Existing bus | 30,000 |

We will make a simplifying assumption that both buses have a remaining useful life of five years, with no salvage value.

Notice that the old bus has a book value of $25,000, but a current sales value of only $10,000. At first glance, the resulting *$15,000 loss* upon disposal appears to be an argument against replacing the old bus. But the cost of the old bus is a **sunk cost** and therefore is *not relevant* to the decision.

The current book value of the old bus is merely what remains of this sunk cost. If the old bus is sold, its book value is offset against the sale proceeds. But if the old bus is kept, its book value will be recognized as depreciation expense over the next five years. The Stars *cannot avoid* recognizing this cost as expense (or loss) *regardless of which decision is made.* From a present-value standpoint, there actually is some *benefit* to recognizing this sunk cost as a loss in the current period because the related *income tax deduction* will occur now, rather than over the remaining life of the bus.

In deciding whether to replace the old bus, the Stars should determine the present value of the *incremental net cash flows* resulting from this action. This present value may be compared with the cost of the new bus to determine whether the proposal will provide the required rate of return.

**Determining the Present Value of Incremental Cash Flows**  To compute the incremental annual cash flows from acquiring the new bus, we must consider both the annual savings in operating costs and the difference in *annual income taxes.* The Stars's annual income tax expense will be affected by purchasing the new bus because of the difference in annual operating expenses and in the annual deductions for depreciation. (To simplify our computations, we will assume the Stars use straight-line depreciation for tax purposes.)

The data in Exhibit 26–7 show that the new bus is expected to produce a $12,000 annual savings in operating costs. However, annual depreciation on the new bus will be $13,000 ($65,000 ÷ 5 years), whereas annual depreciation on the old bus is only $5,000 ($25,000 ÷ 5 years). This $8,000 increase in depreciation expense means that purchasing the new bus will *increase taxable income* by $4,000 per year ($12,000 annual cost savings, less $8,000 in additional depreciation expense). Assuming a tax rate of 40 percent, purchase of the new bus will *increase annual income tax expense* by *$1,600* ($4,000 × 40%). Thus, the incremental annual net cash flows from purchasing the new bus amount to *$10,400* ($12,000 savings in operating costs, less $1,600 in additional income taxes). Exhibit 26–8 shows the declining present value of each year's annual net cash savings in operating costs if the new bus is purchased.

The Stars require a 15 percent return on capital investments. Referring to the annuity table in Exhibit 26–4, we see that the present value of $1 received annually for five years is *3.352.* Therefore, the $10,400 received annually for five years, discounted at 15 percent, has a present value of *$34,861* ($10,400 × 3.352). In addition to the present value of the *annual* cash flows,

Exhibit 26-8  **DECLINING PRESENT VALUES OF THE ANNUAL COST SAVINGS FROM THE NEW LOBSTARS BUS**

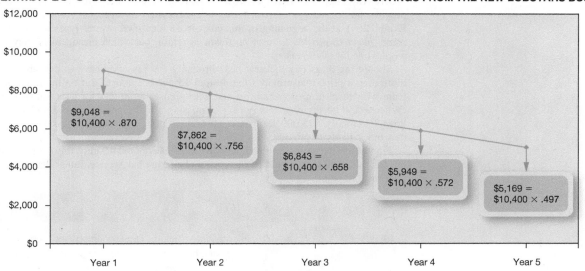

$9,048 =
$10,400 × .870

$7,862 =
$10,400 × .756

$6,843 =
$10,400 × .658

$5,949 =
$10,400 × .572

$5,169 =
$10,400 × .497

however, we should consider two other factors: the $10,000 sale proceeds from the old bus, and the tax savings resulting from the loss on disposal.

The $10,000 proceeds from the sale will be received immediately and, therefore, have a present value of *$10,000*. The $15,000 loss on disposal results in a $6,000 tax savings at the end of the first year ($15,000 × 40%). The present value of $6,000 one year hence, discounted at 15 percent, is *$5,220* ($6,000 × .870), as determined from Exhibit 26–3.

**Summary of Financial Considerations**   We now can determine the net present value of this proposal as follows:

| | |
|---|---|
| Present value of incremental annual cash flows | $ 34,861 |
| Present value of proceeds from sale of old bus | 10,000 |
| Present value of tax savings from loss on disposal | 5,220 |
| Total present value | $ 50,081 |
| Less: Cost of new bus | 65,000 |
| Net present value | $(14,919) |

This proposal fails to provide the Stars with its required minimum return on capital investments of 15 percent. (*Question:* What is the most that the Stars could pay for the new bus and earn a 15 percent return? *Answer:* $50,081, the present value of the cash flows, discounted at 15 percent.)

**YOUR TURN**        **You as a Transportation Manager**

Assume you manage transportation for the LobStars. You have just seen the proposal for acquiring the new bus with its accompanying financial figures. You know that the operating costs for the new bus will not be $18,000 per year but will more likely be $8,000, $12,000, $20,000, $24,000, and $26,000 for years 1 through 5, respectively. Do you have an ethical responsibility to mention this fact, given that operating costs average $18,000 over five years [($8,000 + $12,000 + $20,000 + $24,000 + $26,000) ÷ 5 = $18,000]?

(See our comments on the Online Learning Center Web site.)

**Nonfinancial Considerations**    Just because a capital investment proposal fails to provide the desired rate of return does not necessarily mean that it should be rejected. In Exhibit 26–1 at the beginning of this chapter we identified several types of capital investments likely to provide little or no financial return, but which management may consider worthwhile for other reasons.

Should the Stars buy the new bus? Probably so. Yes, they have to pay about $15,000 more than a price that provides the desired 15 percent return. But on the other hand, the team will travel in greater comfort and with *greater reliability* for a period of *five years*. (What would be the *opportunity cost* of missing a ball game because the old bus breaks down?) Actually, $15,000 seems a small price to pay for the nonfinancial benefits that the new bus is likely to provide.

Finally, has the team considered all of the available options? Surely, this isn't the only used bus for sale. And what would be the cost of chartering bus service, rather than owning their own bus?

**INTERNATIONAL** CASE IN POINT

International factors can be important considerations in capital budgeting. For example, when McDonald's Corporation invested in Brazil and Russia it had to strategically invest in the infrastructure to make its restaurants successful. Management explained the impact of these needed investments as not surprising when the returns in emerging markets proved to be lower than in established markets. The substantial infrastructure investment required to support restaurant growth is higher in less-developed countries.

© The McGraw-Hill Companies, Inc./Barry Barker, photographer/DAL

## BEHAVIORAL CONSIDERATIONS IN CAPITAL BUDGETING

**Learning Objective**

**L05** Explain the behavioral issues involved in capital budgeting and identify how companies try to control the capital budgeting process.

The accuracy of capital budgets is critically dependent on cash flows and project life-span estimates. However, the estimates created by employees involved in capital budgeting need careful consideration for two reasons. First, because the results of the capital budgeting process have serious implications for employees, their estimates may be overly pessimistic or optimistic. Second, capital budgeting involves estimates from many sources within and outside of the company; thus, there are many opportunities for errors to creep into the process.

Pessimistic or optimistic estimates arise because employees are frequently evaluated on outcomes that clearly depend on the amount and type of capital investments the company chooses. For example, the manager of a profit center is likely to be paid a bonus based on the center's profits each quarter. Assume the profit center's profitability depends on the efficiency of currently operating equipment. In providing data for a capital investment proposal for new equipment, that profit center manager may be overly optimistic about the efficiency of the new equipment and overly pessimistic about the projected efficiency of the current equipment in order to persuade management to acquire new equipment.

Because choices among capital budgeting proposals determine future directions of the firm, careful evaluation and aggregation of data are critical. Most capital budgeting proposals require input from a variety of different individuals. For example, in the case of the LobStars bus decision, estimates of the sales prices of the new and old buses, the operating expenses of the new and old buses, and the life spans of the new and old buses are likely to come from various sources. Operating expense information may come from the accountant, sales prices for old and new buses may be gathered from outside of the organization, and the lifespan estimates may come from the bus mechanic. The reliability of these estimates can be a critical factor in the final choices made among capital budget proposals.

Companies establish internal controls for the capital budgeting process to help guard against overly optimistic or pessimistic estimates and aggregation errors. Many companies use routing forms that require all upper-level managers to sign off on large capital budgeting proposals. A finance department's expertise is used to review and complete analyses about the accuracy of estimates. The largest strategic capital investments ordinarily require approval by the board of directors.

In addition, many companies track capital budget projects as they are implemented. Managers compare the projected expenditures with the actual installation and operating costs to identify weaknesses in their planning processes. Capital budget planners, who know that a **capital budget audit** will be undertaken, will be less likely to be overly optimistic or pessimistic about their estimates. Just as you are careful about planning your expenditures from your checking account because you know the bank audits your balance, capital budget planners are more careful when they know an audit of their proposed investment expenditures will be undertaken.

## Concluding Remarks

We now have discussed three methods of evaluating the *financial* aspects of capital investment opportunities. The financial consequences of capital investments are relevant—even if the business has little choice but to make the expenditure.

You probably noticed how income taxes complicated our analysis of decisions about replacing assets. Income taxes *do* complicate business decisions—and in many situations, it is tax considerations that dictate the appropriate course of action. We urge *all* financial decision makers *always to consider the tax consequences* of their actions.

Don't forget that *nonfinancial* considerations drive many business decisions. Businesses must operate in a *socially responsible* manner, which often involves a sacrifice of profitability—especially in the short term. Remember also the concept of *opportunity costs*. There often is a better alternative awaiting discovery by those who are perceptive, innovative, and persistent.

## Ethics, Fraud & Corporate Governance

Throughout this text we have emphasized the growing importance of ethics, fraud, and corporate governance to the practice of accounting and the business community. In this final commentary, we discuss recent developments in these three areas.

Most corporations now have codes of business conduct and ethics that they expect all employees to follow. In fact, public companies whose stock is traded on the New York Stock Exchange or on NASDAQ are required to maintain a code of business conduct and ethics. Moreover, many companies provide training related to their code of conduct and ethics and require employees to certify in writing on a yearly basis that they are in compliance with the code. In addition, as discussed earlier in the text, public companies are required to maintain "whistle-blower hotlines" that enable employees to anonymously report to the audit committee their concerns related to questionable accounting or auditing matters. The greater focus on ethics also has affected academia. Proposals that would require accounting students to complete substantial

training in ethics are being considered and implemented across the country.

Finally, few business topics have received more attention in recent years than the topic of corporate governance. First, given recent abuses in the area of executive pay, the Securities and Exchange Commission has improved the extent and transparency of the required disclosures surrounding executive compensation. In addition, boards of directors, often prodded by institutional investors and/or hedge funds, are more circumspect in providing lavish compensation packages to senior executives, particularly where these compensation packages are not tied to performance.

Second, shareholder activists continue to press for a greater role in choosing the individuals who serve as directors of public companies. A number of shareholder proposals have been introduced that would require an individual to receive a majority of the shareholder votes cast. Some of these shareholder proposals have passed, and some companies have changed their corporate bylaws or corporate governance guidelines to

*(continued)*

require director candidates to receive 50 percent or more of the votes cast in order to serve on the board of directors.

Third, corporate boards are being held to a higher standard of performance and accountability. The outside directors are sued personally, and these directors settle their lawsuits by making payments out of their personal assets. The directors at **The Walt Disney Co.** were sued personally based on allegations that they breached their fiduciary duty in overseeing the compensation package, including severance payments, received by a former senior executive of **Disney.** Finally, a growing body of academic research suggests that individuals who serve on the board of a company with financial reporting problems (e.g., fraud, restatements, etc.) are less likely to be appointed to other corporate boards in the future. As a result, the earning capacity of those individuals is reduced, suggesting that this market-based mechanism may complement legal and regulatory efforts to improve the performance of corporate directors in overseeing company management.

## A Concluding Comment from the Authors

This book has introduced you to the basic concepts of financial accounting, management accounting, and, to a lesser extent, income taxes. We are confident that you will find this background useful throughout your career. However, we also recommend that you continue your study of accounting with additional courses. We particularly recommend a course in cost accounting and an introductory course in taxation.

We appreciate having the opportunity of addressing you through this text. It is indeed a privilege to share our views of accounting and business with so many students.

The writing of this text has taught us much. All of us have had to challenge, research, verify, and rethink much of what we thought we already knew. We hope the experience of this course proves as rewarding to you.

# END-OF-CHAPTER REVIEW

## SUMMARY OF LEARNING OBJECTIVES

**LO1** **Explain the nature of capital investment decisions.** Capital investment decisions generally refer to projects or proposals that require the purchase of plant assets. These decisions are crucial to the long-run financial health of a business enterprise. Not only do they require that resources be committed for long periods of time, but they are also difficult or impossible to reverse once funds have been invested and a project has begun.

**LO2** **Identify nonfinancial factors in capital investment decisions.** Nonfinancial factors may dictate the appropriate course of action. Such factors may include, for example, compliance with laws, corporate image, employee morale, and various aspects of social responsibility. Management must remain alert to such considerations.

**LO3** **Evaluate capital investment proposals using (a) payback period, (b) return on investment, and (c) discounted cash flows.** The payback period is the length of time needed to recover the cost of an investment from the resulting net cash flows. However, this type of investment analysis fails to consider the total life and overall profitability of the investment.

Return on average investment expresses the average estimated net income from the investment as a percentage of the average investment. This percentage represents the rate of return earned on the investment. A shortcoming is that average estimated net income ignores the timing of future cash flows. Therefore, no consideration is given to the time value of money.

Discounting future cash flows determines the net present value of an investment proposal. Proposals with a positive net present value usually are considered acceptable, while proposals with a negative net present value are considered unacceptable. This technique considers both the life of the investment and the timing of future cash flows.

**LO4** **Discuss the relationship between net present value and an investor's required rate of return.** The discount rate used in determining an investment's net present value may be viewed as the investor's minimum required return for that investment. Thus, when an investment's net present value is positive, its expected rate of return exceeds the minimum return required by the investor. Conversely, a negative net present value suggests that an investment's return potential is less than the minimum return required by the investor.

**LO5** **Explain the behavioral issues involved in capital budgeting and identify how companies try to control the capital budgeting process.** Employees may be optimistic or pessimistic in their capital budgeting cash flow estimates because their futures are affected by the selected capital budgeting proposals. Firms audit capital budgeting projects to attempt to control for overly optimistic or pessimistic estimates.

## Key Terms Introduced or Emphasized in Chapter 26

**capital budget audit** (p. 1125)   The process where managers compare the projected expenditures with the actual installation and operating costs of a capital budgeting project to identify weaknesses in their planning processes.

**capital budgeting** (p. 1116)   The process of planning and evaluating proposals for investments in plant assets.

**capital investments** (p. 1116)   Large capital expenditures that typically involve the purchase of plant assets.

**discount rate** (p. 1120)   The minimum required rate of return used by an investor to discount future cash flows to their present value.

**discounted cash flows** (p. 1119)   The present value of future cash flows.

**net present value** (p. 1121)   The excess of the present value of the net cash flows expected from an investment over the amount to be invested. Net present value is one method of ranking alternative investment proposals.

**payback period** (p. 1117)   The length of time necessary to recover the cost of an investment through the cash flows generated by that investment. Payback period is one criterion used in making capital budgeting decisions.

**present value** (p. 1118)   The amount of money today that is considered equivalent to a cash inflow or outflow expected to take place in the future. The present value of money is always less than its future amount, since money on hand today can be invested to become the equivalent of a larger amount in the future.

**return on average investment (ROI)** (p. 1118)   The average annual net income from an investment expressed as a percentage of the average amount invested. Return on average investment is one method of ranking alternative investment proposals according to their profitability.

**sunk cost** (p. 1122)   A cost that has been incurred irrevocably by past actions. Sunk costs are irrelevant to decisions regarding future actions.

# Demonstration Problem

Grover Contracting, Inc., is considering the purchase of a new cement truck costing $150,000. Grover intends to keep the truck for five years before trading it in on a new one. The truck's estimated salvage value at the end of the five-year period is approximately $25,000. The truck is expected to increase annual income and cash flows by the following amounts:

| Year | Increase in Income | Increase in Net Cash Flows |
|------|-------------------|---------------------------|
| 1 | $10,000 | $ 37,500 |
| 2 | 12,000 | 37,500 |
| 3 | 14,000 | 37,500 |
| 4 | 16,000 | 37,500 |
| 5 | 18,000 | 37,500 |
| | $70,000 | $187,500 |

## Instructions

**a.** Compute the payback period associated with this investment.

**b.** Compute the return on average investment of this proposal.

**c.** Compute the net present value of this investment if Grover requires a minimum return of 12 percent.

**d.** Comment on your findings.

## Solution to the Demonstration Problem

**a.** The payback period of the investment is computed as follows:

$$\frac{\text{Amount to Be Invested}}{\text{Estimated Annual Net Cash Flow}} = \frac{\$150,000}{\$37,500} = \underline{\underline{4 \text{ years}}}$$

**b.** The return on average investment may be determined in three steps:

*Step 1: Compute average investment.*

$$\frac{\text{Original Cost} + \text{Salvage Value}}{2} = \frac{\$150,000 + \$25,000}{2} = \underline{\underline{\$87,500}}$$

*Step 2: Compute average estimated net income.*

$$\frac{\text{Total Income}}{\text{Estimated Useful Life}} = \frac{\$70,000}{5 \text{ years}} = \underline{\underline{\$14,000}}$$

*Step 3: Compute average return on investment.*

$$\frac{\text{Average Estimated Net Income}}{\text{Average Investment}} = \frac{\$14,000}{\$87,500} = \underline{\underline{16\%}}$$

**c.** The net present value of the investment is computed as follows:

| | |
|---|---|
| **Refer to Exhibit 26–3** | |
| Present value of salvage value discounted at 12% for 5 years ($25,000 × .567) | $ 14,175 |
| **Refer to Exhibit 26–4** | |
| Present value of net cash flows discounted at 12% for 5 years ($37,500 × 3.605) | 135,188 |
| Total present value of future cash flows | $149,363 |
| Amount to be invested (payable in advance) | 150,000 |
| Net present value of proposed investment | $      (637) |

**d.** Two of the three measures regarding the cement truck investment are encouraging. First, the payback period of four years is less than the truck's estimated life of five years. Second, the return on average investment of 16 percent is greater than Grover's minimum required return of 12 percent. However, a negative net present value of $637 reveals that the truck's return, in present value terms, is actually less than 12 percent. Had the company's minimum required return been 10 percent instead of 12 percent, the net present value of the investment would be positive by $7,688, computed as follows:

| | |
|---|---:|
| **Refer to Exhibit 26–3** | |
| Present value of salvage value discounted at 10% for 5 years ($25,000 × .621) | $ 15,525 |
| **Refer to Exhibit 26–4** | |
| Present value of net cash flows discounted at 10% for 5 years ($37,500 × 3.791) | 142,163 |
| Total present value of future cash flows | $157,688 |
| Amount to be invested (payable in advance) | 150,000 |
| Net present value of proposed investment | $ 7,688 |

Because the net present value of the truck is negative when a discount rate of 12 percent is used and positive when a discount rate of 10 percent is used, we know that the truck's expected return is between 10 percent and 12 percent.

## Self-Test Questions

*The answers to these questions appear on page 1145.*

1. Which of the following capital budgeting measures requires the discounting of an investment's future cash flows?

   **a.** Payback period.

   **b.** Net present value.

   **c.** Return on average investment.

   **d.** All of the above require the discounting of an investment's future cash flows.

2. Which of the following is of least importance in determining whether to replace an old piece of equipment?

   **a.** The incremental costs and revenue associated with the new piece of equipment.

   **b.** The estimated cost of the new piece of equipment.

   **c.** The historical cost of the old piece of equipment.

   **d.** The estimated salvage value of the new piece of equipment.

3. If the net present value of an investment proposal is positive, what conclusions can be drawn? (Identify all correct answers.)

   **a.** The discount rate used is less than the investment's estimated return.

   **b.** The investment's estimated return exceeds the minimum return required by the investor.

   **c.** The discount rate used equals the minimum return required by the investor.

   **d.** The investment generates cash flows with a present value in excess of its cost.

4. Western Mfg. Co. is considering two capital budgeting proposals, each with a 10-year life, and each requiring an initial cash outlay of $50,000. Proposal A shows a higher return on average investment than Proposal B, but Proposal B shows the higher net present value. The most probable explanation is that:

   **a.** Expected cash inflows tend to occur earlier in Proposal B.

   **b.** Total expected cash inflows are greater in Proposal B.

   **c.** The payback period is shorter in Proposal A.

   **d.** The discounted future cash flows approach makes no provision for recovery of the original $50,000 investment.

5. Copy Center is considering replacing its old copying machine, which has a $3,200 book value, with a new one. Discounted cash flow analysis of the proposal to acquire the new machine shows an estimated net present value of $2,800. If the new machine is acquired, the old machine will have no resale value and will be given away. The loss on disposal of the old machine:

   **a.** Is an opportunity cost of purchasing the new machine.

   **b.** Exceeds the net present value of the new machine, indicating that the new machine should not be acquired.

   **c.** Has already been deducted in arriving at the $2,800 net present value of the new machine.

   **d.** Is a sunk cost and is not relevant to the decision at hand, except as it affects the timing of income tax payments.

---

## ASSIGNMENT MATERIAL     Discussion Questions

1. What is *capital budgeting*? Why are capital budgeting decisions crucial to the long-run financial health of a business enterprise?

2. Identify some conditions where upper management might allow some divisions to have a lower required rate of return.

3. What is the major shortcoming of using the payback period as the only criterion in making capital budgeting decisions?

4. Discounting a future cash flow at 15 percent results in a lower present value than does discounting the same cash flow at 10 percent. Explain why.

5. Discounting cash flows takes into consideration one characteristic of the earnings stream that is ignored in the computation of return on average investment. What is this characteristic and why is it important?

6. What nonfinancial considerations should be taken into account regarding a proposal to install a fire sprinkler system in a finished goods warehouse?

7. The present value of an investment depends on the timing of its future cash flows. Explain what this statement means by giving a specific example of two investments that have significant timing differences and discussing the implications of those timing differences.

8. What factors might a company consider in establishing a minimum required return on an investment proposal?

9. A particular investment proposal has a payback period that exceeds the investment's expected life. The investment has no salvage value. Will this proposal's net present value be positive or negative? Explain your answer.

10. Is an investment's average estimated net income used to compute its return on average investment the same thing as the incremental annual cash flows used to compute its net present value? Explain your answer.

11. What can be said about an investment proposal that has a net present value of zero?

12. Depreciation expense does not require payment in cash. However, it is an important consideration in the discounting of an investment's future cash flows. Explain why.

13. What steps can a firm take to ensure that employee estimates of the costs, revenue, and cash flows from a proposed capital investment are not overly optimistic or pessimistic?

14. What are some types of capital investment projects in which nonfinancial factors may outweigh financial factors?

15. Why is it important to consider income tax consequences when deciding whether to replace an asset?

---

## Brief Exercises

connect
|ACCOUNTING

**BRIEF EXERCISE 26.1**

Understanding Payback Period

A company invests $100,000 in plant assets with an estimated 20-year service life and no salvage value. These assets contribute $10,000 to annual net income when depreciation is computed on a straight-line basis. Compute the payback period and explain your computation.

**BRIEF EXERCISE 26.2**

Using Return on Investment to Evaluate Proposals

Doug's Conveyor Systems, Inc., is considering two investment proposals (1 and 2). Data for the two proposals are presented here:

|  | 1 | 2 |
|---|---|---|
| Cost of investment | $98,000 | $98,500 |
| Estimated salvage value | 12,000 | 6,500 |
| Average estimated net income | 13,000 | 10,500 |

Calculate the return on average investment for both proposals.

**BRIEF EXERCISE 26.3**

Comparing NPV and Required Rate of Return

A particular investment proposal has a positive net present value of $20 when a discount rate of 8 percent is used. The same proposal has a negative net present value of $2,000 when a discount rate of 10 percent is used. What conclusions can be drawn about the estimated return of this proposal?

| LO3 | **BRIEF EXERCISE 26.4** Net Present Value Computations | Landry's Tool Supply Corporation is considering purchasing a machine that costs $56,000 and will produce annual cash flows of $19,000 for six years. The machine will be repurchased at the end of six years for $2,000. What is the net present value of the proposed investment? Landry's requires a 12 percent return on all capital investments. |
|---|---|---|
| LO3 | **BRIEF EXERCISE 26.5** Computations for the Payback Period | A company is trying to decide whether to go ahead with an investment opportunity that costs $35,650. The expected incremental cash inflows are $78,000, while the expected incremental cash outflows are $67,500. What is the payback period? |
| LO1 LO2 | **BRIEF EXERCISE 26.6** Capital Investment Challenges | Some types of capital investments have associated cash flows that are very difficult to estimate, while other types of capital investments have associated cash flows that are very easy to estimate. Name two capital investments, one that has associated cash flows that are easy to estimate and one that has associated cash flows that are difficult to estimate. Explain how these two types of investments differ and why the associated cash flows are easier or more difficult to estimate. |
| LO3 LO4 | **BRIEF EXERCISE 26.7** Net Present Value and Required Rate of Return | Assume that the required rate of return for investment projects at Rippenstock Corporation is 12 percent. One department has proposed investment in new equipment with a 10-year life span and a present value of expected future annual cash flows of $120,000. The equipment's initial outlay cost is $125,000 and it has a salvage value of $10,000. Will this investment project meet the required rate of return for the company? |
| LO5 | **BRIEF EXERCISE 26.8** Capital Budgeting Behaviors | Ron Jasper manages a factory for Frombees Inc. A salesperson for new factory equipment has persuaded Ron that the new equipment offered by her company would be less dangerous for the employees and lower the sound level in the factory significantly. Ron believes that employees would be more satisfied with their jobs as a result of reduced danger and lower sound levels. Ron has always said that satisfied employees are more productive. Thus, in making the cash flow estimates for the new equipment, Ron has included increased cash flows from increased productivity. In fact, these estimated increases in productivity are just enough to allow the net present value of the proposal to be positive. Name at least two reasons why the net present value estimates could be optimistic. |
| LO3 | **BRIEF EXERCISE 26.9** Net Present Value Analysis | The Cook County Authority is considering the purchase of a small plane to transport government officials. It is hoped that the plane will save money on travel costs for government employees. Assume the county requires a 10 percent rate of return. If the plane's cost is $250,000 and it can be sold in five years for $75,000, what minimum annual savings in transportation costs is needed in order to make the plane a good investment? |
| LO2 | **BRIEF EXERCISE 26.10** Nonfinancial Investment Concerns | Sam's Gardening Centers has multiple stores in the northeastern United States. Sam's is considering investing in an "online" store. In addition to the identifiable cash flows such as increased sales and the initial costs to invest in software and personnel, other nonfinancial considerations may exist. Identify nonfinancial issues that Sam's should consider. |

## Exercises

| LO1 through LO5 | **EXERCISE 26.1** Accounting Terminology |
|---|---|

The following are 10 technical accounting terms introduced or emphasized in this chapter:

| Net present value | Capital budgeting | Incremental analysis |
|---|---|---|
| Discount rate | Payback period | Present value |
| Sunk cost | Salvage value | Return on average investment |
| Capital budget audit | | |

Each of the following statements may (or may not) describe one of these technical terms. For each statement, indicate the accounting term described, or answer "None" if the statement does not correctly describe any of the terms.

**a.** The examination of differences among revenue, costs, and cash flows under alternative courses of action.

**b.** A cost incurred in the past that cannot be changed as a result of future actions.

**c.** The process of planning and evaluating proposals for investments in plant assets.

**1132**    Chapter 26  Capital Budgeting

d.  The average annual net income from an investment expressed as a percentage of the average amount invested.

e.  The length of time necessary to recover the entire cost of an investment from resulting annual net cash flows.

f.  The present value of an investment's expected future cash flows.

g.  The amount of money today that is considered equivalent to the cash flows expected to take place in the future.

h.  The required rate of return used by an investor to discount future cash flows to their present value.

i.  Often an investment's final cash flows to be considered in discounted cash flow analysis.

**LO1**  **EXERCISE 26.2**
through  Payback Period
**LO3**

Heartland Paper Company is considering the purchase of a new high-speed cutting machine. Two cutting machine manufacturers have approached Heartland with proposals: (1) Toledo Tools and (2) Akron Industries. Regardless of which vendor Heartland chooses, the following incremental cash flows are expected to be realized:

| Year | Incremental Cash Inflows | Incremental Cash Outflows |
|---|---|---|
| 1 | $26,000 | $20,000 |
| 2 | 27,000 | 21,000 |
| 3 | 32,000 | 26,000 |
| 4 | 35,000 | 29,000 |
| 5 | 34,000 | 28,000 |
| 6 | 33,000 | 27,000 |

a.  If the machine manufactured by Toledo Tools costs $27,000, what is its expected payback period?

b.  If the machine manufactured by Akron Industries has a payback period of 66 months, what is its cost?

c.  Which of the machines is most attractive based on its respective payback period? Should Heartland base its decision entirely on this criterion? Explain your answer.

**LO1**  **EXERCISE 26.3**
**LO3**  Understanding Return on Average Investment Relationships

Foz Co. is considering four investment proposals (A, B, C, and D). The following table provides data concerning each of these investments:

|  | A | B | C | D |
|---|---|---|---|---|
| Investment cost | $44,000 | $45,000 | $50,000 | $  ? |
| Estimated salvage value | 8,000 | 5,000 | ? | 4,000 |
| Average estimated net income | 6,000 | ? | 5,400 | 4,500 |
| Return on average investment | ? | 28% | 20% | 15% |

Solve for the missing information pertaining to each investment proposal.

**LO3**  **EXERCISE 26.4**
Discounting Cash Flows

Using the tables in Exhibits 26–3 and 26–4, determine the present value of the following cash flows, discounted at an annual rate of 15 percent:

a.  $10,000 to be received 20 years from today.

b.  $15,000 to be received annually for 10 years.

c.  $10,000 to be received annually for five years, with an additional $12,000 salvage value expected at the end of the fifth year.

d.  $30,000 to be received annually for the first three years, followed by $20,000 received annually for the next two years (total of five years in which cash is received).

**L08**  **EXERCISE 26.5**

Understanding
Net Present Value
Relationships

The following information relates to three independent investment decisions, each with a 10-year life and no salvage value:

|  | A | B | C |
|---|---|---|---|
| Investment cost | $ ? | $141,250 | $80,520 |
| Incremental annual cash inflows | 14,000 | 37,000 | 19,000 |
| Incremental annual cash outflows | 6,000 | ? | 7,000 |
| Discount rate yielding a net present value of zero | 10% | 12% | ? |

Using the present value tables in Exhibits 26–3 and 26–4, solve for the missing information pertaining to each investment proposal.

**L01**  **EXERCISE 26.6**

Analyzing a Capital
Investment Proposal

**L08**

Bowman Corporation is considering an investment in special-purpose equipment to enable the company to obtain a four-year government contract for the manufacture of a special item. The equipment costs $300,000 and would have no salvage value when the contract expires at the end of the four years. Estimated annual operating results of the project are as follows:

| | | |
|---|---|---|
| Revenue from contract sales | | $325,000 |
| Expenses other than depreciation | $225,000 | |
| Depreciation (straight-line basis) | 75,000 | 300,000 |
| Increase in net income from contract work | | $ 25,000 |

All revenue and all expenses other than depreciation will be received or paid in cash in the same period as recognized for accounting purposes. Compute the following for Bowman's proposal to undertake the contract work:

**a.** Payback period.

**b.** Return on average investment.

**c.** Net present value of the proposal to undertake contract work, discounted at an annual rate of 12 percent. (Refer to annuity table in Exhibit 26–4.)

**L01**  **EXERCISE 26.7**

Analyzing a Capital
through Investment Proposal

**L04**

Northwest Records is considering the purchase of Seattle Sound, Inc., a small company that promotes and manages "grunge" bands. The terms of the agreement require that Northwest pay the current owners of Seattle Sound $530,000 to purchase the company. Northwest executives estimate that the investment will generate annual net cash flows of $200,000. They do not feel, however, that demand for grunge music will extend beyond four years. Therefore, they plan to liquidate the entire investment in Seattle Sound at its projected book value of $50,000 at the end of the fourth year. Due to the high risk associated with this venture, Northwest requires a minimum rate of return of 20 percent.

**a.** Compute the payback period for Northwest's proposed investment in Seattle Sound.

**b.** Compute the net present value of the Seattle Sound proposal, using the tables in Exhibits 26–3 and 26–4.

**c.** What nonfinancial factors would you recommend that Northwest executives take into consideration regarding this proposal?

**L01**  **EXERCISE 26.8**

Analyzing a Capital
Investment Proposal

**L03**

Pack & Carry is debating whether to invest in new equipment to manufacture a line of high-quality luggage. The new equipment would cost $900,000, with an estimated four-year life and no salvage value. The estimated annual operating results with the new equipment are as follows:

| | | |
|---|---|---|
| Revenue from sales of new luggage | | $975,000 |
| Expenses other than depreciation | $675,000 | |
| Depreciation (straight-line basis) | 225,000 | (900,000) |
| Increase in net income from the new line | | $ 75,000 |

**1134**     **Chapter 26** Capital Budgeting

All revenue from the new luggage line and all expenses (except depreciation) will be received or paid in cash in the same period as recognized for accounting purposes. You are to compute the following for the investment in the new equipment to produce the new luggage line:

**a.** Annual cash flows.

**b.** Payback period.

**c.** Return on average investment.

**d.** *Total* present value of the expected future annual cash inflows, discounted at an annual rate of 10 percent.

**e.** *Net* present value of the proposed investment discounted at 10 percent.

L01
L02
L05

**EXERCISE 26.9**
Competing Investment Proposals

The division managers of Chester Construction Corporation submit capital investment proposals each year for evaluation at the corporate level. Typically, the total dollar amount requested by the divisional managers far exceeds the company's capital investment budget. Thus, each proposal is first ranked by its estimated net present value as a primary screening criterion.

Jeff Hensel, the manager of Chester's commercial construction division, often overstates the projected cash flows associated with his proposals, and thereby inflates their net present values. He does so because, in his words, "Everybody else is doing it."

**a.** Assume that all the division managers do overstate cash flow projections in their proposals. What would you do if you were recently promoted to division manager and had to compete for funding under these circumstances?

**b.** What controls might be implemented to discourage the routine overstatement of capital budgeting estimates by the division managers?

L01
through
L03
L05

**EXERCISE 26.10**
Replacing Existing Equipment

EnterTech has noticed a significant decrease in the profitability of its line of portable CD players. The production manager believes that the source of the trouble is old, inefficient equipment used to manufacture the product. The issue raised, therefore, is whether EnterTech should (1) buy new equipment at a cost of $120,000 or (2) continue using its present equipment.

It is unlikely that demand for these portable CD players will extend beyond a five-year time horizon. EnterTech estimates that both the new equipment and the present equipment will have a remaining useful life of five years and no salvage value.

The new equipment is expected to produce annual cash savings in manufacturing costs of $34,000, before taking into consideration depreciation and taxes. However, management does not believe that the use of new equipment will have any effect on sales volume. Thus, its decision rests entirely on the magnitude of the potential cost savings.

The old equipment has a book value of $100,000. However, it can be sold for only $20,000 if it is replaced. EnterTech has an average tax rate of 40 percent and uses straight-line depreciation for tax purposes. The company requires a minimum return of 12 percent on all investments in plant assets.

**a.** Compute the net present value of the new machine using the tables in Exhibits 26–3 and 26–4.

**b.** What nonfinancial factors should EnterTech consider?

**c.** If the manager of EnterTech is uncertain about the accuracy of the cost savings estimate, what actions could be taken to double-check the estimate?

L03

**EXERCISE 26.11**
Gains and Losses on Sale of Equipment

Suppose Concrete Suppliers Inc. sells one of its $155,000 concrete trucks, with an original five-year economic life, at the end of Year 3 after taking three years of straight-line depreciation. Concrete Suppliers has a 40 percent tax rate. If the truck is sold for its book value, there is no tax effect. If Concrete Suppliers sells the truck for more or less than its book value, there is a gain or loss that has a tax effect.

**a.** Show the effects on cash flow in Year 3 if the sales price is $80,000.

**b.** Show the effects on cash flow in Year 3 if the sales price is $20,000.

L03

**EXERCISE 26.12**
Depreciation and Cash Flow

Refer to Exercise 26.11. Assume Concrete Suppliers Inc. has assembled the following expected annual income statement data for each of its trucks.

| | |
|---|---|
| Sales. . . . . . . . . . . . . . . . . . . . . . . . . . . . . . . . . . . . . . . . . . . . . . . . . . . . . . . . . . . . . . . | $150,000 |
| Less: Expenses (net of depreciation) . . . . . . . . . . . . . . . . . . . . . . . . . . . . . . . . . . . | (70,000) |
| Depreciation . . . . . . . . . . . . . . . . . . . . . . . . . . . . . . . . . . . . . . . . . . . . . . . . . . . | (35,000) |
| Income before taxes . . . . . . . . . . . . . . . . . . . . . . . . . . . . . . . . . . . . . . . . . . . . . . . . . | $ 45,000 |
| Taxes @ 40% . . . . . . . . . . . . . . . . . . . . . . . . . . . . . . . . . . . . . . . . . . . . . . . . . . . . . . . | (18,000) |
| Net income . . . . . . . . . . . . . . . . . . . . . . . . . . . . . . . . . . . . . . . . . . . . . . . . . . . . . . . . | $ 27,000 |

Analyze the above income statement data for expected cash flow effects each year.

**L02**
**L03**
### EXERCISE 26.13
Net Present Value
Computations

The Radiology Department at St. Joseph's Hospital, a not-for-profit, is considering purchasing a magnetic resonance imaging (MRI) machine. The cost to purchase and install an MRI is approximately $2,000,000. Assume St. Joseph's would like a minimum 8 percent return and that the economic life of the MRI is expected to be 10 years, with no salvage value. Assume that if the MRI is installed, the net cash flows are expected to increase by $300,000 per year. Use Exhibit 26–4 for present value factors.

**a.** Find the NPV of the MRI.

**b.** Should the hospital acquire the MRI?

**c.** What nonfinancial considerations might be important to the MRI investment decision?

**L03**
### EXERCISE 26.14
NPV of Uneven Cash
Flows

Over the next four years, the City of Inditiny, Massachusetts, is expecting the following cash flows from a federal grant: Year 1—$150,000; Year 2—$220,000; Year 3—$250,000; Year 4—$175,000. The city wants to use the grant as collateral for a loan, but it is unsure about its net present value. What is the net present value of the grant if the rate of return is expected to be 5 percent? What if the rate of return is expected to be 8 percent? Use Exhibit 26–3 for your solution.

**L01**
**through**
**L03**
### EXERCISE 26.15
Home Depot's
Present Value of Store
Closing Costs

The section titled "Impairment of Long-Lived Assets" can be found on page A-11 in the Home Depot 2009 financial information in Appendix A. In this section, Home Depot explains procedures used to estimate the carrying value of stores closed. Use this section to answer the following questions:

**a.** Explain how Home Depot decides to close a store?

**b.** What amounts and types or categories of expenses related to the closed stores are recognized?

**c.** Compute the *tax-related* cash flow impact of the charges to SG&A resulting from the closed stores (assume a 35 percent tax rate).

**d.** What nonfinancial factors, related to the store closings, are mentioned by Home Depot? Name other nonfinancial factors you think are important.

## Problem Set A

**L01**
**through**
**L04**
### PROBLEM 26.1A
Capital Budgeting
and Determination
of Annual Net Cash
Flows

Toying With Nature wants to take advantage of children's current fascination with dinosaurs by adding several scale-model dinosaurs to its existing product line. Annual sales of the dinosaurs are estimated at 80,000 units at a price of $6 per unit. Variable manufacturing costs are estimated at $2.50 per unit, incremental fixed manufacturing costs (excluding depreciation) at $45,000 annually, and additional selling and general expenses related to the dinosaurs at $55,000 annually.

To manufacture the dinosaurs, the company must invest $350,000 in design molds and special equipment. Since toy fads wane in popularity rather quickly, Toying With Nature anticipates the special equipment will have a three-year service life with only a $20,000 salvage value. Depreciation will be computed on a straight-line basis. All revenue and expenses other than depreciation will be received or paid in cash. The company's combined federal and state income tax rate is 40 percent.

### Instructions

**a.** Prepare a schedule showing the estimated increase in annual net income from the planned manufacture and sale of dinosaur toys.

**b.** Compute the annual net cash flows expected from this project.

**c.** Compute for this project the (1) payback period, (2) return on average investment, and (3) net present value, discounted at an annual rate of 15 percent. Round the payback period to the nearest tenth of a year and the return on average investment to the nearest tenth of a percent. Use Exhibits 26–3 and 26–4 where necessary.

**1136**    **Chapter 26** Capital Budgeting

L01 **PROBLEM 26.2A**

Analyzing Capital
through Investment Proposals

L04 e**X**cel

Micro Technology is considering two alternative proposals for modernizing its production facilities. To provide a basis for selection, the cost accounting department has developed the following data regarding the expected annual operating results for the two proposals:

|  | Proposal 1 | Proposal 2 |
|---|---|---|
| Required investment in equipment...................... | $360,000 | $350,000 |
| Estimated service life of equipment ...................... | 8 years | 7 years |
| Estimated salvage value................................ | $–0– | $14,000 |
| Estimated annual cost savings (net cash flow)............... | 75,000 | 76,000 |
| Depreciation on equipment (straight-line basis).............. | 45,000 | 48,000 |
| Estimated increase in annual net income.................. | 30,000 | 28,000 |

**Instructions**

a.  For each proposal, compute the (1) payback period, (2) return on average investment, and (3) net present value, discounted at an annual rate of 12 percent. (Round the payback period to the nearest tenth of a year and the return on investment to the nearest tenth of a percent.) Use Exhibits 26–3 and 26–4 where necessary.

b.  On the basis of your analysis in part **a,** state which proposal you would recommend and explain the reasons for your choice.

L01 **PROBLEM 26.3A**

Analyzing Capital
through Investment Proposals

L04

Cartor Industries is evaluating two alternative investment opportunities. The controller of the company has prepared the following analysis of the two investment proposals:

|  | Proposal A | Proposal B |
|---|---|---|
| Required investment in equipment...................... | $220,000 | $250,000 |
| Estimated service life of equipment ...................... | 5 years | 6 years |
| Estimated salvage value................................ | $10,000 | $–0– |
| Estimated annual net cash flow ........................ | 60,000 | 60,000 |
| Depreciation on equipment (straight-line basis).............. | 42,000 | 40,000 |
| Estimated annual net income........................... | 18,000 | 20,000 |

**Instructions**

a.  For each proposed investment, compute the (1) payback period, (2) return on average investment, and (3) net present value, discounted at an annual rate of 10 percent. (Round the payback period to the nearest tenth of a year and the return on investment to the nearest tenth of a percent.) Use Exhibits 26–3 and 26–4 where necessary.

b.  Based on your computations in part **a,** which proposal do you consider to be the better investment? Explain.

L01 **PROBLEM 26.4A**

Capital Budgeting
through Using Multiple Models

L04

Marengo is a popular restaurant located in Chilton Resort. Management feels that enlarging the facility to incorporate a large outdoor seating area will enable Marengo to continue to attract existing customers as well as handle large banquet parties that now must be turned away. Two proposals are currently under consideration. Proposal A involves a temporary walled structure and umbrellas used for sun protection; Proposal B entails a more permanent structure with a full awning cover for use even in inclement weather. Although the useful life of each alternative is estimated to be 10 years, Proposal B results in higher salvage value due to the awning protection. The accounting department of Chilton Resort and the manager of Marengo have assembled the following data regarding the two proposals:

|  | Proposal A | Proposal B |
|---|---|---|
| Required investment................................... | $400,000 | $500,000 |
| Estimated life of fixtures .............................. | 10 years | 10 years |
| Estimated salvage value............................... | $20,000 | $50,000 |
| Estimated annual net cash flow ........................ | 80,000 | 95,000 |
| Depreciation (straight-line basis) ....................... | 38,000 | 45,000 |
| Estimated annual net income........................... | ? | ? |

## Instructions

**a.** For each proposal, compute the (1) payback period, (2) return on average investment, and (3) net present value, discounted at management's required rate of return of 15 percent. (Round the payback period to the nearest tenth of a year and the return on investment to the nearest tenth of a percent.) Use Exhibits 26–3 and 26–4 where necessary.

**b.** On the basis of your analysis in part **a,** state which proposal you would recommend and explain the reasons for your choice.

**LO1**
**PROBLEM 26.5A**
Capital Budgeting
**through** Using Multiple Models
**LO4**

V. S. Yogurt is considering two possible expansion plans. Proposal A involves opening 10 stores in northern California at a total cost of $3,150,000. Under another strategy, Proposal B, V. S. Yogurt would focus on southern California and open six stores for a total cost of $2,500,000. Selected data regarding the two proposals have been assembled by the controller of V. S. Yogurt as follows:

|  | Proposal A | Proposal B |
| --- | --- | --- |
| Required investment ............................... | $3,150,000 | $2,500,000 |
| Estimated life of store locations ........................ | 7 years | 7 years |
| Estimated salvage value .............................. | $–0– | $400,000 |
| Estimated annual net cash flow ........................ | 750,000 | 570,000 |
| Depreciation on equipment (straight-line basis) ............. | 450,000 | 300,000 |
| Estimated annual net income ......................... | ? | ? |

## Instructions

**a.** For each proposal, compute the (1) payback period, (2) return on average investment, and (3) net present value, discounted at management's required rate of return of 15 percent. (Round the payback period to the nearest tenth of a year and the return on investment to the nearest tenth of a percent.) Use Exhibits 26–3 and 26–4 where necessary.

**b.** On the basis of your analysis in part **a,** state which proposal you would recommend and explain the reasoning behind your choice.

**LO3**
**PROBLEM 26.6A**
Analyzing a Capital
Investment Proposal

Pathways Appliance Company is planning to introduce a built-in blender to its line of small home appliances. Annual sales of the blender are estimated at 12,000 units at a price of $35 per unit. Variable manufacturing costs are estimated at $15 per unit, incremental fixed manufacturing costs (other than depreciation) at $60,000 annually, and incremental selling and general expenses relating to the blenders at $50,000 annually.

To build the blenders, the company must invest $260,000 in molds, patterns, and special equipment. Since the company expects to change the design of the blender every four years, this equipment will have a four-year service life with no salvage value. Depreciation will be computed on a straight-line basis. All revenue and expenses other than depreciation will be received or paid in cash. The company's combined state and federal tax rate is 40 percent.

## Instructions

**a.** Prepare a schedule showing the estimated annual net income from the proposal to manufacture and sell the blenders.

**b.** Compute the annual net cash flows expected from the proposal.

**c.** Compute for this proposal the (1) payback period (round to the nearest tenth of a year), (2) return on average investment (round to the nearest tenth of a percent), and (3) net present value, discounted at an annual rate of 15 percent. Use Exhibits 26–3 and 26–4 where necessary.

**LO1**
**PROBLEM 26.7A**
Considering Financial
**through** and Nonfinancial
Factors
**LO4**

Doctors Hanson, Dominick, and Borchard are radiologists living in Fargo, North Dakota. They realize that many of the state's small, rural hospitals cannot afford to purchase their own magnetic resonance imaging devices (MRIs). Thus, the doctors are considering whether it would be feasible for them to form a corporation and invest in their own mobile MRI unit. The unit would be transported on a scheduled basis to more than 100 rural hospitals using an 18-wheel tractor-trailer. The cost of a tractor-trailer equipped with MRI equipment is approximately $1,250,000. The estimated life of the investment is eight years, after which time its salvage value is expected to be no more than $100,000.

The doctors anticipate that the investment will generate incremental revenue of $800,000 per year. Incremental expenses (which include depreciation, insurance, fuel, maintenance, their salaries, and income taxes) will average $700,000 per year. Net incremental cash flows will be reinvested back into the corporation. The only difference between incremental cash flows and incremental income is attributable to depreciation expense. The doctors require a minimum return on their investment of 12 percent.

### Instructions

a. Compute the payback period of the mobile MRI proposal.

b. Compute the return on average investment of the proposal.

c. Compute the net present value of the proposal using the tables in Exhibits 26–3 and 26–4. Comment on what the actual rate of return might be.

d. What nonfinancial factors should the doctors consider in making this decision?

**PROBLEM 26.8A**

Analyzing Competing Capital Investment Proposals

through L04

eXcel

Jefferson Mountain is a small ski resort located in central Pennsylvania. In recent years, the resort has experienced two major problems: (1) unusually low annual snowfalls and (2) long lift lines. To remedy these problems, management is considering two investment proposals. The first involves a $125,000 investment in equipment used to make artificial snow. The second involves the $180,000 purchase of a new high-speed chairlift.

The most that the resort can afford to invest at this time is $200,000. Thus, it cannot afford to fund both proposals. Choosing one proposal over the other is somewhat problematic. If the resort funds the snow-making equipment, business will increase, and lift lines will become even longer than they are currently. If it funds the chairlift, lines will be shortened, but there may not be enough natural snow to attract skiers to the mountain.

The following estimates pertain to each of these investment proposals:

| | Snow-Making Equipment | Chairlift |
|---|---|---|
| Estimated life of investment............................ | 20 years | 36 years |
| Estimated incremental annual revenue of investment........ | $40,000 | $54,000 |
| Estimated incremental annual expense of investment (including taxes and depreciation) .................... | 15,000 | 19,000 |

Neither investment is expected to have any salvage value. Furthermore, the only difference between incremental cash flow and incremental income is attributable to depreciation. Due to inherent risks associated with the ski industry and the resort's high cost of capital, a minimum return on investment of 20 percent is required.

### Instructions

a. Compute the payback period of each proposal.

b. Compute the return on average investment of each proposal.

c. Compute the net present value of each proposal using the tables in Exhibits 26–3 and 26–4.

d. What nonfinancial factors should be considered?

e. Which proposal, if either, do you recommend as a capital investment?

**PROBLEM 26.9A**

Analyzing Competing Capital Investment Proposals

through L05

eXcel

Sonic, Inc., sells business software. Currently, all of its programs come on disks. Due to their complexity, some of these applications occupy as many as seven disks. Not only are the disks cumbersome for customers to load, they are relatively expensive for Sonic to purchase. The company does not intend to discontinue using disks altogether. However, it does want to reduce its reliance on the disk medium.

Two proposals are being considered. The first is to provide software on computer chips. Doing so requires a $300,000 investment in equipment. The second is to make software available through a computerized "software bank." In essence, programs would be downloaded directly from Sonic using telecommunications technology. Customers would gain access to Sonic's mainframe, specify the program they wish to order, and provide their name, address, and credit card information. The software would then be transferred directly to the customer's hard drive, and copies of the user's manual and registration material would be mailed the same day. This proposal requires an initial investment of $240,000.

The following information pertains to the two proposals. Due to rapidly changing technology, neither proposal is expected to have any salvage value or an estimated life exceeding six years.

|  | Computer Chip Equipment | Software Bank Installation |
|---|---|---|
| Estimated incremental annual revenue of investment... | $300,000 | $160,000 |
| Estimated incremental annual expense of investment (including taxes and depreciation) .............. | 250,000 | 130,000 |

The only difference between Sonic's incremental cash flows and its incremental income is attributable to depreciation. A minimum return on investment of 15 percent is required.

**Instructions**

a. Compute the payback period of each proposal.

b. Compute the return on average investment of each proposal.

c. Compute the net present value of each proposal using the tables in Exhibits 26–3 and 26–4.

d. What nonfinancial factors should be considered?

e. Which of Sonic's employees would most likely underestimate the benefits of investing in the software bank? Why?

f. Which proposal, if either, do you recommend Sonic choose?

## Problem Set B

**LO1**
**PROBLEM 26.1B**
Capital Budgeting
**through** and Determination
of Annual Net Cash
**LO4** Flows

Monster Toys is considering a new toy monster called Garga. Annual sales of Garga are estimated at 100,000 units at a price of $8 per unit. Variable manufacturing costs are estimated at $3 per unit, incremental fixed manufacturing costs (excluding depreciation) at $60,000 annually, and additional selling and general expenses related to the monsters at $40,000 annually.

To manufacture the monsters, the company must invest $400,000 in design molds and special equipment. Since toy fads wane in popularity rather quickly, Monster Toys anticipates the special equipment will have a three-year service life with only a $10,000 salvage value. Depreciation will be computed on a straight-line basis. All revenue and expenses other than depreciation will be received or paid in cash. The company's combined federal and state income tax rate is 30 percent.

**Instructions**

a. Prepare a schedule showing the estimated increase in annual net income from the planned manufacture and sale of Garga.

b. Compute the annual net cash flows expected from this project.

c. Compute for this project the (1) payback period, (2) return on average investment, and (3) net present value, discounted at an annual rate of 12 percent. Round the payback period to the nearest tenth of a year and the return on average investment to the nearest tenth of a percent. Use Exhibits 26–3 and 26–4 where necessary.

**LO1**
**PROBLEM 26.2B**
Analyzing Capital
**through** Investment Proposals

**LO4**

Macro Technology is considering two alternative proposals for modernizing its production facilities. To provide a basis for selection, the cost accounting department has developed the following data regarding the expected annual operating results for the two proposals:

|  | Proposal 1 | Proposal 2 |
|---|---|---|
| Required investment in equipment......................... | $400,000 | $380,000 |
| Estimated service life of equipment ...................... | 10 years | 8 years |
| Estimated salvage value.................................. | $–0– | $20,000 |
| Estimated annual cost savings (net cash flow)............... | 80,000 | 82,000 |
| Depreciation on equipment (straight-line basis) .............. | 40,000 | 45,000 |
| Estimated increase in annual net income................... | 40,000 | 37,000 |

**Instructions**

a. For each proposal, compute the (1) payback period, (2) return on average investment, and (3) net present value, discounted at an annual rate of 15 percent. (Round the payback period to the nearest tenth of a year and the return on investment to the nearest tenth of a percent.) Use Exhibits 26–3 and 26–4 where necessary.

b. On the basis of your analysis in part **a**, state which proposal you would recommend and explain the reasons for your choice.

**1140**    Chapter 26  Capital Budgeting

**L01**  **PROBLEM 26.3B**
Analyzing Capital
**through** Investment Proposals
**L04**

Flagg Equipment Company is evaluating two alternative investment opportunities. The controller of the company has prepared the following analysis of the two investment proposals:

|  | Proposal A | Proposal B |
|---|---|---|
| Required investment in equipment ...................... | $260,000 | $280,000 |
| Estimated service life of equipment ...................... | 6 years | 7 years |
| Estimated salvage value ............................... | $20,000 | $–0– |
| Estimated annual net cash flow ........................ | 82,000 | 65,000 |
| Depreciation on equipment (straight-line basis) ............. | 40,000 | 40,000 |
| Estimated annual net income ......................... | 42,000 | 25,000 |

**Instructions**

a.  For each proposed investment, compute the (1) payback period, (2) return on average investment, and (3) net present value, discounted at an annual rate of 15 percent. (Round the payback period to the nearest tenth of a year and the return on investment to the nearest tenth of a percent.) Use Exhibits 26–3 and 26–4 where necessary.

b.  Based on your analysis in part **a,** which proposal do you consider to be the better investment? Explain.

**L01**  **PROBLEM 26.4B**
Capital Budgeting
**through** Using Multiple Models
**L04**

Samba is a popular restaurant located in Brazilton Resort. Management feels that enlarging the facility to incorporate a large outdoor seating area will enable Samba to continue to attract existing customers as well as handle large banquet parties that now must be turned away. Two proposals are currently under consideration. Proposal A involves a temporary walled structure and umbrellas used for sun protection; Proposal B entails a more permanent structure with a full awning cover for use even in inclement weather. Although the useful life of each alternative is estimated to be 10 years, Proposal B results in higher salvage value due to the awning protection. The accounting department of Brazilton Resort and the manager of Samba have assembled the following data regarding the two proposals:

|  | Proposal A | Proposal B |
|---|---|---|
| Required investment ................................. | $300,000 | $310,000 |
| Estimated life of fixtures .............................. | 10 years | 10 years |
| Estimated salvage value ............................. | $10,000 | $40,000 |
| Estimated annual net cash flow ........................ | 75,000 | 70,000 |
| Depreciation (straight-line basis) ....................... | 24,000 | 36,000 |
| Estimated annual net income .......................... | ? | ? |

**Instructions**

a.  For each proposal, compute the (1) payback period, (2) return on average investment, and (3) net present value discounted at management's required rate of return of 10 percent. (Round the payback period to the nearest tenth of a year and the return on investment to the nearest tenth of a percent.) Use Exhibits 26–3 and 26–4 where necessary.

b.  Based on your analysis in part **a,** which proposal would you recommend? Explain the reasons for your choice.

**L01**  **PROBLEM 26.5B**
Capital Budgeting
**through** Using Multiple Models
**L04**

I.C. Cream is considering two possible expansion plans. Proposal A involves opening eight stores in northern Alaska at a total cost of $4,000,000. Under another strategy, Proposal B, I.C. Cream would focus on southern Alaska and open five stores for a total cost of $3,000,000. Selected data regarding the two proposals have been assembled by the controller of I.C. Cream as follows:

|  | Proposal A | Proposal B |
|---|---|---|
| Required investment ................................. | $4,000,000 | $3,000,000 |
| Estimated life of store locations ....................... | 8 years | 8 years |
| Estimated salvage value ............................. | $–0– | $200,000 |
| Estimated annual net cash flow ........................ | 800,000 | 700,000 |
| Depreciation on equipment (straight-line basis) ............. | 500,000 | 350,000 |
| Estimated annual net income .......................... | ? | ? |

**Instructions**

a. For each proposal, compute the (1) payback period, (2) return on average investment, and (3) net present value, discounted at management's required rate of return of 12 percent. (Round the payback period to the nearest tenth of a year and the return on investment to the nearest tenth of a percent.) Use Exhibits 26–3 and 26–4 where necessary.

b. On the basis of your analysis in part **a,** state which proposal you would recommend and explain the reasoning behind your choice.

 **PROBLEM 26.6B**

Analyzing a Capital Investment Proposal

Cafield Appliance Company is planning to introduce a coffee grinder to its line of small home appliances. Annual sales of the grinder are estimated at 15,000 units at a price of $40 per unit. Variable manufacturing costs are estimated at $18 per unit, incremental fixed manufacturing costs (other than depreciation) at $60,000 annually, and incremental selling and general expenses relating to the grinders at $75,000 annually.

To build the grinders, the company must invest $300,000 in molds, patterns, and special equipment. Since the company expects to change the design of the grinder every five years, this equipment will have a five-year service life with no salvage value. Depreciation will be computed on a straight-line basis. All revenue and expenses other than depreciation will be received or paid in cash. The company's combined state and federal tax rate is 30 percent.

**Instructions**

a. Prepare a schedule showing the estimated annual net income from the proposal to manufacture and sell the grinders.

b. Compute the annual net cash flows expected from the proposal.

c. Compute for this proposal the (1) payback period (round to the nearest tenth of a year), (2) return on average investment (round to the nearest tenth of a percent), and (3) net present value, discounted at an annual rate of 12 percent. Use Exhibits 26–3 and 26–4 where necessary.

**L01 PROBLEM 26.7B**

Considering Financial
**through** and Nonfinancial
Factors
**L04**

Doctors Mowtain, Lawrence, and Curley are radiologists living in Yukville, Maine. They realize that many of the state's small, rural hospitals cannot afford to purchase their own magnetic resonance imaging devices (MRIs). The doctors are considering whether it would be feasible for them to form a corporation and invest in their own MRI unit. The unit would be transported on a scheduled basis to more than 80 rural hospitals using an 18-wheel tractor-trailer. The cost of a tractor-trailer equipped with MRI equipment is approximately $1,500,000. The estimated life of the investment is nine years, after which time its salvage value is expected to be no more than $200,000.

The doctors anticipate that the investment will generate incremental revenue of $900,000 per year. Incremental expenses (which include depreciation, insurance, fuel, maintenance, their salaries, and income taxes) will average $800,000 per year. Net incremental cash flows will be reinvested back into the corporation. The only difference between incremental cash flows and incremental income is attributable to depreciation expense. The doctors require a minimum return on their investment of 15 percent.

**Instructions**

a. Compute the payback period of the mobile MRI proposal.

b. Compute the return on average investment of the proposal.

c. Compute the net present value of the proposal using the tables in Exhibits 26–3 and 26–4. Comment on what the actual rate of return might be.

d. What nonfinancial factors should the doctors consider in making this decision?

**L01 PROBLEM 26.8B**

Analyzing Competing
**through** Capital Investment
Proposals
**L04**

Jackson Mountain is a small ski resort located in northern Connecticut. In recent years, the resort has experienced two major problems: (1) unusually low annual snowfalls and (2) long lift lines. To remedy these problems, management is considering two investment proposals. The first involves a $225,000 investment in equipment used to make artificial snow. The second involves the $250,000 purchase of a new high-speed chairlift.

The most that the resort can afford to invest at this time is $320,000. Thus, it cannot afford to fund both proposals. Choosing one proposal over the other is somewhat problematic. If the resort funds the snow-making equipment, business will increase, and lift lines will become even longer than they are currently. If it funds the chairlift, lines will be shortened, but there may not be enough natural snow to attract skiers to the mountain.

The following estimates pertain to each of these investment proposals:

| | Snow-Making Equipment | Chairlift |
|---|---|---|
| Estimated life of investment. . . . . . . . . . . . . . . . . . . . . . . . . | 10 years | 20 years |
| Estimated incremental annual revenue of investment . . . . . . . . | $70,000 | $70,000 |
| Estimated incremental annual expense of investment (including taxes and depreciation) . . . . . . . . . . . . . . . . . . . | 20,000 | 22,000 |

Neither investment is expected to have any salvage value. Furthermore, the only difference between incremental cash flow and incremental income is attributable to depreciation. Due to inherent risks associated with the ski industry and the resort's high cost of capital, a minimum return on investment of 20 percent is required.

**Instructions**

a. Compute the payback period of each proposal.

b. Compute the return on average investment of each proposal.

c. Compute the net present value of each proposal using the tables in Exhibits 26–3 and 26–4.

d. What nonfinancial factors should be considered?

e. Which proposal, if either, do you recommend as a capital investment?

**L01**
**PROBLEM 26.9B**
through
**L05**
Analyzing Competing Capital Investment Proposals

Boom, Inc., sells business software. Currently, all of its programs come on disks. Due to their complexity, some of these applications occupy as many as seven disks. Not only are the disks cumbersome for customers to load, they are relatively expensive for Boom to purchase. The company does not intend to discontinue using disks altogether. However, it does want to reduce its reliance on the disk medium.

Two proposals are being considered. The first is to provide software on memory sticks. Doing so requires a $500,000 investment in duplicating equipment. The second is to make software available through a computerized "program bank." In essence, programs would be downloaded directly from Boom using telecommunications technology. Customers would gain access to Boom's mainframe, specify the program they wish to order, and provide their name, address, and credit card information. The software would then be transferred directly to the customer's hard drive, and copies of the user's manual and registration material would be mailed the same day. The program bank proposal requires an initial investment of $350,000.

The following information pertains to these proposals. Due to rapidly changing technology, neither proposal is expected to have any salvage value or an estimated life exceeding five years.

| | Memory Stick Equipment | Program Bank Installation |
|---|---|---|
| Estimated incremental annual revenue of investment . . . . . | $400,000 | $260,000 |
| Estimated incremental annual expense of investment (including taxes and depreciation) . . . . . . . . . . . . . . . . . | 260,000 | 140,000 |

The only difference between Boom's incremental cash flows and its incremental income is attributable to depreciation. A minimum return on investment of 12 percent is required.

**Instructions**

a. Compute the payback period of each proposal.

b. Compute the return on average investment of each proposal.

c. Compute the net present value of each proposal using the tables in Exhibits 26–3 and 26–4.

d. What nonfinancial factors should be considered?

e. Which of Boom's employees would most likely underestimate the benefits of investing in the program bank? Why?

f. Which proposal, if either, do you recommend Boom choose?

# Critical Thinking Cases

**L02**

**CASE 26.1**

How Much Is That

through Laser in the Window?

**L04**

The management of Metro Printers is considering a proposal to replace some existing equipment with a new highly efficient laser printer. The existing equipment has a current book value of $2,200,000 and a remaining life (if not replaced) of 10 years. The laser printer has a cost of $1,300,000 and an expected useful life of 10 years. The laser printer would increase the company's annual cash flows by reducing operating costs and by increasing the company's ability to generate revenue. Susan Mills, controller of Metro Printers, has prepared the following estimates of the laser printer's effect on annual earnings and cash flow:

| | | |
|---|---|---|
| Estimated increase in annual cash flows (before taxes): | | |
| Incremental revenue ................................... | $140,000 | |
| Cost savings (other than depreciation) ..................... | 110,000 | $250,000 |
| Reduction in annual depreciation expense: | | |
| Depreciation on existing equipment ........................ | $220,000 | |
| Depreciation on laser printer ............................ | 130,000 | 90,000 |
| Estimated increase in income before income taxes ...................... | | $340,000 |
| Increase in annual income taxes (40%) .............................. | | 136,000 |
| Estimated increase in annual net income ............................ | | $204,000 |
| Estimated increase in annual net cash flows | | |
| ($250,000 − $136,000) ....................................... | | $114,000 |

Don Adams, a director of Metro Printers, makes the following observation: "These estimates look fine, but won't we take a huge loss in the current year on the sale of our existing equipment? After the invention of the laser printer, I doubt that our old equipment can be sold for much at all." In response, Mills provides the following information about the expected loss on the sale of the existing equipment:

| | |
|---|---|
| Book value of existing printing equipment ........................... | $2,200,000 |
| Estimated current sales price, net of removal costs ..................... | 200,000 |
| Estimated loss on sale, before income taxes .......................... | $2,000,000 |
| Reduction in current year's income taxes as a result of loss (40%) .......... | 800,000 |
| Loss on sale of existing equipment, net of tax savings ................... | $1,200,000 |

Adams replies, "Good grief, our loss would be almost as great as the cost of the laser itself. Add this $1,200,000 loss to the $1,300,000 cost of the laser, and we're into this new equipment for $2,500,000. I'd go along with a cost of $1,300,000, but $2,500,000 is out of the question."

## Instructions

**a.** Use Exhibits 26–3 and 26–4 to help compute the net present value of the proposal to sell the existing equipment and buy the laser printer, discounted at an annual rate of 15 percent. In your computation, make the following assumptions regarding the timing of cash flows:

1. The purchase price of the laser printer will be paid in cash immediately.

2. The $200,000 sales price of the existing equipment will be received in cash immediately.

3. The income tax benefit from selling the equipment will be realized one year from today.

4. Metro uses straight-line depreciation in its income tax returns as well as its financial statements.

5. The annual net cash flows may be regarded as received at year-end for each of the next 10 years.

**b.** Is the cost to Metro Printers of acquiring the laser printer $2,500,000, as Adams suggests? Explain fully.

**1144**

**L01**
**CASE 26.2**
through Dollars and Cents versus a Sense of Ethics
**L05**

Grizzly Community Hospital in central Wyoming provides health care services to families living within a 200-mile radius. The hospital is extremely well equipped for a relatively small, community facility. However, it does not have renal dialysis equipment for kidney patients. Those patients requiring dialysis must travel as far as 300 miles to receive care.

Several of the staff physicians have proposed that the hospital invest in a renal dialysis center. The minimum cost required for this expansion is $4.5 million. The physicians estimate that the center will generate revenue of $1.15 million per year for approximately 20 years. Incremental costs, including the salaries of professional staff, will average $850,000 annually. Grizzly is exempt from paying any income taxes. The only difference between annual net income and net cash flows is caused by depreciation expense. The center is not expected to have any salvage value at the end of 20 years.

The administrators of the hospital strongly oppose the proposal for several reasons: (1) they do not believe that it would generate the hospital's minimum required return of 12 percent on capital investments, (2) they do not believe that kidney patients would use the facility even if they could avoid traveling several hundred miles to receive treatment elsewhere, (3) they do not feel that the hospital has enough depth in its professional staff to operate a dialysis center, and (4) they are certain that $4.5 million could be put to better use, such as expanding the hospital's emergency services to include air transport by helicopter.

The issue has resulted in several heated debates between the physicians and the hospital administrators. One physician has even threatened to move out of the area if the dialysis center is not built. Another physician was quoted as saying, "All the administrators are concerned about is the almighty dollar. We are a hospital, not a profit-hungry corporation. It is our ethical responsibility to serve the health care needs of central Wyoming's citizens."

**Instructions**

Form small groups of four or five persons. Within each group, designate who will play the role of the hospital's physicians and who will play the role of the hospital's administrators. Then engage in a debate from each party's point of view. Be certain to address the following:

**a.** Financial factors and measures.

**b.** Nonfinancial factors such as (1) ethical responsibility, (2) quality of care issues, (3) opportunity costs associated with alternative uses of $4.5 million, (4) physician morale, and (5) whether a community hospital should be run like a business.

**c.** Measures that could be taken to check for overly optimistic or pessimistic estimates.

**L01**
**CASE 26.3**
International Investments in Outsourcing
**L02**

**L05**

What are the pitfalls to avoid when investing in overseas activities? The following key issues have been identified as important:

- Lower cost offshore does not always mean gains in efficiency.
- Choose your model carefully; either run your own offshore operation or outsource.
- Get your current employees to be supportive, otherwise they can hinder the process.
- Be prepared to invest time and effort because quality control can be challenging.
- Treat your overseas partners as equals in your business dealings.

**Instructions**

**a.** Explain how the above list of key issues in offshore investments can have an impact on future cash flows associated with an offshore investment.

**b.** Discuss the ethical implications of encouraging current employees to help a company shift jobs overseas.

**L01**
**INTERNET CASE 26.4**
Capital Investment History
**L02**

**L05**

JC Penney Company, founded in the early 1900s, has made many significant capital investment decisions throughout its history. Access the JC Penney Web site at the following address:

http://www.jcpenney.net/about/jcp/history.aspx

Locate the JC Penney Milestones.

**Instructions**

**a.** Identify what you would consider to be a major strategic capital investment decision undertaken by JC Penney since 1902.

**b.** For one such decision, discuss the nonfinancial issues that likely would have been considered.

**c.** A common capital investment decision undertaken by retailers is whether to invest funds in a store that is earning less than the desired level of profit (in the hopes that the investment will generate higher profits) or close the location altogether. In evaluating both options, which employee groups would you expect to overstate the benefits of additional investment? Which groups would understate the benefits of additional investment?

*Internet sites are time and date sensitive. It is the purpose of these exercises to have you explore the Internet. You may need to use the Yahoo! search engine http://www.yahoo.com (or another favorite search engine) to find a company's current Web address.*

**L05 CASE 26.5**

Governance and Capital Budgeting Conflicts

**Red Robin Gourmet Burgers** is an upscale restaurant chain in the Northwest. The chain's former chairman, Michael Snyder, encouraged employees to be "unbridled" in everything they did. Unfortunately, Snyder was too unbridled with his use of some of the company's assets. The company reported the issue to the Securities and Exchange Commission, saying that the chairman's improprieties involved "use of chartered aircraft and travel and entertainment expenses, including charitable donations." After an audit of travel logs, Snyder repaid the company $1.25 million. In addition, Snyder owned a large stake in a company that was on opposite sides of transactions with **Red Robin**, a clear violation of the company's code of ethics governing conflicts of interest. Snyder has since stepped down and the company has moved to improve its corporate governance.

**Instructions**

**a.** Explain how governance violations such as those described as taking place at **Red Robin Gourmet Burgers** can have an impact on capital budgeting outcomes.

**b.** Do you believe that improved corporate governance practices can result in improved returns to capital investments in companies? Explain why or why not.

## Answers to Self-Test Questions

**1.** b    **2.** c    **3.** a, b, d    **4.** a    **5.** d

## APPENDIX A

# Home Depot 2009 Financial Statements

A

## Item 8.    Financial Statements and Supplementary Data.

### Management's Responsibility for Financial Statements

The financial statements presented in this Annual Report have been prepared with integrity and objectivity and are the responsibility of the management of The Home Depot, Inc. These financial statements have been prepared in conformity with U.S. generally accepted accounting principles and properly reflect certain estimates and judgments based upon the best available information.

The financial statements of the Company have been audited by KPMG LLP, an independent registered public accounting firm. Their accompanying report is based upon an audit conducted in accordance with the standards of the Public Company Accounting Oversight Board (United States).

The Audit Committee of the Board of Directors, consisting solely of independent directors, meets five times a year with the independent registered public accounting firm, the internal auditors and representatives of management to discuss auditing and financial reporting matters. In addition, a telephonic meeting is held prior to each quarterly earnings release. The Audit Committee retains the independent registered public accounting firm and regularly reviews the internal accounting controls, the activities of the independent registered public accounting firm and internal auditors and the financial condition of the Company. Both the Company's independent registered public accounting firm and the internal auditors have free access to the Audit Committee.

### Management's Report on Internal Control over Financial Reporting

Our management is responsible for establishing and maintaining adequate internal control over financial reporting, as such term is defined in Rule 13a-15(f) promulgated under the Securities Exchange Act of 1934, as amended (the "Exchange Act"). Under the supervision and with the participation of our management, including our Chief Executive Officer and Chief Financial Officer, we conducted an evaluation of the effectiveness of our internal control over financial reporting as of January 31, 2010 based on the framework in *Internal Control—Integrated Framework* issued by the Committee of Sponsoring Organizations of the Treadway Commission (COSO). Based on our evaluation, our management concluded that our internal control over financial reporting was effective as of January 31, 2010 in providing reasonable assurance regarding the reliability of financial reporting and the preparation of financial statements for external purposes in accordance with U.S. generally accepted accounting principles. The effectiveness of our internal control over financial reporting as of January 31, 2010 has been audited by KPMG LLP, an independent registered public accounting firm, as stated in their report which is included on page 30 in this Form 10-K.

/s/    FRANCIS S. BLAKE

**Francis S. Blake**
**Chairman &**
**Chief Executive Officer**

/s/    CAROL B. TOMÉ

**Carol B. Tomé**
**Chief Financial Officer &**
**Executive Vice President – Corporate Services**

## Report of Independent Registered Public Accounting Firm

The Board of Directors and Stockholders
The Home Depot, Inc.:

We have audited the accompanying Consolidated Balance Sheets of The Home Depot, Inc. and subsidiaries as of January 31, 2010 and February 1, 2009, and the related Consolidated Statements of Earnings, Stockholders' Equity and Comprehensive Income, and Cash Flows for each of the fiscal years in the three-year period ended January 31, 2010. These Consolidated Financial Statements are the responsibility of the Company's management. Our responsibility is to express an opinion on these Consolidated Financial Statements based on our audits.

We conducted our audits in accordance with the standards of the Public Company Accounting Oversight Board (United States). Those standards require that we plan and perform the audit to obtain reasonable assurance about whether the financial statements are free of material misstatement. An audit includes examining, on a test basis, evidence supporting the amounts and disclosures in the financial statements. An audit also includes assessing the accounting principles used and significant estimates made by management, as well as evaluating the overall financial statement presentation. We believe that our audits provide a reasonable basis for our opinion.

In our opinion, the Consolidated Financial Statements referred to above present fairly, in all material respects, the financial position of The Home Depot, Inc. and subsidiaries as of January 31, 2010 and February 1, 2009, and the results of their operations and their cash flows for each of the fiscal years in the three-year period ended January 31, 2010, in conformity with U.S. generally accepted accounting principles.

We also have audited, in accordance with the standards of the Public Company Accounting Oversight Board (United States), The Home Depot, Inc.'s internal control over financial reporting as of January 31, 2010, based on criteria established in *Internal Control —Integrated Framework* issued by the Committee of Sponsoring Organizations of the Treadway Commission (COSO), and our report dated March 25, 2010 expressed an unqualified opinion on the effectiveness of the Company's internal control over financial reporting.

/s/ KPMG LLP

Atlanta, Georgia
March 25, 2010

## THE HOME DEPOT, INC. AND SUBSIDIARIES

## CONSOLIDATED STATEMENTS OF EARNINGS

| | Fiscal Year Ended[1] | | |
|---|---|---|---|
| amounts in millions, except per share data | January 31, 2010 | February 1, 2009 | February 3, 2008 |
| NET SALES | $ 66,176 | $ 71,288 | $ 77,349 |
| Cost of Sales | 43,764 | 47,298 | 51,352 |
| GROSS PROFIT | 22,412 | 23,990 | 25,997 |
| Operating Expenses: | | | |
| Selling, General and Administrative | 15,902 | 17,846 | 17,053 |
| Depreciation and Amortization | 1,707 | 1,785 | 1,702 |
| Total Operating Expenses | 17,609 | 19,631 | 18755 |
| OPERATING INCOME | 4,803 | 4,359 | 7,242 |
| Interest and Other (Income) Expense: | | | |
| Interest and Investment Income | (18) | (18) | (74) |
| Interest Expense | 676 | 624 | 696 |
| Other | 163 | 163 | — |
| Interest and Other, net | 821 | 769 | 622 |
| EARNINGS FROM CONTINUING OPERATIONS BEFORE PROVISION FOR INCOME TAXES | 3,982 | 3,590 | 6,620 |
| Provision for Income Taxes | 1,362 | 1,278 | 2,410 |
| EARNINGS FROM CONTINUING OPERATIONS | 2,620 | 2,312 | 4,210 |
| EARNINGS (LOSS) FROM DISCONTINUED OPERATIONS, NET OF TAX | 41 | (52) | 185 |
| NET EARNINGS | $ 2,661 | $ 2,260 | $ 4,395 |
| Weighted Average Common Shares | 1,683 | 1,682 | 1,849 |
| BASIC EARNINGS PER SHARE FROM CONTINUING OPERATIONS | $ 1.56 | $ 1.37 | $ 2.28 |
| BASIC EARNINGS (LOSS) PER SHARE FROM DISCONTINUED OPERATIONS | $ 0.02 | $ (0.03) | $ 0.10 |
| BASIC EARNINGS PER SHARE | $ 1.58 | $ 1.34 | $ 2.38 |
| Diluted Weighted Average Common Shares | 1,692 | 1,686 | 1,856 |
| DILUTED EARNINGS PER SHARE FROM CONTINUING OPERATIONS | $ 1.55 | $ 1.37 | $ 2.27 |
| DILUTED EARNINGS (LOSS) PER SHARE FROM DISCONTINUED OPERATIONS | $ 0.02 | $ (0.03) | $ 0.10 |
| DILUTED EARNINGS PER SHARE | $ 1.57 | $ 1.34 | $ 2.37 |

(1) Fiscal years ended January 31, 2010 and February 1, 2009 include 52 weeks. Fiscal year ended February 3, 2008 includes 53 weeks.

See accompanying Notes to Consolidated Financial Statements.

## THE HOME DEPOT, INC. AND SUBSIDIARIES
## CONSOLIDATED BALANCE SHEETS

| *amounts in millions, except share and per share data* | January 31, 2010 | February 1, 2009 |
|---|---|---|
| **ASSETS** | | |
| Current Assets: | | |
| Cash and Cash Equivalents | $ 1,421 | $ 519 |
| Short-Term Investments | 6 | 6 |
| Receivables, net | 964 | 972 |
| Merchandise Inventories | 10,188 | 10,673 |
| Other Current Assets | 1,321 | 1,192 |
| Total Current Assets | 13,900 | 13,362 |
| Property and Equipment, at cost: | | |
| Land | 8,451 | 8,301 |
| Buildings | 17,391 | 16,961 |
| Furniture, Fixtures and Equipment | 9,091 | 8,741 |
| Leasehold Improvements | 1,383 | 1,359 |
| Construction in Progress | 525 | 625 |
| Capital Leases | 504 | 490 |
| | 37,345 | 36,477 |
| Less Accumulated Depreciation and Amortization | 11,795 | 10,243 |
| Net Property and Equipment | 25,550 | 26,234 |
| Notes Receivable | 33 | 36 |
| Goodwill | 1,171 | 1,134 |
| Other Assets | 223 | 398 |
| **Total Assets** | $ 40,877 | $ 41,164 |
| **LIABILITIES AND STOCKHOLDERS' EQUITY** | | |
| Current Liabilities: | | |
| Accounts Payable | $ 4,863 | $ 4,822 |
| Accrued Salaries and Related Expenses | 1,263 | 1,129 |
| Sales Taxes Payable | 362 | 337 |
| Deferred Revenue | 1,158 | 1,165 |
| Income Taxes Payable | 108 | 289 |
| Current Installments of Long-Term Debt | 1,020 | 1,767 |
| Other Accrued Expenses | 1,589 | 1,644 |
| Total Current Liabilities | 10,363 | 11,153 |
| Long-Term Debt, excluding current installments | 8,662 | 9,667 |
| Other Long-Term Liabilities | 2,140 | 2,198 |
| Deferred Income Taxes | 319 | 369 |
| Total Liabilities | 21,484 | 23,387 |
| **STOCKHOLDERS' EQUITY** | | |
| Common Stock, par value $0.05; authorized: 10 billion shares; issued: 1.716 billion shares at January 31, 2010 and 1.707 billion shares at February 1, 2009; outstanding: 1.698 billion shares at January 31, 2010 and 1.696 billion shares at February 1, 2009 | 86 | 85 |
| Paid-In Capital | 6,304 | 6,048 |
| Retained Earnings | 13,226 | 12,093 |
| Accumulated Other Comprehensive Income (Loss) | 362 | (77) |
| Treasury Stock, at cost, 18 million shares at January 31, 2010 and 11 million shares at February 1, 2009 | (585) | (372) |
| Total Stockholders' Equity | 19,393 | 17,777 |
| **Total Liabilities and Stockholders' Equity** | $ 40,877 | $ 41,164 |

*See accompanying Notes to Consolidated Financial Statements.*

## THE HOME DEPOT, INC. AND SUBSIDIARIES
## CONSOLIDATED STATEMENTS OF STOCKHOLDERS' EQUITY AND COMPREHENSIVE INCOME

| amounts in millions, except per share data | Common Stock Shares | Amount | Paid-In Capital | Retained Earnings | Accumulated Other Comprehensive Income (Loss) | Treasury Stock Shares | Amount | Stockholders' Equity | Total Comprehensive Income |
|---|---|---|---|---|---|---|---|---|---|
| **BALANCE, JANUARY 28, 2007** | 2,421 | $ 121 | $ 7,930 | $ 33,052 | $ 310 | (451) | $(16,383) | $ 25,030 | |
| Cumulative Effect of the Adoption of FIN 48 | — | — | — | (111) | — | — | — | (111) | |
| Net Earnings | — | — | — | 4,395 | — | — | — | 4,395 | $ 4,395 |
| Shares Issued Under Employee Stock Plans | 12 | 1 | 239 | — | — | — | — | 240 | |
| Tax Effect of Sale of Option Shares by Employees | — | — | 4 | — | — | — | — | 4 | |
| Translation Adjustments | — | — | — | — | 455 | — | — | 455 | 455 |
| Cash Flow Hedges, net of tax | — | — | — | — | (10) | — | — | (10) | (10) |
| Stock Options, Awards and Amortization of Restricted Stock | — | — | 206 | — | — | — | — | 206 | |
| Repurchase of Common Stock | — | — | — | — | — | (292) | (10,815) | (10,815) | |
| Retirement of Treasury Stock | (735) | (37) | (2,608) | (24,239) | — | 735 | 26,884 | — | |
| Cash Dividends ($0.90 per share) | — | — | — | (1,709) | — | — | — | (1,709) | |
| Other | — | — | 29 | — | — | — | — | 29 | |
| Comprehensive Income | | | | | | | | | $ 4,840 |
| **BALANCE, FEBRUARY 3, 2008** | 1,698 | $ 85 | $ 5,800 | $ 11,388 | $ 755 | (8) | $ (314) | $ 17,714 | |
| Net Earnings | — | — | — | 2,260 | — | — | — | 2,260 | $ 2,260 |
| Shares Issued Under Employee Stock Plans | 9 | — | 68 | — | — | — | — | 68 | |
| Tax Effect of Sale of Option Shares by Employees | — | — | 7 | — | — | — | — | 7 | |
| Translation Adjustments | — | — | — | — | (831) | — | — | (831) | (831) |
| Cash Flow Hedges, net of tax | — | — | — | — | (1) | — | — | (1) | (1) |
| Stock Options, Awards and Amortization of Restricted Stock | — | — | 176 | — | — | — | — | 176 | |
| Repurchase of Common Stock | — | — | — | — | — | (3) | (70) | (70) | |
| Cash Dividends ($0.90 per share) | — | — | — | (1,521) | — | — | — | (1,521) | |
| Other | — | — | (3) | (34) | — | — | 12 | (25) | |
| Comprehensive Income | | | | | | | | | $ 1,428 |
| **BALANCE, FEBRUARY 1, 2009** | 1,707 | $ 85 | $ 6,048 | $ 12,093 | $ (77) | (11) | $ (372) | $ 17,777 | |
| Net Earnings | — | — | — | 2,661 | — | — | — | 2,661 | $ 2,661 |
| Shares Issued Under Employee Stock Plans | 9 | 1 | 57 | — | — | — | — | 58 | |
| Tax Effect of Sale of Option Shares by Employees | — | — | (2) | — | — | — | — | (2) | |
| Translation Adjustments | — | — | — | — | 426 | — | — | 426 | 426 |
| Cash Flow Hedges, net of tax | — | — | — | — | 11 | — | — | 11 | 11 |
| Stock Options, Awards and Amortization of Restricted Stock | — | — | 201 | — | — | — | — | 201 | |
| Repurchase of Common Stock | — | — | — | — | — | (7) | (213) | (213) | |
| Cash Dividends ($0.90 per share) | — | — | — | (1,525) | — | — | — | (1,525) | |
| Other | — | — | — | (3) | 2 | — | — | (1) | 2 |
| Comprehensive Income | | | | | | | | | $ 3,100 |
| **BALANCE, JANUARY 31, 2010** | 1,716 | $ 86 | $ 6,304 | $ 13,226 | $ 362 | (18) | $ (585) | $ 19,393 | |

*See accompanying Notes to Consolidated Financial Statements.*

## THE HOME DEPOT, INC. AND SUBSIDIARIES
## CONSOLIDATED STATEMENTS OF CASH FLOWS

| | Fiscal Year Ended[1] | | |
| *amounts in millions* | January 31, 2010 | February 1, 2009 | February 3, 2008 |
|---|---|---|---|
| **CASH FLOWS FROM OPERATING ACTIVITIES:** | | | |
| Net Earnings | $ 2,661 | $ 2,260 | $ 4,395 |
| Reconciliation of Net Earnings to Net Cash Provided by Operating Activities: | | | |
| Depreciation and Amortization | 1,806 | 1,902 | 1,906 |
| Impairment Related to Rationalization Charges | — | 580 | — |
| Impairment of Investment | 163 | 163 | — |
| Stock-Based Compensation Expense | 201 | 176 | 207 |
| Changes in Assets and Liabilities, net of the effects of acquisitions and disposition: | | | |
| (Increase) Decrease in Receivables, net | (23) | 121 | 116 |
| Decrease (Increase) in Merchandise Inventories | 625 | 743 | (491) |
| Decrease (Increase) in Other Current Assets | 4 | (7) | 109 |
| Increase (Decrease) in Accounts Payable and Accrued Expenses | 59 | (646) | (465) |
| Decrease in Deferred Revenue | (21) | (292) | (159) |
| (Decrease) Increase in Income Taxes Payable | (174) | 262 | — |
| Decrease in Deferred Income Taxes | (227) | (282) | (348) |
| (Decrease) Increase in Other Long-Term Liabilities | (19) | 306 | 186 |
| Other | 70 | 242 | 271 |
| Net Cash Provided by Operating Activities | 5,125 | 5,528 | 5,727 |
| **CASH FLOWS FROM INVESTING ACTIVITIES:** | | | |
| Capital Expenditures, net of $10, $37 and $19 of non-cash capital expenditures in fiscal 2009, 2008 and 2007, respectively | (966) | (1,847) | (3,558) |
| Proceeds from Sale of Business, net | — | — | 8,337 |
| Payments for Businesses Acquired, net | — | — | (13) |
| Proceeds from Sales of Property and Equipment | 178 | 147 | 318 |
| Purchases of Investments | — | (168) | (11,225) |
| Proceeds from Sales and Maturities of Investments | 33 | 139 | 10,899 |
| Net Cash (Used in) Provided by Investing Activities | (755) | (1,729) | 4,758 |
| **CASH FLOWS FROM FINANCING ACTIVITIES:** | | | |
| (Repayments of) Proceeds from Short-Term Borrowings, net | — | (1,732) | 1,734 |
| Repayments of Long-Term Debt | (1,774) | (313) | (20) |
| Repurchases of Common Stock | (213) | (70) | (10,815) |
| Proceeds from Sales of Common Stock | 73 | 84 | 276 |
| Cash Dividends Paid to Stockholders | (1,525) | (1,521) | (1,709) |
| Other Financing Activities | (64) | (128) | (105) |
| Net Cash Used in Financing Activities | (3,503) | (3,680) | (10,639) |
| Increase (Decrease) in Cash and Cash Equivalents | 867 | 119 | (154) |
| Effect of Exchange Rate Changes on Cash and Cash Equivalents | 35 | (45) | (1) |
| Cash and Cash Equivalents at Beginning of Year | 519 | 445 | 600 |
| Cash and Cash Equivalents at End of Year | $ 1,421 | $ 519 | $ 445 |
| **SUPPLEMENTAL DISCLOSURE OF CASH PAYMENTS MADE FOR:** | | | |
| Interest, net of interest capitalized | $ 664 | $ 622 | $ 672 |
| Income Taxes | $ 2,082 | $ 1,265 | $ 2,524 |

*(1) Fiscal years ended January 31, 2010 and February 1, 2009 include 52 weeks. Fiscal year ended February 3, 2008 includes 53 weeks.*

*See accompanying Notes to Consolidated Financial Statements.*

## NOTES TO CONSOLIDATED FINANCIAL STATEMENTS

### 1. SUMMARY OF SIGNIFICANT ACCOUNTING POLICIES

#### Business, Consolidation and Presentation

The Home Depot, Inc. and its subsidiaries (the "Company") operate The Home Depot stores, which are full-service, warehouse-style stores averaging approximately 105,000 square feet in size. The stores stock approximately 30,000 to 40,000 different kinds of building materials, home improvement supplies and lawn and garden products that are sold to do-it-yourself customers, do-it-for-me customers and professional customers. At the end of fiscal 2009, the Company was operating 2,244 stores, which included 1,976 The Home Depot stores in the United States, including the Commonwealth of Puerto Rico and the territories of the U.S. Virgin Islands and Guam ("U.S."), 179 The Home Depot stores in Canada, 79 The Home Depot stores in Mexico and 10 The Home Depot stores in China. The Consolidated Financial Statements include the accounts of the Company and its wholly-owned subsidiaries. All significant intercompany transactions have been eliminated in consolidation.

#### Fiscal Year

The Company's fiscal year is a 52- or 53-week period ending on the Sunday nearest to January 31. Fiscal years ended January 31, 2010 ("fiscal 2009") and February 1, 2009 ("fiscal 2008") include 52 weeks. The fiscal year ended February 3, 2008 ("fiscal 2007") includes 53 weeks.

#### Use of Estimates

Management of the Company has made a number of estimates and assumptions relating to the reporting of assets and liabilities, the disclosure of contingent assets and liabilities, and reported amounts of revenues and expenses in preparing these financial statements in conformity with U.S. generally accepted accounting principles. Actual results could differ from these estimates.

#### Fair Value of Financial Instruments

The carrying amounts of Cash and Cash Equivalents, Receivables and Accounts Payable approximate fair value due to the short-term maturities of these financial instruments. The fair value of the Company's investments is discussed under the caption "Short-Term Investments" in this Note 1. The fair value of the Company's Long-Term Debt is discussed in Note 11.

#### Cash Equivalents

The Company considers all highly liquid investments purchased with original maturities of three months or less to be cash equivalents. The Company's Cash Equivalents are carried at fair market value and consist primarily of high-grade commercial paper, money market funds and U.S. government agency securities.

#### Short-Term Investments

Short-Term Investments are recorded at fair value based on current market rates and are classified as available-for-sale.

#### Accounts Receivable

The Company has an agreement with a third-party service provider who directly extends credit to customers, manages the Company's private label credit card program and owns the related receivables. We evaluated the third-party entities holding the receivables under the program and concluded that they should not be consolidated by the Company. The agreement with the third-party service provider expires in 2018, with the Company having the option, but no obligation, to purchase the receivables at the end of the agreement. The deferred interest charges incurred by the Company for its deferred financing programs offered to its customers are included in Cost of Sales. The interchange fees charged to the Company for the customers' use of the cards and the profit sharing with the third-party administrator are included in Selling, General and Administrative expenses ("SG&A"). The sum of the three is referred to by the Company as "the cost of credit" of the private label credit card program.

In addition, certain subsidiaries of the Company extend credit directly to customers in the ordinary course of business. The receivables due from customers were $38 million and $37 million as of January 31, 2010 and February 1, 2009, respectively. The Company's valuation reserve related to accounts receivable was not material to the Consolidated Financial Statements of the Company as of the end of fiscal 2009 or 2008.

## Merchandise Inventories

The majority of the Company's Merchandise Inventories are stated at the lower of cost (first-in, first-out) or market, as determined by the retail inventory method. As the inventory retail value is adjusted regularly to reflect market conditions, the inventory valued using the retail method approximates the lower of cost or market. Certain subsidiaries, including retail operations in Canada, Mexico and China, and distribution centers, record Merchandise Inventories at the lower of cost or market, as determined by a cost method. These Merchandise Inventories represent approximately 18% of the total Merchandise Inventories balance. The Company evaluates the inventory valued using a cost method at the end of each quarter to ensure that it is carried at the lower of cost or market. The valuation allowance for Merchandise Inventories valued under a cost method was not material to the Consolidated Financial Statements of the Company as of the end of fiscal 2009 or 2008.

Independent physical inventory counts or cycle counts are taken on a regular basis in each store and distribution center to ensure that amounts reflected in the accompanying Consolidated Financial Statements for Merchandise Inventories are properly stated. During the period between physical inventory counts in stores, the Company accrues for estimated losses related to shrink on a store-by-store basis based on historical shrink results and current trends in the business. Shrink (or in the case of excess inventory, "swell") is the difference between the recorded amount of inventory and the physical inventory. Shrink may occur due to theft, loss, inaccurate records for the receipt of inventory or deterioration of goods, among other things.

## Income Taxes

The Company provides for federal, state and foreign income taxes currently payable, as well as for those deferred due to timing differences between reporting income and expenses for financial statement purposes versus tax purposes. Deferred tax assets and liabilities are recognized for the future tax consequences attributable to temporary differences between the financial statement carrying amounts of existing assets and liabilities and their respective tax bases. Deferred tax assets and liabilities are measured using enacted income tax rates expected to apply to taxable income in the years in which those temporary differences are expected to be recovered or settled. The effect of a change in income tax rates is recognized as income or expense in the period that includes the enactment date.

The Company and its eligible subsidiaries file a consolidated U.S. federal income tax return. Non-U.S. subsidiaries and certain U.S. subsidiaries, which are consolidated for financial reporting purposes, are not eligible to be included in the Company's consolidated U.S. federal income tax return. Separate provisions for income taxes have been determined for these entities. The Company intends to reinvest substantially all of the unremitted earnings of its non-U.S. subsidiaries and postpone their remittance indefinitely. Accordingly, no provision for U.S. income taxes for these non-U.S. subsidiaries was recorded in the accompanying Consolidated Statements of Earnings.

## Depreciation and Amortization

The Company's Buildings, Furniture, Fixtures and Equipment are recorded at cost and depreciated using the straight-line method over the estimated useful lives of the assets. Leasehold Improvements are amortized using the straight-line method over the original term of the lease or the useful life of the improvement, whichever is shorter. The Company's Property and Equipment is depreciated using the following estimated useful lives:

|  | Life |
| --- | --- |
| Buildings | 5–45 years |
| Furniture, Fixtures and Equipment | 3–20 years |
| Leasehold Improvements | 5–45 years |

## Capitalized Software Costs

The Company capitalizes certain costs related to the acquisition and development of software and amortizes these costs using the straight-line method over the estimated useful life of the software, which is three to six years. These costs are included in Furniture, Fixtures and Equipment in the accompanying Consolidated Balance Sheets. Certain development costs not meeting the criteria for capitalization are expensed as incurred.

### Revenues

The Company recognizes revenue, net of estimated returns and sales tax, at the time the customer takes possession of merchandise or receives services. The liability for sales returns is estimated based on historical return levels. When the Company receives payment from customers before the customer has taken possession of the merchandise or the service has been performed, the amount received is recorded as Deferred Revenue in the accompanying Consolidated Balance Sheets until the sale or service is complete. The Company also records Deferred Revenue for the sale of gift cards and recognizes this revenue upon the redemption of gift cards in Net Sales. Gift card breakage income is recognized based upon historical redemption patterns and represents the balance of gift cards for which the Company believes the likelihood of redemption by the customer is remote. During fiscal 2009, 2008 and 2007, the Company recognized $40 million, $37 million and $36 million, respectively, of gift card breakage income. This income is recorded as other income and is included in the accompanying Consolidated Statements of Earnings as a reduction in SG&A.

### Services Revenue

Net Sales include services revenue generated through a variety of installation, home maintenance and professional service programs. In these programs, the customer selects and purchases material for a project and the Company provides or arranges professional installation. These programs are offered through the Company's stores. Under certain programs, when the Company provides or arranges the installation of a project and the subcontractor provides material as part of the installation, both the material and labor are included in services revenue. The Company recognizes this revenue when the service for the customer is complete.

All payments received prior to the completion of services are recorded in Deferred Revenue in the accompanying Consolidated Balance Sheets. Services revenue was $2.6 billion, $3.1 billion and $3.5 billion for fiscal 2009, 2008 and 2007, respectively.

### Self-Insurance

The Company is self-insured for certain losses related to general liability, product liability, automobile, workers' compensation and medical claims. The expected ultimate cost for claims incurred as of the balance sheet date is not discounted and is recognized as a liability. The expected ultimate cost of claims is estimated based upon analysis of historical data and actuarial estimates.

### Prepaid Advertising

Television and radio advertising production costs, along with media placement costs, are expensed when the advertisement first appears. Amounts included in Other Current Assets in the accompanying Consolidated Balance Sheets relating to prepayments of production costs for print and broadcast advertising as well as sponsorship promotions were not material at the end of fiscal 2009 and 2008.

### Vendor Allowances

Vendor allowances primarily consist of volume rebates that are earned as a result of attaining certain purchase levels and advertising co-op allowances for the promotion of vendors' products that are typically based on guaranteed minimum amounts with additional amounts being earned for attaining certain purchase levels. These vendor allowances are accrued as earned, with those allowances received as a result of attaining certain purchase levels accrued over the incentive period based on estimates of purchases.

Volume rebates and certain advertising co-op allowances earned are initially recorded as a reduction in Merchandise Inventories and a subsequent reduction in Cost of Sales when the related product is sold. Certain advertising co-op allowances that are reimbursements of specific, incremental and identifiable costs incurred to promote vendors' products are recorded as an offset against advertising expense. In fiscal 2009, 2008 and 2007, gross advertising expense was $897 million, $1.0 billion and $1.2 billion, respectively, and is included in SG&A. Specific, incremental and identifiable advertising co-op allowances were $105 million, $107 million and $120 million for fiscal 2009, 2008 and 2007, respectively, and were recorded as an offset to advertising expense in SG&A.

### Cost of Sales

Cost of Sales includes the actual cost of merchandise sold and services performed, the cost of transportation of merchandise from vendors to the Company's stores, locations or customers, the operating cost of the Company's sourcing and distribution network and the cost of deferred interest programs offered through the Company's private label credit card program.

The cost of handling and shipping merchandise from the Company's stores, locations or distribution centers to the customer is classified as SG&A. The cost of shipping and handling, including internal costs and payments to third parties, classified as SG&A was $426 million, $501 million and $571 million in fiscal 2009, 2008 and 2007, respectively.

### Impairment of Long-Lived Assets

The Company evaluates its long-lived assets each quarter for indicators of potential impairment. Indicators of impairment include current period losses combined with a history of losses, management's decision to relocate or close a store or other location before the end of its previously estimated useful life, or when changes in other circumstances indicate the carrying amount of an asset may not be recoverable. The evaluation for long-lived assets is performed at the lowest level of identifiable cash flows, which is generally the individual store level.

The assets of a store with indicators of impairment are evaluated by comparing its undiscounted cash flows with its carrying value. The estimate of cash flows includes management's assumptions of cash inflows and outflows directly resulting from the use of those assets in operations, including gross margin on Net Sales, payroll and related items, occupancy costs, insurance allocations and other costs to operate a store. If the carrying value is greater than the undiscounted cash flows, an impairment loss is recognized for the difference between the carrying value and the estimated fair market value. Impairment losses are recorded as a component of SG&A in the accompanying Consolidated Statements of Earnings. When a leased location closes, the Company also recognizes in SG&A the net present value of future lease obligations less estimated sublease income.

As part of its Rationalization Charges, the Company recorded no asset impairment and $84 million of lease obligation costs in fiscal 2009 compared to $580 million of asset impairments and $252 million of lease obligation costs in fiscal 2008. See Note 2 for more details on the Rationalization Charges. The Company also recorded impairments on other closings and relocations in the ordinary course of business, which were not material to the Consolidated Financial Statements in fiscal 2009, 2008 and 2007.

### Goodwill and Other Intangible Assets

Goodwill represents the excess of purchase price over the fair value of net assets acquired. The Company does not amortize goodwill, but does assess the recoverability of goodwill in the third quarter of each fiscal year, or more often if indicators warrant, by determining whether the fair value of each reporting unit supports its carrying value. The fair values of the Company's identified reporting units were estimated using the present value of expected future discounted cash flows.

The Company amortizes the cost of other intangible assets over their estimated useful lives, which range from 1 to 20 years, unless such lives are deemed indefinite. Intangible assets with indefinite lives are tested in the third quarter of each fiscal year for impairment, or more often if indicators warrant. The Company recorded no impairment charges for goodwill or other intangible assets for fiscal 2009, 2008 or 2007.

### Stock-Based Compensation

The per share weighted average fair value of stock options granted during fiscal 2009, 2008 and 2007 was $6.61, $6.46 and $9.45, respectively. The fair value of these options was determined at the date of grant using the Black-Scholes option-pricing model with the following assumptions:

|  | Fiscal Year Ended | | |
|  | January 31, 2010 | February 1, 2009 | February 3, 2008 |
|---|---|---|---|
| Risk-free interest rate | **2.3%** | 2.9% | 4.4% |
| Assumed volatility | **41.5%** | 33.8% | 25.5% |
| Assumed dividend yield | **3.9%** | 3.5% | 2.4% |
| Assumed lives of option | **6 years** | 6 years | 6 years |

### Derivatives

The Company uses derivative financial instruments from time to time in the management of its interest rate exposure on long-term debt and its exposure on foreign currency fluctuations. The Company accounts for its derivative financial instruments in accordance with the Financial Accounting Standards Board Accounting Standards Codification ("FASB ASC") 815-10. The fair value of the Company's derivative financial instruments is discussed in Note 5.

### Comprehensive Income

Comprehensive Income includes Net Earnings adjusted for certain revenues, expenses, gains and losses that are excluded from Net Earnings under U.S. generally accepted accounting principles. Adjustments to Net Earnings and Accumulated Other Comprehensive Income consist primarily of foreign currency translation adjustments.

### Foreign Currency Translation

Assets and Liabilities denominated in a foreign currency are translated into U.S. dollars at the current rate of exchange on the last day of the reporting period. Revenues and expenses are generally translated using average exchange rates for the period and equity transactions are translated using the actual rate on the day of the transaction.

### Segment Information

The Company operates within a single reportable segment primarily within North America. Net Sales for the Company outside of the U.S. were $7.0 billion for fiscal 2009 and were $7.4 billion for fiscal 2008 and 2007. Long-lived assets outside of the U.S. totaled $3.0 billion and $2.8 billion as of January 31, 2010 and February 1, 2009, respectively.

**10-Year Summary of Financial and Operating Results**
**The Home Depot, Inc. and Subsidiaries**

| amounts in millions, except where noted | 10-Year Compound Annual Growth Rate | 2009 | 2008 | 2007[1] |
|---|---|---|---|---|
| *STATEMENT OF EARNINGS DATA[2]* | | | | |
| Net sales | 5.6% | $ 66,176 | $ 71,288 | $ 77,349 |
| Net sales increase (decrease) (%) | — | (7.2) | (7.8) | (2.1) |
| Earnings before provision for income taxes | 0.5 | 3,982 | 3,590 | 6,620 |
| Net earnings | 1.2 | 2,620 | 2,312 | 4,210 |
| Net earnings increase (decrease) (%) | — | 13.3 | (45.1) | (20.1) |
| Diluted earnings per share ($) | 4.5 | 1.55 | 1.37 | 2.27 |
| Diluted earnings per share increase (decrease) (%) | — | 13.1 | (39.6) | (11.0) |
| Diluted weighted average number of common shares | (3.2) | 1,692 | 1,686 | 1,856 |
| Gross margin – % of sales | — | 33.9 | 33.7 | 33.6 |
| Total operating expenses – % of sales | — | 26.6 | 27.5 | 24.3 |
| Interest and other, net – % of sales | — | 1.2 | 1.1 | 0.8 |
| Earnings before provision for income taxes – % of sales | — | 6.0 | 5.0 | 8.6 |
| Net earnings – % of sales | — | 4.0 | 3.2 | 5.4 |
| *BALANCE SHEET DATA AND FINANCIAL RATIOS[3]* | | | | |
| Total assets | 9.1% | $ 40,877 | $ 41,164 | $ 44,324 |
| Working capital | 2.6 | 3,537 | 2,209 | 1,968 |
| Merchandise inventories | 6.4 | 10,188 | 10,673 | 11,731 |
| Net property and equipment | 9.6 | 25,550 | 26,234 | 27,476 |
| Long-term debt | 27.7 | 8,662 | 9,667 | 11,383 |
| Stockholders' equity | 4.6 | 19,393 | 17,777 | 17,714 |
| Book value per share ($) | 7.9 | 11.42 | 10.48 | 10.48 |
| Long-term debt-to-equity (%) | — | 44.7 | 54.4 | 64.3 |
| Total debt-to-equity (%) | — | 49.9 | 64.3 | 75.8 |
| Current ratio | — | 1.34:1 | 1.20:1 | 1.15:1 |
| Inventory turnover[2] | — | 4.1x | 4.0x | 4.2x |
| Return on invested capital (%)[2] | — | 10.7 | 9.5 | 13.9 |
| *STATEMENT OF CASH FLOWS DATA* | | | | |
| Depreciation and amortization | 14.6% | $ 1,806 | $ 1,902 | $ 1,906 |
| Capital expenditures | (9.5) | 966 | 1,847 | 3,558 |
| Payments for businesses acquired, net | (100.0) | — | — | 13 |
| Cash dividends per share ($) | 23.3 | 0.900 | 0.900 | 0.900 |
| *STORE DATA* | | | | |
| Number of stores | 9.2% | 2,244 | 2,274 | 2,234 |
| Square footage at fiscal year-end | 8.9 | 235 | 238 | 235 |
| (Decrease) increase in square footage (%) | — | (1.3) | 1.3 | 4.9 |
| Average square footage per store (in thousands) | (0.3) | 105 | 105 | 105 |
| *STORE SALES AND OTHER DATA* | | | | |
| Comparable store sales increase (decrease) (%)[4][5] | — | (6.6) | (8.7) | (6.7) |
| Weighted average weekly sales per operating store (in thousands) | (4.3)% | $ 563 | $ 601 | $ 658 |
| Weighted average sales per square foot ($) | (4.1) | 279 | 298 | 332 |
| Number of customer transactions | 4.8 | 1,274 | 1,272 | 1,336 |
| Average ticket ($) | 0.8 | 51.76 | 55.61 | 57.48 |
| Number of associates at fiscal year-end[3] | 4.6 | 317,000 | 322,000 | 331,000 |

(1)   *Fiscal years 2007 and 2001 include 53 weeks; all other fiscal years reported include 52 weeks.*

(2)   *Fiscal years 2003 through 2009 include Continuing Operations only. The discontinued operations in fiscal years prior to 2003 were not material. See Note 4 to the Consolidated Financial Statements included in Item 8, "Financial Statements and Supplementary Data."*

(3)   *Amounts for fiscal years 2009, 2008 and 2007 include Continuing Operations only. All amounts in other fiscal years reported include discontinued operations. See Note 4 to the Consolidated Financial Statements included in Item 8, "Financial Statements and Supplementary Data."*

**Appendix A** Home Depot 2009 Financial Statements

*amounts in millions, except where noted*

| | 2006 | 2005 | 2004 | 2003 | 2002 | 2001[1] | 2000 |
|---|---|---|---|---|---|---|---|
| *STATEMENT OF EARNINGS DATA[2]* | | | | | | | |
| Net sales | $ 79,022 | $ 77,019 | $ 71,100 | $ 63,660 | $ 58,247 | $ 53,553 | $ 45,738 |
| Net sales increase (decrease) (%) | 2.6 | 8.3 | 11.7 | 9.3 | 8.8 | 17.1 | 19.0 |
| Earnings before provision for income taxes | 8,502 | 8,967 | 7,790 | 6,762 | 5,872 | 4,957 | 4,217 |
| Net earnings | 5,266 | 5,641 | 4,922 | 4,253 | 3,664 | 3,044 | 2,581 |
| Net earnings increase (decrease) (%) | (6.6) | 14.6 | 15.7 | 16.1 | 20.4 | 17.9 | 11.3 |
| Diluted earnings per share ($) | 2.55 | 2.63 | 2.22 | 1.86 | 1.56 | 1.29 | 1.10 |
| Diluted earnings per share increase (decrease) (%) | (3.0) | 18.5 | 19.4 | 19.2 | 20.9 | 17.3 | 10.0 |
| Diluted weighted average number of common shares | 2,062 | 2,147 | 2,216 | 2,289 | 2,344 | 2,353 | 2,352 |
| Gross margin – % of sales | 33.6 | 33.7 | 33.4 | 31.7 | 31.1 | 30.2 | 29.9 |
| Total operating expenses – % of sales | 22.4 | 21.9 | 22.4 | 21.1 | 21.1 | 20.9 | 20.7 |
| Interest and other, net – % of sales | 0.5 | 0.1 | — | — | (0.1) | — | — |
| Earnings before provision for income taxes – % of sales | 10.8 | 11.6 | 11.0 | 10.6 | 10.1 | 9.3 | 9.2 |
| Net earnings – % of sales | 6.7 | 7.3 | 6.9 | 6.7 | 6.3 | 5.7 | 5.6 |
| *BALANCE SHEET DATA AND FINANCIAL RATIOS[3]* | | | | | | | |
| Total assets | $ 52,263 | $ 44,405 | $ 39,020 | $ 34,437 | $ 30,011 | $ 26,394 | $ 21,385 |
| Working capital | 5,069 | 2,563 | 3,818 | 3,774 | 3,882 | 3,860 | 3,392 |
| Merchandise inventories | 12,822 | 11,401 | 10,076 | 9,076 | 8,338 | 6,725 | 6,556 |
| Net property and equipment | 26,605 | 24,901 | 22,726 | 20,063 | 17,168 | 15,375 | 13,068 |
| Long-term debt | 11,643 | 2,672 | 2,148 | 856 | 1,321 | 1,250 | 1,545 |
| Stockholders' equity | 25,030 | 26,909 | 24,158 | 22,407 | 19,802 | 18,082 | 15,004 |
| Book value per share ($) | 12.71 | 12.67 | 11.06 | 9.93 | 8.38 | 7.71 | 6.46 |
| Long-term debt-to-equity (%) | 46.5 | 9.9 | 8.9 | 3.8 | 6.7 | 6.9 | 10.3 |
| Total debt-to-equity (%) | 46.6 | 15.2 | 8.9 | 6.1 | 6.7 | 6.9 | 10.3 |
| Current ratio | 1.39:1 | 1.20:1 | 1.37:1 | 1.40:1 | 1.48:1 | 1.59:1 | 1.77:1 |
| Inventory turnover[2] | 4.5x | 4.7x | 4.9x | 5.0x | 5.3x | 5.4x | 5.1x |
| Return on invested capital (%)[2] | 16.8 | 20.4 | 19.9 | 19.2 | 18.8 | 18.3 | 19.6 |
| *STATEMENT OF CASH FLOWS DATA* | | | | | | | |
| Depreciation and amortization | $ 1,886 | $ 1,579 | $ 1,319 | $ 1,076 | $ 903 | $ 764 | $ 601 |
| Capital expenditures | 3,542 | 3,881 | 3,948 | 3,508 | 2,749 | 3,393 | 3,574 |
| Payments for businesses acquired, net | 4,268 | 2,546 | 727 | 215 | 235 | 190 | 26 |
| Cash dividends per share ($) | 0.675 | 0.400 | 0.325 | 0.26 | 0.21 | 0.17 | 0.16 |
| *STORE DATA* | | | | | | | |
| Number of stores | 2,147 | 2,042 | 1,890 | 1,707 | 1,532 | 1,333 | 1,134 |
| Square footage at fiscal year-end | 224 | 215 | 201 | 183 | 166 | 146 | 123 |
| (Decrease) increase in square footage (%) | 4.2 | 7.0 | 9.8 | 10.2 | 14.1 | 18.5 | 22.6 |
| Average square footage per store (in thousands) | 105 | 105 | 106 | 107 | 108 | 109 | 108 |
| *STORE SALES AND OTHER DATA* | | | | | | | |
| Comparable store sales increase (decrease) (%)[4][5] | (2.8) | 3.1 | 5.1 | 3.7 | (0.5) | — | 4 |
| Weighted average weekly sales per operating store (in thousands) | $ 723 | $ 763 | $ 766 | $ 763 | $ 772 | $ 812 | $ 864 |
| Weighted average sales per square foot ($) | 358 | 377 | 375 | 371 | 370 | 394 | 415 |
| Number of customer transactions | 1,330 | 1,330 | 1,295 | 1,246 | 1,161 | 1,091 | 937 |
| Average ticket ($) | 58.90 | 57.98 | 54.89 | 51.15 | 49.43 | 48.64 | 48.65 |
| Number of associates at fiscal year-end[3] | 364,400 | 344,800 | 323,100 | 298,800 | 280,900 | 256,300 | 227,300 |

*(4) Includes Net Sales at locations open greater than 12 months, including relocated and remodeled stores. Stores become comparable on the Monday following their 365th day of operation. Comparable store sales is intended only as supplemental information and is not a substitute for Net Sales or Net Earnings presented in accordance with generally accepted accounting principles.*

*(5) Comparable store sales in fiscal years prior to 2002 were reported to the nearest percent.*

## APPENDIX B

# The Time Value of Money
## Future Amounts and Present Values

AFTER STUDYING THIS APPENDIX, YOU SHOULD BE ABLE TO:

*Learning Objectives*

**LO1**  Explain what is meant by the phrase *time value of money*.

**LO2**  Describe the relationships between *present values* and *future amounts*.

**LO3**  Explain three basic ways in which decision makers apply the time value of money.

**LO4**  Compute future amounts and the investments necessary to accumulate future amounts.

**LO5**  Compute the present values of future cash flows.

**LO6**  Discuss accounting applications of the concept of present value.

## The Concept

One of the most basic—and important—concepts of investing is the *time value of money*. This concept is based on the idea that an amount of money available today can be safely invested to accumulate to a larger amount in the future. As a result, an amount of money available today is considered to be equivalent in value to a *larger sum* available at a future date.

In our discussion, we will refer to an amount of money available today as a *present value*. In contrast, an amount receivable or payable at a future date will be described as a *future amount*.

To illustrate, assume that you place $500 in a savings account that earns interest at the rate of 8 percent per year. The balance of your account at the end of each of the next four years is illustrated in Exhibit B–1.

**Learning Objective**
Explain what is meant by the phrase *time value of money*.   L01

**Learning Objective**
Describe the relationships between *present values* and *future amounts*.   L02

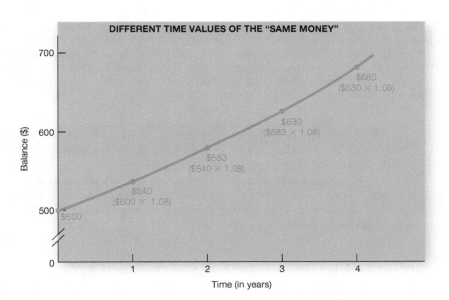

**Exhibit B–1**

**THE VALUES OF MONEY OVER TIME**

 Future values are bigger, but are they worth more? This is the real issue.

These balances represent different time values of your $500 investment. When you first open the account, your investment has a *present value* of only $500. As time passes, the value of your investment increases to the *future amounts* illustrated in the graph. (Throughout this appendix, present values will be illustrated in red, and future amounts will be shown in blue.)

## RELATIONSHIPS BETWEEN PRESENT VALUES AND FUTURE AMOUNTS

The difference between a present value and any future amount is the *interest* that is included in the future amount. We have seen that interest accrues over time. Therefore, the difference between the present value and a future amount depends on *two factors:* (1) the *rate of interest* at which the present value increases and (2) the *length of time* over which interest accumulates. (Notice in our graph, the farther away the future date, the larger the future amount.)

**Present Values Change over Time**    The present value of an investment gradually increases toward the future amount. In fact, when a future date *arrives,* what once was a future amount becomes the present value of the investment. For example, at the end of the first year, $540 will no longer be a future amount—it will be the present value of your savings account.

**The Basic Concept (Stated Several Different Ways)**    Notice that the present value of our savings account is *always less than its future amounts*. This is the basic idea underlying the time value of money. But this idea often is expressed in different ways, including the following:

- A present value is always *less than* a future amount.
- A future amount is always *greater than* a present value.
- A dollar available today is always worth *more* than a dollar that does not become available until a future date.
- A dollar available at a future date is always worth *less* than a dollar that is available today.

Read these statements carefully. All four reflect the idea that a present value is the "equivalent" of a larger number of dollars at a future date. This is what is meant by the time value of money.

## COMPOUND INTEREST

The relationships between present values and future amounts assume that the interest earned on the investment is *reinvested,* rather than withdrawn. This concept often is called *compounding the interest.* Compounding has an interesting effect. Reinvesting the interest causes the amount invested to increase each period. This, in turn, causes more interest to be earned in each successive period. Over a long period of time, an investment in which interest is compounded continuously will increase to surprisingly large amounts.

> **CASE IN POINT**
>
> In 1626, Peter Minuit is said to have purchased Manhattan Island from a group of Indians for $24 worth of "beads, cloth, and trinkets." This episode often is portrayed as an incredible bargain—even a steal. But if the Indians had invested this $24 to earn interest at a compound interest rate of 8 percent, they would have more than enough money today to buy the island back—along with everything on it.

## APPLICATIONS OF THE TIME VALUE OF MONEY CONCEPT

**Learning Objective**

**LO3** Explain three basic ways in which decision makers apply the time value of money.

Investors, accountants, and other decision makers apply the time value of money in three basic ways. These applications are summarized below, along with a typical example.

1. To determine the amount to which an investment will accumulate over time. *Example:* If we invest $5,000 each year and earn an annual rate of return of 10 percent, how much will be accumulated after 10 years?

2. To determine the amount that must be invested every period to accumulate a required future amount. *Example:* We must accumulate a $200 million bond sinking fund over the next 20 years. How much must we deposit into this fund each year, assuming that the fund's assets will be invested to earn an annual rate of return of 8 percent?

3. To determine the present value of cash flows expected to occur in the future. *Example:* Assuming that we require a 15 percent return on our investments, how much can we afford to pay today for new machinery that is expected to reduce production costs by $20,000 per year for the next 10 years?

We will now introduce a framework for answering such questions.

## Future Amounts

A future amount is simply the dollar amount to which a present value *will accumulate* over time. As we have stated, the difference between a present value and a related future amount depends on (1) the interest rate and (2) the period of time over which the present value accumulates.

Starting with the present value, we may compute future amounts through a series of multiplications, as illustrated in our graph in Exhibit B–1. But there are faster and easier ways. For example, many financial calculators are programmed to compute future amounts; you merely enter the present value, the interest rate, and the number of periods. Or you may use a *table of future amounts,* such as Table FA–1 in Exhibit B–2.

### Table FA–1
### Future Value of $1 after *n* Periods

| Number of Periods (*n*) | Interest Rate | | | | | | | | |
|---|---|---|---|---|---|---|---|---|---|
| | **1%** | **1½%** | **5%** | **6%** | **8%** | **10%** | **12%** | **15%** | **20%** |
| 1 | 1.010 | 1.015 | 1.050 | 1.060 | 1.080 | 1.100 | 1.120 | 1.150 | 1.200 |
| 2 | 1.020 | 1.030 | 1.103 | 1.124 | 1.166 | 1.210 | 1.254 | 1.323 | 1.440 |
| 3 | 1.030 | 1.046 | 1.158 | 1.191 | 1.260 | 1.331 | 1.405 | 1.521 | 1.728 |
| 4 | 1.041 | 1.061 | 1.216 | 1.262 | 1.360 | 1.464 | 1.574 | 1.749 | 2.074 |
| 5 | 1.051 | 1.077 | 1.276 | 1.338 | 1.469 | 1.611 | 1.762 | 2.011 | 2.488 |
| 6 | 1.062 | 1.093 | 1.340 | 1.419 | 1.587 | 1.772 | 1.974 | 2.313 | 2.986 |
| 7 | 1.072 | 1.110 | 1.407 | 1.504 | 1.714 | 1.949 | 2.211 | 2.660 | 3.583 |
| 8 | 1.083 | 1.126 | 1.477 | 1.594 | 1.851 | 2.144 | 2.476 | 3.059 | 4.300 |
| 9 | 1.094 | 1.143 | 1.551 | 1.689 | 1.999 | 2.358 | 2.773 | 3.518 | 5.160 |
| 10 | 1.105 | 1.161 | 1.629 | 1.791 | 2.159 | 2.594 | 3.106 | 4.046 | 6.192 |
| 20 | 1.220 | 1.347 | 2.653 | 3.207 | 4.661 | 6.727 | 9.646 | 16.367 | 38.338 |
| 24 | 1.270 | 1.430 | 3.225 | 4.049 | 6.341 | 9.850 | 15.179 | 28.625 | 79.497 |
| 36 | 1.431 | 1.709 | 5.792 | 8.147 | 15.968 | 30.913 | 59.136 | 153.152 | 708.802 |

**Exhibit B-2**

**THE FUTURE VALUE OF $1**

Approach to computing future amount

## THE TABLES APPROACH

A table of future amounts shows the future amount to which *$1* will accumulate over a given number of periods, assuming that it has been invested to earn any of the illustrated interest rates. We will refer to the amounts shown in the body of this table as *factors,* rather than as dollar amounts.

To find the future amount of a present value *greater* than $1, simply multiply the present value by the factor obtained from the table. The formula for using the table in this manner is:

Learning Objective
Compute future amounts and the investments necessary to accumulate future amounts.    L04

Future Amount = Present Value × Factor (from Table FA–1)

Let us demonstrate this approach using the data for our savings account, illustrated in Exhibit B–1. The account started with a present value of $500, invested at an annual interest rate of 8 percent. Thus, the future values of the account in each of the next four years can be computed as follows (rounded to the nearest dollar):

Using the table to compute the amounts in our graph

| Year | Future Amount | Computation (Using Table FA–1) |
|---|---|---|
| 1 | $540 | $500 × 1.080 = $540 |
| 2 | $583 | $500 × 1.166 = $583 |
| 3 | $630 | $500 × 1.260 = $630 |
| 4 | $680 | $500 × 1.360 = $680 |

Computing a future amount is relatively easy. The more interesting question is: How much must we *invest today* to accumulate a required future amount?

### Computing the Required Investment

At the beginning of Year 1, Metro Recycling agrees to create a fully funded pension plan for its employees by the end of Year 5. It is estimated that $5 million will be required to fully fund the pension plan. How much must Metro invest in this plan *today* to accumulate the promised $5 million by the end of Year 5, assuming that payments to the fund will be invested to earn an annual return of 8 percent?

Let us repeat our original formula for computing future amounts using Table FA–1:

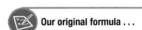

$$\text{Future Amount} = \text{Present Value} \times \text{Factor (from Table FA–1)}$$

In this situation, we *know* the future amount—$5 million. We are looking for the *present value* which, when invested at an interest rate of 8 percent, will accumulate to $5 million in five years. To determine the *present value,* the formula shown above may be restated as follows:

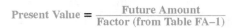

$$\text{Present Value} = \frac{\text{Future Amount}}{\text{Factor (from Table FA–1)}}$$

Referring to Table FA–1, we get a factor of 1.469 at the intersection of five periods and 8 percent interest. Thus, the amount of the required investment at the beginning of Year 1 is $3,403,676 ($5 million ÷ 1.469). Invested at 8 percent, this amount will accumulate to the required $5 million at the end of five years as illustrated in Exhibit B–3.

**Our original formula ...**

**restated to find the present value**

## Exhibit B-3

**THE FUTURE AMOUNT OF A SINGLE INVESTMENT**

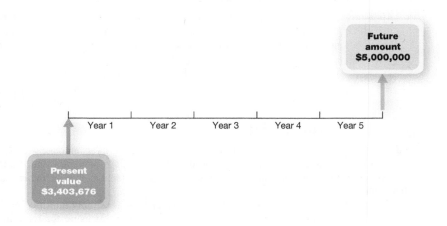

## THE FUTURE AMOUNT OF AN ANNUITY

In many situations, an investor will make a *series* of investment payments rather than a single payment. As an example, assume that you plan to deposit $500 into your savings account at the end of each of the next five years. If the account pays annual interest of 8 percent, what will be the balance in your savings account at the end of the fifth year? Tables, such as Table FA–2 in Exhibit B–4, may be used to answer this question. Table FA–2 presents the future amount of an *ordinary annuity of $1,* which is a series of payments of $1 made at the *end* of each of a specified number of periods.

To find the future amount of an ordinary annuity of payments greater than $1, we simply multiply the amount of the periodic payment by the factor appearing in the table, as shown here:

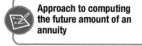

$$\begin{array}{c}\text{Future Amount}\\\text{of an Annuity}\end{array} = \text{Periodic Payment} \times \text{Factor (from Table FA–2)}$$

In our example, a factor of 5.867 is obtained from the table at the intersection of five periods and 8 percent interest. If this factor is multiplied by the periodic payment of $500, we find that your savings account will accumulate to a balance of $2,934 ($500 × 5.867) at the end of

**Approach to computing the future amount of an annuity**

Future Amounts

| Table FA–2 Future Amount of $1 Paid Periodically for *n* Periods | | | | | | | | | |
|---|---|---|---|---|---|---|---|---|---|
| **Number of Periods (n)** | **Interest Rate** | | | | | | | | |
| | **1%** | **1½%** | **5%** | **6%** | **8%** | **10%** | **12%** | **15%** | **20%** |
| 1 | 1.000 | 1.000 | 1.000 | 1.000 | 1.000 | 1.000 | 1.000 | 1.000 | 1.000 |
| 2 | 2.010 | 2.015 | 2.050 | 2.060 | 2.080 | 2.100 | 2.120 | 2.150 | 2.200 |
| 3 | 3.030 | 3.045 | 3.153 | 3.184 | 3.246 | 3.310 | 3.374 | 3.473 | 3.640 |
| 4 | 4.060 | 4.091 | 4.310 | 4.375 | 4.506 | 4.641 | 4.779 | 4.993 | 5.368 |
| 5 | 5.101 | 5.152 | 5.526 | 5.637 | 5.867 | 6.105 | 6.353 | 6.742 | 7.442 |
| 6 | 6.152 | 6.230 | 6.802 | 6.975 | 7.336 | 7.716 | 8.115 | 8.754 | 9.930 |
| 7 | 7.214 | 7.323 | 8.142 | 8.394 | 8.923 | 9.487 | 10.089 | 11.067 | 12.916 |
| 8 | 8.286 | 8.433 | 9.549 | 9.897 | 10.637 | 11.436 | 12.300 | 13.727 | 16.499 |
| 9 | 9.369 | 9.559 | 11.027 | 11.491 | 12.488 | 13.579 | 14.776 | 16.786 | 20.799 |
| 10 | 10.462 | 10.703 | 12.578 | 13.181 | 14.487 | 15.937 | 17.549 | 20.304 | 25.959 |
| 20 | 22.019 | 23.124 | 33.066 | 36.786 | 45.762 | 57.275 | 72.052 | 102.444 | 186.688 |
| 24 | 26.974 | 28.634 | 44.502 | 50.816 | 66.765 | 88.497 | 118.155 | 184.168 | 392.484 |
| 36 | 43.077 | 47.276 | 95.836 | 119.121 | 187.102 | 299.127 | 484.463 | 1014.346 | 3539.009 |

## Exhibit B-4

**FUTURE VALUE OF AN ORDINARY ANNUITY**

five years. Therefore, if you invest $500 at the end of each of the next five years in the savings account, you will accumulate $2,934 at the end of the five-year period.

While computing the future amount of an investment is sometimes necessary, many business and accounting problems require us to determine the *amount of the periodic payments* that must be made to accumulate the required future amount.

**Computing the Required Periodic Payments**  Assume that Ultra Tech Company is required to accumulate $10 million in a *bond sinking fund* to retire bonds payable five years from now. The *bond indenture* requires Ultra Tech to make equal payments to the fund at the end of each of the next five years. What is the amount of the required periodic payment, assuming that the fund will earn 10 percent annual interest? To answer this question, we simply rearrange the following formula for computing the future amount of an annuity:

$$\frac{\text{Future Amount}}{\text{of an Annuity}} = \text{Periodic Payment} \times \text{Factor (from Table FA–2)}$$

 Our original formula . . .

In our example, we know that Ultra Tech is required to accumulate a future amount of $10 million. However, we need to know the amount of the periodic payments that, when invested at 10 percent annual interest, will accumulate to that future amount. To make this calculation, the formula may be restated as follows:

$$\text{Periodic Payment} = \frac{\text{Future Amount of an Annuity}}{\text{Factor (from Table FA–2)}}$$

 restated to find the amount of the periodic payments

The amount of each required payment, therefore, is $1,638,000 ($10 million ÷ 6.105). If payments of $1,638,000 are made at the end of each of the next five years to a bond sinking fund that earns 10 percent annual interest, the fund will accumulate to $10 million, as shown in Exhibit B–5.

## INTEREST PERIODS OF LESS THAN ONE YEAR

In our computations of future amounts, we have assumed that interest is paid (compounded) or payments are made annually. Therefore, in using the tables, we used *annual* periods and an *annual* interest rate. Investment payments or interest payments may be made on a more

## Exhibit B-5 FUTURE AMOUNT OF A SERIES OF INVESTMENTS

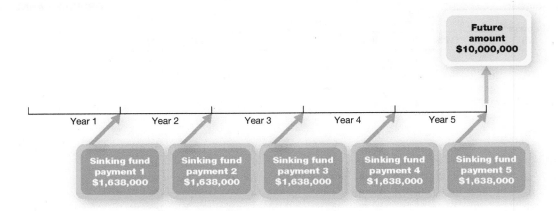

frequent basis, such as monthly, quarterly, or semiannually. Tables FA–1 and FA–2 may be used with any of these payment periods, *but the rate of interest must represent the interest rate for that period.*

As an example, assume that 24 monthly payments are to be made to an investment fund that pays a 12 percent annual interest rate. To determine the future amount of this investment, we would multiply the amount of the monthly payments by the factor from Table FA–2 for 24 periods, using a *monthly* interest rate of 1 percent—the 12 percent annual rate divided by 12 months.

## Present Values

**Learning Objective**
**Compute the present values of future cash flows.**
**L05**

As indicated previously, the present value is *today's* value of funds to be received in the future. While present value has many applications in business and accounting, it is most easily explained in the context of evaluating investment opportunities. In this context, the present value is the amount that a knowledgeable investor would pay *today* for the right to receive an expected future amount of cash. The present value is always *less* than the future amount, because the investor will expect to earn a return on the investment. The amount by which the future cash receipt exceeds its present value represents the investor's profit.

The amount of the profit on a particular investment depends on two factors: (1) the rate of return (called the *discount rate*) required by the investor and (2) the length of time until the future amount will be received. The process of determining the present value of a future cash receipt is called *discounting* the future amount.

To illustrate the computation of present value, assume that an investment is expected to result in a $1,000 cash receipt at the end of one year and that an investor requires a 10 percent return on this investment. We know from our discussion of present and future values that the difference between a present value and a future amount is the return (interest) on the investment. In our example, the future amount would be equal to 110 percent of the original investment, because the investor expects 100 percent of the investment back plus a 10 percent return on the investment. Thus, the investor would be willing to pay *$909* ($1,000 ÷ 1.10) for this investment. This computation may be verified as follows (amounts rounded to the nearest dollar):

| | |
|---|---:|
| Amount to be invested (present value) | $ 909 |
| Required return on investment ($909 × 10%) | 91 |
| Amount to be received in one year (future value) | $1,000 |

As illustrated in Exhibit B–6, if the $1,000 is to be received *two years* in the future, the investor would pay only *$826* for the investment today [($1,000 ÷ 1.10) ÷ 1.10]. This computation may be verified as follows (amounts rounded to the nearest dollar):

| | |
|---|---:|
| Amount to be invested (present value) . . . . . . . . . . . . . . . . . . . . . . . . . . . . . . . . . . . . . | $ 826 |
| Required return on investment in first year ($826 × 10%) . . . . . . . . . . . . . . . . . . . . | 83 |
| Amount invested after one year. . . . . . . . . . . . . . . . . . . . . . . . . . . . . . . . . . . . . . . . . . | $ 909 |
| Required return on investment in second year ($909 × 10%) . . . . . . . . . . . . . . . . . | 91 |
| Amount to be received in two years (future value) . . . . . . . . . . . . . . . . . . . . . . . . . . | $1,000 |

The amount that our investor would pay today, $826, is the present value of $1,000 to be received two years from now, discounted at an annual rate of 10 percent. The $174 difference between the $826 present value and the $1,000 future amount is the return (interest revenue) to be earned by the investor over the two-year period.

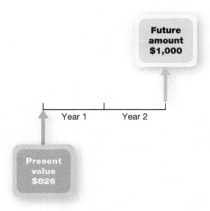

**Exhibit B–6**

**PRESENT VALUE OF $1,000 TO BE RECEIVED IN A SINGLE SUM IN TWO YEARS**

## USING PRESENT VALUE TABLES

Although we can compute the present value of future amounts by a series of divisions, tables are available that simplify the calculations. We can use a table of present values to find the present value of $1 at a specified discount rate and then multiply that value by the future amount as illustrated in the following formula:

**Present Value = Future Amount × Factor (from Table PV–1)**

Referring to Table PV–1 in Exhibit B–7, we find a factor of *.826* at the intersection of two periods and 10 percent interest. If we multiply this factor by the expected future cash receipt of $1,000, we get a present value of *$826* ($1,000 × .826), the same amount computed previously.

Formula for finding present value

## WHAT IS THE APPROPRIATE DISCOUNT RATE?

As explained earlier, the *discount rate* may be viewed as the investor's required rate of return. All investments involve some degree of risk that actual future cash flows may turn out to be less than expected. Investors will require a rate of return that justifies taking this risk. In today's market conditions, investors require annual returns of between 2 percent and 6 percent on low-risk investments, such as government bonds and certificates of deposit. For relatively high-risk investments, such as the introduction of a new product line, investors may expect to earn an annual return of perhaps 15 percent or more. When a higher discount rate is used, the present value of the investment will be lower. In other words, as the risk of an investment increases, its value to investors decreases.

**Exhibit B-7**

**PRESENT VALUE OF $1**

**Table PV-1**
**Present Values of $1 Due in _n_ Periods**

| Number of Periods (_n_) | Discount Rate | | | | | | | | |
|---|---|---|---|---|---|---|---|---|---|
| | **1%** | **1½%** | **5%** | **6%** | **8%** | **10%** | **12%** | **15%** | **20%** |
| 1 | .990 | .985 | .952 | .943 | .926 | .909 | .893 | .870 | .833 |
| 2 | .980 | .971 | .907 | .890 | .857 | .826 | .797 | .756 | .694 |
| 3 | .971 | .956 | .864 | .840 | .794 | .751 | .712 | .658 | .579 |
| 4 | .961 | .942 | .823 | .792 | .735 | .683 | .636 | .572 | .482 |
| 5 | .951 | .928 | .784 | .747 | .681 | .621 | .567 | .497 | .402 |
| 6 | .942 | .915 | .746 | .705 | .630 | .564 | .507 | .432 | .335 |
| 7 | .933 | .901 | .711 | .665 | .583 | .513 | .452 | .376 | .279 |
| 8 | .923 | .888 | .677 | .627 | .540 | .467 | .404 | .327 | .233 |
| 9 | .914 | .875 | .645 | .592 | .500 | .424 | .361 | .284 | .194 |
| 10 | .905 | .862 | .614 | .558 | .463 | .386 | .322 | .247 | .162 |
| 20 | .820 | .742 | .377 | .312 | .215 | .149 | .104 | .061 | .026 |
| 24 | .788 | .700 | .310 | .247 | .158 | .102 | .066 | .035 | .013 |
| 36 | .699 | .585 | .173 | .123 | .063 | .032 | .017 | .007 | .001 |

## THE PRESENT VALUE OF AN ANNUITY

Many investment opportunities are expected to produce annual cash flows for a number of years, instead of one single future cash flow. Let us assume that Camino Company is evaluating an investment that is expected to produce _annual net cash flows of_ $10,000 in _each of the next three years._[1] If Camino Company expects a 12 percent return on this type of investment, it may compute the present value of these cash flows as follows:

| Year | Expected New Cash Flows | × | Present Value of $1 Discounted at 12% | = | Present Value of Net Cash Flows |
|---|---|---|---|---|---|
| 1 | $10,000 | | .893 | | $ 8,930 |
| 2 | 10,000 | | .797 | | 7,970 |
| 3 | 10,000 | | .712 | | 7,120 |
| Total present value of the investment................................ | | | | | $24,020 |

This analysis indicates that the present value of the expected net cash flows from the investment, discounted at an annual rate of 12 percent, amounts to $24,020. This is the maximum amount that Camino Company could afford to pay for this investment and still expect to earn the 12 percent required rate of return, as shown in Exhibit B–8.

In the preceding analysis, we computed the present value of the investment by separately discounting each period's cash flows, using the appropriate factors from Table PV–1. Separately discounting each period's cash flows is necessary only when the cash flows vary in amount from period to period. Since the annual cash flows in our example are _uniform in amount,_ there are easier ways to compute the total present value.

Many financial calculators are programmed to compute the present value of an investment after the interest rate, the future cash flows, and the number of periods have been entered.

---

[1] "Annual net cash flows" normally are the net result of a series of cash receipts and cash payments occurring throughout the year. For convenience, we follow the common practice of assuming that the entire net cash flows for each year occur at _year-end._ This assumption causes relatively little distortion and greatly simplifies computations.

Present Values

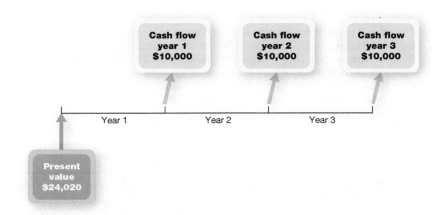

### Exhibit B-8

**PRESENT VALUE OF THREE $10,000 CASH FLOWS DISCOUNTED AT 12%**

Another approach is to refer to a *present value annuity table,* which shows the present value of *$1 to be received each period for a specified number of periods.* An annuity table labeled Table PV–2 appears in Exhibit B–9.[2]

To illustrate the use of Table PV–2, let's return to the example of the investment by Camino Company. That investment was expected to return $10,000 per year for the next three years, and the company's required rate of return was 12 percent per year. Using Table PV–2, we can compute the present value of the investment with the following formula:

**Present Value of an Annuity = Periodic Cash Flows × Factor (from Table PV–2)**

As illustrated in Table PV–2, the present value of $1 to be received at the end of the next three years, discounted at an annual rate of 12 percent, is 2.402. If we multiply 2.402 by the expected future annual cash receipt of $10,000, we get a present value of $24,020, which is the same amount produced by the series of calculations made earlier.

**Formula to find the present value of a series of cash flows**

### Exhibit B-9

**PRESENT VALUE OF AN ORDINARY ANNUITY**

**Table PV–2**
**Present Values of $1 to Be Received Periodically for *n* Periods**

| Number of Periods (*n*) | Discount Rate | | | | | | | | |
|---|---|---|---|---|---|---|---|---|---|
| | 1% | 1½% | 5% | 6% | 8% | 10% | 12% | 15% | 20% |
| 1 | 0.990 | 0.985 | 0.952 | 0.943 | 0.926 | 0.909 | 0.893 | 0.870 | 0.833 |
| 2 | 1.970 | 1.956 | 1.859 | 1.833 | 1.783 | 1.736 | 1.690 | 1.626 | 1.528 |
| 3 | 2.941 | 2.912 | 2.723 | 2.673 | 2.577 | 2.487 | 2.402 | 2.283 | 2.106 |
| 4 | 3.902 | 3.854 | 3.546 | 3.465 | 3.312 | 3.170 | 3.037 | 2.855 | 2.589 |
| 5 | 4.853 | 4.783 | 4.329 | 4.212 | 3.993 | 3.791 | 3.605 | 3.352 | 2.991 |
| 6 | 5.795 | 5.697 | 5.076 | 4.917 | 4.623 | 4.355 | 4.111 | 3.784 | 3.326 |
| 7 | 6.728 | 6.598 | 5.786 | 5.582 | 5.206 | 4.868 | 4.564 | 4.160 | 3.605 |
| 8 | 7.652 | 7.486 | 6.463 | 6.210 | 5.747 | 5.335 | 4.968 | 4.487 | 3.837 |
| 9 | 8.566 | 8.361 | 7.108 | 6.802 | 6.247 | 5.759 | 5.328 | 4.772 | 4.031 |
| 10 | 9.471 | 9.222 | 7.722 | 7.360 | 6.710 | 6.145 | 5.650 | 5.019 | 4.192 |
| 20 | 18.046 | 17.169 | 12.462 | 11.470 | 9.818 | 8.514 | 7.469 | 6.259 | 4.870 |
| 24 | 21.243 | 20.030 | 13.799 | 12.550 | 10.529 | 8.985 | 7.784 | 6.434 | 4.937 |
| 36 | 30.108 | 27.661 | 16.547 | 14.621 | 11.717 | 9.677 | 8.192 | 6.623 | 4.993 |

---

[2] This table is for an *ordinary* annuity, which assumes that the periodic cash flows occur at the *end* of each period.

## DISCOUNT PERIODS OF LESS THAN ONE YEAR

The interval between regular periodic cash flows is called the *discount period*. In our preceding examples, we have assumed cash flows once a year. Often, cash flows occur on a more frequent basis, such as monthly, quarterly, or semiannually. The present value tables can be used with discount periods of any length, *but the discount rate must be for that length of time.* For example, if we use Table PV–2 to find the present value of a series of *quarterly* cash payments, the discount rate must be the *quarterly* rate.

There are many applications of the present value concept in accounting. In the next several pages, we will discuss some of the most important of these applications.

## Valuation of Financial Instruments

**Learning Objective**
**Discuss accounting applications of the concept of present value.**
LO6

Accountants use the phrase *financial instruments* to describe cash, equity investments in another business, and any contracts that call for receipts or payments of cash. (Notice that this phrase applies to all financial assets, as well as most liabilities. In fact, the only common liabilities *not* considered financial instruments are unearned revenue and deferred income taxes.)

Whenever the present value of a financial instrument *differs significantly* from the sum of the expected future cash flows, the instrument is recorded in the accounting records at its *present value*—not at the expected amount of the future cash receipts or payments.

Let us illustrate with a few common examples. Cash appears in the balance sheet at its face amount. This face value *is* a present value—that is, the value of the cash today.

Marketable securities appear in the balance sheet at their *current market values.* These too are present values—representing the amount of cash into which the security can be converted *today.*

Accounts receivable and accounts payable normally appear in the balance sheet at the amounts expected to be collected or paid in the near future. Technically, these are *future amounts,* not present values. But they usually are received or paid within 30 or 60 days. Considering the short periods of time involved, the differences between these future amounts and their present values simply are *not material.*

### INTEREST-BEARING RECEIVABLES AND PAYABLES

When a financial instrument calls for the receipt or payment of interest, the difference between the present value and the future amounts *does* become material. Thus, interest-bearing receivables and payables initially are recorded in accounting records at the *present value* of the future cash flows—also called the "principal amount" of the obligation. This present value often is *substantially less* than the sum of the expected future amounts.

Consider, for example, $100 million in 30-year, 9 percent bonds payable issued at par. At the issuance date, the present value of this bond issue is $100 million—the amount of cash received. But the future payments to bondholders are expected to total *$370* million, computed as follows:

| | |
|---|---:|
| Future interest payments ($100 million × 9% × 30 years) . . . . . . . . . . . . . . . . . | $ 270,000,000 |
| Maturity value of the bonds (due in 30 years) . . . . . . . . . . . . . . . . . . . . . . . . . | 100,000,000 |
| Sum of the future cash payments . . . . . . . . . . . . . . . . . . . . . . . . . . . . . . . . . . | $370,000,000 |

Thus the $100 million issuance price represents the present value of $370 million in future cash payments to be made over a period of 30 years.

In essence, interest-bearing financial instruments are "automatically" recorded at their present values simply because we do not include future interest charges in the original valuation of the receivable or the liability.

### "NON-INTEREST-BEARING" NOTES

On occasion, companies may issue or accept notes that make no mention of interest, or in which the stated interest rates are unreasonably low. If the difference between the present value of such a note and its face amount is *material,* the note initially is recorded at its present value.

To illustrate, assume that on January 1, 2011, Elron Corporation purchases land from U.S. Development Co. As full payment for this land, Elron issues a $300,000 installment note payable, due in three annual installments of $100,000, beginning on December 31, 2011. This note makes *no mention* of interest charges.

Clearly, three annual installments of $100,000 are not the equivalent of $300,000 available today. Elron should use the *present value* of this note—not the face amount—in determining the cost of the land and reporting its liability.

Assume that a realistic interest rate for financing land over a three-year period currently is 10 percent per annum. The present value of Elron's installment note, discounted at 10 percent, is *$248,700* [$100,000, 3-year annuity × 2.487 (from Table PV–2) in Exhibit B–9]. Elron should view this $248,700 as the "principal amount" of this installment note payable. The remaining $51,300 ($300,000 − $248,700) represents interest charges included in the installment payments.

Elron should record the purchase of the land and the issuance of this note as follows:[3]

| | | |
|---|---|---|
| Land . . . . . . . . . . . . . . . . . . . . . . . . . . . . . . . . . . . . . . . . . . . . . . . . . . . . . . . | 248,700 | |
|     Notes Payable. . . . . . . . . . . . . . . . . . . . . . . . . . . . . . . . . . . . . . . . . | | 248,700 |
| Purchased land, issuing a 3-year installment note payable with a present value of $248,700. | | |

(U.S. Development Co. should make similar computations in determining the sales price of the land and the valuation of its note receivable.)

Elron also should prepare an *amortization table* to allocate the amount of each installment payment between interest expense and reduction in the principal amount of this obligation. This table, based on an original unpaid balance of $248,700, three annual payments of $100,000, and an annual interest rate of 10 percent, is illustrated in Exhibit B–10.

**Exhibit B-10**

**AMORTIZATION TABLE FOR A DISCOUNTED NOTE PAYABLE**

| AMORTIZATION TABLE (3-YEAR, $300,000 INSTALLMENT NOTE PAYABLE, DISCOUNTED AT 10% PER ANNUM) | | | | | |
|---|---|---|---|---|---|
| Interest Period | Payment Date | Annual Payment | Interest Expense (10% of the Last Unpaid Balance) | Reduction in Unpaid Balance | Unpaid Balance |
| Issue date | Jan. 1, 2011 | | | | $248,700 |
| 1 | Dec. 31, 2011 | $100,000 | $24,870 | $75,130 | 173,570 |
| 2 | Dec. 31, 2012 | 100,000 | 17,357 | 82,643 | 90,927 |
| 3 | Dec. 31, 2013 | 100,000 | 9,073* | 90,927 | –0– |

*In the last period, interest expense is equal to the amount of the final payment minus the remaining unpaid balance. This compensates for the use of a present value table with factors carried to only three decimal places.

The entry at December 31, 2011, to record the first installment payment will be as follows:

| | | |
|---|---|---|
| Interest Expense . . . . . . . . . . . . . . . . . . . . . . . . . . . . . . . . . . . . . . . . . . | 24,870 | |
| Notes Payable . . . . . . . . . . . . . . . . . . . . . . . . . . . . . . . . . . . . . . . . . . . . | 75,130 | |
|     Cash. . . . . . . . . . . . . . . . . . . . . . . . . . . . . . . . . . . . . . . . . . . . . . . . . | | 100,000 |
| Made annual payment on installment note payable to U.S. Development Co. | | |

---

[3] There is an alternative recording technique that makes use of an account entitled Discount on Notes Payable. This alternative approach produces the same results and will be explained in later accounting courses.

## MARKET PRICES OF BONDS

The market price of bonds may be regarded as the *present value* to bondholders of the future principal and interest payments, discounted at the prevailing market rate of interest at the time of issuance. To illustrate, assume that Driscole Corporation issues $1,000,000 of 10-year, 10 percent bonds when the going market rate of interest is 12 percent. Because bond interest is paid semiannually, we must use 20 *semiannual* periods as the life of the bond issue and a 6 percent *semiannual* market rate of interest in our present value calculations. The discounted present value of the bond's future cash flows, discounted for 20 semiannual periods at 6 percent, is $885,500, computed as follows:

| | |
|---|---:|
| Present value of future principal payments: | |
|   $1,000,000 due after 20 semiannual periods, discounted at 6%: | |
|     $1,000,000 × .312 (from Table PV–1) . . . . . . . . . . . . . . . . . . . . . . . . . . . . . | $312,000 |
| Present value of future interest payments: | |
| $50,000 per period ($1,000,000 × 10% × ½) for 20 semiannual periods, | |
|   discounted at 6%: $50,000 × 11.470 (from Table PV–2) . . . . . . . . . . . . . . . . | 573,500 |
| Expected issuance price of bond issue . . . . . . . . . . . . . . . . . . . . . . . . . . . . . . | $885,500 |

Note that, because the market rate of interest exceeds the bond's coupon rate, the bonds are issued at a $114,500 discount ($1,000,000 face value − $885,500 issue price). Thus, we know that these bonds were sold to an underwriter at 88.55 (meaning 88.55 percent of their face value).

As illustrated in Chapter 10, the entire amount of the discount is debited to an account titled Discount on Bonds Payable at the time the bonds are issued. The entry to record the issuance of this bond is:

| | | |
|---|---:|---:|
| Cash . . . . . . . . . . . . . . . . . . . . . . . . . . . . . . . . . . . . . . . . . . . . . . . . . . . . . . | 885,500 | |
| Discount on Bonds Payable. . . . . . . . . . . . . . . . . . . . . . . . . . . . . . . . . . . | 114,500 | |
|   Bonds Payable . . . . . . . . . . . . . . . . . . . . . . . . . . . . . . . . . . . . . . . . . | | 1,000,000 |
| Issued 10%, 10-year bonds with $1,000,000 face value to an | | |
|   underwriter at a price of 88.55. | | |

When the bonds mature in 10 years, Driscole must pay bondholders the *full* $1 million face value of the bond issue, or $114,500 *more* than it received at the time the bonds were issued. As discussed in Chapter 10, the additional $114,500 due at maturity represents a portion of the company's total *interest expense* that must be amortized over the 10-year life of the bond. Thus, Driscole will incur interest expense of $55,725 every six months, computed as follows:

| | |
|---|---:|
| Semiannual interest *payment* (1,000,000 × 10% × ½) . . . . . . . . . . . . . . . . . . . . . | $50,000 |
| Add:  Semiannual amortization of bond discount | |
|     ([$114,500 ÷ 10 years] × ½) . . . . . . . . . . . . . . . . . . . . . . . . . . . . . . . . . . | 5,725 |
| Semiannual interest expense . . . . . . . . . . . . . . . . . . . . . . . . . . . . . . . . . . . . . | $55,725 |

The entry to record $55,725 of semiannual interest expense is:

| | | |
|---|---:|---:|
| Bond Interest Expense . . . . . . . . . . . . . . . . . . . . . . . . . . . . . . . . . . . . . . . . | 55,725 | |
|   Cash . . . . . . . . . . . . . . . . . . . . . . . . . . . . . . . . . . . . . . . . . . . . . . . . . . | | 50,000 |
|   Discount on Bonds Payable . . . . . . . . . . . . . . . . . . . . . . . . . . . . . . . . . | | 5,725 |
| To record semiannual interest expense and to recognize | | |
|   six months' amortization of the $114,500 discount | | |
|   on 10-year bonds payable. | | |

Notice that, while the amortization of the discount increases semiannual interest expense by $5,725, it does not require an immediate cash outlay. The $114,500 of additional interest expense for the *entire* 10-year period will not be paid until the bonds mature.

## CAPITAL LEASES

We briefly discuss capital leases in Chapter 10, but do not illustrate the accounting for these instruments. This appendix gives us an opportunity to explore this topic in greater detail.

A capital lease is regarded as a sale of the leased asset by the lessor to the lessee. At the date of this sale, the lessor recognizes sales revenue equal to the *present value* of the future lease payments receivable, discounted at a realistic rate of interest. The lessee also uses the present value of the future payments to determine the cost of the leased asset and the valuation of the related liability.

To illustrate, assume that, on December 1, Pace Tractor uses a *capital lease* to finance the sale of a tractor to Kelly Grading Co. The tractor was carried in Pace Tractor's perpetual inventory records at a cost of $15,000. Terms of the lease call for Kelly Grading Co. to make *24* monthly payments of *$1,000* each, beginning on December 31. These lease payments include an interest charge of *1 percent* per month. At the end of the 24-month lease, title to the tractor will pass to Kelly Grading Co. at no additional cost.

### Accounting by the Lessor (Pace Tractor)   Table PV–2 shows that the present value of $1 to be received monthly for 24 months, discounted at 1 percent per month, is 21.243. Therefore, the present value of the 24 future lease payments is $1,000 × 21.243, or *$21,243*. Pace Tractor should record this capital lease as a sale of the tractor at a price equal to the present value of the lease payments, as follows:

| | | |
|---|---|---|
| Lease Payments Receivable (net) ............................. | 21,243 | |
| Sales ..................................................... | | 21,243 |
| Financed sale of a tractor to Kelly Grading Co. using a capital lease requiring 24 monthly payments of $1,000. Payments include a 1% monthly interest charge. | | |
| Cost of Goods Sold ........................................ | 15,000 | |
| Inventory ............................................. | | 15,000 |
| To record cost of tractor sold under capital lease. | | |

Notice that the sales price of the tractor is only $21,243, even though the gross amount to be collected from Kelly Grading Co. amounts to $24,000 ($1,000 × 24 payments). The difference between these two amounts, $2,757, will be recognized by Pace Tractor as interest revenue over the term of the lease.

To illustrate the recognition of interest revenue, the entry on December 31 to record collection of the first monthly lease payment (rounded to the nearest dollar) will be:

| | | |
|---|---|---|
| Cash ...................................................... | 1,000 | |
| Interest Revenue ........................................ | | 212 |
| Lease Payments Receivable (net).......................... | | 788 |
| Received first lease payment from Kelly Grading Co.: $1,000 lease payment received, less $212 interest revenue ($21,243 × 1%), equals $788 reduction in lease payments receivable. | | |

After this first monthly payment is collected, the present value of the lease payments receivable is reduced to $20,455 ($21,243 original balance, less $788). Therefore, the interest revenue earned during the *second* month of the lease (rounded to the nearest dollar) will be *$205* ($20,455 × 1%).[4]

---

[4] Both Pace Tractor and Kelly Grading Co. would prepare *amortization tables* showing the allocation of each lease payment between interest and the principal amount due.

### Accounting by the Lessee (Kelly Grading Co.)

Kelly Grading Co. also should use the present value of the lease payments to determine the cost of the tractor and the amount of the related liability, as follows:

| | | |
|---|---|---|
| Leased Equipment | 21,243 | |
|    Lease Payments Obligation | | 21,243 |

To record acquisition of a tractor through a capital lease from
Pace Tractor. Terms call for 24 monthly payments of $1,000,
which include a 1% monthly interest charge.

The entry on December 31 to record the first monthly lease payment (rounded to the nearest dollar) will be:

| | | |
|---|---|---|
| Interest Expense | 212 | |
| Lease Payments Obligation | 788 | |
|    Cash | | 1,000 |

To record first monthly lease payment to Pace Tractor:
$1,000 lease payment, less $212 interest expense ($21,243 × 1%),
equals $788 reduction in lease payments obligation.

## OBLIGATIONS FOR POSTRETIREMENT BENEFITS

As we explain in Chapter 10, any unfunded obligation for postretirement benefits appears in the balance sheet at the *present value* of the expected future cash outlays to retired employees. The computation of this present value is so complex that it is performed by a professional actuary. But the present value of this obligation normally is far less than the expected future payments, as the cash payments will take place many years in the future.

**ASSIGNMENT MATERIAL** ## Discussion Questions

1. Explain what is meant by the phrase *time value of money.*

2. Explain why the present value of a future amount is always *less* than the future amount.

3. Identify the two factors that determine the difference between the present value and the future amount of an investment.

4. Describe three basic investment applications of the concept of the time value of money.

5. Briefly explain the relationships between present value and
(**a**) the length of time until the future cash flow occurs, and
(**b**) the discount rate used in determining present value.

6. Define *financial instruments*. Explain the valuation concept used in initially recording financial instruments in financial statements.

7. Are normal accounts receivable and accounts payable financial instruments? Are these items shown in the balance sheet at their present values? Explain.

8. Assuming no change in the expected amount of future cash flows, what factors may cause the present value of a financial instrument to change? Explain fully.

## Problems

**PROBLEM B.1**

Using Future Amount Tables

Use Table FA–1 (in Exhibit B–2) and Table FA–2 (in Exhibit B–4) to determine the future amounts of the following investments:

**a.** $20,000 is invested for 10 years, at 6 percent interest, compounded annually.

**b.** $100,000 is to be received five years from today, at 10 percent annual interest.

**c.** $10,000 is invested in a fund at the end of each of the next 10 years, at 8 percent interest, compounded annually.

**d.** $50,000 is invested initially, plus $5,000 is invested annually at the end of each of the next three years, at 12 percent interest, compounded annually.

**L03**  **PROBLEM B.2**
Bond Sinking Fund
**L04**

Tilman Company is required by a bond indenture to make equal annual payments to a bond sinking fund at the end of each of the next 20 years. The sinking fund will earn 8 percent interest and must accumulate to a total of $500,000 at the end of the 20-year period.

**Instructions**

**a.** Calculate the amount of the annual payments.

**b.** Calculate the total amount of interest that will be earned by the fund over the 20-year period.

**c.** Make the general journal entry to record redemption of the bond issue at the end of the 20-year period, assuming that the sinking fund is recorded on Tilman's accounting records at $500,000 and bonds payable are recorded at the same amount.

**d.** What would be the effect of an increase in the rate of return on the required annual payment? Explain.

**L01**  **PROBLEM B.3**
Using Present Value
Tables
**L02**

**L05**

Use Table PV–1 (in Exhibit B–7) and Table PV–2 (in Exhibit B–9) to determine the present values of the following cash flows:

**a.** $15,000 to be paid annually for 10 years, discounted at an annual rate of 6 percent. Payments are to occur at the end of each year.

**b.** $9,200 to be received today, assuming that the money will be invested in a two-year certificate of deposit earning 8 percent annually.

**c.** $300 to be paid monthly for 36 months, with an additional "balloon payment" of $12,000 due at the end of the thirty-sixth month, discounted at a monthly interest rate of 1½ percent. The first payment is to be one month from today.

**d.** $25,000 to be received annually for the first three years, followed by $15,000 to be received annually for the next two years (total of five years in which collections are received), discounted at an annual rate of 8 percent. Assume collections occur at year-end.

**L03**  **PROBLEM B.4**
Present Value and
Bond Prices
**L05**

**L06**

On June 30 of the current year, Rural Gas & Electric Co. issued $50,000,000 face value, 9 percent, 10-year bonds payable, with interest dates of December 31 and June 30. The bonds were issued at a discount, resulting in an effective *semiannual* interest rate of 5 percent.

**Instructions**

**a.** Compute the issue price for the bond that results in an effective semiannual interest rate of 5 percent. (Hint: Discount both the interest payments and the maturity value over 20 semiannual periods.)

**b.** Prepare a journal entry to record the issuance of the bonds at the sales price you computed in part **a.**

**c.** Explain why the bonds were issued at a discount.

**L03**  **PROBLEM B.5**
Valuation of a Note
Payable
**L05**

**L06**

On December 1, Showcase Interiors purchased a shipment of furniture from Colonial House by paying $10,500 cash and issuing an installment note payable in the face amount of $28,800. The note is to be paid in 24 monthly installments of $1,200 each. Although the note makes no mention of an interest charge, the rate of interest usually charged to Showcase Interiors in such transactions is 1½ percent per month.

**Instructions**

**a.** Compute the present value of the note payable, using a discount rate of 1½ percent per month.

**b.** Prepare the journal entries in the accounts of Showcase Interiors on:

    **1.** December 1, to record the purchase of the furniture (debit Inventory).

    **2.** December 31, to record the first $1,200 monthly payment on the note and to recognize interest expense for one month by the effective interest method. (Round interest expense to the nearest dollar.)

**c.** Show how the liability for this note would appear in the balance sheet at December 31. (Assume that the note is classified as a current liability.)

L08 **PROBLEM B.6**
Capital Leases: A
L05 Comprehensive
Problem

L06

Custom Truck Builders frequently uses long-term lease contracts to finance the sale of its trucks. On November 1, 2011, Custom Truck Builders leased to Interstate Van Lines a truck carried in the perpetual inventory records at $33,520. The terms of the lease call for Interstate Van Lines to make 36 monthly payments of $1,400 each, beginning on November 30, 2011. The present value of these payments, after considering a built-in interest charge of 1 percent per month, is equal to the regular $42,150 sales price of the truck. At the end of the 36-month lease, title to the truck will transfer to Interstate Van Lines.

**Instructions**

**a.** Prepare journal entries for 2011 in the accounts of Custom Truck Builders on:

  **1.** November 1, to record the sale financed by the lease and the related cost of goods sold. (Debit Lease Payments Receivable for the $42,150 present value of the future lease payments.)

  **2.** November 30, to record receipt of the first $1,400 monthly payment. (Prepare a compound journal entry that allocates the cash receipt between interest revenue and reduction of Lease Payments Receivable. The portion of each monthly payment recognized as interest revenue is equal to 1 percent of the balance of the account Lease Payments Receivable, at the beginning of that month. Round all interest computations to the nearest dollar.)

  **3.** December 31, to record receipt of the second monthly payment.

**b.** Prepare journal entries for 2011 in the accounts of Interstate Van Lines on:

  **1.** November 1, to record acquisition of the leased truck.

  **2.** November 30, to record the first monthly lease payment. (Determine the portion of the payment representing interest expense in a manner parallel to that described in part **a.**)

  **3.** December 31, to record the second monthly lease payment.

  **4.** December 31, to recognize depreciation on the leased truck through year-end. Compute depreciation expense by the straight-line method, using a 10-year service life and an estimated salvage value of $6,150.

**c.** Compute the net carrying value of the leased truck in the balance sheet of Interstate Van Lines at December 31, 2011.

**d.** Compute the amount of Interstate Van Lines's lease payment obligation at December 31, 2011.

L05 **PROBLEM B.7**
Valuation of a Note
L06 Receivable with an
Unrealistic Interest
Rate

On December 31, Richland Farms sold a tract of land, which had cost $930,000, to Skyline Developers in exchange for $150,000 cash and a five-year, 4 percent note receivable for $900,000. Interest on the note is payable annually, and the principal amount is due in five years. The accountant for Richland Farms did not notice the unrealistically low interest rate on the note and made the following entry on December 31 to record this sale.

| | | |
|---|---|---|
| Cash . . . . . . . . . . . . . . . . . . . . . . . . . . . . . . . . . . . . . . . . . . . . . . . . | 150,000 | |
| Notes Receivable. . . . . . . . . . . . . . . . . . . . . . . . . . . . . . . . . . . . . . . | 900,000 | |
|    Land . . . . . . . . . . . . . . . . . . . . . . . . . . . . . . . . . . . . . : . . . . . . . . . | | 930,000 |
|    Gain on Sale of Land . . . . . . . . . . . . . . . . . . . . . . . . . . . . . . . . . . . | | 120,000 |
| Sold land to Skyline Developers in exchange for cash and five-year note with interest due annually. | | |

**Instructions**

a. Compute the present value of the note receivable from Skyline Developers at the date of sale, assuming that a realistic rate of interest for this transaction is 12 percent. (Hint: Consider both the annual interest payments and the maturity value of the note.)

b. Prepare the journal entry on December 31 to record the sale of the land correctly. Show supporting computations for the gain or loss on the sale.

c. Explain what effects the error made by Richland Farms's accountant will have on (**1**) the net income in the year of the sale and (**2**) the combined net income of the next five years. Ignore income taxes.

# Forms of Business Organization

Learning Objectives

**AFTER STUDYING THIS APPENDIX, YOU SHOULD BE ABLE TO:**

**LO1** Describe the basic characteristics of a sole proprietorship.

**LO2** Identify factors to consider in evaluating the profitability and liquidity of a sole proprietorship.

**LO3** Describe the basic characteristics of a general partnership and of partnerships that limit personal liability.

**LO4** Describe the basic characteristics of a corporation.

**LO5** Account for corporate income taxes; explain the effects of these taxes on before-tax profits and losses.

**LO6** Account for the issuance of capital stock.

**LO7** Explain the nature of retained earnings, account for dividends, and prepare a statement of retained earnings.

**LO8** Explain why the financial statements of a corporation are interpreted differently from those of an unincorporated business.

**LO9** Discuss the principal factors to consider in selecting a form of business organization.

**LO10** Allocate partnership net income among the partners.

c

## IMPORTANCE OF BUSINESS FORM

The legal form of a business organization is an important consideration not only when the business is first formed but also throughout its operating life. The form of an enterprise affects its ability to raise capital, the relationship between the organization and its owners, and the security of both creditors' and owners' claims. Three primary forms of business organization are generally found in the United States—sole proprietorships, partnerships, and corporations.

Corporations carry out the majority of business activity, and as a result, that form of business organization is the primary focus of this textbook. Sole proprietorships and partnerships are also important, however, because they represent the largest numbers of business organizations in the United States. This appendix supplements the introductory coverage of sole proprietorships and partnerships presented earlier in the text, as well as expanding the coverage of corporations as the dominant form of business organization.

## Sole Proprietorships

A **sole proprietorship** is an unincorporated business owned by one person. Proprietorships are the most common form of business organization because they are so easy to start.

Creating a sole proprietorship requires *no authorization* from any governmental agency. Often the business requires little or no investment of capital. For example, a youngster with a paper route, baby-sitting service, or lawn-mowing business is a sole proprietorship. On a larger scale, sole proprietorships are widely used for farms, service businesses, small retail stores, restaurants, and professional practices, such as medicine, law, and public accounting.

A sole proprietorship provides an excellent model for demonstrating accounting principles because it is the simplest form of business organization. But in the business world, you will seldom encounter financial statements for these organizations.

Most sole proprietorships are relatively small businesses with few—if any—financial reporting obligations. Their needs for accounting information consist primarily of data used in daily business operations—the balance in the company's bank account and the amounts receivable and payable. In fact, many sole proprietorships do not prepare formal financial statements unless some special need arises, such as information to support bank loans.

### THE CONCEPT OF THE SEPARATE BUSINESS ENTITY

For accounting purposes, and consistent with one of the basic accounting principles, we treat every business organization—including a sole proprietorship—as an entity separate from the other activities of its owner. This enables us to measure the performance of the business separately from the other financial affairs of its owner.

In the eyes of the law, however, a sole proprietorship is *not* an entity separate from its owner. Under the law, the proprietor is the "entity," and a sole proprietorship merely represents some of this individual's financial activities. The fact that a sole proprietorship and its owner legally are one and the same explains many of the distinctive characteristics of this form of organization.

### CHARACTERISTICS OF A SOLE PROPRIETORSHIP

Among the key characteristics of sole proprietorships are:

- *Ease of formation.* (This explains why these organizations are so common.)
- *Business assets actually belong to the proprietor.* Because the business is not a legal entity, it cannot own property. The business assets actually belong to the *proprietor,* not to the business. Therefore, the proprietor may transfer assets in or out of the business *at will.*
- *The business pays no income taxes.* Federal tax laws do not view a sole proprietorship as separate from the other financial activities of its owner. Therefore, the proprietorship *does not* file an income tax return or pay income taxes. Instead, the *owner* must include the income of the business in his or her *personal* federal income tax return.
- *The business pays no salary to the owner.* The owner of a sole proprietorship is not working for a salary. Rather, the owner's compensation consists of the entire net income

**Learning Objective**
Describe the basic
characteristics of a sole
proprietorship.

(or net loss) of the business. Any money withdrawn from the business by its owner should be recorded in the owner's *drawing* account, *not* recognized as salaries expense.

- *The owner is personally liable for the debts of the business*. This concept, called **unlimited personal liability,** is too important to be treated as just one item in a list. It deserves special attention.

## UNLIMITED PERSONAL LIABILITY

The owner of a sole proprietorship is *personally responsible* for all of the company's debts. Thus, a business "mishap," such as personal injuries stemming from business operations, may result in enormous personal liability for the business owner.[1]

Unlimited personal liability is the greatest *disadvantage* to this form of organization. Other forms of business organization provide owners with some means of limiting their personal liability for business debts—but not the sole proprietorship. If business operations entail a risk of substantial liability, the owner should consider another form of business organization.

## ACCOUNTING PRACTICES OF SOLE PROPRIETORSHIPS

In the balance sheet of a sole proprietorship, total owner's equity is represented by the balance in the owner's **capital account.** Investments of assets by the owner are recorded by crediting this account. Withdrawals of assets by the owner are recorded by debiting the owner's **drawing account.** At the end of the accounting period, the drawing account and the Income Summary account are closed into the owner's capital account and presented as a single amount.

The only financial reporting obligation of many sole proprietorships is the information that must be included in the owner's personal income tax return. For this reason, some sole proprietorships base their accounting procedures on *income tax rules,* rather than generally accepted accounting principles.

## EVALUATING THE FINANCIAL STATEMENTS OF A PROPRIETORSHIP

**Learning Objective**

**LO2**  Identify factors to consider in evaluating the profitability and liquidity of a sole proprietorship.

**The Adequacy of Net Income**    Sole proprietorships do not recognize any salary expense relating to the owner, nor any interest expense on the capital that the owner has invested in the business. Thus, if the business is to be considered successful, its net income should *at least* provide the owner with reasonable compensation for any personal services and equity capital that the owner has provided to the business.

In addition, the net income of a sole proprietorship should be adequate to compensate the owner for taking significant *risks*. Many small businesses fail. The owner of a sole proprietorship has *unlimited personal liability* for the debts of the business. Therefore, if a sole proprietorship sustains large losses, the owner can lose *much more* than the amount of his or her equity investment.

In summary, the net income of a sole proprietorship should be sufficient to compensate the owner for three factors: (1) personal services rendered to the business, (2) capital invested, and (3) the degree of financial risk that the owner is taking.

**Evaluating Liquidity**    For a business organized as a *corporation,* creditors often base their lending decisions on the relationships between assets and liabilities in the corporation's balance sheet. But if the business is organized as a sole proprietorship, the balance sheet is less useful to creditors.

Remember, the assets listed in the balance sheet are owned by the *proprietor,* not by the business. The owner can transfer assets in and out of the business at will. Also, it is the *owner* who is financially responsible for the company's debts. Therefore, the ability of a sole proprietorship to pay its debts depends on the *financial strength of the owner,* not on the relationships among the assets and liabilities appearing in the company's balance sheet.

---

[1] Injuries sustained by employees or customers have often resulted in multimillion-dollar liabilities for the business organization. The judgments against a business that result from litigation may exceed available insurance coverage. A sole proprietorship should always carry substantial malpractice and general liability insurance to protect the owner from losing personal assets.

The financial strength of a sole proprietor may be affected by many things that *do not appear* in the financial statements of the business. For example, the owner may have great personal wealth—or overwhelming personal debts.

In summary, creditors of a sole proprietorship should look past the balance sheet of the business. The real issue is the debt-paying ability of the *owner*. Creditors of the business may ask the owner to supply *personal* financial information. They also may investigate the owner's credit history, using such credit-rating agencies as TRW.

**A Word of Caution**    In Chapter 1, we discussed several factors that *promote the integrity* of the financial statements of publicly owned companies. Among these safeguards are the structure of internal control, audits by independent accountants, federal securities laws, and the competence and integrity of the professional accountants.

Let us stress that these safeguards apply to the **public information** distributed by publicly owned companies. However, they often *do not* apply to financial information provided by small businesses.

Small businesses may not have the resources—or the need—to establish sophisticated internal control structures. The financial information that they develop usually is *not* audited. Federal securities laws apply only to companies that are publicly owned. And the accounting records of a sole proprietorship often are maintained by the owner, who may have little experience in accounting.

## Partnerships

A **partnership** is an unincorporated business owned by two or more *partners.*[2] A partnership often is referred to as a *firm.*

Partnerships are the *least* common form of business organization, but they are widely used for professional practices, such as medicine, law, and public accounting.[3] Partnerships also are used for many small businesses, especially those that are family-owned. Most partnerships are small businesses—but certainly not all.

For accounting purposes, we view a partnership as an entity separate from the other activities of its owners. But under the law, the partnership is *not* separate from its owners. Rather, the law regards the partners as personally—*and jointly*—responsible for the activities of the business.

The assets of a partnership do not belong to the business—they belong jointly to all of the partners. Unless special provisions are made, each partner has unlimited personal liability for the debts of the business. The partnership itself pays no income taxes, but the partners include their respective shares of the firm's income in their *personal* income tax returns.

From a legal standpoint, partnerships have *limited lives*. A partnership ends upon the withdrawal or death of an existing partner. Admission of a new partner terminates the previous partnership and creates a new legal entity. However, this is only a legal distinction. Most partnerships have *continuity of existence* extending beyond the participation of individual partners. Partnership agreements often have provisions that make the retirement of partners and the admission of new partners *routine events* that do not affect the operations of the business.

The term *partnership* actually includes three distinct types of organizations: general partnerships, limited partnerships, and limited liability partnerships. We will begin our discussion with the characteristics of *general partnerships*.

### GENERAL PARTNERSHIPS

In a general partnership, each partner has rights and responsibilities similar to those of a sole proprietor. For example, each **general partner** can withdraw cash and other assets from the

**Learning Objective**

Describe the basic characteristics of a general partnership and of partnerships that limit personal liability.

LO3

---

[2] A partner may be either an individual or a corporation.

[3] Some state laws prohibit professional practices from incorporating. Therefore, professional practices with more than one owner *must* operate as partnerships.

business at will.[4] Also, each partner has the full authority of an owner to negotiate contracts binding upon the business. This concept is called **mutual agency.** Every partner also has *unlimited personal liability* for the debts of the firm.

Combining the characteristics of unlimited personal liability and mutual agency makes a general partnership a potentially risky form of business organization. Assume, for example, that you enter into a general partnership with Tom Jones. You agree to split profits and losses "50–50." While you are on vacation, Jones commits the partnership to a contract that it simply does not have the resources to complete. Your firm's failure to complete the contract causes large financial losses to the customer. The customer sues your firm and is awarded a judgment of $5 million by the court.

Jones has few financial resources and declares personal bankruptcy. The holder of the judgment against your firm can hold *you personally liable for the whole $5 million.* The fact that you and Jones agreed to split everything "50–50" does *not* lessen your personal liability to the partnership's creditors. You may have a legal claim against Jones for his half of this debt, but so what? Jones is bankrupt.

In summary, general partnerships involve the same unlimited personal liability as sole proprietorships. This risk is intensified, however, because you may be held financially responsible for your partner's actions, as well as for your own.

## PARTNERSHIPS THAT LIMIT PERSONAL LIABILITY

Over the years, state laws have evolved to allow modified forms of partnerships, including limited partnerships and limited liability partnerships. The purpose of these modified forms of partnerships is to *place limits* on the potential liability of individual partners.

### Limited Partnerships

A **limited partnership** has one or more general partners and one or more limited partners. The general partners are partners in the traditional sense, with unlimited personal liability for the debts of the business and the right to make managerial decisions.

The **limited partners** are basically passive investors. They share in the profits and losses of the business, but they do not participate actively in management and are *not* personally liable for debts of the business. Thus, if the firm has financial troubles, the losses incurred by the limited partners are limited to the amounts they have invested in the business.

In the past, limited partnerships were widely used for various investment ventures, such as drilling for oil, developing real estate, or making a motion picture. These businesses often lost money—at least in the early years; if they were profitable, the profits came in later years.

For such ventures, the limited partnership concept had great appeal to investors. Limited partners could include their share of any partnership net loss in their personal income tax returns, offsetting taxable income from other sources. And as *limited* partners, their financial risk was limited to the amount of their equity investment.

Recent changes in tax laws have greatly restricted the extent to which limited partners may offset partnership losses against other types of income. For this reason, there are fewer limited partnerships today than in the past. But in many cases, investors today can obtain similar tax benefits if the business venture is organized as an *S Corporation,* a form of business organization discussed later in this appendix.

### Limited Liability Partnerships

A **limited liability partnership** is a relatively new form of business organization. States traditionally have required professionals, such as doctors, lawyers, and accountants, to organize their practices either as sole proprietorships or as partnerships. The purpose of this requirement was to ensure that these professionals had unlimited liability for their professional activities.

Over the years, many professional partnerships have grown in size. Several public accounting firms, for example, now have thousands of partners and operate in countries all over the

---

[4] Title to real estate is held in the name of the partnership and, therefore, cannot be sold or withdrawn by any partner at will.

world. Also, lawsuits against professional firms have increased greatly in number and in dollar amount. To prevent these lawsuits from bankrupting innocent partners, the concept of the limited liability partnership has emerged. In this type of partnership, each partner has unlimited personal liability for his or her *own* professional activities, but not for the actions of other partners. Unlike a limited partnership, all of the partners in a limited liability partnership may participate in management of the firm.

## ACCOUNTING PRACTICES OF PARTNERSHIPS

In most respects, partnership accounting is similar to that in a sole proprietorship—except there are more owners. As a result, a separate capital account and a separate drawing account are maintained for each partner.

Partnerships, like sole proprietorships, recognize no salaries expense for services provided to the organization by the partners. Amounts paid to partners are recorded in the partner's drawing account.

The statement of owner's equity is replaced by a **statement of partners' equity,** which shows separately the changes in each partner's capital account.[5] A typical statement of partners' equity appears in Exhibit C–1.

| BLAIR AND CROSS STATEMENT OF PARTNERS' EQUITY FOR THE YEAR ENDED DECEMBER 31, 2011 | | | |
|---|---|---|---|
| | Blair | Cross | Total |
| Balances, Jan. 1, 2011 | $160,000 | $160,000 | $320,000 |
| Add: Additional Investments | 10,000 | 10,000 | 20,000 |
| Net Income for the Year | 30,000 | 30,000 | 60,000 |
| Subtotals | $200,000 | $200,000 | $400,000 |
| Less: Drawings | 24,000 | 16,000 | 40,000 |
| Balances, Dec. 31, 2011 | $176,000 | $184,000 | $360,000 |

**Exhibit C–1**

**STATEMENT OF PARTNERS' EQUITY**

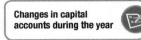

Changes in capital accounts during the year

**Allocating Net Income among the Partners**    A special feature of a partnership is the need to *allocate* the firm's net income among its partners. Allocating partnership net income means computing each partner's share of total net income (or loss) and crediting (or debiting) this amount to the partner's capital account.

This allocation of partnership income is simply a bookkeeping entry, made as the Income Summary account is closed into the various partners' capital accounts. It *does not* involve any distributions of cash or other assets to the partners.

The amount that an individual partner *withdraws* during the year may *differ substantially* from the amount of partnership net income allocated to that partner. All partners pay personal income taxes on the amount of partnership income *allocated* to them—*not* on the amount of assets withdrawn.

Partners have great freedom in deciding how to allocate the firm's net income among themselves. In the absence of prior agreement, state laws generally provide for an *equal split* among the partners. But this seldom happens. Partners usually agree in advance how the firm's net income will be allocated.

Various features of partnership accounting, including the allocation of net income, are illustrated later in this appendix.

**The Importance of a Partnership Contract**    Every partnership needs a carefully written **partnership contract,** prepared before the firm begins operation. This contract is an *agreement among the partners* as to their rights and responsibilities. It spells out the

---

[5] In firms with a large number of partners, this statement is condensed to show only the changes in *total* partners' equity.

responsibilities of individual partners, how net income will be divided between or among the partners, and the amounts of assets that partners are allowed to withdraw.

A partnership contract does not prevent disputes from arising among the partners, but it does provide a contractual foundation for their resolution.

## EVALUATING THE FINANCIAL STATEMENTS OF A PARTNERSHIP

**The Adequacy of Net Income**    The net income of a partnership is similar to that of a sole proprietorship. It represents the partners' compensation for (1) personal services, (2) invested capital, and (3) assumption of the risks of ownership. Also, the reported net income is a pretax amount because the partnership itself pays no income tax.

The services and capital provided by individual partners may vary, as may the degree of financial risk assumed. Therefore, it is quite difficult to evaluate the income of a partnership. Rather, the individual partners must separately evaluate their *respective shares* of the partnership net income in light of their personal contributions to the firm. Some partners may find the partnership quite rewarding, while others may consider their share of the partnership net income inadequate.

**Evaluating Liquidity**    The balance sheet of a partnership is more meaningful than that of a sole proprietorship. This is because there are legal distinctions between partnership assets, which are jointly owned, and the personal assets of individual partners. Another reason is that personal responsibility for business debts may *not* extend to all of the partners.

Creditors should understand the distinctions among the types of partnerships. In a general partnership, all partners have unlimited personal liability for the debts of the business. This situation affords creditors the maximum degree of protection. In a limited partnership, only the *general partners* have personal liability for these obligations. In a limited liability partnership, liability for negligence or malpractice extends only to those partners directly involved.

## Corporations

Nearly all large businesses—and many small ones—are organized as corporations. There are many more sole proprietorships than corporations; but in dollar volume of business activity, corporations hold an impressive lead. Because of the dominant role of the corporation in our economy, it is important for everyone interested in business, economics, or politics to have an understanding of corporations and their accounting policies.

## WHAT IS A CORPORATION?

Learning Objective

**L04  Describe the basic characteristics of a corporation.**

A **corporation** is a *legal entity,* having an existence separate and distinct from that of its owners. The owners of a corporation are called **stockholders** (or shareholders), and their ownership is evidenced by transferable shares of **capital stock.**

A corporation is more difficult and costly to form than other types of organizations. The corporation must obtain a *charter* from the state in which it is formed, and it must receive authorization from that state to issue shares of capital stock. The formation of a corporation usually requires the services of an attorney.

As a separate legal entity, a corporation may own property in its own name. The assets of a corporation belong to the corporation itself, not to the stockholders. A corporation has legal status in court—it may sue and be sued as if it were a person. As a legal entity, a corporation may enter into contracts, is *responsible for its own debts,* and *pays income taxes* on its earnings.

On a daily basis, corporations are run by *salaried professional managers,* not by their stockholders.[6] Thus, the stockholders are primarily investors, rather than active participants in the business.

---

[6] In many cases, the managers and stockholders are one and the same. That is, managers may own stock, and stockholders may be hired into management roles. Ownership of stock, however, does not *automatically* give the shareholder managerial authority.

The top level of a corporation's professional management is the **board of directors.** These directors are *elected by the stockholders* and are responsible for hiring the other professional managers. In addition, the directors make major policy decisions, including the extent to which profits of the corporation are distributed to stockholders.

The fact that directors are elected by the stockholders means that a stockholder—or group of stockholders—owning more than 50 percent of the company's stock effectively controls the corporation. These controlling stockholders have the voting power to elect the directors, who in turn set company policies and appoint managers and corporate officers.

The transferability of corporate ownership, together with professional management, gives corporations a greater *continuity of existence* than other forms of organization. Individual stockholders may sell, give, or bequeath their shares to someone else without disrupting business operations. Thus, a corporation may continue its business operations *indefinitely,* without regard to changes in ownership.

In Exhibit C–2 we contrast the corporate form of business with a sole proprietorship and a general partnership.

| Characteristics of Forms of Business Organizations | | | |
|---|---|---|---|
| | **Sole Proprietorship** | **General Partnership** | **Corporation** |
| 1. Legal status | Not a separate legal entity | Not a separate legal entity | Separate legal entity |
| 2. Liability of owners for business debts | Personal liability for business debts | Personal liability for partnership debts | No personal liability for corporate debts |
| 3. Accounting status | Separate entity | Separate entity | Separate entity |
| 4. Tax status | Income taxable to owner | Income taxable to partners | Files a corporate tax return and pays income taxes on its earnings |
| 5. Persons with managerial authority | Owner | Every partner | Hires professional managers |
| 6. Continuity of the business | Entity ceases with retirement or death of owner | New partnership is formed with a change in partners | Indefinite existence that is not affected by the exchange of ownership shares |

**Exhibit C–2**

**COMPARISON OF BUSINESS ORGANIZATIONS**

## STOCKHOLDERS' LIABILITY FOR DEBTS OF A CORPORATION

The second item in Exhibit C–2—the liability of owners for business debts—deserves special attention. Stockholders in a corporation have *no personal liability* for the debts of the business. If a corporation fails, stockholders' potential losses are limited to the amount of their equity in the business.

To investors in large companies—and to the owners of many small businesses—**limited personal liability** is the *greatest advantage* of the corporate form of business organization.

Creditors, too, should understand that shareholders are not personally liable for the debts of a corporation. Creditors have claims against only the *assets of the corporation,* not the personal assets of the corporation's owners.

## WHAT TYPES OF BUSINESSES CHOOSE THE CORPORATE FORM OF ORGANIZATION?

The answer, basically, is *all kinds.*

When we think of corporations, we often think of large, well-known companies such as IBM, Procter & Gamble, and AT&T. Indeed, almost all large businesses are organized as corporations. Limited shareholder liability, transferability of ownership, professional management, and continuity of existence make the corporation the best form of organization for pooling the resources of a great many equity investors.

The stocks of these large corporations are traded (bought and sold by investors) on organized securities markets, such as the New York Stock Exchange and the National Association of Securities Dealers Automated Quotations (NASDAQ). Companies whose shares are traded on these exchanges are said to be **publicly owned corporations** because anyone may purchase their stock.

When you purchase stock through an exchange, you normally are acquiring the shares from *another investor* (stockholder), not from the corporation itself. The existence of organized stock exchanges is what makes the stock in publicly owned corporations readily transferable.

Not all corporations, however, are large and publicly owned. Many small businesses are organized as corporations. In fact, many corporations have *only one stockholder.* Corporations whose ownership shares are not publicly traded are said to be **closely held corporations.**

Generally accepted accounting principles are basically the same for all types of business organizations. Because of the legal characteristics of corporations, however, there are significant differences in the ways these organizations account for income taxes, salaries paid to owners, owners' equity, and distributions of profits to their owners.

## ACCOUNTING FOR CORPORATE INCOME TAXES

**Learning Objective**

**L05** Account for corporate income taxes; explain the effects of these taxes on before-tax profits and losses.

One of the principal differences between a corporation and an *unincorporated business* is that the corporation must pay income taxes on its earnings.

Corporate income taxes usually are payable in four quarterly installments. If the company is to properly "match" income taxes with the related revenue, **income tax expense** should be recognized in the periods in which the taxable income is *earned*. This is accomplished by making an *adjusting entry* at the end of each accounting period.

Total income tax expense for the year cannot be accurately determined until the corporation completes its annual income tax return. But the income tax expense for each accounting period can be *reasonably estimated* by applying the current *tax rate* to the company's *taxable income*. This relationship is summarized below:

$$\begin{array}{c}\textbf{Taxable Income}\\ \textbf{(determined according}\\ \textbf{to tax regulations)}\end{array} \times \begin{array}{c}\textbf{Tax Rate}\\ \textbf{(set by law)}\end{array} = \begin{array}{c}\textbf{Income Tax}\\ \textbf{Expense}\end{array}$$

**Taxable income** is computed in conformity with *income tax regulations,* not generally accepted accounting principles. In this introductory discussion, we will assume that taxable income is equal to **income before income tax**—a subtotal that often appears in a corporate income statement. Income before income tax is simply total revenue less all expenses *other than* income tax expense.[7]

Tax rates vary depending on the amount of taxable income. Also, Congress may change these rates from one year to the next. For purposes of illustration, we will assume a corporate tax rate of *40 percent* to include the effects of both federal and state income taxes.

To illustrate the recognition of income tax expense, assume that, in November, Warren, Inc., earns income before tax of $50,000. The month-end adjusting entry to recognize the related income tax would be:

**Adjusting entry to accrue income taxes for the month**

| | | |
|---|---|---|
| Income Tax Expense............................................. | 20,000 | |
|    Income Tax Payable....................................... | | 20,000 |
| To record estimated income tax expense on income earned in November ($50,000 × 40%). | | |

---

[7] In most cases, *income before tax* provides a reasonable approximation of *taxable income,* but differences in the determination of income before income tax and taxable income do exist. We discuss significant differences between these subtotals at various points throughout this textbook, although an in-depth discussion of this topic is deferred to more advanced accounting courses.

Income tax payable is a current liability that will appear in Warren's balance sheet. The presentation of income tax expense in the company's November income statement is illustrated in Exhibit C–3:

| WARREN, INC. CONDENSED INCOME STATEMENT FOR THE MONTH ENDED NOVEMBER 30, 2011 | |
| --- | --- |
| Net sales. | $550,000 |
| Cost of goods sold | 350,000 |
| Gross profit. | $200,000 |
| Expenses (other than income taxes—detail not shown) | 150,000 |
| Income before income tax | $ 50,000 |
| Income tax expense | 20,000 |
| Net income | $ 30,000 |

**Exhibit C–3**

**CONDENSED INCOME STATEMENT**

**Notice income taxes appear separately from other expenses**

Income tax expense differs from other business expenses in that income taxes do not help generate revenue. For this reason, income tax is often shown separately from other expenses in the income statement—following a subtotal such as Income (or Loss) Before Income Tax. In an income statement, income tax expense often is termed *provision for income taxes*.

### Income Tax in *Unprofitable* Periods
What happens to income tax expense when *losses* are incurred? In these situations, the company may recognize a negative amount of income tax expense. The adjusting entry to record income tax in an unprofitable accounting period consists of a *debit* to Income Tax Payable and a *credit* to Income Tax Expense.

"Negative" income tax expense means that the company expects to recover from the government some of the income tax recognized as expense in earlier profitable periods.[8] A negative (credit) balance in the Income Tax Expense account is offset against the amount of the before-tax loss, as shown below:

| Partial Income Statement—for an *Unprofitable* Period | |
| --- | --- |
| Income (loss) before income tax. | $(100,000) |
| Income tax benefit (recovery of previously recorded tax) | 40,000 |
| Net loss | $ (60,000) |

**Income tax benefit reduces a pretax loss**

We have seen that income tax expense *reduces* the amount of before-tax *profits*. Notice now that an income tax *benefit*—representing tax refunds—*reduces the amount of a pretax loss*. Thus, income tax reduces the amounts of *both* profits and losses.

If the Income Taxes Payable account has a *negative (debit) balance* at year-end, it is reclassified in the balance sheet as an *asset,* called "Income Tax Refund Receivable."

## SALARIES PAID TO OWNERS

We have made the point that unincorporated businesses record payments to their owners as *drawings,* not as salaries expense. But the owners of a corporation cannot make withdrawals of corporate assets. Also, many of a corporation's employees—perhaps thousands—may also be stockholders. Therefore, corporations make *no distinction* between employees who are stockholders and those who are not. All salaries paid to employees (including employee/stockholders) are recognized by the corporation as *salaries expense.*

---

[8] Tax refunds are limited to taxes paid in recent years. In this introductory discussion, we assume the company has paid sufficient taxes in prior periods to permit full recovery of any negative tax expense relating to a loss in the current period.

## OWNERS' EQUITY IN A CORPORATE BALANCE SHEET

In every form of business organization, there are two basic *sources* of owners' equity: (1) investment by the owners and (2) earnings from profitable operations. State laws require corporations to distinguish in their balance sheets between the amounts of equity arising from each source.

To illustrate, assume the following:

- On January 4, 2009, Mary Foster and several investors started Mary's Cab Co., a closely held corporation, by investing $100,000 cash. In exchange, the corporation issued to these investors 10,000 shares of its capital stock.
- It is now December 31, 2011. Over its three-year life, Mary's Cab Co. has earned total net income of $180,000, of which $60,000 has been distributed to the stockholders as *dividends.*

The stockholders' equity section of the company's 2011 balance sheet follows:

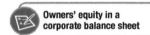

**Owners' equity in a corporate balance sheet**

| Stockholders' equity: | |
| --- | --- |
| Capital stock | $100,000 |
| Retained earnings | 120,000 |
| Total stockholders' equity | $220,000 |

The Capital Stock account represents the $100,000 invested in the business by Mary Foster and the other stockholders. This amount often is described as "invested capital," or "paid-in capital."

The $120,000 shown as **retained earnings** represents the *lifetime earnings* of the business, less the amount of cash representing those earnings that has been *distributed to the stockholders as dividends* (that is, $180,000 in net income, less $60,000 in dividends, equals $120,000). Retained earnings often are described as "earned capital."

## THE ISSUANCE OF CAPITAL STOCK

**Learning Objective**

**L08** Account for the issuance of capital stock.

When a corporation receives cash or other assets from its owners, in a sale of capital stock, it records these investment transactions by crediting the Capital Stock account.

For example, the entry made by Mary's Cab Co. to record the issuance of 10,000 shares of capital stock in exchange for $100,000 cash is:

**Entry to record issuance of capital stock**

| | | |
| --- | --- | --- |
| Cash | 100,000 | |
| Capital Stock | | 100,000 |
| Issued 10,000 shares of capital stock for cash. | | |

## RETAINED EARNINGS

**Learning Objective**

**L07** Explain the nature of retained earnings, account for dividends, and prepare a statement of retained earnings.

Retained earnings represent the owners' equity created through profitable operation of the business. Earning net income causes the balance in the Retained Earnings account to increase. However, many corporations follow a policy of *distributing to their stockholders* some of the resources generated by profitable operations. These distributions are termed **dividends.**

Dividends *reduce* both total assets and stockholders' equity (similar to drawings in an unincorporated business). The reduction in stockholders' equity is reflected by decreasing the balance in the Retained Earnings account. Retained earnings also are reduced by any *net losses* incurred by the business.

Notice that the balance of the Retained Earnings account does *not* represent the net income or net loss of one specific accounting period. Rather, it represents the *cumulative* net income (or net loss) of the business to date, *less* any amounts that have been distributed to the stockholders as dividends. In short, retained earnings represent the earnings that have been *retained* in the corporation. Some of the largest corporations have become large by consistently retaining in the business most of the resources generated by profitable operations.

Remember, retained earnings are *an element of owners' equity.* The owners' equity in a business *does not* represent cash or any other asset. The amount of cash owned by a corporation appears in the *asset section* of the balance sheet, *not* in the stockholders' equity section.

## ACCOUNTING FOR DIVIDENDS

The owners of a corporation may not withdraw profits from the business at will. Instead, distributions of cash or other assets to the stockholders must be formally authorized—or *declared*—by the company's board of directors. These formal distributions are termed *dividends.* By law, dividends must be distributed to all stockholders *in proportion to the number of shares owned.*

A dividend is officially declared by the board of directors on one date, and then is paid (distributed) in the near future. To illustrate, assume that on December 1, 2011, the directors of Mary's Cab Co. declare a regular quarterly dividend of 50 cents per share on the 10,000 shares of outstanding capital stock. The board's resolution specifies that the dividend will be paid on December 15 to stockholders of record on December 10.

Two entries are required: one on December 1 to record the *declaration* of the dividend, and the other on December 15 to record payment:

| | | | |
|---|---|---|---|
| Dec. 1 | Dividends ............................................... | 5,000 | |
| |     Dividends Payable..................................... | | 5,000 |
| | Declared a dividend of 50 cents per share payable Dec. 15 to stockholders of record on Dec. 10. | | |
| 15 | Dividends Payable ..................................... | 5,000 | |
| |     Cash ................................................. | | 5,000 |
| | Paid dividend declared on Dec. 1. | | |

Entry to record the declaration of a dividend ...

and the entry to record its payment

Notice that at the *declaration date,* December 1, there is no reduction in assets. But the stockholders' right to receive the dividend is recognized as a liability. This liability is discharged on the *payment date,* December 15, when the dividend checks are actually mailed to stockholders. No entry is required on the date of record, December 10.

At the end of the period, the Dividends account is closed into the Retained Earnings account.

## CLOSING ENTRIES AND THE STATEMENT OF RETAINED EARNINGS

### Updating the Retained Earnings Account for Profits, Losses, and Dividends
To review, the amount of retained earnings is increased by earning net income; it is reduced by incurring net losses and by declaring dividends. In the accounting records, these changes are recorded by *closing* the balances in the Income Summary account and Dividends account into the Retained Earnings account.

To illustrate, assume that at January 1, 2011, Mary's Cab Co. had retained earnings of *$80,000.* During the year, the company earned net income of *$60,000* and paid four quarterly dividends totaling *$20,000.* These entries at December 31 close the Income Summary and Dividends accounts:

| | | |
|---|---|---|
| Income Summary.......................................... | 60,000 | |
|     Retained Earnings ...................................... | | 60,000 |
| To close the Income Summary account at the end of a profitable year. | | |

Net income increases retained earnings

| | | |
|---|---|---|
| Retained Earnings......................................... | 20,000 | |
|     Dividends ............................................. | | 20,000 |
| To close the Dividends account, thereby reducing retained earnings by the amount of dividends declared during the year. | | |

If the corporation had incurred a *net loss* for the year, the Income Summary account would have had a debit balance. The entry to close the account then would have involved a *debit* to Retained Earnings, which would *reduce* total stockholders' equity, and a *credit* to the Income Summary account.

**The Statement of Retained Earnings**   Corporations prepare a **statement of retained earnings,** summarizing the changes in the amount of retained earnings over the year.[9] A statement of retained earnings for Mary's Cab Co. is in Exhibit C–4. The last line of the statement represents the amount of retained earnings that will appear in the company's year-end balance sheet.

**Exhibit C–4**

**STATEMENT OF RETAINED EARNINGS**

| MARY'S CAB CO.<br>STATEMENT OF RETAINED EARNINGS<br>FOR THE YEAR ENDED DECEMBER 31, 2011 | |
| --- | --- |
| Retained earnings, Jan. 1, 2011 | $ 80,000 |
| Net income for the year | 60,000 |
| Subtotal | $140,000 |
| Less: Dividends | 20,000 |
| Retained earnings, Dec. 31, 2011 | $120,000 |

## EVALUATING THE FINANCIAL STATEMENTS OF A CORPORATION

**Learning Objective**

**LO8** Explain why the financial statements of a corporation are interpreted differently from those of an unincorporated business.

**The Adequacy of Net Income**   In some respects, the financial statements of a corporation are *easier* to evaluate than those of an unincorporated business. For example, the income of an *unincorporated* business represents compensation to the owners for three distinct factors:

1. Services rendered to the business.
2. Capital invested in the business.
3. The risks of ownership, which often include unlimited personal liability.

But this is *not the case* with a corporation. If stockholders render services to the business, they are compensated with a salary. The corporation recognizes this salary as an expense in the computation of its net income. Therefore, the net income does *not* serve as compensation to the owners for personal services rendered to the business.

Also, stockholders' financial risk of ownership is limited to the amount of their investment. Thus, the net income of a corporation represents simply the *return on the stockholders' financial investment.* The stockholder need only ask, "Is this net income sufficient to compensate me for risking the amount of my investment?" This makes it relatively easy for stockholders to compare the profitability of various corporations in making investment decisions.

Remember also that stockholders *do not* report their respective shares of the corporate net income in their personal income tax returns. However, they must pay personal income taxes on the amount of any dividends received.[10]

**Evaluating Liquidity**   When extending credit to an *unincorporated* business, creditors often look to the liquidity of the individual *owners,* rather than that of the business entity. This is because the owners often are personally liable for the business debts. But in lending funds to a corporation, creditors generally look only to the *business entity* for repayment. Therefore, the financial strength of the business organization becomes much more important when the business is organized as a corporation.

---

[9] Many corporations instead prepare a *statement of stockholders' equity,* which shows the changes in *all* stockholders' equity accounts over the year. A statement of stockholders' equity is illustrated and discussed in Chapter 12.

[10] An exception to this rule is S Corporations, which we discuss shortly.

### Small Corporations and Loan Guarantees

Small, closely held corporations often do not have sufficient financial resources to qualify for the credit they need. In such cases, creditors may require one or more of the company's stockholders to personally guarantee (or co-sign) specific debts of the business entity. By co-signing debts of the corporation, the individual stockholders *do become personally liable for the debts if the corporation fails to make payment.*

## THE CONCEPT—AND THE PROBLEM— OF "DOUBLE TAXATION"

*Unincorporated businesses* do not pay income taxes. Instead, each owner pays *personal income taxes* on his or her share of the business net income.

Corporations, in contrast, must pay *corporate income taxes* on their taxable income. In addition, the stockholders must pay *personal income taxes* on the dividends they receive. As a result, corporate earnings may end up being *taxed twice:* once to the corporation as the income is earned and then again to the stockholders when the profits are distributed as dividends.

This concept of taxing a corporation's earnings at two levels is often called **double taxation.** Together, these two levels of taxation can consume as much as *60 percent to 70 percent* of a corporation's before-tax income. Few businesses would be able to raise equity capital if investors indeed expected to face such a high overall tax rate. Therefore, careful **tax planning** is *absolutely essential* in any business organized as a corporation.

There are several ways to avoid the full impact of double taxation. For example, corporations always should pay *salaries* to stockholders who work in the business. These salaries are taxable to the stockholders, but they are expenses of the business and therefore reduce the corporation's taxable income. Also, the taxation of dividends can be avoided entirely if the corporation *retains* its profits, rather than distributing them as dividends.

There are legal limits, however, on the extent to which taxes can be avoided by a corporation retaining its earnings rather than distributing them to stockholders. If a corporation exceeds these limits, it may be required to pay a supplemental tax.

## S CORPORATIONS

Tax laws allow many small, closely held corporations a special tax status under Subchapter S of the tax code.[11] Corporations that qualify for this special tax treatment are called **S Corporations.**

S Corporations *do not* pay corporate income taxes; nor do stockholders pay *personal* income taxes on the amounts of dividends received. Instead, each stockholder pays personal income taxes on his or her share of the corporate net income. The net income of an S Corporation is taxed in the same manner as that of a *partnership.*

S Corporation status is most advantageous in the following situations:

- A profitable corporation plans to distribute most of its earnings as dividends. In this case, organization as an S Corporation avoids the problem of *double taxation.*
- A new corporation is expected to incur *net losses* in its early years of operation. Ordinarily, net losses incurred by a corporation have *no effect* on the stockholders' personal income tax returns. But if the business is organized as an S Corporation, stockholders *may* deduct their share of any net business loss in their personal income tax returns.

From a tax standpoint, S Corporation status may greatly benefit the owners of a closely held corporation. Owners of small businesses should consider this form of organization.

S Corporations are a special case, not the norm. Unless we specifically state otherwise, you should assume that all corporations used in our examples and assignment materials are regular corporations, not S Corporations.

---

[11] An S Corporation must have 75 or fewer stockholders, all of whom are individuals and residents of the United States. Thus, while one corporation generally may own stock in another, it may *not* be a stockholder in an S Corporation.

**Learning Objective**

**L09**  Discuss the principal factors to consider in selecting a form of business organization.

# Selecting an Appropriate Form of Business Organization

Anyone planning to start a business should give careful thought to the form of organization. Among the factors most often considered are:

- The personal liability of the owner(s) for business debts.
- Income tax considerations.
- The need to raise large amounts of equity capital.
- The owners' need for flexibility in withdrawing assets from the business.
- Whether all owners are to have managerial authority.
- The need for continuity in business operations, despite future changes in ownership.
- The ease and cost of forming the business.

## INCORPORATING AN ESTABLISHED BUSINESS

Often a business starts out as a sole proprietorship or partnership, but as it grows larger, it is reorganized as a closely held corporation. Eventually, the business may "go public," meaning that it issues stock to the general public and its shares are traded on an organized stock exchange.

When an existing business is reorganized as a corporation, the corporation is a *new business entity.* The valuation of the corporation's assets and liabilities is based on their *current market value* when the new entity is established, not on their values in the accounting records of the previous business entity.

Assume, for example, that Devin Ryan has long owned and operated a sole proprietorship called Ryan Engineering. In January, Ryan decides to *incorporate* his business. He obtains a corporate charter and transfers to the new corporation all of the assets used in his sole proprietorship. The new corporation also assumes responsibility for all of the proprietorship's business debts. In exchange for these net assets (assets less liabilities), Ryan receives 20,000 shares of capital stock in the new corporation.

The following table lists the assets, liabilities, and owner's equity of the sole proprietorship at the date the new business is formed. The left-hand column indicates the amounts of these items in the proprietorship's accounting records. The right-hand column indicates the *current market value* of these items on this date. (In each column, owner's equity is equal to total assets less total liabilities.)

| | Amount in Proprietorship's Accounting Records | Current Market Value |
|---|---|---|
| Cash ............................................... | $ 30,000 | $ 30,000 |
| Accounts Receivable ................................ | 75,000 | 60,000 |
| Inventory ......................................... | 10,000 | 15,000 |
| Land .............................................. | 40,000 | 100,000 |
| Building .......................................... | 60,000 | 50,000 |
| Equipment ......................................... | 70,000 | 80,000 |
| Notes Payable ..................................... | 55,000 | 55,000 |
| Accounts Payable .................................. | 20,000 | 20,000 |
| Owner's Equity ................................... | 210,000 | 260,000 |

The entry to establish a new set of records for the business as a corporation based on the values of the assets received and the liabilities assumed is as follows:

| | | |
|---|---:|---:|
| Cash | 30,000 | |
| Accounts Receivable | 60,000 | |
| Inventory | 15,000 | |
| Land | 100,000 | |
| Building | 50,000 | |
| Equipment | 80,000 | |
| Notes Payable | | 55,000 |
| Accounts Payable | | 20,000 |
| Capital Stock | | 260,000 |
| Acquired assets and assumed liabilities of Ryan Engineering; issued 20,000 shares of capital stock in exchange. | | |

**Entries to record the formation of a partnership**

A publicly owned corporation receives cash only when it first sells shares of stock to the investing public (called an "initial public offering," or IPO). Future trading of these securities takes place between individual investors and has no direct impact on the company's cash flows. Yet publicly owned corporations are extremely concerned about growth trends in the market value of their outstanding securities.

Why is this? There are several reasons. First, corporations monitor closely the current market value of their securities because current stock performance directly influences the ability to raise equity capital in the future (through new public offerings). Second, poor stock performance often signals that a company is experiencing financial difficulty. This, in turn, often makes it difficult for the company to obtain credit and may even make potential customers reluctant to buy the goods or services it sells. Finally, a growing number of corporations include stock options in their executive compensation plans. If the market price of the company's stock falls below a certain value, these options become worthless. When this happens, key executives often lose motivation to stay with the company and make the decision to take their "intellectual capital" elsewhere.

## SUPPLEMENTAL TOPIC

### Partnership Accounting—A Closer Look

There are a number of unique aspects of partnership accounting. In this section, we describe opening the accounts of a new partnership, additional investments and withdrawals by owners, allocating partnership net income among the partners, and closing the accounts at year-end.

## OPENING THE ACCOUNTS OF A NEW PARTNERSHIP

When a partner contributes assets other than cash, a question always arises as to the value of such assets. The valuations assigned to noncash assets should be their *fair values* at the date of transfer to the partnership. The valuations assigned must be agreed to by all partners.

To illustrate the opening entries for a newly formed partnership, assume that on January 1, 2009, Joan Blair and Richard Cross, who operate competing retail stores, decide to form a partnership by consolidating their two businesses. A capital account is opened for each partner and credited with the agreed valuation of the *net assets* (total assets less total liabilities) that the partner contributes. The journal entries to open the accounts of the partnership of Blair and Cross are as follows:

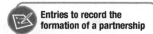
**Entries to record the formation of a partnership**

| | | |
|---|---|---|
| Cash .......................................................... | 40,000 | |
| Accounts Receivable ...................................... | 60,000 | |
| Inventory .................................................... | 90,000 | |
|     Accounts Payable ...................................... | | 30,000 |
|     Joan Blair, Capital ..................................... | | 160,000 |
| To record the investment by Joan Blair in the partnership of Blair and Cross. | | |
| Cash .......................................................... | 10,000 | |
| Inventory .................................................... | 60,000 | |
| Land .......................................................... | 60,000 | |
| Building ...................................................... | 100,000 | |
|     Accounts Payable ...................................... | | 70,000 |
|     Richard Cross, Capital ................................. | | 160,000 |
| To record the investment by Richard Cross in the partnership of Blair and Cross. | | |

Accounting in a partnership is similar to that in a sole proprietorship, except that separate capital accounts are maintained for each partner. These capital accounts show for each partner the amounts invested, the amounts withdrawn, and the appropriate share of partnership net income. In brief, each partner is provided with a history of his or her equity in the firm.

Separate *drawing accounts* also are maintained for each partner. These drawing accounts are debited to record all withdrawals of cash or other assets, including the use of partnership funds to pay a partner's personal debts.

**Additional Investments**   Assume that after six months of operation the firm is in need of more cash, and the partners make additional investments of $10,000 each on July 1. These additional investments are credited to the capital accounts as shown below:

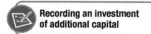
**Recording an investment of additional capital**

| | | |
|---|---|---|
| Cash .......................................................... | 20,000 | |
|     Joan Blair, Capital ..................................... | | 10,000 |
|     Richard Cross, Capital ................................. | | 10,000 |
| To record additional investments. | | |

**Closing the Accounts of a Partnership at Year-End**   At the end of the accounting period, the balance in the Income Summary account is closed into the partners' capital accounts. The profits or losses of a partnership may be divided among the partners in *any manner agreed upon* by the partners in their partnership agreement.

In our illustration, let us assume that Blair and Cross have agreed to share profits equally. (We will discuss other profit-and-loss sharing arrangements later in this section.) Assuming that the partnership earns net income of $60,000 in the first year of operations, the entry to close the Income Summary account is as follows:

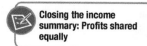
**Closing the income summary: Profits shared equally**

| | | |
|---|---|---|
| Income Summary ........................................... | 60,000 | |
|     Joan Blair, Capital ..................................... | | 30,000 |
|     Richard Cross, Capital ................................. | | 30,000 |
| To divide net income for the year in accordance with partnership agreement to share profits equally. | | |

The next step in closing the accounts is to transfer the balance of each partner's drawing account to his or her Capital account. Assuming that withdrawals during the year amounted to $24,000 for Blair and $16,000 for Cross, the entry at December 31 to close the drawing accounts is as follows:

| | | |
|---|---|---|
| Joan Blair, Capital | 24,000 | |
| Richard Cross, Capital | 16,000 | |
| Joan Blair, Drawing | | 24,000 |
| Richard Cross, Drawing | | 16,000 |
| To transfer debit balances in partners' drawing accounts to their respective capital accounts. | | |

> Closing the partners' drawing accounts to their capital accounts

### Income Statement for a Partnership

The income statement for a partnership differs from that of a sole proprietorship in only one respect: A final section may be added to show the division of the net income between the partners, as illustrated in Exhibit C–5 for the firm of Blair and Cross. The income statement of a partnership is consistent with that of a sole proprietorship in showing no income taxes expense and no salaries relating to services rendered by partners.

**BLAIR AND CROSS**
**INCOME STATEMENT**
**FOR THE YEAR ENDED DECEMBER 31, 2011**

| | | |
|---|---|---|
| Sales | | $600,000 |
| Cost of goods sold | | 400,000 |
| Gross profit on sales | | $200,000 |
| Operating expenses: | | |
| Selling expenses | $100,000 | |
| General & administrative expenses | 40,000 | 140,000 |
| Net income | | $ 60,000 |
| Division of net income: | | |
| To Joan Blair (50%) | $ 30,000 | |
| To Richard Cross (50%) | 30,000 | $ 60,000 |

**Exhibit C–5**
**INCOME STATEMENT**

### Statement of Partners' Equity

The partners usually want an explanation of the change in their capital accounts from one year-end to the next. The statement of partners' equity for Blair and Cross appears in Exhibit C–6 (this statement also was illustrated in Exhibit C–1):

**BLAIR AND CROSS**
**STATEMENT OF PARTNERS' EQUITY**
**FOR THE YEAR ENDED DECEMBER 31, 2011**

| | Blair | Cross | Total |
|---|---|---|---|
| Balances, Jan. 1, 2011 | $160,000 | $160,000 | $320,000 |
| Add: Additional Investments | 10,000 | 10,000 | 20,000 |
| Net Income for the Year | 30,000 | 30,000 | 60,000 |
| Subtotals | $200,000 | $200,000 | $400,000 |
| Less: Drawings | 24,000 | 16,000 | 40,000 |
| Balances, Dec. 31, 2011 | $176,000 | $184,000 | $360,000 |

**Exhibit C–6**
**STATEMENT OF PARTNERS' EQUITY**

The balance sheet of Blair and Cross would show the capital balance for each partner, as well as the total equity of $360,000.

# ALLOCATING PARTNERSHIP NET INCOME AMONG THE PARTNERS

Profits earned by partnerships compensate the owners for (1) personal services rendered to the business, (2) capital invested in the business, and (3) assuming the risks of ownership. Recognition of these three factors is helpful in developing an equitable plan for the division of partnership profits.

If one partner devotes full time to the business while another devotes little or no time, the difference in the partners' contributions of time and effort should be reflected in the profit-sharing agreement. If one partner possesses special skills, the profit-sharing agreement should reward this partner's talent. Also, partners may each provide different amounts of capital to the business entity. Again, the differences in the value of the partners' contributions to the business should be reflected in the profit-and-loss sharing agreement.

To recognize the particular contributions of each partner to the business, partnership profit-and-loss sharing agreements often include salary allowances to partners and interest on the balances of partners' capital accounts. These "salaries" and "interest" are *not expenses* of the business; rather, they are *steps in the computation made to divide partnership net income among the partners.*

In the preceding illustrations of the partnership of Blair and Cross, we assumed that the partners invested equal amounts of capital, rendered equal services, and divided net income equally. We are now ready to consider cases in which the partners invest *unequal* amounts of capital and services. Partners can share net income or loss in any manner they choose; however, most profit-sharing agreements fall under one of the following types:

1. A fixed ratio. The fixed ratio method has already been illustrated in the example of the Blair and Cross partnership, in which profits were shared equally, that is, 50 percent and 50 percent. Partners may agree upon any fixed ratio such as 60 percent and 40 percent, or 70 percent and 30 percent.
2. Salary allowances to the partners, with remaining net income or loss divided in a fixed ratio.
3. Interest allowances on partners' capital balances, with remaining net income or loss divided in a fixed ratio.
4. Salary allowances to the partners, interest allowances on partners' capital balances, and remaining net income or loss divided in a fixed ratio.

All these methods of sharing partnership net income are intended to recognize differences in the personal services rendered by partners and in the amounts of capital invested in the firm.

In the illustrations that follow, the assumption is made that beginning balances in the partners' capital accounts are Brooke Adams, $160,000, and Ben Barnes, $40,000. At year-end, the Income Summary account shows a credit balance of $96,000, representing the net income for the year.

### Salaries to Partners, with Remainder in a Fixed Ratio    Because partners often contribute different amounts of personal services, partnership agreements often provide for partners' salaries as a factor in the division of profits.

For example, assume that Adams and Barnes agree to annual salary allowances of $12,000 for Adams and $60,000 for Barnes. These salaries, which total $72,000 per year, are agreed upon by the partners in advance. Of course, the net income of the business is not likely to be exactly $72,000 in a given year. Therefore, the profit-and-loss sharing agreement should also specify a fixed ratio for dividing any profit or loss remaining after giving consideration to the agreed-upon salary allowances. We will assume that Adams and Barnes agree to divide any remaining profit or loss equally.

The division of the $96,000 in partnership net income between Adams and Barnes is illustrated in the schedule shown in Exhibit C–7. The first step is to allocate to each partner his or her agreed-upon salary allowance. This step allocates $72,000 of the partnership net income. The remaining $24,000 is then divided in the agreed-upon fixed ratio (50–50 in this example).

| Division of Partnership Net Income | | | |
|---|---|---|---|
| | **Adams** | **Barnes** | **Net Income** |
| Net income to be divided . . . . . . . . . . . . . . . . . . . . . . . . | | | $96,000 |
| Salary allowances to partners. . . . . . . . . . . . . . . . . . . | $12,000 | $60,000 | (72,000) |
| Remaining income after salary allowances . . . . . . . . . . . . . . . . . . . . . . . . . . . . . . . . . . | | | $24,000 |
| Allocated in a fixed ratio: | | | |
| Adams (50%) . . . . . . . . . . . . . . . . . . . . . . . . . . . . . . | 12,000 | | |
| Barnes (50%) . . . . . . . . . . . . . . . . . . . . . . . . . . . . . | | 12,000 | (24,000) |
| Total share to each partner . . . . . . . . . . . . . . . . . . . . | $24,000 | $72,000 | $ –0– |

### Exhibit C-7

**DISTRIBUTION OF PARTNERSHIP NET INCOME**

Profit sharing: Salary allowances and remainder in a fixed ratio

Under this agreement, Adams's share of the $96,000 profit amounts to $24,000 and Barnes's share amounts to $72,000. The entry to close the Income Summary account would be:

| | | |
|---|---|---|
| Income Summary . . . . . . . . . . . . . . . . . . . . . . . . . . . . . . . . . . . . . . . . . . . . . . . . | 96,000 | |
| Brooke Adams, Capital . . . . . . . . . . . . . . . . . . . . . . . . . . . . . . . . . . . . . . | | 24,000 |
| Ben Barnes, Capital . . . . . . . . . . . . . . . . . . . . . . . . . . . . . . . . . . . . . . . . | | 72,000 |
| To close the Income Summary account by crediting each partner with agreed-upon salary allowance and dividing the remaining profits equally. | | |

Notice that the allocation of partnership income is used in this closing entry

The salary allowances used in dividing partnership net income are sometimes misinterpreted, even by the partners. These salary allowances are merely an agreed-upon device for dividing net income; they are *not expenses* of the business and are *not recorded in any ledger account.* A partner is considered an owner of the business, not an employee. In a partnership, the services that a partner renders to the firm are assumed to be rendered in anticipation of earning a share of the profits, not a salary.

The amount of cash or other assets that a partner withdraws from the partnership may be greater than or less than the partner's salary allowance. Even if a partner decides to withdraw an amount of cash equal to his or her "salary allowance," the withdrawal should be recorded by debiting the partner's drawing account, *not by debiting an expense account.* Let us repeat the main point: *"Salary allowances" to partners should not be recorded as expenses of the business.*[12]

### Interest Allowances on Partners' Capital, with Remainder in a Fixed Ratio

Next we shall assume a business situation in which the partners spend very little time in the business and net income depends primarily on the amount of money invested. The profit-sharing plan then might emphasize invested capital as a basis for the first step in allocating income.

For example, assume that Adams and Barnes had agreed that both partners are to be allowed interest at *15 percent* on their beginning capital balances, with any remaining profit or loss to be divided equally. Net income to be divided is $96,000, and the beginning capital balances are Adams, *$160,000,* and Barnes, *$40,000.* Exhibit C–8 shows the distribution of partnership net income in this case.

---

[12] Some exceptions to this general rule will be discussed in more advanced accounting courses.

## Exhibit C–8

**DISTRIBUTION OF PARTNERSHIP NET INCOME**

Profit sharing: Interest on capital and remainder in a fixed ratio

| Division of Partnership Net Income | | | |
|---|---|---|---|
| | Adams | Barnes | Net Income |
| Net income to be divided . . . . . . . . . . . . . . . . . . . . . . . . . | | | $96,000 |
| Interest allowances on beginning capital: | | | |
| Adams ($160,000 × 15%) . . . . . . . . . . . . . . . . . . . . . | $24,000 | | |
| Barnes ($40,000 × 15%) . . . . . . . . . . . . . . . . . . . . . | | $ 6,000 | |
| Total allocated as interest allowances . . . . . . . . . . | | | (30,000) |
| Remaining income after interest allowances . . . . . . . . . . . . . . . . . . . . . . . . . . . . . . . . | | | $66,000 |
| Allocated in a fixed ratio: | | | |
| Adams (50%) . . . . . . . . . . . . . . . . . . . . . . . . . . . . . . | 33,000 | | |
| Barnes (50%) . . . . . . . . . . . . . . . . . . . . . . . . . . . . . . | | 33,000 | (66,000) |
| Total share to each partner . . . . . . . . . . . . . . . . . . . . | $57,000 | $39,000 | $ –0– |

The entry to close the Income Summary account in this example would be:

Each partners' capital account is increased by his or her share of partnership net income

| | | |
|---|---|---|
| Income Summary . . . . . . . . . . . . . . . . . . . . . . . . . . . . . . . . . . . . . . . . . . . | 96,000 | |
| Brooke Adams, Capital . . . . . . . . . . . . . . . . . . . . . . . . . . . . . . . . . . . | | 57,000 |
| Ben Barnes, Capital . . . . . . . . . . . . . . . . . . . . . . . . . . . . . . . . . . . . | | 39,000 |

To close the Income Summary account by crediting each partner with interest at 15% on beginning capital and dividing the remaining profits equally.

## Salary Allowances, Interest on Capital, and Remainder in a Fixed Ratio

The preceding example took into consideration the difference in amounts of capital provided by Adams and Barnes but ignored any difference in personal services performed. In the next example, we shall assume that the partners agree to a profit-sharing plan providing for salaries and for interest on beginning capital balances. Salary allowances, as before, are authorized at $12,000 for Adams and $60,000 for Barnes. Beginning capital balances are $160,000 for Adams and $40,000 for Barnes. Partners are to be allowed interest at 10 percent on their beginning capital balances, and any profit or loss remaining after authorized salary and interest allowances is to be divided equally. Exhibit C–9 shows the distribution of partnership net income under this agreement.

## Exhibit C–9

**DISTRIBUTION OF PARTNERSHIP NET INCOME**

Profit sharing: Salaries, interest, and remainder in a fixed ratio

| Division of Partnership Net Income | | | |
|---|---|---|---|
| | Adams | Barnes | Net Income |
| Net income to be divided . . . . . . . . . . . . . . . . . . . . . . . . . | | | $96,000 |
| Salary allowances to partners . . . . . . . . . . . . . . . . . . . . | $12,000 | $60,000 | (72,000) |
| Income after salary allowances . . . . . . . . . . . . . . . . . . | | | $24,000 |
| Interest allowances on beginning capital: | | | |
| Adams ($160,000 × 10%) . . . . . . . . . . . . . . . . . . . . . | 16,000 | | |
| Barnes ($40,000 × 10%) . . . . . . . . . . . . . . . . . . . . . | | 4,000 | |
| Total allocated as interest allowances . . . . . . . . . . | | | (20,000) |
| Remaining income after salary and interest allowances . . . . . . . . . . . . . . . . . . . . . . . . . . . . | | | $ 4,000 |
| Allocated in a fixed ratio: | | | |
| Adams (50%) . . . . . . . . . . . . . . . . . . . . . . . . . . . . . . | 2,000 | | |
| Barnes (50%) . . . . . . . . . . . . . . . . . . . . . . . . . . . . . . | | 2,000 | (4,000) |
| Total share to each partner . . . . . . . . . . . . . . . . . . . . | $30,000 | $66,000 | $ –0– |

The journal entry to close the Income Summary account in this case will be:

| | | |
|---|---|---|
| Income Summary ........................................... | 96,000 | |
|     Brooke Adams, Capital ..................................... | | 30,000 |
|     Ben Barnes, Capital ...................................... | | 66,000 |
| To close the Income Summary account by crediting each partner with authorized salary and interest at 10% on beginning capital, and dividing the remaining profits equally. | | |

### Authorized Salary and Interest Allowance in Excess of Net Income

In the preceding example the total of the authorized salaries and interest was $92,000 and the net income to be divided was $96,000. Suppose that the net income had been only $50,000. How should the division have been made?

If the partnership contract provides for salaries and interest on invested capital, these provisions are to be followed even though the net income for the year is *less* than the total of the authorized salaries and interest. If the net income of the firm of Adams and Barnes amounted to only $50,000, this amount would be allocated as shown in Exhibit C–10.

| Division of Partnership Net Income | Adams | Barnes | Net Income |
|---|---|---|---|
| Net income to be divided ..................... | | | $ 50,000 |
| Salary allowances to partners ................... | $12,000 | $60,000 | (72,000) |
| Residual loss after salary allowances ............. | | | $(22,000) |
| Interest allowances on beginning capital: | | | |
|   Adams ($160,000 × 10%) .................... | 16,000 | | |
|   Barnes ($40,000 × 10%) ..................... | | 4,000 | |
|     Total allocated as interest allowances .......... | | | (20,000) |
| Residual loss after salary and interest allowances ................................. | | | $(42,000) |
| Allocated in a fixed ratio: | | | |
|   Adams (50%) ............................ | (21,000) | | |
|   Barnes (50%) ............................ | | (21,000) | 42,000 |
| Total share to each partner ................... | $ 7,000 | $43,000 | $ –0– |

**Exhibit C–10**

**DISTRIBUTION OF PARTNERSHIP NET INCOME**

Authorized salary and interest allowances in excess of net income

Unless she is thoroughly familiar with the terms of the partnership contract, Adams certainly will be surprised at her allocation of net income for this accounting period. The allocation formula caused Adams to actually be allocated income of only $7,000 for the period, while Barnes was allocated net income of $43,000. The entry to close the Income Summary will be as follows:

| | | |
|---|---|---|
| Income Summary........................................... | 50,000 | |
|     Brooke Adams, Capital ..................................... | | 7,000 |
|     Ben Barnes, Capital ...................................... | | 43,000 |
| To close the Income Summary account by crediting each partner with authorized salary and interest at 10% on beginning capital, and dividing the residual loss equally. | | |

Had the net income of the firm been even less, say, $30,000, Adams would actually have been allocated a *negative* amount, as shown in Exhibit C–11.

Exhibit C–11

**DISTRIBUTION OF PARTNERSHIP NET INCOME**

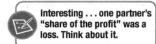

Interesting . . . one partner's "share of the profit" was a loss. Think about it.

| Division of Partnership Net Income | Adams | Barnes | Net Income |
|---|---|---|---|
| Net income to be divided ..................... | | | $ 30,000 |
| Salary allowances to partners .................. | $12,000 | $60,000 | (72,000) |
| Residual loss after salary allowances ............. | | | $(42,000) |
| Interest allowances on beginning capital: | | | |
|   Adams ($160,000 × 10%) .................... | 16,000 | | |
|   Barnes ($40,000 × 10%) ..................... | | 4,000 | |
|     Total allocated as interest allowances .......... | | | (20,000) |
| Residual loss after salary and interest allowances ................................. | | | $(62,000) |
| Allocated in a fixed ratio: | | | |
|   Adams (50%) ........................... | (31,000) | | |
|   Barnes (50%) ........................... | | (31,000) | 62,000 |
| Total share to each partner .................... | $ (3,000) | $33,000 | $ –0– |

---

## Discussion Questions

1. Terry Hanson owns Hanson Sporting Goods, a retail store organized as a sole proprietorship. He also owns a home that he purchased for $200,000 but that is worth $250,000 today. (Hanson has a $140,000 mortgage against this house.) Explain how this house and mortgage should be classified in the financial statements of Hanson Sporting Goods.

2. Jane Miller is the proprietor of a small manufacturing business. She is considering the possibility of joining in partnership with Tom Bracken, whom she considers to be thoroughly competent and congenial. Prepare a brief statement outlining the advantages and disadvantages of the potential partnership to Miller.

3. What is meant by the term *mutual agency*?

4. A real estate development business is managed by two experienced developers and is financed by 50 investors from throughout the state. To allow maximum income tax benefits to the investors, the business is organized as a partnership. Explain why this type of business probably would be a limited partnership rather than a regular partnership.

5. What factors should be considered when comparing the net income figure of a partnership to that of a corporation of similar size?

6. Susan Reed is a partner in Computer Works, a retail store. During the current year, she withdraws $45,000 in cash from this business and takes for her personal use inventory costing $3,200. Her share of the partnership net income for the year amounts to $39,000. What amount must Reed report on her personal income tax return?

7. Distinguish between corporations and partnerships in terms of the following characteristics:
   a. Owners' liability for debts of the business.
   b. Transferability of ownership interest.
   c. Continuity of existence.
   d. Federal taxation on income.

8. Explain the meaning of the term *double taxation* as it applies to corporate profits.

9. What factors should be considered in drawing up an agreement as to the way in which income shall be shared by two or more partners?

10. Partner John Young has a choice to make. He has been offered by his partners a choice between no salary allowance and a one-third share in the partnership income or a salary of $16,000 per year and a one-quarter share of residual profits. Write a brief memorandum explaining the factors he should consider in reaching a decision.

---

## PROBLEMS

 **L03 PROBLEM C.1**
Partnership Transaction
**L10**

E-Z Manufacturing Company is a partnership among Yolando Gonzales, Willie Todd, and Linda Yeager. The partnership contract states that partnership profits will be split equally among the three partners. During the current year Gonzales withdrew $25,000, Todd withdrew $23,000, and Yeager withdrew $30,000. Net income of E-Z Manufacturing Company amounted to $180,000.

a. Calculate each partner's share of net income for the period.

b. Describe the effects, if any, that partnership operations would have on the individual tax returns of the partners.

c. Prepare a statement of partners' equity for the year. Assume that partners' capital accounts had beginning balances of $50,000, $60,000, and $40,000 for Gonzales, Todd, and Yeager, respectively.

**LO6**

**PROBLEM C.2**

Analysis of Equity

**LO7**

Shown below are the amounts from the stockholders' equity section of the balance sheets of Wasson Corporation for the years ended December 31, 2010 and 2011.

|  | 2011 | 2010 |
|---|---|---|
| Stockholders' equity: |  |  |
| Capital Stock .......................................... | $ 50,000 | $ 30,000 |
| Retained Earnings ..................................... | 200,000 | 180,000 |
| Total stockholders' equity ............................ | $250,000 | $210,000 |

a. Calculate the amount of additional investment that the stockholders made during 2011.

b. Assuming that the corporation declared and paid $10,000 in dividends during 2011, calculate the amount of *net income* earned by the corporation during 2011.

c. Explain the significance of the $200,000 balance of retained earnings at December 31, 2011.

**LO10**

**PROBLEM C.3**

Division of
Partnership Income

Guenther and Firmin, both of whom are CPAs, form a partnership, with Guenther investing $100,000 and Firmin, $80,000. They agree to share net income as follows:

1. Salary allowances of $80,000 to Guenther and $50,000 to Firmin.

2. Interest allowances at 15 percent of beginning capital account balances.

3. Any partnership earnings in excess of the amount required to cover the interest and salary allowances to be divided 60 percent to Guenther and 40 percent to Firmin.

The partnership net income for the first year of operations amounted to $247,000 before interest and salary allowances. Show how this $247,000 should be divided between the two partners. Use a three-column schedule of the type illustrated in Exhibit C–9. List on separate lines the amounts of interest, salaries, and the residual amount divided.

**LO3**

**PROBLEM C.4**

Analysis of
Partnership Accounts

Hot Dog Shack is a fast-food restaurant that is operated as a partnership of three individuals. The three partners share profits equally. The following selected account balances are for the current year before any closing entries are made:

|  | Debit | Credit |
|---|---|---|
| Glen, Capital ............................................... |  | 55,000 |
| Chow, Capital .............................................. |  | 60,000 |
| West, Capital ............................................... |  | 5,000 |
| Glen, Drawing ............................................. | 15,000 |  |
| Chow, Drawing ............................................ | 15,000 |  |
| West, Drawing ............................................. | 30,000 |  |
| Income Summary ......................................... |  | 90,000 |

**Instructions**

On the basis of this information, answer the following questions and show any necessary computations.

a. How much must each of the three partners report on his individual income tax return related to this business?

b. Prepare a Statement of Partners' Equity for the current year ended December 31. Assume that no partner has made an additional investment during the year.

c. Assuming that each of the partners devotes the same amount of time to the business, why might Glen and Chow consider the profit-sharing agreement to be inequitable?

d. Which factors should the partners consider when evaluating whether the profit from the partnership is adequate?

**PROBLEM C.5**

Stockholders' Equity Transactions

The Top Hat, Inc., is a chain of magic shops that is organized as a corporation. During the month of June, the stockholders' equity accounts of The Top Hat were affected by the following events:

**June  3**   The corporation sold 1,000 shares of capital stock at $20 per share.

**June 10**   The corporation declared a 25 cents per share dividend on its 20,000 shares of outstanding capital stock, payable on June 23.

**June 23**   The corporation paid the dividend declared on June 10.

**June 30**   The Income Summary account showed a credit balance of $60,000; the corporation's accounts are closed monthly.

**Instructions**

a.   Prepare journal entries for each of the above events in the accounts of The Top Hat. Include the entries necessary to close the Income Summary and Dividends accounts.

b.   Prepare a statement of retained earnings for June. Assume that the balance of retained earnings on May 31 was $520,000.

through

**PROBLEM C.6**

Stockholders' Equity Transactions—More Challenging

William Bost organized Frontier Western Wear, Inc., early in 2010. On January 15, the corporation issued to Bost and other investors 40,000 shares of capital stock at $20 per share.

After the revenue and expense accounts (except Income Tax Expense) were closed into the Income Summary account at the end of 2010, the account showed a before-tax profit of $120,000. The income tax rate for the corporation is 40 percent. No dividends were declared during the year.

On March 15, 2011, the board of directors declared a cash dividend of 50 cents per share, payable on April 15.

**Instructions**

a.   Prepare the journal entries for 2010 to (1) record the issuance of the common stock, (2) record the income tax liability at December 31, and (3) close the Income Tax Expense account.

b.   Prepare the journal entries in 2011 for the declaration of the dividend on March 15 and payment of the dividend on April 15.

c.   Operations in 2011 resulted in an $18,000 *net loss*. Prepare the journal entries to close the Income Summary and Dividends accounts at December 31, 2011.

d.   Prepare the stockholders' equity section of the balance sheet at December 31, 2011. Include a separate supporting schedule showing your determination of retained earnings at that date.

**PROBLEM C.7**

Stockholders' Equity Section

The two cases described below are independent of each other. Each case provides the information necessary to prepare the stockholders' equity section of a corporate balance sheet.

a.   Early in 2009, Wesson Corporation was formed with the issuance of 50,000 shares of capital stock at $5 per share. The corporation reported a net loss of $32,000 for 2009, and a net loss of $12,000 in 2010. In 2011 the corporation reported net income of $90,000 and declared a dividend of 50 cents per share.

b.   Martin Industries was organized early in 2007 with the issuance of 100,000 shares of capital stock at $10 per share. During the first five years of its existence, the corporation earned a total of $800,000 and paid dividends of 25 cents per share each year on the common stock.

**Instructions**

Prepare the stockholders' equity section of the corporate balance sheet for each company for the year ending December 31, 2011.

**PROBLEM C.8**

Comparison of Proprietorship with Corporation

S & X Co. is a retail store owned solely by Paul Turner. During the month of November, the equity accounts were affected by the following events:

**Nov.  9**   Turner invested an additional $15,000 in the business.

**Nov. 15**   Turner withdrew $1,500 for his salary for the first two weeks of the month.

**Nov. 30**   Turner withdrew $1,500 for his salary for the second two weeks of the month.

**Nov. 30**   S & X distributed $1,000 of earnings to Turner.

## Instructions

**a.** Assuming that the business is organized as a sole proprietorship:

    **1.** Prepare the journal entries to record the above events in the accounts of S & X.

    **2.** Prepare the closing entries for the month of November. Assume that after closing all of the revenue and expense accounts the Income Summary account has a balance of $5,000.

    Hint: Record the investment in a separate capital account and the withdrawals (salary) in a separate drawing account. Close the drawing account into the capital account as part of the closing entries.

**b.** Assuming that the business is organized as a corporation:

    **1.** Prepare the journal entries to record the above events in the accounts of S & X. Assume that the distribution of earnings on November 30 was payment of a dividend that was declared on November 20.

    **2.** Prepare the closing entries for the month of November. Assume that after closing all of the revenue and expense accounts (except Income Tax Expense) the Income Summary account has a balance of $2,000. Before preparing the closing entries, prepare the entries to accrue income tax expense for the month and to close the Income Tax Expense account to the Income Summary account. Assume that the corporate income tax rate is *30 percent.*

**c.** Explain the causes of the differences in net income between S & X as a sole proprietorship and S & X as a corporation.

**d.** Describe the effects of the business operations on Turner's individual income tax return, assuming that the business is organized as (**1**) a sole proprietorship and (**2**) a corporation.

---

**L010**  **PROBLEM C.9**

Formation of a Partnership

The partnership of Avery and Kirk was formed on July 1, when George Avery and Dinah Kirk agreed to invest equal amounts and to share profits and losses equally. The investment by Avery consists of $30,000 cash and an inventory of merchandise valued at $56,000.

Kirk also is to contribute a total of $86,000. However, it is agreed that her contribution will consist of the transfer of both the assets of her business and its liabilities (listed below). A list of the agreed values of the various items as well as their carrying values on Kirk's records follows. Kirk also contributes enough cash to bring her capital account to $86,000.

| | Investment by Kirk | |
| --- | --- | --- |
| | **Balances on Kirk's Records** | **Agreed Value** |
| Accounts Receivable | $81,680 | $79,600 |
| Inventory | 11,400 | 12,800 |
| Office Equipment (net) | 14,300 | 9,000 |
| Accounts Payable | 24,800 | 24,800 |

## Instructions

**a.** Draft entries (in general journal form) to record the investments of Avery and Kirk in the new partnership.

**b.** Prepare the beginning balance sheet of the partnership (in report form) at the close of business July 1, reflecting the above transfers to the firm.

**c.** On the following June 30 after one year of operation, the Income Summary account showed a credit balance of $74,000, and the Drawing account for each partner showed a debit balance of $31,000. Prepare journal entries to close the Income Summary account and the Drawing accounts at June 30.

---

**L010**  **PROBLEM C.10**

Sharing Partnership Net Income: Various Methods

A comedy club called Comedy Today was organized as a partnership with Abbott investing $80,000 and Martin investing $120,000. During the first year, net income amounted to $110,000.

## Instructions

**a.** Determine how the $110,000 net income would be divided under each of the following three independent assumptions as to the agreement for sharing profits and losses. Use schedules of the type illustrated in this chapter to show all steps in the division of net income between the partners.

1. Net income is to be divided in a fixed ratio: 40 percent to Abbott and 60 percent to Martin.

2. Interest at 15 percent to be allowed on beginning capital investments and balance to be divided equally.

3. Salaries of $36,000 to Abbott and $56,000 to Martin; interest at 15 percent to be allowed on beginning capital investments; balance to be divided equally.

b. Prepare the journal entry to close the Income Summary account, using the division of net income developed in part **a(3)**.

---

**LO10**  **PROBLEM C.11**

Dividing Partnership Profit and Loss

Rothchild Furnishings, Inc., has three partners—Axle, Brandt, and Conrad. At the beginning of the current year their capital balances were: Axle, $180,000; Brandt, $140,000; and Conrad, $80,000. The partnership agreement provides that partners shall receive salary allowances as follows: Axle, $10,000; Brandt, $50,000; and Conrad, $28,000. The partners shall also be allowed 12 percent interest annually on their capital balances. Residual profit or loss is to be divided: Axle, one-half; Brandt, one-third; and Conrad, one-sixth.

### Instructions

Prepare separate schedules showing how income will be divided among the three partners in each of the following cases. The figure given in each case is the annual partnership net income or loss to be allocated among the partners. Round calculations to the nearest dollar.

a. Income of $526,000.

b. Income of $95,000.

c. Loss of $32,000.

---

**LO1**

**LO4**

**LO5**

**LO9**

**PROBLEM C.12**

Who Gets the Prime Cut? Tax Planning and Pitfalls

Alan Weber originally started Prime Cuts, a small butcher shop, as a sole proprietorship. Then he began advertising in gift catalogs, and his company quickly grew into a large mail-order business. Now Prime Cuts sends meat and seafood all over the world by overnight mail.

At the beginning of the current year, Weber reorganized Prime Cuts as a corporation—with himself as the sole stockholder. This year, the company earned $1 million before income taxes. (For the current year, the corporate income tax rate is *40 percent*. Weber's *personal* income is taxed at the rate of *45 percent*.)

With respect to salaries and withdrawals of assets, Weber continued the same policies as when the business had been a sole proprietorship. Although he personally runs the business, he draws no salary. He explains, "Why should I draw a salary? Nowadays, I have plenty of income from other sources. Besides, a salary would just reduce the company's profits—which belong to me."

In recent years, Weber had made monthly transfers from the business bank account to his personal bank account of an amount equal to the company's monthly net income. After Prime Cuts became a corporation, he continued making these transfers by declaring monthly dividends.

### Instructions

a. Without regard to income taxes, identify several reasons why it might be *advantageous* for Weber to have incorporated this business.

b. Compute the portion of the company's $1 million pretax income that Weber would have retained after income taxes if Prime Cuts *had remained a sole proprietorship*.

c. Compute the portion of this $1 million before-tax income that Weber will retain after income taxes, given that Prime Cuts *is now a corporation*.

d. Explain the meaning of the term *double taxation*.

e. Discuss several ways that Weber legally might have reduced the overall "tax bite" on his company's before-tax earnings.

---

**LO10**  **PROBLEM C.13**

Developing an Equitable Plan for Dividing Partnership Income

Juan Ramirez and Jimmy Smith are considering forming a partnership to engage in the business of aerial photography. Ramirez is a licensed pilot, is currently earning $48,000 a year, and has $50,000 to invest in the partnership. Smith is a professional photographer who is currently earning $30,000 a year. He has recently inherited $70,000, which he plans to invest in the partnership.

Both partners will work full-time in the business. After careful study, they have estimated that expenses are likely to exceed revenue by $10,000 during the first year of operations. In the second year, however, they expect the business to become profitable, with revenue exceeding expenses by an estimated $90,000. (Bear in mind that these estimates of expenses do not include any salaries or interest to the partners.) Under present market conditions, a fair rate of return on capital invested in this type of business is 20 percent.

### Instructions

a. On the basis of this information, prepare a brief description of the income-sharing agreement that you would recommend for Ramirez and Smith. Explain the basis for your proposal.

b. Prepare a separate schedule for each of the next two years showing how the estimated amounts of net income would be divided between the two partners under your plan. (Assume that the original capital balances for both partners remain unchanged during the two-year period. This simplifying assumption allows you to ignore the changes that would normally occur in capital accounts as a result of divisions of profits, or from drawings or additional investments.)

c. Write a brief statement explaining the differences in allocation of income to the two partners and defending the results indicated by your income-sharing proposal.